THE MEANING OF DIFFERENCE

THE MEANING OF DIFFERENCE

American Constructions of Race, Sex and Gender, Social Class, and Sexual Orientation

A Text/Reader

SECOND EDITION

Karen E. Rosenblum
George Mason University

Toni-Michelle C. Travis
George Mason University

Boston Burr Ridge, IL Dubuque, IA Madison, WI New York San Francisco St. Louis
Bangkok Bogotá Caracas Lisbon London Madrid
Mexico City Milan New Delhi Seoul Singapore Sydney Taipei Toronto

McGraw-Hill Higher Education 

A Division of The ***McGraw-Hill*** *Companies*

The Meaning of Difference
American Constructions of Race, Sex and Gender, Social Class, and Sexual Orientation

This book is printed on acid-free paper.

2 3 4 5 6 7 8 9 0 FGR/FGR 0 9 8 7 6 5 4 3 2 1 0

ISBN 0-07-229602-X

Editorial director: *Phillip A. Butcher*
Sponsoring editor: *Sally Constable*
Developmental editor: *Katherine Blake*
Marketing manager: *Leslie A. Kraham*
Project manager: *Christina Thornton-Villagomez*
Senior production supervisor: *Lori Koetters*
Coordinator freelance design: *Mary L. Christianson*
Freelance cover designer: *Maureen McCutcheon*
Supplement coordinator: *Marc Mattson*
Compositor: *GAC Indianapolis*
Typeface: *10.5/12 Times Roman*
Printer: *Quebecor Printing Book Group/Fairfield*

Library of Congress Cataloging-in-Publication Data

The meaning of difference : American constructions of race, sex and gender, social class, and sexual orientation / [editors] Karen E. Rosenblum, Toni-Michelle Travis. -- 2nd ed.
p. cm.
Includes bibliographical references and index.
ISBN 0-07-229602-X (pbk.)
1. United States--Social conditions--1980- 2. Pluralism (Social sciences)--United States. I. Rosenblum, Karen Elaine. II. Travis, Toni-Michelle, 1947-
HN59.2.M44 2000
306′.0973--dc21 99-34828

http://www.mhhe.com

ABOUT THE AUTHORS

KAREN E. ROSENBLUM is associate professor of sociology and vice president for University Life at George Mason University in Fairfax, Virginia. She is a former director of Women's Studies and of the Women's Studies Research and Resource Center, and a faculty member in Cultural Studies. Professor Rosenblum received her Ph.D. in sociology from the University of Colorado, Boulder. Her areas of research and teaching include sex and gender, language, and deviance.

TONI-MICHELLE C. TRAVIS is associate professor of government and politics at George Mason University in Fairfax, Virginia. She is also a faculty member in the Women's Studies and African-American Studies programs. Professor Travis received her Ph.D. in political science from the University of Chicago. Her areas of research and teaching include race and gender in political participation and urban politics. She has served as president of the National Capital Area Political Science Association and the Women's Caucus of the American Political Science Association. She hosts "Capital Regional Roundtable," a cable television show, and is a frequent commentator on Virginia politics.

KAREN [illegible] is associate professor of [illegible] and [illegible] George Mason University [illegible]

[illegible]

TONI-MICHELLE [illegible] TRAVIS is associate professor of government and politics at George Mason University in [illegible] Virginia. [illegible] Women [illegible] American [illegible] Political Science Association [illegible]

[illegible]

CONTENTS

PREFACE

For us, this book is not simply a reader. Rather, it is an attempt to move forward in understanding how race, sex, sexual orientation, social class, and other significant social categories are formulated in American culture. We hope that after reading this volume, students will see the world differently and faculty will feel better able to expand the scope and structure of their courses.

Our aim in *The Meaning of Difference* is to offer a conceptual framework by which to understand the social construction of difference. That perspective is provided in the three framework essays that structure the book. The first essay describes how categories of difference are *created,* the second considers the *experience* of difference, and the third examines the *meanings* assigned to difference by law, politics, and public policy; the economy; science; popular culture; and language. Each framework essay is followed by a set of readings that illustrate and extend the concepts developed in the essay. The readings were specifically selected because of their applicability to multiple groups. For example, Deborah Tannen's discussion of women as a "marked category" can be used to consider how people of color and the poor are also "marked." Similarly, M. Annette Jaimes's article on the "blood quantum" required to classify one as Native American can be applied to a discussion of the criteria people use to classify one another as gay or straight. Throughout, our premise is that similar processes operate when we "see" differences of color, gender, class, and sexual orientation, and that these processes likely also apply to other statuses, such as disability. We hope that this encompassing, conceptual approach makes this book more than "just another reader."

Several other features distinguish the material presented here. Rather than focusing on one or two types of difference, we have tried to provide scope and equal representation. The chapter on Supreme Court decisions offers an accessible and historically contexted discussion of the origins of public policy. The text has also been designed with an eye toward the pedagogic difficulties that accompany this material: When the topic is simultaneously race, sex and gender, social class, and homophobia, no one group can be easily cast as victim or victimizer.

This second edition offers 26 new readings as well as more readings overall. Topically, this means we have extended coverage to mixed-race people, Native Americans, and those who are disabled. While the focus of the book remains on race, sex, social class, and sexual orientation, we believe the extension of the conceptual framework to disability breaks new ground in understanding how difference is constructed. A list of key concepts at the beginning of each framework essay makes the material more accessible. The chapter on Supreme Court decisions discusses a recent case on affirmative action in higher education admissions, *Hopwood v. Texas.* Jamey Piland, a colleague at Trinity College in Washington, D.C., has used the book in several interdisciplinary courses, and from that experience has produced an insightful *Instructor's Manual* that focuses especially on how to teach this material.

Many colleagues and friends have helped us clarify the ideas we present here. David W. Haines provided a thoughtful critique of the framework essays and continues to be a source of conceptual and technical guidance. Theodore W. Travis provided insight on Supreme Court decisions, their relationship to social values, and their impact on American society. The second edition benefited enormously from the comments of colleagues who have used the volume: Victoria Rader, Rose Pascarell, and Jamey Piland—master teachers all.

We owe special thanks to our students at George Mason University and Simmons College for sharing their experiences, to Simmons faculty members for their review and critique, and to Bernadette O'Leary for her general assistance and commitment to keeping us on track. We are particularly grateful to Beth Omansky Gordon for convincing us to expand our framework to include disability. Thanks also go to John Ameer of Simmons College for his compilation of video and film titles, which is included in the Instructor's Manual. Many thanks to Nancy Murphy for keeping the administrative side of Karen's life in order during the completion of this edition. Katherine Blake at McGraw-Hill provided considerable and much-appreciated support. For the second edition, we again convey our appreciation to Joan Lester and the Equity Institute in Emeryville, California, for their understanding of the progress that can be made through a holistic analysis.

McGraw-Hill proved itself as committed to a thorough review process for the second edition as it did for the first, again putting together a panel of accomplished scholars with broad expertise: Judith Baker, Ithaca College; James Fenelon, John Carroll University; Anne Onyekwuluje, Western Kentucky University; Shaunna Scott, University of Kentucky; Sarah Soule, University of Arizona; Mindy Stombler, Texas Tech University; and Pamela Ann Quiroz, University of Massachusetts–Amherst. All offered detailed, insightful, and invaluable critiques, and we are much in their debt.

THE MEANING OF DIFFERENCE

CONSTRUCTING CATEGORIES OF DIFFERENCE

FRAMEWORK ESSAY I: KEY CONCEPTS

aggregate To combine or lump together (verb); something composed of different elements (noun). (See pages 11–14.)

constructionism The perspective that reality cannot be separated from the way a culture makes sense of it—that meaning is "constructed" through social, political, legal, scientific, and other practices. From this perspective, differences among people are created through social processes. (See pages 2–5.)

dichotomize To divide into two parts and to see those parts as mutually exclusive. (See page 14.)

differential undercount In the census, undercounting more of one group than of another. (See pages 9–10.)

disaggregate To separate something into its constituent elements. (See pages 11–14.)

essential identity An identity that is treated as core to a person. Essential identities can be attributed to people even when they are inconsistent with actual behavior. (See page 20.)

essentialism The perspective that reality exists independently of our perception of it, that we perceive the meaning of the world rather than construct that meaning. From this perspective, there are real and important (essential) differences among categories of people. (See pages 2–5.)

ethnic group, ethnicity An ethnic group is composed of people with a shared national origin or ancestry and shared cultural characteristics, such as language. For example, Polish Americans, Italian Americans, Chinese Americans, and Haitian Americans are ethnic groups. "African American" can be considered a racial category, but also an ethnicity (given the shared history of slavery). (See page 16.)

gender Masculinity and femininity; the acting out of the behaviors thought to be appropriate for a particular sex. (See page 21.)

master status A status that has a profound effect on one's life, that dominates or overwhelms the other statuses one occupies. In contemporary American society, race, sex, sexual orientation, social class, and ability/disability function as master statuses, but other statuses—such as religion—do not. For example, race strongly affects occupational status, income, health, and longevity. Religion may have a similar impact in other cultures. (See page 2.)

Other A usage designed to refer to those considered profoundly unlike oneself. (See pages 23–25.)

panethnic An ethnic classification that spans national-origin identities. (See page 12.)

race The conception that people can be classified into coherent groups based on skin color, hair texture, shape of head, eyes, nose, and lips. (See pages 16–18.)

sex The categories of male and female. (See page 21.)

status A position in society. Individuals occupy multiple statuses simultaneously, such as occupational, kinship, and educational statuses. (See page 2.)

stigma An attribute for which someone is considered bad, unworthy, or deeply discredited. (See pages 25–26.)

FRAMEWORK ESSAY

This book deals with the social construction of difference as it operates in American conceptions of race, sex and gender, social class, and sexual orientation. These categories, so often taken for granted, will be systematically questioned throughout the text.

Race, sex, class, and sexual orientation may be described as *master statuses.* In everyday speech, the term *status* conveys prestige. In most social science literature and in this text, however, a status is understood as a position or slot in a social structure. For example, office manager is an occupational status, college graduate is an educational status, and cousin is a kinship status. At any point in time, each of us occupies multiple statuses; that is, one may be an office manager, a college graduate, and a cousin simultaneously. Among these statuses, master statuses are those that "in most or all social situations will overpower or dominate all other statuses. . . . Master status influences every other aspect of life, including personal identity" (Marshall, 1994:315).

In this text we will examine the similarities in the master statuses of race, sex, social class, and sexual orientation. The circumstances of African Americans, Latinos, and Asian Americans differ in many ways, just as the experiences of racial minorities differ from those of sexual orientation minorities. Nonetheless, similar processes are at work when we "see" differences of color, gender, class, and sexual orientation. The impacts of these statuses on people's lives also have important commonalities. Indeed, we will suggest that many of the same processes occur in the operation of other master statuses, such as disability.

In preparing this volume, we noticed that talk about racism, sexism, homophobia,[1] and class status seemed to be everywhere—film, music, news reports, talk shows, sermons, and scholarly publications—and that the topics carried considerable intensity. These are controversial subjects; thus, readers may have strong reactions to this volume. Two perspectives—essentialism and constructionism—are core to the book and should help you understand your own reaction to the material.

The Essentialist and Constructionist Orientations

The difference between the *constructionist* and *essentialist* orientations is illustrated in the tale of the three umpires, first apparently told by social psychologist Hadley Cantril:

> Hadley Cantril relates the story of three baseball umpires discussing their profession. The first umpire said, "Some are balls and some are strikes, and I call them as they are." The second replied, "Some's balls and some's strikes, and I call 'em as I sees 'em." The third thought about it and said, "Some's balls and some's strikes, but they ain't nothing 'till I calls 'em." (Henshel and Silverman, 1975:26)

---

[1]The term *homophobia* was coined in 1973 by psychologist George Weinberg to describe an irrational fear of, or anger toward, homosexuals. While the psychological application has been abandoned, the word remains in common use to describe a strong opposition to or rejection of same-sex relationships. The term leaves much to be desired, but the alternative that has emerged, *heterosexism,* is not yet in conventional usage. *Heterosexism* has been defined as the presumption that all people are heterosexual and that heterosexuality is the only acceptable form of sexual expression.

The first umpire in the story takes an essentialist position. In arguing that "I call them as they are," he indicates his assumption that balls and strikes are entities that exist in the world independently of his perception of them. For this umpire, "balls" and "strikes" are easily identified, mutually exclusive categories, and he is a neutral observer of them. This umpire "regards knowledge as objective and independent of mind, and himself as the impartial reporter of things 'as they are' " (Pfuhl, 1986:5). For this essentialist umpire, balls and strikes exist in the world; he simply observes their presence.

Thus, the essentialist orientation presumes that the items in a category all share some "essential" quality, their "ball-ness" or "strike-ness." For essentialists, the categories of race, sex, sexual orientation, and social class identify significant, empirically verifiable differences among people. From the essentialist perspective, racial categories exist apart from any social processes; they are objective categories of real difference among people.

The second umpire is somewhat removed from pure essentialism. His statement, "I call 'em as I sees 'em," conveys the belief that while an independent, objective reality exists, it is subject to interpretation. For him the world contains balls and strikes, but individuals may have different perceptions about which is which.

The third umpire, who says "they ain't nothing 'till I calls 'em," is a constructionist. He operates from the belief that "conceptions such as 'strikes' and 'balls' have no meaning except that given them by the observer" (Pfuhl, 1986:5). For this constructionist umpire, reality cannot be separated from the way a culture makes sense of it; strikes and balls do not exist until they are constructed through social processes. From this perspective, difference is created rather than intrinsic to a phenomenon. Social processes, such as those in political, legal, economic, scientific, and religious institutions, create differences, determine that some differences are more important than others, and assign particular meanings to those differences. From this perspective, the way a society defines difference among its members tells us more about that society than the people so classified. This book operates from the constructionist perspective, since it examines how we have arrived at our race, sex, sexual orientation, and social class categories.

Few of us have grown up as constructionists. More likely, we are essentialists who believe that master statuses such as race or sex encompass clear-cut, unchanging, and in some way meaningful differences. Still, not everyone is an essentialist. Those from mixed racial or religious backgrounds are familiar with the ways in which identity is not clear-cut. They grow up understanding how definitions of self vary with the context; how others try to define one as belonging in a particular category; and how in many ways, one's very presence calls prevailing classification systems into question. For example, being asked "What are you?" is a common experience among mixed-race people. Such experiences make evident the social constructedness of racial identity.

Most of us are unlikely to be exclusively essentialist or constructionist. As authors we have taken the constructionist perspective, but we still relied on essentialist terms we ourselves find problematic. The irony of questioning the idea of race but still talking about "blacks," "whites," and "Asians," or of rejecting a dualistic approach to sexual identity while still using the terms "gay" and "straight," has not escaped us. Indeed, throughout our discussion we have used the currently favored essentialist phrase "sexual orientation" over the more constructionist "sexual preference."[2]

Further, there is a serious risk that a text such as this falsely identifies people on the basis of either their sex, race, sexual orientation, or social class, despite the fact that master statuses are not parts of a person broken off from one another like the segments of a Tootsie Roll (Spelman, 1988). All of us are always simultaneously all of our master statuses, and it is that complex package that exists in the world. While Section I of the readings may make it seem as if these were separable statuses, they are not. Indeed, even the concept of master status suggests that there can be only one dominating status, though we would reject that position.

Both constructionism and essentialism can be found in the social sciences. We present constructionism as a useful approach to contemporary master status formulations, but essentialism has nonetheless been a critical element in the development of modern science. It has been the basis of probability theory and statistics (Hilts, 1973), and it forms the bedrock for most social scientific research.

Both perspectives also are evident in social movements, and those movements sometimes shift from one perspective to the other over time. Some feminists have held the essentialist belief that women and men are inherently different, as have most of those opposed to feminism. The constructionist view that sexual identity is chosen dominated the gay rights movement of the 1970s (Faderman, 1991), but today most members of that movement take the essentialist approach that sexual identity is something one is born with, whereas those opposed to gay relationships take the constructionist view that it is chosen. In this case, the use of language often signals which perspective is being used. For example, sexual *preference* conveys active, human decision making with the possibility of change (constructionism), while sexual *orientation* implies something fixed and inherent to a person (essentialism). Opinion polls show an increasing percentage of Americans believe homosexuality is something one is born with. In 1977, 13 percent indicated they believed that to be the case; in 1998, 31 percent agreed with that statement (Berke, 1998).

In telling the life story of a friend, journalist Darryl Rist explained the shift to a more essentialist approach on the part of gay rights activists as a response to heightened prejudice against same-sex relationships:

> [Chris Yates's parents were] . . . Pentecostal ministers who had tortured his adolescence with Christian cures for sexual perversity. Shock and aversion therapies under born-again doctors and gruesome exorcisms of sexual demons by spirit-filled preachers had culminated in a plan to have him castrated by a Mexican surgeon who touted the procedure as a way to make the boy, if not straight, at least sexless. Only then had the terrified son rebelled.
>
> Then, in the summer of 1991, the journal *Science* reported anatomical differences between the brains of homosexual and heterosexual men. . . . The euphoric media—those

[2]The phrase "sexual identity" may now be replacing "sexual orientation." It could be used in either an essentialist or a constructionist way.

> great purveyors of cultural myths—drove the story wildly. Every major paper in the country headlined the discovery smack on the front page. . . . Like many others, I suspect, Chris Yates's family saw in this newly reported sexual science a way out of its wrenching impasse. After years of virtual silence between them and their son, Chris's parents drove several hundred miles to visit him and ask for reconciliation. Whatever faded guilt they might have felt for the family's faulty genes was nothing next to the reassurance that neither by a perverse upbringing nor by his own iniquity was Chris or the family culpable for his urges and actions. "We could never have condoned this if you could do something to change it. But when we finally understood that you were *born* that way, we knew we'd been wrong. We had to ask your forgiveness." (Rist, 1992:425–26)

It is understandable that those under attack would find essentialist orientations appealing, just as the expansiveness of constructionist approaches would be appealing in more tolerant eras. Still, both perspectives can be used to justify discrimination, since people can be persecuted for the choices they make as well as for the "genes" they were born with.

Why have we spent so much time describing the essentialist and constructionist perspectives? Discussions about race, sex, sexual orientation, and social class generate such great intensity partly because they involve the clash of essentialist and constructionist assumptions. Essentialists are likely to view categories of people as "essentially" different in some important way; constructionists are likely to see these differences as socially created and arbitrary. An essentialist asks what causes people to be different; a constructionist asks about the origin and consequence of the categorization system itself. While arguments about the nature and cause of racism, sexism, homophobia, and poverty are disputes about power and justice, from the perspective of essentialism and constructionism they are also disputes about what differences in color, sexuality, and social class *mean.*

The constructionist approach has one clear advantage, however. It is from that perspective that one understands that all the talk about race, sex, sexual orientation, and social class has a profound significance. Such talk is not simply *about* difference and similarity; it is itself the *creation* of difference and similarity. In the sections that follow, we will examine how categories of people are named, dichotomized, and stigmatized—all toward the construction of difference.

Naming

Difference is constructed first by naming categories of people. Therefore, constructionists pay special attention to the names people use to refer to themselves and others—the points at which new names are asserted, the negotiations that surround the use of particular names, and those occasions when people are grouped together or separated out.

Asserting a Name Both individuals and categories of people face similar issues in the assertion of a name. A change of name involves, to some extent, the claim of a new identity. For example, one of our colleagues wanted to be called by her first name rather than by its abbreviated version because the diminutive had come to seem childish to her. It took a few rounds of reminding people that this was her new name, and with most that was adequate. One colleague, however, argued that he could not adapt to the new name; she would just have to tolerate his continued use of the nickname. This was a small but public battle about who had the power to name whom. Did she have the power to enforce her own naming, or did he have the power to name her despite her wishes? Eventually, she won.

A more disturbing example was a young woman who wanted to keep her "maiden" name after she married. Her fiancé agreed with her decision, recognizing that he would be reluctant to give up his name were the tables turned. When his mother heard of this possibility, however, she was outraged. In her mind, a rejection of her family's name was a rejection of her family. She urged her son to reconsider getting married. (We do not know how this story ended.)

Thus, asserting a name can create social conflict. On both a personal and societal level, naming can involve the claim of a particular identity and the rejection of others' power to impose a name. For example, is one Native American, American Indian, or Sioux; African American or black; girl or woman; Asian American or Japanese American; gay or homosexual; Chicano, Mexican American, Mexican, Latino, Hispanic, Spanish American, or Hispaño?

> Geographically, *Hispanic* is preferred in the Southeast and much of Texas. New Yorkers use both *Hispanic* and *Latino.* Chicago, where no nationality has attained a majority, prefers *Latino.* In California, the word *Hispanic* has been barred from the Los Angeles *Times,* in keeping with the strong feelings of people in the community. Some people in New Mexico prefer *Hispaño.* Politically, *Hispanic* belongs to the right and some of the center, while *Latino* belongs to the left and the center. Historically, the choice went from *Spanish* or *Spanish-speaking* to *Latin American, Latino,* and *Hispanic.* (Shorris, 1992:xvi–xvii)

Deciding what name to use for a category of people is no easy task. It is unlikely that all members of the category use the same name; the name members use for one another may not be acceptable for outsiders to use; nor is it always advisable to ask what name a person prefers. We once saw an old friend become visibly angry when asked whether he preferred the term *black* or *African American.* "Either one is fine with me," he replied, "*I* know what *I* am." To him, the question meant that he was being seen as a member of a category, not as an individual.

Because naming may involve a redefinition of self, an assertion of power, and a rejection of others' ability to impose an identity, social change movements often lay claim to a new name, and opponents to the movement may signal their opposition by continuing to use the old name. For example, *black* emerged in opposition to *Negro* as the Black Power movement sought to distinguish itself from the more moderate Martin Luther King wing of the civil rights movement. The term *Negro* had itself been put forward by influential leaders W. E. B. Du Bois and Booker T. Washington as a rejection of the term "colored" that had dominated the mid- to late 19th century. "[D]espite its association with racial epithets, 'Negro' was defined to stand for a new way of thinking about Blacks" (Smith, 1992:497–98). Similarly, in 1988 Ramona H. Edelin, president of the National Urban Coalition, proposed that *African American* be substituted for *black,* and now both terms are in use (Smith,

1992).[3] Ironically, *people of color* is now a common reference to all nonwhite Americans, while *colored people* remains offensive to many African Americans.

Each of these changes—from *Negro* to *black* to *African American*—was first promoted by activists as a way to demonstrate their commitment to change and militance. Similar themes are reflected in the history of the terms *Chicano* and *Chicanismo.* Although the origin of the terms is unclear, the principle was the same. As reporter Ruben Salazar wrote in the 1960s, "a chicano is a Mexican-American with a non-Anglo image of himself" (Shorris, 1992:101).

In the gay rights movement, the term *homosexual* was first coined in 1869 by a Hungarian physician who was seeking to have such relationships recognized as a medical problem rather than a criminal one. The term was adopted by the medical and psychological literature of the time, which, as Jonathan Katz explains in Reading 12, depicted all nonprocreative sex as pathological. When activists of the 1960s rejected the pathological characterization, they rejected the name associated with it as well, substituting *gay* for *homosexual.* Presently *gay* is used both as a generic term encompassing men and women and as a specific reference to men.[4]

The 1990 founding of Queer Nation may signal the demise of *gay,* however. This use of *queer*—as in the slogan "We're here. We're queer. Get used to it."—attempts to transform an epithet into a label of pride and militance. Nonetheless, use of the word is also debated within the gay community. Some argue that it reflects the internalization of homophobic attitudes, while others argue that it is appropriately defiant of straight culture.

Just as each of these social movements has involved a public renaming that proclaims pride, the women's movement has asserted *woman* as a replacement for *girl.* The significance of these two terms was revealed by a student who described a running feud with her roommate. The student preferred the word *woman,* arguing that the application of the word *girl* to females past adolescence was insulting. Her female roommate just as strongly preferred the term *girl* and regularly applied it to the females she knew. Each of them had such strong feelings on the matter that they clearly would not be roommates much longer.

How could these two words destroy their relationship? It appears that English speakers use the terms *girl* and *woman* to refer to quite different qualities. *Woman* (like *man*) is understood to convey adulthood, power, and sexuality; *girl* (like *boy*) connotes youth, powerlessness, and irresponsibility (Richardson, 1988). Thus, the two roommates were asserting quite different places for themselves in the world. One claimed adulthood; the other saw herself as not having achieved adulthood.

---

[3]Thus, one can find Black Studies, Afro-American Studies, and African American Studies programs in universities across the country.

[4]In the 17th century, *gay* became associated with an addiction to social pleasure, dissipation, and loose morality, and was used to refer to female prostitutes (e.g., "gay girl"). The term was apparently first used in reference to a male homosexual in 1925 in Australia. "It may have been both the connotations of femininity and those of immorality that led American homosexuals to adopt the title 'gay' with some self-irony in the 1920s. The slogan 'Glad to be Gay,' adopted by both female and male homosexuals, and the naming of the Gay Liberation Front, which was born from the Stonewall resistance riots following police raids on homosexual bars in New York in 1969, bear witness to a greater self-confidence" (Mills, 1989:102).

This is the explanation offered by many females: It is not so much that they like being *girls,* as that they value youth and/or do not yet feel justified in calling themselves *women.* Yet this is precisely the identity the women's movement has put forward: "We cannot be girls anymore, we must be women."

Creating Categories of People While individuals or groups may assert names for themselves, governments have the power to create categories of people. These categories usually draw on conventional practices, but operate somewhat independently of them. The recent history of the questions asked by the U.S. Census illustrates this process.

Every census since 1790 has included a question about race. In 1970, the options for race were "white, Negro or black, American Indian (with a request to 'print the name of the enrolled or principal tribe'), Japanese, Chinese, Filipino, Hawaiian, Korean, and Other." The head of the household was directed to select only one option for each household member. Census data had always been critical to the functioning of American government; the apportionment of seats in the U.S. House of Representatives and the distribution of federal funding to states and localities are based on those data. By the 1970s, however, the information on race was increasingly understood as critical to eliminating discrimination. Such data, the newly formed U.S. Commission on Civil Rights argued, was necessary to monitor equal access in housing, education, and employment. In addition,

> There were the civil rights movement and its offshoots such as the Mexican-American Brown Power movement. In addition, the federal government initiated the War Against Poverty and the Great Society programs. These movements and programs stated clearly that poor minority groups had a legitimate claim to better conditions in cities. Several of the social welfare programs of President Johnson's Great Society distributed dollars by means of statistically driven grant-in-aid formulas. The proliferation of federal grants programs and the cities' increasing dependence upon them tended to heighten the political salience of census statistics. Such formulas often incorporated population size, as measured or estimated by the Census Bureau, as a major factor. By 1978 there were more than one hundred such programs, covering a wide range of concerns, from preschool education (Headstart) to urban mass transportation (U.S. Congress, 1978). . . . [T]he single most commonly used data source was the decennial census. (Choldin, 1994:27–8)

In all, the census offered an important source of information for the courts, Congress, and local entities to gauge the extent of discrimination and monitor civil rights enforcement.

To improve the collection of data on race, the Commission on Civil Rights reviewed agency practices and found that six categories were in use: White, Negro/Black, Spanish Surnamed, American Indian, Oriental, and Other. These categories were not scientific—"these designations do not refer strictly to race, color, national or ethnic origin" (U.S. Commission on Civil Rights, 1973:38)—but the commission argued they were nonetheless what the general public understood to be *minority groups.* "The federal emphasis was clearly on minority status in a legal sense. Minority group status did not derive from a specific race or ethnicity *per se,* but on the treatment of race and ethnicity to confer a privileged, disadvantaged, or equitable status and to gauge representation and under-representation" (Tamayo Lott, 1998:37). The aim of data collection was to determine the extent of discrimination, not to identify all population categories.

Based on its review, the commission recommended that the Office of Management and Budget (OMB) develop governmentwide standards for the collection of data on race and ethnicity, reasoning that OMB could ensure that federal agencies would monitor whether their programs "reached minority beneficiaries on an equitable basis" (Tamayo Lott, 1998:37). The development of these standards actually had begun earlier by the Federal Interagency Committee on Education at the request of the Department of Health, Education, and Welfare. Using this information, in 1977 OMB issued "Statistical Policy Directive No. 15," which established standard categories and definitions for all federal agencies, including the Bureau of the Census. Directive No. 15 defined five basic racial and ethnic categories: American Indian or Alaskan Native, Asian or Pacific Islander, Hispanic, Negro or Black, and White.

> The choice of four racial categories and one ethnic category redefined the United States beyond a White and non-White classification and even beyond a White and Black classification. The new classification facilitated the enumeration of a multiracial and multicultural population. . . . The particular status of Hispanics was recognized in two ways. Hispanic was the only choice for the ethnic category. Furthermore . . . Black and White Hispanics were enumerated as Hispanics. To avoid duplicated counts, the Black and White categories excluded Hispanics. (Tamayo Lott, 1998:54)

The Hispanic/non-Hispanic ethnicity question (which in the 1990 census read: "Is this person of Spanish/Hispanic origin? If yes, Mexican, Mexican American, Chicano? Puerto Rican? Cuban? Other Spanish/Hispanic?") was added at the recommendation of the census bureau's Hispanic Advisory Committee to correct for the *differential undercount* (undercounting more people in one category than in another) of the Hispanic population. Undercounting primarily affects low-income, non-English-speaking residents of inner cities. This is the case because the poor often lack stable residences and are thus difficult to reach, more likely to be illiterate or non-English speakers (there was no Spanish-language survey until the 1990 census), and more likely to be illegal immigrants afraid to respond to such a government questionnaire. The Constitution requires a count of all the people in the United States, not just those who are citizens or legal residents.

Undercounting is a long-standing problem. "[T]he net underenumeration of non-Whites has been and continues to be much greater than for Whites. In 1960, for example, among all males, 2.8 percent of White males were underenumerated compared to 10.9 percent of non-White males. . . . In the 1990 Census, Blacks were undercounted by 4.8 percent, Hispanics by 5.2 percent, American Indians and Alaskan Natives by 5 percent, and Asians and Pacific Islanders by 3.1 percent" (Tamayo Lott, 1998:32). Census data affect the distribution of billions of dollars of federal aid for "everything from feeding the poor to running mass transit systems" (Espiritu, 1992: 116). For example, federal funding for the construction of homes for the poor, child care centers, and social service programs for the elderly are tied to population, as is state aid for neighborhood rehabilitation and school construction. Thus, undercounting remains an important fiscal and political issue. For the year 2000 census, the federal government proposed supplementing the traditional head count with statistical sampling techniques such as those used in opinion polls. This would provide an estimate of the number and demographic characteristics of those who did not respond to the census. In a 5-to-4 decision in 1999, the Supreme Court barred the use of these methods for determining the nation's population and the apportionment of congressional seats. However, it left open the possibility of using these methods in the allocation of federal funding and in political redistricting within the states.

By the 1990 census, 16 choices were listed under the four major racial categories: (1) white; (2) Black or Negro; (3) American Indian (with a request to "print the name of the enrolled or principal tribe"), Eskimo, or Aleut; and (4) under the category *Asian or Pacific Islander,* Chinese, Filipino, Hawaiian, Korean, Vietnamese, Japanese, Asian Indian, Samoan, Guamanian, Other Asian or Pacific Islander (with a request to print the race), and Other race (with a request to print the race). As always, respondents were instructed to select only *one* option. This classification system was coming under increasing attack for failing to reflect accurately the nation's diversity and for excluding those who considered themselves multiracial. Four years of review, public comment, and field testing led OMB to the following changes in Directive No. 15 and the census (Office of Management and Budget, 1997):

- The 2000 census will not offer a multiracial option, but people will be free to mark more than one racial category. Answers to the race question will be tabulated for those in each single race category and for those reporting in each of the possible combinations. (About 1 percent of respondents reported themselves as multiracial when they were given that option in field tests of trial census questions.)
- *Black* will be changed to *Black or African American.*
- The category *Asian or Pacific Islander* will be broken into two, one called *Asian* and the other called *Native Hawaiian or Other Pacific Islander.*
- *Asian* will include "any of the original peoples of the Far East, Southeast Asia, or the Indian subcontinent including, for example, Cambodia, China, India, Japan, Korea, Pakistan, the Philippine Islands, Thailand, and Vietnam."
- *Native Hawaiian or Other Pacific Islander* will include the original peoples of Hawaii, Guam, Samoa, or other Pacific Islands, and the Pacific Islander groups reported in the 1990 census.
- The ethnicity question will use both the terms *Hispanic* and *Latino.* For the future, OMB is considering allowing respondents to indicate that they have both Hispanic and non-Hispanic background (analogous to the option of marking more than one race category).
- The Hispanic/Latino origin question will precede the race question, and the number of respondents in each racial category who are Hispanic or Latino will be reported separately.

- An *Arab* or *Middle Eastern* category will not be added. The public comment process did not indicate agreement on a definition for this category, but OMB will continue research on this option. Arab or Middle Eastern peoples will continue to be categorized as white.
- The term *American Indian* will not be changed to *Native American.*
- Those identifying themselves as Central and South American Indians will be classified as *American Indian.*
- *Alaska Native* will replace *Alaskan Native, Eskimo, and Aleut.*

When considering official counts of the population, we must be careful not to assume that what is counted is real. While census data contribute to the essentialist view that the world is populated by distinct, scientifically defined categories of people, this brief history demonstrates that not even those who collect the data make that assumption; rather, census categories have been based on constructionist premises. As OMB warns,

> The racial and ethnic categories set forth in the standards should not be interpreted as being primarily biological or genetic in reference. Race and ethnicity may be thought of in terms of social and cultural characteristics as well as ancestry. (Office of Management and Budget, 1997:2)
>
> There are no clear, unambiguous, objective generally agreed-upon definitions of the terms "race" and "ethnicity." Cognitive research shows that respondents are not always clear on the differences between race and ethnicity. There are differences in terminology, group boundaries, attributes and dimensions of race and ethnicity. . . .
>
> [The Directive No. 15 categories] do not represent objective "truth" but rather are ambiguous social constructs and involve subjective and attitudinal issues. (Office of Management and Budget, 1995:44680)

Aggregating and Disaggregating Federal identification policies collapsed various national-origin groups into four categories: Hispanics or Latinos, Native Americans, Blacks, and Asian or Pacific Islanders. This process *aggregated* categories of people; that is, it combined, or "lumped together," different groups. In their answers to the census questions, Puerto Ricans, Mexican Americans, and Cubans all became "Latino" is some sense.

But the groups that were now lumped together had historically regarded one another as different, and thus in people's everyday lives the aggregate category was likely to *disaggregate,* or fragment, into its constituent national-origin elements.

While one might think that *Hispanic* or *Asian American* are terms used for self-identification, it appears that is often not the case. In the United States, "Mexicans, Puerto Ricans, and Cubans have little interaction with each other, most do not recognize that they have much in common culturally, and they do not profess strong affection for each other" (de la Garza et al., 1992:14). Thus, it is not surprising that a survey of the Latino population concludes that "respondents do not primarily identify as members of an Hispanic or Latino community. . . . [Rather, they] overwhelmingly prefer to identify by national origin . . ." (de la Garza et al., 1992:13). While members of these groups share common positions on many domestic policy issues, they do not appear to share a commitment to Spanish-language maintenance, common cultural traditions, or religiosity (de la Garza et al., 1992). In short, the category *Latino/Hispanic* exists primarily, but not exclusively, from the perspective of non-Latinos.

While the classification *Hispanic* offers at least a commonality in Spanish as a shared language in the country of origin, among those sharing the category *Asian American* are groups with different languages, cultures, and religions and sometimes centuries of hostility. In all, the category *Asian American* is based on geography rather than on any cultural, racial, linguistic, or religious commonalities. "Asian Americans are those who come from a region of the world that *the rest of the world* has defined as Asia" (Hu-Dehart, 1994).[5]

Aggregate classifications such as Latino or Asian American were not simply the result of federal classifications, however. Student activists inspired by the Black Power and civil rights movements first proposed the terms. As Yen Le Espiritu describes in Reading 5, college students coined the identifier *Asian American* in response to "the similarity of [their] experiences and treatment." *Asian American* is an example of a *panethnic* term, that is, a classification that spans national-origin identities. Panethnicity is "the development of bridging organizations and solidarities among subgroups of ethnic collectivities that are often seen as homogeneous by outsiders. . . . Those . . . groups that, from an outsider's point of view, are most racially homogeneous are also the groups with the greatest panethnic development" (Lopez and Espiritu, 1990:219–20).

Panethnicity is both useful and unstable. "The elites representing such groups find it advantageous to make political demands by using the numbers and resources panethnic formations can mobilize. The state, in turn, can more easily manage claims by recognizing and responding to large blocs as opposed to dealing with the specific claims of a plethora of ethnically defined interest groups" (Omi, 1996:180). At the same time, competition and historic antagonisms make such alliances unstable. "At times it is advantageous to be in a panethnic bloc, and at times it is desirable to mobilize along particular ethnic lines" (Omi, 1996:181).

For the categories *Native American* and *African American,* the aggregate classification was the direct result of conquest and enslavement.

---

[5]In census classifications, *Asian* includes Chinese, Filipino, Japanese, Asian Indian, Korean, Vietnamese, Cambodian, Hmong, Laotian, Thai; *Other Asian* includes Bangladeshi, Bhutanese, Bornean, Burmese, Celebesian, Ceram, Indochinese, Indonesian, Iwo-Jiman, Javanese, Malayan, Maldivian, Nepali, Okinawan, Pakistani, Sikkim, Singaporean, Sri Lankan, and Sumatran. The category *Pacific Islander* includes Hawaiian, Samoan, and Guamian; *Other Pacific Islander* includes Carolinian, Fijan, Kosraean, Melanesian, Micronesian, Northern Mariana Islander, Palauan, Papua New Guinean, Ponapean, Polynesian, Solomon Islander, Tahitian, Tarawa Islander, Tokelauan, Tongan, Trukese, and Yapese.

In 1980, Asian Indians successfully lobbied to change their census classification from white to Asian American by reminding Congress that historically immigrants from India had been classed as Asian. With other Asians, those from India had been barred from immigration by the 1917 Immigration Act, prohibited from becoming naturalized citizens until 1946, and denied the right to own land by the 1920 Alien Land Law. Indeed, in 1923 the U.S. Supreme Court (in *Thind*) ruled that Asian Indians were non-white, and could therefore have their U.S. citizenship nullified (Espiritu, 1992:124–25). Thus, in the bulk of their experience in the United States, Asian Indians had been classed as Asian.

> The "Indian," like the European, is an idea. The notion of "Indians" was invented to distinguish the indigenous peoples of the New World from Europeans. The "Indian" is the person on shore, outside of the boat. . . . There [were] hundreds of cultures, languages, ways of living in Native America. The place was a model of diversity at the time of Columbus's arrival. Yet Europeans did not see this diversity. They created the concept of the "Indian" to give what they did see some kind of unification, to make it a single entity they could deal with, because they could not cope with the reality of 400 different cultures. (Mohawk, 1992: 440)[6]

Conquest made "Indians" out of a heterogeneity of tribes and nations that had been distinctive on linguistic, religious, and economic grounds. It was not only that Europeans had the unifying concept of "Indian" in mind—after all, they were sufficiently aware of cultural differences to generate an extensive body of tribally specific treaties. It was also that conquest itself—encompassing as it did the appropriation of land, the forging and violation of treaties, and the implementation of policies that forced relocation—structured the lives of Native Americans along common lines. While contemporary Native Americans still identify themselves by tribal ancestry, just as those called Asian American and Latino identify themselves by national origin, their shared experience of conquest also forged the common identity reflected in the collective name, *Native American.*

Similarly, the capture, purchase, and forced relocation of Africans, and their experience of being moved from place to place as personal property, created the category now called *African American.* This experience forged a single people from those who had been culturally diverse; it produced an "oppositional racial consciousness," that is, a unity-in-opposition (Omi and Winant, 1994). "Just as the conquest created the 'native' where once there had been Pequot, Iroquois, or Tutelo, so too it created the 'black' where once there had been Asante or Ovimbundu, Yoruba or Bakongo" (Omi and Winant, 1994:66).

Even the categories of gay and straight, male and female, and poor and middle class are aggregations that presume a commonality by virtue of shared master status. For example, the category *gay and lesbian* assumes that sharing a sexual orientation binds people together despite all the issues that might divide them as men and women, people of different colors, or people of different social classes. And, just as in the cases we have previously discussed, alliances of gay and lesbian people can be expected to come together and separate out in response to social circumstances.

Still, our analysis has so far ignored one category of people. From whose perspective do the categories of Native American, Asian American, African American, and Latino/Hispanic exist? Since "difference" is always "difference *from,*" from

---

[6]The idea of "Europe" and the "European" is also a constructed, aggregate category. "Physically, Europe is not a continent. Where is the water separating Europe from Asia? It is culture that separates Europe from Asia. Western Europe roughly comprises the countries that in the Middle Ages were Latin Christendom, and Eastern Europe consists of those countries that in the Middle Ages were Eastern Orthodox Christendom. It was about 1257 A.D. when the Pope claimed hegemony over the secular emperors in Western Europe and formulated the idea that Europeans, that Christians, were a unified ethnicity even though they spoke many different languages" (Mohawk, 1992:439–40).

whose perspective is "difference" determined? Who has the power to define "difference"? If "we" are in the boat looking at "them," who precisely are "we"?

Every perspective on the social world emerges from a particular vantage point, a particular social location. Ignoring who the "us" is in the boat treats that place as if it were just the view "anyone" would take. Historically, the people in the boat were European; contemporarily, they are white Americans. As Ruth Frankenberg frames it in Reading 6, in America "whites are the nondefined definers of other people," "the unmarked marker of others' differentness." Failing to identify the "us" in the boat means that "white culture [becomes] the unspoken norm," a category that is powerful enough to define others while itself remaining invisible. Indeed, Frankenberg argues that those with the most power in a society are best positioned to have their own identities left unnamed, thus masking their power.

The term *androcentrism* describes the world as seen from a male-centered perspective. By analogy, one may also describe a *Eurocentric* and *heterocentric* perspective. To some extent, regardless of their sex, race, or sexual orientation, all Americans operate from an andro-, Euro-, and heterocentric perspective since these are the guiding assumptions of the culture. Recognizing these perspectives as historically and culturally located makes it possible to evaluate their adequacy.

Dichotomizing

Many forces promote the construction of aggregate categories of people. Frequently, these aggregates are built as *dichotomies.* To dichotomize is not only to divide something into two parts; it is also to see those parts as mutually exclusive and in opposition. Dichotomization encourages the sense that there are two and only two categories, that everyone fits easily in one or the other, and that the categories stand in opposition to each other. In contemporary American culture, we appear to treat the master statuses of race, sex, class, and sexual orientation as if each embodied "us" and "them"—as if people could be easily sorted into two mutually exclusive, opposed groupings.[7]

Dichotomizing Race The clearest example of dichotomization is provided by the "one-drop rule" discussed by F. James Davis in Reading 1. American social practices dictate that a person with any traceable African heritage is classified as black. While in other cultures people of mixed racial ancestry might be defined as "mixed," the American one-drop rule specifically denies that possibility. As Davis describes, the one-drop rule is an informal social practice strongly supported by both blacks and whites, and reaffirmed by the Supreme Court as recently as 1986.

The life stories of biracial and multiracial celebrities such as Jasmine Guy, Jennifer Beals, Halle Berry, Mariah Carey, Paula Abdul, and Tiger Woods give evidence of both the continued application of the one-drop rule and its potential unraveling. In Reading 2, Jon Michael Spencer describes the recent activism of members of biracial families. While their lobbying did not succeed in adding a

[7]Springer and Deutsch (1981) coined the term *dichotomania* to describe the current belief that there are male and female sides of the brain. We think that term also fits our discussion here.

multiracial classification to the year 2000 census, the effort certainly contributed to the census's historic move toward the recognition of multiple racial ancestries.

The black/white dichotomy is an abiding and rigidly enforced one, but different regions and historical periods have also produced their own two-part distinctions. In the Southwest the divide has been between Anglos and Latinos, and on parts of the West Coast it is between Asian Americans and whites. Each of these variations, however, is an instance of America's most encompassing and historic dichotomization: that of whites and nonwhites.

While three racial categories—*white, Negro,* and *Indian*—were identified throughout the 19th century (Omi and Winant, 1994), all were located within the white/nonwhite dichotomy. In 1854, the California Supreme Court in *People v. Hall* held that blacks, mulattos, Native Americans, and Chinese were "not white" and therefore could not testify for or against a white man in court (Takaki, 1993:205–6). (Hall, a white man, had been convicted of killing a Chinese man on the testimony of one white and three Chinese witnesses; the Supreme Court overturned the conviction.) Mexican residents of the southwest territories ceded to the United States in the 1848 Treaty of Guadalupe Hidalgo, however, "were defined as a white population and accorded the political-legal status of 'free white persons'" (Omi and Winant, 1994). European immigrants were initially treated as nonwhite, or at least not-yet-white. In turn, they lobbied for their own inclusion in American society on the basis of the white/nonwhite distinction.

> [Immigrants struggled to] equate whiteness with Americanism in order to turn arguments over immigration from the question of who was foreign to the question of who was white. . . . Immigrants could not win on the question of who was foreign. . . . But if the issue somehow became defending "white man's jobs" or "white man's government" . . . [they] could gain space by deflecting debate from nativity, a hopeless issue, to race, an ambiguous one. . . . After the Civil War, the new-coming Irish would help lead the movement to bar the relatively established Chinese from California, with their agitation for a "white man's government," serving to make race, and not nativity, the center of the debate and to prove the Irish white. (Roediger, 1994:189–90)

Historically, *American* has meant white, as many Americans of Asian ancestry learn when they are complimented on their English—a compliment that presumes that someone who is Asian could not be a native-born American.[8] For example,

> A white woman from New Jersey once raved to William Wong of the *Oakland Tribune* about a wonderful new Vietnamese restaurant in her town: "We were there the other night and we were the only Americans there." Wong noted with regret: "She probably meant the only white people." (Takaki, 1989:6)

Novelist Toni Morrison would describe this as a story about "how *American* means *white*":

---

[8]Since the historic American ban on Asian immigration remained in place until 1965, it is nonetheless the case that a high proportion of Asian Americans are foreign born. The 1990 census indicated that 66 percent of the Asian American population was foreign born. This figure, however, masks a considerable range. Among Japanese Americans, only 32 percent were foreign born, while that was the case for 83 percent of Vietnamese Americans (Hirschman, 1996).

> Deep within the word "American" is its association with race. To identify someone as South African is to say very little; we need the adjective "white" or "black" or "colored" to make our meaning clear. In this country it is quite the reverse. American means white, and Africanist people struggle to make the term applicable to themselves with . . . hyphen after hyphen after hyphen. (Morrison, 1992:47)

Because *American* means *white,* those who are not white are presumed to be recent arrivals and often told to go "back where they came from." In America, we appear to operate within the dichotomized *racial* categories of American/non-American—these are racial categories, because they effectively mean white/nonwhite.

But what exactly *is* race? First, we need to distinguish race from *ethnicity.* Social scientists define *ethnic groups* as categories of people who are distinctive on the basis of national origin, language, and cultural practices. As Robert Blauner explains in Reading 23, "members of an ethnic group hold a set of common memories that make them feel that their customs, culture, and outlook are distinctive." Thus, racial categories encompass different ethnic groups. For example, the racial category *white* includes ethnic groups such as Irish, Italian, and Polish Americans. Unfortunately, many fail to recognize ethnic distinctions among people of color. For example, not all blacks in the United States are African American; some are Haitian, Jamaican, or Nigerian.

The term *race* first appeared in the Romance languages of Europe in the Middle Ages to refer to breeding stock (Smedley, 1993). A "race" of horses described common ancestry and a distinctive appearance or behavior. *Race* appears to have been first applied to New World peoples by the Spanish in the 16th century. Later it was adopted by the English, again in reference to people of the New World, and generally came to mean "people," "nation," or "variety." By the late 18th century, "when scholars became more actively engaged in investigations, classifications, and definitions of human populations, the term 'race' was elevated as the one major symbol and mode of human group differentiation employed extensively for non-European groups and even those in Europe who varied in some way from the subjective norm" (Smedley, 1993:39).

Though elevated to the level of science, the concept of race continued to reflect its origins in animal breeding. Farmers and herders had used the concept to describe stock bred for particular qualities; scholars used it to suggest that human behaviors could also be inherited. "Unlike other terms for classifying people . . . the term 'race' places emphasis on innateness, on the inbred nature of whatever is being judged" (Smedley, 1993:39). Like animal breeders, scholars also presumed that appearance revealed something about potential behavior. Just as the selective breeding of animals entailed the ranking of stock by some criteria, scholarly use of the concept of race involved the ranking of humans. Differences in skin color, hair texture, and the shape of head, eyes, nose, lips, and body were developed into an elaborate hierarchy of merit and potential for "civilization."

The idea of race emerged among all the European colonial powers, although their conceptions of it varied. However, only the British in North America and South Africa constructed a system of rigid, exclusive racial categories and a social order *based on race,* a "racialized social structure" (Omi and Winant, 1994). "[S]kin color variations in many regions of the world and in many societies have been imbued with some degree of social value or significance, but color prejudice or preferences do not of themselves amount to a fully evolved racial worldview . . ." (Smedley, 1993:25).

This racialized social structure—which in America produced a race-based system of slavery and subsequently a race-based distribution of political, legal, and social rights—was a historical first. "Expansion, conquest, exploitation, and enslavement have characterized much of human history over the past five thousand years or so, but none of these events before the modern era resulted in the development of ideologies or social systems based on race" (Smedley, 1993:25, 15). While differences of color had long been noted, societies had never been built on those differences.

As scientists assumed that race differences involved more than simply skin color or hair texture, they sought the biological distinctiveness of racial categories—but with little success. In the early 20th century, anthropologists looked to physical features such as height, stature, and head shape to distinguish the races, only to learn that these are affected by environment and nutrition. Later the search turned to genetic traits carried in the blood, only to find that those cannot be correlated with conventional racial classifications. Even efforts to reach a consensus about how many races exist or what specific features distinguish them from one another are problematic. As one anthropologist has put it, "Classifying people by color is very much like classifying cars by color. Those in the same classification look alike . . . but the classification tells you nothing about the hidden details of construction or about how the cars or people will perform" (Cohen, 1998:12).

> If our eyes could perceive more than the superficial, we might find race in chromosome 11: there lies the gene for hemoglobin. If you divide humankind by which of two forms of the gene each person has, than equatorial Africans, Italians and Greeks fall into the "sickle-cell race"; Swedes and South Africa's Xhosas (Nelson Mandela's ethnic group) are in the healthy hemoglobin race. Or do you prefer to group people by whether they have epicanthic eye folds, which produce the "Asian" eye? Then the !Kung San (Bushmen) belong with the Japanese and Chinese. . . . [D]epending on which traits you pick, you can form very surprising races. Take the scooped-out shape of the back of the front teeth, a standard "Asian" trait. Native Americans and Swedes have these shovel-shaped incisors, too, and so would fall in the same race. Is biochemistry better? Norwegians, Arabians, north Indians and the Fulani of northern Nigeria . . . fall into the "lactase race" (the lactase enzyme digests milk sugar). Everyone else—other Africans, Japanese, Native Americans—form the "lactase-deprived race" (their ancestors did not drink milk from cows or goats and hence never evolved the lactase gene). How about blood types, the familiar A, B, and O groups? Then Germans and New Guineans, populations that have the same percentages of each type, are in one race; Estonians and Japanese comprise a separate one for the same reason. . . . The dark skin of Somalis and Ghanaians, for instance, indicates that they evolved under the same selective force (a sunny climate). But that's all it shows. It does *not* show that they are any more closely related in the sense of sharing more genes than either is to Greeks. Calling Somalis and Ghanaians "black" therefore sheds no further light on their evolutionary history and implies—wrongly—that they are more closely related to each other than either is to

> someone of a different "race." . . . If you pick at random any two "blacks" walking along the street, and analyze their 23 pairs of chromosomes, you will probably find that their genes have less in common than do the genes of one of them with that of a random "white" person. (Begley, 1995:67, 68)

The "no-race" position now dominates the fields of physical anthropology and human genetics (Cohen, 1998). This perspective argues that "(1) Biological variability exists but this variability does not conform to the discrete packages labeled races. (2) So-called racial characteristics are not transmitted as complexes. (3) Races do not exist because isolation of groups has been infrequent; populations have always interbred" (Lieberman, 1968:128). Still, few scholars outside of anthropology seem to have been affected by this knowledge.

> [I]t does not appear that this debate [about the existence of race] has had widespread impact on professionals in the fields of medicine, psychology, sociology, history, or political science. . . . [I]t will suffice to point out that virtually all scholars who write about "race and intelligence" assume that the "races" which they study are distinguished on the basis of biologically relevant criteria. So accepted is this fact that most scholars engaged in such research never consider it necessary to justify their assignment of individuals to this or that "race." . . . [Thus], the layman who reads the literature on race and racial groupings is justified in assuming that the existent typologies have been derived through the application of theories and methods current in disciplines concerned with the biological study of human variation. Since the scientific racial classifications which a layman finds in the literature are not too different from popular ones, he can be expected to feel justified in the maintenance of his views on race. (Marshall, 1993:117, 121)

In all, the primary significance of race is as a *social* concept: We "see" it, we expect it to tell us something significant about a person, and we organize social policy, law, and the distribution of wealth, power, and prestige around it. From the essentialist position, race is assumed to exist independently of our perception of it; it is assumed to significantly distinguish people from one another. From the constructionist perspective, race exists because we have created it as a meaningful category of difference among people.

Dichotomizing Sexual Orientation Many similarities exist in the construction of race and sexual orientation. First, both are often dichotomized—into black/white, white/nonwhite, or gay/straight—and individuals are expected to fit easily into one category or the other. While popular discussion of bisexuality is increasing and some gay organizations have added the term to their title, the depth of support for this third category is not yet clear. For example, many people publicly assert that bisexuals either are "really" gay (Pope and Reynolds, 1991) or are heterosexuals who are merely experimenting with same-sex relationships. In either case, the accepted options are still only gay or straight.

Scientists have sought biological differences between gay and straight people just as they have looked for such differences between the "races." In Reading 13, Barbara Sherman Heyl notes that such research is intrinsically suspect, since we are unlikely to find any biological structure or process that *all* gay people share but *no* straight people have. Still, the conviction that such differences must exist propels the search and leads to the naive acceptance of questionable findings (as Gilbert Zicklin describes in Reading 41).

As with race, sexual orientation appears more straightforward than it is. Because sexuality encompasses physical, social, and emotional attraction, as well as actual sexual behavior, fantasies, and self-identity (Klein, 1978), determining one's sexual orientation may involve emphasizing one of these features over the others. Just as the system of racial classification asks people to pick *one* race, the sexual orientation system requires that all the different aspects of sexuality be distilled into one of two possible choices.

For example, an acquaintance described the process by which he came to self-identify as gay. In high school and college he had dated and been sexually active with women, but his relations with men had always been more important to him. He looked to men for emotional and social gratification and for relief from "gender games" he felt required to play with women. He had been engaged to be married, but when that ended he spent his time exclusively with other men. Eventually he established a sexual relationship with another man and came to identify himself as gay. His experience reflects the varied dimensions of sexuality and shows the resolution of those differences by choosing a single sexual identity. Rather than say "I used to be straight but I am now gay," he described himself as always "really" having been gay.

Alfred Kinsey's landmark survey of American sexual practices, described by Barbara Sherman Heyl in Reading 13,[9] showed that same-sex experience was more common than had been assumed, and that sexual practices could change over the lifespan. Kinsey suggested that instead of thinking about "homosexuals" and "heterosexuals" as if these were two discrete categories of people, we should recognize that sexual behavior exists along a continuum from those who are exclusively heterosexual to those who are exclusively gay.

Further, there is no necessary correspondence between identity and sexual behavior. Someone who self-identifies as gay is still likely to have had some heterosexual experience; someone who self-identifies as straight may have had some same-sex experience; and even someone with no sexual experience can lay claim to being gay or straight. Identity is not always directly tied to behavior. Indeed, a person who self-identifies as gay may have had *more* heterosexual experience than someone who self-identifies as straight. This distinction between identity and experience was underscored by the results of a 1994 survey, the most comprehensive American sex survey since Kinsey's. Only 2.8 percent of the men and 1.4 percent of the women identified themselves as gay, but an additional 7.3 percent and 7.2 percent, respectively, reported a same-sex experience or attraction (Michael, 1994).

One last analogy between the construction of race and sexual orientation bears discussion. Most Americans would not question the logic of this sentence: "Tom has

---

[9]Heyl's article is titled "Homosexuality: A Social Phenomenon." The subtitle conveys Heyl's constructionist orientation, since in sociological theory the term *phenomenon* emphasizes the constructed dimension of social life. Heyl is not using the term to indicate something extraordinary or unusual.

been monogamously married for 30 years and had a dozen children, but I think he's *really* gay." In a real-life illustration of the same logic, a young man and woman were often seen kissing on our campus. When this became the subject of a class discussion, a suggestive ripple of laughter went through the room: Everyone "knew" that the young man was really gay.

How could they "know" that? For such conclusions to make sense, we must believe that someone could be gay irrespective of his or her actual behavior. Just as it is possible in this culture for one to be "black" even if one looks "white," apparently one may be gay despite acting straight. Just as "black" can be established by any African heritage, "gay" is apparently established by displaying any behavior thought to be associated with gays. Indeed, "gay" can be "established" by reputation alone, by a failure to demonstrate heterosexuality, or even by the demonstration of an overly aggressive heterosexuality. In all, "gay" can be assigned no matter what one actually does. Sociologist Jack Katz (1975) explains this as the imposition of an *essential identity,* that is, an identity assigned to an individual *irrespective of his or her actual behavior,* as in "I know she's a genius even though she's flunking all her courses." Because "gay" is understood as an essential identity in our culture, it can be assigned no matter what one's behavior. Because no behavior can ever prove one is *not* gay, this label is an extremely effective mechanism of social control.

In all, several parallels exist between race and sexual orientation classifications. With both, we assume there are a limited number of possibilities—usually two, but no more than three—and we assume individuals can be easily fit into one or another of these options. We treat both race and sexual orientation categories as encompassing populations that are internally homogeneous and profoundly dissimilar from each other. For both, this presumption of difference has prompted a wide-ranging search for the biological distinctiveness of the categories. Different races or sexual orientations are judged superior and inferior to one another, and members of each category historically have been granted unequal legal and social rights. Finally, we assume that sexual orientation, like color, tells us something meaningful about a person.

Dichotomizing Class Although the case is less clear-cut, social class is often reduced to a dichotomy between the poor and the vast middle class. This dichotomy is treated as reflecting individual merit.

Americans, more than people of other nationalities, explain success and failure in terms of *individual merit* rather than economic or social forces (Morris and Williamson, 1982). As Richard Kahlenberg and Ronald Mincey describe (in Readings 10 and 11, respectively), an emphasis on individual values, attributes, and lifestyle—rather than unemployment, discrimination, or a changing economy—has long characterized popular opinion and research on social class. Americans are prone to think that those who are financially successful have become so on the basis of their merit and those who fail do so by virtue of their faults. Indeed, many talk about social class as if it were just the result of personal values or attitudes. Surveys indicate that over half of the American public believe "that lack of effort by the poor was the principal reason for poverty, or a reason at least equal to any that was beyond a person's control. . . . Popular majorities did not consider any other factor to be a very important cause of poverty—not low wages, or a scarcity of jobs, or discrimination, or even sickness" (Schwarz and Volgy, 1992:11).

This attribution of poverty and wealth to individual merit hides the complex reality of American social class. It ignores those who work but earn less than the poverty line—a group estimated to be as high as 12 million workers (Schwarz and Volgy, 1992). It also defines those in the highest income brackets as "really just like the rest of us," that is, middle class. Although Americans are aware of a broad range of social class differences (Jackman and Jackman, 1983; Vanneman and Cannon, 1987), the widespread conviction that one's station in life reflects one's merit in many ways overwhelms this awareness. In a strikingly essentialist formulation, social class standing is taken to reveal one's essential nature and merit. Two presumably homogeneous and distinct categories are constructed: the poor and the rest of us.

Because social class is seldom discussed in American society, the vocabulary for talking about it is not well developed. Indeed, it appears that we often substitute race for class. For example, the common assumption that people of color are poor and whites well-off simply applies the dichotomy of race to the arena of social class. Just as the American/non-American distinction functions to mean white/nonwhite, the middle class/poor dichotomy is often understood to mean white/nonwhite.

Dichotomizing Sex First, to distinguish the terms *sex* and *gender, sex* refers to females and males—that is, to chromosomal, hormonal, anatomical, and physiological differences—and *gender* describes the socially constructed roles associated with each sex. Gender is learned; it is the culturally and historically specific acting out of "masculinity" and "femininity." The term is often used erroneously as being synonymous with sex. For example, newspapers describe what are really sex differences in voting as gender differences. In these Framework Essays, however, the distinction between the two terms will be maintained.

While the approach may be unsettling, sex can be understood as a socially created dichotomy much like race, sexual orientation, or gender. Readings 7 and 8 by developmental geneticist Anne Fausto-Sterling and anthropologist Walter Williams describe the belief in Western culture that there are two, and only two, sexes and that all individuals can be clearly identified as one or the other (Kessler and McKenna, 1978). But like sexual orientation, sex refers to a complex set of attributes—anatomical, chromosomal, hormonal, physiological—that may sometimes be inconsistent with one another or with individuals' sense of their own identity. This was illustrated by a Spanish athlete who is anatomically female, but in a pregame genetic test was classified as male. On the basis of that test, she was excluded from the 1985 World University Games. She was then reclassed as female in 1991, when the governing body for track-and-field contests abandoned genetic testing and returned to physical inspection. As the gynecologist for the sports federation noted, "about 1 in 20,000 people has genes that conflict with his or her apparent gender" (Lemonick, 1992).

Just as with race and sexual orientation, membership is assigned to one or the other sex category regardless of inconsistent or ambiguous evidence. Indeed, the conviction that there ought to be consistency between the physical and psychological dimensions of sex propels some people into sex change surgery in an effort to produce a body consistent with their self-identities. Others will pursue psychotherapy to find an identity consistent with their bodies. In either case, it makes more sense to us to use surgery and therapy to create consistency than to accept inconsistency: a man who feels like a woman must become a woman rather than just being a man who feels like a woman.

The Social Construction of Disability

Our discussion of race, sexual orientation, sex, and social class has emphasized that each of these categories encompasses a continuum of behavior and characteristics rather than a finite set of discrete or easily separated groupings. It has also stressed that difference is a social creation—that differences of color or sex, for example, have no meaning other than what is attributed to them.

Can the same be said about ability and disability, which also qualify as master statuses? It is often assumed that people are easily classed as able-bodied or disabled, but that is no more true in this case than it is for the other master statuses. The comments of sociologist Irving Zola show how our use of statistics contributes to the misconception of ability/disability as fixed and dichotomous.

> The way we report statistics vis-à-vis disability and disease is generally misleading. If we speak of ratio figures for a particular disease as 1 in 8, 1 in 14, etc., we perpetuate what Rene Dubos (1961) once called "The Mirage of Health." For these numbers convey that if 1 person in 10 *does get* a particular disease, that 9 out of 10 *do not.* This means, however, only that those 9 people do not get *that* particular disease. It does not mean that they are disease-free, nor are they likely to be so. . . .
>
> Similarly deceptive is the now-popular figure of "43 million people with a disability" . . . for it implies that there are over 200 million Americans without a disability. . . . But the metaphor of being but a banana-peel slip away from disability is inappropriate. The issue of disability for individuals . . . is not *whether* but *when,* not so much *which one* but *how many* and *in what combination.* (Zola, 1993:18)

However, recognizing an ability/disability dichotomy as illogical may be easier than understanding the case that disability is socially constructed. The latter case, which has emerged in the disability rights movement, is made by Michelle Fine and Adrienne Asch in Reading 18 and Michael Oliver in Reading 41. Rather than treating disability as a defect within an individual, this approach argues that disability is created by physical and social environments. While individuals may be "impaired," it is the environment that disables them.

For example, disability is created by environments that lack the physical design or social supports that would make life worth living.

> Larry McAfee was aged 34 when a motorcycle accident resulted in complete paralysis and the need to use a ventilator. His insurance benefit (of $1 million) enabled him to employ personal care attendants in his own home for a period after his accident but when this ran out he was forced to enter a nursing home. He decided life wasn't worth living and tried turning his respirator off but couldn't cope with the feeling of suffocation. So he

> petitioned the courts to be allowed to be sedated while someone else unplugged his breathing apparatus. . . .
>
> Yet when, as a result of the publicity, McAfee received an outpouring of support from disability activists, he decided to delay the decision to take his own life. What he really wanted was to live in his own home and get a job. . . .
>
> It is not the physical disability itself but the social and economic circumstances of the experience which can lead to a diminished quality of life. (Morris, 1991:40–41)

Not only is disability the result of disabling environments, but the categories of disability are themselves socially constructed. "Epilepsy, illness, disease, and disability are not 'givens' in nature . . . but rather *socially constructed* categories that emerge from the interpretive activities of people acting together in social situations" (Schneider, 1988:65). Learning disabilities are an example of this process.

> Before the late 1800s when observers began to write about "word blindness," and, more significantly, before the mid-1960s when educators and others began to popularize learning disability, it did not exist. Learning disability did not exist as a means for making sense of difficulties people experienced in learning groups (Coles, 1987). Even the human variation (i.e., the learning difficulties) to which it refers has not existed for most of human history. However, today almost 2 million students are served as learning disabled, more than are served through any other disability category (U.S. Department of Education, 1990:12). (Higgins, 1992:9)

While both abled and disabled individuals participate in the social construction of disability, they do not do so on an equal basis. Cultural concepts such as dependence and independence—which bear heavily on judgments about what constitutes a disability—are most often imposed on disabled people by those not so identified.

> In terms of the physical world, none of us—whether disabled or not—is completely independent in the sense that we rely on nothing and nobody. However, the meaning of our dependence on others and on the physical world is determined by both its socio-economic and ideological context. For example, we all depend on water coming out of the tap when we turn it on, while a disabled person depends on someone to help her get dressed in the morning. However, when non-disabled people talk about water coming out of the tap, the issue is whether the water company is reliable; when they talk about [a disabled person] being dependent on an assistant, the issue for them is what they see as her helplessness created by her physical limitations. (Morris, 1991:137–38)

In both these ways—physical and conceptual—we create disability. "Through our beliefs and our behaviors, through our policies and our practices, we make disability (Albrecht, 1981:275; Ferguson, 1987). Through interpersonal, organizational, and social activities, we make disability (Bogdan and Biklen, 1977). In all areas of social life we make and remake disability" (Higgins, 1992:6).

Constructing the "Other"

We have seen how the complexity of a population may be reduced to aggregates and then to a simplistic dichotomy. Aggregation assumes that those who share a master status are alike in "essential" ways. It ignores the multiple and conflicting statuses an individual inevitably occupies. Dichotomization especially promotes the image of a mythical *Other* who is not at all like "us." Whether in race, sex, sexual orientation, or social class, dichotomization yields a vision of "them" as profoundly different. Ultimately, dichotomization results in stigmatizing those who are less powerful. It provides the grounds for whole categories of people to become the objects of contempt.

Constructing "Others" as Profoundly Different The expectation that Others are profoundly different can be seen most clearly in the significance that has been attached to sex differences. In this case, biological differences between males and females have been the grounds from which to infer an extensive range of nonbiological differences. Women and men are assumed to differ from each other in behavior, perception, and personality, and such differences are used to argue for different legal, social, and economic roles and rights. The expectation that men and women are not at all alike is so widespread that we often talk about them as members of the "opposite" sex; indeed, it is not unusual to talk about the "war" between the sexes.

While this assumption of difference undergirds everyday life as well as scientific research, as Susan Basow describes in Reading 9, few significant differences in behavior, personality, or even physical ability have been found between men and women of any age. The lack of difference between women and men is especially striking given the degree to which we are all socialized. Thus, while boys and girls, and men and women, are often socialized to be different as well as treated differently, this does not mean they inevitably *become* different. Even though decades of research have confirmed few differences, the search for difference continues and, as Basow suggests, may even have been intensified by the failure to find many differences.

The same expectation that the Other differs in personality or behavior emerges in race, class, and sexual orientation classifications. Race differences are expected to involve more than just differences of color, those who are "gay" or "straight" are expected to differ in more ways than just their sexual orientation, while the poor and middle class are expected to differ in more than just economic standing. In each case, scientific research is directed toward finding such differences.

Sanctioning Those Who Associate with the "Other" There are also similarities in the sanctions against those who cross race, sex, class, or sexual orientation boundaries. Parents sometimes disown children who marry outside of their racial or social class group, just as they often sever connections with children who are gay. Those who associate with the Other are also in danger of being labeled a member of that category.

For example, during Reconstruction the fear of an invisible black ancestry was pervasive among southern whites, since that heritage would subject them to nascent segregation. "Concern about people passing as white became so great that even behaving like blacks or willingly associating with them were often treated as more important than any proof of actual black ancestry" (Davis, 1991:56). Thus, southern whites who associated with blacks ran the risk of being defined as black.

A contemporary parallel can be found in gay/straight relations. Those who associate with gays and lesbians or defend gay rights are often presumed—by gays and straights alike—to be gay. Many men report that when they object to homophobic remarks, they simply become the target of them. Indeed, the prestige of young men in fraternities and other all-male groups often rests on a willingness to disparage women and gays (Sanday, 1990).

Similarly, few contemporary reactions are as strongly negative as that against men who appear feminine. Because acting like a woman is so disparaged, boys learn at an early age to control their behavior or suffer public humiliation. This ridicule has its greatest effect on young men; the power and prestige usually available to older men reduces their susceptibility to such accusations. There is a long list of behavior young men must avoid for fear of being called feminine or gay: Don't be too emotional, watch how you sit, don't move your hips when you walk, take long strides, don't put your hands on your hips, don't talk too much, don't let your voice show emotion, don't be too compliant or eager to please, etc.

Because effeminate men are often assumed to be gay, they become targets for verbal and physical abuse. The popular linkage of effeminate behavior with a gay sexual orientation is so strong that it may be the primary criterion most people use to decide who is gay: A "masculine" man must be straight, a "feminine" man must be gay. But gender and sexual orientation are *separate* phenomena. Knowing that someone is a masculine man or a feminine woman does not tell us what that person's sexual orientation is—indeed, our guesses are most likely to be "false negatives"; that is, we are likely to falsely identify someone as straight. Since we do not know who around us is gay, we cannot accurately judge how gay people behave.

In the world of mutual Othering, being labeled one of "them" is a remarkably effective social control mechanism. Boys and men control their behavior so that they are not called gay. Members of racial and ethnic groups maintain distance from one another to avoid the criticism that might be leveled by members of their own and other groups. These social controls are effective because all parties are willing to enforce them.

Stigma

In the extreme, those depicted as Other may be said to be *stigmatized.* The stigmatization of whole categories of people is the outcome of large-scale social and historical processes.

The term *stigma* comes from ancient Greece, where it meant a "bodily sign designed to expose something unusual and bad about the moral status of [an individual]" (Goffman, 1963:1). Such signs were "cut or burnt into the body to advertise that the bearer was a slave, a criminal, or a blemished person, ritually polluted, to be avoided, especially in public places" (Goffman, 1963:1). Stigmatized people are those "marked" as bad, unworthy, and polluted because of the category they belong to, for example, their race, sex, sexual orientation, or social class category. The core assumption behind stigma is that internal merit is revealed through external features—for the Greeks, that a brand or a cut showed the moral worth of the person. This is not an unusual linkage; for example, physically attractive people are often assumed to possess a variety of positive attributes (Adams, 1982). Because they look good, it is thought they must *be* good.

Such judgments of worth based on membership in certain categories have a self-fulfilling potential. Those who are judged superior by virtue of their membership in some acceptable category are given more opportunity to prove their worth; those who are judged less worthy by virtue of membership in a stigmatized category have a difficult time establishing their merit no matter what they do. For example, experimental evidence from social psychology indicates that many whites perceive blacks as incompetent, regardless of evidence to the contrary: White subjects were "reluctant or unable to recognize that a black person is higher or equal in intelligence compared to themselves" (Gaertner and Dovidio, 1986:75). This would explain why many whites react negatively to affirmative action programs. If they cannot conceive of black applicants as being more qualified than whites, they will see such programs as only mandates to hire the less qualified.

Stigma involves objectification as well as devaluation. *Objectification* means treating people as if they were objects, members of a category rather than possessors of individual characteristics. In objectification, the "living, breathing, complex individual" ceases to be seen or valued (Allport, 1958:175). In its extreme, those who are objectified are "viewed as having no other noteworthy status or identity. When that point is reached a person becomes *nothing* but 'a delinquent,' 'a cripple,' 'a homosexual,' 'a black,' 'a woman.' The indefinite article 'a' underlines the depersonalized nature of such response" (Schur, 1984:30–31).

Examples of Stigmatized Master Statuses: Women and the Poor Sociologist Edwin Schur argues that since women are subject to both objectification and devaluation, they are stigmatized. First, considering objectification, Schur argues that women are seen

> as all alike, and therefore substitutable for one another; as innately passive and object-like; as easily ignored, dismissed, trivialized, treated as childlike, and even as a nonperson; as having a social standing only through their attachments to men (or other non-stigmatized groups); and as a group which can be easily victimized through harassment, violence, and discrimination. (Schur, 1984:33)

Objectification occurs when women are thought of as generally indistinguishable from one another, as for example when someone says, "Let's get the woman's angle on this story"; or "Tonight I'm going to get one of these women in bed with me." In these statements, one woman stands for "any woman"; they are all the same, interchangeable.

African Americans, Latinos, Asian Americans, and gay/lesbian people are often similarly treated as indistinguishable from one another. Indeed, hate crimes have been defined by this quality of interchangeability, such as the attack on any black family that moves into a neighborhood or the assault on any woman or man who looks gay. Hate crimes are also marked by excessive brutality, personal violence rather than property destruction, and are likely to have been perpetrated by multiple offenders—all of which indicate that the victims have been objectified (Levin and McDevitt, 1993).

Some members of stigmatized categories objectify themselves in the same ways that they are objectified by others. Thus, women may evaluate their own worth in terms of physical appearance. In the process of self-objectification, a woman "joins the spectators of herself"; that is, she views herself as if from the outside, as if she were nothing more than what she looked like (Berger, 1963:50). This sense of making an object of oneself was captured by a cereal commercial in which a bikini-clad woman posed before a mirror. She had lost weight for an upcoming vacation and was imagining herself as a stranger on the beach might see her. Thus, she succeeded in making an object of herself. While physical appearance is also valued for men, it rarely takes precedence over all other qualities. Rather, men are more likely to be objectified in terms of wealth and power.

In addition to being objectified, there is a strong case that American women as a category remain devalued, a conclusion drawn from the characteristics most frequently attributed to men and women. Research conducted over the last 40 years has documented a remarkable consistency in those attributes. Both sexes are described as possessing valued qualities, but the characteristics attributed to men are more valued in the culture as a whole. For example, the female-valued characteristics include being talkative, gentle, religious, aware of the feelings of others, security oriented, and attentive to personal appearance. Male-valued traits include being aggressive, independent, unemotional, objective, dominant, active, competitive, logical, adventurous, and direct (Basow, 1992).[10] (Remember that these attributes are only people's beliefs about sex differences.)

In many ways, the characteristics attributed to women are inconsistent with core American values. While American culture values achievement, individualism, and action—all understood as male attributes—women are expected to subordinate their personal interests to the family and to be passive and patient (Richardson, 1977). In all, "women are asked to become the kind of people that this culture does not value" (Richardson, 1977:11). Thus, it is more acceptable for women to display masculine traits, since these are culturally valued, than it is for men to display less-valued feminine characteristics. Men who are talkative, gentle, religious, aware of the feelings of others, security oriented, and attentive to personal appearance are much maligned. In contrast, women may be independent, unemotional, objective, dominant, active, competitive, logical, adventurous, and direct with less negative consequences. The characteristics we attribute to women are not valued for everyone, unlike the characteristics attributed to men.

Much of what we have described about the stigmatization of women applies to the poor as well. Indeed, being poor is a much more obviously shameful status than being female. The category *poor* is intrinsically devalued. It is presumed there is

---

[10]"Compared with White women, Black women are viewed as less passive, dependent, status conscious, emotional and concerned about their appearance. . . . Hispanic women tend to be viewed as more 'feminine' than White women in terms of submissiveness and dependence. . . . [A] similar stereotype holds for Asian women, but with the addition of exotic sexuality. . . . Native-American women typically are stereotyped as faceless . . . drudges without any personality. . . . Jewish women are stereotyped as either pushy, vain 'princesses' or overprotective, manipulative 'Jewish mothers' . . . working-class women are stereotyped as more hostile, confused, inconsiderate and irresponsible than middle-class women . . . and lesbians are stereotyped as possessing masculine traits" (Basow, 1992:4).

little commendable to be said about poor people; "they" are primarily constructed as a "problem." Poor people are also objectified; they are described as "*the* poor," as if they were all alike, substitutable for and interchangeable with one another.

> Most of the writing about poor people, even by sympathetic observers, tells us that they are different, truly strangers in our midst: Poor people think, feel, and act in ways unlike middle-class Americans. . . .
>
> We can think about poor people as "them" or as "us." For the most part, Americans have talked about "them." Even in the language of social science, as well as in ordinary conversation and political rhetoric, poor people usually remain outsiders, strangers to be pitied or despised, helped or punished, ignored or studied, but rarely full citizens, members of a larger community on the same terms as the rest of us. They are . . . "those people," objects of curiosity, analysis, prurience, or compassion, not subjects who construct their own lives and history. Poor people seem cardboard cutouts, figures in single dimension, members of inferior categories, rarely complex, multifaceted, even contradictory in the manner of other persons. (M. Katz, 1989:6, 126)

Like women, poor people are not expected to display attributes valued in the culture as a whole.

Stereotypes about People in Stigmatized Master Statuses Finally, in an effort to capture the general features of what "we" say about "them," let us consider five common stereotypes about individuals in stigmatized master statuses.

First, they are presumed to lack the values the culture holds dear. Neither women nor those who are poor, gay, black, Asian American, or Hispanic are expected to be independent, unemotional, objective, dominant, active, competitive, logical, adventurous, or direct. Stigmatized people are presumed to lack precisely those values that nonstigmatized people are expected to possess.

Second, stigmatized people are likely to be seen as a problem (Adam, 1978; Wilson and Gutierrez, 1985). Certainly black, Latino, and Native American men and women, gay and lesbian people of all colors, white women, and people living in poverty are constructed as *having* problems and *being* problems. Often the implication is that they are responsible for all of "our" problems. While there are occasions for the celebration of the historic contributions of such groups to the culture, little in the public discourse lauds their current contributions. Indeed, those in stigmatized categories are often constructed as *nothing but a problem,* as if they had no life or existence apart from those problems. This was illustrated by a black student who described her shock at hearing white students describe her middle-class neighborhood as a "ghetto."

Ironically, this depiction of stigmatized people as nothing but a problem is often accompanied by the trivialization of those problems. For example, "a majority of voting Americans believe that Asian Americans are not discriminated against" (U.S. Commission on Civil Rights, 1992) despite evidence of racial harassment and employment discrimination (Feagin and Feagin, 1999). Despite the annual participation of hundreds of thousands of people in Gay Pride marches throughout the country, television footage typically focuses on the small number in drag. Whites' opinion that blacks prefer welfare to supporting themselves (a 1992 poll showed

78 percent of whites affirming that view) similarly trivializes the experience of poverty (Thornton and Whitman, 1992). The pervasive belief that women and men are now treated equally in employment dismisses the wage gap that continues to characterize male/female earnings, as Andrew Hacker describes in Reading 37. Thus, the problems that stigmatized categories of people create for those in privileged statuses are highlighted, while the problems they experience are discounted.

Third, people in stigmatized master statuses are stereotyped as lacking self-control; they are characterized as being lustful, immoral, and carriers of disease (Gilman, 1985, 1991). Currently, such accusations hold center stage in the depictions of gay men, but historically such charges have been leveled at African American, Latino, and Asian American men (e.g., Chinese immigrants in the late 19th century). Poor women and women of color have been and continue to be depicted as promiscuous, and poor men and women are presumed to be morally irresponsible.

Fourth, people in stigmatized categories are often marked as having too much or too little intelligence, and in either case as tending to deception or criminality. Many stigmatized categories of people have been assumed to use their "excessive" intelligence to unfair advantage. This was historically the case for Jews, and now appears to be the case for Asian American college students.

> [T]he educational achievement of Asian American students was, and continues to be, followed by a wave of reaction. The image of Asian Americans as diligent super-students has often kindled resentment in other students. Sometimes called "damned curve raisers," a term applied first to Jewish students at elite East Coast colleges during the 1920s and 1930s, Asian American students have increasingly found themselves taking the brunt of campus racial jokes. (Takagi, 1992:60)

Fifth, people in stigmatized categories are often depicted as both childlike and savagely brutal. Historically, characterizations of Native Americans, enslaved Africans, and Chinese immigrants reflected these conceptions. Currently, the same is true for the poor in their representation as both pervasively violent and irresponsible. A related depiction of women as both "virgins and whores" has been well documented in historical and contemporary scholarship.

Perhaps because people in stigmatized master statuses are stereotyped as deviant, it appears that those who commit violence against them are unlikely to be punished. For example, "major offenses *against* women which we *profess* to consider deviant, in practice have been responded to with much ambivalence" (Schur, 1984:7). As another example, "of the 16,000 executions in U.S. history, only thirty cases involved a white sentenced for killing a black" (Smolowe, 1991:68). One way to recognize a stigmatized category of people is that the violence directed at them is not treated seriously (Schur, 1984).

Overall, individuals in stigmatized master statuses are represented as not only physically distinctive but in their behavior and attitudes as the antithesis of the culture's desired attributes. They do not operate from cultural values. They are problems; they are immoral and disease ridden; their intelligence is questionable; they are childlike and savage. Such characterizations serve to dismiss claims of discrimination and unfair treatment, affirming that those in stigmatized categories deserve such treatment, that they are themselves responsible for their plight. Indeed, many of these stereotypes are now applied to teenagers, whom the media depict as violent, reckless, hypersexed, ignorant, out of control, and the cause of society's problems (Males, 1994).

A Final Comment

It is disheartening to think of oneself as a member of a stigmatized group, just as it is disheartening to think of oneself as thoughtlessly perpetuating stigma. Still, there are at least two important points of hopefulness here. First, the characteristics attributed to stigmatized groups are similar across a great variety of master statuses. Thus, there is the relief of impersonality because the stigmatized characteristics are not tied to the actual characteristics of any particular group. Second, people who are stigmatized have often formed alliances with those who are not stigmatized to successfully lobby against these attributions.

As we said at the outset of this essay, our hope is to provide you with a framework by which to make sense of what sex, race, social class, and sexual orientation mean in contemporary American society. Clearly, these categorizations are complex; they are tied to issues of emotional intensity that are in many ways uniquely American; and they have consequences that are both mundane and dramatic. From naming, to aggregating, to dichotomizing, and ultimately to stigmatizing, difference has a meaning for us. The readings in Section I explore the construction of these categorizations; the readings in Section II examine how we experience them; and the readings in Section III address the meaning that is attributed to difference.

REFERENCES

Adam, Barry. 1978. *The Survival of Domination.* New York: Elsevier.

Adams, Gerald R. 1982. Physical Attractiveness. *In the Eye of the Beholder: Contemporary Issues in Stereotyping,* edited by A. G. Miller, 253–304. New York: Praeger.

Albrecht, Gary L. 1981. Cross-National Rehabilitation Policies: A Critical Assessment. *Cross-National Rehabilitation Policies: A Sociological Perspective,* edited by G. Albrecht, 269–77. Beverly Hills, CA: Sage.

Allport, Gordon. 1958. *The Nature of Prejudice.* Garden City, NY: Doubleday Anchor.

Basow, Susan A. 1992. *Gender: Stereotypes and Roles.* 3d ed. Pacific Grove, CA: Brooks/Cole Publishing.

Begley, Sharon. 1995. Three Is Not Enough. *Newsweek,* February 13, 1995, 67–69.

Berger, Peter L. 1963. *Invitation to Sociology: A Humanistic Perspective.* Garden City, NY: Doubleday Anchor.

Berke, Richard. 1998. Chasing the Polls on Gay Rights. *New York Times,* August 2, 4:3.

Bogdan, Robert, and Douglas Biklen. 1977. Handicapism. *Social Policy,* 7:14–19.

Choldin, Harvey M. 1986. Statistics and Politics: The "Hispanic Issue" in the 1980 Census. *Demography,* 23:403–18.

______. 1994. *Looking for the Last Percent: The Controversy over Census Undercounts.* New Brunswick, NJ: Rutgers University Press.

Cohen, Mark Nathan. 1998. *Culture of Intolerance: Chauvinism, Class, and Racism in the United States.* New Haven, CT: Yale University Press.

Coles, Gerald. 1987. *The Learning Mystique: A Critical Look at "Learning Disabilities."* New York: Pantheon.

Conrad, Peter, and Joseph W. Schneider. 1980. *Deviance and Medicalization: From Badness to Sickness.* Philadelphia: Temple University Press.

Davis, F. James. 1991. *Who Is Black? One Nation's Rule.* University Park, PA: Pennsylvania State University Press.

de la Garza, Rudolfo O., Louis DeSipio, F. Chris Garcia, John Garcia, and Angelo Falcon. 1992. *Latino Voices: Mexican, Puerto Rican, and Cuban Perspectives on American Politics.* Boulder, CO: Westview Press.

Dubos, Rene. 1961. *Mirage of Health.* Garden City, NY: Anchor Books.

Espiritu, Yen Le. 1992. *Asian American Panethnicity: Bridging Institutions and Identities.* Philadelphia: Temple University Press.

Faderman, Lillian. 1991. *Odd Girls and Twilight Lovers: A History of Lesbian Life in Twentieth-Century America.* New York: Penguin Books.

Feagin, Joe R., and Clairece Booher Feagin. 1999. *Racial and Ethnic Relations.* 6th ed. Upper Saddle River, NJ: Prentice-Hall.

Ferguson, Philip M. 1987. The Social Construction of Mental Retardation. *Social Policy,* 18:51–52.

Gaertner, Samuel L., and John F. Dovidio. 1986. The Aversive Form of Racism. *Prejudice, Discrimination, and Racism,* edited by John F. Dovidio and Samuel L. Gaertner, 61–89. Orlando, FL: Academic Press.

Gilman, Sander. 1991. *The Jew's Body.* New York: Routledge.

———. 1985. *Difference and Pathology: Stereotypes of Sexuality, Race, and Madness.* Ithaca, NY: Cornell University Press.

Goffman, Erving. 1963. *Stigma: Notes on the Management of Spoiled Identity.* Englewood Cliffs, NJ: Prentice-Hall.

Gordon, Margaret T., and Stephanie Riger. 1989. *The Female Fear.* New York: The Free Press.

Henshel, Richard L., and Robert A. Silverman. 1975. *Perceptions in Criminology.* New York: Columbia University Press.

Higgins, Paul C. 1992. *Making Disability: Exploring the Social Transformation of Human Variation.* Springfield, IL: Charles C. Thomas.

Hilts, V. 1973. Statistics and Social Science. *Foundations of Scientific Method in the Nineteenth Century,* edited by R. Giere and R. Westfall, 206–33. Bloomington, IN: Indiana University Press.

Hirschman, Charles. 1996. Studying Immigrant Adaptation from the 1990 Population Census: From Generational Comparisons to the Process of "Becoming American." *The New Second Generation,* edited by A. Portes, 54–81. New York: Russell Sage Foundation.

Hu-Dehart, Evelyn. 1994. Asian/Pacific American Issues in American Education. Presentation at the 7th Annual National Conference on Race and Ethnicity in American Higher Education, Atlanta, sponsored by The Southwest Center for Human Relations Studies, University of Oklahoma, College of Continuing Education.

Jackman, Mary R., and Robert W. Jackman. 1983. *Class Awareness in the United States.* Berkeley, CA: University of California Press.

Katz, Jack. 1975. Essences as Moral Identities: Verifiability and Responsibility in Imputations of Deviance and Charisma. *American Journal of Sociology,* 80:1369–90.

Katz, Michael B. 1989. *The Undeserving Poor: From the War on Poverty to the War on Welfare.* New York: Pantheon Books.

Kessler, Suzanne J., and Wendy McKenna. 1978. *Gender: An Ethnomethodological Approach.* New York: John Wiley & Sons.
Kinsey, Alfred, Wardell Pomeroy, and Clyde Martin. 1948. *Sexual Behavior in the Human Male.* Philadelphia: W. B. Saunders.
Klein, Fritz. 1978. *The Bisexual Option.* New York: Arbor House.
Lemonick, Michael. 1992. Genetic Tests under Fire. *Time,* February 24, 65.
LeVay, Simon. 1991. A Difference in Hypothalmic Structure between Heterosexual and Homosexual Men. *Science,* 253:1034–37.
Levin, Jack, and Jack McDevitt. 1993. *Hate Crimes.* New York: Plenum Press.
Lieberman, Leonard. 1968. A Debate over Race: A Study in the Sociology of Knowledge. *Phylon,* 29:127–41.
Lopez, David, and Yen Espiritu. 1990. Panethnicity in the United States: A Theoretical Framework. *Ethnic and Racial Studies,* 13:198–224.
Males, Mike. 1994. Bashing Youth: Media Myths about Teenagers. *Extra!,* March/April, 8–11.
Marshall, Gloria. 1993. Racial Classifications: Popular and Scientific. *The "Racial" Economy of Science: Toward a Democratic Future,* edited by Sandra Harding, 116–27. Bloomington, IN: Indiana University Press (Originally published 1968).
Marshall, Gordon. 1994. *The Concise Oxford Dictionary of Sociology.* Oxford, UK: Oxford University Press.
Michael, Robert T. 1994. *Sex in America: A Definitive Survey.* Boston: Little, Brown.
Mills, Jane. 1989. *Womanwords: A Dictionary of Words about Women.* New York: Henry Holt.
Mohawk, John. 1992. Looking for Columbus: Thoughts on the Past, Present and Future of Humanity. *The State of Native America: Genocide, Colonization, and Resistance,* edited by M. Annette Jaimes, 439–44. Boston: South End Press.
Morris, Jenny. 1991. *Pride against Prejudice: Transforming Attitudes to Disability.* Philadelphia: New Society Publishers.
Morris, Michael, and John B. Williamson. 1982. Stereotypes and Social Class: A Focus on Poverty. *In the Eye of the Beholder,* edited by Arthur G. Miller, 411–65. New York: Praeger.
Morrison, Toni. 1992. *Playing in the Dark.* New York: Vintage.
Office of Management and Budget. 1995. Standards for the Classification of Federal Data on Race and Ethnicity Notice. *Federal Register* 60:44674–693.
———. October 1997. *Revisions to the Standards for the Classification of Federal Data on Race and Ethnicity.* Washington, DC: U.S. Government Printing Office.
Omi, Michael. 1996. Racialization in the Post–Civil Rights Era. *Mapping Multiculturalism,* edited by A. Gordon and C. Newfield, 178–85. Minneapolis: University of Minnesota Press.
———, and Howard Winant. 1994. *Racial Formation in the United States.* New York: Routledge.
Pfuhl, Erdwin H. 1986. *The Deviance Process.* 2d ed. Belmont, CA: Wadsworth.
Pope, Raechele L., and Amy L. Reynolds. 1991. Including Bisexuality: It's More Than Just a Label. *Beyond Tolerance: Gays, Lesbians, and Bisexuals on Campus,* edited by Nancy J. Evans and Vernon A. Wall, 205–11. Alexandria, VA: American College Personnel Association.
Richardson, Laurel. 1977. *The Dynamics of Sex and Gender: A Sociological Perspective.* New York: Harper and Row.

———. 1988. *The Dynamics of Sex and Gender: A Sociological Perspective.* 3d ed. New York: Harper and Row.

Rist, Darrell Yates. 1992. Are Homosexuals Born That Way? *The Nation,* 255:424–29.

Roediger, David. 1994. *Towards the Abolition of Whiteness.* London: Verso.

Sanday, Peggy Reeves. 1990. *Fraternity Gang Rape.* New York: New York University Press.

Schneider, Joseph W. 1988. Disability as Moral Experience: Epilepsy and Self in Routine Relationships. *Journal of Social Issues,* 44:63–78.

Schur, Edwin. 1984. *Labeling Women Deviant: Gender, Stigma, and Social Control.* New York: Random House.

Schwarz, John E., and Thomas J. Volgy. 1992. *The Forgotten Americans.* New York: W. W. Norton.

Shipman, Pat. 1994. *The Evolution of Racism: Human Differences and the Use and Abuse of Science.* New York: Simon and Schuster.

Shorris, Earl. 1992. *Latinos: A Biography of the People.* New York: W. W. Norton.

Smedley, Audrey. 1993. *Race in North America: Origin and Evolution of a Worldview.* Boulder, CO: Westview Press.

Smith, Tom W. 1992. Changing Racial Labels: From "Colored" to "Negro" to "Black" to "African American." *Public Opinion Quarterly,* 56:496–514.

Smolowe, Jill. 1991. Race and the Death Penalty. *Time,* April 29, 68–69.

Spelman, Elizabeth. 1988. *Inessential Woman.* Boston: Beacon Press.

Springer, S. P., and G. Deutsch. 1981. *Left Brain, Right Brain.* San Francisco: Freeman.

Steinberg, Stephen. 1989. *The Ethnic Myth: Race, Ethnicity, and Class in America.* Boston: Beacon Press.

Takagi, Dana Y. 1992. *The Retreat from Race: Asian-American Admission and Racial Politics.* New Brunswick, NJ: Rutgers University Press.

Takaki, Ronald. 1989. *Strangers from a Different Shore: A History of Asian Americans.* New York: Penguin.

———. 1990. *Iron Cages: Race and Culture in 19th-Century America.* New York: Oxford University Press.

———. 1993. *A Different Mirror.* Boston: Little Brown.

Tamayo Lott, Juanita. 1998. *Asian Americans: From Racial Category to Multiple Identities.* Walnut Creek, CA: Altamira Press.

Thornton, Jeannye, and David Whitman. 1992. Whites' Myths about Blacks. *U.S. News and World Report,* November 9, 41–44.

U.S. Commission on Civil Rights. 1973. *To Know or Not to Know: Collection and Use of Racial and Ethnic Data in Federal Assistance Programs.* Washington, DC: U.S. Government Printing Office.

———. 1992. *Civil Rights Issues Facing Asian Americans in the 1990s.* Washington, DC: U.S. Government Printing Office.

U.S. Department of Education, 1990. *To Assure the Free Appropriate Public Education of All Handicapped Children: Twelfth Annual Report to Congress on the Implementation of the Education of the Handicapped Act.* Washington, DC: U.S. Government Printing Office.

Vanneman, Reeve, and Lynn Weber Cannon. 1987. *The American Perception of Class.* Philadelphia: Temple University Press.

Weinberg, George. 1973. *Society and the Healthy Homosexual.* Garden City, NY: Anchor.

Wilson, II, Clint, and Felix Gutierrez. 1985. *Minorities and the Media.* Beverly Hills: Sage.

Zola, Irving K. 1993. Disability Statistics, What We Count and What It Tells Us: A Personal and Political Analysis. *Journal of Disability Policy Studies,* 4:10–37.

What Is Race?

READING 1

Who Is Black? One Nation's Definition

F. James Davis

In a taped interview conducted by a blind, black anthropologist, a black man nearly ninety years old said: "Now you must understand that this is just a name we have. I am not black and you are not black either, if you go by the evidence of your eyes. . . . Anyway, black people are all colors. White people don't look all the same way, but there are more different kinds of us than there are of them. Then too, there is a certain stage [at] which you cannot tell who is white and who is black. Many of the people I see who are thought of as black could just as well be white in their appearance. Many of the white people I see are black as far as I can tell by the way they look. Now, that's it for looks. Looks don't mean much. The things that makes us different is how we think. What we believe is important, the ways we look at life" (Gwaltney, 1980:96).

How does a person get defined as a black, both socially and legally, in the United States? What is the nation's rule for who is black, and how did it come to be? And so what? Don't we all know who is black, and isn't the most important issue what opportunities the group has? Let us start with some experiences of three well-known American blacks—actress and beauty pageant winner Vanessa Williams, U.S. Representative Adam Clayton Powell, Jr., and entertainer Lena Horne.

For three decades after the first Miss America Pageant in 1921, black women were barred from competing. The first black winner was Vanessa Williams of Millwood, New York, crowned Miss America in 1984. In the same year the first runner-up—Suzette Charles of Mays Landing, New Jersey—was also black. The viewing public was charmed by the television images and magazine pictures of the beautiful and musically talented Williams, but many people were also puzzled. Why was she being called black when she appeared to be white? Suzette Charles, whose ancestry appeared to be more European than African, at least looked like many of the "lighter blacks." Notoriety followed when Vanessa Williams resigned because of the impending publication of some nude photographs of her taken before the pageant, and Suzette Charles became Miss America for the balance of 1984. Beyond the troubling question of whether these young women could have won if they had looked "more black," the publicity dramatized the nation's definition of a black person.

Some blacks complained that the Rev. Adam Clayton Powell, Jr., was so light that he was a stranger in their midst. In the words of Roi Ottley, "He was white to all appearances, having blue eyes, an aquiline nose, and light, almost blond, hair" (1943:220), yet he became a bold, effective black leader—first as minister of the Abyssinian Baptist Church of Harlem, then as a New York city councilman, and finally as a U.S. congressman from the state of New York. Early in his activist career he led 6,000 blacks in a march on New York City Hall. He used his power in Congress to fight for civil rights legislation and other black causes. In 1966, in Washington, D.C., he convened the first black power conference.

In his autobiography, Powell recounts some experiences with racial classification in his youth that left a lasting impression on him. During Powell's freshman year at Colgate University, his roommate did not know that he was a black until his father, Adam Clayton Powell, Sr., was invited to give a chapel talk on Negro rights and problems, after which the roommate announced

F. James Davis is professor emeritus of sociology at Illinois State University.

that because Adam was a Negro they could no longer be roommates or friends.

Another experience that affected Powell deeply occurred one summer during his Colgate years. He was working as a bellhop at a summer resort in Manchester, Vermont, when Abraham Lincoln's aging son Robert was a guest there. Robert Lincoln disliked blacks so much that he refused to let them wait on him or touch his luggage, car, or any of his possessions. Blacks who did got their knuckles whacked with his cane. To the great amusement of the other bellhops, Lincoln took young Powell for a white man and accepted his services (Powell, 1971:31–33).

Lena Horne's parents were both very light in color and came from black upper-middle-class families in Brooklyn (Horne and Schickel, 1965; Buckley, 1986). Lena lived with her father's parents until she was about seven years old. Her grandfather was very light and blue-eyed. Her fair-skinned grandmother was the daughter of a slave woman and her white owner, from the family of John C. Calhoun, well-known defender of slavery. One of her father's great-grandmothers was a Blackfoot Indian, to whom Lena Horne has attributed her somewhat coppery skin color. One of her mother's grandmothers was a French-speaking black woman from Senegal and never a slave. Her mother's father was a "Portuguese Negro," and two women in his family had passed as white and become entertainers.

Lena Horne's parents had separated, and when she was seven her entertainer mother began placing her in a succession of homes in different states. Her favorite place was in the home of her Uncle Frank, her father's brother, a red-haired, blue-eyed teacher in a black school in Georgia. The black children in that community asked her why she was so light and called her a "yellow bastard." She learned that when satisfactory evidence of respectable black parents is lacking, being light-skinned implies illegitimacy and having an underclass white parent and is thus a disgrace in the black community. When her mother married a white Cuban, Lena also learned that blacks can be very hostile to the white spouse, especially when the "black" mate is very light. At this time she began to blame the confused color line for her childhood troubles. She later endured much hostility from blacks and whites alike when her own second marriage, to white composer-arranger Lennie Hayton, was finally made public in 1950 after three years of keeping it secret.

Early in Lena Horne's career there were complaints that she did not fit the desired image of a black entertainer for white audiences, either physically or in her style. She sang white love songs, not the blues. Noting her brunette-white beauty, one white agent tried to get her to take a Spanish name, learn some Spanish songs, and pass as a Latin white, but she had learned to have a horror of passing and never considered it, although Hollywood blacks accused her of trying to pass after she played her first bit part in a film. After she failed her first screen test because she looked like a white girl trying to play black-face, the directors tried making her up with a shade called "Light Egyptian" to make her look darker. The whole procedure embarrassed and hurt her deeply. . . .

Other light mulatto entertainers have also had painful experiences because of their light skin and other caucasoid features. Starting an acting career is never easy, but actress Jane White's difficulties in the 1940s were compounded by her lightness. Her father was NAACP leader Walter White. Even with dark makeup on her ivory skin, she did not look like a black person on the stage, but she was not allowed to try out for white roles because blacks were barred from playing them. When she auditioned for the part of a young girl from India, the director was enthusiastic, although her skin color was too light, but higher management decreed that it was unthinkable for a Negro to play the part of an Asian Indian (White, 1948:338). Only after great perseverance did Jane White make her debut as the educated mulatto maid Nonnie in the stage version of Lillian Smith's *Strange Fruit* (1944). . . .

THE ONE-DROP RULE DEFINED

As the above cases illustrate, to be considered black in the United States not even half of one's ancestry must be African black. But will one-fourth do, or one-eighth, or less? The nation's answer to the question "Who is black?" has long been that a black is any person with *any* known African black ancestry (Myrdal, 1944:113–18; Berry and Tischler, 1978:97–98; Williamson, 1980:1–2). This definition reflects the long experience with slavery and later with Jim Crow segregation. In the South it became known as the "one-drop rule," meaning that a single drop of "black blood" makes a person a black. It is also known as the "one black ancestor rule," some courts have called it the "traceable amount rule," and anthropologists call it the "hypo-descent rule," meaning that racially mixed persons are assigned the status of the subordinate group (Harris, 1964:56). This definition emerged from the American South to become the nation's definition, generally accepted by whites and blacks alike (Bahr, Chadwick, and Stauss, 1979:27–28). Blacks had no other choice. This American cultural definition of blacks is taken for granted as readily by judges, affirmative action officers, and black protesters as it is by Ku Klux Klansmen.

Let us not be confused by terminology. At present the usual statement of the one-drop rule is in terms of "black blood" or black ancestry, while not so long ago it referred to "Negro blood" or ancestry. The term "black" rapidly replaced "Negro" in general usage in the United States as the black power movement peaked at the end of the 1960s, but the black and Negro populations are the same. The term "black" is used [here] for persons with any black African lineage, not just for unmixed members of populations from sub-Saharan Africa. The term "Negro," which is used in certain historical contexts, means the same thing. Terms such as "African black," "unmixed Negro," and "all black" are used here to refer to unmixed blacks descended from African populations.

We must also pay attention to the terms "mulatto" and "colored." The term "mulatto" was originally used to mean the offspring of a "pure African Negro" and a "pure white." Although the root meaning of mulatto, in Spanish, is "hybrid," "mulatto" came to include the children of unions between whites and so-called "mixed Negroes." For example, Booker T. Washington and Frederick Douglass, with slave mothers and white fathers, were referred to as mulattoes (Bennett, 1962:255). To whatever extent their mothers were part white, these men were more than half white. Douglass was evidently part Indian as well, and he looked it (Preston, 1980:9–10). Washington had reddish hair and gray eyes. At the time of the American Revolution, many of the founding fathers had some very light slaves, including some who appeared to be white. The term "colored" seemed for a time to refer only to mulattoes, especially lighter ones, but later it became a euphemism for darker Negroes, even including unmixed blacks. With widespread racial mixture, "Negro" came to mean any slave or descendant of a slave, no matter how much mixed. Eventually in the United States, the terms mulatto, colored, Negro, black, and African American all came to mean people with any known black African ancestry. Mulattoes are racially mixed, to whatever degree, while the terms black, Negro, African American, and colored include both mulattoes and unmixed blacks. These terms have quite different meanings in other countries.

Whites in the United States need some help envisioning the American black experience with ancestral fractions. At the beginning of miscegenation between two populations presumed to be racially pure, quadroons appear in the second generation of continuing mixing with whites, and octoroons in the third. A quadroon is one-fourth African black and thus easily classed as black in the United States, yet three of this person's four grandparents are white. An octoroon has seven white great-grandparents out of eight and usually looks white or almost so. Most parents of black

American children in recent decades have themselves been racially mixed, but often the fractions get complicated because the earlier details of the mixing were obscured generations ago. Like so many white Americans, black people are forced to speculate about some of the fractions—one-eighth this, three-sixteenths that, and so on. . . .

PLESSY, PHIPPS, AND OTHER CHALLENGES IN THE COURTS

Homer Plessy was the plaintiff in the 1896 precedent-setting "separate-but-equal" case of *Plessy v. Ferguson* (163 U.S. 537). This case challenged the Jim Crow statute that required racially segregated seating on trains in interstate commerce in the state of Louisiana. The U.S. Supreme Court quickly dispensed with Plessy's contention that because he was only one-eighth Negro and could pass as white he was entitled to ride in the seats reserved for whites. Without ruling directly on the definition of a Negro, the Supreme Court briefly took what is called "judicial notice" of what it assumed to be common knowledge: that a Negro or black is any person with any black ancestry. (Judges often take explicit "judicial notice" not only of scientific or scholarly conclusions, or of opinion surveys or other systematic investigations, but also of something they just assume to be so, including customary practices or common knowledge.) This has consistently been the ruling in the federal courts, and often when the black ancestry was even less than one-eighth. The federal courts have thus taken judicial notice of the customary boundary between two sociocultural groups that differ, on the average, in physical traits, not between two discrete genetic categories. In the absence of proof of a specific black ancestor, merely being known as a black in the community has usually been accepted by the courts as evidence of black ancestry. The separate-but-equal doctrine established in the Plessy case is no longer the law, as a result of the judicial and legislative successes of the civil rights movement, but the nation's legal definition of who is black remains unchanged.

State courts have generally upheld the one-drop rule. For instance, in a 1948 Mississippi case a young man, Davis Knight, was sentenced to five years in jail for violating the anti-miscegenation statute. Less than one-sixteenth black, Knight said he was not aware that he had any black lineage, but the state proved his great-grandmother was a slave girl. In some states the operating definition of black has been limited by statute to particular fractions, yet the social definition—the one-drop rule—has generally prevailed in case of doubt. Mississippi, Missouri, and five other states have had the criterion of one-eighth. Virginia changed from one-fourth to one-eighth in 1910, then in 1930 forbade white intermarriage with a person with any black ancestry. Persons in Virginia who are one-fourth or more Indian and less than one-sixteenth African black are defined as Indians while on the reservation but as blacks when they leave (Berry, 1965:26). While some states have had general race classification statutes, at least for a time, others have legislated a definition of black only for particular purposes, such as marriage or education. In a few states there have even been varying definitions for different situations (Mangum, 1940:38–48). All states require a designation of race on birth certificates, but there are no clear guidelines to help physicians and midwives do the classifying.

Louisiana's latest race classification statute became highly controversial and was finally repealed in 1983 (Trillin, 1986:77). Until 1970, a Louisiana statute had embraced the one-drop rule, defining a Negro as anyone with a "trace of black ancestry." This law was challenged in court a number of times from the 1920s on, including an unsuccessful attempt in 1957 by boxer Ralph Dupas, who asked to be declared white so that a law banning "interracial sports" (since repealed) would not prevent him from boxing in the state. In 1970 a lawsuit was brought on behalf of a child whose ancestry was allegedly only one two-hundred-fifty-sixth black, and the legislature revised its law. The 1970 Louisiana statute defined a black as someone whose ancestry is more than one thirty-second black (La. Rev. Stat. 42:267). Adverse publicity about this law was widely disseminated during the Phipps trial in 1983 (discussed below), filed as *Jane Doe v. State of Louisiana.* This case was decided in a district court in May 1983, and in June the legislature abolished its one thirty-second statute and gave parents the right to designate the race of newborns, and even to change classifications on birth certificates if they can prove the child is white by a "preponderance of the evidence." However, the new statute in 1983 did not abolish the "traceable amount rule" (the one-drop rule), as demonstrated by the outcomes when the Phipps decision was appealed to higher courts in 1985 and 1986.

The history in the Phipps (Jane Doe) case goes as far back as 1770, when a French planter named Jean Gregoire Guillory took his wife's slave, Margarita, as his mistress (Model, 1983:3–4). More than two centuries and two decades later, their great-great-great-great-granddaughter, Susie Guillory Phipps, asked the Louisiana courts to change the classification on her deceased parents' birth certificates to "white" so she and her brothers and sisters could be designated white. They all looked white, and some were blue-eyed blonds. Mrs. Susie Phipps had been denied a passport because she had checked "white" on her application although her birth certificate designated her race as "colored." This designation was based on information supplied by a midwife, who presumably relied on the parents or on the family's status in the community. Mrs. Phipps claimed that this classification came as a shock, since she had always thought she was white, had lived as white, and had twice married as white. Some of her relatives, however, gave depositions saying they considered themselves "colored," and the lawyers for the state claimed to have proof that Mrs. Phipps is three-thirty-seconds black (Trillin, 1986:62–63, 71–74). That was more than enough "blackness" for the district court in 1983 to declare her parents, and thus Mrs. Phipps and her siblings, to be legally black.

In October and again in December 1985, the state's Fourth Circuit Court of Appeals upheld the district court's decision, saying that no one can change the racial designation of his or her parents or anyone else's (479 So. 2d 369). Said the majority of the court in its opinion: "That appellants might today describe themselves as white does not prove error in a document which designates their parents as colored" (479 So. 2d 371). Of course, if the parents' designation as "colored" cannot be disturbed, their descendants must be defined as black by the "traceable amount rule." The court also concluded that the preponderance of the evidence clearly showed that the Guillory parents were "colored." Although noting expert testimony to the effect that the race of an individual cannot be determined with scientific accuracy, the court said the law of racial designation is not based on science, that "individual race designations are purely social and cultural perceptions and the evidence conclusively proves those subjective perspectives were correctly recorded at the time the appellants' birth certificates were recorded" (479 So. 2d 372). At the rehearing in December 1985, the appellate court also affirmed the necessity of designating race on birth certificates for public health, affirmative action, and other important public programs and held that equal protection of the law has not been denied so long as the designation is treated as confidential.

When this case was appealed to the Louisiana Supreme Court in 1986, that court declined to review the decision, saying only that the court "concurs in the denial for the reasons assigned by the court of appeals on rehearing" (485 So. 2d 60). In December 1986 the U.S. Supreme Court was equally brief in stating its reason for refusing to review the decision: "The appeal is dismissed for want of a substantial federal question" (107 Sup. Ct. Reporter, interim ed. 638). Thus, both the final court of appeals in Louisiana and the highest court of the United States saw no reason to disturb the application of the one-drop rule in the lawsuit brought by Susie Guillory Phipps and her siblings.

CENSUS ENUMERATION OF BLACKS

When the U.S. Bureau of the Census enumerates blacks (always counted as Negroes until 1980), it does not use a scientific definition, but rather the one accepted by the general public and by the courts. The Census Bureau counts what the nation wants counted. Although various operational instructions have been tried, the definition of black used by the Census Bureau has been the nation's cultural and legal definition: all persons with any known black ancestry. Other nations define and count blacks differently, so international comparisons of census data on blacks can be extremely misleading. For example, Latin American countries generally count as black only unmixed African blacks, those only slightly mixed, and the very poorest mulattoes. If they used the U.S. definition, they would count far more blacks than they do, and if Americans used their definition, millions in the black community in the United States would be counted either as white or as "coloreds" of different descriptions, not as black.

Instructions to our census enumerators in 1840, 1850, and 1860 provided "mulatto" as a category but did not define the term. In 1870 and 1880, mulattoes were officially defined to include "quadroons, octoroons, and all persons having any perceptible trace of African blood." In 1890 enumerators were told to record the *exact* proportion of the "African blood," again relying on visibility. In 1900 the Census Bureau specified that "pure Negroes" be counted separately from mulattoes, the latter to mean "all persons with some trace of black blood." In 1920 the mulatto category was dropped, and black was defined to mean any person with any black ancestry, as it has been ever since.

In 1960 the practice of self-definition began, with the head of household indicating the race of its members. This did not seem to introduce any noticeable fluctuation in the number of blacks, thus indicating that black Americans generally apply the one-drop rule to themselves. One exception is that Spanish-speaking Americans who have black ancestry but were considered white, or some designation other than black, in their place of origin generally reject the one-drop rule if they can. American Indians with some black ancestry also generally try to avoid the rule, but those who leave the reservation are often treated as black. At any rate, the 1980 census count showed that self-designated blacks made up about 12 percent of the population of the United States.

No other ethnic population in the nation, including those with visibly non-caucasoid features, is defined and counted according to a one-drop rule. For example, persons whose ancestry is one-fourth or less American Indian are not generally defined as Indian unless they want to be, and they are considered assimilating Americans who may even be proud of having some Indian ancestry. The same implicit rule appears to apply to Japanese Americans, Filipinos, or other peoples from East Asian nations and also to Mexican Americans who have Central American Indian ancestry, as a large majority do. For instance, a person whose ancestry is one-eighth Chinese is not defined as just Chinese, or East Asian, or a member of the mongoloid race. The United States certainly does not apply a one-drop rule to its white ethnic populations either, which include both national and religious groups. Ethnicity has often been confused with racial biology and not just in Nazi Germany. Americans do not insist that an American with a small fraction of Polish ancestry be classified as a Pole, or that someone with a single remote Greek ancestor be designated Greek, or that someone with any trace of Jewish lineage is a Jew and nothing else.

It is interesting that, in *The Passing of the Great Race* (1916), Madison Grant maintained that the one-drop rule should be applied not only to blacks but also to all the other ethnic groups he considered biologically inferior "races," such as Hindus, Asians in general, Jews, Italians, and other Southern and Eastern European peoples. Grant's book went through four editions, and he and others succeeded in getting Congress to pass the national origins quota laws of the early 1920s. This racist quota legislation sharply curtailed immigration from everywhere in the world except Northern and Western Europe and the Western Hemisphere, until it was repealed in 1965. Grant and other believers in the racial superiority of their own group have confused race with ethnicity. They consider miscegenation with any "inferior" people to be the ultimate danger to the survival of their own group and have often seen the one-drop rule as a crucial component in their line of defense. Americans in general, however, while finding other ways to discriminate against immigrant groups, have rejected the application of the drastic one-drop rule to all groups but blacks.

UNIQUENESS OF THE ONE-DROP RULE

Not only does the one-drop rule apply to no other group than American blacks, but apparently the rule is unique in that it is found only in the United States and not in any other nation in the world. In fact, definitions of who is black vary quite sharply from country to country, and for this reason people in other countries often express consternation about our definition. James Baldwin relates a revealing incident that occurred in 1956 at the Conference of Negro-African Writers and Artists held in Paris. The head of the delegation of writers and artists from the United States was John Davis. The French chairperson introduced Davis and then asked him why he considered himself Negro, since he certainly did not look like one. Baldwin wrote, "He *is* a Negro, of course, from the remarkable legal point of view which obtains in the United States, but more importantly, as he tried to make clear to his interlocutor, he was a Negro by choice and by depth of involvement—by experience, in fact" (1962:19).

The phenomenon known as "passing as white" is difficult to explain in other countries or to foreign students. Typical questions are: "Shouldn't Americans say that a person who is passing as white *is* white, or nearly all white, and has previously been passing as black?" or "To be consistent, shouldn't you say that someone who is one-eighth white is passing as black?" or "Why is there so much concern, since the so-called blacks who pass take so little negroid ancestry with them?" Those who ask such questions need to realize that "passing" is so much more a social phenomenon than a biological one, reflecting the nation's unique definition of what makes a person black. The concept of "passing" rests on the one-drop rule and on folk beliefs about race and miscegenation, not on biological or historical fact.

The black experience with passing as white in the United States contrasts with the experience of other ethnic minorities that have features that are clearly non-caucasoid. The concept of passing applies only to blacks—consistent with the nation's unique definition of the group. A person who is one-fourth or less American Indian or Korean or Filipino is not regarded as passing if he or she intermarries and joins fully the life of the dominant community, so the minority ancestry need not be hidden. It is often suggested that the key reason for this is that the physical differences between these other groups and whites are less pronounced than the physical differences between African blacks and whites, and therefore are less threatening to whites. However, keep in mind that the one-drop rule and anxiety about passing originated during slavery and later received powerful reinforcement under the Jim Crow system.

For the physically visible groups other than blacks, miscegenation promotes assimilation, despite barriers of prejudice and discrimination during two or more generations of racial mixing. As noted above, when ancestry in one of these racial minority groups does not exceed one-fourth, a person is not defined solely as a member of that group. Masses of white European immigrants have climbed the class ladder not only through education but also with the help of close personal relationships in the dominant community, intermarriage, and ultimately full cultural and social assimilation. Young people tend to marry people they meet in the same informal social circles (Gordon, 1964:70–81). For visibly noncaucasoid minorities other than blacks in the United States, this entire route to full assimilation is slow but possible.

For all persons of any known black lineage, however, assimilation is blocked and is not promoted by miscegenation. Barriers to full opportunity and participation for blacks are still formidable, and a fractionally black person cannot escape these obstacles without passing as white and cutting off all ties to the black family and community. The pain of this separation, and condemnation by the black family and community, are major reasons why many or most of those who could pass as white choose not to. Loss of security within the minority community, and fear and distrust of the white world are also factors.

It should now be apparent that the definition of a black person as one with any trace at all of black African ancestry is inextricably woven into the history of the United States. It incorporates beliefs once used to justify slavery and later used to buttress the castelike Jim Crow system of segregation. Developed in the South, the definition of "Negro" (now black) spread and became the nation's social and legal definition. Because blacks are defined according to the one-drop rule, they are a socially constructed category in which there is wide variation in racial traits and therefore not a race group in the scientific sense. However, because that category has a definite status position in the society it has become a self-conscious social group with an ethnic identity.

The one-drop rule has long been taken for granted throughout the United States by whites and blacks alike, and the federal courts have taken "judicial notice" of it as being a matter of common knowledge. State courts have generally upheld the one-drop rule, but some have limited the definition to one thirty-second or one-sixteenth or one-eighth black ancestry, or made other limited exceptions for persons with both Indian and black ancestry. Most Americans seem unaware that this definition of blacks is extremely unusual in other countries, perhaps even unique to the United States, and that Americans define no other minority group in a similar way. . . .

REFERENCES

Bahr, Howard M., Bruce A. Chadwick, and Joseph H. Stauss. 1979. *American Ethnicity.* Lexington, Mass.: D.C. Heath & Co.

Baldwin, James. 1962. *Nobody Knows My Name.* New York: Dell Publishing Co.

Bennett, Lerone, Jr. 1962. *Before the Mayflower: A History of the Negro in America 1619–1962.* Chicago: Johnson Publishing Co.

Berry, Brewton. 1965. *Race and Ethnic Relations.* 3rd ed. Boston: Houghton Mifflin Co.

Berry, Brewton, and Henry L. Tischler. 1978. *Race and Ethnic Relations.* 4th ed. Boston: Houghton Mifflin Co.

Buckley, Gail Lumet. 1986. *The Hornes: An American Family.* New York: Alfred A. Knopf.

Gordon, Milton M. 1964. *Assimilation in American Life.* New York: Oxford University Press.

Grant, Madison. 1916. *The Passing of the Great Race.* New York: Scribner.

Gwaltney, John Langston. 1980. *Drylongso: A Self-Portrait of Black America.* New York: Vintage Books.

Harris, Melvin. 1964. *Patterns of Race in the Americas.* New York: W. W. Norton.

Horne, Lena, and Richard Schickel. 1965. *Lena.* Garden City, N.Y.: Doubleday & Co.

Mangum, Charles Staples, Jr. 1940. *The Legal Status of the Negro in the United States.* Chapel Hill: University of North Carolina Press.

Model, F. Peter, ed. 1983. "Apartheid in the Bayou." *Perspectives: The Civil Rights Quarterly* 15 (Winter–Spring), 3–4.

Myrdal, Gunnar, assisted by Richard Sterner and Arnold M. Rose. 1944. *An American Dilemma.* New York: Harper & Bros.

Ottley, Roi. 1943. *New World A-Coming.* Cleveland: World Publishing Co.

Powell, Adam Clayton, Jr. 1971. *Adam by Adam: The Autobiography of Adam Clayton Powell, Jr.* New York: Dial Press.

Preston, Dickson J. 1980. *Young Frederick Douglass: the Maryland Years.* Baltimore: Johns Hopkins University Press.

Trillin, Calvin. 1986. "American Chronicles: Black or White." *New Yorker,* April 14, 1986, pp. 62–78.

White, Walter. 1948. *A Man Called White: The Autobiography of Walter White.* New York: Viking Press.

Williamson, Joel. 1980. *New People: Miscegenation and Mulattoes in the United States.* New York: The Free Press.

PERSONAL ACCOUNT

A Wonderful Opportunity

I was one among many—growing up and being educated in a stable, loving, supportive Black community—who was informed of a wonderful opportunity that lay ahead for me.

My neighborhood school would be closed and I, and others like me, would have the "honor" and "privilege" of being transported to the suburbs to go to school where everything would be "bigger and better": bigger gym, bigger lunchroom, better teachers, better equipment, better books, "better" people. It would be a great opportunity for me, and others like me, to "better" ourselves.

This land of "bigger and better" was located atop one of the many hills surrounding the city of Pittsburgh, Pennsylvania, a hill pregnant with fear, ignorance, and hate. It was not long after my arrival in this land that I, and others like me, would be greeted, verbally and visually, with that welcoming term of endearment, "nigger."

During my stay in this land of "bigger and better" (mid-seventies through early eighties, grades 6 through 12) this hill gave birth, on several occasions, to a human wall of hate brandishing weapons of intimidation: lead pipes, baseball bats, vicious dogs, and vicious racial epithets. Those of us who were targets of this intimidation did what anyone would do when an assault against one's humanity is launched. We masked our fear with anger-bravado-attitude and defiance. A hostile confrontation ensued. Some of us were chased by dogs, some were attacked with pipes and chains, some were injured when buses were turned over while occupied, some were hit and cut by rocks being thrown at buses as they attempted to descend the hill.

No one effectively intervened on our behalf. Our parents' response was to be defiant, to send us back up the hill determined not to have their children denied access to that "wonderful opportunity." The parents of our combatants responded by aligning themselves on the hill with their children. Thus, busing for integration was transformed into busing for confrontation. . . . Welcome to the Suburbs.

I would have liked for both groups of parents (Black and White) to have realized that the political, ideological, and social battle for and against integration left in the middle a group of kids battling (literally) each other. This physical battle strained and/or dissolved newly formed friendships. The mental battle shattered a child's sense of self and fostered feelings of inadequacy, inferiority, and hatred of others (and self) in a young person previously insulated from such a penetrating and devastating psychological ambush. What an "opportunity."

R.M.A.

READING 2

The New Colored People

Jon Michael Spencer

Black people and white people had intermixed in Africa and Europe long before the New World—"America"—was ever "discovered." Thus, black was never purely black, and white was never purely white, and our uses of these racial designations has been merely relative. While race has some relationship to biological makeup, it is primarily a sociopolitical construct, one that was created and has been maintained and modified by the powerful to sustain their group as a privileged caste. In the United States the powerful have done such a thorough job at sewing the idea of race into the social fabric of the nation, that Americans have always treated race as though it were something that defined the very nature of people. Americans have especially treated race as though it defined the essence of black and white people, who generally have been viewed as opposites during the course of their shared history in the New World.

Because black and white people have been viewed as pure opposites, Americans have been confused about the consequence of black and white intermixing (miscegenation). For part of American history, on and off between 1870 and 1920, the term "mulatto" was used to describe people of this particular interracial mixture. In 1920 the category "mulatto" was dropped and "black" was used to cover everyone with any known black ancestry. By including mulattoes under the category of black, it was clear (and has been clear ever since) that "black" and its earlier synonyms no longer denoted a people who were "pure." Rather, it referred to a people who were not white and who had at least "one drop" of black "blood."

Jon Michael Spencer is professor of American studies and professor of music at the University of Richmond.

The acceptance of the "one-drop rule" by black people (the rule that says "one drop" of black blood makes one black) was more than merely a passive internalizing of the system of oppression fashioned by the powerful. Certainly race is a tool of oppression in the hand of the powerful. But, unable to escape from racial labeling, blacks chose to wield race for their liberation by nurturing a sense of common identity and then fashioning unified social and political action. Thus, the ideas of "black pride" and "black power" of the 1960s, logical successors to the New Negro movement that came to wide public attention in the 1920s, brought lighter- and darker-skinned blacks into even closer alliance. Thus, in 1960, when the United States Bureau of the Census commenced the practice of the head of the household defining the race of its members, there was no significant change in the numbers of blacks reported. Even with the coming of the biracial baby boom that started after the last antimiscegenation laws were repealed in 1967, the result was an increase in the number of blacks in the United States.

When the 1970s came, rather than the country moving away from racial categorization, where people are judged by the content of their character rather than by the color of their skin, the sociopolitical construct of race became even more interwoven into the societal fabric. Some scholars blame this on the establishment of a federal document called Statistical Directive No. 15. Issued by the Office of Management and Budget (OMB), Directive No. 15 provides standard classifications for recording, collecting, and presenting data on race and ethnicity at the federal level, so that data acquired by one agency can be used by other agencies for their particular purposes. The current consequence of Directive No. 15 is that there exists a tension between racial identification as requisite for the legal protection of minorities and, on the other hand, racial identification as a traditional tool that whites have used to maintain power by relegating certain races to particular levels of the social ladder.

The history of Directive No. 15 began in 1973 when Caspar Weinberger, then the Secretary of Health, Education, and Welfare, asked the Federal Interagency Committee on Education (FICE) to develop standards for classifying race and ethnicity. The ad hoc committee started its work in 1974, and in 1977 the OMB adopted the FICE recommendations almost verbatim. From that point on there would be, according to Statistical Directive No. 15, four racial groups recognized by the United States government—White, Black, Asian and Pacific Islander, and American Indian and Alaskan Native. The instructions of Directive No. 15 to the parents of those biracial baby boomers of the late 1960s and beyond is that they are to select the racial category that most closely reflects the way their community sees them: "The category which most closely reflects the individual's recognition in his community should be used for purposes of reporting on persons who are of mixed racial and/or ethnic origins."

The census data gathered in compliance with Directive No. 15 are for the purposes of tracking demographic shifts in the country. For instance, we can see that between 1980 and 1990 the black population increased 13 percent, from 26.5 million people to 29.9 million. The white population increased 6 percent, up to 199.7 million people, making up 80.3 percent of the entire population. In addition to tracking demographic shifts of this kind, the census permits the government to be able to measure the racial makeup of the country in order to develop the appropriate public policies and federal services. For instance, the data have been used to address the requirements of the civil rights laws—establishing and evaluating federal affirmative action plans and desegregation plans in schools, and evaluating workforce participation and state redistricting plans for the protection of minority voting rights. Even the Center for Control of Diseases uses the categories of Directive No. 15 to do research on whether certain segments of the population are susceptible to certain diseases. Indeed, a great many programs intended to counter historical and systemic discrimination require demographic information about racial and ethnic groups. Thus, a careful counting of the population has become increasingly important over the last several decades, especially due to the demands on dwindling government resources.

As a result of the racial classification system of Directive No. 15 and societal custom that labeled mixed-race blacks as monoracially black, African Americans became the largest minority group in the United States. Because of the laws that more or less protected those that the classification system identified as black, African Americans increasingly became a political presence to be reckoned with. Much of that political clout was harnessed and organized by the black church, which was the spiritual backbone to the cohesiveness of the black community.

Notwithstanding this black cohesiveness and despite the seemingly important legal and programmatic uses of the data on race and ethnicity collected by the Census Bureau, there is some tension between having racial categories that serve the legislative and programmatic needs of the federal government and having categories that reflect the self-perception of American citizens.[1] There is a growing population of Americans who feel Directive No. 15 props up traditional notions of bigotry with regard to "race mixing" and that this is detrimental to the offspring of such interracial unions.[2] These people believe the four racial groups established by the federal government do not permit mixed-race people to have a name that recognizes their mixed racial parentage. The census instructions directing them to select the racial category most closely reflecting the way their "community" sees them may seem rather liberal, but the "community"—whether black or white, segregated or integrated—has traditionally seen mixed-race blacks as monoracially black.

Many of the complainants who want a change in Directive No. 15 are the people of the biracial baby boom that resulted from the doubling of interracial marriages (from 1 percent to 2 percent) and the tripling of interracial births (from 1 percent to 3 percent) between 1970 and 1990. In 1990, the year the multiracial movement especially picked up momentum, the Census Bureau received a substantial number of inquiries from persons of mixed-race background and from parents in interracial marriages, who did not want to identify themselves or their children monoracially. Whereas in 1970 only 720,000 people (less than one-half of 1 percent of the population) indicated some other category on the census, in 1990 ten million people (about 4 percent of the entire population) checked the official "other" category, which first appeared that year. Of the 8 million write-ins under the "other" category, 253,000 people gave such identifications as "multiracial" or "interracial" or specifically as "black-white" or "Asian-white," and so forth.[3] In most cases the Census Bureau simply reassigned these individuals (those who had specified their biracial makeup) under monoracial categories. For instance, while people who wrote "multiracial" or "biracial" were left in the "other" race classification, those who wrote "white-black" were classified as white and those who wrote "black-white" were classified as black.[4] Those who wrote "creole" on the 1990 census were also classified as black.

Since 1990 the growth in the number of interracial marriages and births has continued to increase, as has the growth in the number of advocacy groups for interracial couples and mixed-race people. Today, most states have support groups for interracial families and mixed-race individuals, and there are two national magazines that address the blessings and curses of interracial living. These advocacy groups and magazines have helped organize the frustrations of interracial parents and mixed-race people into the multiracial movement, which seeks an appropriate and recognized racial identity for mixed-race people.

We should understand that mixed-race people are not the only ones who view themselves different from what the government calls them, and that the multiracialists are not the only ones trying to convince the OMB to modify the racial categories on Directive No. 15. For instance, the Census Bureau and the OMB have received suggestions that the term "African American" be substituted for "Black," that "Native American" be substituted for "American Indian,"[5] and that "European American"[6] be substituted for "White." A number of organizations representing Arab Americans wish to see their constituency removed from the "white" category.

Louis Massery, an Arab American attorney from Boston who testified before the OMB as a representative of the Arab Anti-Discrimination Committee, said Arabs and other Middle Easterners who are American citizens are the only groups from the Third World who do not hold protected status as minorities. Massery also argued that classifying Arab Americans as if they were a white European ethnic group is absurd, since the Arab world neither lies in Europe nor traces its ancestry to Europe.[7] Hamzi Moghrabi, representing the Colorado branch of the Arab Anti-Discrimination Committee, told the OMB that by identifying Arab Americans as white they are denied the benefits of a minority group. He said Arabs are a people whose history and culture are ridiculed by whites in the nation's classrooms and whose well-being is threatened by the bigotry and hate crimes of whites.[8]

A result of the effort of some Arabs not to be classified as white is that there are now some white groups that would like to eliminate the "white" classification. They seek this change because the category of white has, since the 1970 census, included North Africans and Southwest Asians along with European Americans.* Perhaps this suggests a possible change for the better in white self-perception. . . . The term "European American" was coined after the official end of segregation. However, whites may

**Editors' note:* Asian Indians were reclassified as Asian in 1980.

also prefer "European-American" to further protect white "purity" and privilege.

The attempt to protect white purity and privilege seems to be favored by those whites who feel that the term "white" is no longer synonymous with "European American."[9] For instance, Dale Warner, representing Irish, Scottish, and Welsh groups before the OMB, said his constituency does not want to be classified as white because it includes peoples originating from North Africa and Southwest Asia (the Middle East).[10] Joseph Fallon, who testified similarly before the OMB as a representative of the National European American Society and the Society for German-American Studies, said that "European American" would refer specifically to Americans whose ethnic origins derive from peoples of Europe, such as the English, Germans, Irish, Italians, and Polish.[11] . . .

Gerhard Holford, co-moderator of the Conference of Americans of Germanic Heritage, also wants the category of white eliminated because of the political and social ideology the term carries. First, Holford argues that few of the people categorized by the government as white really consider their culture, language, or history to be "white culture," "white language," or "white history." "If anything," he remarks, "the notion of whiteness is a political idea or a state of mind." To this Holford adds that from time to time the idea of whiteness has been a factor in both pro-white and anti-white political movements, but due to changes in political ideas and states of mind the number of people identifying themselves as white has decreased.[12] Among these changed political ideas and states of mind, according to Holford, is the idea of white supremacy. Many European Americans reject the term "white," he argues, because of the stereotype that suggests that any people calling themselves by that name are white supremacists. For similar reasons, Holford suggests that the Conference of Americans of Germanic Heritage advocates omitting references to a "majority race" in Directive No. 15, in that such a term suggests that the white race is more dominant, superior, and more powerful than the other races that are not white.[13]

Another representative of this view, Donald Freiberg, a San Jose attorney, submitted a written testimony to the OMB, which said of the term "European American" what blacks have long said about the term "African American": "It enriches us with a history, culture, and continent of origin. Other groups choose a continental label because they wish to embody more than a mere color. European Americans wish to do the same, yet we are constantly slapped with a bland, lifeless color 'white' that we did not choose." Freiberg also said that the term "European American" would permit whites to distance themselves from the likes of David Duke, the Louisiana politician who uses the term "white" in a way that implies white supremacy.[14]

These efforts at racial name changes are part of the context in which the multiracial movement is situated. While certain groups feel they want an identity more fitting than the "white" label, the multiracialists now feel that people of mixed racial ancestry deserve a fitting appellation since they are the country's least recognized people in a period when racial and ethnic pride and cultural awareness are at an all-time high.[15]

Aware of the complaints of the various groups of Americans who wish to have a federal name change, Thomas Sawyer, chair of the House subcommittee that addressed the census, said that the problem with the categories of Directive No. 15 is that they have remained constant at a time when the country is changing in significant ways.[16] Indeed, today's reality of greater interaction between the existing racial categories suggests to many people a need for modification, not to mention that those interacting across racial lines and those offspring who are the product of that interaction are developing a new self-perception.

The increased interaction across racial lines and the new self-perception that mixed-race people have of themselves descended on most Americans so quickly that we have not had much time to think about the possible consequences. Indeed, views have changed so rapidly that it was just a few years ago, in 1991, that sociologist F. James Davis concluded that the "one-drop rule" was here to stay for the foreseeable future. Davis raised a question about whether or not a change in the "one-drop rule" might not result in the adoption of one of the world's other status rules for mixed-race people (such as in South Africa). He answered that the potential for the establishment of a "middle-minority position" that has occurred in other parts of the world, even in the early history of this country, "seems to be nil."[17] Davis summarizes, "We can only conclude that none of the world's known alternatives to the American definition of who is black now seems at all likely to be given serious consideration in the United States."[18] Perhaps in 1991 most Americans would have come to the same conclusion as Davis, but today a movement is spreading among the community of interracial parents and their mixed-race offspring whose goal is to see "multiracial" established as a new racial classification on the United States census for the year 2000. If this does not happen, then efforts will likely be made to reach this goal in 2010.

Some may be surprised by the rapid rise of the multiracial movement. After all, the Census Bureau has been trying to accommodate those who wish to identify themselves in myriad ways by allowing them to check the category "other" and write in a racial identification not included in the standard classifications. Furthermore, many of us know mixed-race people who prefer the "other" category—people like Roy Harrison, founder of a California support and advocacy group called Mixed Race People of Color. Harrison testified at the OMB hearings that he prefers "other" because it allows him to be more specific.[19] Nonetheless, for the multiracialists the "other" category is unsatisfactory in that it signifies a nonidentity that relegates mixed-race people to nonpersonhood. In addition, some of the multiracialists do not like the fact that the Bureau recategorizes those "others" into the four principal monoracial categories. This reclassification becomes necessary because "other" is used in the census but not in those administrative records that need to know who those "others" are. Since the figures gathered by the census are used to enforce certain legislation that depends on precise numbers, the Bureau cannot leave nearly 10 million "others" outside the standard racial categories.

The multiracialists who are challenging the one-drop rule prefer the word "multiracial" over "biracial" because there are many instances where a person's ancestry includes more than two racial or ethnic groups. Some prefer "colored," a name that for a time referred only to mulattoes (especially lighter ones) but later was used to identify all blacks. Some South African coloureds would like mixed-race Americans to join them in using the name "coloured" because of the similarity they see between mixed-race Americans and themselves as mixed-race South Africans. . . .

Thus there is a parallel between the mixed-race people in the United States and the coloured people in South Africa. If some of the multiracialists get their way, the multiracial classification they seek could be the beginning of a global pan-colouredism, where "brown" (mixed-race) peoples take their place along white and black peoples of the world. Because the multiracial movement may have national and global significance, it may surprise us that we did not see it coming long before now. But some movements seem to work that way: we do not see them coming, but when they are here we can see that they were coming all along. This multiracial movement, then, was no sudden development, even though sociologist F. James Davis had not yet seen it coming only a few years earlier in 1991.

NOTES

1. Katherine Wallman, Office of Management and Budget, Public Hearing(s) on Standards for the Classification of Federal Data on Race and Ethnicity, July 11, 1994, 4–5.
2. Carlos A. Fernandez, Review of Federal Measurements of Race and Ethnicity, Hearings before the Subcommittee on Census, Statistics and Postal Personnel of the Committee on Post Office and Civil Service, House of Representatives, 103rd Congress, June 30, 1993 (Washington, D.C.: U.S. Government Printing Office, 1994), 134.
3. Harry A. Scarr (Acting Director of the Bureau of the Census), Review of Federal Measurements of Race and Ethnicity, April 14, 1993, 10. See also Christine C. Iijima Hall, "Coloring Outside the Lines," in Maria P. P. Root, ed., *Racially Mixed People in America* (Newbury Park, Calif.: Sage, 1992), 327.
4. Scarr, Review of Federal Measurements of Race and Ethnicity, 10.
5. Scarr, Review of Federal Measurements of Race and Ethnicity; Katherine Wallman, Office of Management and Budget, Public Hearing(s), 2.
6. Dale Warner, Office of Management and Budget, Public Hearing(s), July 14, 1994, 78.
7. Louis Massery, Office of Management and Budget, Public Hearing(s), July 7, 1994, 51, 57.
8. Hamzi Moghrabi, Office of Management and Budget, Public Hearing(s), July 11, 1994, 9, 51. See also Beesan Barghouti (representing the Arab-American Institute in Washington), Office of Management and Budget, Public Hearing(s), July 11, 1994, 16–17.
9. Joseph E. Fallon, Office of Management and Budget, Public Hearing(s), July 7, 1994, 14.
10. Warner, Office of Management and Budget, Public Hearing(s), 78.
11. Fallon, Office of Management and Budget, Public Hearing(s), 15.
12. Gerhard Holford, Office of Management and Budget, Public Hearing(s), July 14, 1994, 81.
13. Holford, Office of Management and Budget, Public Hearing(s), 82.
14. Donald H. Freiberg, Office of Management and Budget, Public Hearing(s), July 14, 1994, n.p.
15. Letter to the Editor, *Interrace,* May/June 1992, 7.
16. Thomas Sawyer, on Wayne Olney, host, "Racial Categories on the Next Census: Should They Be Changed or Should They Be Eliminated Altogether," on *Which Way L.A.?* KCRW Radio, Santa Monica College, California.
17. F. James Davis, *Who Is Black?: One Nation's Definition* (University Park: Pennsylvania State University Press, 1991), 181.
18. Davis, *Who Is Black?,* 184.
19. Roy Harrison, Office of Management and Budget, Public Hearing(s), July 14, 1994, 133.

REFERENCES

Davis, F. James. *Who Is Black?: One Nation's Definition.* University Park: Pennsylvania State University Press, 1991.

Hall, Christine C. Iijima. "Coloring Outside the Lines." In Maria P. P. Root, ed., *Racially Mixed People in America.* Newbury Park, Calif.: Sage, 1992.

Letters to the Editor. *Interrace,* May/June 1992, 5–7.

Office of Management and Budget, Public Hearing(s) on Standards for the Classification of Federal Data on Race and Ethnicity, July 7 (Boston), July 11 (Denver), July 14 (San Francisco), July 18 (Honolulu), 1994.

Olney, Wayne, host. "Racial Categories on the Next Census: Should They Be Changed or Should They Be Eliminated Altogether." On *Which Way L.A.?* KCRW Radio, Santa Monica College, California, August 4, 1994.

Review of Federal Measurements of Race and Ethnicity. Hearings before the Subcommittee on Census, Statistics and Postal Personnel of the Committee on Post Office and Civil Service, House of Representatives, 103rd Congress, First Session, April 17, June 30, July 29, November 3, 1993. Washington, D.C.: U.S. Government Printing Office, 1994.

Root, Maria P. P., ed. *Racially Mixed People in America.* Newbury Park, Calif.: Sage, 1992.

READING 3

Federal Indian Identification Policy

M. Annette Jaimes

I'm forever being asked not only my "tribe," but my "percentage of Indian blood." I've given the matter a lot of thought, and find I prefer to make the computation based on all of me rather than just the fluid coursing through my veins. Calculated in this way, I can report that I am precisely 52.5 pounds Indian—about 35 pounds Creek and the remainder Cherokee—88 pounds Teutonic, 43.5 pounds some sort of English, and the rest "undetermined." Maybe the last part should just be described as "human." It all seems rather silly as a means of assessing who I am, don't you think?

Ward Churchill
Creek/Cherokee Métis, 1991

The question of my "identity" often comes up. I think I must be a mixed-blood. I claim to be male, although only one of my parents was male.

Jimmie Durham
Cherokee, 1991

By all accepted standards of international jurisprudence and human decency, American Indian peoples whose territory lies within the borders of the United States hold compelling legal and moral rights to be treated as fully sovereign nations. It is axiomatic that any such national entity is inherently entitled to exercise the prerogative of determining for itself the criteria by which its citizenry, or "membership," is to be recognized by other sovereign nations. This is a principle that applies equally to superpowers such as the U.S. and to non-powers such as Grenada and Monaco. In fact, it is a tenet so widely understood and imbedded in international law, custom, and convention that it bears no particular elaboration here.

M. Annette Jaimes is a lecturer in American Indian studies at the University of Colorado, Boulder.

Contrary to virtually universal practice, the United States has opted to preempt unilaterally the rights of many North American indigenous nations to engage in this most fundamental level of internal decisionmaking. Instead, in pursuit of the interests of their own state rather than those of the nations that are thereby affected, federal policymakers have increasingly imposed "Indian identification standards" of their own design. Typically centering upon a notion of "blood quantum"—not especially different in its conception from the eugenics code once adopted by nazi Germany in its effort to achieve "racial purity," or currently utilized by South Africa to segregate Blacks and "coloreds"—this aspect of U.S. policy has increasingly wrought havoc with the American Indian sense of nationhood (and often the individual sense of self) over the past century. This chapter offers a brief analysis of the motivations underlying this federal usurpation of the American Indian expression of sovereignty and points out certain implications of it.

FEDERAL OBLIGATIONS

The more than 370 formally ratified treaties entered into by the United States with various Indian nations represent the basic real estate documents by which the federal government now claims legal title to most of its land base. In exchange for the lands ceded by Indians, the United States committed itself to the permanent provision of a range of services to Indian populations (i.e., the citizens of the Indian nations with which the treaty agreements were reached), which would assist them in adjusting their economies and ways of life to their newly constricted territories. For example, in the 1794 Treaty with the Oneida (also affecting the Tuscarora and Stockbridge Indians), the United States guaranteed provision of instruction "in the arts of the miller and sawyer," as well as regular annuities paid in goods and cash, in exchange for a portion of what is now the state of New York.[1] Similarly, the 1804 Treaty with the Delaware extended assurances of technical instruction in agriculture and the mechanical arts, as well as annuities.[2] As Evelyn C. Adams frames it:

> Treaties with the Indians varied widely, stipulating cash annuities to be paid over a specified period of time or perpetually; rations and clothing, farming implements and domestic animals, and instruction in agriculture along with other educational opportunities. . . . [And eventually] the school supplemented the Federal program of practical teaching.[3]

The reciprocal nature of such agreements received considerable reinforcement when it was determined, early in the 19th century, that "the enlightenment and civilization of the Indian" might yield—quite aside from any need on the part of the United States to honor its international obligations—a certain utility in terms of subordinating North America's indigenous peoples to Euroamerican domination. Secretary of War John C. Calhoun articulated this quite clearly in 1818:

> By a proper combination of force and persuasion, of punishment and rewards, they [the Indians] ought to be brought within the pales of law and civilization. Left to themselves, they will never reach that desirable condition. Before the slow operation of reason and experience can convince them of its superior advantages, they must be overwhelmed by the mighty torrent of our population. Such small bodies, with savage customs and character, cannot, and ought not, to be allowed to exist in an independent society. Our laws and manners ought to supersede their present savage manners and customs . . . their [treaty] annuities would constitute an ample school fund; and education, comprehending as well as the common arts of life, reading, writing, and arithmetic, ought not to be left discretionary with the parents. . . . When sufficiently advanced in civilization, they would be permitted to participate in such civil and political rights as the respective States.[4]

The utter cynicism involved in Calhoun's position—that of intentionally using the treaty instruments by which the United States conveyed recognition of Indian sovereignty as the vehicle with which to destroy that same sovereignty—speaks for itself. The more important point for purposes of this study, however, is that by 1820 U.S. strategic interests had congealed around the notion of extending federal obligations to Indians. The tactic was therefore continued throughout the entirety of the period of U.S. internal territorial conquest and consolidation.[5] By 1900, the federal obligations to Indian nations were therefore quite extensive.

FINANCIAL FACTORS

As Vine Deloria, Jr., has observed:

> The original relationship between the United States government and American Indian [nations] was one of treaties. Beginning with the establishment of federal policy toward Indians in the Northwest Ordinance of 1787, which pledged that the utmost good faith would be exercised toward the Indian [nations], and continuing through many treaties and statutes, the relationship has gradually evolved into a strange and stifling union in which the United States has become responsible for all the programs and policies affecting Indian communities.[6]

What this meant in practice was that the government was being required to underwrite the cost of a proliferating bureaucratic apparatus overseeing "service delivery" to Indians, a process initiated on April 16, 1818, with the passage of an act (*U.S. Statutes at Large,* 13:461) requiring the placement of a federal agent with each Indian nation, to serve as liaison and to "administer the discharge of Governmental obligations thereto." As the number of Indian groups with which the United States held relations had increased, so too had the number of "civilizing" programs and services undertaken, ostensibly in their behalf. This was all well and good during the time-span when it was seen as a politico-military requirement, but by the turn of the century this need had passed. The situation was compounded by the fact that the era of Indian population decline engendered by war and disease had also come to an end; the population eligible for per capita benefits, which had been reduced to a quarter-million by the 1890s, could be expected to rebound steadily in the 20th century. With its land base secured, the United States was casting about for a satisfactory mechanism to avoid paying the ongoing costs associated with its acquisition.

The most obvious route to this end, of course, lay in simply and overtly refusing to comply with the terms of the treaties, thus abrogating them.[7] The problems in this regard were, however, both two-fold and extreme. First, the deliberate invalidation of the U.S. treaties with the Indians would (obviously) tend to simultaneously invalidate the legitimacy which the country attributed to its occupancy of much of North America. Second, such a move would immediately negate the useful and carefully nurtured image the U.S. had cultivated of itself as a country of progressive laws rather than raw force. The federal government had to appear to continue to meet its commitments, while at the same time avoiding them, or at least containing them at some acceptable level. A devious approach to the issue was needed.

This was found in the so-called "blood quantum" or "degree of Indian blood" standard of American Indian identification which had been adopted by Congress in 1887 as part of the General Allotment Act. The function of this piece of legislation was to expedite the process of Indian "civilization" by unilaterally dissolving their collectively (i.e., nationally) held reservation land holdings. Reservation lands were reallocated in accordance with the "superior" (i.e., Euroamerican) concept of property: *individually* deeded land parcels, usually of 160 acres each. Each Indian, identified as being those documentably of *one-half or more Indian blood,* was entitled to receive title in fee of such a parcel; all others were simply disenfranchised altogether. Reserved Indian land which remained unallotted after all "blooded" Indians had received their individual parcels was to be declared "surplus" and opened up for non-Indian use and occupancy.

Needless to say, there were nowhere near enough Indians meeting the Act's genetic requirements to absorb by individual parcel the quantity of acreage involved in the formerly reserved land areas. Consequently, between 1887 and 1934, the aggregate Indian land base within the U.S. was "legally" reduced from about 138 million acres to about 48 million.[8] Moreover, the allotment process itself had been manipulated in such a way that the worst reservation acreage tended to be parceled out to Indians, while the best was opened to non-Indian homesteading and corporate use; nearly 20 million of the acres remaining in Indian hands by the latter year were arid or semi-arid, and thus marginal or useless for agricultural purposes.[9]

By the early 1900s, then, the eugenics mechanism of the blood quantum had already proven itself such a boon in the federal management of its Indian affairs that it was generally adapted as the "eligibility factor," triggering entitlement to any federal service from the issuance of commodity rations to health care, annuity payments, and educational benefits. If the government could not repeal its obligations to Indians, it could at least act to limit their number, thereby diminishing the cost associated with underwriting their entitlements on a per capita basis. Concomitantly, it must have seemed logical that if the overall number of Indians could be kept small, the administrative expenses involved in their service programs might also be held to a minimum. Much of the original impetus toward the federal preemption of the sovereign Indian prerogative of defining "who's Indian," and the standardization of the racist degree-of-blood method of Indian identification, derived from the budgetary considerations of a federal government anxious to avoid paying its bills.

OTHER ECONOMIC FACTORS

As the example of the General Allotment Act clearly demonstrates, economic determinants other than the mere outflow of cash from the federal treasury figure into the federal utilization of the blood quantum. The huge windfall of land expropriated by the United States as a result of the act was only the tip of the iceberg. For instance, in constricting the acknowledged size of Indian populations, the government could technically meet its obligations to reserve "first rights" to water usage for Indians while simultaneously siphoning off artificial "surpluses" to non-Indian agricultural, ranching, municipal, and industrial use in the arid west.[10] The same principle pertains to the assignment of fishing quotas in the Pacific Northwest, a matter directly related to the development of a lucrative non-Indian fishing industry there.[11]

By the 1920s, it was also becoming increasingly apparent that much of the agriculturally worthless terrain left to Indians after allotment lay astride rich deposits of natural resources such as coal, copper, oil, and natural gas; later in the century, it was revealed that some 60 percent of all "domestic" uranium reserves also lay beneath reservation lands. It was therefore becoming imperative, from the viewpoint of federal and corporate economic planners, to gain unhindered access to these assets. Given that it would have been just as problematic to simply seize the resources as it would have been to abrogate the treaties, another expedient was required. This assumed the form of legislation unilaterally extending the responsibilities of citizenship (though not all the rights; Indians are still regulated by about 5,000 more laws than other citizens) over all American Indians within the United States.

> Approximately two-thirds of the Indian population had citizenship conferred upon them under the 1877 Allotment Act, as a condition of the allotment of their holdings. . . . [In 1924] an act of Congress [8 U.S.C.A. 1402 (a) (2)] declared all Indians to be citizens of the United States and of the states in which they resided. . . .[12]

The Indian Citizenship Act greatly confused the circumstances even of many of the blooded and federally certified Indians insofar as it was held to bear legal force, and to carry legal obligations, whether or not any given Indian or group of Indians wished to be a U.S. citizen. As for the host of non-certified, mixed-blood people residing in the U.S., their status was finally "clarified"; they had been definitionally absorbed into the American mainstream at the stroke of the congressional pen. And, despite the fact that the act technically left certified Indians occupying the status of citizenship in their own indigenous nation as well as in the U.S. (a "dual form" of citizenship so awkward as to be sublime), the juridical door had been opened by which the weight of Indian obligations would begin to accrue more to the U.S. than to themselves. Resource negotiations would henceforth be conducted between "American citizens" rather than between representatives of separate nations, a context in which federal and corporate arguments "for the greater good" could be predicted to prevail.

In 1934, the effects of the citizenship act were augmented by the passage of the Indian Reorganization Act. The expressed purpose of this law was finally and completely to usurp the traditional mechanisms of American Indian governance (e.g., the traditional chiefs, council of elders, etc.), replacing them with a system of federally approved and regulated "tribal councils." These councils, in turn, were consciously structured more along the lines of corporate boards than of governmental entities. As Section 17 of the IRA, which spells out the council functions, puts the matter:

> [An IRA charter] may convey to the incorporated tribe the power to purchase, take by gift, or bequest, or otherwise, own, hold, manage, operate, and dispose of property of every description, real and personal, including the power to purchase restricted Indian lands and to issue in exchange for corporate property, and such further powers as may be incidental to the conduct of corporate business, not inconsistent with the law.

Indeed, since the exercise of such typical governmental attributes as jurisdiction over criminal law had already been stripped away from the councils by legislation such as the 1885 Major Crimes Act, there has been very little for the IRA form of Indian government to do *but* sign off on leasing and other business arrangements with external interests. The situation was and is compounded by the fact that grassroots Indian resistance to the act's "acceptance" on many reservations was overcome by federal manipulation of local referenda.[13] This has left the IRA governments in the position of owing Washington rather than their supposed constituents for whatever legitimacy they may possess. All in all, it was and is a situation made to order for the rubber-stamping of plans integral to U.S. economic development at the direct expense of Indian nations and individual Indian people. This is readily borne out by the fact that, as of 1984, American Indians received, on the average, less than 20 percent of the market royalty rates (i.e., the rates paid to non-Indians) for the extraction of minerals from their land. As Winona LaDuke observes:

> By official census counts, there are only about 1½ million Indians in the United States. By conservative estimates a quarter of all the low sulphur coal in the United States lies under our reservation land. About 15 percent of all the oil and natural gas lies there, as well as two-thirds of the uranium. 100 percent of all U.S. uranium production since 1955 has been on Indian land. And we have a lot of copper, timber, water rights and other resources too. By any reasonable estimation, with this small number of people and vast amount of resources, we should be the richest group in the United States. But we are the poorest. Indians have the lowest per capita income of any population group in the U.S. We have the highest rate of unemployment and the lowest level of educational attainment. We have the highest rates of malnutrition, plague disease, death by exposure and infant mortality. On the other hand, we have the shortest life-span. Now, I think this says it all. Indian wealth is going somewhere, and that somewhere is definitely not to Indians. I don't know your definition of colonialism, but this certainly fits into mine.[14]

In sum, the financial advantages incurred by the United States in its appropriation of the definition of Indian identity have been neatly joined to even more powerful economic motivators during this century. The previously noted reluctance of the federal government to pay its bills cannot be uncoupled from its desire to profit from the resources of others.

CONTEMPORARY POLITICAL FACTORS

The utilization of treaties as instruments by which to begin the subordination of American Indian nations to U.S. hegemony, as well as subsequent legislation, such as the Major Crime Act, the General Allotment Act, and the Termination Act, all carry remarkably clear political overtones. This, to be sure, is the language of the colonizer and the colonized, to borrow a phrase from Albert Memmi,[15] and in each case the federal manipulation of the question of American Indian identity has played its role. These examples, however, may rightly be perceived as being both historical and parts of the "grand scheme" of U.S. internal colonialism (or "Manifest Destiny," as it was once called).

Today, the function of the Indian identity question appears to reside at the less rarified level of maintaining the status quo. First, it goes to the matter of keeping the aggregate number of Indians at less than 1 percent of the overall U.S. population and thus devoid of any potential electoral power. Second, and perhaps of equal importance, it goes to the classic "divide and conquer" strategy of keeping Indians at odds with one another, even within their own communities. As Tim Giago, conservative editor of the *Lakota Times,* asks:

> Don't we have enough problems trying to unite without . . . additional headaches? Why must people be categorized as full-bloods, mixed-bloods, etc? Many years ago, the Bureau of Indian Affairs decided to establish blood quanta for the purpose of [tribal] enrollment. At that time, blood quantum was set at one-fourth degree for enrollment. Unfortunately, through the years this caused many people on the

> reservation to be categorized and labeled . . . [The] situation [is] created solely by the BIA, with the able assistance of the Department of Interior.[16]

What has occurred is that the limitation of federal resources allocated to meeting U.S. obligations to American Indians has become so severe that Indians themselves have increasingly begun to enforce the race codes excluding the genetically marginalized from both identification as Indian citizens and consequent entitlements. In theory, such a posture leaves greater per capita shares for all remaining "bona fide" Indians. But, as American Indian Movement activist Russell Means has pointed out:

> The situation is absurd. Our treaties say nothing about your having to be such-and-such a degree of blood in order to be covered . . . when the federal government made its guarantees to our nations in exchange for our land, it committed to provide certain services to us as we defined ourselves. As nations, and as a *people*. This seems to have been forgotten. Now we have Indian people who spend most of their time trying to prevent other Indian people from being recognized as such, just so that a few more crumbs—crumbs from the federal table—may be available to them, personally. I don't have to tell you that this isn't the Indian way of doing things. The Indian way would be to get together and demand what is coming to each and every one of us, instead of trying to cancel each other out. We are acting like colonized peoples, like subject peoples. . . .[17]

The nature of the dispute has followed the classic formulation of Frantz Fanon, wherein the colonizer contrives issues which pit the colonized against one another, fighting viciously for some presumed status within the colonial structure, never having time or audacity enough to confront their oppressors.[18] In the words of Stella Pretty Sounding Flute, a member of the Crow Creek band of Lakota, "My grandmother used to say that Indian blood was getting all mixed up, and some day there would be a terrible mess. . . . [Now] no matter which way we turn, the white man has taken over."[19]

The problem, of course, has been conscientiously exacerbated by the government through its policies of leasing individual reservation land parcels to non-Indians, increasingly "checkerboarding" tribal holdings since 1900. Immediate economic consequences aside, this has virtually ensured that a sufficient number of non-Indians would be residents in reservations, and that intermarriage would steadily result. During the 1950s, the federal relocation program—in which reservation-based Indians were subsidized to move to cities, where they might be anticipated as being subsumed within vastly larger non-Indian populations—accelerated the process of "biological hybridization." Taken in combination with the ongoing federal insistence that "Indianness" could be measured only by degree of blood, these policies tend to speak for themselves. Even in 1972 when, through the Indian Education Act (86 *Stat.* 334), the government seemed finally to be abandoning the blood quantum, there was a hidden agenda. As Lorelei DeCora (Means), a former Indian education program coordinator, put it:

> The question was really one of control, whether Indians would ever be allowed to control the identification of their own group members or citizens. First there was this strict blood quantum thing, and it was enforced for a hundred years, over the strong objections of a lot of Indians. Then, when things were sufficiently screwed up because of that, the feds suddenly reverse themselves completely, saying it's all a matter of self-identification. Almost anybody who wants to can just walk in and announce that he or she is Indian—no familiarity with tribal history, or Indian affairs, community recognition, or anything else really required—and, under the law, there's not a lot that Indians can do about it. The whole thing is suddenly just . . . really out of control. At that point, you really did have a lot of people showing up claiming that one of their ancestors, seven steps removed, had been some sort of "Cherokee princess." And we were obliged to accept that, and provide services. Hell, if all of that was real, there are more Cherokees in the world than there are Chinese.[20]

Predictably, Indians of all perspectives on the identity question reacted strongly against such gratuitous dilution of themselves. The result was a broad rejection of what was perceived as "the federal attempt to convert us from being the citizens of our own sovereign nations into benign members of some sort of all-purpose U.S. 'minority group,' without sovereign rights."[21] For its part, the government, without so much as a pause to consider the connotations of the word "sovereign" in this connection, elected to view such statements as an *Indian* demand for resumption of the universal application of the blood-quantum standard. Consequently, the Reagan administration, during the 1980s, set out to gut the Indian Education Act[22] and to enforce degree-of-blood requirements for federal services, such as those of the Indian Health Service.[23]

An even clearer example of the contemporary reassertion of eugenics principles in federal Indian identification policies came under the Bush administration. On November 30, 1990, Public Law 101-644 (104 *Stat.* 4662) went into effect. Grotesquely described as "an Act to promote development of Indian arts and crafts," the statute legally restricts definition of American Indian artists to those possessing a federally issued "Certificate of Degree of Indian Blood"—derogatorally referred to as "pedigree slips" by opponents—or those certified as such by "federally recognized tribes" or the "Alaska Native Corporation." Excluded are not only those who fall below blood-quantum requirements, but anyone who has, for politico-philosophical reasons, refused to cooperate with federal pretensions to define for itself who will and who will not be considered a member and citizen of a recognized indigenous nation. Further, the entire populations of federally unrecognized nations such as the populous Lumbees of North Carolina, Abenakis of Vermont, and more than 200 others, are simply written out of existence even in terms of their internal membership identification as Indians.

In order to put "teeth" into the legislation, Congress imposed penalties of up to $1 million in fines and as much as fifteen years in a federal prison for anyone not meeting its definition to "offer to display for sale or to sell any good, with or without a Government trademark, which . . . suggests it is Indian produced." For galleries, museums, and other private concerns to display as "Indian arts or crafts" the work of any person not meeting the federal definition of Indian-ness, a fine of up to $5 million is imposed. Under such conditions, the Cherokee National Museum in Muskogee, Oklahoma was forced to close its doors when it was discovered that even the late Willard Stone—a talented sculptor, creator of the Great Seal of the Cherokee Nation, and a probable "full blood"—had never registered himself as a bona fide Indian according to federal standards.[24] At this juncture, things have become such a welter of confusion that:

> The Federal government, State governments and the Census Bureau all have different criteria for defining "Indians" for statistical purposes, and even Federal criteria are not consistent among Federal agencies. For example, a State desiring financial aid to assist Indian education receives the aid only for the number of people with one-quarter or more Indian blood. For preference in hiring, enrollment records from a Federally recognized tribe are required. Under regulations for law and order, anyone of "Indian descent" is counted as an Indian. If the Federal criteria are inconsistent, State guidelines are [at this point] even more chaotic. In the course of preparing this report, the Commission contacted several States with large Indian populations to determine their criteria. Two States accept the individual's own determination. Four accept individuals as Indian if they were "recognized in the community" as Native Americans. Five use residence on a reservation as criteria. One requires one-quarter blood, and still another uses the Census Bureau definition that Indians are who they say they are.[25]

This, without doubt, is a situation made to order for conflict, among Indians more than anyone else. Somehow, it is exceedingly difficult to imagine that the government would wish to see things turn out any other way.

IMPLICATIONS

The eventual outcome of federal blood-quantum policies can be described as little other than genocidal in their final implications. As historian Patricia Nelson Limerick recently summarized the process:

> Set the blood quantum at one-quarter, hold to it as a rigid definition of Indians, let intermarriage proceed as it had for centuries, and eventually Indians will be defined out of existence. When that happens, the federal government will be freed of its persistent "Indian problem."[26]

Already, this conclusion receives considerable validation in the experience of the Indians of California, such as the Juaneño. Pursuant to the "Pit River Consolidated Land Settlement" of the 1970s, in which the government purported to "compensate" many of the small California bands for lands expropriated during the course of non-Indian "settlement" in that state (at less than 50 cents per acre), the Juaneño and a number of other "Mission Indians" were simply declared to be "extinct." This policy was pursued despite the fact that substantial numbers of such Indians were known to exist, and that the government was at the time issuing settlement checks to them. The tribal rolls were simply ordered closed to *any* new additions, despite the fact that many of the people involved were still bearing children, and their population might well have been expanding. It was even suggested in some instances that children born after an arbitrary cutoff date should be identified as "Hispanic" or "Mexican" in order that they benefit from federal and state services to minority groups.[27]

When attempting to come to grips with the issues raised by such federal policies, the recently "dissolved" California groups, as well as a number of previously unrecognized ones such as the Gay Head Wampanoags (long described as extinct), confronted a Catch-22 situation worthy of Joseph Heller. This rested in the federal criteria for recognition of Indian existence to the present day:

1. An Indian is a member of any federally recognized Indian Tribe. To be federally recognized, an Indian Tribe must be comprised of Indians.
2. To gain federal recognition, an Indian Tribe must have a land base. To secure a land base, an Indian Tribe must be federally recognized.[28]

As Shoshone activist Josephine C. Mills put it in 1964, "There is no longer any need to shoot down Indians in order to take away their rights and land [or to wipe them out] . . . legislation is sufficient to do the trick legally."[29]

The notion of genocidal implications in all this receives firm reinforcement from the increasing federal propensity to utilize residual Indian land bases as dumping grounds for many of the more virulently toxic by-products of its advanced technology and industry.[30] By the early '70s, this practice had become so pronounced that the Four Corners and Black Hills regions, two of the more heavily populated locales (by Indians) in the country, had been semi-officially designated as prospective "National Sacrifice Areas" in the interests of projected U.S. energy development.[31] This, in turn, provoked Russell Means to observe that such a move would turn the Lakota, Navajo, Laguna, and other native nations into "national sacrifice peoples."[32]

AMERICAN INDIAN RESPONSE

Of late, there have been encouraging signs that American Indians of many perspectives and political persuasions have begun to arrive at common conclusions regarding the use to which the federal government had been putting their identity and the compelling need for Indians to finally reassert complete control over this vital aspect of their lives. For instance, Dr. Frank

Ryan, a liberal and rather establishmentarian Indian who has served as the director of the federal Office of Indian Education, began during the early 1980s to reach some rather hard conclusions about the policies of his employers. Describing the federal blood-quantum criteria for benefits eligibility in the educational arena as "a racist policy," Ryan went on to term it nothing more than "a shorthand method for denying Indian children admission to federal schools [and other programs]."[33] He concluded that, "The power to determine tribal membership has always been an essential attribute of inherent tribal sovereignty," and called for abolition of federal guidelines on the question of Indian identity without *any* lessening of federal obligations to the individuals and groups affected.[34] The question of the (re)adoption of blood-quantum standards by the Indian Health Service, proposed during the '80s by the Reagan administration, has served as even more of a catalyst. The National Congress of American Indians, never a bastion of radicalism, took up the issue at its 43rd Annual Convention, in October 1986. The NCAI produced a sharply worded statement rejecting federal identification policy:

> [T]he federal government, in an effort to erode tribal sovereignty and reduce the number of Indians to the point where they are politically, economically and culturally insignificant, [is being censured by] many of the more than 500 Indian leaders [attending the convention].[35]

The statement went on to condemn:

> . . . a proposal by the Indian Health Service to establish blood quotas for Indians, thus allowing the federal government to determine who is Indian and who is not, for the purpose of health care. Tribal leaders argue that *only* the individual tribe, not the federal government, should have this right, and many are concerned that this debate will overlap [as it has, long since] into Indian education and its regulation as well [emphasis added].[36]

Charles E. Dawes, Second Chief of the Ottawa Indian Tribe of Oklahoma, took the convention position much further at about the same time:

> What could not be completed over a three hundred year span [by force of arms] may now be completed in our life-span by administrative law. . . . What I am referring to is the continued and expanded use of blood quantum to determine eligibility of Indian people for government entitlement programs . . . [in] such areas as education, health care, management and economic assistance . . . [obligations] that the United States government imposed upon itself in treaties with sovereign Indian nations. . . . We as tribal leaders made a serious mistake in accepting [genetic] limits in educational programs, and we must not make the same mistake again in health programs. On the contrary, we must fight any attempt to limit any program by blood quantum every time there is mention of such a possibility . . . we simply cannot give up on this issue—ever. . . . Our commitment as tribal leaders must be to eliminate any possibility of *genocide* for our people by administrative law. We must dedicate our efforts to insuring that . . . Native American people[s] will be clearly identified without reference to blood quantum . . . and that our sovereign Indian Nations will be recognized as promised [emphasis added].[37]

On the Pine Ridge Reservation in South Dakota, the Oglala Lakota have become leaders in totally abandoning blood quantum as a criterion for tribal enrollment, opting instead to consider factors such as residency on the reservation, affinity to and knowledge of, as well as service to the Oglala people.[38] This follows the development of a recent "tradition" of Oglala militancy in which tribal members played a leading role in challenging federal conceptions of Indian identity during the 1972 Trail of Broken Treaties takeover of BIA headquarters in Washington, and seven non-Indian members of the Vietnam Veterans Against the War were naturalized as citizens of the "Independent Oglala Nation" during the 1973 siege of Wounded Knee.[39] In 1986, at a meeting of the United Sioux Tribes in Pierre, South Dakota, Oglala representatives lobbied the leaders of other Lakota reservations to broaden their own enrollment criteria beyond federal norms. This is so, despite recognition that "in the past fifty years, since the Indian Reorganization Act of 1934, tribal leaders have been reluctant to recognize blood from individuals from other tribes [or any one else]."[40]

In Alaska, the Haida have produced a new draft constitution which offers a full expression of indigenous sovereignty, at least insofar as the identity of citizenry is concerned. The Haida draft begins with those who are now acknowledged as members of the Haida nation and posits that all those who marry Haidas will also be considered eligible for naturalized citizenship (just as in any other nation). The children of such unions would also be Haida citizens from birth, regardless of their degree of Indian blood, and children adopted by Haidas would also be considered citizens.[41] On Pine Ridge, a similar "naturalization" plank had surfaced in the 1983 TREATY platform upon which Russell Means attempted to run for the Oglala Lakota tribal presidency before being disqualified at the insistence of the BIA.[42]

An obvious problem that might be associated with this trend is that even though Indian nations have begun to recognize their citizens by their own standards rather than those of the federal government, the government may well refuse to recognize the entitlement of unblooded tribal members to the same services and benefits as any other. In fact, there is every indication that this is the federal intent, and such a disparity of "status" stands to heighten tensions among Indians, destroying their fragile rebirth of unity and solidarity before it gets off the ground. Federal policy in this regard is, however, also being challenged.

Most immediately, this concerns the case of Dianne Zarr, an enrolled member of the Sherwood Valley Pomo Band of Indians, who is of less than one-quarter degree of Indian blood. On September 11, 1980, Zarr filed an application for higher educational grant benefits, and was shortly rejected as not meeting quantum requirements. Zarr went through all appropriate appeal procedures before filing, on July 15, 1983, a suit in federal court, seeking to compel award of her benefits. This was denied by the district court on April 2, 1985. Zarr appealed and, on September 26, 1985, the lower court was reversed on the basis of the "Snyder Act" (25 U.S.C. S297), which precludes discrimination based solely on racial criteria.[43] Zarr received her grant, setting a very useful precedent for the future.

Still, realizing that the utility of the U.S. courts will necessarily be limited, a number of Indian organizations have recently begun to seek to bring international pressure to bear on the federal government. The Indian Law Resource Center, National Indian Youth Council, and, for a time, the International Indian Treaty Council have repeatedly taken Native American issues before the United Nations Working Group on Indigenous Populations (a component of the U.N. Commission on Human Rights) in Geneva, Switzerland, since 1977. Another forum that has been utilized for this purpose has been the Fourth Russell International Tribunal on the Rights of the Indians of the Americas, held in Rotterdam, Netherlands, in 1980. Additionally, delegations from various Indian nations and organizations have visited, often under auspices of the host governments, more than thirty countries during the past decade.[44]

CONCLUSION

The history of the U.S. imposition of its standards of identification upon American Indians is particularly ugly. Its cost to Indians has involved millions of acres of land, the water by which to make much of this land agriculturally useful, control over vast mineral resources that might have afforded them a comfortable standard of living, and the ability to form themselves into viable and meaningful political blocks at any level. Worse, it has played a prominent role in bringing about their generalized psychic disempowerment; if one is not allowed even to determine for one's self, or within one's peer group, the answer to the all-important question "Who am I?," what possible personal power can one feel s/he possesses? The negative impact, both physically and psychologically, of this process upon succeeding generations of Native Americans in the United States is simply incalculable.

The blood-quantum mechanism most typically used by the federal government to assign identification to individuals over the years is as racist as any conceivable policy. It has brought about the systematic marginalization and eventual exclusion of many more Indians from their own cultural/national designation than it has retained. This is all the more apparent when one considers that, while one-quarter degree of blood has been the norm used in defining *Indian-ness,* the quantum has varied from time to time and place to place; one-half blood was the standard utilized in the case of the Mississippi Choctaws and adopted in the Wheeler-Howard Act; one sixty-fourth was utilized in establishing the Santee rolls in Nebraska. It is hardly unnatural, under the circumstances, that federal policy has set off a ridiculous game of one-upmanship in Indian Country: "I'm more Indian than you" and "You aren't Indian enough to say (or do, or think) that" have become common assertions during the second half of the 20th century.

The restriction of federal entitlement funds to cover only the relatively few Indians who meet quantum requirements, essentially a cost-cutting policy at its inception, has served to exacerbate tensions over the identity issue among Indians. It has established a scenario in which it has been perceived as profitable for one Indian to cancel the identity of her/his neighbor as means of receiving her/his entitlement. Thus, a bitter divisiveness has been built into Indian communities and national policies, sufficient to preclude our achieving the internal unity necessary to offer any serious challenge to the status quo. At every turn, U.S. practice vis-à-vis American Indians is indicative of an advanced and extremely successful system of colonialism.

Fortunately, increasing numbers of Indians are waking up to the fact that this is the case. The recent analysis and positions assumed by such politically diverse Indian nations, organizations, and individuals as Frank Ryan and Russell Means, the National Congress of American Indians and the Indian Law Resource Center, the Haida and the Oglala are a very favorable sign. The willingness of the latter two nations simply to defy federal standards and adopt identification and enrollment policies in line with their own interests and traditions is particularly important. Recent U.S. court decisions, such as that in the *Zarr* case, and growing international attention and concern over the circumstances of Native Americans are also hopeful indicators that things may be at long last changing for the better.

We are currently at a crossroads. If American Indians are able to continue the positive trend in which we reassert our sovereign prerogative to control the criteria of our own membership, we may reasonably assume that we will be able to move onward, into a true process of decolonization and reestablishment of ourselves as functioning national entities. The alternative, of course, is that we will fail, continue to be duped into bickering over the question of "who's Indian" in light of federal guidelines, and thus facilitate not only our own continued subordination, expropriation, and colonization, but ultimately our own statistical extermination.

NOTES

1. Kappler, Charles J., ed., *Indian Treaties, 1778–1883,* Interland Publishing Co., New York, (Second Printing) 1973, pp. 3–5.
2. Ibid., pp. 7–9.
3. Adams, Evelyn C., *American Indian Education: Government Schools and Economic Progress,* King's Crown Press, New York, 1946, pp. 30–31.
4. Calhoun is quoted in *American State Papers: Indian Affairs* (Volume II), Wilmington, Delaware, 1972, pp. 183–4.
5. The bulk of the obligations in question were established prior to Congress' 1871 suspension of

treaty-making with "the tribes" (Title 25, Section 71, U.S. Code). Additional obligations were undertaken by the federal government thereafter by "agreement" and as part of its ongoing agenda of completing the socio-political subordination of Indians, with an eye toward their eventual "assimilation" into the dominant culture and polity.

6. Deloria, Vine, Jr., "The Place of Indians In Contemporary Education," *American Indian Journal,* Vol. 2, No. 21, February, 1976, p. 2.
7. This strategy was actually tried in the wake of the passage of the House Concurrent Resolution 108 in June 1953. Predictably, the federal dissolution of American Indian nations such as the Klamath and Menominee so tarnished the U.S. image that implementation of the policy was shortly suspended (albeit the law remains on the books).
8. Collier, John, *Memorandum, Hearings on H.B. 7902 Before the House Committee on Indian Affairs,* (73rd Cong., 2d Sess.), U.S. Department of the Interior, Washington, D.C., 1934, pp. 16–18.
9. Deloria, Vine, Jr., and Clifford M. Lytle, *American Indians, American Justice,* University of Texas Press, Austin, 1983, p. 10.
10. See Hundley, Norris C., Jr., "The Dark and Bloody Ground of Indian Water Rights," in Roxanne Dunbar Ortiz and Larry Emerson, eds., *Economic Development in Indian Reservations,* University of New Mexico Press, Albuquerque, 1979.
11. See American Friends Service Committee, *Uncommon Controversy: Fishing Rights of the Muckleshoot, Puyallup, and Nisqually Indians,* University of Washington Press, Seattle, 1970. Also see Cohen, Fay G., *Treaties on Trial: The Continuing Controversy over Northwest Indian Fishing Rights,* University of Washington Press, Seattle, 1986.
12. League of Women Voters, *Indian Country,* Publication No. 605, Washington, D.C., 1977, p. 24.
13. Probably the best overview of the IRA process may be found in Deloria, Vine, Jr., and Clifford M. Lytle, *The Nations Within: The Past and Future of American Indian Sovereignty,* Pantheon Press, New York, 1984; on referenda fraud, see Chapter 11.
14. LaDuke, Winona, presentation at International Women's Week activities, University of Colorado at Boulder, March 13, 1984; tape on file.
15. Memmi, Albert, *The Colonizer and the Colonized,* Beacon Press, Boston, 1967.
16. Giago, Tim, "Blood Quantum Is a Degree of Discrimination," *Notes From Indian Country,* Vol. 1, State Publishing Co., Pierre, SD, 1984, p. 337.
17. Means, Russell, speech at the law school of the University of Colorado at Boulder, April 19, 1985; tape on file.
18. See Fanon, Frantz, *The Wretched of the Earth,* Grove Press, New York, 1966.
19. Quoted in Martz, Ron, "Indians decry verification plan for federally-funded health care," *Cox News Service,* Pierre, SD, October 7, 1986.
20. DeCora (Means), Lorelei, statement on radio station KILI, Porcupine, SD, October 12, 1986.
21. Means, Ted, statement before the South Dakota Indian Education Association, Pierre, SD, November 16, 1975.
22. See Jones, Richard, *American Indian Policy: Selected Major Issues in the 98th Congress,* Issue Brief No. 1B83083, Library of Congress, Government Division, Washington, D.C. (updated version, February 6, 1984), pp. 3–4.
23. Martz, op. cit.
24. Nichols, Lyn, "New Indian Art Regulations Shut Down Muskogee Museum," *San Francisco Examiner,* December 3, 1990.
25. American Indian Policy Review Commission, *Final Report,* Vol. 1, May 17, 1977, U.S. Government Printing Office, Washington, D.C., 1977, p. 89.
26. Limerick, Patricia Nelson, *The Legacy of Conquest: The Unbroken Past of the American West,* W. W. Norton and Co., New York, 1987, p. 338.
27. The author is an enrolled Juaneño, as is her eldest son. Her younger son, born after the closing of the Juaneño rolls, is not "federally recognized" as an Indian, despite the fact that his genealogy, cultural background, etc., is identical to that of his brother. The "suggestions" mentioned in the text were made to the author by a federal employee in 1979. The Juaneño band in California, in the 1990s, is initiating federal recognition procedures.
28. Native American Consultants, Inc., *Indian Definition Study,* contracted pursuant to P.L. 95-561, Title IV, Section 1147, submitted to the Office of the Assistant Secretary of Education, U. S. Department of Education, Washington, D.C., January 1980, p. 2.
29. Quoted in Armstrong, Virginia I., *I Have Spoken: American History Through the Voices of Indians,* Pocket Books, New York, 1975, p. 175.

PERSONAL ACCOUNT

Shopping With A Friend

My best friend and I decided that we wanted to take pictures together in the photo booth in our local mall. Taking pictures meant buying new outfits. So we decided to go shopping at a center downtown one day after school. We picked a store and began our search.

We browsed for a bit before deciding to try on two items each. That afternoon, there was only one sales associate working. My friend and I had to wait for what seemed like five minutes before we could get her attention to request to use the dressing room. She quickly checked what we had and handed us a ticket listing the number of clothing items. She motioned for us to go into the dressing room as she continued her telephone conversation.

While we were trying on our clothes, my friend suddenly realized that she had to be home within the next half-hour. That meant we had to hurry up because we had to catch the bus. We put the clothes back on the hangers and left the dressing room. We tried to get the sales associate's attention to show her that we had returned the clothes to the rack outside the dressing room, but she was too involved in her telephone conversation to notice us.

On our way out, my friend wanted to stop briefly in the adjoining store. Shortly after we entered, I felt a hand on *my* shoulder. A security guard was standing directly behind me. He said to me in a very authoritative voice, "Come with me, please." He brought me back to the store we had just left. My friend followed. The sales associate approached us and said to me in a very accusatory tone of voice, "Where are the clothes that you tried on?" At that point, my heart was pounding. She thinks I stole the clothes, I thought to myself. I just prayed that the clothes were still where I left them. Otherwise, it would be my word again against hers. I walked toward the rack. At first I did not see them. That happens sometimes in panicky situations. Thank God my best friend saw them and said, "They are right there." I handed the clothes to the sales associate, who snatched them away and left in a huff. No apology, no thank you, nothing.

I have often heard the saying "Nothing is a black-or-white issue." My situation was obviously the exception. In terms of black and white, I am black, my best friend appears to be white—although she is black and white—and the sales associate is white. That explains why I was questioned and not my friend.

What bothers me most is that the sales associate truly felt that she did not owe me an apology. She considered her actions to be completely justified. I would not have been as mad if she had told the security guard that *two* teenage girls might have stolen some clothing, but she did not do that. She singled me out simply because I am black. In addition, my best friend looked at the situation as merely a misunderstanding, Also, she could not be supportive in an empathetic way because she had never been subjected to that kind of treatment. Although it happened three years ago, retelling the story still brings back all the anger, embarrassment, and frustration that I felt on that day.

Rashonda Ambrose

30. See Churchill, Ward, "American Indian Lands: The Native Ethic amid Resource Development," *Environment,* Vol. 28, No. 6, July/August 1986, pp. 12–17, 28–33.
31. Ibid.
32. Means, Russell, "The Same Old Song," in Ward Churchill, ed., *Marxism and Native Americans,* South End Press, Boston, 1983, p. 25.
33. Ryan, Frank A., *A Working Paper Prepared for the National Advisory Committee on Indian Education,* Paper No. 071279, Harvard American Indian Education Program, Harvard University Graduate School of Education, Cambridge, MA, July 18, 1979, p. 3.
34. Ibid., pp. 41–44.
35. Quoted in Martz, Ron, "Indians maintain U.S. trying to erode tribal sovereignty: cultural insignificance said to be goal," *Cox News Service,* Pierre, SD, October 26, 1986.
36. Quoted in Martz, Ron, "Indians decry verification plan for federally-funded health care," *Cox News Service,* Pierre, SD, October 26, 1986.
37. Dawes, Charles E., "Tribal leaders see danger in use of blood quantum as eligibility standard," *The Uset Calumet,* Nashville, TN, February/March, 1986, pp. 7–8.
38. "Indians decry verification plan for federally-funded health care," op. cit.

39. On the Trail of Broken Treaties challenge, see Editors, *BIA, I'm Not Your Indian Any More, Akwesasne Notes,* Mohawk Nation via Rooseveltown, NY, 1973, p. 78. On VVAW naturalization, see Burnette, Robert, and John Koster, *The Road to Wounded Knee,* Bantam Books, New York, 1974, p. 238.
40. "Indians maintain U.S. trying to erode tribal sovereignty," op. cit.
41. Draft, Haida Constitution, circa 1982, xerox copy provided to the author by Pam Colorado.
42. *TREATY: The Campaign of Russell Means for the Presidency of the Oglala Sioux Tribe,* Porcupine, SD, 1982, p. 3.
43. *Zarr v. Barlow, et al.,* No. 85-2170, U.S. Ninth Circuit Court of Appeals, District Court for the Northern District of California, Judge John P. Vukasin presiding.
44. These have included Austria, Cuba, Nicaragua, Poland, East Germany, Hungary, Rumania, Switzerland, Algeria, Grenada, El Salvador, Colombia, Tunisia, Libya, Syria, Jordan, Iran, the Maori of New Zealand, New Aotara (Australia), Belize, Mexico, Costa Rica, Guinea, Kenya, Micronesia, the USSR, Finland, Norway, Sweden, Canada, Great Britain, Netherlands, France, Belgium, Japan, West Germany, Bulgaria, Yugoslavia, and Papua (New Guinea). The list here is undoubtedly incomplete.

READING 4

La Raza and the Melting Pot: A Comparative Look at Multiethnicity

Carlos A. Fernández

LATIN AMERICA: LA RAZA CÓSMICA[1]

. . . The year 1992 marks the 500th anniversary of the accidental discovery of the Americas by Columbus under the sponsorship of the Catholic Spanish monarchs Isabella and Fernando. In the United States, we refer to the commemoration of this discovery as Columbus Day. In parts of Latin America, however, they celebrate El Día de la Raza (the Day of the [New Mixed] Race). The different names for the same observance illustrate one of the most fundamental cultural, historical, and even philosophical differences between the United States and Latin America, namely, the way we view race and interracial mixture.[2]

Many Americans are unaware of the "racial" history of Latin America. Evidence for this can be found in the fact that people of Latin American origin or ancestry are included as "Whites" in the U.S. Census, and since about 1980 have come to be referred to as "Hispanic," that is, European (Muñoz, 1989). What is the truth of the matter?

Mexico and Mexicans

. . . The racial history of Mexico out of which Mexican Americans have emerged starts with Native Americans. An estimated 25 million Native Americans, the largest concentration in the hemisphere, lived in the region of Mexico and Central America at the time of the Spanish invasion (MacLachlan & Rodríguez O, 1980). The Spanish eventually conquered the Mexica[3] (Aztec) capital city, Tenochtitlán, in 1522, not by superior arms, nor by disease, which took its heavy toll later, but by their ability to muster a huge army of non-Mexica indigenous peoples eager to rid themselves of their reputedly oppressive overlords. The conquest of the Aztec empire was not just a Spanish conquest, but also a Spanish-led indigenous revolt (White, 1971).

Upon the Spanish-Indian alliance's success, the Spanish soldiery and the Native American ruling classes, including what remained of the Mexicas, established mutually agreeable social and political ties, secured in many cases by intermarriage with noble families. The first mestizos born of these relationships were not products of rape; they were acknowledged as "Spanish" or "Creoles" by their Spanish fathers. Of course, the ordinary Native

---

No biographical material available.

Americans who constituted the masses of the people were not privy to any of these transactions. Indeed, rape and concubinage befell many indigenous commoner women; their children became the first "illegitimate" mestizos. During this early era, the "purely" Spanish constituted approximately 3–5% of the total population, and never grew beyond an estimated 10% throughout the subsequent history of Mexico (MacLachlan & Rodríguez O, 1980; Morner, 1970).

From the beginning of Spanish colonialism, Indian slaves in large numbers were employed in the silver mines. In 1523, the first foreign-origin slaves were introduced to Mexico, mainly as servants. These first slaves were a collection of Spanish Moslems—Arabs, Berbers, Moors (a mixed people of Arab, Berber, and Black African ancestry)—and *ladino* Blacks, that is, Blacks who had been slaves in Spain or one of its colonies prior to arriving in Mexico (MacLachlan & Rodríguez O, 1980). With the opening up of the large coastal plantations, however, the Spanish turned to the principal region in the world where slaves were being offered for sale in significant numbers at the time, the coast of Africa.

The number of African slaves increased dramatically in Mexico between 1530 and 1700. By the middle of the eighteenth century, African and part-African people were the second largest component of the Mexican population. Only the Native Americans had a larger population. Several individuals of acknowledged part-African ancestry played prominent roles in Mexican history; for example, the Independence hero Vicente Guerrero, for whom a state is named (MacLachlan & Rodríguez O, 1980).

Toward the end of the eighteenth century, the mestizo population began to increase more rapidly. By 1800, it overtook the African and part-African groups, who were increasingly absorbed into the mestizo population. By 1900, the mestizos had become the largest ethnic group in Mexico.

Although the 1921 census was the last in which racial classifications were used in Mexico, some estimates are that mestizos (which in practice became a catchall term for all mixtures) today constitute some 85–90% of the Mexican population and Native Americans some 8–10%, with Europeans, mainly Spanish, making up the rest of the total (Morner, 1970). These estimates are highly suspect, however, a fact generally acknowledged by Mexican demographers, because *Indian* has come to mean "someone who speaks an Indian language" or who "lives like an Indian," that is, who is poor. The fact is, many biological Indians have become cultural mestizos who speak Spanish, and hence are regarded as mestizos. There are also many "Indians" and "Spanish" who are actually of mixed ancestry (Morner, 1970). This ambiguity serves to highlight the absurdity and practical irrelevance of racial categories in Mexico today. . . .

LA RAZA CÓSMICA VERSUS THE MELTING POT

The prevailing attitude toward race among the masses throughout Latin America might be summarized as comparative indifference. Of course, this is far from concluding that the region is the exaggerated stereotype of a "racial paradise." Indeed, by observing the disproportion of darker people in the lower classes and of lighter people in the upper classes, one might be led to conclude that race is at least as much of an active principle in Latin America as it is in the United States. But this is not quite true. For example, how is it that the Mexicans could elect a full-blooded Indian, Benito Juárez, as their president around the time of the U.S. Civil War? How is it that Peruvians of today elected an Asian their president? Many Mexican and other Latin American leaders have been and are of mixed blood. Then what explains the apparent tie between race and class in Latin America?

Many sociologists have long noted that in the absence of effective countermeasures, poverty and wealth alike tend to be inherited (Harris, 1971, chap. 18). Thus in Latin America the caste form of racism that was the hallmark of its colonial past has become ensconced, even though legal racial discrimination has long since been done away with. Add to this the blurring of racial lines on a large scale over hundreds of years, such that customary forms of discrimination based on actual ancestry have been rendered impotent. Taken together, these factors are what is usually meant by the observation that the race question in Latin America has by and large been transformed into a socioeconomic issue (Morner, 1970).

It needs to be said, however, that active remnants of attitudinal racism persist. One of these presents itself as "colorism" or even "featurism," neither of which requires proof of actual ancestry to be operative. Professor G. Reginald Daniel of the University of California, Los Angeles, very aptly terms this phenomenon a "recapitulation of racism" (personal communication, February 1991). To what extent this attitude affects whatever social mobility is available to poor people of any phenotype in Latin America remains to be definitively measured. Some evidence for it can be seen in the disproportion of European-looking models and actors in the Latin American media, although another, probably coexistent, explanation for this is that, for socioeconomic reasons, access to the media is easier for the predominantly lighter elite. There is also a conservative tendency to ape the European and U.S. media.

Another remnant of racism can be heard in many derogatory expressions that include the term *indio* (or other, usually vulgar, terms for Black). Though originally directed at *indios,* these epithets have become generalized insults often used even by their supposed objects, the purely racist feeling having been muted or lost (as, for instance, we might use the expression "welshed"). However, in those districts where Native American communities remain relatively intact, such as in the Yucatán, the Andes, and the many isolated mountain settlements throughout Latin America, these expressions still carry their hard edge and reflect a real, present-day situation of unresolved interethnic conflict and outright oppression.

In the United States, it is the biological aspect of race and racial mixture that is essential to racist thinking, quite apart from any other consideration. This attitude finds expression in the failure of our society and its institutions officially to acknowledge racial mixture, potentially the basis for a unifying national identity and a crucial step for breaking down traditional lines of social separation. Such an important omission unnecessarily contributes to the perpetuation of ethnic divisiveness in U.S. society.

HISTORICALLY EVOLVED CULTURAL FACTORS

Since both the United States and Latin America came into existence from the same expansionary impulse of a Europe reawakening out of medievalism, what might explain the contrasting attitudes regarding race and race mixture?

Sex Ratio Differences

An important difference between the Anglo-dominated colonization of North America and the Iberian conquest of Central and South America was that the Spanish and Portuguese came primarily as soldiers and priests, while the British (and Dutch) came as religious rebels and farmers. That is to say, the Iberians had proportionally fewer of their countrywomen with them than did the Anglos. Thus sexual relations occurred more frequently between the Iberians and the indigenous and African slave women, and, consequently, the numbers of "mixed" people began to increase in Latin America relative to Anglo America right from the outset.

Because interracial unions were less common in Anglo America, their rare occurrence was regarded as aberrational and, hence, in a religiously puritanical milieu where anything unusual was cause for alarm, deeply sinful. On the other hand, while the Catholic church was not at all tolerant of any sexual relations outside of marriage, interracial sexual relations within the bounds of marriage were permitted and at times even encouraged. Nevertheless, the vast majority of interracial sexual relations occurred outside of marriage in Latin America, to the extent that the very terms for a mixed person, *mestizo* and *mulato,* became synonyms for *bastard.*[4] In Mexico, use of the term *mestizo* was not really legitimized until the Revolution of 1910. Today it is regarded by most Mexicans as an honorable badge of national identity (if it is given any thought at all) (Páz, 1950/1961).

Racial Classifications

Another striking difference between Anglo and Latin America can be seen in the systems of racial classification. In Anglo America, no mixed category has ever existed officially, except as a means for assigning all people of any discernible African ancestry to the status of "Negro." This principle of classifying Blacks has been referred to as the "one-drop rule." In common parlance, terms such as *mulatto, Eurasian,* and *half-breed* (or simply *breed*) have been used, but never adopted as ongoing racial categories.[5] This institutional refusal to make a place for a racially mixed identity is strong evidence for the visceral abhorrence of race mixture in U.S. culture. Further evidence can be seen in that peculiar rule of "check one box only" with which multiethnic children and adults are constantly confronted (which parent and heritage shall be denied today?)

In Latin America, on the other hand, elaborate racial taxonomies gained official recognition from the outset, drawing on Spain's own national experience. Some of these have already been mentioned. In the Spanish colonies, these *casta* designations became distinct identities unto themselves, with legal rights as well as disabilities attaching to each.[6] Most, if not all, of Spain's colonies abolished the *casta* system upon their independence. Classifications based on race persisted in some official documents, but discriminatory application of laws based on race was forbidden, something that did not occur in the United States until the middle of the twentieth century. Today, given the large degree of mixture in the Latin American countries, racial classifications are virtually meaningless and hence, for the most part, are no longer used. . . .

The Native Americans, North and South

The difference in the size and nature of the Native American populations in Anglo and Latin America also helps account for the emergence of different attitudes about race. In that part of North America in which the English, Dutch, and others settled, the indigenous peoples were by and large nomadic or seminomadic and not very numerous. Moreover, the socioeconomic and technological distance between the settlers and the indigenous peoples they encountered allowed the settlers from England and other parts of Northwestern Europe to regard surviving Native Americans as savages, mere objects of the wilderness to be moved out of the way. The Anglos, for the most part, felt they had little reason to respect Native Americans (notwithstanding later maudlin stories about the "noble savage"), nor did they feel any need to compromise with them, or to abide by the few compromises that were made.

Entire peoples were segregated, forcibly removed, or exterminated. The occasional exceptions to this history of genocide are few and far between. Although some intermarriage occurred, and some native peoples managed to survive in various desperate, ingenious, and often fortuitous ways, the major outcome was the virtual disappearance of Native Americans as a significant part of North American society.

In those parts of the Americas to which the Spanish came, particularly Mexico and Peru, the indigenous peoples lived a settled, advanced (even by European standards) agricultural life with large cities and developed class systems. They were also very numerous, despite the estimated disease mortality rate of nearly 90% following the first contacts with Europeans.

Eliminating them, even if the idea had occurred to the Spanish, would probably have been impossible. Instead, the Spanish found it advantageous to graft their feudal society onto the semifeudal structures of the Native American civilizations already in place. Spaniards, in the absence of their countrywomen, married into Indian ruling-class families, thereby acquiring key kinship ties to the various peoples composing the Mexican and Incan empires. In short, the Spanish integrated themselves and their culture into communities of civilized (defined as above, in terms of relative technological and socioeconomic development) peoples. Instead of genocide, they opted for a more profitable (and brutally exploitative) *modus vivendi.*

In contrast to the Anglo settlers, many, though not all, of the Spanish came to regard the Native Americans as people rather than savages.[7] The Catholic church itself eventually recognized this and, in theory at least, maintained that an Indian could become the spiritual equal of a Spaniard, if only he or she converted to Christianity. Of course, there was no question about who was superior in secular life, but the very idea of making a place for the Native American in Spanish colonial society demonstrated an attitude far different from the outright genocidal policies carried out further to the north. This difference resulted in a greater permissiveness in the Iberians regarding miscegenation, an attitude that was to some extent generalized to include Africans.

Race Consciousness and "Scientific" Racism

A major ideological difference between the United States and Latin America respecting race and race consciousness is a result of the development of "race theory," a pseudoscientific expression of social Darwinism in the nineteenth century. It is this theory and concept of race to which most Americans have become accustomed, particularly in the form of the "three-race theory" (King, 1981; Stepan, 1982). It is also the basis of modern racism.[8]

Whereas the idea that the human species might be divided up into distinct subspecies marked by skin color or other superficial features had occurred before, it was not until the scientific revolution that accompanied the Industrial Revolution in Europe and North America that such divisions were elevated to the status of "science." The first outstanding proponent of the race theory was the Count Gobineau, a petty French noble among whose occupations had been an ambassadorship in Rio de Janeiro from 1868 to 1870. Of that stay, he once wrote, revealingly: "This is not a country to my taste. An entirely Mulatto population, corrupted in body and soul, ugly to a terrifying degree" (quoted in Morner, 1967). His *Essay on the Inequality of the Human Races* became the starting point for a long line of intellectual racists, culminating in the atrocities of the Nazi death camps (Biddess, 1970). Other Europeans and Americans of European ancestry took up the race theory with relish, perhaps noting how conveniently it displaced onto "nature" human responsibility for discriminatory laws and practices, the drawing of territorial borders, the annexation and government of non-Europeans in the interests of overseas commercial empires, and so forth.

Today, most anthropologists reject traditional race theory, though their continued occasional use of its terminology betrays its stubborn influence, and remains a source of ongoing debate. Reputable anthropologists will typically use the alternative term *population* to refer to groupings of humans having various genetic frequencies. But these groups are predefined by the researcher, their boundaries changing depending on what it is that he or she wishes to study. When discussing the very real sociocultural distinctions that exist among human societies, terms such as *tribe, ethnic group, class,* and *religion* are preferred. These labels do not suffer from the disabilities of the term *race* because they are acknowledged to be artifices of humankind, with no pretense or implication of being "natural."

In the nineteenth century, pseudoscientific concepts of race had a decisive influence on the public mind in Europe and the United States, an influence that continues right down to the present. On the other hand, though race theory was disseminated and discussed among the intelligentsia in Latin America, it never caught on among the masses of the people in the same way as it did here. The reasons for this different receptivity have much to do with the various historically evolved cultural factors reviewed above.

Demographic Differences

The outcome of the differing conditions outlined above brings us finally to the most important difference between Latin and Anglo America with regard to race: the fact that people of mixed racial ancestry came to form a much greater proportion of the population in Latin America than in Anglo America. This simple fact meant that, in varying degrees, race was neutralized as a significant social issue (or at least transformed into a class issue) throughout much of Latin America while it remains one of the most salient features of North American life.

Mexican Americans in the Melting Pot

The United States is poised to integrate the greatest diversity of ethnic groups across all traditional "race" lines that the world has yet seen. As the "browning of America" accelerates through the course of the next few decades, the question of race in all its dimensions will have to be resolved. With their numbers rapidly growing, Mexican Americans, together with their Latino cousins, will undoubtedly exercise an increasing influence on the future development of U.S. culture. Indeed, that influence has already occurred in our folk culture—witness the all-American cowboy, originally the *vaquero,* the Mexican mestizo ranch hand of what is now the American Southwest.

But perhaps the most important contribution is yet to come, that is, in the reshaping of our attitudes about race and especially about race mixture. As the bearers of Latin America's historico-cultural experience and familiar with the ways of U.S. society, Mexican Americans are uniquely positioned to upset the traditional Anglo-American taboo against "race mixing" by merely reaffirming their heritage. Concretely, Chicanos and their Latino cousins are also favorably positioned to mediate alliances among the various racial and ethnic groups that make up the U.S. population, something the African American group, for all its accomplishments, could not do, defined as it was (and is still) by the dominant White culture. Latinos, and especially Mexican Americans, have been conditioned by their history, however imperfectly and unevenly, to accept racial ambiguity and mixture as "normal." This attitude might be of enormous benefit to all of us in the United States. First, the race question may be neutralized and energies redirected to other pressing socioeconomic issues. Second, the principle of *mestizaje,* or "multicultural synthesis," as a social norm, a truer expression of the old melting-pot thesis, can free us all from the limits of ethnocentrism by opening us up to a wider repertoire of cultural elements, thereby stimulating our creativity to the fullest. From this, we can reap economic as well as psychological benefits. As a society, we will then be especially well suited to shape the ongoing emergence of a truly global community.

Unfortunately, it must be noted here that the pervasiveness of U.S. culture in Latin America as well as the assimilation of Latin American immigrants into it within this country has had some effect of instilling U.S.-style race consciousness. Thus some Latin Americans will adopt views against intermarriage or repeat what racist Whites say about African and Asian Americans, or even Latin Americans of nationalities different from their own.[9] There are also some who will insist on the purity of their Spanish ancestry and culture, by which they mean White, European ancestry, especially if they are phenotypically light-skinned, even though, for most, such hoped-for purity is extremely dubious.[10] The self-proclaimed "Hispanic" who has definite African or Native American features is particularly absurd and foolish.

Which way will the Latino community go? Nonracial ethnocentrism? Anglo conformity? *Hispanidad? Indigenismo?* Afrocentrism? Or *mestizaje?* The decision must be made. In this society, deeply scarred by racism, evading the issue will prove useless. Latinos cannot avoid the reality of their mixed identity without losing themselves. In the process of asserting their mixed identity, Mexican Americans and other Latinos will have little choice but to challenge traditional American race thinking.[11]

CONCLUSION

Whether we in the United States change our attitudes as a society or not, the numbers of "mixed," "blended," "brown," "cosmic," "melded," or simply *multiethnic* people will grow, in both numbers and complexity. Moreover, our global society is rapidly becoming a union of all cultures, the old cultures not dying, but living on in new forms. It is in the minds of the multiethnic children that the new culture of the future world society is being synthesized. There will be no place for racism or ethnocentrism in this new world, because the multiethnic children cannot hate or disrespect their parents and their heritage without sacrificing their own personal integrity and peace of mind.

What will happen in this future world of race or ethnic irrelevance? As many have speculated, national cultures may indeed disappear as independent entities, to be replaced not by the homogeneous-monotony specter we often hear about (really what narrow cultural nationalism is about—rigid, forced conformity to an ideal, monolithic cultural standard), but by a society that recognizes and respects diversity at the level of the individual.

The fulfillment of the melting-pot and *La Raza Cósmica*—ideals and realities on the continents of the Western Hemisphere—these will form the real New World for all humankind.

NOTES

1. *La Raza Cósmica* is the title of an essay by the Mexican philosopher and educator Jose Vasconcelos (1925/1979), in which he proclaims and extolls the spiritual virtues that may ensue from the fact that America—in particular, Latin America—has become the site of the first large-scale mixture of "races" in the world. As Minister of Education he took every opportunity to foster a unified Mexican identity. Vasconcelos was responsible for the motto of the National Autonomous University of Mexico (my father's alma mater): "Por mi raza, el espíritu se hablará" (Through my race [the mixed race], the spirit shall speak).
2. Of course, any discussion of race or racial mixing presumes the existence of "race" or, more specifically, the existence of the particular concept of race that holds sway in the popular consciousness.
3. *Mexica* (pronounced meshEEca), besides being the origin of the name for the country of Mexico, is also the probable origin of *Chicano,* a slang term for Mexican Americans popularized in the 1960s. In colonial times, many in the Spanish upper class did not consider themselves "Mexican," that is, Indian or mestizo. Thus they might refer to ordinary Mexicans derogatorily as *xicanos.* The usage was carried over into the United States, where Mexican American youths transformed *Chicano* into a term of pride and defiance.
4. The number of terms for the various mixtures of peoples in Latin America far exceeds the two mentioned here. In fact, the race terminology in popular usage and adopted into law by many states in the United States is directly derived from the Spanish: *Negro* (from the Spanish word for *black*), *mulatto* (from the Spanish *mulato,* which means mule, meaning half Black and half White), *quadroon* (from the Spanish *cuarterón,* or one-quarter Black), *octoroon* (from the Spanish *octorón,* or one-eighth Black), *zambo* (from the Spanish *zambo,* or Black and Indian), and *maroon* (from the Spanish *cimarrón,* or runaway Black slave). Many other terms were also used, including *coyote, pardo, castizo, morisco, lobo,* and

chino. Collectively, the mixed groups were called *castas* (castes). See O'Crouley (1774/1972) and Woodbridge (1948).

5. The U.S. Census, for example, included mulatto and quadroon during some censuses, but not consistently, and certainly with no bearing on the legal rights of the people so designated.
6. *Casta* was a term midway in meaning between "estate" and "race." To the extent it meant race it had a spiritual or ethnic sense rather than the genetic sense to which we are accustomed (Castro, 1971).
7. The question of Native American humanity was the subject of a famous debate in Valladolid, Spain, between Bartolomé de las Casas and Juan Ginés de Sepúlveda during the sixteenth century. Sepúlveda invoked Aristotle's thesis that some people are naturally slaves. Las Casas argued that slavery and generally brutal treatment of Native Americans violated Christian principles. Las Casas won the debate, and the Laws of the Indies resulted. Unfortunately, Las Casas's solution to Native American slavery was African slavery, a view that he later apparently recanted. That any controversy existed at all during this early period says much about Spanish attitudes regarding race compared with those of other Europeans (including their fellow Iberians, the Portuguese) of that or subsequent times. For an excellent examination of this famous debate, see Hanke (1959/1970).
8. I contend that in its most essential sense, racism is a system of thinking, an *ideology,* based on the concept of race.
9. In March 1989, 82% of "Hispanic" men who got married married Hispanic women, while 85% of "Hispanic" women married Hispanic men. The Mexican intermarriage rate was nearly the same as the overall "Hispanic" rate, while it was actually higher (28%) for Puerto Rican men (see U.S. Bureau of the Census, 1990).
10. Even if this is true in any given instance, Spaniards and Spanish culture are a mixture anyway, including the ancestry of Black Africans, Gypsies (from India), and Semites (Jews, Arabs, and Phoenicians), as well as Romans, Celts, Germans, Greeks, Berbers, Basques, and probably more. Today, there are even many mestizo and *mulato* immigrants from Latin America resident in Spain.
11. Interestingly, more than 96% of the 9.8 million people who declined to choose a particular race by checking the "other race" box on the 1990 census forms were "Hispanics" (J. García, demographic analyst, U.S. Bureau of the Census, Ethnic and Hispanic Branch, personal communication, May 1991).

REFERENCES

Biddess, M. D. (1970). *Father of racist ideology: The social and political thought of Count Gobineau.* New York: Weybright & Talley.

Castro, A. (1971). *The Spaniards: An introduction to their history.* Berkeley: University of California Press.

Hanke, L. (1970). *Aristotle and the American Indians: A study in race prejudice in the modern world.* Bloomington: Indiana University Press. (Original work published 1959).

Harris, M. (1971). *Culture, man and nature.* New York: Thomas Y. Crowell.

King, J. C. (1981). *The biology of race.* Berkeley: University of California Press.

MacLachlan, C. M., & Rodríguez O, J. E. (1980). *The forging of the cosmic race: A reinterpretation of colonial Mexico.* Berkeley: University of California Press.

Morner, M. (1967). *Race Mixture in the History of Latin America.* Boston: Little, Brown

Morner, M. (Ed.). (1970). *Race and class in Latin America.* New York: Columbia University Press.

Muñoz, C., Jr. (1989). *Youth, identity, power: The Chicano movement.* London: Verso.

O'Crouley, P. (1972). *A description of the kingdom of New Spain in 1774.* San Francisco: John Howell. (Original work published 1774).

Páz, O. (1961). *The labyrinth of solitude: Life and thought in Mexico* (L. Kemp, Trans.). New York: Grove. (Original work published 1950).

Stepan, N. (1982). *The idea of race in science.* Hamden, CT: Archon.

U.S. Bureau of the Census. (1990). *The Hispanic population in the United States: March 1989* (Current Population Reports, Series P-20, No. 444). Washington DC: Government Printing Office.

U.S. Bureau of the Census. (1991, March 11). *U.S. Department of Commerce news* (Publication No.

CB91-100). Washington, DC: Government Printing Office.

Vasconcelos, J. (1979). *La raza cósmica* (D. T. Jaen, Trans.). Los Angeles: California State University, Centro de Publicaciones. (Original work published 1925)

White, J. M. (1971). *Cortés and the downfall of the Aztec empire.* New York: St. Martin's.

Woodbridge, H. C. (1948). Glossary of names in colonial Latin America for crosses among Indians, Negros and Whites. *Journal of the Washington Academy of Sciences, 38,* 353–362.

READING 5

Asian American Panethnicity

Yen Le Espiritu

Arriving in the United States, nineteenth-century immigrants from Asian countries did not think of themselves as "Asians." Coming from specific districts in provinces in different nations, Asian immigrant groups did not even consider themselves Chinese, Japanese, Korean, and so forth, but rather people from Toisan, Hoiping, or some other district in Guandong Province in China or from Hiroshima, Yamaguchi, or some other prefecture in Japan. Members of each group considered themselves culturally and politically distinct. Historical enmities between their mother countries further separated the groups even after their arrival in the United States. Writing about early Asian immigrant communities, Eliot Mears (1928:4) reported that "it is exceptional when one learns of any entente between these Orientals." However, non-Asians had little understanding or appreciation of these distinctions. For the most part, outsiders accorded to Asian peoples certain common characteristics and traits that were essentially supranational (Browne 1985:8–9). Indeed, the exclusion acts and quotas limiting Asian immigration to the United States relied upon racialist constructions of Asians as homogeneous (Lowe 1991:28).

Mindful that whites generally lump all Asians together, early Asian immigrant communities sought to "keep their images discrete and were not above denigrating, or at least approving the denigration of, other Asian groups" (Daniels 1988:113). It was not until the late 1960s, with the advent of the Asian American movement, that a pan-Asian consciousness and constituency were first formed. To build political unity, college students of Asian ancestry heralded their common fate—the similarity of experiences and treatment that Asian groups endured in the United States (Omi and Winant 1986:105). In other words, the pan-Asian concept, originally imposed by non-Asians, became a symbol of pride and a rallying point for mass mobilization by later generations. This [discussion] examines the social, political, and demographic factors that allowed pan-Asianism to take root in the 1960s and not earlier.

ETHNIC "DISIDENTIFICATION"

Before the 1960s, Asians in this country frequently practiced ethnic disidentification, the act of distancing one's group from another group so as not to be mistaken and suffer the blame for the presumed misdeeds of that group (Hayano 1981:162). Faced with external threats, group members can either intensify their solidarity or they can distance themselves from the stigmatized segment. Instead of uniting to fight anti-Asian forces, early Asian immigrant communities often disassociated themselves from the targeted group so as not to be mistaken for members of it and suffer any possible negative consequences (Hayano 1981:161; Daniels 1988:113). Two examples of ethnic disidentification among Asians in this country occurred during the various anti-Asian exclusion movements and during World War II. These incidents are instructive not only as evidence of ethnic disidentification but also as documentation of the pervasiveness of

Yen Le Espiritu is professor of ethnic studies, University of California, San Diego.

racial lumping. Precisely because of racial lumping, persons of Asian ancestry found it necessary to disassociate themselves from other Asian groups.

Exclusion Movements

Beginning with the first student laborers in the late nineteenth century, Japanese immigrants always differentiated themselves from Chinese immigrants. Almost uniformly, Japanese immigrants perceived their Chinese counterparts in an "unsympathetic, negative light, and often repeated harsh American criticisms of the Chinese" (Ichioka 1988:191). In their opinion, the Chinese came from an inferior nation; they also were lower-class laborers, who had not adapted themselves to American society. In 1892, a Japanese student laborer described San Francisco's Chinatown as "a world of beasts in which . . . exists every imaginable depravity, crime, and vice" (cited in Ichioka 1988:191).

Indeed, the Japanese immigrants were a more select group than their Chinese counterparts. The Japanese government viewed overseas Japanese as representatives of their homeland. Therefore, it screened prospective emigrants to ensure that they were healthy and literate and would uphold Japan's national honor (Takaki 1989:46).

More important, Japanese immigrants distanced themselves from the Chinese because they feared that Americans would lump them together. Aware of Chinese exclusion, Japanese immigrant leaders had always dreaded the thought of Japanese exclusion. To counteract any negative association, Japanese immigrant leaders did everything possible to distinguish themselves from the Chinese immigrants (Ichioka 1988:250). For example, to separate themselves from the unassimilable Chinese laborers, some Japanese immigrant leaders insisted that their Japanese workers wear American work clothes and even eat American food (Ichioka 1988:185). In 1901, the Japanese in California distributed leaflets requesting that they be differentiated from the Chinese (tenBroek, Barnhart, and Matson 1970:23).

However, under the general rubric Asiatic, the Japanese inherited the painful experiences of the Chinese.[1] All the vices attributed to the Chinese were transferred to these newest Asian immigrants (Browne 1985). Having successfully excluded Chinese laborers, organized labor once again led the campaign to drive out the Japanese immigrants. In 1904, the American Federation of Labor adopted its first anti-Japanese resolution. Charging that the Japanese immigrants were as undesirable as the Chinese, the unions' resolution called for the expansion of the 1902 Chinese Exclusion Act to include Japanese and other Asian laborers. By mid-1905, the labor unions of California had joined forces to establish the Asiatic Exclusion League (Hill 1973:52–54; Ichioka 1988:191–192).

Since the Japanese immigrants considered themselves superior to the Chinese, they felt indignant and insulted whenever they were lumped together with them. In 1892, a Japanese immigrant wrote in the *Oakland Enquirer* that he wished "to inveigh with all my power" against American newspapers that compared the Japanese to "the truly ignorant class of Chinese laborers and condemned them as bearers of some mischievous Oriental evils" (cited in Ichioka 1988:192). Instead of joining with the Chinese to fight the anti-Asian exclusion movement, some Japanese leaders went so far as to condone publicly the exclusion of the Chinese while insisting that the Japanese were the equals of Americans (Daniels 1988:113). Above all else, Japanese immigrant leaders wanted Japanese immigration to be treated on the same footing as European immigration (Ichioka 1988:250).

In the end, Japanese attempts at disidentification failed. With the passage of the 1924 Immigration Act, Japanese immigration was effectively halted. This act contained two provisions designed to stop Japanese immigration. The first barred the immigration of Japanese wives even if their husbands were United States citizens. The second prohibited the immigration of aliens ineligible for citizenship. Because the Supreme Court had ruled in 1922 that persons of

Japanese ancestry could not become naturalized citizens, this provision effectively closed the door on Japanese and most other Asian immigration (U.S. Commission on Civil Rights 1986:8–9). The Japanese immigrants felt doubly affronted by the 1924 act because it ranked them, not as the equals of Europeans, but on the same level as the lowly Chinese, the very people whom they themselves considered inferior (Ichioka 1988:250). Thus, despite all their attempts to disassociate themselves from the Chinese, with the passage of the act, the Japanese joined the Chinese as a people deemed unworthy of becoming Americans. Little did they foresee that, in less than two decades, other Asian groups in America would disassociate themselves from the Japanese.

World War II and Japanese Internment

Immediately after the bombing of Pearl Harbor, the incarceration of Japanese Americans began. On the night of December 7, the Federal Bureau of Investigation (FBI) began taking into custody persons of Japanese ancestry who had connections to the Japanese government. Working on the principle of guilt by association, the security agencies simply rounded up most of the Issei (first-generation) leaders of the Japanese community. Initially, the federal government differentiated between alien and citizen Japanese Americans, but this distinction gradually disappeared. In the end, the government evacuated more than 100,000 persons of Japanese ancestry into concentration camps, approximately two-thirds of whom were American-born citizens. It was during this period that the Japanese community discovered that the legal distinction between citizen and alien was not nearly so important as the distinction between white and yellow (Daniels 1988:ch. 6).

Like the Japanese, the Chinese understood the importance of the distinction between white and yellow. Fearful that they would be targets of anti-Japanese activities, many persons of Chinese ancestry, especially in the West, took to wearing buttons that proclaimed positively "I'm Chinese." Similarly, many Chinese shopkeepers displayed signs announcing, "This is a Chinese shop." Some Chinese immigrants even joined the white persecution with buttons that added "I hate Japs worse than you do" (Daniels 1988:205; Takaki 1989:370–371). The small Korean and Filipino communities took similar actions. Because of Japan's occupation of Korea at the time, being mistaken as Japanese particularly angered Koreans in the United States. Cognizant of Asian lumping, the United Korean Committee prepared identification cards proclaiming "I am Korean." During the early months of the war, women wore Korean dresses regularly to distinguish themselves from the Japanese (Melendy 1977:158; Takaki 1989:365–366). Similarly, persons of Filipino ancestry wore buttons proclaiming "I am a Filipino" (Takaki 1989:363).

Given the wars between their mother countries and Japan, it is not surprising that the Chinese, Koreans, and Filipinos distanced themselves from the Japanese. But their reactions are instructive not only as examples of ethnic disidentification but also as testimonies to the pervasiveness of racial lumping. Popular confusion of the various Asian groups was so prevalent that it was necessary for Chinese, Filipinos, and Koreans to don ethnic clothing and identification buttons to differentiate themselves from the Japanese. Without these *visible* signs of ethnicity, these three Asian groups would probably have been mistaken for Japanese by anti-Japanese forces. As Ronald Takaki (1989:370) reported, Asian groups "remembered how they had previously been called 'Japs' and how many whites had lumped all Asians together." But there are also examples of how Asian groups united when inter-Asian cooperation advanced their common interests.

Inter-Asian Labor Movements

The most notable example of inter-Asian solidarity was the 1920 collaboration of Japanese and Filipino plantation laborers in Hawaii. In the beginning, plantation workers had organized in terms of national origins. Thus, the Japanese belonged to the Japanese union and the Filipinos to the Filipino union. In the early 1900s, an ethnically based strike seemed sensible to Japanese plantation laborers because they represented about 70 percent of the entire work force. Filipinos constituted less than 1 percent. However, by 1920, Japanese workers represented only 44 percent of the labor force, while Filipino workers represented 30 percent. Japanese and Filipino union leaders understood that they would have to combine to be politically and economically effective (Johanessen 1950:75–83; Takaki 1989:152).

Because together they constituted more than 70 percent of the work force in Oahu, the 1920 Japanese-Filipino strike brought plantation operations to a sudden stop. Although the workers were eventually defeated, the 1920 strike was the "first major interethnic working-class struggle in Hawaii" (Takaki 1989:154).[2] Subsequently, the Japanese Federation of Labor elected to become an interethnic union. To promote a multiethnic class solidarity, the new union called itself the Hawaii Laborers Association (Takaki 1989:154–155).

Although the 1920 strike was a de facto example of pan-Asian cooperation, this cooperation needs to be distinguished from the post-1960 pan-Asian solidarity. The purported unifying factor in 1920 was a common class status, not a shared cultural or racial background (Takaki 1989:154). This class solidarity is different from the large-scale organization of ethnicity that emerged in the late 1960s. For most Asian Americans, the more recent development represents an enlargement of their identity system, a circle beyond their previous national markers of identity. True, like working-class unions, panethnic groups are interest groups with material demands (Glazer and Moynihan 1963; Bonacich and Modell 1980). However, unlike labor unions, panethnic groups couch their demands in ethnic or racial terms—not purely in class terms. In other words, their ethnicity is used as a basis for the assertion of collective claims, many but not all of which are class based.

SOCIAL AND DEMOGRAPHIC CHANGES: SETTING THE CONTEXT

. . . Before 1940, the Asian population in the United States was primarily an immigrant population. Immigrant Asians faced practical barriers to pan-Asian unity. Foremost was their lack of a common language. Old national rivalries were another obstacle, as many early Asian immigrants carried the political memories and outlook of their homelands. For example, Japan's occupation of Korea resulted in pervasive anti-Japanese sentiments among Koreans in the United States. According to Brett Melendy (1977:155), "Fear and hatred of the Japanese appeared to be the only unifying force among the various Korean groups through the years." Moreover, these historical enmities and linguistic and cultural differences reinforced one another as divisive agents.

During the postwar period, due to immigration restrictions and the growing dominance of the second and third generations, American-born Asians outnumbered immigrants. The demographic changes of the 1940s were pronounced. During this decade, nearly twenty thousand Chinese American babies were born. For the first time, the largest five-year cohort of Chinese Americans was under five years of age (Kitano and Daniels 1988:37). By 1960, approximately two-thirds of the Asian population in California had been born in the United States (Ong 1989:5–8). As the Asian population became a native-born community, linguistic and cultural differences began to blur. Although they had attended Asian-language schools, most American-born Asians possessed only a limited knowledge of their ethnic language (Chan 1991:115). By 1960, with English as the common language, persons from different Asian backgrounds were able to communicate with one another (Ling 1984:73), and in so doing create a common identity associated with the United States.

Moreover, unlike their immigrant parents, native-born and American-educated Asians could muster only scant loyalties to old world ties. Historical antagonisms between their mother countries thus receded in importance (Wong 1972:34). For example, growing up in America, second-generation Koreans "had difficulty feeling the painful loss of the homeland and understanding the indignity of Japanese domination" (Takaki 1989:292). Thus, while the older generation of Koreans hated all Japanese, "their children were much less hostile or had no concern at all" (Melendy 1977:156). As a native-born Japanese American community advocate explained, "By 1968, we had a second generation. We could speak English; so there was no language problem. And we had little feelings of historical animosity" (Kokubun interview).

As national differences receded in subjective importance, generational differences widened. For the most part, American-born Asians considered themselves to have more in common with other American-born Asians than they did with foreign-born compatriots.[3] According to a third-generation Japanese American who is married to a Chinese American, "As far as our experiences in America, I have more things in common than differences with a Chinese American. Being born and raised here gives us something in common. We have more in common with each other than with a Japanese from Japan, or a Chinese from China" (Ichioka interview). Much to their parents' dismay, young Asian Americans began to choose their friends and spouses from other Asian groups. . . .

Before World War II, Asian immigrant communities were quite distinct entities, isolated from one another and from the larger society. Because of language difficulties, prejudice, and lack of business opportunities elsewhere, there was little chance for Asians in the United States to live outside their ethnic enclaves (Yuan 1966:331). Shut out of the mainstream of American society, the various immigrant groups struggled separately in their respective Chinatowns, Little Tokyos, or Manilatowns. Stanford Lyman (1970:57–63) reported that the early Chinese and Japanese communities in the western states had little to do with one another—either socially or politically . . .

Economic and residential barriers began to crumble after World War II. The war against Nazism called attention to racism at home and discredited the notions of white superiority. The fifteen years after the war was a period of largely positive change as civil rights statutes outlawed racial discrimination in employment as well as housing (Daniels 1988:ch. 7). Popular attitudes were also changing. Polls taken during World War II showed a distinct hostility toward Japan: 74 percent of the respondents favored either killing off all Japanese, destroying Japan as a political entity, or supervising it. On the West Coast, 97 percent of the people polled approved of the relocation of Japanese Americans. In contrast, by 1949, 64 percent of those polled were either friendly or neutral toward Japan (Feraru 1950).

During the postwar years, Asian American residential patterns changed significantly. Because of the lack of statistical data,[4] a longitudinal study of the changing residential patterns of Asian Americans cannot be made. However, descriptive accounts of Asian American communities indicate that these enclaves declined in the postwar years. Edwin Hoyt (1974:94) reported that in the 1940s, second-generation Chinese Americans moved out of the Chinatowns. Although they still came back to shop or to see friends, they lived elsewhere. In 1940, Rose Hum Lee found twenty-eight cities with an area called Chinatown in the United States. By 1955, Peter Sih found only sixteen (Sung 1967:143–144). New York's Chinatown exemplifies the declining significance of Asian ethnic enclaves. In 1940, 50 percent of the Chinese in New York City lived in its Chinatown; by 1960, less than one-third lived there (Yuan 1966:331). Similarly, many returning Japanese Americans abandoned their prewar settlement in old central cities and joined the migration to suburbia (Daniels 1988:294). In the early 1970s, Little Tokyo in Los Angeles remained a bustling Japanese American center, "but at night the shop owners [went] home to the houses in the suburbs" (Hoyt 1974:84). . . .

Moreover, recent research on suburban segregation indicates that the level of segregation between certain Asian American groups is often less than that between them and non-Asians. . . . Though not comprehensive, these studies together suggest that Asian residential segregation declined in the postwar years.

As various Asian groups in the United States interacted, they became aware of common problems and goals that transcended parochial interests and historical antagonisms. One recurrent problem was employment discrimination. According to a 1965 report published by the California Fair Employment Practices Commission, for every $51 earned by a white male Californian, Japanese males earned $43 and Chinese males $38—even though Chinese and Japanese American men had become slightly better educated than the white majority (Daniels 1988:315). Moreover, although the postwar period marked the first time that well-trained Chinese and Japanese Americans could find suitable employment with relative ease, they continued to be passed over for promotion to administrative and supervisory positions (Kitano and Daniels 1988:47). Asians in the United States began to see themselves as a group that shared important common experiences: exploitation, oppression, and discrimination (Uyematsu 1971).

Because inter-Asian contact and communication were greatest on college campuses, pan-Asianism was strongest there (Wong 1972:33–34). Exposure to one another and to the mainstream society led some young Asian Americans to feel that they were fundamentally different from whites. Disillusioned with the white society and alienated from their traditional communities, many Asian American student activists turned to the alternative strategy of pan-Asian unification (Weiss 1974:69–70).

THE CONSTRUCTION OF PAN-ASIAN ETHNICITY

Although broader social struggles and internal demographic changes provided the impetus for the Asian American movement, it was the group's politics—confrontational and explicitly pan-Asian—that shaped the movement's content. Influenced by the internal colonial model, which stresses the commonalities among "colonized groups," college students of Asian ancestry declared solidarity with fellow Asian Americans—and with other Third World[5] minorities (Blauner 1972:ch. 2). Rejecting the label "Oriental," they proclaimed themselves "Asian American." Through pan-Asian organizations, publications, and Asian American studies programs, Asian American activists built pan-Asian solidarity by pointing out their common fate in American society. The pan-Asian concept enabled diverse Asian American groups to understand their "unequal circumstances and histories as being related" (Lowe 1991:30).

From "Yellow" to "Asian American"

Following the example of the Black Power movement, Asian American activists spearheaded their own Yellow Power movement to seek "freedom from racial oppression through the power of a consolidated yellow people" (Uyematsu 1971:12). In the summer of 1968, more than one hundred students of diverse Asian backgrounds attended an "Are You Yellow?" conference at UCLA to discuss issues of Yellow Power, identity, and the war in Vietnam (Ling 1989:53). In 1970, a new pan-Asian organization in northern California called itself the "Yellow Seed" because "Yellow [is] the common bond between Asian-Americans and Seed symboliz[es] growth as an individual and as an alliance" (Masada 1970). This "yellow" reference was dropped when Filipino Americans rejected the term, claiming that they were brown, not yellow (Rabaya 1971:110; Ignacio 1976:84). At the first Asian American national conference in 1972, Filipino Americans "made it clear to the conferees that we were 'Brown Asians'" by forming a Brown Asian Caucus (Ignacio 1976:139–141). It is important to note, however, that Filipino American activists did not reject the term "yellow" because they objected to the pan-Asian framework. Quite the contrary, they rejected it because it allegedly excluded them from that grouping (Rabaya 1971:110).

. . . Asian American activists also rejected *Oriental* because the term conjures up images of "the sexy Susie Wong, the wily Charlie Chan, and the evil Fu Manchu" (Weiss 1974:234). It is also a term that smacks of European colonialism and imperialism: *Oriental* means "East"; Asia is "east" only in relationship to Europe, which was taken as the point of reference (Browne 1985). To define their own image and to claim an *American* identity, college students of Asian ancestry coined the term *Asian American* to "stand for all of us Americans of Asian descent" (Ichioka interview). While *Oriental* suggests passivity and acquiescence, *Asian Americans* connotes political activism because an Asian American "gives a damn about his life, his work, his beliefs, and is willing to do almost anything to help Orientals become Asian Americans" (cited in Weiss 1974:234).

The account above suggests that the creation of a new name is a significant symbolic move in constructing an ethnic identity. In their attempt to forge a pan-Asian identity, Asian American activists first had to coin a composite term that would unify and encompass the constituent groups. Filipino Americans' rejection of the term "yellow" and the activists' objection to the cliché-ridden *Oriental* forced the group to change its name to Asian American. . . .

Pan-Asian Organizations

Influenced by the political tempo of the 1960s, young Asian Americans began to join such organizations as the Free Speech Movement at the University of California at Berkeley, Students for a Democratic Society, and the Progressive Labor Party. However, these young activists "had no organization or coalition to draw attention to themselves as a distinct group" (Wong 1972:33). Instead, they participated as individuals—often at the invitation of their white or black friends (Chin 1971:285; Nakano 1984:3–4). While Asian American activists subscribed to the integrationist ideology of the 1960s and 1970s social movements, they also felt impotent and alienated. There was no structure to uphold their own identity. As an example, when the Peace and Freedom Party was formed on the basis of black and white coalitions, Asian American activists felt excluded because they were neither black nor white (Wong 1972:34; Yoshimura 1989:107).

In the late 1960s, linking their political views with the growth of racial pride among their ranks, Asian Americans already active in various political movements came together to form their own organizations (Nakano 1984:3–4). Most of the early pan-Asian organizations were college based. In 1968, activists at the University of California, Berkeley founded one of the first pan-Asian political organizations: the Asian American Political Alliance (AAPA). According to a co-founder of the organization, its establishment marked the first time that the term "Asian American" was used nationally to mobilize people of Asian descent (Ichioka interview). . . .

By the mid-1970s, *Asian American* had become a familiar term (Lott 1976:30). Although first coined by college activists, the pan-Asian concept began to be used extensively by professional and community spokespersons to lobby for the health and welfare of Americans of Asian descent. In addition to the local and single-ethnic organizations of an earlier era, Asian American professionals and community activists formed national and pan-Asian organizations such as the Pacific/Asian Coalition and the Asian American Social Workers (Ignacio 1976:162; Kuo 1979:283–284). Also, Asian American caucuses could be found in national professional organizations such as the American Public Health Association, the American Sociological Association, the American Psychological Association, the

American Psychiatric Association, and the American Librarians Association (Lott 1976:31). Commenting on the "literally scores of pan-Asian organizations" in the mid-1970s, William Liu (1976:6) asserted that "the idea of pan-Asian cooperation [was] viable and ripe for development." . . .

THE LIMITS OF PAN-ASIANISM

Although pan-Asian consolidation certainly has occurred, it has been by no means universal. For those who wanted a broader political agenda, the pan-Asian scope was too narrow and its racial orientation too segregative (Wong 1972:33; Lowe 1991:39). For others who wanted to preserve ethnic particularism, the pan-Asian agenda threatened to remove second- and third-generation Asians "from their conceptual ties to their community" (R. Tanaka 1976:47). These competing levels of organization mitigated the impact of pan-Asianism.

Moreover, pan-Asianism has been primarily the ideology of native-born, American-educated, and middle-class Asians. Embraced by students, artists, professionals, and political activists, pan-Asian consciousness thrived on college campuses and in urban settings. However, it barely touched the Asian ethnic enclaves. When the middle-class student activists carried the enlarged and politicized Asian American consciousness to the ethnic communities, they encountered apprehension, if not outright hostility (Chan 1991:175). Conscious of their national origins and overburdened with their day-to-day struggles for survival, most community residents ignored or spurned the movement's political agenda (P. Wong 1972:34). Chin (1971:287) reported that few Chinatown residents participated in any of the pan-Asian political events. Similarly, members of the Nisei-dominated Japanese American Citizens League "were determined to keep a closed mind and maintain their negative stereotype" of the members of the Asian American Political Alliance (J. Matsui 1968:6). For their part, young Asian American activists accused their elders of having been so whitewashed that they had deleted their experiences of prejudice and discrimination from their history (Weiss 1974:238). Because these young activists were not rooted in the community, their base of support was narrow and their impact upon the larger society often limited (Wong 1972:37; Nishio 1982:37).

Even among those who were involved in the Asian American movement, divisions arose from conflicting sets of interests as subgroups decided what and whose interests would be addressed. Oftentimes, conflicts over material interests took on ethnic coloration, with participants from smaller subgroups charging that "Asian American" primarily meant Chinese and Japanese American, the two largest and most acculturated Asian American groups at the time (Ignacio 1976:220; Ling 1984:193–195). For example, most Asian American Studies programs did not include courses on other Asian groups, but only on Chinese and Japanese. Similarly, the Asian American women's movement often subsumed the needs of their Korean and Filipina members under those of Chinese and Japanese women (Ling 1984:193–195). Chinese and Japanese Americans also were the instructors of Asian American ethnic studies directors and staff members of many Asian American projects,[6] and advisory and panel members in many governmental agencies (Ignacio 1976:223–224).

The ethnic and class inequality within the pan-Asian structure has continued to be a source of friction and mistrust, with participants from the less dominant groups feeling shortchanged and excluded. The influx of the post-1965 immigrants and the tightening of public funding resources have further deepened the ethnic and class cleavages among Asian American subgroups.

CONCLUSION

The development of a pan-Asian consciousness and constituency reflected broader societal developments and demographic changes, as well as the group's political agenda. By the late

1960s, pan-Asianism was possible because of the more amicable relationships among the Asian countries, the declining residential segregation among diverse Asian groups in America, and the large number of native-born, American-educated political actors. Disillusioned with the larger society and estranged from their traditional communities, third- and fourth-generation Asian Americans turned to the alternative strategy of pan-Asian unification. Through pan-Asian organizations, media, and Asian American Studies programs, these political activists assumed the role of "cultural entrepreneurs" consciously creating a community of culture out of diverse Asian peoples.[7] This process of pan-Asian consolidation did not proceed smoothly nor did it encompass all Asian Americans. Ethnic chauvinism, competition for scarce resources, and class cleavages continued to divide the subgroups. However, once established, the pan-Asian structure not only reinforced the cohesiveness of already existing networks but also expanded these networks. Although first conceived by young Asian American activists, the pan-Asian concept was subsequently institutionalized by professionals and community groups, as well as government agencies. The confrontational politics of the activists eventually gave way to the conventional and electoral politics of the politicians, lobbyists, and professionals, as Asian Americans continued to rely on the pan-Asian framework to enlarge their political capacities.

NOTES

1. On the other hand, due to the relative strength of Japan in the world order, Japanese immigrants at times received more favorable treatment than other Asian immigrants. For example, in 1905, wary of offending Japan, national politicians blocked an attempt by the San Francisco Board of Education to transfer Japanese students from the public schools reserved for white children to the "Oriental" school serving the Chinese (Chan 1991: 59).
2. Although many Korean laborers were sympathetic to the 1920 strike, because of their hatred for the Japanese, they did not participate. As the Korean National Association announced, "We do not wish to be looked upon as strikebreakers, but we shall continue to work in the plantation and we are opposed to the Japanese in everything" (cited in Melendy 1977: 164).
3. The same is true with other racial groups. For example, American-born Haitians are more like their African American peers than like their Haitian parents (Woldemikael 1989: 166).
4. Ideally, residential patterns should be analyzed at the census tract level. However, this analysis cannot be done because Asians were not tabulated by census tracts until the 1980 census.
5. During the late 1960s, in radical circles, the term *third world* referred to the nation's racially oppressed people.
6. For example, the staff of the movement publication *Gidra* were predominantly Japanese Americans.
7. For a discussion of the role of "cultural entrepreneurs," see Cornell (1988*b*).

REFERENCES

Blauner, Robert. 1972. *Racial Oppression in America.* New York: Harper & Row.

Bonacich, Edna, and John Modell. 1980. *The Economic Basis of Ethnic Solidarity: A Study of Japanese Americans.* Berkeley: University of California Press.

Browne, Blaine T. 1985. "A Common Thread: American Images of the Chinese and Japanese, 1930–1960." Ph.D. dissertation, University of Oklahoma.

Chan, Sucheng. 1991. *Asian Americans: An Interpretive History.* Boston: Twayne.

Chin, Rocky. 1971. "NY Chinatown Today: Community in Crisis." Pp. 282–295 in *Roots: An Asian American Reader,* edited by Amy Tachiki, Eddie Wong, and Franklin Odo. Los Angeles: UCLA Asian American Studies Center.

Cornell, Stephen. 1988*a*. *The Return of the Native: American Indian Political Resurgence.* New York: Oxford University Press.

______. 1988*b*. "Structure, Content, and Logic in Ethnic Group Formation." Working Paper series,

Center for Research on Politics and Social Organization, Department of Sociology, Harvard University.

Daniels, Roger. 1971. *Concentration Camps USA: Japanese Americans and World War II.* Hinsdale, Ill.: Dryden Press.

______. 1988. *Asian America: Chinese and Japanese in the United States since 1850.* Seattle: University of Washington Press.

Feraru, Arthur N. 1950. "Public Opinions Polls on Japan." *Far Eastern Survey* 19 (10): 101–103.

Glazer, Nathan, and Daniel Patrick Moynihan. 1963. *Beyond the Melting Pot: The Negroes, Puerto Ricans, Jews, Italians, and Irish of New York City.* Cambridge, Mass.: M.I.T. Press.

Hayano, David M. 1981. "Ethnic Identification and Disidentification: Japanese-American Views of Chinese-Americans." *Ethnic Groups* 3 (2): 157–171.

Hill, Herbert. 1973. "Anti-Oriental Agitation and the Rise of Working-Class Racism." *Society* 10 (2): 43–54.

Hoyt, Edwin P. 1974. *Asians in the West.* New York: Thomas Nelson.

Ichioka, Yuji. 1988. *The Issei: The World of the First Generation Japanese Americans, 1885–1924.* New York: Free Press.

Ignacio, Lemuel F. 1976. *Asian Americans and Pacific Islanders (Is There Such an Ethnic Group?)* San Jose: Filipino Development Associates.

Johanessen, Edward L. H. 1950. *The Labor Movement in the Territory of Hawaii.* M.A. thesis, University of California, Berkeley.

Kitano, Harry H. L., and Roger Daniels. 1988. *Asian Americans: Emerging Minorities.* Englewood Cliffs, N.J.: Prentice-Hall.

Kuo, Wen H. 1979. "On the Study of Asian-Americans: Its Current State and Agenda." *Sociological Quarterly* 20 (Spring): 279–290.

Ling, Susie Hsiuhan. 1984. "The Mountain Movers: Asian American Women's Movement in Los Angeles." M.A. thesis, University of California, Los Angeles.

______. 1989. "The Mountain Movers: Asian American Women's Movement in Los Angeles." *Amerasia Journal* 15 (1): 51–67.

Liu, William. 1976. "Asian American Research: Views of a Sociologist." *Asian Studies Occasional Report,* no. 2.

Lott, Juanita Tamayo. 1976. "The Asian American Concept: In Quest of Identity." *Bridge,* November, pp. 30–34.

Lowe, Lisa. 1991. "Heterogeneity, Hybridity, Multiplicity: Marking Asian American Differences." *Diaspora* 1: 24–44.

Lyman, Stanford M. 1970. *The Asian in the West.* Reno and Las Vegas: Desert Research Institute, University of Nevada.

Masada, Saburo. 1970. "Stockton's Yellow Seed." *Pacific Citizen,* 9 October.

Massey, Douglas S., and Nancy A. Denton. 1987. "Trends in the Residential Segregation of Blacks, Hispanics, and Asians, 1970–1980." *American Sociological Review* 52 (December): 802–825.

Matsui, Jeffrey. 1968. "Asian Americans." *Pacific Citizen,* 6 September.

Mears, Eliot Grinnell. 1928. *Resident Orientals on the American Pacific Coast.* New York: Arno Press.

Melendy, H. Brett. 1977. *Asians in America: Filipinos, Koreans, and East Indians.* Boston: Twayne.

Nakano, Roy. 1984. "Marxist Leninist Organization in the Asian American Community: Los Angeles, 1969–79." Unpublished student paper, UCLA.

Nishio, Alan. 1982. "Personal Reflections on the Asian National Movements." *East Wind,* Spring/Summer, pp. 36–38.

Omi, Michael, and Howard Winant. 1986. *Racial Formation in the United States: From the 1960s to the 1980s.* New York: Routledge and Kegan Paul.

Ong, Paul. 1989. "California's Asian Population: Past Trends and Projections for the Year 2000." Los Angeles: Graduate School of Architecture and Urban Planning.

Rabaya, Violet. 1971. "I Am Curious (Yellow?)." Pp. 110–111 in *Roots: An Asian American Reader,* edited by Amy Tachiki, Eddie Wong, and Franklin Odo. Los Angeles: UCLA Asian American Studies Center.

Sung, Betty Lee. 1967. *Mountain of Gold: The Story of the Chinese in America.* New York: Macmillan.

Takaki, Ronald. 1989. *Strangers from a Different Shore: A History of Asian Americans.* Boston: Little, Brown.

Tanaka, Ron. 1976. "Culture, Communication, and the Asian Movement in Perspective." *Journal of Ethnic Studies* 4 (1): 37–52.

tenBrock, J., E. N. Barnhart, and F. W. Matson. 1970.

Prejudice, War, and the Constitution. Berkeley: University of California Press.

U.S. Commission on Civil Rights. 1986. *Recent Activities against Citizens and Residents of Asian Descent.* Washington, D.C.: U.S. Government Printing Office.

Uyematsu, Amy. 1971. "The Emergence of Yellow Power in America." Pp. 9–13 in *Roots: An Asian American Reader,* edited by Amy Tachiki, Eddie Wong, and Franklin Odo. Los Angeles: UCLA Asian American Studies Center.

Weiss, Melford S. 1974. *Valley City: A Chinese Community in America.* Cambridge, Mass.: Schenkman.

Woldemikael, Tekle Mariam. 1989. *Becoming Black Americans: Haitians and American Institutions in Evanston, Illinois.* New York: AMS Press.

Wong, Paul. 1972. "The Emergence of the Asian-American Movement." *Bridge* 2 (1): 33–39.

Yoshimura, Evelyn. 1989. "How I Became an Activist and What It All Means to Me." *Amerasia Journal* 15 (I): 106–109.

Yuan, D. Y. 1966. "Chinatown and Beyond: The Chinese Population in Metropolitan New York." *Phylon* 23 (4): 321–332.

PERSONAL ACCOUNT

I Thought My Race Was Invisible

In a conversation with a close friend, I noticed that I am, to her, a representative of my entire racial category. To put things in perspective, my friend Janet and I have been friends for eight years. During this period, it has come up that I am a third-generation Japanese-American who has no ties to being Japanese other than a couple of sushi dishes I learned how to make from my grandmother. Nonetheless, whenever a question regarding "Asians" comes up, she comes to me as if I can provide the definitive answer to every Asian mystery.

Yesterday Janet asked me if there is a cultural reason why Asians "always drive so slow." Not having noticed that Asians drive slowly (in fact, I have noticed a number of Asians who actually exceed the speed limit), I commented that perhaps they are law-abiding citizens. She said that must explain it: "They are used to following the law." I thought, "Am I one of 'they'?" but didn't comment further. Before we switched subjects, she noted that she "knew there had to be a cultural reason" for their driving.

Janet then told me about a Vietnamese woman at the Hair Cuttery who cut her husband's hair. As is normal, her husband talked to the woman as she worked on his hair; he asked her what she did before working at the Hair Cuttery. She said that she used to work in the fields in California (i.e., she was a field hand). Janet told me of the healthy respect that she and her husband had for a woman who worked in the fields, put herself through cosmetology school, moved East, and became a professional hairstylist. She commented that "Blacks" should follow her example and work instead of complaining of their lot in life.

This conversation was interesting and a bit startling. Janet is a good friend who shares many interests with me. What I realized from this conversation, and in remembering others that were similar, is that she feels that I am a representative of the whole Asian race. Not only is this unrealistic, but it is surprising that she would imagine I could answer for my race given my lack of real cultural exposure. In relaying the story of the Vietnamese woman, I had a sense that she was complimenting me, and my race, for the industriousness "we" demonstrate. It seems to me that she approved of the "typically" Asian way of working (quietly, so as not to insult or offend), even though this woman was probably underpaid and overworked in her field hand job. While she approved of her reticence, Janet did not approve of "Black" complaints.

I realize that to Janet, I will always be Asian. I had not really thought about it before, but I never think of Janet as White; her race is invisible to me. I had thought that my race was invisible too; however, I realize now that I will always be the "marked" friend. This saddens me a bit, but I accept it with the knowledge that she is a close friend. Nonetheless, it is unfortunate to think that even between friends, race is an issue.

Sherri H. Pereira

READING 6

Whiteness as an "Unmarked" Cultural Category

Ruth Frankenberg

> America's supposed to be the melting pot. I know that I've got a huge number of nationalities in my blood, but how do I—what do I call myself? And hating this country as I do, I don't like to say I'm an American. Even though it is what I am. I hate identifying myself as only an American, because I have so much objections to Americans' place in the world. I don't know how I felt about that when I was growing up, but I never—I didn't like to pledge allegiance to the flag. . . . Still, at this point in my life, I wonder what it is that somebody with all this melting pot blood can call their own. . . .
>
> Especially growing up in the sixties, when people *did* say "I'm proud to be Black," "I'm proud to be Hispanic," you know, and it became very popular to be proud of your ethnicity. And even feminists, you know, you could say, "I'm a woman," and be proud of it. But there's still a majority of the country that can't say they are proud of anything!

Suzie Roberts's words powerfully illustrate the key themes . . . that stirred the women I interviewed as they examined their own identities: what had formed them, what they counted as (their own or others') cultural practice(s), and what constituted identities of which they could be proud.* This [discussion] explores perceptions of whiteness as a location of culture and identity, focusing mainly on white feminist . . . women's views and contrasting their voices with those of more politically conservative women. . . .

[M]any of the women I interviewed, including even some of the conservative ones, appeared to be self-conscious about white power and racial inequality. In part because of their sense of the links and parallels between white racial dominance in the United States and U.S. domination on a global scale, there was a complex interweaving of questions about race and nation—whiteness and Americanness—in these women's thoughts about white culture. Similarly, conceptions of racial, national, and cultural belonging frequently leaked into one another.

On the one hand, then, these women's views of white culture seemed to be distinctively modern. But at the same time, their words drew on much earlier historical moments and participated in long-established modes of cultural description. In the broadest sense, Western colonial discourses on the white self, the nonwhite Other, and the white Other too, were very much in evidence. These discourses produced dualistic conceptualizations of whiteness versus other cultural forms. The women thus often spoke about culture in ways that reworked, and yet remained tied to, "older" forms of racism.

For a significant number of young white women, being white felt like being cultureless. Cathy Thomas, in the following description of whiteness, raised many of the themes alluded to by other feminist and race-cognizant women. She described what she saw as a lack of form and substance:

> . . . the formlessness of being white. Now if I was a middle western girl, or a New Yorker, if I had a fixed regional identity that was something palpable, then I'd be a white New Yorker, no doubt, but I'd still be a New Yorker. . . . Being a Californian, I'm sure it has its hallmarks, but to me they were invisible. . . . If I had an ethnic base to identify from, if I was even Irish American, that would have been something formed, if I was a working-class woman, that would have been something formed. But to be a Heinz 57 American, a white, class-confused American, land of the Kleenex type American, is so formless in and of itself. It only takes shape in relation to other people.

Whiteness as a cultural space is represented here as amorphous and indescribable, in contrast

---

Ruth Frankenberg is associate professor of American studies at the University of California, Davis.

*Between 1984 and 1986 I interviewed 30 white women, diverse in age, class, region of origin, sexuality, family situation and political orientation, all living in California at the time of the interviews.

with a range of other identities marked by race, ethnicity, region, and class. Further, white culture is viewed here as "bad" culture. In fact, the extent to which identities can be named seems to show an inverse relationship to power in the U.S. social structure. The elisions, parallels, and differences between characterizations of white people, Americans, people of color, and so-called white ethnic groups will be explored [here].

Cathy's own cultural positioning seemed to her impossible to grasp, shapeless and unnameable. It was easier to know others and to know, with certainty, what one was *not.* Providing a clue to one of the mechanisms operating here is the fact that, while Cathy viewed New Yorkers and midwesterners as having a cultural shape or identity, women from the East Coast and the Midwest also described or mourned their own seeming lack of culture. The self, where it is part of a dominant cultural group, does not have to name itself. In this regard, Chris Patterson hit the nail on the head, linking the power of white culture with the privilege not to be named:

> I'm probably at the stage where I'm beginning to see that you can come up with a definition of white. Before, I didn't know that you could turn it around and say, "Well what *does* white mean?" One thing is, it's taken for granted. . . . [To be white means to] have some sort of advantage or privilege, even if it's something as simple as not having a definition.

The notion of "turning it around" indicates Chris's realization that, most often, whites are the nondefined definers of other people. Or, to put it another way, whiteness comes to be an unmarked or neutral category, whereas other cultures are specifically marked "cultural."

Many of the women shared the habit of turning to elements of white culture as the unspoken norm. This assumption of a white norm was so prevalent that even Sandy Alvarez and Louise Glebocki, who were acutely aware of racial inequality as well as being members of racially mixed families, referred to "Mexican" music versus "regular" music, and regular meant "white."

Similarly, discussions of race difference and cultural diversity at times revealed a view in which people of color actually embodied difference and whites stood for sameness. Hence, Margaret Phillips said of her Jamaican daughter-in-law that: "She *really* comes with diversity." In spite of its brevity, and because of its curious structure, this short statement says a great deal. It implicitly designates whiteness as norm, and Jamaicans as having or bearing with them "differentness." At the risk of being crass, one might say that in this view, diversity is to the daughter-in-law as "the works" is to a hamburger—added on, adding color and flavor, but not exactly essential. Whiteness, seen by many of these women as boring, but nonetheless definitive, could also follow this analogy. This mode of thinking about "difference" expresses clearly the double-edged sword of a color- and power-evasive repertoire, apparently valorizing cultural difference but doing so in a way that leaves racial and cultural hierarchies intact.

For a seemingly formless entity, then, white culture had a great deal of power, difficult to dislodge from its place in white consciousness as a point of reference for the measuring of others. Whiteness served simultaneously to eclipse and marginalize others (two modes of making the other inessential). Helen Standish's description of her growing-up years in a small New England town captured these processes well. Since the community was all white, the differences at issue were differences between whites. (This also enables an assessment of the links between white and nonwhite "marked" cultures.) Asked about her own cultural identity, Helen explained that "it didn't seem like a culture because everyone else was the same." She had, however, previously mentioned Italian Americans in the town, so I asked about their status. She responded as follows, adopting at first the voice of childhood:

> They are different, but I'm the same as everybody else. They speak Italian, but everybody else in the U.S. speaks English. They eat strange, different food, but I eat the same kind of food as everybody else in the U.S. . . . The way I was brought up was

to think that everybody who was the same as me were "Americans," and the other people were of "such and such descent."

Viewing the Italian Americans as different and oneself as "same" serves, first, to marginalize, to push from the center, the former group. At the same time, claiming to be the same as everyone else makes other cultural groups invisible or eclipses them. Finally, there is a marginalizing of all those who are not like Helen's own family, leaving a residual, core or normative group who are the true Americans. The category of "American" represents simultaneously the normative and the residual, the dominant culture and a nonculture.

Although Helen talked here about whites, it is safe to guess that people of color would not have counted among the "same" group but among the communities of "such and such descent" (Mexican American, for example). Whites, within this discursive repertoire, became conceptually the real Americans, and only certain kinds of whites actually qualified. Whiteness and Americanness both stood as normative and exclusive categories in relation to which other cultures were identified and marginalized. And this clarifies that there are two kinds of whites, just as there are two kinds of Americans: those who are truly or only white, and those who are white but also something more—or is it something less?

In sum, whiteness often stood as an unmarked marker of others' differentness—whiteness not so much void or formlessness as norm. I associate this construction with colonialism and with the more recent assymetrical dualisms of liberal humanist views of culture, race, and identity. For the most part, this construction views nonwhite cultures as lesser, deviant, or pathological. However, another trajectory has been the inverse: conceptualizations of the cultures of peoples of color as somehow better than the dominant culture, perhaps more natural or more spiritual. These are positive evaluations of a sort, but they are equally dualistic. Many of the women I interviewed saw white culture as less appealing and found the cultures of the "different" people more interesting. As Helen Standish put it:

[We had] Wonder bread, white bread. I'm more interested in, you know, "What's a bagel?" in other people's cultures rather than my own.

The claim that whiteness lacks form and content says more about the definitions of culture being used than it does about the content of whiteness. However, I would suggest that in describing themselves as cultureless these women are in fact identifying specific kinds of unwanted absences or presences in their own culture(s) as a generalized lack or nonexistence. It thus becomes important to look at what they *did* say about the cultural content of whiteness.

Descriptions of the content of white culture were thin, to say the least. But despite the paucity of signifiers, there was a great deal of consistency across the narratives. First, there was naming based on color, the linking of white culture with white objects—the clichéd white bread and mayonnaise, for example. Freida Kazen's identification of whiteness as "bland," together with Helen Standish's "blah," also signified paleness or neutrality. The images connote several things—color itself (although exaggerated, and besides, bagels are usually white inside, too), lack of vitality (Wonder bread is highly processed), and homogeneity. However, these images are perched on a slippery slope, at once suggesting "white" identified as a color (though an unappealing one) and as an absence of color, that is, white as the unmarked marker.

Whiteness was often signified in these narratives by commodities and brands: Wonder bread, Kleenex, Heinz 57. In this identification whiteness came to be seen as spoiled by capitalism, and as being linked with capitalism in a way that other cultures supposedly are not. Another set of signifiers that constructed whiteness as uniquely tainted by capitalism had to do with the "modern condition": Dot Humphrey described white neighborhoods as "more privatized," and Cathy Thomas used "alienated" to describe her cultural condition. Clare Traverso added to this theme, mourning her own feeling of lack of identity, in contrast with images of her husband's Italian American background (and here, Clare is again talking about perceived differences between whites):

> Food, old country, mama. Stories about a grandmother who can't speak English. . . . Candles, adobe houses, arts, music. [It] has emotion, feeling, belongingness that to me is unique.

In linking whiteness to capitalism and viewing nonwhite cultures as untainted by it, these women were again drawing on a colonial discourse in which progress and industrialization were seen as synonymous with Westernization, while the rest of the world is seen as caught up in tradition and "culture." In addition, one can identify, in white women's mourning over whiteness, elements of what Raymond Williams has called "pastoralism," or nostalgia for a golden era now gone by (but in fact, says Williams, one that never existed).[1]

The image of whiteness as corrupted and impoverished by capitalism is but one of a series of ways in which white culture was seen as impure or tainted. White culture was also seen as tainted by its relationship to power. For example, Clare Traverso clearly counterposed white culture and white power, finding it difficult to value the former because of the overwhelming weight of the latter:

> The good things about whites are to do with folk arts, music. Because other things have power associated with them.

For many race-cognizant white women, white culture was also made impure by its very efforts to maintain race purity. Dot Humphrey, for example, characterized white neighborhoods as places in which people were segregated by choice. For her, this was a good reason to avoid living in them.

The link between whiteness and domination, however, was frequently made in ways that both artificially isolated culture from other factors and obscured economics. For at times, the traits the women envied in Other cultures were in fact at least in part the product of poverty or other dimensions of oppression. Lack of money, for example, often means lack of privacy or space, and it can be valorized as "more street life, less alienation." Cathy Thomas's notion of Chicanas' relationship to the kitchen ("the hearth of the home") as a cultural "good" might be an idealized one that disregards the reality of intensive labor.

Another link between class and culture emerged in Louise Glebocki's reference to the working-class Chicanos she met as a child as less pretentious, "closer to the truth," more "down to earth." And Marjorie Hoffman spoke of the "earthy humor" of Black people, which she interpreted as, in the words of Langston Hughes, a means of "laughing to keep from crying." On the one hand, as has been pointed out especially by Black scholars and activists, the positions of people of color at the bottom of a social and economic hierarchy create the potential for a critique of the system as a whole and consciousness of the need to resist.[2] From the standpoint of race privilege, the system of racism is thus made structurally invisible. On the other hand, descriptions of this kind leave in place a troubling dichotomy that can be appropriated as easily by the right as by the left. For example, there is an inadvertent affinity between the image of Black people as "earthy" and the conservative racist view that African American culture leaves African American people ill equipped for advancement in the modern age. Here, echoing essentialist racism, both Chicanos and African Americans are placed on the borders of "nature" and "culture."

By the same token, often what was criticized as "white" was as much the product of middle-class status as of whiteness as such. Louise Glebocki's image of her fate had she married a white man was an image of a white-collar, nuclear family:

> Him saying, "I'm home, dear," and me with an apron on—ugh!

The intersections of class, race, and culture were obscured in other ways. Patricia Bowen was angry with some of her white feminist friends who, she felt, embraced as "cultural" certain aspects of African American, Chicano, and Native American cultures (including, for example, artwork or dance performances) but would reject as "tacky" (her term) those aspects of daily life that communities of color shared with working-class whites, such as the stores and supermarkets of poor neighborhoods. This, she felt, was tantamount to a selective expansion of middle-class aesthetic horizons, but not to true antiracism or to comprehension of the cultures of people of color. Having herself grown up in a white working-class family, Pat also felt that middle-class white feminists were able to use selective engagement to avoid addressing their class privilege.

I have already indicated some of the problems inherent in this kind of conceptualization, suggesting that it tends to keep in place dichotomous constructions of "white" versus Other cultures, to separate "culture" from other dimensions of daily life, and to reify or strip of history *all* cultural forms. There are, then, a range of issues that need to be disentangled if we are to understand the location of "whiteness" in the terrain of culture. It is, I believe, useful to approach this question by means of a reconceptualization of the concept of culture itself. A culture, in the sense of the set of rules and practices by means of which a group organizes itself and its values, manners, and worldview—in other words, culture as "a field articulating the life-world of subjects . . . and the structures created by human activity"[3]—is an indispensable precondition to any individual's existence in the world. It is nonsensical in terms of this kind of definition to suggest that anyone could actually have "no culture." But this is not, as I have suggested, the mode of thinking about culture that these women are employing.

Whiteness emerges here as inextricably tied to domination partly as an effect of a discursive "draining process" applied to both whiteness and Americanness. In this process, any cultural practice engaged in by a white person that is not identical to the dominant culture is automatically counted as either "not really white"—and, for that matter, not really American, either—(but rather of such and such descent), or as "not really cultural" (but rather "economic"). There is a slipperiness to whiteness here: it shifts from "no culture" to "normal culture" to "bad culture" and back again. Simultaneously, a range of marginal or, in Trinh T. Minh-ha's terminology, "bounded" cultures are generated. These are viewed as enviable spaces, separate and untainted by relations of dominance or by linkage to other structures or systems. By contrast, whiteness is conceived as axiomatically tied to dominance, to economics, to political structures. In this process, both whiteness and nonwhiteness are reified, made into objects rather than processes, and robbed of historical context and human agency. As long as the discussion remains couched in these terms, a critique of whiteness remains a double-edged sword: for one thing, whiteness remains normative because there is no way to name the cultural practices associated with it *as* cultural. Moreover, as I have suggested, whether whiteness is viewed as artificial and dominating (and therefore "bad") or civilized (and therefore "good"), whiteness and all varieties of nonwhiteness continue to be viewed as ontologically different from one another.

A genuine sadness and frustration about the meaning of whiteness at this moment in history motivated these women to decry white culture. It becomes important, then, to recognize the grains of truth in their views of white culture. It is important to acknowledge their anger and frustration about the meaning of whiteness as we reach toward a politicized analysis of culture that is freer of colonial and pastoral legacies.

The terms "white" and "American" as these women used them signified domination in international and domestic terms. This link is both accurate and inaccurate. While it is true that, by and large, those in power in the United States are white, it is also true that not all those who are white are in power. Nor is the axiomatic linkage between Americanness and power accurate, because not all Americans have the same access to power. At the same time, the link between whiteness, Americanness, and power *are* accurate because, as we have seen, the terms "white" and "American" both function discursively to exclude people from normativity—including white people "of such and such descent." But here we need to distinguish between the fates of people of color and those of white people. Notwithstanding a complicated history, the boundaries of Americanness and whiteness have been much more fluid for "white ethnic" groups than for people of color.

There have been border skirmishes over the meaning of whiteness and Americanness since the inception of those terms. For white people, however, those skirmishes have been resolved through processes of assimilation, not exclusion. The late nineteenth and early twentieth centuries in the United States saw a systematic push toward the cultural homogenization of whites carried out through social reform movements and the schools. This push took place alongside the expansion of industrial capitalism, giving rise to the sense that whiteness signifies the production and consumption of commodities under capitalism.[4] But recognition of this history should not be translated into an assertion that whites were stripped of culture (for to do that would be to continue to adhere to a colonial view of "culture"). Instead one must argue that certain cultural practices replaced others. Were one to undertake a history of this "generic" white culture, it would fragment into a thousand tributary elements, culturally specific religious observances, and class survival mechanisms as well as mass-produced commodities and mass media.

There are a number of dangers inherent in continuing to view white culture as no culture. Whiteness appeared in the narratives to function as both norm or core, that against which everything else is measured, and as residue, that which is left after everything else has been named. A far-reaching danger of whiteness coded as "no culture" is that it leaves in place whiteness as defining a set of normative cultural practices against which all are measured and into which all are expected to fit. This normativity has underwritten oppression from the beginning of colonial expansion and has had impact in multiple ways: from the American pioneers' assumption of a norm of private property used to justify appropriation of land that within their worldview did not have an owner, and the ideological construction of nations like Britain as white,[5] to Western feminism's Eurocentric shaping of its movements and institutions. It is important for white feminists not to continue to participate in these processes.

And if whiteness has a history, so do the cultures of people of color, which are worked on, crafted, and created, rather than just "there." For peoples of color in the United States, this work has gone on as much in the context of relationships to imperialism and capitalism as has the production of whiteness, though it has been premised on exclusion and resistance to exclusion more than on assimilation. Although not always or only forged in resistance, the visibility and recognition of the cultures of U.S. peoples of color in recent times *is* the product of individual and collective struggle. Only a short time has elapsed since those struggles made possible the introduction into public discourse of celebration and valorization of their cultural forms. In short, it is important not to reify any culture by failing to acknowledge its createdness, and not to view it as always having been there in unchanging form.

Rather than feeling "cultureless," white women need to become conscious of the histories and specificities of our cultural positions, and of the political, economic, and creative fusions that form all cultures. The purpose of such an exercise is not, of course, to reinvert the dualisms and valorize whiteness so much as to develop a clearer sense of where and who we are.

NOTES

1. Raymond Williams, *The Country and the City* (New York: Oxford University Press, 1978).
2. The classic statement of this position is W. E. B. Du Bois's concept of the "double consciousness" of Americans of African descent. Two recent feminist statements of similar positions are Patricia Hill Collins, *Black Feminist Thought: Knowledge, Consciousness, and the Politics of Empowerment* (Boston: Unwin Hyman, 1990); and Aida Hurtado, "Relating to Privilege: Seduction and Rejection in the Subordination of White Women and Women of Color," *Signs* 14, no. 4:833–55.
3. Paul Gilroy, *There Ain't No Black In The Union Jack*. London: Hutchinson, 1987.
4. See, for example, Winthrop Talbot, ed., *Americanization* (New York: H. W. Wilson, 1917), esp. Sophonisba P. Breckinridge, "The Immigrant Family," 251–52; Olivia Howard Dunbar, "Teaching the Immigrant Woman," 252–56, and North American Civic League for Immigrants, "Domestic Education among Immigrants," 256–58; and Kathie Friedman Kasaba, " 'To Become a Person': The Experience of Gender, Ethnicity and Work in the Lives of Immigrant Women, New York City, 1870–1940," doctoral dissertation. Department of Sociology, State University of New York, Binghamton, 1991. I am indebted to Katie Friedman Kasaba for these references and for her discussions with me about working-class European immigrants to the United States at the turn of this century.
5. Gilroy, *There Ain't No Black In The Union Jack*.

What Is Sex? What Is Gender?

READING 7

The Five Sexes

Why Male and Female Are Not Enough

Anne Fausto-Sterling

In 1843 Levi Suydam, a twenty-three-year-old resident of Salisbury, Connecticut, asked the town board of selectmen to validate his right to vote as a Whig in a hotly contested local election. The request raised a flurry of objections from the opposition party, for reasons that must be rare in the annals of American democracy: it was said that Suydam was more female than male and thus (some eighty years before suffrage was extended to women) could not be allowed to cast a ballot. To settle the dispute a physician, one William James Barry, was brought in to examine Suydam. And, presumably upon encountering a phallus, the good doctor declared the prospective voter male. With Suydam safely in their column the Whigs won the election by a majority of one.

Barry's diagnosis, however, turned out to be somewhat premature. Within a few days he discovered that, phallus notwithstanding, Suydam menstruated regularly and had a vaginal opening. Both his/her physique and his/her mental predispositions were more complex than was first suspected. S/he had narrow shoulders and broad hips and felt occasional sexual yearnings for women. Suydam's "feminine propensities, such as a fondness for gay colors, for pieces of calico, comparing and placing them together, and an aversion for bodily labor, and an inability to perform the same, were remarked by many," Barry later wrote. It is not clear whether Suydam lost or retained the vote, or whether the election results were reversed.

Anne Fausto-Sterling is professor of biology and medicine at Brown University.

Western culture is deeply committed to the idea that there are only two sexes. Even language refuses other possibilities; thus to write about Levi Suydam I have had to invent conventions—*s/he* and *his/her*—to denote someone who is clearly neither male nor female or who is perhaps both sexes at once. Legally, too, every adult is either man or woman, and the difference, of course, is not trivial. For Suydam it meant the franchise; today it means being available for, or exempt from, draft registration, as well as being subject, in various ways, to a number of laws governing marriage, the family and human intimacy. In many parts of the United States, for instance, two people legally registered as men cannot have sexual relations without violating anti-sodomy statutes.

But if the state and the legal system have an interest in maintaining a two-party sexual system, they are in defiance of nature. For biologically speaking, there are many gradations running from female to male; and depending on how one calls the shots, one can argue that along that spectrum lie at least five sexes—and perhaps even more.

For some time medical investigators have recognized the concept of the intersexual body. But the standard medical literature uses the term *intersex* as a catch-all for three major subgroups with some mixture of male and female characteristics: the so-called true hermaphrodites, whom I call herms, who possess one testis and one ovary (the sperm- and egg-producing vessels, or gonads); the male pseudohermaphrodites (the "merms"), who have testes and some aspects of the female genitalia but no ovaries; and the female pseudohermaphrodites (the "ferms"), who have ovaries and some aspects of the male genitalia but lack testes. Each of those categories is in itself complex; the percentage of male and female characteristics, for instance, can vary enormously among members of the same subgroup. Moreover, the inner lives of the people in each subgroup—their special needs and their problems, attractions and repulsions—have gone unexplored by science. But on the basis of what is known about them I suggest that the three intersexes, herm, merm and ferm, deserve to be considered additional sexes each in its own right. Indeed, I would argue further that sex is a vast, infinitely malleable continuum that defies the constraints of even five categories.

Not surprisingly, it is extremely difficult to estimate the frequency of intersexuality, much less the frequency of each of the three additional sexes: it is not the sort of information one volunteers on a job application. The psychologist John Money of Johns Hopkins University, a specialist in the study of congenital sexual-organ defects, suggests intersexuals may constitute as many as 4 percent of births. As I point out to my students at Brown University, in a student body of about 6,000 that fraction, if correct, implies there may be as many as 240 intersexuals on campus—surely enough to form a minority caucus of some kind.

In reality though, few such students would make it as far as Brown in sexually diverse form. Recent advances in physiology and surgical technology now enable physicians to catch most intersexuals at the moment of birth. Almost at once such infants are entered into a program of hormonal and surgical management so that they can slip quietly into society as "normal" heterosexual males or females. I emphasize that the motive is in no way conspiratorial. The aims of the policy are genuinely humanitarian, reflecting the wish that people be able to "fit in" both physically and psychologically. In the medical community, however, the assumptions behind that wish—that there be only two sexes, that heterosexuality alone is normal, that there is one true model of psychological health—have gone virtually unexamined.

The word *hermaphrodite* comes from the Greek names Hermes, variously known as the messenger of the gods, the patron of music, the controller of dreams or the protector of livestock, and Aphrodite, the goddess of sexual love and beauty. According to Greek mythology, those two gods parented Hermaphroditus, who at age fifteen became half male and half female when his body fused with the body of a nymph he fell in love with. In some true hermaphrodites the testis and the ovary grow separately but bilaterally; in others they grow together within the same organ, forming an ovo-testis. Not infrequently, at least one of the gonads functions quite well, producing either sperm cells or eggs, as well as functional levels of the sex hormones—androgens or estrogens. Although in theory it might be possible for a true hermaphrodite to become both father and mother to a child, in practice the appropriate ducts and tubes are not configured so that egg and sperm can meet.

In contrast with the true hermaphrodites, the pseudohermaphrodites possess two gonads of the same kind along with the usual male (XY) or female (XX) chromosomal makeup. But their external genitalia and secondary sex characteristics do not match their chromosomes. Thus merms have testes and XY chromosomes, yet they also have a vagina and a clitoris, and at puberty they often develop breasts. They do not menstruate, however. Ferms have ovaries, two X chromosomes and sometimes a uterus, but they also have at least partly masculine external genitalia. Without medical intervention they can develop beards, deep voices and adult-size penises. . . .

Intersexuality itself is old news. Hermaphrodites, for instance, are often featured in stories about human origins. Early biblical scholars believed Adam began life as a hermaphrodite and later divided into two people—a male and a female—after falling from grace. According to Plato there once were three sexes—male, female and hermaphrodite—but the third sex was lost with time.

Both the Talmud and the Tosefta, the Jewish books of law, list extensive regulations for people of mixed sex. The Tosefta expressly forbids hermaphrodites to inherit their fathers' estates (like daughters), to seclude themselves with women (like sons) or to shave (like men). When hermaphrodites menstruate they must be isolated from men (like women); they are disqualified from serving as witnesses or as priests (like women), but the laws of pederasty apply to them.

In Europe a pattern emerged by the end of the Middle Ages that, in a sense, has lasted to the present day: hermaphrodites were compelled to choose an established gender role and stick with it. The penalty for transgression was often death. Thus in the 1600s a Scottish hermaphrodite living as a woman was buried alive after impregnating his/her master's daughter.

For questions of inheritance, legitimacy, paternity, succession to title and eligibility for certain professions to be determined, modern Anglo-Saxon legal systems require that newborns be registered as either male or female. In the U.S. today sex determination is governed by state laws. Illinois permits adults to change the sex recorded on their birth certificates should a physician attest to having performed the appropriate surgery. The New York Academy of Medicine, on the other hand, has taken an opposite view. In spite of surgical alterations of the external genitalia, the academy argued in 1966, the chromosomal sex remains the same. By that measure, a person's wish to conceal his or her original sex cannot outweigh the public interest in protection against fraud.

During this century the medical community has completed what the legal world began—the complete erasure of any form of embodied sex that does not conform to a male–female, heterosexual pattern. Ironically, a more sophisticated knowledge of the complexity of sexual systems has led to the repression of such intricacy.

In 1937 the urologist Hugh H. Young of Johns Hopkins University published a volume titled *Genital Abnormalities, Hermaphroditism and Related Adrenal Diseases.* The book is remarkable for its erudition, scientific insight and openmindedness. In it Young drew together a wealth of carefully documented case histories to demonstrate and study the medical treatment of such "accidents of birth." Young did not pass judgment on the people he studied, nor did he attempt to coerce into treatment those intersexuals who rejected that option. And he showed unusual even-handedness in referring to those people who had had sexual experiences as both men and women as "practicing hermaphrodites."

One of Young's more interesting cases was a hermaphrodite named Emma who had grown up as a female. Emma had both a penis-size clitoris and a vagina, which made it possible for him/her to have "normal" heterosexual sex with both men and women. As a teenager Emma had had sex with a number of girls to whom s/he was deeply attracted; but at the age of nineteen s/he had married a man. Unfortunately, he had given Emma little sexual pleasure (though he had had no complaints), and so throughout that marriage and subsequent ones Emma had kept girlfriends on the side. With some frequency s/he had pleasurable sex with them. Young describes his subject as appearing "to be quite content and even happy." In conversation Emma occasionally told him of his/her wish to be a man, a circumstance Young said would be relatively easy to bring about. But Emma's reply strikes a heroic blow for self-interest:

> Would you have to remove that vagina? I don't know about that because that's my meal ticket. If you did that, I would have to quit my husband and go to work, so I think I'll keep it and stay as I am. My husband supports me well, and even though I don't have any sexual pleasure with him, I do have lots with my girlfriends.

Yet even as Young was illuminating intersexuality with the light of scientific reason, he was beginning its suppression. For his book is also an extended treatise on the most modern surgical and hormonal methods of changing intersexuals into either males or females. Young may have differed from his successors in being less judgmental and controlling of the patients and their families, but he nonetheless supplied the foundation on which current intervention practices were built.

By 1969, when the English physicians Christopher J. Dewhurst and Ronald R. Gordon wrote *The Intersexual Disorders,* medical and surgical approaches to intersexuality had neared a state of rigid uniformity. It is hardly surprising that such a hardening of opinion took place in the era of the feminine mystique—of the post-Second World War flight to the suburbs and the strict division of family roles according to sex. That the medical consensus was not quite universal (or perhaps that it seemed poised to break apart again) can be gleaned from the near-hysterical tone of Dewhurst and Gordon's book, which contrasts markedly with the calm reason of Young's founding work. Consider their opening description of an intersexual newborn:

> One can only attempt to imagine the anguish of the parents. That a newborn should have a deformity . . . [affecting] so fundamental an issue as the very sex of the child . . . is a tragic event which immediately conjures up visions of a hopeless psychological misfit doomed to live always as a sexual freak in loneliness and frustration.

Dewhurst and Gordon warned that such a miserable fate would, indeed, be a baby's lot should the case be improperly managed; "but fortunately," they wrote, "with correct management the outlook is infinitely better than the poor parents—emotionally stunned by the event—or indeed anyone without special knowledge could ever imagine."

Scientific dogma has held fast to the assumption that without medical care hermaphrodites are doomed to a life of misery. Yet there are few empirical studies to back up that assumption, and some of the same research gathered to build a case for medical treatment contradicts it. Francies Benton, another of Young's practicing hermaphrodites, "had not worried over his condition, did not wish to be changed, and was enjoying life." The same could be said of Emma, the opportunistic hausfrau. Even Dewhurst and Gordon, adamant about the psychological importance of treating intersexuals at the infant stage, acknowledged great success in "changing the sex" of older patients. They reported on twenty cases of children reclassified into a different sex after the supposedly critical age of eighteen months. They asserted that all the reclassifications were "successful," and they wondered then whether reregistration could be "recommended more readily than [had] been suggested so far."

The treatment of intersexuality in this century provides a clear example of what the French historian Michel Foucault has called biopower. The knowledge developed in biochemistry, embryology, endocrinology, psychology and surgery has enabled physicians to control the very sex of the human body. The multiple contradictions in that kind of power call for some scrutiny. On the one hand, the medical "management" of intersexuality certainly developed as part of an attempt to free people from perceived psychological pain (though whether the pain was the patient's, the parents' or the physician's is unclear). And if one accepts the assumption that in a sex-divided culture people can realize their greatest potential for happiness and productivity only if they are sure they belong to one of only two acknowledged sexes, modern medicine has been extremely successful.

On the other hand, the same medical accomplishments can be read not as progress but as a mode of discipline. Hermaphrodites have unruly bodies. They do not fall naturally into a binary classification; only a surgical shoehorn can put them there. But why should we care if a "woman," defined as one who has breasts, a vagina, a uterus and ovaries and who menstruates, also has a clitoris large enough to penetrate the vagina of another woman? Why should we care if there are people whose biological equipment enables them to have sex "naturally" with both men and women? The answers seem to lie in a cultural need to maintain clear distinctions between the sexes. Society mandates the control of intersexual bodies because they blur and bridge the great divide. Inasmuch as hermaphrodites literally embody both sexes, they challenge traditional beliefs about sexual difference: they possess the irritating ability to live sometimes as one sex and sometimes the other, and they raise the specter of homosexuality.

But what if things were altogether different? Imagine a world in which the same knowledge that has enabled medicine to intervene in the management of intersexual patients has been placed at the service of multiple sexualities. Imagine that the sexes have multiplied beyond currently imaginable limits. It would have to be a world of shared powers. Patient and physician, parent and child, male and female, heterosexual and homosexual—all those oppositions and others would have to be dissolved as sources of division. A new ethic of medical treatment would arise, one that would permit ambiguity in a culture that had overcome sexual division. The central mission of medical treatment would be to preserve life. Thus hermaphrodites would be concerned primarily not about whether they can conform to society but about whether they might develop potentially life-threatening conditions—hernias, gonadal tumors, salt imbalance caused by adrenal malfunction—that sometimes accompany hermaphroditic development. In my ideal world medical intervention for intersexuals would take place only rarely before the age of reason; subsequent treatment would be a cooperative venture between physician, patient and other advisers trained in issues of gender multiplicity.

I do not pretend that the transition to my utopia would be smooth. Sex, even the supposedly "normal," heterosexual kind, continues to cause untold anxieties in Western society. And certainly a culture that has yet to come to grips—religiously and, in some states, legally—with the ancient and relatively uncomplicated reality of homosexual love will not readily embrace intersexuality. No doubt the most troublesome arena by far would be the rearing of children. Parents, at least since the Victorian era, have fretted, sometimes to the point of outright denial, over the fact that their children are sexual beings.

All that and more amply explains why intersexual children are generally squeezed into one of the two prevailing sexual categories. But what would be the psychological consequences of taking the alternative road—raising children as unabashed intersexuals? On the surface that tack seems fraught with peril. What, for example, would happen to the intersexual child amid the unrelenting cruelty of the school yard? When the time came to shower in gym class, what horrors and humiliations would await the intersexual as his/her anatomy was displayed in all its nontraditional glory? In whose gym class would s/he register to begin with? What bathroom would s/he use? And how on earth would Mom and Dad help shepherd him/her through the mine field of puberty?

In the past thirty years those questions have been ignored, as the scientific community has, with remarkable unanimity, avoided contemplating the alternative route of unimpeded intersexuality. But modern investigators tend to overlook a substantial body of case histories, most of them compiled between 1930 and 1960, before surgical intervention became rampant. Almost without exception, those reports describe children who grew up knowing they were intersexual (though they did not advertise it) and adjusted to their unusual status. Some of the studies are richly detailed—described at the level of gym-class showering (which most intersexuals avoided without incident); in any event, there is not a psychotic or a suicide in the lot.

Still, the nuances of socialization among intersexuals cry out for more sophisticated analysis. Clearly, before my vision of sexual multiplicity can be realized, the first openly intersexual children and their parents will have to be brave pioneers who will bear the brunt of society's growing pains. But in the long view—though it could take generations to achieve—the prize might be a society in which sexuality is something to be celebrated for its subtleties and not something to be feared or ridiculed.

READING 8

The Berdache Tradition

Walter L. Williams

Because it is such a powerful force in the world today, the Western Judeo-Christian tradition is often accepted as the arbiter of "natural" behavior of humans. If Europeans and their descendant nations of North America accept something as normal, then anything different is seen as abnormal. Such a view ignores the great diversity of human existence.

This is the case for the study of gender. How many genders are there? To a modern Anglo-American, nothing might seem more definite than the answer that there are two: men and women. But not all societies around the world agree with Western culture's view that all humans are either women or men. The commonly accepted notion of "the opposite sex," based on anatomy, is itself an artifact of our society's rigid sex roles.

Among many cultures, there have existed different alternatives to "man" or "woman." An alternative role in many American Indian societies is referred to by anthropologists as *berdache*. . . The role varied from one Native American culture to another, which is a reflection of the vast diversity of aboriginal New World societies. Small bands of hunter-gatherers existed in some areas, with advanced civilizations of farming peoples in other areas. With hundreds of different languages, economies, religions, and social patterns existing in North America alone, every generalization about a cultural tradition must acknowledge many exceptions.

This diversity is true for the berdache tradition as well, and must be kept in mind. My statements should be read as being specific to a particular

Walter L. Williams is professor of anthropology at the University of Southern California.

culture, with generalizations being treated as loose patterns that might not apply to peoples even in nearby areas.

Briefly, a berdache can be defined as a morphological male who does not fill a society's standard man's role, who has a nonmasculine character. This type of person is often stereotyped as effeminate, but a more accurate characterization is androgyny. Such a person has a clearly recognized and accepted social status, often based on a secure place in the tribal mythology. Berdaches have special ceremonial roles in many Native American religions, and important economic roles in their families. They will do at least some women's work, and mix together much of the behavior, dress, and social roles of women and men. Berdaches gain social prestige by their spiritual, intellectual, or craftwork/artistic contributions, and by their reputation for hard work and generosity. They serve a mediating function between women and men, precisely because their character is seen as distinct from either sex. They are not seen as men, yet they are not seen as women either. They occupy an alternative gender role that is a mixture of diverse elements.

In their erotic behavior berdaches also generally (but not always) take a nonmasculine role, either being asexual or becoming the passive partner in sex with men. In some cultures the berdache might become a wife to a man. This male-male sexual behavior became the focus of an attack on berdaches as "sodomites" by the Europeans who, early on, came into contact with them. From the first Spanish conquistadors to the Western frontiersmen and the Christian missionaries and government officials, Western culture has had a considerable impact on the berdache tradition. In the last two decades, the most recent impact on the tradition is the adaptation of a modern Western gay identity.

To Western eyes berdachism is a complex and puzzling phenomenon, mixing and redefining the very concepts of what is considered male and female. In a culture with only two recognized genders, such individuals are gender nonconformist, abnormal, deviant. But to American Indians, the institution of another gender role means that berdaches are not deviant—indeed, they do conform to the requirements of a custom in which their culture tells them they fit. Berdachism is a way for society to recognize and assimilate some atypical individuals without imposing a change on them or stigmatizing them as deviant. This cultural institution confirms their legitimacy for what they are.

Societies often bestow power upon that which does not neatly fit into the usual. Since no cultural system can explain everything, a common way that many cultures deal with these inconsistencies is to imbue them with negative power, as taboo, pollution, witchcraft, or sin. That which is not understood is seen as a threat. But an alternative method of dealing with such things, or people, is to take them out of the realm of threat and to sanctify them.[1] The berdaches' role as mediator is thus not just between women and men, but also between the physical and the spiritual. American Indian cultures have taken what Western culture calls negative, and made it a positive; they have successfully utilized the different skills and insights of a class of people that Western culture has stigmatized and whose spiritual powers have been wasted.

Many Native Americans also understood that gender roles have to do with more than just biological sex. The standard Western view that one's sex is always a certainty, and that one's gender identity and sex role always conform to one's morphological sex is a view that dies hard. Western thought is typified by such dichotomies of groups perceived to be mutually exclusive: male and female, black and white, right and wrong, good and evil. Clearly, the world is not so simple; such clear divisions are not always realistic. Most American Indian worldviews generally are much more accepting of the ambiguities of life. Acceptance of gender variation in the berdache tradition is typical of many native cultures' approach to life in general.

Overall, these are generalizations based on those Native American societies that had an accepted role for berdaches. Not all cultures recognized such a respected status. Berdachism in aboriginal North America was most established among tribes in four areas: first, the Prairie and western Great Lakes, the northern and central Great Plains, and the lower Mississippi Valley; second, Florida and the Caribbean; third, the Southwest, the Great Basin, and California; and fourth, scattered areas of the Northwest, western Canada, and Alaska. For some reason it is not noticeable in eastern North America, with the exception of its southern rim. . . .

AMERICAN INDIAN RELIGIONS

Native American religions offered an explanation for human diversity by their creation stories. In some tribal religions, the Great Spiritual Being is conceived as neither male nor female but as a combination of both. Among the Kamia of the Southwest, for example, the bearer of plant seeds and the introducer of Kamia culture was a man-woman spirit named Warharmi.[2] A key episode of the Zuni creation story involves a battle between the kachina spirits of the agricultural Zunis and the enemy hunter spirits. Every four years an elaborate ceremony commemorates this myth. In the story a kachina spirit called *ko'lhamana* was captured by the enemy spirits and transformed in the process. This transformed spirit became a mediator between the two sides, using his peacemaking skills to merge the differing lifestyles of hunters and farmers. In the ceremony, a dramatic reenactment of the myth, the part of the transformed *ko'lhamana* spirit, is performed by a berdache.[3] The Zuni word for berdache is *lhamana,* denoting its closeness to the spiritual mediator who brought hunting and farming together.[4] The moral of this story is that the berdache was created by the deities for a special purpose, and that this creation led to the improvement of society. The continual reenactment of this story provides a justification for the Zuni berdache in each generation.

In contrast to this, the lack of spiritual justification in a creation myth could denote a lack of tolerance for gender variation. The Pimas, unlike most of their Southwestern neighbors, did not respect a berdache status. *Wi-kovat,* their derogatory word, means "like a girl," but it does not signify a recognized social role. Pima mythology reflects this lack of acceptance, in a folk tale that explains male androgyny as due to Papago witchcraft. Knowing that the Papagos respected berdaches, the Pimas blamed such an occurrence on an alien influence.[5] While the Pimas' condemnatory attitude is unusual, it does point out the importance of spiritual explanations for the acceptance of gender variance in a culture.

Other Native American creation stories stand in sharp contrast to the Pima explanation. A good example is the account of the Navajos, which presents women and men as equals. The Navajo origin tale is told as a story of five worlds. The first people were First Man and First Woman, who were created equally and at the same time. The first two worlds that they lived in were bleak and unhappy, so they escaped to the third world. In the third world lived two twins, Turquoise Boy and White Shell Girl, who were the first berdaches. In the Navajo language the word for berdache is *nadle,* which means "changing one" or "one who is transformed." It is applied to hermaphrodites—those who are born with the genitals of both male and female—and also to "those who pretend to be *nadle,*" who take on a social role that is distinct from either men or women.[6]

In the third world, First Man and First Woman began farming, with the help of the changing twins. One of the twins noticed some clay and, holding it in the palm of his/her hand, shaped it into the first pottery bowl. Then he/she formed a plate, a water dipper, and a pipe. The second twin observed some reeds and began to weave them, making the first basket. Together they shaped axes and grinding stones from rocks, and hoes from bone. All these new inventions made the people very happy.[7]

The message of this story is that humans are dependent for many good things on the inventiveness of *nadle*. Such individuals were present from the earliest eras of human existence, and their presence was never questioned. They were part of the natural order of the universe, with a special contribution to make.

Later on in the Navajo creation story, White Shell Girl entered the moon and became the Moon Bearer. Turquoise Boy, however, remained with the people. When First Man realized that Turquoise Boy could do all manner of women's work as well as women, all the men left the women and crossed a big river. The men hunted and planted crops. Turquoise Boy ground the corn, cooked the food, and weaved cloth for the men. Four years passed with the women and men separated, and the men were happy with the *nadle*. Later, however, the women wanted to learn how to grind corn from the *nadle,* and both the men and the women had decided that it was not good to continue living separately. So the women crossed the river and the people were reunited.[8]

They continued living happily in the third world, until one day a great flood began. The people ran to the highest mountaintop, but the water kept rising and they all feared they would be drowned. But just in time, the ever-inventive Turquoise Boy found a large reed. They climbed upward inside the tall hollow reed, and came out at the top into the fourth world. From there, White Shell Girl brought another reed, and they climbed again to the fifth world, which is the present world of the Navajos.[9]

These stories suggest that the very survival of humanity is dependent on the inventiveness of berdaches. With such a mythological belief system, it is no wonder that the Navajos held *nadle* in high regard. The concept of the *nadle* is well formulated in the creation story. As children were educated by these stories, and all Navajos believed in them, the high status accorded to gender variation was passed down from generation to generation. Such stories also provided instructions for *nadle* themselves to live by. A spiritual explanation guaranteed a special place for a person who was considered different but not deviant.

For American Indians, the important explanations of the world are spiritual ones. In their view, there is a deeper reality than the here-and-now. The real essence or wisdom occurs when one finally gives up trying to explain events in terms of "logic" and "reality." Many confusing aspects of existence can better be explained by actions of a multiplicity of spirits. Instead of a concept of a single god, there is an awareness of "that which we do not understand." In Lakota religion, for example, the term *Wakan Tanka* is often translated as "god." But a more proper translation, according to the medicine people who taught me, is "The Great Mystery."[10]

While rationality can explain much, there are limits to human capabilities of understanding. The English language is structured to account for cause and effect. For example, English speakers say, "It is raining," with the implication that there is a cause "it" that leads to rain. Many Indian languages, on the other hand, merely note what is most accurately translated as "raining" as an observable fact. Such an approach brings a freedom to stop worrying about causes of things, and merely to relax and accept that our human insights can go only so far. By not taking ourselves too seriously, or overinflating human importance, we can get beyond the logical world.

The emphasis of American Indian religions, then, is on the spiritual nature of all things. To understand the physical world, one must appreciate the underlying spiritual essence. Then one can begin to see that the physical is only a faint shadow, a partial reflection, of a supernatural and extrarational world. By the Indian view, everything that exists is spiritual. Every object—plants, rocks, water, air, the moon, animals, humans, the earth itself—has a spirit. The spirit of one thing (including a human) is not superior to the spirit of any other. Such a view promotes a sophisticated ecological awareness of the place that humans have in the larger environment. The function of religion is not to try to condemn or to change what exists, but to accept the realities of the world and to appreciate their contributions to life. Everything that exists has a purpose.[11]

One of the basic tenets of American Indian religion is the notion that everything in the universe is related. Nevertheless, things that exist are often seen as having a counterpart: sky and earth, plant and animal, water and fire. In all of these polarities, there exist mediators. The role of the mediator is to hold the polarities together, to keep the world from disintegrating. Polarities exist within human society also. The most important category within Indian society is gender. The notions of Woman and Man underlie much of social interaction and are comparable to the other major polarities. Women, with their nurturant qualities, are associated with the earth, while men are associated with the sky. Women gatherers and farmers deal with plants (of the earth), while men hunters deal with animals.

The mediator between the polarities of woman and man, in the American Indian religious explanation, is a being that combines the elements of both genders. This might be a combination in a physical sense, as in the case of hermaphrodites. Many Native American religions accept this phenomenon in the same way that they accept other variations from the norm. But more important is their acceptance of the idea that gender can be combined in ways other than physical hermaphroditism. The physical aspects of a thing or a person, after all, are not nearly as important as its spirit. American Indians use the concept of a person's *spirit* in the way that other Americans use the concept of a person's *character*. Consequently, physical hermaphroditism is not necessary for the idea of gender mixing. A person's character, their spiritual essence, is the crucial thing.

THE BERDACHE'S SPIRIT

Individuals who are physically normal might have the spirit of the other sex, might range somewhere between the two sexes, or might have a spirit that is distinct from either women or men. Whatever category they fall into, they are seen as being different from men. They are accepted spiritually as "Not Man." Whichever option is chosen, Indian religions offer spiritual explanations. Among the Arapahos of the Plains, berdaches are called *haxu'xan* and are seen to be that way as a result of a supernatural gift from birds or animals. Arapaho mythology recounts the story of Nih'a'ca, the first *haxu'xan.* He pretended to be a woman and married the mountain lion, a symbol for masculinity. The myth, as recorded by ethnographer Alfred Kroeber about 1900, recounted that "These people had the natural desire to become women, and as they grew up gradually became women. They gave up the desires of men. They were married to men. They had miraculous power and could do supernatural things. For instance, it was one of them that first made an intoxicant from rainwater."[12] Besides the theme of inventiveness, similar to the Navajo creation story, the berdache role is seen as a product of a "natural desire." Berdaches "gradually became women," which underscores the notion of woman as a social category rather than as a fixed biological entity. Physical biological sex is less important in gender classification than a person's desire—one's spirit.

The myths contain no prescriptions for trying to change berdaches who are acting out their desires of the heart. Like many other cultures' myths, the Zuni origin myths simply sanction the idea that gender can be transformed independently of biological sex.[13] Indeed, myths warn of dire consequences when interference with such a transformation is attempted. Prince Alexander Maximilian of the German state of Wied, traveling in the northern Plains in the 1830s, heard a myth about a warrior who once tried to force a berdache to avoid women's clothing. The berdache resisted, and the warrior shot him with an arrow. Immediately the berdache disappeared, and the warrior saw only a pile of stones with his arrow in them. Since then, the story concluded, no intelligent person would try to coerce a berdache.[14] Making the point even more directly, a Mandan myth told of an Indian who tried to force *mihdacke* (berdaches) to give up their distinctive dress and status, which led the spirits to punish many people with death. After that, no Mandans interfered with berdaches.[15]

With this kind of attitude, reinforced by myth and history, the aboriginal view accepts human diversity. The creation story of the Mohave of the Colorado River Valley speaks of a time when people were not sexually differentiated. From this perspective, it is easy to accept that certain individuals might combine elements of masculinity and femininity.[16] A respected Mohave elder, speaking in the 1930s, stated this viewpoint simply: "From the very beginning of the world it was meant that there should be [berdaches], just as it was instituted that there should be shamans. They were intended for that purpose."[17]

This elder also explained that a child's tendencies to become a berdache are apparent early, by about age nine to twelve, before the child reaches puberty: "That is the time when young persons become initiated into the functions of their sex. . . . None but young people will become berdaches as a rule."[18] Many tribes have a public ceremony that acknowledges the acceptance of berdache status. A Mohave shaman related the ceremony for his tribe: "When the child was about ten years old his relatives would begin discussing his strange ways. Some of them disliked it, but the more intelligent began envisaging an initiation ceremony." The relatives prepare for the ceremony without letting the boy know of it. It is meant to take him by surprise, to be both an initiation and a test of his true inclinations. People from various settlements are invited to attend. The family wants the community to see it and become accustomed to accepting the boy as an *alyha.*

On the day of the ceremony, the shaman explained, the boy is led into a circle: "If the boy showed a willingness to remain standing in the circle, exposed to the public eye, it was almost certain that he would go through with the ceremony. The singer, hidden behind the crowd, began singing the songs. As soon as the sound reached the boy he began to dance as women do." If the boy is unwilling to assume *alyha* status, he would refuse to dance. But if his character—his spirit—is *alyha,* "the song goes right to his heart and he will dance with much intensity. He cannot help it. After the fourth song he is proclaimed." After the ceremony, the boy is carefully bathed and receives a woman's skirt. He is then led back to the dance ground, dressed as an *alyha,* and announces his new feminine name to the crowd. After that he would resent being called by his old male name.[19]

Among the Yuman tribes of the Southwest, the transformation is marked by a social gathering, in which the berdache prepares a meal for the friends of the family.[20] Ethnographer Ruth Underhill, doing fieldwork among the Papago Indians in the early 1930s, wrote that berdaches were common among the Papago Indians, and were usually publicly acknowledged in childhood. She recounted that a boy's parents would test him if they noticed that he preferred female pursuits. The regular pattern, mentioned by many of Underhill's Papago informants, was to build a small brush enclosure. Inside the enclosure they placed a man's bow and arrows, and also a woman's basket. At the appointed time the boy was brought to the enclosure as the adults watched from outside. The boy was told to go inside the circle of brush. Once he was inside, the adults "set fire to the enclosure. They watched what he took with him as he ran out and if it was the basketry materials, they reconciled themselves to his being a berdache."[21]

What is important to recognize in all of these practices is that the assumption of a berdache role was not forced on the boy by others. While adults might have their suspicions, it was only when the child made the proper move that he was considered a berdache. By doing woman's dancing, preparing a meal, or taking the woman's basket he was making an important symbolic gesture. Indian children were not stupid, and they knew the implications of these ceremonies beforehand. A boy in the enclosure could have left without taking anything, or could have taken both the man's and the woman's tools. With the community standing by watching, he was well aware that his choice would mark his assumption of berdache status. Rather than being seen as an involuntary test of his reflexes, this ceremony may be interpreted as a definite statement by the child to take on the berdache role.

Indians do not see the assumption of berdache status, however, as a free will choice on the part of the boy. People felt that the boy was acting out his basic character. The Lakota shaman Lame Deer explained:

> They were not like other men, but the Great Spirit made them *winktes* and we accepted them as such. . . . We think that if a woman has two little ones growing inside her, if she is going to have twins, sometimes instead of giving birth to two babies they have formed up in her womb into just one, into a half-man/half-woman kind of being. . . . To us a man is what nature, or his dreams, make him. We accept him for what he wants to be. That's up to him.[22]

While most of the sources indicate that once a person becomes a berdache it is a lifelong status, directions from the spirits determine everything. In at least one documented case, concerning a nineteenth-century Klamath berdache named Lele'ks, he later had a supernatural experience that led him to leave the berdache role. At that time Lele'ks began dressing and acting like a man, then married women, and eventually became one of the most famous Klamath chiefs.[23] What is important is that both in assuming berdache status and in leaving it, supernatural dictate is the determining factor.

DREAMS AND VISIONS

Many tribes see the berdache role as signifying an individual's proclivities as a dreamer and a visionary. . . .

Among the northern Plains and related Great Lakes tribes, the idea of supernatural dictate through dreaming—the vision quest—had its highest development. The goal of the vision quest is to try to get beyond the rational world by sensory deprivation and fasting. By depriving one's body of nourishment, the brain could escape from logical thought and connect with the higher reality of the supernatural. The person doing the quest simply sits and waits for a vision. But a vision might not come easily; the person might have to wait for days.

The best way that I can describe the process is to refer to my own vision quest, which I experienced when I was living on a Lakota reservation in 1982. After a long series of prayers and blessings, the shaman who had prepared me for the ceremony took me out to an isolated area where a sweat lodge had been set up for my quest. As I walked to the spot, I worried that I might not be able to stand it. Would I be overcome by hunger? Could I tolerate the thirst? What would I do if I had to go to the toilet? The shaman told me not to worry, that a whole group of holy people would be praying and singing for me while I was on my quest.

He had me remove my clothes, symbolizing my disconnection from the material world, and crawl into the sweat lodge. Before he left me I asked him, "What do I think about?" He said, "Do not think. Just pray for spiritual guidance." After a prayer he closed the flap tightly and I was left in total darkness. I still do not understand what happened to me during my vision quest, but during the day and a half that I was out there, I never once felt hungry or thirsty or the need to go to the toilet. What happened was an intensely personal experience that I cannot and do not wish to explain, a process of being that cannot be described in rational terms.

When the shaman came to get me at the end of my time, I actually resented having to end it. He did not need to ask if my vision quest were successful. He knew that it was even before seeing me, he explained, because he saw an eagle circling over me while I underwent the quest. He helped interpret the signs I had seen, then after more prayers and singing he led me back to the others. I felt relieved, cleansed, joyful, and serene. I had been through an experience that will be a part of my memories always.

If a vision quest could have such an effect on a person not even raised in Indian society, imagine its impact on a boy who from his earliest years had been waiting for the day when he could seek his vision. Gaining his spiritual power from his first vision, it would tell him what role to take in adult life. The vision might instruct him that he is going to be a great hunter, a craftsman, a warrior, or a shaman. Or it might tell him that he will be a berdache. Among the Lakotas, or Sioux, there are several symbols for various types of visions. A person becomes *wakan* (a sacred person) if she or he dreams of a bear, a wolf, thunder, a buffalo, a white buffalo calf, or Double Woman. Each dream results in a different gift, whether it is the power to cure illness or wounds, a promise of good hunting, or the exalted role of a *heyoka* (doing things backward).

A white buffalo calf is believed to be a berdache. If a person has a dream of the sacred Double Woman, this means that she or he will have the power to seduce men. Males who have a vision of Double Woman are presented with female tools. Taking such tools means that the male will become a berdache. The Lakota word *winkte* is composed of *win,* "woman," and *kte,* "would become."[24] A contemporary Lakota berdache explains, "To become a *winkte,* you have a medicine man put you up on the hill, to search for your vision. You can become a *winkte* if you truly are by nature. You see a vision of the White Buffalo Calf Pipe. Sometimes it varies. A vision is like a scene in a movie."[25] Another way to become a *winkte* is to have a vision given by a *winkte* from the past.[26] . . .

By interpreting the result of the vision as being the work of a spirit, the vision quest frees the person from feeling responsible for his transformation. The person might even claim that the change was done against his will and without his control. Such a claim does not suggest a negative attitude about berdache status, because it is common for people to claim reluctance to fulfill their spiritual duty no matter what vision appears to them. Becoming any kind of sacred person involves taking on various social responsibilities and burdens.[27] . . .

A story was told among the Lakotas in the 1880s of a boy who tried to resist following his vision from Double Woman. But according to Lakota informants "few men succeed in this effort after having taken the strap in the dream." Having rebelled against the instructions given him by the Moon Being, he committed suicide.[28] The moral of that story is that one should not resist spiritual guidance, because it will lead only to grief. In another case, an Omaha young man told of being addressed by a spirit as "daughter," whereupon he discovered that he was unconsciously using feminine styles of speech. He tried to use male speech patterns, but could not. As a result of this vision, when he returned to his people he resolved himself to dress as a woman.[29] Such stories function to justify personal peculiarities as due to a fate over which the individual has no control.

Despite the usual pattern in Indian societies of using ridicule to enforce conformity, receiving instructions from a vision inhibits others from trying to change the berdache. Ritual explanation provides a way out. It also excuses the community from worrying about the cause of that person's difference, or the feeling that it is society's duty to try to change him.[30] Native American religions, above all else, encourage a basic respect for nature. If nature makes a person different, many Indians conclude, a mere human should not undertake to counter this spiritual dictate. Someone who is "unusual" can be accommodated without being stigmatized as "abnormal." Berdachism is thus not alien or threatening; it is a reflection of spirituality.

NOTES

1. Mary Douglas, *Purity and Danger* (Baltimore: Penguin, 1966), p. 52. I am grateful to Theda Perdue for convincing me that Douglas's ideas

apply to berdachism. For an application of Douglas's thesis to berdaches, see James Thayer, "The Berdache of the Northern Plains: A Socioreligious Perspective," *Journal of Anthropological Research 36* (1980): 292–93.

2. E. W. Gifford, "The Kamia of Imperial Valley," *Bureau of American Ethnology Bulletin 97* (1931): 12.
3. By using present tense verbs in this text, I am not implying that such activities are necessarily continuing today. I sometimes use the present tense in the "ethnographic present," unless I use the past tense when I am referring to something that has not continued. Past tense implies that all such practices have disappeared. In the absence of fieldwork to prove such disappearance, I am not prepared to make that assumption, on the historic changes in the berdache tradition.
4. Elsie Clews Parsons, "The Zuni La' Mana," *American Anthropologist 18* (1916): 521; Matilda Coxe Stevenson, "Zuni Indians," *Bureau of American Ethnology Annual Report 23* (1903): 37; Franklin Cushing, "Zuni Creation Myths," *Bureau of American Ethnology Annual Report 13* (1894): 401–3. Will Roscoe clarified this origin story for me.
5. W. W. Hill, "Note on the Pima Berdache," *American Anthropologist 40* (1938): 339.
6. Aileen O'Bryan, "The Dine': Origin Myths of the Navaho Indians," *Bureau of American Ethnology Bulletin 163* (1956): 5; W. W. Hill, "The Status of the Hermaphrodite and Transvestite in Navaho Culture," *American Anthropologist 37* (1935): 273.
7. Martha S. Link, *The Pollen Path: A Collection of Navajo Myths* (Stanford: Stanford University Press, 1956).
8. O'Bryan, "Dine'," pp. 5, 7, 9–10.
9. Ibid.
10. Lakota informants, July 1982. See also William Powers, *Oglala Religion* (Lincoln: University of Nebraska Press, 1977).
11. For this admittedly generalized overview of American Indian religious values, I am indebted to traditionalist informants of many tribes, but especially those of the Lakotas. For a discussion of native religions see Dennis Tedlock, *Finding the Center* (New York: Dial Press, 1972); Ruth Underhill, *Red Man's Religion* (Chicago: University of Chicago Press, 1965); and Elsie Clews Parsons, *Pueblo Indian Religion* (Chicago: University of Chicago Press, 1939).
12. Alfred Kroeber, "The Arapaho," *Bulletin of the American Museum of Natural History 18* (1902–7): 19.
13. Parsons, "Zuni La' Mana," p. 525.
14. Alexander Maximilian, *Travels in the Interior of North America, 1832–1834,* vol. 22 of *Early Western Travels,* ed. Reuben Gold Thwaites, 32 vols. (Cleveland: A. H. Clark, 1906), pp. 283–84, 354. Maximilian was quoted in German in the early homosexual rights book by Ferdinand Karsch-Haack, *Das Gleichgeschlechtliche Leben der Naturvölker* (The same-sex life of nature peoples) (Munich: Verlag von Ernst Reinhardt, 1911; reprinted New York: Arno Press, 1975), pp. 314, 564.
15. Oscar Koch, *Der Indianishe Eros* (Berlin: Verlag Continent, 1925), p. 61.
16. George Devereux, "Institutionalized Homosexuality of the Mohave Indians," *Human Biology 9* (1937): 509.
17. Ibid., p. 501.
18. Ibid.
19. Ibid., pp. 508–9.
20. C. Daryll Forde, "Ethnography of the Yuma Indians," *University of California Publications in American Archaeology and Ethnology 28* (1931): 157.
21. Ruth Underhill, *Social Organization of the Papago Indians* (New York: Columbia University Press, 1938), p. 186. This story is also mentioned in Ruth Underhill, ed., *The Autobiography of a Papago Woman* (Menasha, Wisc.: American Anthropological Association, 1936), p. 39.
22. John Fire and Richard Erdoes, *Lame Deer, Seeker of Visions* (New York: Simon and Schuster, 1972), pp. 117, 149.
23. Theodore Stern, *The Klamath Tribe: A People and Their Reservation* (Seattle: University of Washington Press, 1965), pp. 20, 24; Theodore Stern, "Some Sources of Variability in Klamath Mythology," *Journal of American Folklore 69* (1956): 242ff; Leshe Spier, *Klamath Ethnography* (Berkeley: University of California Press, 1930), p. 52.
24. Clark Wissler, "Societies and Ceremonial Associations in the Oglala Division of the Teton

Dakota," *Anthropological Papers of the American Museum of Natural History 11,* pt. 1 (1916): 92; Powers, *Oglala Religion,* pp. 57–59.

25. Ronnie Loud Hawk, Lakota informant 4, July 1982.
26. Terry Calling Eagle, Lakota informant 5, July 1982.
27. James S. Thayer, "The Berdache of the Northern Plains: A Socioreligious Perspective," *Journal of Anthropological Research 36* (1980): 289.
28. Fletcher, "Elk Mystery," p. 281.
29. Alice Fletcher and Francis La Flesche, "The Omaha Tribe," *Bureau of American Ethnology Annual Report 27* (1905–6): 132.
30. Harriet Whitehead offers a valuable discussion of this element of the vision quest in "The Bow and the Burden Strap: A New Look at Institutionalized Homosexuality in Native North America," in *Sexual Meanings,* ed. Sherry Ortner and Harriet Whitehead (Cambridge: Cambridge University Press, 1981), pp. 99–102. See also Erikson, "Childhood," p. 329.

READING 9

Gender Stereotypes and Roles

Susan Basow

ALL-OR-NONE CATEGORIZING

The all-or-none categorizing of gender traits is misleading. People just are not so simple that they either possess all of a trait or none of it. This is even more true when trait dispositions for groups of people are examined. Part a of Figure 1 illustrates what such an all-or-none distribution of the trait "strength" would look like: all males would be strong, all females weak. The fact is, most psychological and physical traits are distributed according to the pattern shown in Part b of Figure 1 with most people possessing an average amount of that trait and fewer people having either very much or very little of that trait.

To the extent that females and males may differ in the average amount of the trait they possess (which needs to be determined empirically), the distribution can be characterized by *overlapping normal curves,* as shown in Part c of Figure 1. Thus, although most men are stronger than most women, the shaded area indicates that some men are weaker than some women and vice versa. The amount of overlap of the curves generally is considerable. Another attribute related to overlapping normal curves is that differences within one group are usually greater than the differences between the two groups. Thus, more variation in strength occurs within a group of men than between the average male and the average female. . . . For example, although males on the average may be more aggressive than females on the average, greater differences may be found among males than between males and females. . . .

Susan Basow is professor of psychology at Lafayette College.

FIGURE 1 **Three types of distribution for the trait "strength."**

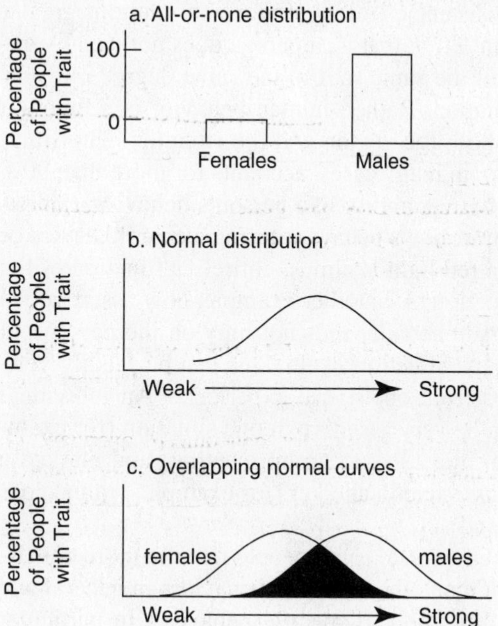

This concept of overlapping normal curves is critically important in understanding gender stereotypes because it undermines the basis of most discriminatory regulations and laws. Although most men are stronger than most women, denying women access to jobs requiring strength simply on the basis of sex is unjustified, because some women are stronger than some men (see shaded area in Part c of Figure 1). Thus, if most of the stereotypic traits are actually distributed in normal curves along a continuum (that is, people may be more or less dominant, more or less submissive) rather than distributed in an all-or-none fashion—dominant or submissive—then setting up two opposite and distinct lists of traits for females and males is entirely inappropriate and misleading. . . .

Strong debate exists over whether personality can be viewed in trait terms altogether. Despite their popularity, trait theories of personality have little empirical validity (see, for example, Chaplin & Goldberg, 1985). People are simply not as consistent in their behavior across a variety of situations as one might like to believe. Mischel (1968) concludes that cross-situational consistencies rarely produce correlations greater than +.30; that is, a person does not usually exhibit the same trait to the same degree in every situation. Rather, human behavior is a function of both the person and the situation. The situation, in many cases, accounts for more than 90% of the variability in a person's behavior. For example, one's behavior during a church service or at a red light is almost entirely a function of the situation. As another example, how assertively a person acts depends not only on the person but on the situation itself. This can be readily verified from one's own experience. An individual can be very assertive in one situation (for example, in a class or group meeting) and markedly unassertive in another (for example, with a close friend).

Of course, some people may be more consistent than others in their behaviors in general and with respect to specific behaviors in particular (D. Bem & Allen, 1974). That is, some people may generally be more predictable than others across a wide range of situations. For example, people who strongly identify with a sex role are more predictable because they more often act according to sex role expectations than people who don't identify with such a role (S. L. Bem, 1975, 1985). And some people are more consistent than others with respect to a particular behavior (for example, "You can always count on Mary to be assertive"). On the whole, however, the trait approach to personality needs to be modified. Specific people interact with specific situations and produce specific behaviors; generalized traits rarely apply.

With reference to gender stereotypes, then, it can be concluded that (1) people cannot be viewed simply as collections of consistent traits, because situations also are important; (2) males and females specifically cannot be viewed as having unique traits that are opposite each other; and (3) whatever attributes are thought of as distinctly masculine or feminine are also possessed by at least some members of the other sex. . . .

SEX TYPING AND ANDROGYNY

Research in the mid-1970s on the degree to which individuals were sex-typed (that is, conformed to gender stereotypes) led to a redefinition of the older concept of androgyny. Since the two sets of personality traits viewed as stereotypically masculine (active-instrumental traits) and stereotypically feminine (nurturant-expressive traits) were statistically independent (that is, the way an individual scored on one set of traits was unrelated to the way she or he scored on the other set of traits), terms were needed to describe individuals who were high on both sets of traits and others who were low on both. Sandra Bem (1974, 1975, 1976) and others (for example, Spence & Helmreich, 1978) used the term *androgynous* to describe those individuals who scored high on both active-instrumental traits (such as assertiveness, self-reliance, and independence) and nurturant-expressive traits (such as understanding, compassion, and affection). These people were different from masculine-sex-typed individuals (high on instrumental-active traits, low on nurturant-expressive traits), feminine-sex-typed individuals (high on nurturant-expressive traits, low on instrumental-active traits), and *undifferentiated* individuals (those who scored low on both sets of traits) (Spence, Helmreich, & Stapp, 1974). Figure 2 presents this fourfold classification. One virtue of this fourfold typology is that it separates biological sex from psychological sex typing. Any person can be masculine-sex-typed, feminine-sex-typed, androgynous, or undifferentiated.

Being androgynous does not mean being neuter or imply anything about one's sexual orientation. Rather, it describes the degree of flexibility a person has regarding gender-stereotypic behaviors. The complex characteristics of androgynous individuals can be evidenced, depending on the situation, all in a single act or only in a number of different acts. Thus, a person may be an empathic listener when a friend has a problem, an assertive leader propelling a group to action, and an assertive and sensitive boss when an employee needs to be fired. . . .

The percentage of people who could be classified as androgynous varies as a function of many factors: the specific population studied, the measuring instrument and the scoring procedure used, and even the year in which a study is done. For example, males seem to have increased their level of androgyny during the 1970s compared to the 1960s, whereas females showed higher levels of androgyny in the 1960s (Heilbrun & Schwartz, 1982). One should note that there are no absolute cutoff points for the categories of androgynous and sex-typed individuals. Rather, the cutoffs typically are based on the median scores of a particular sample. The vast majority of studies have been conducted on college populations. In general, about 40% of all college students describe themselves as possessing traits viewed as more characteristic of their sex than of the other (that is, traditionally sex-typed). (See Figure 2.) About one-fourth of college populations are classified as androgynous (somewhat more females than males). Another 20% are characterized as undifferentiated (that is, low in both sets of traits). Finally, about 10% describe themselves as possessing traits viewed as more characteristic of the other sex than of their own (that is, cross-sex-typed). Thus, more than half of all college students are *not* traditionally sex-typed, although more males than females possess instrumental traits (masculine-sex-typed and androgynous) and more females than males possess expressive traits (feminine-sex-typed and androgynous).

Among other populations, degree of sex typing is unclear. There is evidence of increasing androgyny as people reach middle age. Racial differences in sex typing may also exist. One study of young adult women, most of whom had completed high school, found that the Black women had higher instrumentality scores than the White women (Binion, 1990). In terms of sex typing, more Black women (37%) than White women (16%) fell in the androgynous category, whereas more White women (38%) than Black women (28%) fell in the undifferentiated category. Again, we must be careful not to generalize from young, primarily White, well-educated individuals to the entire population.

FIGURE 2 Fourfold classification of sex typing. Numbers are percentages of college students who typically fall into each cell. From S. L. Bem, 1981a.

Femininity \ Masculinity	Low	High
Low	Undifferentiated 18% females 27% males	Masculine 12% females 42% males
High	Feminine 39% females 12% males	Androgynous 30% females 20% males

More recently, Sandra Bem (1981b, 1985, 1987) has reconceptualized androgyny and sex typing to refer to cognitive schemata rather than personality types. Sex-typed individuals seem to be more aware than non-sex-typed individuals (both the androgynous and the undifferentiated) of gender and such gender-related issues as the number of men and women in a room, whether the topic discussed is masculine or feminine, and whether an occupation is gender-appropriate or not (Frable, 1989; Frable & Bem, 1985; J. B. Miller, 1984; C. J. Mills, 1983). Thus, sex typing may refer to the process of construing reality in terms of gender. Non-sex-typed individuals seem less ready to impose a gender-based classification system on reality.

The concept of androgyny, when first articulated, was hailed by some as a signpost leading the way toward gender equality and deplored by others as signifying the end of sex differentiation and thus the end of the world. Neither extreme view now seems justified. The concepts of sex typing and androgyny do have some utility in helping us understand how and why some males and females differ on some behaviors. For example, more behavioral differences exist between feminine-sex-typed and masculine-sex-typed people than between women and men as social groups, because most men and women are *not* traditionally sex-typed. This finding explains why there are so few strong gender differences in behavior at the same time that it suggests why we *think* there are (because we *expect* most men to be masculine-sex-typed and most women to be feminine-sex-typed). These concepts also emphasize the importance of looking for factors other than biology to account for gender differences.

For all its value, the concept of androgyny still has its limitations. Theoretically, androgyny may be a self-defeating concept in the sense that it depends on the existence of two separate sets of traits—masculine and feminine. Thus, it may serve to perpetuate the gender stereotypes themselves. One solution to this problem is to refer to masculine and feminine traits by their qualities—instrumental-agentic and expressive-nurturant—rather than by their stereotyped labels (Spence, 1983; Spence & Helmreich, 1980). Another solution is to go beyond the concept of androgyny altogether and speak in terms of sex role transcendence (Rebecca, Hefner, & Olenshansky, 1976).

A related problem is whether these two sets of traits adequately distinguish what is feminine from what is masculine (J. Archer, 1989; Deaux & Kite, 1987; Locksley & Colten, 1979). As we've already noted, gender refers to more than simply personality traits and indeed, to more personality traits than can be summarized by the terms *instrumental* and *expressive*. Gender and sex typing are multidimensional constructs, and bidimensional measures, such as the Bem Sex-Role Inventory (S. L. Bem, 1974, 1981a) or the Personal Attributes Questionnaire (Spence & Helmreich, 1978; Spence, Helmreich, & Stapp, 1974) are not sufficient. They tell us something but not everything we need to know about gender.

Another issue is whether androgyny is actually a unique type (an interaction between instrumental and expressive traits) or just the sum of its parts—that is, a linear combination of instrumental and expressive traits. Research suggests that androgyny does not have unique predictive power (J. A. Hall & Taylor, 1985; Lubinski, Tellegen, & Butcher, 1983). For example, with respect to self-esteem, creativity, and psychological adjustment, it is high scores on the instrumental-agentic trait scale that are beneficial (true of both masculine-sex-typed individuals and androgynous individuals), not high scores on both scales (Harrington & Andersen, 1981; Whitley, 1984, 1988a). Thus, the androgynous "ideal" may turn out to be a traditionally masculine one (Morawski, 1987). We need to understand why that is, and explanations in terms of personality traits alone will not help us.

Finally, a host of empirical problems have been raised with respect to measuring androgyny and sex typing. Different scales do not all seem to measure the same thing (A. C. Baldwin, Critelli, Stevens, & Russell, 1986; F. R. Wilson & Cook, 1984). Different scoring methods yield different results (for example, Handal & Salit, 1985). Sex-typing scales seem to measure more than two different factors (for example, Marsh et al., 1989; Pedhazur & Tetenbaum, 1979). Different researchers use different definitions of androgyny (for example, Heilbrun & Mulqueen, 1987). Sex-typing categories do not always predict stereotypic attitudes and beliefs (for example, J. Archer, 1989; Beauvais & Spence, 1987; Binion, 1990). And sex-typing categories do not always predict behavior (Lubinski et al., 1983; Myers & Gonda, 1982).

Many of these problems stem from inadequate understanding of the nature of androgyny and overly general use of the term (Morawski, 1987; Sedney, 1989). On the whole, however, if we view androgyny as a limited but valid construct whose parameters are still being explored, we will have a useful tool with which to understand some of the research on gender. We should not expect sex typing and androgyny, however, to be the only explanatory tools we will need. The concepts of power or status and the importance of situational determinants still play pivotal roles in any exploration of gender, since gender is not primarily a psychological variable but a socially constructed one. Psychologists have a tendency to overlook the latter variables, whereas sociologists have a tendency to overlook the former ones. Since gender is right at the intersection of the two fields, we need to keep as broad a perspective as possible. . . .

RESEARCH PROBLEMS

. . . Although research problems are liable to occur in any research area, the areas of sex comparisons and gender-related behaviors are particularly vulnerable to such problems, because these areas are very personal and in many ways, political. . . .

Problems can occur in one or more areas of any research project: the basic assumptions of the researchers, choice of subjects, experimental design and methodology, and interpretation of the results. We will look at each in turn.

Basic Assumptions

All experimenters bring certain assumptions to bear on their research, mainly because as human beings we cannot help but be influenced by our personal experiences and the sociohistorical contexts in which we live. Perhaps the most basic problem in examining the research on gender is the underlying assumption that *sex differences exist* and that *these differences are important* (see Hare-Mustin & Marecek, 1990, and Rhode, 1990, for theoretical explorations of this assumption). As A. Kaplan and Bean (1976) point out, because researchers study areas already thought to reflect male-female differences, such as hormonal cyclicity, the data reflecting these differences may be exaggerated. For example, much research has been done on the effect of female hormone cyclicity on moods; very little has been done on the effect of male hormones. The implication is that hormones play a larger role in female behavior than they do in male behavior. Similarly, Petersen (1983) observed that as research reveals fewer sex differences in cognitive abilities than previously had been thought, more and more research is done on the few remaining areas that do suggest a gender difference. Thus, we get an exaggerated picture of a male-female dichotomy and a limited understanding of the full range of human potential.

This emphasis on sex differences, as opposed to similarities, is further perpetuated by the policy of most journals to publish only statistically significant findings. The null hypothesis, meaning that there is no difference between groups, can never be proved. The strongest statement that can be made is that the null hypothesis cannot be rejected. Therefore, findings reflecting no difference usually do not get reported in the literature. Additionally, because journals have limited space, they have to reject a high percentage of submitted articles, and they naturally tend to accept those with positive findings. . . .

Another basic assumption in research on gender is that *sex differences can be attributed to either nature* (that is, biology—the essentialist position) *or nurture* (that is, the environment—the constructivist position). Even calling this topical area "*sex* differences" suggests that the underlying reason for any differences found is likely to be biological (related to sex) rather than cultural (related to gender). As many writers have noted, it is nearly impossible to separate the influences of biology and environment in humans because socialization begins at birth, and humans have such a tremendous capacity for learning. Gender identity is formed through a complex interaction of biological, psychological, and sociocultural factors. All these factors need to be taken into account when examining human behavior. The upsurge of interest in sociobiological theories since 1975 demonstrates that belief in pure biological determinism still has appeal (see Bleier, 1984, and Fausto-Sterling, 1985, for critiques). An interactionist perspective is needed, and we must determine the way this interaction operates for various behavior patterns in various contexts.

The third basic assumption influencing research is that *what males do is the norm;* what females do, if it is different from what males do, is deviant. Thus McClelland and colleagues (1953) based an entire theory of achievement motivation primarily on male subjects. The fact that this theory does not fit females as well as males should have made the validity and generalizability of the theory suspect but did not. Similarly, Kohlberg (1969) based a theory of moral development almost entirely on male subjects; females have been shown not to conform to his theory as well (Gilligan, 1982). Indeed, Grady (1981) reports that males appear as subjects in research nearly twice as often as do females. The important point here is that theories based solely or primarily on males have been generalized to all people even though the theories may not fit 51% of the human race. When women's behaviors and thoughts are included, the theories themselves frequently must be revised drastically. Such work already has begun.

Hare-Mustin and Marecek (1988) have analyzed the degree to which researchers have defined gender in terms of difference. They have noted two tendencies: the exaggeration of difference, which they call *alpha bias* (such as viewing men as instrumental, women as expressive); and the minimization of difference, which they call *beta bias* (such as ignoring women's greater child-care responsibilities in research on workplace productivity). Both biases support the existing gender hierarchy by making what is male normative and by focusing on individuals rather than on the power differential embedded within the organization of society (see also M. Fine & Gordon, 1989; A. S. Kahn & Yoder, 1989). . . .

The assumptions that we have just reviewed all fit in with a positivist empiricist model of research in psychology, one that restricts analysis to a few clearly observable units of behavior. Such a model shapes research questions, findings, and interpretations. Yet this model ignores the inevitable effects of social constructs, such as status and power, on the research process itself. Mary Gergen (1988) and others (for example, M. Fine & Gordon, 1989; Unger, 1983, 1989; Wittig, 1989) suggest a more reflexive model of research, which requires an understanding of the reciprocal and interactive relationship that exists between the person and reality, and therefore between the experimenter and the "subject." The researcher, together with the persons being researched, exists within a specific cultural and historical setting. Such settings affect the entire research enterprise. For example, the assumption that men are the sexual aggressors and women are sexually passive has affected scientific research on the process of conception (E. Martin,

1991). The egg traditionally has been depicted as passively awaiting "penetration" by active sperm (like Sleeping Beauty), whereas recent biological research finally has acknowledged that both the egg and the sperm play active roles in conception. . . .

Choice of Subjects

Research problems arise in choosing whom to study. Some researchers have used animals, because human experimentation in the biological area presents serious ethical and practical problems. The choice of which animals to study, however, is often a product of the experimenter's assumptions and biases. Donna Haraway (1989) forcefully demonstrates how the study of primates has reflected gender politics. For example, rhesus monkeys, who show different behaviors by sex, are studied more frequently than gibbons, who do not show such differences; yet gibbons are evolutionarily closer to humans than rhesus monkeys (Rosenberg, 1973). The generalizability of findings from animals is also questionable, because humans are unique in their development of the neocortex and in the plasticity of their behavior. Human behavior is extremely modifiable by experience. Although there may be similarities in behavior between humans and animals, the antecedents of behaviors may be quite different. It is curious, in this regard, to note the overwhelming number of studies on aggression that have used nonprimates, particularly rats and mice, and have generalized their findings to humans. (See Bleier, 1979, for an excellent discussion of this topic.)

Subjects may be selected to fit preexisting assumptions. For example, in examining the effect of menopause on women, one study simply excluded from the sample all women who worked outside the home, apparently on the grounds that such women were deviant (Van Hecke, Van Keep, & Kellerhals, 1975). Similarly, studies of attachment in infants nearly always look at mothers rather than fathers, on the assumption that infant-mother attachment is more important. Another example of bias in subject selection is the fact that 90% of all research on aggression has used male subjects, whereas females have been involved in only half the studies (McKenna & Kessler, 1977). As noted previously, males more often are used to represent all human beings, despite the frequent importance of gender as regards the topic studied. Indeed, significant self-selection may occur in some studies. Signorella and Vegega (1984) have found that women are most interested in signing up for experiments on "feminine" topics, such as revealing feelings and moods, whereas men are most interested in signing up for experiments on "masculine" topics, such as power and competition. Results from such studies may be biased and thus limited in generalizability.

Studying people with some abnormality or who need some form of treatment also is problematic, because by definition, these are individuals whose development differs from normal. Women who consult doctors for menstrual problems, for example, are a select group and cannot be assumed to represent women in general. People with inconsistent sex characteristics may be treated differently by their parents from other children, and research may be designed to specifically highlight their differences (for example, Stoller, 1968). Such problems limit the generalizability of findings.

Most research has used White, North American, middle-class, presumedly heterosexual subjects, which severely limits the generalizability of findings. For example, "women" have been found to be less assertive than "men," but this finding is not necessarily true for Black women and Black men (K. A. Adams, 1983; Reid, 1984). Who then is meant by the terms *women and men?* Elizabeth Spelman (1988) and others argue that we must become aware of our (usually hidden) assumptions about who represents the norm. As pointed out previously, each of us is embedded in a complex social matrix with respect to gender, race or ethnicity, class, sexual preference, able-bodiedness, and so on. Not only must researchers learn to stop privileging White, middle-class, heterosexual, Christian norms, but they must also actively seek out other groups to study (for example, Cannon, Higginbotham, & Leung, 1988; Scarr, 1988). The relative impossibility of speaking for all women or all men when the differences within each sex or gender group are enormous must constantly be borne in mind.

Some behaviors seem to be situation- or age-specific. Yet the vast majority of social psychological studies published in the mid-1980s were conducted on college students, especially within an experimental laboratory (Lykes & Stewart, 1986; Sears, 1986). We are left with a great deal of information about a select group of young men and women in atypical situations and very little information about the majority of men and women in natural situations. We therefore are likely to have an incomplete view regarding the great complexity of human behavior as it occurs outside the laboratory. Even the gender of the researcher/experimenter has been shown to be a very influential contextual variable, yet it is rarely even reported (Basow & Howe, 1987; Rumenik, Capasso, & Hendrick, 1977). Also not frequently reported is age of subject in topical areas where age may be influential. For example, menstrual problems appear to be age-related (Golub & Harrington, 1981). Clearly, such variables are important to control and need to be borne in mind when generalizations are made from research findings.

A major problem in many studies is the lack of an adequate control group. For example, female behavior during the menstrual cycle has been extensively studied but rarely compared to male behavior during a similar length of time. When men and women are compared (for example, on mood and behavioral variability over a four-week period), no differences are found (Dan, 1976; McFarlane, Martin, & Williams, 1988; J. S. Stein & Yaworsky, 1983). Thus, studies that focus on mood changes only in women distort the nature of the findings.

Design

As we have seen, feminist critiques of psychological research have emphasized the importance of getting outside the experimental laboratory and exploring issues of gender in more naturalistic contexts with a more diverse population than predominantly White middle-class college students. This is important because different methodologies will lead to different types of results. We now know that quantitatively oriented experimental research tends to minimize findings of gender differences (beta bias), whereas qualitatively oriented clinical research tends to maximize findings of gender differences (alpha bias) (M. Crawford, 1988). The point is not to determine which finding is "correct" but to understand how gender operates within different contexts. The increased use of different methodologies is apparent in feminist journals but, unfortunately, not in mainstream ones (M. Fine & Gordon, 1989; Lykes & Stewart, 1986). Thus the transformative potential of feminist methodology in the social sciences is not being realized (M. Crawford & Marecek, 1989).

Other problems afflict research design: lack of precise objective definitions of the behavior studied, selective perception of raters, and shifting anchor points. This last problem refers to the fact that we often evaluate male and female behavior differently. For example, what is seen as active for a boy may be different from what is seen as active for a girl. The use of different definitions of a behavior as a function of the sex of the ratee also may be a function of the sex of the rater. For example, men and women may use different definitions of "active behavior." Imprecise measures of behavior may also limit a study's findings. Besides the premenstrual syndrome having various definitions, actual physiological measures of cycle phase have varied enormously from study to study, some relying on self-reports, others relying on varying physiological measurements taken at varying intervals (Parlee, 1973).

Using an appropriate baseline, or standard, when measuring gender differences is imperative but not frequently found. For example, with respect to the menstrual cycle, it may be as accurate to posit a follicular phase (midcycle) syndrome of positive traits and behaviors as to posit a premenstrual syndrome of negative traits and behaviors (McFarlane et al., 1988; Parlee, 1973). Yet we hear far more of the latter than the former.

Three research designs used in studying sex differences should be examined particularly carefully since each has serious limitations:

1. *Correlation studies* do not demonstrate causation, although they are frequently interpreted that way by unsophisticated readers and, at times, by researchers themselves. Thus, a correlation between anxiety and the premenstrual phase has led many to assume that hormones determine mood in females, although such a relation may be caused by a third variable such as expectation of amount of flow (Paige, 1971). The causation also may occur in the opposite direction. For example, anxiety can bring on menstruation (see Parlee, 1973).
2. *Retrospective questionnaires* suffer from reliance on an individual's memory. For example, complaints of mood impairment during or before menstruation typically are found when mood is assessed retrospectively, but not when mood is assessed daily (for example, McFarlane et al., 1988). Questionnaires also may selectively lead the respondent to provide certain information—for example, by asking only about negative mood changes as a function of menstrual phase.
3. *Self-reports or observations* are affected by people's need to respond in a socially desirable way. As an example, men may be reluctant to admit mood changes because such changes contradict societal gender stereotypes. These methods also have a problem with selective perception or selective reporting by the respondent. For example, only negative mood changes may be observed in or admitted by women because that is the cultural and/or the reporter's expectation (McFarland, Ross, & DeCourville, 1989; D. N. Ruble, 1977).

An important problem in all psychological research, especially in this area, is the effect on the results of the experimenter's beliefs. Robert Rosenthal (1966; Rosenthal & Jacobson, 1968) has ingeniously demonstrated that in unconscious, nonverbal ways, experimenters can influence the outcome of an experiment to conform to the experimental hypotheses. Thus, in studies in which the experimenter expects to find moods varying with menstrual phase, she or he may indeed find them (Moos et al., 1969). Because most researchers have been male, they unconsciously may have misperceived certain situations with humans and animals to put males in the better light. For example, Harry Harlow's (1962, 1965) research with monkeys has contributed a great deal to our understanding of attachment behavior. But reading some of Harlow's observations of the behavior of monkeys sometimes resembles viewing a soap opera with females "scheming" and acting "helpless" and males acting "intelligently" and "strongly." (See also Hrdy, 1986.) This brings us to the question of interpretation.

Interpretation

Statistical reporting and analysis are often a function of an experimenter's hypotheses and biases. To illustrate, although Dalton (1969) found that 27% of her female subjects got poorer grades before menstruation than at ovulation, she ignored the 56% who had no changes and the 17% who actually improved.

Another reporting problem arises in reviews such as that by Maccoby and Jacklin (1974).

Although the reviewed studies varied greatly in quality, the results were simply tabulated without giving greater emphasis to the better research. Therefore, a finding of a high percentage of studies reporting no difference in an area may be due to there being no difference, or it may be due to a large number of inadequate experiments. . . .

Interpretation of scientific facts has sometimes determined the facts themselves. Recent feminist examinations of the history of science reveal numerous illustrations of gender, race, and class prejudices (Bleier, 1988; Hubbard, 1990; Katz, 1988; Russett, 1989; Sayers, 1987). For example, Shields (1975) found that when the frontal lobes of the brain were regarded as the main area of intellectual functioning, research studies found men had larger frontal lobes, relative to the parietal lobes, than women. When parietal lobes were regarded as more important, the findings themselves changed. Men now were found to have relatively larger parietal lobes, relative to their frontal lobes, than women. Today, there is no firm evidence of sex differences in brain structures or proportions, so interest has turned to sex differences in brain organization, following a predictable pattern. When men were thought to be less lateralized than women, that was thought to be the superior organization. When men were thought to have more brain lateralization than women, then *that* was thought to be the superior organization. . . .

SUMMARY

. . . In examining the studies on female and male behaviors and characteristics, one must be aware of the many research problems that can invalidate the results. Science is constructed by people, and people are never value-free or impervious to social forces. As Sue Rosser (1988) notes, until our society is neutral with respect to gender, class, race, and sexual preference, it is impossible to assume that science will be. Therefore, it is incumbent upon all researchers to understand how the social context influences the research process. With this caution in mind, we will examine the current findings.

CURRENT FINDINGS

Aside from the physical area, few clear-cut differences between males and females have been found. Males, compared to females, tend to be more physically vulnerable, physically active, aggressive, power-oriented, and sexually active. Males have a slight edge in visual-spatial and quantitative skills after childhood, and they tend to dominate verbal and nonverbal communications. Females, compared to males, tend to mature faster and to be more people-oriented, more prosocial, and more emotionally expressive. Females have cyclic hormonal production after puberty and are capable of multiple orgasms. They may have a slight edge on some verbal tasks.

Far more numerous than the areas of gender difference are the areas in which no overall differences have been found or where differences are unclear because of the importance of situational factors. These areas include intelligence, memory, cognitive styles, creativity, temperament, empathy, nurturance, altruism, morality, assertiveness, achievement, and sexual responsiveness.

To give a clearer sense of how much the sexes differ, the magnitudes of the average gender differences can be compared. . . . Gender differences can be divided into small, moderate, and large effects. Most of the small gender differences . . . are cognitive ones: overall verbal ability, SAT verbal scores, overall math ability, problem solving, computation skills, and spatial visualization. Small gender differences are also found in balance, social smiling (child), and noncompliance. Of small to moderate size . . . are gender differences in spatial perception (before age 18), helping others, democratic leadership style, aggression (by adults), and approval of intercourse in serious relationships. Of moderate size . . . are gender differences in activity level, grammar, SAT math scores, decoding skill, body expressiveness, and aggression (all ages). Of moderate to large size . . . are gender differences in dash, spatial perception (after age 18), mental rotations, social smiling (adult), gaze, and speech errors. Large gender differences . . . are found for only a few comparisons: height, throwing distance, facial expressiveness, and approval of sexual intercourse without love.

From these comparisons, it's obvious that the gender differences we are examining are mostly of small to moderate size—large enough to be noticed but not large enough to provide a basis for statements (such as "all men are more aggressive than all women") or job applicant choice. As Eagly (1987) notes, the meaning of the size of any particular gender difference is a function of the value attached to it. For example, if people value quantitative skills, then the slight edge males may have in these skills may seem very important. If people don't value facial expressiveness, then even the large advantage females have in this area will be viewed as unimportant.

Furthermore, situational and individual variability in most of these behaviors is enormous. . . . Gender differences can be either magnified or minimized by situational factors, such as whether the person is observed by others or whether the research is conducted in the laboratory or in a natural setting. Individual factors, such as age, class, beliefs, and sex-typing category, also affect results. In general, masculine- and feminine-sex-typed individuals show stereotypical gender differences to a greater degree than androgynous or undifferentiated males and females. Another factor affecting results is the date of the research. Cognitive gender differences, in particular, have become smaller over time, probably due to changes in early childhood socialization and expectations.

In looking at explanations of the differences, social factors (roles, status, expectations, and learning history) seem to be the most powerful influences on gender differences, although biological predispositions may play a role in some cases (for example, aggression and nurturance). Even in these cases, however, nature and nurture interact, with environmental-social factors usually overpowering biological factors, shaping the behavior to conform to cultural expectations. We are all born with different physical, intellectual, and emotional potential, but these differences are not distributed by gender. The potentials that become actualized depend on the environment and the roles in which we are raised. And social factors and roles do differ on the basis of gender. Indeed, gender differences are maximized in situations in which gender roles are made salient, such as among strangers who are being observed, the traditional research design. Gender also serves as a stimulus cue for others; that is, people perceive and react to an individual depending upon that person's biological sex.

The question remains as to why the gender stereotypes remain and are so strongly believed when gender differences, to the extent that they exist, are relatively small and highly variable. To understand the tenacity of stereotypes, one needs to understand the nature of the stereotypes themselves. Once believed, stereotypes become confirmed and strengthened whenever someone behaves in the expected way. For example, whenever a female expresses fearfulness, an observer may remark, "That's just like a woman." The observer's belief in the stereotype then becomes stronger. On the other hand, when someone acts in a way contrary to the observer's expectation, instead of weakening the stereotype, the behavior in question is more likely to go unnoticed or to be classified as an exception. Thus, if a female does not act fearful, an observer might simply brush off the observation as unusual ("Oh, she's different"), if an observation is made at all. The stereotype itself remains inviolate and protected from refutation. Thus, we have the case where active athletic behavior on the part of girls is called atypical ("tomboyish") even though the majority of girls behave that way.

Another reason for the strength and persistence of stereotypes is that men and women tend to hold different roles, both in the home and in the workplace. The roles inhabited by women tend to be low-status and to involve nurturant-communal behaviors (mother, homemaker, nurse). Conversely, the roles inhabited by men tend to be high-status and to involve agentic-instrumental behaviors (paid employee, boss, political leader). Thus, in real life, women generally engage in more prosocial behaviors than men, and men generally engage in more power-related behaviors than women, but this apparent *sex* difference actually is a *role* difference. To the general observer, however, these different behaviors seem to confirm the stereotypes. The same is true with regard to sexual scripts and sexual behaviors. That is, males and females are given different scripts to follow, but when they follow the scripts, their behaviors are viewed as reflecting innate differences.

To challenge stereotypes, we need to get to the individual before he or she learns them; that is, we need to change the content of our gender socialization. In particular, we need to change the assignment of males and females to different social roles.

REFERENCES

Adams, K. A. (1983). Aspects of social context as determinants of black women's resistance to challenges. *Journal of Social Issues, 39,* 69–78.

Archer, J. (1989). The relationship between gender-role measures: A review. *British Journal of Social Psychology, 28,* 173–184.

Baldwin, A. C., Critelli, J. W., Stevens, L. C., & Russell, S. (1986). Androgyny and sex role measurement: A personal construct approach. *Journal of Personality and Social Psychology, 51,* 1081–1088.

Basow, S. A. & Howe, K. G. (1987). Evaluations of college professors: Effects of professors' sex-type and sex, and students' sex. *Psychological Reports, 60,* 671–678.

Beauvais, C., & Spence, J. T. (1987). Gender, prejudice, and categorization. *Sex Roles, 16,* 89–100.

Bem, D., & Allen, A. (1974). On predicting some of the people some of the time: The search for cross-situational consistencies in behavior. *Psychological Review, 81,* 506–520.

Bem, S. L. (1974). The measurement of psychological androgyny. *Journal of Consulting and Clinical Psychology, 42,* 155–162.

Bem, S. L. (1975). Sex role adaptability: One consequence of psychological androgyny. *Journal of Personality and Social Psychology, 31,* 634–643.

Bem, S. L. (1976). Probing the promise of androgyny. In A. Kaplan & J. Bean (Eds.), *Beyond sex role stereotypes: Readings toward a psychology of androgyny* (pp. 47–62). Boston: Little, Brown.

Bem, S. L. (1981a). *Bem Sex-Role Inventory, professional manual.* Palo Alto, CA: Consulting Psychologists Press.

Bem, S. L. (1981b). Gender schema theory: A cognitive account of sex typing. *Psychological Review, 88,* 354–364.

Bem, S. L. (1985). Androgyny and gender schema theory: A conceptual and empirical integration. In T. B. Sonderegger (Ed.), *Nebraska Symposium on Motivation, 1984: Psychology and gender,* Vol. 32 (pp. 179–226). Lincoln, NE: University of Nebraska Press.

Bem, S. L. (1987). Gender schema theory and the romantic tradition. In P. Shaver & C. Hendrick (Eds.), *Sex and gender* (pp. 251–271). Newbury Park, CA: Sage.

Binion, V. J. (1990). Psychological androgyny: A Black female perspective. *Sex Roles, 22,* 487–507.

Bleier, R. (1979). Social and political bias in science: An examination of animal studies and their generalizations to human behaviors and evolution. In E. Tobach & B. Rosoff (Eds.), *Genes and gender II* (pp. 49–69). Staten Island: Gordian Press.

Bleier, R. (1984). *Science and gender: A critique of biology and its theories on women.* New York: Pergamon Press.

Bleier, R. (1988). A decade of feminist critiques in the natural sciences. *Signs: Journal of Women in Culture and Society, 14,* 186–195.

Cannon, L. W., Higginbotham, E., & Leung, M. L. A. (1988). Race and class bias in qualitative research on women. *Gender and Society, 2,* 449–462.

Chaplin, W. F., & Goldberg, L. R. (1985). A failure to replicate the Bem and Allen study of individual differences in cross-situational consistency. *Journal of Personality and Social Psychology, 47,* 1074–1090.

Crawford, M. (1988). Agreeing to differ: Feminist epistemologies and women's ways of knowing. In M. Crawford & M. Gentry (Eds.), *Gender and thought: Psychological perspectives* (pp. 128–145). New York: Springer-Verlag.

Crawford, M., & Marecek, J. (1989). Psychology reconstructs the female: 1968–1988. *Psychology of Women Quarterly, 13,* 147–165.

Dalton, K. (1969) *The menstrual cycle.* New York: Pantheon.

Dan, A. J. (1976). Patterns of behavioral and mood variation in men and women: Variability and the menstrual cycle. *Dissertation Abstracts International, 37,* 3145B–3146B.

Deaux, K., & Kite, M. E. (1987). Thinking about gender. In B. B. Hess & M. M. Ferree (Eds.), *Analyzing gender: A handbook of social science research* (pp. 92–117). Newbury Park, CA: Sage.

Eagly, A. H. (1987). *Sex differences in social behavior: A social-role interpretation.* Hillsdale, NJ: Erlbaum.

Fausto-Sterling, A. (1985). *Myths of gender: Biological theories about women and men.* New York: Basic Books.

Fine, M., & Gordon, S. M. (1989). Feminist transformations of/despite psychology. In M. Crawford & M. Gentry (Eds.), *Gender and thought: Psychological perspectives* (pp. 146–174). New York: Springer-Verlag.

Frable, D. E. S. (1989). Sex typing and gender ideology: Two facets of the individual's gender psychology that go together. *Journal of Personality and Social Psychology, 56,* 95–108.

Frable, D. E. S., & Bem, S. L. (1985). If you're gender-schematic, all members of the opposite sex look alike. *Journal of Personality and Social Psychology, 49,* 459–468.

Gergen, M. M. (1988). Building a feminist methodology. *Contemporary Social Psychology, 13*(2), 47–53.

Gilligan, C. (1982). *In a different voice: Psychological theory and women's development.* Cambridge, MA: Harvard University Press.

Golub, S., & Harrington, D. M. (1981). Premenstrual and menstrual mood changes in adolescent women. *Journal of Personality and Social Psychology, 41,* 961–965.

Grady, K. E. (1981). Sex bias in research design. *Psychology of Women Quarterly, 5,* 628–636.

Hall, J. A., & Taylor, M. C. (1985). Psychological androgyny and the masculinity × femininity interaction. *Journal of Personality and Social Psychology, 49,* 429–435.

Handal, P. J., & Salit, E. D. (1985). Gender-role classification and demographic relationships: A function of type of scoring procedures. *Sex Roles, 12,* 411–419.

Haraway, D. (1989). *Primate visions: Gender, race, and nature in the world of modern science.* New York: Routledge.

Harding, S. (Ed.). (1987). *Feminism and methodology: Social science issues.* Bloomington: Indiana University Press.

Hare-Mustin, R. T., & Marecek, J. (1988). The meaning of difference: Gender theory, postmodernism, and psychology. *American Psychologist, 43,* 455–464.

Hare-Mustin, R. T., & Marecek, J. (1990). *Making a difference: Psychology and the construction of gender.* New Haven: Yale University Press.

Harlow, H. F. (1962). The heterosexual affectional system in monkeys. *American Psychologist, 17,* 1–9.

Harlow, H. F. (1965). Sexual behavior in the rhesus monkeys. In F. A. Beach (Ed.), *Sex and behavior.* New York: Wiley.

Harrington, D. M., & Andersen, S. M. (1981). Creativity, masculinity, femininity, and three models of psychological androgyny. *Journal of Personality and Social Psychology, 41,* 744–757.

Heilbrun, A. B., Jr., & Mulqueen, C. M. (1987). The second androgyny: A proposed revision in adaptive priorities for college women. *Sex Roles, 17,* 187–207.

Heilbrun, A. B., Jr., & Schwartz, H. L. (1982). Sex-gender differences in level of androgyny. *Sex Roles, 8,* 201–214.

Hrdy, S. B. (1986). Empathy, polyandry, and the myth of the coy female. In R. Bleier (Ed.), *Feminist approaches to science* (pp. 119–146). New York: Pergamon Press.

Hubbard, R. (1990). *The politics of women's biology.* New Brunswick, NJ: Rutgers University Press.

Kahn, A. S., & Yoder, J. D. (1989). The psychology of women and conservatism: Rediscovering social change. *Psychology of Women Quarterly, 13,* 417–432.

Kaplan, A., & Bean, J. P. (1976). From sex stereotypes to androgyny: Considerations of societal and individual change. In A. Kaplan & J. Bean (Eds.), *Beyond sex-role stereotypes* (pp. 383–392). Boston: Little, Brown.

Katz, S. (1988). Sexualization and the lateralized brain: From craniometry to pornography. *Women's Studies International Forum, 11,* 29–41.

Kohlberg, L. (1969). Stage and sequence: The cognitive-developmental approach to socialization. In D. A. Goslin (Ed.), *Handbook of socialization and research* (pp. 347–480). Chicago: Rand McNally.

Locksley, A., & Colten, M. E. (1979). Psychological androgyny: A case of mistaken identity? *Journal of Personality and Social Psychology, 37,* 1017–1031.

Lubinski, D., Tellegen, A., & Butcher, J. N. (1983). Masculinity, femininity, and androgyny viewed and assessed as distinct concepts. *Journal of Personality and Social Psychology, 44,* 428–439.

Lykes, M. B., & Stewart, A. J. (1986). Evaluating the feminist challenge to research in personality and social psychology: 1963–1983. *Psychology of Women Quarterly, 10,* 393–412.

Maccoby, E. E., & Jacklin, C. N. (1974). *The psychology of sex differences.* Stanford, CA: Stanford University Press.

Marsh, H. W., Antill, J. K., & Cunningham, J. D. (1989). Masculinity and femininity: A bipolar construct and independent constructs. *Journal of Personality, 57,* 625–663.

Martin, E. (1991). The egg and the sperm: How science has constructed a romance based on stereotypical male-female roles. *Signs: Journal of Women in Culture and Society, 16,* 485–501.

McClelland, D. C., Atkinson, J. W., Clark, R. A., & Lowell, E. G. (1953). *The achievement motive.* New York: Appleton-Century-Crofts.

McFarland, C., Ross, M., & DeCourville, N. (1989). Women's theories of menstruation and biases in recall of menstrual symptoms. *Journal of Personality and Social Psychology, 57,* 522–531.

McFarlane, J., Martin, C. L., & Williams, T. M. (1988). Mood fluctuations: Women versus men and menstrual versus other cycles. *Psychology of Women Quarterly, 12,* 201–223.

McKenna, W., & Kessler, S. (1977). Experimental design as a source of sex bias in social psychology. *Sex Roles, 3,* 117–128.

Miller, J. B. (1984). *The development of women's sense of self* (Work in Progress, No. 12). Wellesley, MA: Wellesley College, The Stone Center.

Mills, C. J. (1983). Sex-typing and self-schemata effects on memory and response latency. *Journal of Personality and Social Psychology, 45,* 163–172.

Mischel, W. (1968). *Personality and assessment.* New York: Wiley.

Moos, R., Kopell, B., Melges, F., Yalum, I., Lunde, D., Clayton, R., & Hamburg, D. (1969). Variations in symptoms and mood during the menstrual cycle. *Journal of Psychosomatic Research, 13,* 37–44.

Morawski, J. G. (1987). The troubled quest for masculinity, femininity, and androgyny. In P. Shaver & C. Hendrick (Eds.), *Sex and gender* (pp. 44–69). Newbury Park, CA: Sage.

Myers, A. M., & Gonda, G. (1982). Empirical validation of the Bem Sex-Role Inventory. *Journal of Personality and Social Psychology, 43,* 304–318.

Paige, K. E. (1971). The effects of oral contraceptives on affective fluctuations associated with the menstrual cycle. *Psychosomatic Medicine, 33,* 515–537.

Parlee, M. B. (1973). The premenstrual syndrome. *Psychological Bulletin, 80,* 454–465.

Pedhazur, E. J., & Tetenbaum, T. J. (1979). Bem Sex Role Inventory: A theoretical and methodological critique. *Journal of Personality and Social Psychology, 37,* 996–1016.

Petersen, A. C. (1983). *The development of sex-related differences in achievement.* Invited address at the meeting of the American Psychological Association, Anaheim.

Rebecca, M., Hefner, R., & Olenshansky, B. (1976). A model of sex role transcendence. *Journal of Social Issues, 32*(3), 197–206.

Reid, P. T. (1984). Feminism versus minority group identity: Not for Black women only. *Sex Roles, 10,* 247–255.

Rhode, D. L. (1990). Definitions of difference. In D. L. Rhode (Ed.), *Theoretical perspectives on sexual difference* (pp. 197–212). New Haven: Yale University Press.

Rosenberg, M. (1973). The biological basis for sex role stereotypes. *Contemporary Psychoanalysis, 9,* 374–391.

Rosenthal, R. (1966). *Experimenter effects in behavioral research.* New York: Appleton-Century-Crofts.

Rosenthal, R., & Jacobson, L. (1968). *Pygmalion in the classroom: Teacher expectations and pupils' intellectual development.* New York: Holt, Rinehart & Winston.

Rosser, S. V. (1988). Good science: Can it ever be gender-free? *Women's Studies International Forum, 11,* 13–19.

Ruble, D. N. (1977). Premenstrual symptoms: A reinterpretation. *Science, 197,* 291–292.

Rumenik, D. K., Capasso, D. R., & Hendrick, C. (1977). Experimenter sex effects in behavioral research. *Psychological Bulletin, 84,* 852–877.

Russett, C. E. (1989). *Sexual science: The Victorian construction of womanhood.* Cambridge, MA: Harvard University Press.

Sayers, J. (1987). Science, sexual difference, and feminism. In B. B. Hess & M. M. Ferree (Eds.), *Analyzing gender: A handbook of social science research* (pp. 68–91). Newbury Park, CA: Sage.

Scarr, S. (1988). Race and gender as psychological variables: Social and ethical issues. *American Psychologist, 43,* 56–59.

Sears, D. O. (1986). College sophomores in the laboratory: Influences of a narrow data base on social psychology's view of human nature. *Journal of Personality and Social Psychology, 51,* 515–530.

Sedney, M. A. (1989). Conceptual and methodological sources of controversies about androgyny. In R. Unger (Ed.), *Representations: Social constructions of gender* (pp. 126–144). Amityville, NY: Baywood.

Shields, S. (1975). Functionalism, Darwinism, and the psychology of women: A study in social myth. *American Psychologist, 30,* 739–754.

Signorella, M. L., & Vegega, M. E. (1984). A note on gender stereotyping of research topics. *Personality and Social Psychology Bulletin, 10,* 107–109.

Spelman, E. V. (1988). *Inessential woman. Problems of exclusion in feminist thought.* Boston: Beacon Press.

Spence, J. T. (1983). Commenting on Lubinski, Tellegen, and Butcher's "Masculinity, femininity, and androgyny viewed and assessed as distinct concepts." *Journal of Personality and Social Psychology, 44,* 440–446.

Spence, J. T., & Helmreich, R. (1978) *Masculinity and femininity: The psychological dimensions, correlates, and antecedents.* Austin: University of Texas Press.

Spence, J. T., & Helmreich, R. L. (1980). Masculine instrumentality and feminine expressiveness: Their relationships with sex role attitudes and behavior. *Psychology of Women Quarterly, 5,* 147–163.

Spence, J. T., Helmreich, R., & Stapp, J. (1974). The Personal Attributes Questionnaire: A measure of sex role stereotyping and masculinity and femininity. *JSAS selected documents in psychology* (Ms. No. 617).

Stein, J. S., & Yaworsky, K. B. (1983, August). *Menstrual cycle and memory for affective and neutral words.* Paper presented at the meeting of the American Psychological Association, Anaheim.

Stoller, R. J. (1968). *Sex and gender: On the development of masculinity and femininity.* New York: Science House.

Unger, R. K. (1983). Through the looking glass: No wonderland yet! (The reciprocal relationship between methodology and models of reality.) *Psychology of Women Quarterly, 8,* 9–32.

Unger, R. K. (1989). Sex, gender, and epistemology. In M. Crawford & M. Gentry (Eds.), *Gender and thought: Psychological perspectives* (pp. 17–35). New York: Springer-Verlag.

Van Hecke, M. T., Van Keep, P. A., & Kellerhals, J. M. (1975). The aging women. *Acts Obstictrica et Gynecologia, 51,* Scandinavica Supplement, 17–27.

Whitley, B. E., Jr. (1984). Sex-role orientation and psychological well-being: Two meta-analyses. *Sex Roles, 12,* 207–225.

Whitley, B. E., Jr. (1987). The relationship of sex role orientation to heterosexuals' attitudes toward homosexuals. *Sex Roles, 17,* 103–113.

Whitley, B. E., Jr. (1988a). Masculinity, femininity, and self-esteem: A multitrait-multimethod analysis. *Sex Roles, 18,* 419–432.

Wilson, F. R., & Cook, E. P. (1984). Concurrent validity of four androgyny instruments. *Sex Roles, 11,* 813–837.

Wittig, M. A. (1989, August). *Frameworks for a feminist psychology of gender: Reconciling scientific and feminist values.* Paper presented at the meeting of the American Psychological Association, New Orleans.

PERSONAL ACCOUNT

He Hit Her

I was raised in Charleston, South Carolina, a city where racial and class lines are both evident and defined by street address. I had been taught all my life that black people were different than "us" and were to be feared, particularly in groups.

One summer afternoon when I was eighteen or nineteen, I was sitting in my car at a traffic light at the corner of Cannon and King streets, an area on the edge of the white part of the peninsular city, but progressively being inhabited by more and more blacks. It was hot, had been for weeks, and the sticky heat of South Carolina can be enraging by itself.

As I waited at the light, a young black couple turned the corner on the sidewalk and began to walk towards where I was sitting. The man was yelling and screaming and waving his arms about his head. The woman, a girl really, looked scared and was walking and trying to ignore his tirade. Perhaps it was her seeming indifference that finally did it, perhaps the heat, I don't know. As they drew right up next to my car though, he hit her. He hit her on the side of her head, open palmed, and her head bounced off the brick wall of the house on the corner and she sprawled to the ground, dazed and crying. The man stood over her, shaking his fist and yelling.

I looked around at the other people in cars around me, mostly whites, and at the other people on the sidewalks, mostly blacks, and I realized as everyone gaped that no one was going to do anything, no one was going to help, and neither was I. I don't think it was fear of the man involved that stopped me; rather, I think it was fear generated by what I had been told about the man that stopped me. Physically I was bigger than he was and I knew how to handle myself in a fight: I worked as a bouncer in a nightclub. What I was afraid of was what I had been told about blacks: that *en masse,* they hated whites, and that given the opportunity they would harm me. I was afraid getting out of the car in that neighborhood would make me the focus of the fight and in a matter of time I would be pummeled by an angry black crowd. Also in my mind were thoughts of things I had heard voiced as a child: "They are different. Violence is a part of life for them. They beat, stab, and shoot each other all the time, and the women are just as bad as the men." So I sat and did nothing. The light changed and I pulled away.

The incident has haunted me over the last almost fifteen years. I have often thought about it and felt angry when I did. I believe that as I examined it over time the woman who had been hit, the victim, became less and less prominent, and the black man and myself more prominent. Then I had an epiphany about it.

What bothered me about the incident was not that a man had hit a woman and I had done nothing to intervene, not even to blow my horn, but that a man had hit a woman and I had done nothing to intervene and that this reflected on me as a man. "Men don't hit women, and other men don't let men hit women," was also part of my masculinity training as a boy. There was a whole list of things that "real" men did and things that "real" men didn't do, and somewhere on there was this idea that men didn't let other men hit women. I realized that the incident haunted me not because a man had hit a woman, but because my lack of response was an indictment of *my* masculinity. The horror had become that I was somehow less of a man because of my inaction. Part of the dichotomy that this set up was the notion that the black man had done something to *me,* not to the woman he hit, and it was here that my anger lay. I wonder how this influenced my perception of black men I encountered in the future.

Tim Norton

READING 10

How Much Social Mobility Exists in the United States?

Richard D. Kahlenberg

. . . The key empirical question is this: how close do we come to providing genuine equal opportunity today, to providing an equal start as well as an open road? If, as Lyndon Johnson said, ability is not just the product of birth but the product of family and community and schooling, do our various social programs give children born into different economic circumstances substantive equal opportunity?

Some Americans are satisfied that we have achieved genuine equal opportunity. Unlike race, they say, class is mutable. They point to people like Ross Perot and to Bill Clinton—the quintessential meritocratic president, "son of a salesman and a nurse," whose "ticket out of Hot Springs was high scores on college entrance exams"—as evidence that in this country class is a matter of choice, not fate.[1] While various economic classes obviously exist in America, the very real possibility of social mobility—the temporary nature of class—makes the term "classless society" highly appropriate. In this way, the United States is different from Europe, the argument runs. Invoked is Tocqueville's observation that "among democratic peoples new families continually rise from nothing while others fall, and nobody's position is quite stable. The woof of time is ever being broken and the track of past generations lost."[2] And since Tocqueville's time, social mobility has increased, it is argued, with the growth of free public education, inexpensive state colleges, and the rise of standardized tests, which remove the prejudice of class.[3] The government already spends billions of dollars every year on programs like Head Start to provide equal starts. (Some, of course, argue that these programs are too generous and advocate cutting them back.) We have, they say, done the best we can to provide equal opportunity for each younger generation without mandating equal result for the older generation. (A few conservatives even argue that the extent to which children of the poor largely end up poor themselves, and rich parents tend to have kids who grow up rich, is not itself evidence of unequal opportunity but rather a manifestation of genetic differences between the rich and poor.) . . .

But statistically speaking, the evidence is quite strong that social mobility is limited, that privilege tends to perpetuate itself. And while we have made great strides in providing greater opportunity through social programs, there are numerous real-life barriers that remain unaddressed by current public policy. Finally, the genetic argument, that the poor are poor because they are of lesser genetic stock, is simply not supported by the scientific evidence.[4]

First, how much intergenerational mobility is there? How many sons and daughters of the poor or working class become wealthy, compared with the sons and daughters of the rich? How typical is Bill Clinton's or Ross Perot's story? The question has been the subject of a wealth of studies. Though most focus on boys, similar questions can be asked of girls.[5] Here are some relevant findings:

- In 1979 Northwestern University's Christopher Jencks found: "If we define 'equal opportunity' as a situation in which sons born into different families have the same chances of success, our data show that America comes nowhere near achieving it. . . . The sons of the most advantaged fifth could expect to earn 150 to 186 percent of the national average, while the sons of the least advantaged fifth could expect to earn 56 to 67 percent of the national

Richard D. Kahlenberg is a fellow at the Center for National Policy.

average." Occupationally, the same pattern emerges. Writes Jencks: "Sons from the most favored fifth of all families had predicted Duncan scores [measuring occupational status on a scale of 0 to 96] of about 64, while sons from the least favored fifth of all families have predicted scores of about 16." Jencks also found that "those who do well economically typically owe almost half of their occupational advantage and 55 to 85 percent of their earnings advantage to family background."[6]

- John Brittain of the Brookings Institution found that a son in the bottom 10 percent is predicted to have an income less than half the income of a son born into the top 10 percent. Sons born in the top 5 percent could expect to earn more than three times that earned by the bottom 5 percent. . . .
- The sociologists Peter Blau and Otis Dudley Duncan, who pioneered mobility studies, found that in 1962 males studied between 25 and 64 had a 10.2 percent chance of being salaried professionals, but if their fathers had been salaried professionals, the chance was 31.9 percent; if their fathers had been farm laborers, the chance was 1.9 percent.[7]
- Samuel Bowles and Herbert Gintis found that even when controlling for ability (which itself is influenced by class advantages), children from the top 10 percent of income are twenty-seven times as likely as children from the bottom 10 percent to themselves end up in the top 10 percent of the income bracket. Of one thousand children born into the bottom tenth, only four will make it to the top tenth.[8]
- In 1991 the economist David Zimmerman, now at Williams College, found that only 12 percent of boys born into the bottom quartile rose as adults to the top quartile. Sixty-nine percent were in the lower half. Zimmerman found that sons received a 4 percent advantage for every 10 percent that their father's income exceeded the average.[9]
- In 1992 the University of Michigan's Gary Solon found that if a boy is born into the bottom 5 percent of the economic distribution, his chance of staying in the bottom fifth is one in two, his chance of rising above the median is only one in four, and his chance of making the top fifth is one in twenty.[10]

Historians have also found that the amount of social mobility in the United States has been greatly exaggerated.[11] And while America is supposed to be the quintessential nation of equal opportunity, a number of studies have found that our level of social mobility is not much different than that of the class-conscious countries of Europe. The sociologists Seymour Martin Lipset and Reinhard Bendix, for example, found that opportunities to rise were not greater for Americans than for Europeans.[12] Zimmerman's 1991 study confirmed this phenomenon, finding the correlation between father's and son's incomes almost identical for the United States and Britain.[13] And while one might expect the degree of social mobility and opportunity to have increased over time, as social programs have grown, the National Research Council found that in recent years opportunities for upward mobility have actually declined for low-income people.[14]

These figures are likely to strike many readers as wrong. We are always hearing about people who started with nothing and built up a fortune, the immigrant who came to America with no education or money and has children and grandchildren who went on to great success. But we tend to hear more about exceptional success stories than about routine failures.[15] In addition, equal opportunity seems more prevalent than it is because *absolute* and *relative* mobility are often confused: absolute mobility involves general progress in education and material success across generations; relative mobility measures whether people born into different classes in the same generation have equal shots at success. When there is educational progress across society, the son of a high school graduate is more likely to go to college (absolute mobility), but he does not necessarily keep up with the son of the college graduate who does postgraduate work (relative mobility). To test whether equal opportunity exists, we need to know the degree of relative mobility—the degree to which the sons of street sweepers do as well, not as their fathers, but as the sons of lawyers. Until recently, our nation has had a great deal of absolute mobility, which has masked the lack of relative mobility.[16]

REAL LIFE BARRIERS REMAIN UNADDRESSED

In analyzing the vast class-based environmental differences that bombard American children and adolescents, we begin by pointing to the enormous differences in family wealth. Despite the New Deal, the Fair Deal, the New Frontier, the Great Society, and on and on, enormous inequalities persist. At each stage of childhood—from birth to elementary school to high school to college—the chances are decidedly unequal for individuals who are born with the same talents and work at the same level of effort. We first turn to the enormous differences in income and wealth among American families and then look at how well the various government initiatives to provide greater equal opportunity have worked.

Family Differences

Since its founding, our nation has been considered more egalitarian than Europe, not only because of our supposedly high rates of social mobility but also because—as Tocqueville noted—we have a broad, solid middle class.[17] But today, as Labor Secretary Robert Reich notes, "we have the most unequal distribution of income of any industrial nation in the world."[18]

In 1993 the top one-fifth of the American public took home almost as much income as the bottom 80 percent. The differential between the top and bottom fifth was more than 13:1.[19] The gap has been growing over the past fifteen years. Between 1979 and 1993, according to the Labor Department, real family income for the top 20 percent increased by 18 percent, while the bottom 20 percent saw a 17 percent decline.[20] Income inequality is at its highest rate since the Census Bureau began keeping records in 1947.[21]

In the workplace, pay gaps skyrocketed. In 1979 American chief executive officers made on average 29 times as much as the average manufacturing worker. In 1985 the multiple was 40, by 1988 the figure was 93 times as much—prompting even *Business Week* to question the disparity.[22] But the gap continued to grow, and by 1990 CEOs earned 113 times the wage of the average worker; by 1995 the multiple was 150. By comparison, Japanese and German CEOs continue to have a pay differential similar to those of U.S. executives in 1979—between twenty and thirty-five times the wage of the average worker.[23]

Wealth differences are even more pronounced than income differences. According to the congressional Joint Economic Committee (JEC), the top 10 percent of the American population owns two-thirds of net wealth, while the bottom 90 percent owns one-third.[24] A 1983 Federal Reserve study, which focused specifically on financial assets, found that the top 2 percent held 54 percent of assets, that the top 10 percent held 86 percent of assets, and that a majority of Americans (the bottom 55 percent) had no net fungible assets.[25] The MIT economist Lester Thurow found in 1987 that the Forbes 400 list of the richest Americans had "effective control" over "40 percent of all fixed, nonresidential private capital in the United States."[26]

Conservatives have justified these inequalities as merely reflecting inequality of *result,* arguing that what matters is not the ultimate degree of inequality but whether the gains were obtained fairly, in a system of equal opportunity.[27] The problem, of course, is that vast inequality of parental result translates, necessarily, into unequal opportunities for the next generation. . . .

Equalizers Don't Equalize

Some conservatives, while conceding that children grow up in very different families, would argue that there is not much we can do about that, and that our country evens out the different family environments by the time a teenager leaves his family in three significant ways. We provide (a) a progressive tax system and welfare state, which eliminate gross inequalities; (b) free public education through age eighteen; and (c) a system of standardized tests, which allow the naturally smart to advance, irrespective of class prejudice. Do these equalizers equalize opportunity?

One would think, with all our social reforms—a stiff inheritance tax, progressive marginal tax rates, and welfare payments to the poor—that America has done a fairly good job of addressing inequality of wealth and income. But the evidence suggests the opposite. According to the Brookings Institution's John A. Brittain, "The relative gap between rich and poor in America has remained substantially impervious to egalitarian public policy." Even when marginal tax rates reach 91 percent, Brittain says, the *after-tax* income of the top 10 percent "consistently averages around twenty times that of the lowest tenth." Great wealth has survived nominally high estate taxes as well, he says: the top 1 percent continues to hold 25 percent of all personal wealth "decade after decade."[28] MIT's Lester Thurow has come to similar conclusions about the minimal effect of transfer payments and gift and inheritance taxes on inequality of wealth and income in the United States.[29] The Center on Budget and Policy Priorities, using Congressional Budget Office (CBO) data, found that "the richest 1 percent of all Americans now receive nearly as much income *after taxes* as the bottom 40% of Americans combined. Stated another way, the richest 2.5 million people now have nearly as much income as the 100 million Americans with the lowest income."[30] Between 1980 and 1990, after-tax income inequality rose faster than inequality measured before taxes.[31] Of the twenty-four leading industrial countries, only Australia and Turkey have lower tax rates than the United States.[32] The argument here is not that all incomes should be equal, but that children continue to be born into strikingly different economic circumstances under existing efforts at redistribution.

Public education is supposed to be the great democratizer. As John Dewey envisioned it, rich and poor would come together and share the common schooling available to all. But are the schools today a model for promoting equality of opportunity? Dozens of studies have looked at this question, and most conclude that schools tend to reproduce the existing social hierarchy.[33] The problem, notes the *New Republic*'s Mickey Kaus, is that "common access to schooling isn't the same thing as access to common schooling."[34] At the most basic level, we lack equal educational funding: there are often large gaps in per-pupil expenditure between poor and wealthy school districts.[35] The federal government's effort to provide greater funding to poor school districts through Chapter I of the Elementary and Secondary Education Act of 1965 has had a limited impact. While the federal government provides more than $6 billion a year through the program, federal spending amounts to only $6 of every $100 spent on public education.[36] The money is spread thinly: some 93 percent of the nation's school districts receive Chapter I funds.[37] And attempts by the Clinton administration to focus the money more clearly on poor districts in 1994 were largely blocked by representatives of wealthier districts.[38]

Some conservatives point out that James Coleman's landmark 1966 study, *Equality of Educational Opportunity,* found that school funding is a small determinant of educational achievement. But the weight of evidence confirms the commonsense notion that school funding does make a difference.[39] Indeed, the Coleman report argued for *greater* funding for schools with high concentrations of poverty than for schools with wealthier populations, to compensate for the disadvantage that students from poor backgrounds bring to school and for the additional disadvantage of attending school with other poor students.[40] Coleman found that poor black sixth graders in middle-class schools were twenty months ahead of poor black sixth graders in poor schools. The same was true of poor white sixth graders.[41] Overall, Coleman reported, "attributes of other students account for far more variation in the achievement of minority group children than do attributes of staff."[42]

So in America, poor students are at a triple disadvantage: they come from disadvantaged family environments; they go to schools with high concentrations of poverty; and instead of receiving much more funding per pupil to make up for those two disadvantages, they often receive less. On top of these disadvantages, add a fourth: even in schools with some socioeconomic mix, poor students are likely to be segregated from the more affluent students through tracking. Without getting into the merits of the debate over the value of tracking, we do know that tracking is widespread—83 percent of school districts use it—and that it undercuts some of the equal opportunity potential of public schools.[43]

In sum, the current public educational system, far from tending to compensate for unequal starting places, tends to legitimatize and freeze socioeconomic status. Even the conservative economist Milton Friedman acknowledges:

> At the elementary and secondary level, the quality of schooling varies tremendously: outstanding in some wealthy suburbs of major metropolises, excellent or reasonably satisfactory in many small towns and rural areas, incredibly bad in the inner cities of major metropolises. The education, or rather the uneducation, of black children from low income families is undoubtedly the greatest disaster area in public education and its most devastating failure. This is doubly tragic for it has always been the official ethic of public schooling that it was the poor and the oppressed who were its greatest beneficiaries.[44]

This was the central insight of the Coleman report: far from removing the handicaps that come from varying family backgrounds, public schools actually accentuate them. As children progress through their school years, the initial gap between children from high-status and low-status families does not close but actually widens.[45]

Thus far, we have limited our discussion to public schools, but it is, of course, the right of wealthy parents to opt out of the public schools entirely, to buy what they see as superior opportunities for their children. Although the elite preparatory schools like to say they have opened up their doors and are more democratic, make no mistake as to whose children predominate. According to one study, two-thirds of the students at the twenty top prep schools had parents whose income was three times the national median, while almost half the student families had incomes four times the national median.[46] At one prep school, 40 percent of the students' parents were listed in the Social Register, a status claimed by .00265 percent of American families.[47]

Besides public education, the college board exams are meant to be the great democratizers. When you take an SAT, what counts is brains and effort, not race or social class. But many who have looked at the issue more closely conclude, as the journalist James Fallows has, that "in most instances, the tests simply ratify earlier advantage—that as engines of mobility, they have sputtered and died."[48]

It is not surprising that the accumulation of profound advantages and disadvantages we have outlined leave their mark on academic achievement, including the College Board exam. We know that these tests do not simply measure innate intelligence but significantly reflect class and family background. Indeed, the designers of the SAT themselves concede: "The SAT measures developed verbal and mathematical reasoning abilities that are involved in successful academic work in college; it is not a test of some inborn and unchanging ability."[49] Indeed, in 1993 the College Board changed the name of the SAT from the Scholastic Aptitude Test to the Scholastic Assessment Test, to dispel the impression "that the SAT measures something that is innate and impervious to change regardless of effort or instruction."[50]

To add insult to injury, affluent students in recent years have compounded their advantage with SAT preparation courses. While the Educational Testing Service (ETS) once held that coaching had no impact on scores, the debate has now shifted to the question not of whether but of how much coaching can help.[51] And there is little question that the courses benefit the affluent disproportionately.[52]

While much ink has been spilled on the disparate racial impact of the SAT, researchers have found that the class impact is profound—and that, indeed, the racial impact is in part a reflection of the class impact. This has been consistently true over time. Thus, in the mid-1970s the mean income at each level of SAT performance painted a striking picture, as it did in 1985.[53] In 1994, according to the College Board, SAT scores broke down as follows[54]

SAT Scores by Family Income

Family Income	Combined SAT Score
Less than $10,000	766
$10,000–20,000	812
$20,000–30,000	856
$30,000–40,000	885
$40,000–50,000	911
$50,000–60,000	929
$60,000–70,000	948
$70,000 or more	1000

Not once does the correlation make a false step.[55] Overall, as the National Academy of Sciences (NAS) points out, children from the top socioeconomic 20 percent on average score at the 65th percentile, while the bottom socioeconomic 20 percent scores on average at the 35th percentile.[56]

None of this is to say the test is itself biased, since it makes no claim to measure "innate" natural intelligence plus effort. The test is meant to predict freshman year grades, and since rich kids (through no doing of their own) have access to much better training than do poor kids, one would expect the "learned ability," and ability to do well in college, to be higher for the rich. The bias, then, appears not to be in the tests per se but rather reflects our entire social structure. The SATs have, in turn, an enormous impact on who gets into selective colleges, and who gets into selective colleges has a large impact on who gets ahead in America.[57]. . .

It is true that on grounds of efficiency, we normally care only about who can do the best job, not who has faced the most obstacles. . . . If a corporate board is deciding between two fifty-year-olds for the position of chief executive officer, efficiency surely dictates that the board choose the individual who has a track record of producing the most; past record, in this case, is a fairly accurate predictor of future achievement. However, when we are dealing with adolescents who are beginning their adulthood, there is a strong efficiency argument for looking at obstacles faced, to get a better assessment of long-term potential. A poor applicant from the inner city who scores 1000 on the SAT surely has more potential than a wealthy student with private tutors who scores 1050. Indeed, one study found that the most successful Harvard graduates were those with lower SATs from blue-collar backgrounds.[58] In deciding between two eighteen-year-olds who have applied for an entry-level position or for admission to a competitive university, the future potential is less well known; looking beyond the track record to consider the obstacles faced is surely relevant to determining long-run potential. A seventeen- or eighteen-year-old taking the SAT has three-quarters of her life ahead of her. If there is a time to factor in obstacles, this is it.[59]

Second, it is highly appropriate, for reasons of moral desert, to correct for a teenager's class position. While sociologists and policy makers will debate the extent to which an adult's economic class is mutable—Republicans stressing the role of individual initiative and Democrats the role of environmental forces—all agree that for children and adolescents, their class position is essentially not theirs but that of their parents.[60] Adolescents are, of course, responsible for their own actions, but they are not responsible for their class or socioeconomic status, or for the disadvantages that stem from that status. A teenager from a lower-class background should get the benefit of a preference; only those who as individuals work hard and apply themselves should advance from within the group to whom such preferences are awarded. Because the class-based obstacles and disadvantages that face adolescents are not in any sense of their own making, a preference correcting for that unfair and immutable condition makes perfect moral sense. Those who work hard and do fairly well despite obstacles do deserve a hand up, and failure to offer that hand is to underestimate the long-run potential of such adolescents. . . .

NOTES

1. Paul Glastris, "Life Among the 'Meritocrats,'" *U.S. News and World Report,* September 6, 1993, 30.
2. Tocqueville, *Democracy in America,* 507.
3. William Angoff, quoted in Fallows, "The Tests and the 'Brightest,'" 43.
4. The genetic argument, revived by publication of *The Bell Curve* in 1994, says that relative social mobility is small, not because there is inequality of opportunity, but because poor people are, in the aggregate, less innately intelligent and pass on their genetic deficiencies to their children. Michael Young's meritocratic nightmare is upon us, the argument says; see Murray and Herrnstein, *The Bell Curve,* 51. In the 1940s, Murray and Herrnstein argue, to say someone was poor did not say much about them; today, however, given the advances toward meritocracy, the poor "are likely to be disproportionately those who suffer not only bad luck but also a lack of energy, thrift, farsightedness, determination—and brains" (129). The "powerful trend toward meritocracy," which Herrnstein saw coming back in 1971, has made Young look very "prescient"; Herrnstein, "I.Q.," 44–45, 63. Murray and Herrnstein say the chief concern is not achieving meritocracy but coming to terms with the "merging of the cognitive elite with the affluent"; *The Bell Curve,* 509.

   To buy the argument that social mobility levels are simply a reflection of genetic differences—a claim even Murray and Herrnstein do not fully make—one must believe that (a) we live in a perfect meritocracy, so that rich parents are rich because they are smarter; (b) rich children do well because they have their parents' smart genes, as opposed to having superior chances to develop their talents; and (c) children succeed in replicating their parents' positions, again, based on the perfect workings of the meritocracy in the next generation. Most of the evidence points in the opposite direction.

   The first and third assumptions—that a meritocracy exists in both generations—is at least as weak as the argument that intelligence is based on nature, not nurture. Studies by Christopher Jencks and by Bowles, Gintis, and Nelson suggest that IQ plays a fairly small role in who gets ahead; see Jencks, *Inequality,* 7–8 ("there is almost as much economic inequality among those who score high on standardized tests as in the general population"); see also Jencks, *Who Gets Ahead,* 121, but see 73–75; Bowles and Nelson, "The 'Inheritance of IQ,'" 44 (arguing that while a child's IQ does matter, a child's socioeconomic background matters more in predicting ultimate adulthood status). In all, Bowles and Nelson found that "the genetic inheritance of IQ plays a minor role in the process of intergenerational educational and economic status transmission" (40). Likewise, in 1984 Hunter and Hunter found that cognitive test scores fail to explain 72 percent of the variance in job ratings; see Ira T. Kaplan, "Hugging the Middle of the Bell Curve," *Wall Street Journal,* November 7, 1994, A15.

   Indeed, while Murray and Herrnstein worry about the rise of the meritocracy, there is evidence that in some areas we are becoming *less* meritocratic—that young Americans are becoming, in Kevin Phillips's words, "the first generation to receive—or not to receive—much of their economic opportunity from family inheritance, not personal achievement"; *Boiling Point,* 190–92 (noting that among individuals ages 35–39, an astounding 86 percent of net worth in 1986 came from their parents, up from 56 percent in 1973). In the area of college admissions, as Steven Waldman notes, between 1982 and 1989 the percentage of students at private colleges and universities hailing from well-to-do families increased from 50 percent to

63 percent; "How Washington Tries to Strangle Even the Best Ideas," *Washington Monthly* (January–February 1995): 28. This could be a stunningly rapid, genetically driven convergence of the wealthy and the cognitive elite, but it looks more like old-fashioned unequal opportunity at work.

The second assumption—rich kids do well for genetic reasons—is also highly problematic. There has been a broad debate for centuries on the question of the heritability of intelligence; the debate is unresolved to this day. Today most studies say intelligence among individuals is 50 percent hereditary, Murray and Herrnstein say 60 percent, while other studies indicate 70 percent; see Gina Kolata, "Study Raises the Estimate of Inherited Intelligence," *New York Times,* October 12, 1990, A22 (reporting that the Minnesota twins study found 70 percent genetic differences while "previous studies had suggested that about 50 percent of the differences in scores were inherited").

Two factors work against the creation of genetic castes. First, setting aside the role of environment, the genetic transmission of intelligence is itself complicated. As Adrian Woolridge, author of *Measuring the Mind,* points out, "The random element in Mendelian inheritance combined with regression to the mean insured that children would differ in significant ways from their parents"; "Bell Curve Liberals," *New Republic* (February 27, 1995): 22. Herrnstein himself conceded the existence of "regression toward the mean," a genetic phenomenon in which there is a "tendency for children to be closer to the general population average (in this case, IQ 100) than their parents. And in fact, *very bright* parents have children who tend to be merely *bright,* while *very dull* parents tend to have them merely *dull*"; "I.Q.," 58. And we all know marriages (say, Marilyn and Dan Quayle) in which partners may be of different IQs.

Second, even if we agree with Murray and Herrnstein's estimate that 60 percent of intelligence is inherited, that leaves an enormous role to environment. "Forty percent variability based on environment would make intelligence an exceptionally pliant trait," notes the former Harvard evolutionary biology professor Evan Balaban; quoted in Gregg Easterbrook, "The Case against the Bell Curve," *Washington Monthly* (December 1994): 25. "If IQ swings by 40 percent owing to circumstances and life experiences," adds Gregg Easterbrook, "then human society has more control over intelligence than virtually anything else in its genetic inheritance" (25). Arthur Jensen, a leading proponent of the genetic school, concedes that there are "great and relatively untapped reservoirs of mental ability in the disadvantaged"; quoted in Sowell, *Race and Culture,* 169.

In sum, then, both links in the argument that genetics accounts for the reproduction of economic inequality are weak. Even Murray and Herrnstein concede that (a) we are not a pure meritocracy, so that the socioeconomic status a child is born into has an impact on his life chances separate from IQ (*The Bell Curve,* 135), and (b) IQ is not a pure measure of raw genetic ability, because IQ itself is affected by socioeconomic background. Thus, they argue, "improvements in the economic circumstances of blacks, in the quality of the schools they attend, in better public health, and perhaps also diminishing racism," may explain the closing gap between black and white IQ observed over the past few decades (270–71). Indeed, for these reasons, Murray and Herrnstein themselves argue for a form of class preference for disadvantaged students (475). As we shall see, the environmental differences based on wealth are quite dramatic; far from proving the genetic superiority of the rich, the scores merely confirm what we would expect.

5. See Rossides, *Social Stratification,* 20.
6. Jencks, *Who Gets Ahead?,* 82–83, 82, 81.
7. See Blau and Duncan, *The American Occupational Structure,* 28. Blau and Duncan were generally fairly sanguine about occupational mobility in the United States, but they noted that short-distance mobility was more common than long-distance mobility, and that much of the occupational gain was due to an expansion in the higher professions (36–37). In 1972, Duncan, teaming up this time with David L. Featherman and Beverly Duncan, wrote: "The absolute number of able young men and women of lower socioeconomic origins who are 'wasted' is striking"; Duncan, Featherman, and Duncan, *Socioeconomic Background and Achievement,* 257.
8. Bowles and Gintis, "IQ in the United States Class Structure," cited in DeLone, *Small Futures,* 209.

9. Zimmerman study cited in Frances Ann Burns, "Income Study Says, Like Father, Like Son," *Los Angeles Times,* March 17, 1991, A34. See also Zimmerman, "Regression Toward Mediocrity in Economic Status," 409.
10. Solon, "Intergenerational Income Mobility," 404, 403.
11. Historians have made several findings. Edward Pessen of the City University of New York argues that Tocqueville and others who claimed to see great social mobility in America "mistook appearances for reality"; *Social Mobility,* 57. Pessen's study found that "only about 2 percent of the Jacksonian era's urban economic elite appear to have actually been born poor, with no more than about 6 percent of middling social and economic status" (112). In New York, Pessen found that 95 percent of the city's wealthiest one hundred were born into families of wealth or high status, 3 percent were from middling families, and 2 percent were born poor. Pessen found the same pattern in Boston and Philadelphia (113).

    In his study of lawyers in early nineteenth-century America, Gary B. Nash found that most were born to wealth. Between 1800 and 1805, 72 percent were from upper-class backgrounds, 16 percent were middle-class, and only 12 percent were lower-class; "The Social Origins of Antebellum Lawyers," in Pessen, *Social Mobility,* 108.

    Harvard's Stephen Thernstrom found in his study of Bostonians from 1880 to 1970 that "all in all, it was very helpful indeed to a man's career to come from a family headed by a professional or a prosperous businessman." Offspring of upper white-collar workers "were overrepresented in upper white-collar jobs by about 400 percent as compared with lower white-collar sons, 650 percent as compared with skilled sons, and 1200 percent as compared with the sons of unskilled or semiskilled fathers"; *The Other Bostonians,* 89–90.

    Even the hallowed notion that some of our presidents were born in log cabins turns out to be largely mythical. In Pessen's study of American presidents, he found that only one, Andrew Johnson, came from the bottom 50 percent of the economic strata; *Log Cabin Myth,* 69–70; see also Michael Kelly, "The President's Past," *New York Times Magazine* (July 31, 1994): 20ff, on President Clinton's "comfortable" background.
12. See Lipset and Bendix, *Social Mobility,* 12–13.
13. The correlation in the United States was 0.4, while the correlation in Britain was 0.45, "only slightly more"; Zimmerman quoted in Burns, "Income Study," A34. Kahl and Gilbert cite seven different studies finding similar rates of social mobility in the United States and other advanced industrial societies, all of "which contradicts the myth that the United States has a society much more open than others"; *The American Class Structure* (1987), 161.
14. National Research Council, *A Common Destiny,* 4.
15. Poor children who grow up to be successful businesspeople, said one economist, "have always been more conspicuous in American history books than in American history"; Pessen, *Log Cabin Myth,* 172–73. We hear more about success partly because our culture is attuned to it. As the writer Katherine Newman points out, "No one ever talks about the Pilgrims who gave up and headed back to England"; *Falling from Grace,* 8. Just as African Americans are rightly annoyed when whites cite Colin Powell as evidence that racism has been eradicated, so the poor and working class are rightly annoyed when Ross Perot is cited as proof that anyone can rise from humble origins to be a billionaire.
16. The end of World War II, says Jeff Greenfield, "triggered the swiftest, broadest rise in living standards any society has ever known": median family income doubled between 1947 and 1973; quoted in Phillips, *Boiling Point,* 223; see also Barry Bluestone, "The Inequality Express," *American Prospect* (Winter 1994): 82. Occupationally, progress was also largely a result of absolute mobility. Stephan Thernstrom found that "32 percent of Boston's males held white-collar jobs of some kind in 1880, 51 percent in 1970; the proportion of professionals, a mere 3 percent in 1880 increased sevenfold during the period, while unskilled-labor jobs shrank from 15 percent of the total to 5 percent"; *The Other Bostonians,* 49–51. Nationally, between 1940 and 1970 the number of professional and technical jobs for men increased 192 percent, while the jobs for nonfarm laborers declined 32 percent; Census Bureau statistics cited in Kahl and Gilbert, *The American Class Structure* (1987), 163. The average level of education also rose astronomically as the proportion of

people earning college degrees increased fifteen times between 1900 and 1990; Census Bureau statistics cited in Murray and Herrnstein, *The Bell Curve,* 29–33.

All this absolute mobility is good and important, but it tells us little about equal opportunity and, indeed, obscures the question of whether people have equal life chances. Because the standard of living has until recently risen swiftly, a child born into the 25th percentile of income could do twice as well as his parents (having, say, two cars instead of one) but would not have moved up in relative terms and still be in the 25th percentile. For our purposes—knowing the degree to which people are handicapped or advantaged by their social origins—absolute mobility merely confuses the issue. So how much mobility is relative as opposed to absolute? When controlling for absolute mobility, the researcher Joseph Kahl found that only 20 percent of American males exceed the status of their fathers by individual effort; see Kahl, *The American Class Structure* (1957). And most of these do not climb very far; see Chester, *Inheritance, Wealth, and Society,* 8.

17. Tocqueville, *Democracy in America,* 9.
18. Quoted in Spencer Rich, "Number of Poor Americans Increases to 39.3 Million," *Washington Post,* October 7, 1994, A1.
19. See Census Bureau statistics cited in ibid., A18. The upper 20 percent took home 48.2 percent of income. The bottom fifth took in 3.6 percent.
20. Labor Department statistics cited in Rick Wartzman, "A Clinton Potion to Restore Middle Class Love, Brewed by Labor Secretary, Stresses Job Training," *Wall Street Journal,* January 11, 1995, A16.
21. Rattner, "GOP Ignores Income Inequality," A22.
22. Phillips, *The Politics of Rich and Poor,* 179–80.
23. Phillips, *Boiling Point,* 63; and Rattner, "GOP Ignores Income Inequality," A22.
24. Revised JEC figures cited in Phillips, *The Politics of Rich and Poor,* 11.
25. Rose, *Social Stratification,* 21–22. See also Mishel and Simon, *The State of Working America,* iii–iv.
26. Cited in Lapham, *Money and Class,* 22.
27. See, e.g., Rep. Richard K. Armey, "Income Mobility and the U.S. Economy: Open Society or Caste System?," Joint Economic Committee of Congress, January 1992.
28. Brittain, *The Inheritance of Economic Status,* 6.
29. Thurow, *The Zero Sum Society,* 155–56, 172.
30. Quoted in Johnson, *Divided We Fall,* 36–37.
31. Rattner, "GOP Ignores Income Inequality," A22.
32. See David S. Broder, "Are We Really Overtaxed?," *Washington Post,* April 23, 1995, C7, citing statistics of the Organization for Economic Cooperation and Development.
33. See Alwin and Thornton, "Family Origins and the Schooling Process," 784.
34. Kaus, *The End of Equality,* 52. Kaus cites Ira Katznelson and Margaret Weir, *Schooling for All: Class, Race, and the Decline of the Democratic Ideal* (New York: Basic Books, 1985), 214.
35. In the 1973 case of *San Antonio v. Rodriguez,* the Supreme Court upheld disparate public school spending: a wealthy district in Texas spent more than one and a half times what a poorer district did (counting state, local, and federal contributions)—$356 versus $594 per pupil; see *San Antonio v. Rodriguez,* 12–13. Fifteen years later, when lawyers for the poor brought suit under the Texas state constitution, the gap between the richest and poorest per pupil expenditure had grown to $2,112 versus $19,333. The 100 poorest districts averaged $2,978 per student, and the 100 richest averaged $7,233; *Edgewood Independent School District v. Kirby,* 777 SW2d 391, 392–93 (Tex. 1989) (*Edgewood 1*); see also Taylor, "The Continuing Struggle," 1705. On Long Island, New York, where a similar suit was tried in 1991, the spending disparity ranged from $17,435 per pupil to $7,305 per pupil; see Judges, "Bayonets for the Wounded," 699. In New Jersey, the site of ongoing lawsuits, Camden spent $4,184 per pupil, and Princeton spent $8,344; see John B. Judis, "A Taxing Governor," *New Republic* (October 15, 1990): 24; see also Valerie Strauss, "Disparity Between City, Suburban Schools: Almost $440 a Student," *Washington Post,* September 28, 1994, A20.

State courts have begun to strike down unequal funding as violative of state constitutions in Texas, California, New Jersey, Kentucky, Montana, and elsewhere; see, e.g., *Serrano v. Priest,* 18 Cal. 3d 728, 557 P2d 929, 135 *Cal. Rptr.* 345 (1976); see also Taylor, "The Continuing Struggle," 1704, 1707. But the progress is uneven; as of 1994, fourteen states had struck down funding mechanisms, but fourteen had seen mechanisms upheld; see Curriden, "Unequal Education at Issue," *ABA Journal,* May 1994, 36. And even where legal victories are claimed, the progress is often very slow. In New Jersey, legal wrangling over equal funding has gone on for a quarter-century. Strong voter resistance to Governor Jim Florio's attempt to equalize funding has given governors in other states ample reason to delay and circumvent court orders as long as possible.

36. Taylor, "The Continuing Struggle," 1706. See also David Broder, "Getting Serious about Schools," *Washington Post,* February 20, 1994, C7.
37. See Broder, "Getting Serious about Schools."
38. See Kenneth J. Cooper, "$13 Billion Education Bill Clears House; Senate Is Likely to Vote on It Next Week," *Washington Post,* October 1, 1994, A4; Associated Press, "Senate Passes $12 Billion in Federal Education Aid," *Washington Post,* August 3, 1994, A3; and Broder, "Getting Serious about Schools." Forty-three percent of funds now go to the bottom 25 percent of school districts. Clinton wanted them to get 50 percent. In the *San Antonio v. Rodriguez* case, the federal grant did reduce the spending disparity somewhat, but a substantial gap remained: from $310 per pupil before federal aid to $238 afterwards; *San Antonio v. Rodriguez,* 12–13.
39. Conservatives are partially right to cite Coleman for the proposition that there is a weak correlation between school spending and test scores; see Mosteller and Moynihan, *Educational Opportunity,* 15–16; see also George F. Will, "Meaningless Money Factor," *Washington Post,* September 12, 1993, C7. But there is empirical support in the academic literature for the commonsense notion that spending money does matter; see Ogbu, *Minority Education and Caste,* 52–53 (citing review of seventeen studies); see also *San Antonio v. Rodriguez,* 83 (Marshall dissenting) (citing two studies conflicting with the Coleman report). The Texas Supreme Court also found that money mattered. "The amount of money spent on a student's education has a real and meaningful impact on the educational opportunity offered that student," the court found; *Edgewood I,* 393. It is obvious, the court said, that money can purchase better equipment and more books, provide lower teacher-student ratios and dropout prevention services, and attract and retain better teachers.

    If it were true that money made no difference in the quality of education, why would wealthy school districts fight so much to keep their edge? Why in the *San Antonio* case did we see amicus briefs filed by the nation's wealthiest school districts, from Beverly Hills to Bloomfield Hills and Grosse Pointe?; see *San Antonio v. Rodriguez,* 85 (Marshall dissenting). During the litigation over equal expenditure in New Jersey, the superintendent in the wealthy South Brunswick area was asked what he would do if he had to live on the budget of the low-income Trenton area. Kozol reports: "The superintendent tells the court that such a cut would be an 'absolute disaster.' He says that he 'would quit' before he would accept it. If such a cut were made, he says, class size would increase about 17 percent; nursing, custodial and other staff would have to be reduced; the district would stop purchasing computers and new software; it would be unable to paint the high school, would cut back sports, drop Latin and German, and reduce supplies to every school"; *Savage Inequalities,* 168.
40. See Edmund Gordon, "Toward Defining Equality of Educational Opportunity," in Mosteller and Moynihan, *Educational Opportunity,* 427; see also Kozol, *Savage Inequalities,* 2–5, 205. We do not insist that firefighters spend equal amounts of time on a house that is burning and a neighboring house that is not; nor do we argue that a doctor must provide equal attention to two patients, one with a cold, the other in critical condition in the emergency room; see Gross, *Discrimination in Reverse,* 19. As William Taylor points out, the object of Chapter I was to have federal money supplement, not equalize; the extra money was needed for disadvantaged students; "The Continuing Struggle," 1706.
41. Christopher S. Jencks, "The Coleman Report and the Conventional Wisdom," in Mosteller and Moynihan, *Educational Opportunity,* 87. And the relationship was linear: poor students in working-class schools "fell neatly in between"; ibid.
42. Coleman, quoted in Mosteller and Moynihan, *Educational Opportunity,* 20.
43. See "Note: Teaching Inequality" (*Harvard Law Review*), 1318.

44. Friedman and Friedman, *Free to Choose,* 151.
45. Summarized in Kahl and Gilbert, *The American Class Structure* (1987), 170.
46. Kingston and Lewis, *High Status Track,* xi.
47. Caroline Hodges Persell and Peter W. Cookson, Jr., "Chartering and Bartering: Elite Education and Social Reproduction," in ibid., 30, 42.
48. Fallows, "The Tests and the 'Brightest,'" 46.
49. See Fallows, "The Tests and the 'Brightest,'" 43.
50. Mary Jordan, "SAT Changes Name, but It Won't Score 1600 with Critics," *Washington Post,* March 27, 1993, A7.
51. According to the *New York Times,* ETS officials "now concede that their previous public posture that tests are not coachable was less than accurate"; Edward B, Fiske, "Nader's Challenge to Testing," *New York Times,* January 15, 1980, C4. For a summary of ETS's internal study by Pike and Evans, see Owen, *None of the Above,* 96–97, finding a 33-point increase from a coaching course above and beyond increases attributable to practice and growth. Nancy Cole reviews five studies and finds an average combined gain of 47 points on the SAT; "The Implications Of Coaching for Ability Testing," in NAS, *Ability Testing II,* 402–10. See also Slack and Porter's review of studies, which found a combined mean gain of 62 points; "The Scholastic Aptitude Test," 161.
52. A Federal Trade Commission study found that those who were coached "were heavily concentrated in the upper income brackets"; Nairn and Associates, *The Reign of ETS,* 98. And the founder of the Princeton Review SAT preparation course, John Katzman, readily acknowledges, "Most of our kids are wealthy." His students "have an advantage to begin with. And we're moving them up another level"; quoted in Owen, *None of the Above,* 138–39. While the National Academy of Sciences says it has no evidence that commercial coaching is more effective than "free coaching" in schools, it notes that even the latter retains a class bias, since "school-based coaching is more generally available in schools with many college-bound students than it is in those with fewer such students"; see Nancy Cole, "The Implications of Coaching for Ability Testing," 402–10.
53. College Board, *College Bound Seniors,* 1973–74, Table 21, 27, cited in Nairn and Associates, *The Reign of ETS,* 201. See also Fallows, "The Tests and the 'Brightest,'" 47; and Fallows, *More Like Us,* 163–64.
54. See College Board, *College Bound Seniors: 1994 Profile of SAT and Achievement Test Takers,* 7.
55. Fallows, "The Tests and the 'Brightest,'" 47.
56. Robert Linn, "Ability Testing: Individual Differences, Prediction, and Differential Prediction," in NAS, *Ability Testing II,* 363.
57. The College Board likes to argue that its own test is not that important: the SAT is only one factor used in admissions, they argue, and on average public four-year colleges accept 80 percent of applicants and private four-year colleges accept 70 percent. At elite colleges, however, acceptance rates can go below 20 percent; Rodney Skager, "On the Use and Importance of Tests of Ability in Admission to Postsecondary School," in NAS, *Ability Testing II,* 292–93, 294, 307. Only two selective institutions nationwide—Bates and Bowdoin—do not consider the SAT at all; see Michael Kirst and Henry Rowen, "Scrap the SATs for Achievement Tests," *Washington Post,* September 16, 1994, A27. And an NAS study found that the SAT ranks second only to grades as an admissions criteria. In law school, the LSAT is often more important than grades; Skager, "On the Use and Importance of Tests of Ability," 307. Moreover, the College Board's general figures on acceptance rates ignore the powerful indirect impact of the SATs. Many students with low scores will assume their scores are a valid indicator of their long-run potential (if not their very self-worth) and, with the help of a high school guidance counselor, will "face the facts of life" and adjust their aspirations. As the NAS study points out, applicant self-selection can play a major role in acceptance rates; the academy notes that "one distinguished private institution accepts 80 percent of its applicants because mainly academically outstanding students choose to apply" (293). Relying on the SAT, high school counselors across the country guide poor and working-class students away from selective colleges, predicting, accurately, that they would simply be rejected if they applied.

The result is that the wealthy—who score better and do not face uncertainties about financial aid—are dramatically more likely to attend high-status schools. In 1984, 13.7 percent of freshman nationwide came from families with income exceeding $50,000, while among the twenty-eight most selective colleges and universities, the figure was over 50 percent. While 4 percent of freshman nationwide came from families with incomes exceeding $100,000, more than 20 percent of freshman at the elite colleges came from that background; Kingston and Lewis, *High Status Track,* xii. In 1986, while less than 20 percent of American families made $50,000 or more, 31 percent of families of freshman students did, as did more than 60 percent of families with freshman at highly selective private colleges. Only one in twelve students at highly selective private universities came from families with incomes below $20,000 (at a time when the national median income was $28,000) (111). At Berkeley, for example, in the fall of 1987 only 22 percent of the freshman class came from families with income at or below the national median. The median income for freshman families was $53,500, compared with $30,000 for the national population; Karabel, *Freshman Admissions at Berkeley,* 53.

Moreover, attendance at selective universities matters greatly in determining who gets ahead. While it is true that many bright students may attend nonselective public universities and go on to do quite well, the evidence confirms that going to a high-prestige college brings a greater return. Kingston and Lewis found that the lay wisdom is right: where one goes does matter; *High Status Track,* 148. Forty-three percent of the Harvard class of 1940, for example, are now worth more than $1 million; Larew "Why Are Droves . . . ," 12. The median family income of the Harvard class of 1968 is $135,000 and the median net worth is $500,000; James K. Glassman, "Crimson and Closure," *New Republic* (July 11, 1994): 14. Almost 30 percent of the Harvard-Radcliffe class of 1970 had become millionaires by 1995; see Jonathan D. Canter, "'Stock of the Puritans': 1970 Issue," *Harvard* (September–October 1995): 26. A 1992 study by Duke University's Philip Cook and Cornell's Robert Frank says the common-sense notion that students from elite universities get the best-paying jobs is more true than ever; Reuters, "Graduates of Elite Schools Increasingly Get Top Jobs," *Chicago Tribune,* August 19, 1992, C1. They cite a *Fortune* survey of CEOs that found that one in ten had attended just seven elite schools (ibid., C1). In Yale Professor George W. Pierson's exhaustive study, *The Education of American Leaders: Comparative Contributions of U.S. Colleges and Universities,* graduates of elite universities were heavily overrepresented among "elder statesmen" in the professions, in scholarship, in politics, and in business. Looking at *Who's Who,* Pierson found that one of twenty-five graduates of Harvard, Yale, and Princeton were recognized, compared with one in 145 for state universities as a whole; cited in Klitgaard, *Choosing Elites,* 123–24.

58. See David K. Shipler, "My Equal Opportunity, Your Free Lunch," *New York Times,* March 5, 1995, sect. 4, pp. 1, 16. See also Hugh Price, "Affirmative Action: Quality, Not Quotas," *Wall Street Journal,* August 18, 1995, A10.
59. As Derek Bok points out, the case for racial preferences in faculty hiring is weaker than in student admissions because "we can make better judgements about who is better than whom when we hire people for jobs. They are older, they have track records. . . . We really are guessing with students"; Derek Bok, interview with *Harvard Political Review* (Spring 1985): 9.
60. As an individual grows older, she may, with effort, attempt to improve her economic position so that over time class becomes more mutable than race. But even Charles Murray concedes, "There is no such thing as an undeserving five-year-old"; *Losing Ground,* 223. In constitutional terms, the Court has recognized that illegitimacy is a semisuspect class precisely because children are not themselves to blame for their status; see *Trimble v. Gordon,* 430 US 762, 770 (1977)—illegitimate children "can affect neither their parent's conduct nor their own status"—and *Weber v. Aetna,* 164, 175; "Imposing disabilities on the . . . child is contrary to the basic concept of our system that legal burdens should bear some direct relationship to individual responsibility and wrongdoing."

READING 11

The Underclass: Concept, Controversy, and Evidence

Ronald B. Mincy

POVERTY BEFORE THE WAR ON POVERTY

Observers can interpret the underclass literature from two historical perspectives: first, as part of a long-standing tradition of seeking to distinguish the deserving from the undeserving poor; and second, as an attempt to restore balance and breadth to poverty research and policy analysis and to create an interdisciplinary framework for the study of poverty.

Michael Katz (1989) prefers the first interpretation. He argues that distinguishing two groups among the poor is a centuries-old tradition used to justify who will receive limited public and private charity. The yardsticks for distinguishing between the two groups vary with place and time. Under Elizabethan poor laws, for example, members of a community would provide for neighbors, but not for strangers. By another yardstick, communities would provide for their feeble, infirm, or mentally ill members, but not for the able-bodied. According to Katz, values and attitudes are modern yardsticks for distinguishing groups among the poor. In the 1980s Americans resolved to end support for members of a welfare culture that was believed to condone idleness and dependency. Katz argues, therefore, that "underclass" is merely a modern euphemism for the undeserving poor.

Restoring ideological balance and conceptual breadth to poverty research and policy analysis is the second historical perspective for interpreting the underclass literature. Today the conventional view of the ideal antipoverty program is one that places family income above some social minimum. Such a simple approach was not always prominent. Beginning in the late 1950s, anthropologists and sociologists such as Edward Banfield (1958), Michael Harrington (1962), and Oscar Lewis (1966) began to apply their work on rural poverty to urban sociology. There were important differences among these authors, but all emphasized the values, attitudes, and lifestyles of a "poverty class," including work patterns and family formation (Haveman, 1987). They also made similar assumptions about a "culture of poverty" that could influence individual choices. They argued that the cumulative effect of values and attitudes of the poverty class could affect the behavior of members of that class in ways likely to keep their incomes low. This analysis implied that, to be effective, antipoverty strategies would have to influence the values, attitudes, and culture of the members of the poverty class, so that they would make decisions that would alleviate income poverty.

Ironically, the literature surrounding the Moynihan Report (U.S. Department of Labor, 1965) comes closest to modern underclass literature because it recognized the importance of constraints on individual choices and viewed those choices comprehensively. Daniel Patrick Moynihan, then Assistant Secretary of Labor, based much of his analysis on the work of historians and urban sociologists, including black scholars such as E. Franklin Frazier (1939, 1962) and Kenneth Clark (1965), and recognized racism as a key constraint that shaped black choices leading to high black poverty rates. He argued that patterns of family formation, emerging from slavery, destroyed the capacity of blacks to sustain two-parent families. He also saw racism, operating through employment discrimination, as the cause of high black male unemployment rates. Finally, Moynihan emphasized that unemployment undermined the position of black males in their families and communities, which contributed to high delinquency rates among black youth.

Ronald B. Mincy is a senior program officer at the Ford Foundation.

Like the modern underclass literature, Moynihan viewed the problems of the black community as a whole, not in isolation. Borrowing a phrase from Kenneth Clark, Moynihan described these joint problems (including unemployment, drug use, delinquency, and especially out-of-wedlock childbearing) as a "tangle of pathologies." Journalists' accounts of Moynihan's work emphasized this culturally loaded interpretation of the social problems in the black community. They ignored the attention that Moynihan and others who rejected the culture of poverty thesis (for example, Gans, 1968; Valentine, 1968; Rainwater, 1968) paid to racism and unemployment. The Moynihan Report thus raised the ire of the civil rights community and of black scholars in particular. Drug use, delinquency, and out-of-wedlock childbearing among blacks became taboo subjects for liberal social scientists until the early 1980s (Wilson, 1987).

At the same time that liberal social scientists withdrew from discussions of multiple social problems among urban blacks, the War on Poverty led to an expansion in research on the economics of poverty (Haveman, 1987). Economists in the Johnson administration defined this war to be an economic one. The critical tasks for social scientists were to describe the composition of the poverty population and to determine how many people were poor so that analysts could assess the effectiveness of the War on Poverty.

The conceptual framework of the economist was much narrower than the complex conceptual framework of the sociologist and the anthropologist. First, economists focused on a single dimension, income poverty. Government analysts had already begun to use $3,000 as a measure of income poverty, and the Orshansky index, an income level based on household consumption and nutritional standards, was soon adopted as the official government poverty standard. Nevertheless, economists undertook extensive research on alternative ways of measuring economic well-being and inequality. Although these measures were conceptually complex, the data needed to compute them were more readily available than the data needed to measure the dimensions of poverty discussed in the sociological and anthropological literature.

Second, when economists thought about social policy intervention, they emphasized the agents and routes most natural to their discipline and, in their judgment, most easily manipulated by policymakers: individuals, not classes or communities. They also emphasized incentives more frequently than values, attitudes, and institutional constraints. The major strategies underlying the War on Poverty reflected these emphases. These strategies included economic growth to expand employment opportunities for the poor and improvements in the human capital of the poor adults and children, programs under the Manpower Development and Training Act, Head Start, Upward Bound, and Title I of the Elementary and Secondary Education Act, and so on. The Community Action Program, however, a third major part of the War on Poverty, attempted to provide the poor, especially minorities, improved access to the institutions that would promote upward social mobility.

Conservatives filled the void left by the economists and liberal social scientists who retreated from discussions of the nonincome dimensions of poverty (Wilson, 1987; Katz, 1989). In the early 1980s, conservative policy analysts built upon the culture of poverty thesis by arguing that Great Society programs actually increased poverty. These programs allegedly weakened incentives to work; undermined traditional American values among the inner-city poor; and encouraged drug abuse, indolence, delinquency, and promiscuity (Gilder, 1981; Murray, 1984).[1] Economists' studies of labor-supply responses, especially studies based on the negative income tax experiments, did not support the first assertion, and a flurry of studies quickly undermined assertions about the effects of changes in the value of government expenditures (Danziger and Gottschalk, 1985; Burtless, 1986; Pencavel,

1986). These reports, however, were not enough to overcome the influence of conservative policy analysts and journalists, whose writing on deteriorating inner-city conditions also emphasized cultural explanations. Together these analysts and members of the media fueled a growing uneasiness that there was something desperately wrong in America's inner cities and that Great Society programs, along with a developing welfare culture, were at fault (Aponte, 1988).

THE CORE UNDERCLASS HYPOTHESES

Research on the underclass emerged against this background, as several analysts proposed hypotheses that challenged the explanations offered by journalists and conservatives. William Julius Wilson (1987) developed the most comprehensive set of hypotheses, and his work has dominated the emerging research.[2]

Wilson's Theory of the Underclass

Wilson developed four related hypotheses to explain the growth of poverty and social problems in black urban ghettos. These hypotheses dealt with changing employment opportunities, declines in black marriage rates, selective out-migration from ghetto areas, and neighborhood (or contagion) effects. Together they offered an internally consistent theory that avoided arguments about racism, discrimination, and cultural pathologies and suggested changes in government policies.

Changing Employment Opportunities Wilson's hypothesis concerning the role of changing employment opportunities involved three component hypotheses. These hypotheses emphasized demand-side forces that combined to increase joblessness among inner-city black workers. He gave first place to a hypothesis about structural changes, that is, changes in the industrial and occupational composition of urban employment, that reduced the demand for low-skilled labor.[3] These structural changes hurt low-skilled black men the most. Urban employment grew in white-collar and clerical occupations that tended to require some postsecondary schooling or specialized training, and the black inner-city work force lacked the skills to match the needs of a growing number of urban employers. Hence the term *skills mismatch. Spatial mismatch* and *slow economic growth* were the other demand-side hypotheses in Wilson's view of changing employment opportunities. Wilson hypothesized that employers of low-skilled workers, especially in manufacturing, were moving their operations away from the inner city. Employers were also paying wages that, net of transportation costs, discouraged blacks from commuting. Finally, Wilson hypothesized that low-skilled blacks were more often working in manufacturing industries that were most vulnerable to the high local unemployment rates that prevailed in many northern cities during most of the 1970s.[4]

Declines in Black Marriage Rates Next, Wilson hypothesized that joblessness and low wages among inner-city black men led to increased poverty and several other social problems. For example, black men who could not support themselves in mainstream jobs turned to hustling, including criminal activity and drug selling. Rising numbers of female-headed and welfare-dependent families were the other major social problems that Wilson hoped to explain. According to Charles Murray (1984), increases in the real value of benefits under Aid to Families with Dependent Children had caused the social problems. To counter this argument, Wilson and Kathryn Neckerman (1986) asserted that structural changes reduced the number of *marriageable (that is, employed) males* in inner-city neighborhoods. This decline lowered marriage rates and increased out-of-wedlock births and welfare dependency.

Selective Out-Migration For Wilson, the most important policies linked to the underclass were not welfare but equal employment opportunity, affirmative action, and fair housing laws that disproportionately benefited working- and middle-class blacks. He hypothesized that increased income and greater access to suburban housing enabled working- and middle-class blacks to leave inner-city ghettos in the 1970s. This *selective out-migration* resulted in an increasing concentration of poverty and other social problems.

Neighborhood Effects Finally, Wilson hypothesized that selective out-migration had three important consequences for low-skilled blacks. First, a larger proportion of the families that remained in inner-city ghettos had poverty-level incomes and related social problems. Second, inner-city residents were isolated from upwardly mobile role models, neighborhood institutions, and social networks that could help them move into the mainstream. Third, inner-city residents were isolated from important sources of resistance to social problems such as crime, out-of-wedlock parenting, and dropping out of high school. Individuals, especially children, surrounded by poverty and social problems and removed from mainstreaming institutions, were more likely to make choices leading to their own poverty and social disadvantage. These *neighborhood* (or *contagion*) *effects* helped to explain the rapid growth of poverty and social problems.

Other Underclass Hypotheses

Although Wilson provided the most comprehensive theoretical framework to reinterpret cultural and public policy explanations for the underclass, there were other hypotheses. These hypotheses involved the availability of low-skilled employment, the causes of declining black marriage rates, and race.

Wilson portrayed low-skilled blacks as the victims of reduced demand for low-skilled labor. Lawrence Mead, by contrast, argued that low-skilled immigrants had maintained high employment levels despite the additional handicap of language (Wilson and Mead, 1987). The difference, Mead said, was that immigrants rarely relied on Great Society programs to sustain their incomes, even if they did not work. Blacks, who were raised in welfare-dependent families, were accustomed to receiving government support, with no corresponding social obligation (Mead, 1986, 1992). They therefore refused the unpleasant, low-paying jobs that were abundantly available.

Wilson also minimized the role of discrimination as a cause of the social problems evident among inner-city blacks. The major references to employment and housing discrimination were in regard to its reduction, at least for working- and middle-class blacks. Not only did Wilson minimize the role of discrimination, but he rejected race-conscious policies among potential solutions. These policies, he argued, had limited potential for political support and ignored the confluence of race and class that caused the underclass. Instead, Wilson recommended active government intervention to stimulate full employment and balanced economic growth. This universal approach would benefit inner-city blacks and others.

Other analysts argued that race-conscious policies were still needed. Douglas Massey (1990) argued that blacks and many Puerto Ricans shared two attributes that increased poverty rates in their neighborhoods in the 1970s. The first attribute was skin color; many Puerto Ricans are black. The second attribute was geographic concentration in the northern and midwestern cities that experienced both structural change and high rates of segregation against blacks. The structural changes reduced incomes of low-skilled workers. Segregation, however, spatially concentrated these income declines in black and Puerto Rican neighborhoods. Continued efforts to reduce housing segregation were therefore needed to prevent future increases in the concentration of black and Puerto Rican poverty.

William Darity and Samuel Myers (1983) also argued that race-conscious policies were still critical. They were among the first to recognize that nonmarriage was the distinguishing feature of the increase in black female-headed families. They argued that changing demographic constraints—more than welfare or earnings trends—were the dominant explanations of nonmarriage among black women. The most important demographic constraints were increases in black male mortality and incarceration, which represented the long-term results of racism. These constraints reduced the ratio of males to females and hence marriage rates. Nearly a decade later, high rates of mortality, nonmarriage, and incarceration among black males are receiving increased attention by mainstream scholars (Sampson, 1987; Testa, 1991; Freeman, 1992).

Meanwhile, Darity and Myers have proposed an alternative to Wilson's structural thesis about underclass formation. Their thesis offers a more pessimistic interpretation of structural change, the rising mortality and institutionalization of black males, increasing numbers of black females who never marry, the growth of female-headed black families, and the role of the black middle class.

First, in contrast to Wilson's argument that macrostructural changes have inadvertently weakened the labor market status of low-skilled black males, Darity and Myers see a different process: "The structuralism we embrace is one wherein race is central; and where the changes in industrial society—from traditional capitalism towards a managerial age—by design eliminate the need for the very class of persons Wilson and others call the underclass" (Darity et al., 1990, p. 42). Black males (presumably, low-skilled black males) thus became a superfluous source of labor.

A provocative volume edited by Darity and colleagues supports this view of the marginalization of black males. The authors' arguments include a review of historical evidence suggesting differential enforcement of criminal law, which has resulted in staggering incarceration rates among young black males. The authors also discuss the role of the military draft, which has exposed many young black males to military bases, where laws against the use, sale, and possession of drugs have not been adequately enforced. They even implicate the supply-side emphasis of U.S. drug policy, which has maintained high prices for illegal drugs that lure young black males into criminal activity.

Second, according to Wilson, selective out-migration isolated blacks in the underclass from working- and middle-class blacks. By inference, it would seem helpful if blacks in the underclass were reintegrated with blacks from other classes, perhaps by strengthening the institutions within the black community where such integration could take place. Darity and Myers, however, are more skeptical about the role of the black middle class. In their view,

> Much of the middle-class has emerged as a component of the new managerial elite. And, it is the managerial class that is supervising the control and regulation of the unwanted surplus. Thus, in the case of crime and violence, Wilson sees the middle-class as helping to instill values and behaviors that curb individual pathologies. Darity-Myers see members of the middle-class as supporting the means for further control and institutionalization of the unwanted, superfluous inner-city residents, creating further marginalization of many young black males, and thereby increasing observed pathologies like crime and violence. (Darity et al., 1990, p. 43)

Increases in public-sector employment among middle-class blacks have placed them in settings where they are service providers and custodians of the black underclass. These positions include prison guards, welfare caseworkers, probation officers, teachers in ghetto schools, and directors and staff of community development corporations and community-based service agencies. As recent arrivals in these institutional settings, members of the black middle class may be insecure and therefore likely to distance themselves from the black underclass and to respond to them in unsympathetic ways (Anderson, 1990; Farkas et al., 1990). Middle-class blacks, however, also operate civil rights and community-based service organizations committed to supporting lower-income blacks. In recent years, for example, the National Urban League has provided leadership in the youth service community to increase male responsibility programs targeting young black males from high-risk environments. The movement to develop Africentric Rites of Passage programs, targeting the same population, has been led by the National Association of Black Social Workers. And the National Center for Neighborhood Enterprise, a leader in the movement to empower low-income black communities, emerged out of the civil rights movement.

Although Darity and Myers do not detail the policy implications of their structural theses, one thing is clear. Policies that ignore the legacy of racism in this country have no hope of ameliorating the (black) underclass. The policy implications of class conflict within the black community may seem even more intractable, but they are a less immediate concern. The movement of blacks into the middle class and the managerial elite undoubtedly creates new class tensions within the black community, or exacerbates old tensions (Brown and Erie, 1981). It is probably too early to tell, however, whether the net effect of this development on the black underclass is positive or negative.

Wilson provided a consistent theoretical framework to explain why the underclass emerged. Although the empirical support for his arguments came from analyses of data that failed to control for other changes that could have accounted for the same phenomena, his work has stimulated a flood of more rigorous empirical tests of the underlying hypotheses.

EVIDENCE CONCERNING WILSON'S THEORY OF THE UNDERCLASS

Since 1985 many quantitative studies have tested the four core hypotheses in Wilson's theory of the underclass. Analysts generally agree that changing employment opportunities have decreased black employment. Studies also offer qualified support for the hypotheses concerning selective out-migration and neighborhood effects, but little support for the hypothesis concerning black male joblessness and marriage.

Changing Labor Market Opportunities

Studies generally support the hypothesis that skills mismatches have hurt black male employment. In the 1970s and 1980s urban areas, especially in the Northeast and North-Central regions, lost jobs in industries that formerly paid high wages to low-skilled workers (Kasarda, 1989). Many service jobs were lost, as well. This loss in particular reduced the opportunities for black male youths to enter the labor market, because the first jobs most young people can get are service jobs; indeed, the most severe declines in labor market status occurred among black male youth (Johnson and Oliver, 1991).

The quantitative evidence also supports Wilson's theory concerning spatial mismatches. Low-skilled blacks remained in central-city areas; employers moved to the suburbs. Inner-city blacks thus lost access to employment to a greater degree than did whites and suburban blacks (Holzer, 1991). Studies have also found that black earnings and employment probabilities are hurt when blacks must commute long distances to work (see, for example, Ihlanfeldt and Sjoquist, 1989).

Even more important than skills and spatial mismatches has been the decline in the wages of low-skilled workers. Since the early 1970s wages of less-skilled workers have declined and, especially during the 1980s, employers increased pay differentials between workers with and without college training and between workers with more and less experience (Blackburn, Bloom, and Freeman, 1990; Katz and Murphy, 1990; Levy and Murnane, 1992). These trends are industrywide. Further, wage reductions for workers with less skill, less education, and less experience account for most of the reduction in labor market participation among these workers since the early 1970s (Juhn, 1992).

Finally, the literature strongly supports the notion that local unemployment rates have increased black male joblessness. Black youths living in metropolitan areas with tight labor markets had higher earnings and lower unemployment rates than black youths living in metropolitan areas with slack labor markets (Bound and Freeman, 1990; Cain and Finnie, 1990; Freeman, 1991).

Declines in Black Marriage

Studies of marriage trends provide little support for the marriageable-male hypothesis. There has been a long-term decline in black marriages since the early 1950s, despite fluctuating black male employment throughout this period (Jencks, 1988; Ellwood and Crane, 1990). In addition, marriage rates have declined for high-skilled and employed black men as well as for the low-skilled and the jobless (Lerman, 1989; Ellwood and Crane, 1990). Studies also show that the declining labor market status of men can account for only a fraction of the secular decline in black (or white) marriage rates (Ellwood and Rodda, 1991; Mare and Winship, 1991; Hoffman, Duncan, and Mincy, 1991).

Out-Migration of Middle-Income Blacks

Most studies support the selective out-migration hypothesis, at least for large northern cities. Edward Gramlich and Deborah Laren (1991) examined the selective out-migration hypothesis directly.[5] They found that rich black families left poor black neighborhoods, and that some poor black families replaced them. The poverty rates therefore increased in poor black neighborhoods.

Other studies examined the selective out-migration hypothesis indirectly. Andrew Kavee and Michael White (1990) analyzed net migration from Chicago neighborhoods between 1970 and 1980. They found that the higher the percentage of blacks in a given neighborhood, the lower the percentage of blacks in that neighborhood with at least a high school diploma. Richard Greene (1991) examined trends in population and poverty rates in metropolitan areas and concluded that in large northern cities, population declined and poverty increased. This scenario is consistent with selective out-migration. Paul Jargowsky (1991) studied changes in black household income and changes in the sorting of black low- and high-income households across neighborhoods ("neighborhood sorting"). He concluded that, at least in the large northern cities, neighborhood sorting accounted for about half the increase in black ghetto poverty. He emphasized, however, that his study ignored the effects of racial segregation, without which "there would be no ghetto poverty" (p. 20).

Massey and colleagues have forcefully made this point. Massey accepted the role of spatial, structural, and macroeconomic changes in lowering black household income, but rejected the selective out-migration hypothesis. With colleagues, he presented three kinds of evidence against this hypothesis: (1) black segregation does not decline with black income and education; (2) interclass segregation among blacks is lower than interclass segregation among other minority groups; and (3) levels and changes in black poverty have no effect on black interclass segregation (Massey and Denton, 1988; Massey and Eggers, 1990). Massey (1990) illustrated the confluence of racial and class segregation using a careful simulation model. This model showed that rates of racial and class segregation helped to confine the effects of declining black incomes to black neighborhoods that were already poor in 1980. The result was rising concentrations of black poverty and of correlates such as crime, welfare dependency, and female-headed families.

Neighborhood Effects

Empirical research on neighborhood effects is at an early stage. Studies have mostly examined the effects that peers and neighbors have on the decisions of teenagers regarding crime, employment and earnings, educational attainment, and sexual behavior. There have been only a few studies, however, that include even minimal controls for family background characteristics when estimating the effects of peer and neighbor characteristics on these decisions. Such controls are important because community amenities, including the attributes of one's neighbors, are part of the bundle of goods and services that people purchase with housing. Those with higher incomes can more easily afford housing in neighborhoods in which most households have at least one employed person.

The few studies with such controls provide selective and mixed support for peer and neighbor effects. Christopher Jencks and Susan Mayer (1990) found little evidence of peer or neighborhood effects on crime and drug use; Anne Case and Lawrence Katz (1990), however, reported that the number of crimes committed by neighboring youth and their use of alcohol and illegal drugs had significant and positive effects on similar choices by sample respondents. Jencks and Mayer also found that peers significantly affected academic achievement.

Studies of employment indicate that the higher the percentage of unemployed males and welfare recipients in a given neighborhood, the fewer hours a person in that neighborhood will tend to work. None of the neighborhood quality indices significantly affected wages or total earnings, however (Datcher, 1982; Corcoran et al., 1990). This finding is consistent with an interpretation of social isolation that Wilson (1991) accepts: that inner-city youth find labor market entry difficult because they have few adult contacts who can provide information and referrals about job vacancies.

Peers and neighbors most strongly affect choices about childbearing. The more female students at a given school who have had (or thought they would have) a child out of wedlock, the more likely it is that a teenage girl who attends that school will become an unmarried mother (Abrahamse, Morrison, and Waite, 1988). The more male-headed or two-parent families, professional and managerial workers, and families with incomes exceeding thirty thousand dollars in a given neighborhood, the less likely it is that a teenage girl who lives in that neighborhood will become an unmarried mother (Case and Katz, 1990; Brooks-Gunn et al., 1991; Crane, 1991). The higher the proportion of families headed by women and receiving AFDC in a given neighborhood, the more likely it is that girls growing up in that neighborhood will remain single and receive AFDC by age twenty-five, although these results vary by race (Hoffman, Duncan, and Mincy, 1991). Finally, the higher the neighborhood poverty rate in a given neighborhood, the less likely it is that teenage girls in that neighborhood will use contraceptives and the more likely it is that they will become pregnant (Hogan and Kitagawa, 1985).

Ethnographic Evidence and Wilson's Theory of the Underclass

Quantitative studies have two important shortcomings for underclass research. First, they leave certain important issues about neighborhood (and other) effects unresolved, because they tell us little about the mechanisms through which these effects occur. Second, quantitative studies reveal little about illegal acts such as assaults, burglary, drug use, and drug selling. Even when outcomes do not involve illegal acts, individuals may be reluctant to report accurately acts that violate social norms (delaying childbirth until marriage, for example).[6] Survey data on several outcomes related to the underclass are therefore generally unavailable. Without these survey data, quantitative studies cannot test hypotheses about the underclass. The findings of recent ethnographic and small sample research, however, provide helpful insights about these outcomes and the mechanisms through which neighborhood effects operate.

Unlike quantitative researchers, ethnographers focus on groups in communities; it is natural for them to study multiple outcomes for a demographic group in particular community settings (for example, young males in ghettos). Much ethnographic research involves peer groups.

Ethnographic evidence supports Wilson's hypotheses about the underclass. Most ethnographers conclude that macrostructural changes are a leading cause of increasing joblessness, crime, violence, and drug selling among less-skilled males, a conclusion that is consistent with Wilson's hypothesis about changing employment opportunities. These changes, as well as declines in entry-level wages, prolong peer group association and gang participation among white, black, Chicano, and Puerto Rican teenage and young-adult males. Further, ethnographic studies find that young men "hustle" when high-paying employment is unavailable (Williams and Kornblum, 1985; Hagedorn, 1988; Taylor, 1989; Anderson, 1990; Jarret, 1990; Bourgois, 1991; Fagan, 1992). Hustling can mean being idle, working "off the books" for an otherwise legal firm, or selling books, clothing, jewelry, and artwork (sometimes hand crafted) on the street, but it also includes involvement in petty crime and drug selling at various levels. Another conclusion of ethnographic research is that joblessness reduces marriage rates. Elijah Anderson (1989, 1990) and Mercer Sullivan (1989), for example, argue that young minority males do not legitimate out-of-wedlock births through marriage when they lack jobs paying wages high enough to support a family. Families and communities, moreover, do not pressure young couples to marry under these circumstances and sometimes oppose marriage plans involving males who are poor prospects.

Ethnographers also conclude, like Wilson, that peer groups affect choices about health, education, sexuality, substance abuse, and criminal behavior, although parental supervision plays an important mediating role. Anderson (1990) describes the development of peer groups among black female teenagers in ghetto neighborhoods. Sex is a recurring theme in girls' peer group conversations, ranging from who is "going with" whom to who is having sex with whom to who is having a baby with whom. This environment orients peer group members to early sexual intercourse; they become the "fast" young girls that boys in the neighborhood prey upon (Anderson, 1989). Such a peer group is generally ignorant about contraception and the risks of early sexual intercourse, and early pregnancies are inevitable. Not all young girls in ghetto neighborhoods, however, face this outcome. Girls from more "decent" and stable ghetto families, like most girls in most communities, are prepared for marriage and family under the watchful eyes of their mothers, older female relatives, and older female friends (Anderson, 1989; Jarret, 1990).[7]

Ethnographic research provides important clues about the operation of neighborhood effects and the reasons some young residents of poor and underclass areas participate in crime. In seeking to explain these effects, many observers focus on the absence of middle-class adult role models in poor or underclass areas. The ethnographic literature, by contrast, suggests that peer groups may be the more important mechanism through which neighborhood effects operate, at least for youth. Even if young people are surrounded by adult high school drop-outs, the commitment of their peers to schooling may play a bigger role in their academic performance and prospects of graduating. The conventional wisdom sees rigid boundaries between teenagers in school (or young adults working in low-wage jobs) and youth or young adults who are idle or involved in crime. The ethnographic literature, however, suggests that youth and young adults with slim prospects for stable, high-paying, mainstream jobs engage in a variety of activities to make money. Youth or young adults may be engaged in various sorts of hustling in the same month that they attend school, look for work, or work in an unstable, low-paying job. Studies relying on small-scale survey data also find that drug selling is a part-time activity for some youth and young adults otherwise engaged in mainstream activities such as attending school or working in low-wage employment (Brounstein et al., 1990; Reuter, McCoun, and Murphy, 1990). . . .

NOTES

1. See Katz (1989) for an extended historical discussion of the political history of the poverty debate in economics, law, philosophy, and political science.
2. The Social Science Citation Index in 1992 listed 355 papers citing Wilson's book *The Truly Disadvantaged: The Inner City, the Underclass, and Public Policy* (1987).
3. The displacement of low-skilled workers by structural economic changes is what Myrdal (1963) had in mind when he introduced the term "underclass" to American social policy debates.
4. Wilson also mentioned demographic changes, especially increases in the number of women entering the labor force. This created a labor surplus economy in which employers could be selective about whom they hired. Given their low skills, black males were less able to compete.
5. Gramlich and Laren (1991) actually studied the migration patterns of persons in persistently poor, middle-income, and rich families. A family was persistently poor if a three-, five-, or seven-year average of its income-to-needs ratio fell below 1.25. A family was persistently middle class if a three-, five-, or seven-year average of its income-to-needs ratio fell between 1.24 and 3.00. A family was persistently rich if a three-, five-, or seven-year average of its income-to-needs ratio exceeded 3.00. Neighborhood classifications were based on Census definitions. A poor neighborhood had a poverty rate of 30 percent or more; a middle-class neighborhood had a poverty rate between 10 and 30 percent; a rich neighborhood had a poverty rate below 10 percent.
6. For example, although out-of-wedlock birth rates are rising, most children are born to married couples. Never-married single mothers may therefore prefer to claim that they are widows or divorcees. And because marriage rates among white women, educated women, and higher-income women are higher, and these women are more likely to have the resources for abortions, the tendency to misreport out-of-wedlock fertility may be higher among these women.
7. Anderson (1990) uses the term "decent" to describe families with two parents, or families with a strong single mother and supportive relatives, who strictly supervise their children from early childhood through adolescence. "Fast girls" refers to girls who are socialized in a street peer group and who have sexual intercourse early in their adolescence.

REFERENCES

Abrahamse, Allan F., Peter Morrison, and Linda J. Waite. 1988. "Beyond Stereotypes: Who Becomes a Teenage Mother?" RAND Corporation, Santa Monica, Calif. Mimeo.

Anderson, Elijah. 1989. "Sex Codes and Family Life Among Poor Inner-City Youths." *Annals of the American Academy of Political and Social Science* 501 (January): 59–78.

———. 1990. *Streetwise: Race, Class, and Change in an Urban Community.* Chicago: University of Chicago Press.

Aponte, Robert. 1988. "Conceptualizing the Underclass: An Alternative Perspective." Paper presented at the annual meetings of the American Sociological Association, August 26, Atlanta.

Banfield, Edward C. 1958 (2nd ed., 1970). *The Unheavenly City.* Boston: Little, Brown.

Blackburn, McKinley L., David E. Bloom, and Richard B. Freeman. 1990. "Why Has the Economic Position of Less-Skilled Workers Deteriorated in the United States?" In *A Future of Lousy Jobs,* ed. Gary Burtless. Washington, D.C.: Brookings Institution.

Bound, John, and Richard B. Freeman. 1990. "What Went Wrong? The Erosion of the Relative Earnings and Employment of Young Black Men in the 1980s." National Bureau of Economic Research, Cambridge, Mass., November. Mimeo.

Bourgois, Philippe. 1991. "In Search of Respect: The New Service Economy and the Crack Alternative in

Spanish Harlem." Russell Sage Foundation, New York, May. Mimeo.

Brooks-Gunn, Jeanne, Greg J. Duncan, Pam Kato, and Naomi Sealand. 1991. "Do Neighborhoods Influence Child and Adolescent Behavior?" Paper presented at the biennial meeting of the Society for Research on Child Development, April, Seattle.

Brounstein, Paul J., Harry P. Hatry, David M. Altschuler, and Louis H. Blair. 1990. "Substance Abuse and Delinquency among Inner-City Adolescent Males." Urban Institute Report 90-3, Washington, D.C.

Brown, Michael K., and Steven P. Eric. 1981. "Blacks and the Legacy of the Great Society: The Economic and Political Impact of Federal Social Policy." *Public Policy* 29 (3, Summer): 299–330.

Burtless, Gary. 1986. "The Work Response to a Guaranteed Income: A Survey of Experimental Evidence." In *Lessons from the Income Maintenance Experiments,* ed. Alicia A. Munnell. Boston: Federal Reserve Bank of Boston.

Cain, Glen G., and Ross E. Finnie. 1990. "The Black-White Difference in Youth Employment: Evidence for Demand-Side Factors." *Journal of Labor Economics* 8 (1, pt. 2): S364–S395.

Case, Anne C., and Lawrence F. Katz. 1990. "The Company You Keep: The Effects of Family and Neighborhood on Disadvantaged Youths." National Bureau of Economic Research, Cambridge, Mass., July. Mimeo.

Clark, Kenneth B. 1965. *Dark Ghetto: Dilemmas of Social Power.* New York: Harper and Row.

Corcoran, Mary, Roger H. Gordon, Deborah Laren, and Gary Solon. 1990. "Effects of Family and Community Background on Men's Economic Status." Paper presented at the Joint Center for Political and Economic Studies/HHS Forum on Models of the Underclass, March 8–9, Washington, D.C.

Crane, Jonathan. 1991. "The Epidemic Theory of Ghettos and Neighborhood Effects on Dropping Out and Teenage Childbearing." *American Journal of Sociology* 96 (5, March): 1126–1159.

Danziger, Sheldon, and Peter Gottschalk. 1985. "The Poverty of *Losing Ground.*" *Challenge* (May–June): 32–38.

Darity, William A., Jr., and Samuel L. Myers, Jr. 1983. "Changes in Black Family Structure: Implication for Welfare Dependency." *American Economic Review* 73 (May): 59–64.

Darity, William A., Jr., Samuel L. Myers, Jr., William Sabol, and Emmet D. Carson. 1990. "Microeconomic vs. Structural Models of the Underclass." Paper presented at the Joint Center for Political and Economic Studies/HHS Forum on Models of the Underclass, March 8–9, Washington, D.C.

Darity, William A., Jr., Samuel L. Myers, Jr., William Sabol, and Emmet D. Carson. Forthcoming. *Race and Unwantedness: Essays on the Black Underclass.* New York: Garland Publications.

Datcher, Linda. 1982. "Effects of Community and Family Background on Achievement." *Review of Economics and Statistics* 64: 32–41.

Ellwood, David T., and Jonathan Crane. 1990. "Family Change among Black Americans." *Journal of Economic Perspectives* 4 (4, Fall): 65–84.

Ellwood, David T., and David T. Rodda. 1991. "The Hazards of Work and Marriage: The Influence of Male Employment on Marriage Rates." Malcolm Wiener Center for Social Policy, John F. Kennedy School of Government, Harvard University, March. Mimeo.

Fagan, Jeffery. 1992. "Drug Selling and Licit Income in Distressed Neighborhoods: The Economic Lives of Street-Level Drug Users and Sellers." In *Drugs, Crime, and Social Isolation: Barriers to Urban Opportunity,* ed. Adele V. Harrell and George E. Peterson. Washington, D.C.: Urban Institute Press.

Farkas, George, Robert P. Grobe, Daniel Sheehan, and Yuan Shuan. 1990. "Cultural Resources and School Success: Gender, Ethnicity, and Poverty Groups within an Urban School District." *American Sociological Review* 55 (February): 127–142.

Frazier, E. Franklin. 1939. *The Negro in the United States.* Chicago: University of Chicago Press.

______. 1962. *Black Bourgeoisie.* New York: Collier Books.

Freeman, Howard E., Linda H. Aiken, Robert J. Blendon, and Christopher R. Covey. 1990. "Uninsured Working-Age Adults: Characteristics and Consequences." *Health Services Research* 24 (February): 811–824.

Freeman, Richard B. 1991. "Employment and Earnings of Disadvantaged Young Men in a Labor Shortage Economy." In *The Urban Underclass,* ed.

Christopher Jencks and Paul E. Peterson, Washington, D.C.: Brookings Institution.

———. 1992. "Crime and the Employment of Disadvantaged Youths." In *Urban Labor Markets and Job Opportunity,* ed. George E. Peterson and Wayne Vroman. Washington, D.C.: Urban Institute Press.

Gans, Herbert J. 1968. "Culture and Class in the Study of Poverty: An Approach to Anti-Poverty Research." In *On Understanding Poverty: Perspectives from the Social Sciences,* ed. Daniel P. Moynihan. New York: Basic Books.

Gilder, George. 1981. *Wealth and Poverty.* New York: Basic Books.

Gramlich, Edward, and Deborah Laren. 1991. "Geographical Mobility and Persistent Poverty." Paper presented at the Conference on Urban Labor Markets and Labor Mobility, Airlie House, Va., March 7–8.

Green, Richard. 1991. "Poverty Area Diffusion: The Depopulation Hypothesis Examined." *Urban Geography* 12 (6, November–December): 526–541.

Hagedorn, John M. 1988. *People and Folks: Gangs, Crime, and the Underclass in a Rustbelt City.* Chicago: Lake View Press.

Harrington, Michael. 1962. *The Other America: Poverty in the United States.* New York: Macmillan.

Haveman, Robert H. 1987. *Poverty Policy and Poverty Research: The Great Society and the Social Sciences.* Madison: University of Wisconsin Press.

Hoffman, Saul D., Greg J. Duncan, and Ronald B. Mincy. 1991. "Marriage and Welfare Use among Young Women: Do Labor Market, Welfare, and Neighborhood Factors Account for Declining Rates of Marriage among Black and White Women?" Paper presented at the annual meetings of the American Economic Association, New Orleans, December.

Hogan, Dennis P., and Evelyn M. Kitagawa. 1985. "The Impact of Social Status, Family Structure, and Neighborhood on the Fertility of Black Adolescents." *American Journal of Sociology* 90: 825–855.

Holzer, Harry J. 1991. "The Spatial Mismatch Hypothesis: What Has the Evidence Shown?" *Urban Studies* 28 (4, February): 104–122.

Ihlanfeldt, Keith R., and David L. Sjoquist. 1989. "The Impact of Job Decentralization on the Economic Welfare of Central City Blacks." *Journal of Urban Economics* 26: 110–130.

Jargowsky, Paul A. 1991. "Ghetto Poverty: Economic vs. Spatial Factors." Paper presented at the annual meeting of the Association for Public Policy Analysis and Management, Bethesda, Md., October.

Jarret, Robin L. 1990. "A Comparative Examination of Socialization Patterns among Low-Income African Americans, Chicanos, Puerto Ricans, and Whites: A Review of the Ethnographic Literature." Social Science Research Council, New York, May. Mimeo.

Jencks, Christopher. 1988. "Deadly Neighborhoods." *New Republic* (June): 23–32.

Jencks, Christopher, and Susan Mayer. 1990. "Residential Segregation, Job Proximity, and Black Job Opportunities." In *Inner-City Poverty in the United States,* ed. Lawrence E. Lynn, Jr., and Michael G. H. McGeary. Washington, D.C.: National Academy Press.

Johnson, James H., and Melvin L. Oliver. 1991. "Economic Restructuring and Black Male Joblessness in U.S. Metropolitan Areas." *Urban Geography* 12 (6): 542–562.

Juhn Chinhui. 1992. "The Decline of Male Labor Market Participation: The Role of Declining Market Opportunities." *Quarterly Journal of Economics* 107: 79–122.

Kasarda, John D. 1989. "Urban Industrial Transition and the Underclass." *Annals of the American Academy of Political and Social Science* 501 (January): 26–47.

Katz, Lawrence F., and Kevin M. Murphy. 1990. "Changes in Relative Wages, 1963–1987: Supply and Demand Factors." National Bureau of Economic Research, Cambridge, Mass., April. Mimeo.

Katz, Michael B. 1989. *The Undeserving Poor: From the War on Poverty to the War on Welfare.* New York: Pantheon Books.

Kavee, Andrew, and Michael J. White. 1990. "The Outmigration of Educated Blacks from Inner Cities." Paper presented at the annual meeting of the Association for Public Policy Analysis and Management, San Francisco, October.

Lerman, Robert I. 1989. "Employment Opportunities of Young Men and Family Formation." *American Economic Review* 79 (May): 62–66.

Levy, Frank, and Richard J. Murnane. 1992. "U.S. Earnings Levels and Earnings Inequality: A Review of Recent Trends and Proposed Explanations." *Journal of Economic Literature* 30: 1333–1381.

Lewis, Oscar. 1966. "The Culture of Poverty." *Scientific American* 215: 19–25.

Mare, Robert D., and Christopher Winship. 1991. "Socioeconomic Change and the Decline of Marriage for Blacks and Whites." In *The Urban Underclass,* ed. Christopher Jencks and Paul E. Peterson. Washington, D.C.: Brookings Institution.

Massey, Douglas S. 1990. "American Apartheid: Segregation and the Making of the Underclass." *American Journal of Sociology* 96 (2): 329–357.

Massey, Douglas S., and Nancy A. Denton. 1988. "The Dimensions of Residential Segregation." *Social Forces* 67: 281–315.

Massey, Douglas S., and Mitchell L. Eggers. 1990. "The Ecology of Inequality: Minorities and the Concentration of Poverty." *American Journal of Sociology* 95: 1153–1188.

Mead, Lawrence M. 1988. "The Hidden Jobs Debate." *Public Interest* 91 (Spring): 40–58.

______. 1992. *The New Politics of Poverty: The Working Poor in America.* New York: Basic Books.

Murray, Charles. 1984. *Losing Ground: American Social Policy, 1950–1980.* New York: Basic Books.

Myrdal, Gunnar. 1957. *Economic Theory and Under-Developed Regions.* London: Duckworth.

Pencavel, John. 1986. "Labor Supply of Men: A Survey." In *Handbook of Labor Economics,* vol. 1, ed. Orley Ashenfelter and Richard Layer. Amsterdam and New York: North-Holland.

Rainwater, Lee. 1968. "The Problem of Lower-Class Culture and Poverty—War Strategy." In *On Understanding Poverty: Perspectives from the Social Sciences,* ed. Daniel P. Moynihan. New York: Basic Books.

Reuter, Peter, Robert McCoun, and Patrick Murphy. 1990. *Money from Crime: A Study of the Economics of Drug Dealing in Washington, D.C.* Santa Monica, Calif.: Rand Corporation.

Sampson, Robert. 1987. "Urban Black Violence: The Effect of Male Joblessness and Family Disruption." *American Journal of Sociology* 93: 348–382.

Sullivan, Mercer L. 1989. "Absent Fathers in the Inner City." *Annals of the American Academy of Political and Social Science* 501 (1, January): 48–58.

Taylor, Carl S. 1989. *Dangerous Society.* East Lansing: Michigan State University Press.

Testa, Mark. 1991. "Male Joblessness, Nonmarital Parenthood, and Marriage." Paper presented at the Urban Poverty and Family Life Conference, University of Chicago, October 10–12.

U.S. Department of Labor, Office of Policy Planning and Research. 1965. *The Negro Family: The Case for National Action.* Daniel Patrick Moynihan. Washington, D.C.: U.S. Government Printing Office.

Valentine, Charles A. 1968. *Culture and Poverty: Critique and Counter-Proposals.* Chicago: University of Chicago Press.

Williams, Terry M., and William Kornblum. 1985. *Growing up Poor.* Lexington, Mass.: Lexington Books.

Wilson, William Julius. 1987. *The Truly Disadvantaged: The Inner City, the Underclass, and Public Policy.* Chicago: University of Chicago Press.

______. 1991. "Studying Inner-City Social Dislocations: The Challenge of Public Agenda Research—1990 Presidential Address." *American Sociological Review* 56 (February): 1–14.

Wilson, William Julius, and Lawrence M. Mead. 1987. "The Obligation to Work and the Availability of Jobs: A Dialogue between Lawrence M. Mead and William Julius Wilson." *Focus* (newsletter of the Institute for Research on Poverty) 10 (2, Summer): 11–19.

Wilson, William Julius, and Kathryn M. Neckerman. 1986. "Poverty and Family Structure: The Widening Gap between Evidence and Public Policy Issues." In *Fighting Poverty: What Works and What Doesn't,* ed. Sheldon H. Danziger and Daniel H. Weinberg. Cambridge, Mass.: Harvard University Press.

PERSONAL ACCOUNT

I Am a Pakistani Woman

I am a Pakistani woman, raised in the U.S. and Canada, and often at odds with the western standard of beauty.

As a child in Nova Scotia and later growing up in New York and Indiana, I was proud of my uniqueness. On traditional Pakistani and Muslim holidays, I got to wear bright, fun clothes from my country and colorful jewelry. I had a whole rich tradition of my own to celebrate in addition to Christmas and Easter. However, as I started school, I somehow came to realize that being different wasn't so great—that in other people's viewpoint, I looked strange and acted funny. I learned the importance of fitting in and behaving like the other girls. This involved dressing well, giggling a lot, and having a superior, but flirtatious attitude toward boys. I was very outgoing and had very good grades, so outwardly I was able to "assimilate" with some success. But my sister, who was quiet and reticent, often took the brunt of other children's cruelty. I realize how proud and ashamed I was of my heritage when I look at my relationship with my family.

A lesson I learned early on in the U.S. was that being beautiful took a lot of money. It is painful, as an adult, for me to consider the inexorable, never-ending pressure that my father was under to embody the dominant, middle-class cultural expressions of masculinity, as in success at one's job, making a big salary, and owning status symbols. I resented him so much then for being a poor, untenured professor and freelance writer. I wanted designer clothes, dining out at nice restaurants, and a big allowance. Instead, I had a deeply spiritual thinker, writer, and theologian for a dad. I love(d) him and am so very grateful for what he's taught me, but as a child I didn't think of him as a success.

The prettiest girls in school all had a seemingly endless array of outfits, lots of makeup and perfume, and everything by the "right" designers. I hated my mom for making many of my clothes and buying things on sale (and my mom was a great seamstress). I hungrily read about Brooke Shields's seemingly perfect life, with her excursions to expensive restaurants and appointments with personal trainers at exclusive spas. I felt a sense of hopelessness that I could never have the resources or opportunities necessary to compete, to be beautiful.

Instead I found safety in conformity. When I was in high school, the WASPy, preppy look was hot; it represented the epitome of success and privilege in America. I worked hard to purchase a wardrobe of clothes with a polo-horse insignia, by many hours at an after-school job. I tried to hide my exotic look behind Khakis, boat shoes, hair barrettes, and pearl studs. There was comfort in conformity. I saw the class "sex symbol" denigrated for wearing tight dresses and having a very well-developed body for a sixteen-year-old, and the more unique dressers dismissed as frivolous, trendy, and more than a little eccentric. You couldn't be too pretty, too ugly, too different—you had to just blend in.

Though I did it well, I perpetually felt like an imposter. This rigidly controlled, well-dressed preppy going through school with good grades in advanced placement classes in no way represented what I felt to be my true essence.

Hoorie I. Siddique

What Is Sexual Orientation?

READING 12

The Invention of Heterosexuality

Jonathan Ned Katz

In the United States, in the 1890s, the "sexual instinct" was generally identified as a *procreative* desire of men and women. But that reproductive ideal was beginning to be challenged, quietly but insistently, in practice and theory, by a new *different-sex pleasure* ethic. According to that radically new standard, the "sexual instinct" referred to men's and women's erotic desire for each other, *irrespective of its procreative potential.* Those two, fundamentally opposed, sexual moralities informed the earliest American definitions of "heterosexuals" and "homosexuals." Under the old procreative standard, the new term

Jonathan Ned Katz has written for the *Village Voice,* the *Nation,* and the *Advocate.*

heterosexual did not, at first, always signify the normal and good.

The earliest-known use of the word *heterosexual* in the United States occurs in an article by Dr. James G. Kiernan, published in a Chicago medical journal in May 1892.[1]

Heterosexual was not equated here with normal sex, but with perversion—a definitional tradition that lasted in middle-class culture into the 1920s. Kiernan linked heterosexual to one of several "abnormal manifestations of the sexual appetite"—in a list of "sexual perversions proper"—in an article on "Sexual Perversion." Kiernan's brief note on depraved heterosexuals attributed their definition (incorrectly, as we'll see) to Dr. Richard von Krafft-Ebing of Vienna.

These heterosexuals were associated with a mental condition, "psychical hermaphroditism." . . . Heterosexuals experienced so-called male erotic attraction to females *and* so-called female erotic attraction to males. That is, these heterosexuals periodically felt "inclinations to both sexes."[2] The hetero in these heterosexuals referred *not* to their interest in *a different sex,* but to their desire for *two different sexes.* Feeling desire inappropriate, supposedly, for their sex, these heterosexuals were guilty of what we now think of as gender and erotic deviance.

Heterosexuals were also guilty of reproductive deviance. That is, they betrayed inclinations to "abnormal methods of gratification"—modes of ensuring pleasure without reproducing the species. They also demonstrated "traces of the normal sexual appetite"—a touch of the desire to reproduce.

Dr. Kiernan's article also included the earliest-known U.S. publication of the word *homosexual.* The "pure homosexuals" he cited were persons whose "general mental state is that of the opposite sex." These homosexuals were defined explicitly as gender benders, rebels from proper masculinity and femininity. In contrast, his heterosexuals deviated explicitly from gender, erotic, and procreative norms. In their American debut, the abnormality of heterosexuals appeared to be thrice that of homosexuals.[3]. . .

KRAFFT-EBING'S *PSYCHOPATHIA SEXUALIS*

The new term *hetero-sexual* next appeared early in 1893, in the first U.S. publication, in English, of *Psychopathia Sexualis, with Especial Reference to Contrary Sexual Instinct: A Medico-Legal Study,* by Richard von Krafft-Ebing, "Professor of Psychiatry and Neurology at the University of Vienna."[4] This book would appear in numerous later U.S. editions, becoming one of the most famous, influential texts on "pathological" sexuality.[5] Its disturbing (and fascinating) examples of a sex called sick began quietly to define a new idea of a sex perceived as healthy.[6]

In this primer, the "pathological sexual instinct" and "contrary sexual instinct" are major terms referring to non-procreative desire. Their opposite, called, simply, "sexual instinct," is reproductive. But that old procreative norm was no longer as absolute for Krafft-Ebing as it was for Kiernan. . . .

In the heat of different-sex lust, declares Krafft-Ebing, men and women are not usually thinking of baby making: "In sexual love the real purpose of the instinct, the propagation of the species, does not enter into consciousness."[7] An unconscious procreative "purpose" informs his idea of "sexual love." . . . Placing the reproductive aside in the unconscious, Krafft-Ebing created a small, obscure space in which a new pleasure norm began to grow.

Krafft-Ebing's procreative, sex-differentiated, and erotic "sexual instinct" was present by definition in his term *hetero-sexual*—his book introduced that word to many Americans. A hyphen between, Krafft-Ebing's "hetero" and "sexual" newly spliced sex-difference and eroticism to constitute a pleasure defined explicitly by the different sexes of its parties. His hetero-sexual, unlike Kiernan's, does not desire two sexes, only one, different, sex.

Krafft-Ebing's term *hetero-sexual* makes no *explicit* reference to reproduction, though it always implicitly includes reproductive desire. Always, therefore, his hetero-sexual implicitly signifies erotic normality. His twin term, *homosexual,* always signifies a same-sex desire, pathological because non-reproductive.

Contrary to Kiernan's earlier attribution, Krafft-Ebing consistently uses hetero-sexual to mean normal sex. In contrast, for Kiernan, and some other late-nineteenth- and early-twentieth-century sexologists, a simple reproductive standard was absolute: The hetero-sexuals in Krafft-Ebing's text appeared guilty of procreative ambiguity, thus of perversion.

These distinctions between sexual terms and definitions are historically important, but complex, and may be difficult for us to grasp. Our own society's particular, dominant heterosexual norm also helps to cloud our minds to other ways of categorizing.

Readers such as Dr. Kiernan might also understand Krafft-Ebing's hetero-sexuals to be perverts by association. For the word *hetero-sexual,* though signifying normality, appears often in the Viennese doctor's book linked with the non-procreative perverse—coupled with "contrary sexual instinct," "psychical hermaphroditism," "homo-sexuality," and "fetichism."

For example, Krafft-Ebing's first use of "hetero-sexual" occurs in a discussion of several case histories of "hetero- and homo-sexuality" in which "a certain kind of attire becomes a fetich."[8] The hetero-sexual premieres, with the homo-sexual, as clothes fetishist. . . .

Krafft-Ebing's use of the word *hetero-sexual* to mean a normal different-sex eroticism marked in discourse a first historic shift away from the centuries-old procreative norm. His use of the terms *hetero-sexual* and *homo-sexual* helped to make sex difference and eros the basic distinguishing features of a new linguistic, conceptual, and social ordering of desire. His hetero-sexual and homo-sexual offered the modern world two sex-differentiated eroticisms, one normal and good, one abnormal and bad, a division which would come to dominate our twentieth-century vision of the sexual universe. . . .

NOTES

1. Dr. James G. Kiernan, "Responsibility in Sexual Perversion," *Chicago Medical Recorder* 3 (May 1892), 185–210; "Read before the Chicago Medical Society, March 7, 1892," but it's difficult to imagine him reading his footnote on Krafft-Ebing. Kiernan's note on 197–98 cites Krafft-Ebing's classifications in *Psychopathia Sexualis,* "Chaddock's translation" (no date). The U.S. publication in 1893 of C. G. Chaddock's translation of Krafft-Ebing's *Psychopathia Sexualis* followed Kiernan's article (see backnote 4 below). So there's some confusion about the exact source of Kiernan's brief note on Krafft-Ebing's terms "hetero-sexual" and "homo-sexual." Perhaps Kiernan saw a prepublication version of Chaddock's translation. It's also possible that Kiernan had seen some earlier article by Krafft-Ebing or the English translation by F. J. Rebman of the 10th German edition of Krafft-Ebing's *Psychopathia Sexualis,* published in London in 1889 (I have not inspected that edition). Kiernan seems to have based his brief gloss on Krafft-Ebing's definition of the heterosexual and homosexual on a superficial reading of pages 222–23 of the 1893 edition of Chaddock's translation of *Psychopathia Sexualis,* paragraphs numbered 1–4.
2. Mental hermaphrodites experienced, sometimes, the "wrong" feelings for their biological sex; their erotic desire was improperly inverted. A moral judgment founded the ostensibly objective, scientific concept of psychical hermaphroditism.

   Kiernan's idea of "psychical hermaphroditism" is not exactly the same as the attraction we now label "bisexual," referring as we do to the sex of the subject and the two different sexes to which he or she is attracted. Psychical hermaphroditism referred to mental gender, while our bisexuality refers to the sex of a sex partner. Mental hermaphroditism might lead to both sexes as erotic partners, but the term laid the cause in the mental gender of the subject (like the concept of inversion). Our bisexuality does not involve any necessary link to mental gender. I am grateful to Lisa Duggan for this clarification.

3. But heterosexuals' appearance of triple the abnormality of homosexuals was deceiving. For Kiernan, the gender deviance of homosexuals *implied* that they were also, simultaneously, rebels from a procreative norm and an erotic norm. But it's significant that Kiernan explicitly stresses homosexuals' gender rebellion, not their erotic or reproductive deviancy. George Chauncey, Jr., discusses the late-nineteenth-century stress on gender inversion in "From Sexual Inversion to Homosexuality: Medicine and the Changing Conceptualization of Female Deviance," *Salmagundi* 56–59 (Fall–Winter 1983), 114–46.
4. R. von Krafft-Ebing, *Psychopathia Sexualis, with Especial Reference to Contrary Sexual Instinct: A Medico-Legal Study,* trans. Charles Gilbert Chaddock (Philadelphia: F. A. Davis, 1893), from the 7th and revised German ed.; preface dated November 1892. Hereafter cited as Krafft-Ebing. The U.S. Copyright Office received and registered this edition on February 16, 1893 (Copyright Office to Katz, May 25, 1990).

   This book's year of publication is confused, because its copyright page and its preface are dated 1892, while its title page lists the year of publication as 1893. *The National Union Catalogue of Pre-1956 Publications* says this edition was first published in 1892, and the first citation of "hetero-sexual" listed in the *Oxford English Dictionary* (1976 Supplement, p. 85) is to this edition of Krafft-Ebing, attributed to 1892. That year is incorrect. Although it was evidently prepared by November 1892, the date of its preface, it was not officially published until 1893.

   For Krafft-Ebing and his *Psychopathia* see Peter Gay, *The Bourgeois Experience: Victoria to Freud, Volume II, The Tender Passion* (NY: Oxford University Press, 1986), 221, 223–24, 226, 229, 230–32, 286, 338, 350; Gert Hekma, "A History of Sexology: Social and Historical Aspects of Sexuality," in Jan Bremmer, ed., *From Sappho to De Sade: Moments in the History of Sexuality* (first published 1989; NY: Routledge, 1991), 173–93; and Arnold I. Davidson, "Closing Up the Corpses: Diseases of Sexuality and the Emergence of the Psychiatric Style of Reasoning," in George Boolos, ed., *Meaning and Method: Essays in Honor of Hilary Putnam* (NY: Cambridge University Press, 1990), 295–325. I am also greatly indebted to talks with Harry Oosterhuis and an advance copy of his paper "Richard von Krafft-Ebing's Step-Children of Nature: Psychiatry and the Making of Modern Sexual Identity," presented as a talk at the Second Carleton Conference on the History of the Family, May 12, 1994, in Ottawa, Canada.
5. Krafft-Ebing's focus, as a psychiatrist, on disturbed mental states contrasts with the earlier nineteenth-century focus of neurologists on disturbed brains. I thank Lisa Duggan for this comment.
6. In this text the doctor's descriptions of sex sickness and sex health replaced the old, overtly moral judgments about bad sex and good sex, introducing the modern medical model of sexuality to numbers of Americans.
7. Krafft-Ebing 9.
8. Krafft-Ebing 169.

READING 13

Homosexuality: A Social Phenomenon

Barbara Sherman Heyl

. . . This article focuses primarily on the theoretical debates over how best to explain the "condition" of homosexuality, once Western culture had conceptualized it that way. Is there something "essential" that makes homosexuals who they are, or has the identity grown out of social interaction? The sociological view tends to see homosexuality as a social construction, both at the

Barbara Sherman Heyl is professor of sociology at Illinois State University.

macro level—where society defines what homosexual behavior means within its cultural boundaries, and at the micro level—where the individual, in interaction with others, acquires his or her own personal sense of a sexual identity.

VIEWING HOMOSEXUAL BEHAVIOR IN ITS SOCIETAL CONTEXT

Cross-Cultural Variations

If patterns of sexual behavior and the meanings given to them are products of the social, cultural, and historical context out of which they developed, then we can expect them to vary cross-culturally. Recently published research has documented homosexual behavior in different parts of the world and in different time periods; the behavior was found to be interconnected with the social relationships and cultural beliefs of the societies under study (Callender & Kochems, 1983; Dover, 1978; Herdt, 1981; Whitam & Mathy, 1986). These cross-cultural data allow us to compare different types of social organization and division of labor, and how they promote particular forms of homosexual behavior, as well as affect social responses to such behavior (Adam, 1985; Herdt, 1984).

. . . The kinship-structured society of Sambia in New Guinea included homosexual relations between older men and younger boys; the relations are ritualized and in a sense obligatory. This pattern was found in other societies on the eastern islands of Melanesia, as well as in southern New Guinea, and has been termed the "Melanesian" model by Barry Adam (1985). There are several characteristics of Melanesian-model societies that are influential in shaping the ritualized homosexuality that exists in those cultures. For example, these societies exhibit a high degree of gender separation and inequality (Herdt, 1984). Adam (1985) notes that "men and women have separate residences, pathways, crops, foods and rites" (see Allen, 1967). Women are viewed as important for reproductive and labor purposes, but are considered by males to have a polluting influence on young males. As a result of this belief, males "develop a complex and extended system of magical practices to rescue boys from impure contact with their mothers and convert them into men. This conversion is not easy and typically involves the seclusion of youths during which time they are fed and 'grown' by older men" (Adam, 1985, pp. 25, 26).

Thus, in Melanesian societies the homosexual patterns are age-graded, with the older males contributing their semen to the younger males as a way of giving them "manhood," initiating them into warrior groups, and making them strong (Herdt, 1984, pp. 59–64, 181–183). Semen is highly valued as necessary not only in creating life but also as a way of "binding the male line" (Adam, 1985, p. 27). The young men are required to ingest semen from older males in order to become part of the lineage of their past male ancestors. A related but different method of masculinizing boys is practiced among the Sambia of New Guinea. These people segregate young boys from women by sending them to forest lodges for ten to fifteen years. During this seclusion the boys pass through a series of rites, including frequent fellatio practiced between the younger and older boys (Herdt, 1984). After the initiation procedures are completed the males are expected to marry women and to end homosexual behavior.

Separating the young males from any contact with women produces a stage of enforced bachelorhood that all Melanesian males must pass through in order to become adult males. Adam (1985) notes that this separation allows the adult males exclusive rights to "use women's productive and reproductive power for their own use" (p. 20). Thus, the bachelorhood status and its accompanying rituals facilitate the maintenance of social control by the older males over both the young men and the women. Since homosexual behavior in Melanesian societies is routine and obligatory as part of the social organization of these societies, it is not perceived as deviant or abnormal behavior. Clearly, we cannot label this behavior according to our norms or view these men as "homosexuals"—a term that derives from our Western culture (see Herdt, 1984; Stoller, 1980).

Western Culture: Developing a Category of Homosexuality

Most Western cultures have not built overt homosexual behavior into their accepted and obligatory social roles; indeed homosexual behavior has long been discouraged and repressed. Not only has the Judeo-Christian religion taken a strong stand against homosexual behavior, but secular laws have prohibited acts of sodomy as well. There have been variations in this generally negative history; for example, the famous French Penal Code of 1791 did decriminalize homosexual acts between consenting adults (Greenberg & Bystryn, 1984). However, public opinion in nineteenth century Europe and the United States remained hostile to overt homosexual behavior.

In the late eighteenth and early nineteenth centuries the category of homosexuality emerged as a way of describing a condition and the homosexual as a type of person (Foucault, 1978; Richardson, 1984, p. 80). Until that time the moral and legal debates on homosexual behavior had centered on just that—behavior. The shift in focus defined homosexuality as a "state of being" that could exist prior to and without any overt homosexual act and, from somewhere inside the person, compelled a lifelong habitual preference for same-sex partners. Homosexuals became a highly stigmatized category of persons. (It should become clear now why it is inappropriate to use this term to describe the Melanesian males.)

Greenberg and Bystryn (1984) propose that one explanation for this conceptual development was the new capitalism of nineteenth century Europe and the United States which increased competition among men, sharpened the sexual division of labor, and strengthened the ideology of the family. Foucault (1978) and Weeks (1981) relate the conceptual development to the rise in the early nineteenth century of a "scientific" interest in sexual behavior. The medical profession, as part of the scientific community of this period, played a significant role in defining homosexuality by depicting it as a medical pathology or abnormality (Greenberg & Bystryn, 1984; Richardson, 1984).

EFFORTS SINCE THE NINETEENTH CENTURY TO EXPLAIN HOMOSEXUALITY

Shifts in the Major Theoretical Approaches to Homosexuality

The category of "homosexual," once it had been created, demanded an explanation. The first theoretical approach came from the biological/medical model, well established by the late nineteenth century and viewed as the key to understanding homosexuality as well as a wide variety of other perceived social problems, such as crime, alcoholism, retardation, and insanity. Physicians helped instill the idea that homosexuals were stricken by something beyond their control. The medicalization of homosexuality meant that homosexuals were subjected to efforts to cure them with such "therapeutic" interventions as castration, sterilization, and commitment to mental health facilities (Greenberg & Bystryn, 1984, p. 41). These developments launched the debates that continued into 1950s and 1960s over how one could define the biological or mental characteristic that placed "homosexuals" in a different category from the rest of the population; "was homosexuality congenital or acquired, ineradicable or susceptible to cure?" (Weeks, 1981, p. 86).

A second theoretical approach emerged in the early twentieth century that shifted attention to the psychological state of the individual and conceptualized homosexuality as a *sexual orientation* toward members of the same sex as sexual and love objects. Sigmund Freud's (1905; 1931) writings influenced this shift. His theory of homosexuality included the premise that humans came into the world with a capacity to be sexually attracted to both sexes. Richardson (1984) notes that Freud's "concept of bisexuality was based on evidence that embryological remnants of the anatomical characteristics of the opposite sex, however rudimentary, are present in all individuals" (p. 81). Freud's theory of psychosexual development assumed that the normal process of libidinal development resulted in a heterosexual orientation. Homosexuality resulted from the development in the individual, beginning in early childhood, of a fixed and fundamental "sexual orientation" guiding the individual into later homosexual behavior. Thus, both the biological/medical model and the psychological/sexual orientation model posit that there is some "essential" trait about the person that explains his or her homosexuality.

An important turning point in these discussions came from the 1948 Kinsey studies of sexuality in the United States. This nationwide survey of self-reported sexual behavior revealed a much wider involvement in homosexual behavior in the male population than had been previously thought. The study also documented shifting patterns of such involvement over the life span of individual men. As Kinsey and his co-authors note (Kinsey, Pomeroy, & Martin, 1948), "The histories which have been available in the present study make it apparent that the heterosexuality or homosexuality of many individuals is not an all-or-none proposition" (p. 638). This conclusion supported Kinsey's decision to propose a continuum of categories to describe experience in a given age period in the individual's life, ranging from exclusively heterosexual experiences (category 0) to exclusively homosexual experiences (category 6), with five categories in between reflecting varying proportions of same-sex and opposite-sex sexual experiences.

The Kinsey continuum would allow researchers to more accurately describe the experiences of the population with respect to sexual partners than was allowed by the previous assumption that one could easily divide the population into two groups—the heterosexuals and the homosexuals. If behavior was to be an indicator of who could be considered "the homosexuals," then where on the continuum do we draw the line? Were the homosexuals only those who fit into category 6 (exclusively homosexual experiences), or did they include anyone from category 1 (had had only incidental homosexual contact, while having predominantly heterosexual experiences) through category 6? Additionally, Kinsey's data included reports by individuals of their psychic responses to members of the same and opposite sex, and these feelings varied across a continuum and across the life span of the respondents as well.

Kinsey's research posed a major challenge to both previous theoretical approaches. If either the biological or sexual orientation theories were true, how was one to explain changing patterns of homosexual behavior over the life span of one individual? By documenting diversity in lifestyles, sexual behavior patterns, and emotions, Kinsey promoted consideration by other researchers of the individual's own definition of self as relevant data in the debate on how to identify "the homosexual." This new consideration focuses attention again on homosexuality as a state of being—but this time, as Richardson (1984) states "It is, however, a different form of 'being' than previously conceived where the fundamental question was what caused a person to develop into a homosexual. The new question is: How does the state of being a person who *self-identifies as homosexual* come about?" (p. 83).

A third theoretical approach to homosexuality focused on this new question and was dominant in sociology in the United States and Britain from the 1960s to the present. It is known as the labeling interactionist perspective and derives from symbolic interactionism (Weeks, 1981, p. 94). It views the category of homosexuality as a product of the meanings we give the term in our Western culture (social process at the macro level), and sees the individuals who fit the category as those who have come to identify themselves as homosexuals (the result of social process at the micro level). This interactionist or social constructionist perspective allows for considering identity separate from behavior, which proved helpful in interpreting the Kinsey data. For example, since the Kinsey data documented gradations of heterosexual and homosexual experiences within the lives of individuals, then if sexual identity was a direct result of sexual behavior, we would expect all those who had engaged in both homosexual and heterosexual sexual activities to identify themselves as bisexual. Data indicate that such is not the case (Blumstein & Schwartz 1976, Humphreys, 1975, Paul, 1984). One explanation is that an identity as a bisexual is stigmatized by both the heterosexual and homosexual populations, so that many fewer people consider themselves "bisexual" than would be expected given their actual sexual behavior (Golden, 1987, pp. 30–31). Explaining homosexuality from the third perspective meant understanding how individuals arrived at a point where they identified themselves as homosexuals.

Research on the Causes of Homosexuality

Each of the three theoretical approaches discussed above has generated research designed to test the proposed explanation of homosexuality. Much of the resulting research was designed to reveal the ultimate causal explanation of homosexuality. Such a search is based on a belief that the category of "homosexual" consists of people who have some essential characteristic in common that differentiates them from "the heterosexuals" in the society. Just phrasing the problem in this way points to the difficulty a researcher would have locating such a characteristic. Both homosexual and heterosexual categories include people of very diverse backgrounds, personalities, and lifestyles. Even if researchers were able to divide the total population into two distinct and separate groups—homosexual and heterosexual—and discover a common characteristic of all homosexuals that was not characteristic of any heterosexual, the researcher still would have to be careful about announcing that this factor explained the "homosexuality" of the one group. The factor, depending on its nature, might well have developed as a *result* of living out a homosexual lifestyle. But in spite of the difficulties, such research has continued on the premise that something definite will emerge to explain why "homosexuals" are who they are.

Research from the biological or medical model has enjoyed particularly strong appeal since, if a particular gene or hormonal pattern could be found to explain homosexuality, then everyone could know definitively who the homosexuals were and why. The factor would solve issues of who or what is responsible for the condition, and the medical profession might even be able to "help" those found with this condition. Such is the seduction of the biological model. Indeed, biologists and geneticists have for decades searched for the biological key to homosexuality, but such an answer has been elusive.

First, the scientific basis of the research has changed. Biological research on homosexuality conducted during the 1940s or earlier has been thoroughly discredited now on grounds of incomplete understanding of genes and hormones, as well as faulty research designs (Richardson, 1981). Scientific understanding of human biology has developed significantly in recent decades, and technological developments have also facilitated more precise measurement of the sex hormones. However, in spite of these advances, a second set of methodological problems remain. For example, there continues to be a lack of data on the standards of biological characteristics that can appropriately be used as a basis for measurement of differences or deviations, repeated failure to find statistical differences between the "homosexuals" and the control groups, problems in identifying who belongs appropriately in what group (often the heterosexual sample is composed of men the researcher assumes to be heterosexual), failure to include any data on women, while still drawing conclusions about women, and the fact that hormones are influenced by many factors in the subject's world, including stress.

A third problem with the medical model is that it is based on the unwarranted assumption that biology can explain sexuality. Ricketts (1984) notes, that "explanations of a direct cause-and-effect relationship between biological factors and sexual orientation falter because they cannot embrace the complexity and variety of human sexual behavior" (p. 88). Given the diversity of ways in which humans can and do experience their sexuality, including changes in sexual behavior, attractions, and fantasies, it is not surprising that the careful assessment of the biological research results in the conclusion that this research has contributed little to our understanding of sexual identity (Hoult, 1984; Ricketts, 1984; Richardson, 1981). In spite of these research conclusions, the belief that there is a genetic or biochemical explanation for homosexuality still appears frequently in today's media and among the general population.

Research from the second theoretical approach views "sexual orientation" as "a relatively enduring psychological characteristic of the individual, largely determined in early life" (Richardson, 1984, p. 84). Researching the cause of a homosexual "sexual orientation" required documenting early learning experiences and the influences of family relationships on the young "pre-homosexual." Psychologists and psychoanalysts conducted such research by using their homosexual clients in psychotherapy as their source of data. Critics of such research have noted a number of methodological difficulties (see Browning, 1984; Richardson, 1981). First, when researchers draw samples solely from therapy clients, their data come from homosexuals who are likely different from other homosexuals who have not sought out psychotherapy. Second, research conclusions were reached without comparing the data on homosexuals with a control group of heterosexuals. Third, since the psychological researchers attempted to document the existence of a deep-seated, family-oriented sexual orientation, the data came from retrospective accounts. Not only is it difficult for adults to recall accurately events they experienced as children, but the retelling of those events, as well as descriptions of family relationships, can be influenced by their present circumstances and identity, the therapy process itself, and available knowledge about homosexuality. Fourth, most research was conducted with male clients only.

As the criticisms noted above gained recognition, research was conducted that included homosexuals not in therapy and compared their family backgrounds and personality data to heterosexuals, also not in therapy, who were interviewed and given the same questionnaires and standard personality tests as the homosexuals. One hypothesis had been that a homosexual orientation developed from a particular family structure involving a "dominant" mother and a "weak" or absent father. The use of the comparison group of heterosexuals was important in undermining this "explanation" of homosexuality, since there were heterosexuals whose family histories also revealed this pattern (e.g., see Marmor, 1965). Indeed, no single "family constellation" or other pattern, such as the child having identified more with one parent than the other, could be found to explain the adult lifestyle of homosexuality (Bell, Weinberg, & Hammersmith, 1981a; Hooker, 1969; Siegelman, 1974).

Gradually a body of research data accumulated, based on nonpatient and noninstitutionalized homosexual populations that showed that "most lesbians and gay men were remarkably similar to heterosexuals with the exception of their sexual preference" (Browning, 1984, p. 20). Researchers found that homosexuals did not constitute a clinical category. These conclusions led the American Psychiatric Association in 1973 to remove homosexuality from its manual that lists the known pathological clinical conditions. In

1974 the American Psychological Association took the same step.

Since the research from the first two theoretical perspectives failed to identify any biological or psychological factors that could differentiate homosexuals as a separate category from heterosexuals, then homosexuality could not be explained as a biological or psychological phenomenon. The third theoretical approach suggested that homosexuality was a social phenomenon—in that both the category and its contents, "the homosexuals," developed out of social process. The researcher from this approach acknowledges that the individual comes packaged with specific biological characteristics and, in the process of living through early childhood and adolescence, the individual has many experiences that contribute to his or her psychosexual development and individual personality. To develop a sexual identity, however, the individual picks out certain personal characteristics and past experiences as significant, while excluding others. The responses of other people to the individual are an integral part of the process. The individual takes these responses, as well as his or her own feelings about the experiences, into account when he or she assesses the experiences later for clues as to who he or she "really" is. Research from this approach to homosexuality focused on the social process of acquiring a sexual identity, and the next section is devoted to examining these efforts.

HOMOSEXUALITY AS A STATE OF IDENTITY

The question of how and when and under what conditions someone would or could acquire an identity as a homosexual was posed as a genuinely sociological question, and the research into this question benefited greatly from the interactionist perspective in sociology during the 1960s and 1970s. Proponents of this perspective assert that the development of one's personal identity (how an individual answers privately the question of "Who am I?") is an ongoing life process and takes place in a social context. The individual develops a sense of self in relation to major aspects of life, such as work and sex. For example, we develop an occupational or professional identity out of our experiences related to work and our interpretations, utilizing feedback from others, regarding who we are in our work roles. We develop a sexual identity out of all the experiences we have had involving sexuality and the meanings we attach to these experiences. Sexual identity summarizes our sense of self as sexual beings. Sexual orientation or sexual preference is one component of sexual identity that expresses our attraction to members of the same or opposite sex.

From this perspective sexual identity is a social construction. This is not the same as saying one's identity is freely chosen. We are, from this perspective, a product of all we have been through, including experiences which we may not have enjoyed or chosen, but experienced nonetheless. Out of these events and our feelings about them, we try to make sense out of what our life has been and who we are. The process may seem complicated but is remarkably ordinary. Gagnon (1977) notes "people become sexual in the same way they become everything else. Without much reflection, they pick up directions from their social environment" (p. 2). If this is descriptive of sexuality generally, then it also applies to homosexuality more specifically.

Given the premise of a gradual learning of sexual behavior patterns and identities, how does the social scientist conduct research on such a long drawn-out process involving interaction between the personal and the social? And how, if one perceives the culture as providing strong encouragement for heterosexuality (some view it as "compulsory heterosexuality"; see Adrienne Rich, 1980), can one gradually develop a homosexual identity?

One research strategy that derived from the labeling/interactionist tradition focuses on efforts to discover and document what stages of development an individual goes through in the process of acquiring a sexual identity. Beginning in the mid-1970s researchers used intensive interviews with self acknowledged gay males and lesbians to attempt to identify crucial stages or turning-point experiences in the process of reaching a homosexual identity. Following other developmental models, these models typically have an assumption of linear development. The process begins with no sexual identity or a presumption of heterosexuality and passes through experiences in a middle phase that could include some or all of the following: increasing awareness of attraction to members of the same sex, increasing knowledge about the category of "homosexual," sexual involvement with same-sex partners, and self-labeling as homosexual. The final stage of development consists of the individual's acceptance of a strong lesbian or gay male identity. (See especially, Plummer, 1975; Troiden, 1979, 1988; Gramick, 1984; Sophie, 1986.)

One of the problems with a linear model is that it is assumed that those who reach the final stage have all passed through the same series of steps. Research designed to document "stage-sequential models," however, revealed diversity as well as patterns; the more specific the stages or steps were in a given model, the less likely the stages matched the experiences of the different individuals under study (Sophie, 1986, p. 50). . . .

Multiple Dimensions of a Homosexual Identity

The research on identity development documented not only that individuals followed different paths for reaching new identities, but also that identities, once formed, were not always as stable and permanent as people had thought they would be. Golden (1987) concludes "that the assumption that we inherently strive for congruence between our sexual feelings, activities, and identities may not be warranted, and that given the fluidity of sexual feelings, congruence may not be an achievable state" (p. 31). Thus, behavior, emotions, and identities do not necessarily develop into stable packages that can be easily labeled as heterosexual, gay or lesbian, or even bisexual, even though the individual or the society or the gay community might desire such consistency. Both researchers and therapists should be cautious about categorizing under familiar labels people who may in fact be growing and changing their identities. This is not to say that all identities are unstable; many individuals develop a strong and stable sense of self that serves as a guide and source of comfort to their behavior and life choices. But others continue to consider new information about themselves and may be more or less aware that where they are at any point in time is just one step in an ongoing developmental process. Thus, undergoing periods of questioning one's sexual identity may occur at various points in the life cycle. . . .

As researchers and therapists alike are acknowledging the different combinations of components of identity, they can watch for patterns. One pattern that was expected from Freudian theory and one which still shows up in views among the general population is not a pattern at all. The expected pattern was that gender identity—one's own sense of being male or female—would predict one's sexual preference. Freud's theory assumed that "gender inversion" helped explain homosexuality. Consequently, researchers have looked to see if homosexual males had acquired female gender identities, and if lesbians had male gender identities. Although the research has found that a small proportion of homosexual respondents indicate cross-gender identity, Luria (1979) notes, "Male homosexuals almost universally feel they are males, and female homosexuals virtually all feel they are women" (p. 179; see also Storms, 1980; Harry, 1982; Bell, Weinberg, & Hammersmith, 1981a, p. 188). . . .

Sexual Preference and Gender Role Behavior

Gender role behavior, or simply gender role, refers to patterns of behavior or activities routinely expected of a particular gender. Thus, males are expected to engage in masculine behavior patterns, thereby assuming a male gender role. However, individuals may develop a preference for the traditional activities of the opposite gender, and gender role preference may vary separately from either gender identity or sexual identity. Harry (1982) has diagrammed the various combinations, noting, for example, that a heterosexual male with a male gender identity could have a feminine gender role preference. He is, thus, biologically male, views himself as a male, but has a preference for activities routinely associated with women. Since this is behavior, it could be expressed in many different ways, such as through a pattern of effeminate behavior, cross-dressing, or by taking a job in a traditionally female occupation.

Cross-dressing and interest in cross-gender activities during childhood have been reported by adult homosexuals significantly more often than by adult heterosexuals. For example, in the Bell, Weinberg, and Hammersmith (1981b) study, 68 percent of the white homosexual males reported that they were "Not at all" or "Very little" interested in "boys' activities (e.g., baseball, football)" during grade school compared with 11 percent of the white heterosexual males. The matching statistics for black homosexual males were 37 percent compared with 4 percent for black heterosexual males. The homosexual males, more often than heterosexual males, reported that they had enjoyed stereotypical girls' activities, such as playing house, hopscotch, and jacks. Harry (1982) saw these results as replicating his own research findings. Similar differences were found for the female respondents. Seventy-one percent of the white homosexual women reported they "Very much" enjoyed playing typical boys' activities (e.g., baseball, football) compared with 28 percent of the white heterosexual women. The homosexual respondents also reported having cross-dressed and pretending to be the opposite gender more often than the heterosexual respondents did (Bell, Weinberg, & Hammersmith, 1981a). The Bell et al. (1981a) research concludes that "a child's display of gender nonconformity greatly increases the likelihood of that child's becoming homosexual regardless of his or her family background and regardless of how much the child identifies with either parent" (p. 189). The researchers note, however, that gender nonconformity was not characteristic of most of the homosexual respondents and was reported by a minority of heterosexuals (Bell et al., 1981a, p. 188).

. . . We are unable to draw a straight line from behavior patterns or even gender role preferences to sexual preference. . . . Clearly, the environment of prejudice and hostility towards homosexuality has an impact on the process of acquiring a sexual identity—be it homosexual or heterosexual. Herek (1985) notes that the influence may also flow the other way—that the process of developing an identity helps reinforce hostility; thus, "individuals also may gain a sense of who they are by clarifying what they are not" (p. 149). Particularly as homosexuals have developed a stronger sense of themselves as a group, heterosexuals may have developed more of an identity as well. Indeed, as lesbian and gay communities have become more visible and organized, the opposition to them has also become more visible and organized. The in-group gets its identity by contrasting itself with the out-group, and the conflict promotes cohesion within both groups. This fundamental social process is one which sociology has documented as one of its earliest contributions to understanding society. In the case of homosexuality, however, we must recall that the negative label from society came long before persons so labeled organized themselves into a group. . . .

CONCLUSION

. . . I have argued here that the meanings given to behavior and to people who engage in that behavior derive from the culture and structure of the society involved. The major theoretical debate discussed in the chapter is whether or not those who fit our cultural category of "homosexuals" have something that defines their essence as homosexuals or are very much like everyone else except for their sexual preference, which was acquired over their lifespan in the same way as their other identities and in the same way as heterosexual identities. At least one theorist, Kenneth Plummer proposes that we consider both positions to be quite possibly correct. For example, a sexual orientation may be a kind of "essence," formed early in childhood and affecting later choices. Plummer (1981) notes,

> while some people develop restrictive and rigid orientations, others may be open and flexible, while still others may develop no "orientations" at all. . . . Likewise identities are—in all likelihood—highly variable throughout social encounters; but while for some people this may mean drastic restructuring of self conceptions at critical turning points in life, others may develop relatively stable identities at early moments in life and use these as foci to orientate most future contact. (p. 72)

Thus, diversity of experience is a key here; individuals have different ways of coping with life's experiences and different routes for arriving at a place where they feel comfortable with who they are and what they like best. But through it all, the learning and becoming take place within a social environment highly affected by the rules and guidelines of the culture at hand. And it should be remembered that cultural expectations can and do change. The process of forming and maintaining a positive homosexual identity can be especially complex and problematic in the face of conflicting pressures, definitions and attitudes, as the concerns and priorities of the gay community and the surrounding culture change over time.

REFERENCES

Adam, B.D. (1985). Age, structure, and sexuality: Reflections on the anthropological evidence on homosexual relations. *Journal of Homosexuality, 11* (3/4). 19–33.

Adam, B.D. (1987). *The rise of a gay and lesbian movement.* Boston: Twayne Publishers.

Allen, M.R. (1967). *Male cults and secret initiations in Melanesia.* Melbourne, Australia: Melbourne University Press.

Bell, A.P., Weinberg, M.S., & Hammersmith, S.K. (1981a). *Sexual preference: Its development in men and women.* Bloomington, IN: Indiana University Press.

Bell, A.P., Weinberg, M.S., & Hammersmith, S.K. (1981b). *Sexual preference: Statistical appendix.* Bloomington, IN: Indiana University Press.

Blumstein, P.W. & Schwartz, P. (1976). Bisexuality in women. *Archives of Sexual Behavior, 5,* 171–181.

Browning, C. (1984). Changing theories of lesbianism: Challenging the stereotypes. In T. Darty & S. Potter (Eds.), *Women-identified women* (pp. 11–30). Palo Alto, CA: Mayfield.

Callendar, C., & Kochems, L. (1983). The North American berdache. *Current Anthropology, 24,* 443–470.

Dover, K.J. (1978). *Greek homosexuality.* New York: Vintage Books.

Foucault, M. (1978). *The history of sexuality. Volume 1: An introduction.* New York: Random House.

Freud, S. (1905/1953). Three essays on the theory of sexuality. *Standard edition of the complete psychological works of Sigmund Freud, 7,* 136. London: Hogarth Press. (Originally published 1905).

Freud, S. (1931/1961). Female sexuality. *Standard edition of the complete psychological works of Sigmund Freud, 21,* 223. London: Hogarth Press. (Originally published 1931).

Gagnon, J.H. (1977). *Human sexualities.* Illinois: Scott, Foresman.

Golden, C. (1987). Diversity and variability in women's sexual identities. In Boston Lesbian Psychologies Collective (Eds.), *Lesbian psychologies: Explorations and Challenges* (pp. 18–34). Urbana, IL: University of Illinois Press.

Gramick, J. (1984). Developing a lesbian identity. In T. Darty & S. Potter (Eds.), *Women-identified women* (pp. 31–44). Palo Alto, CA: Mayfield.

Greenberg, D.F., & Bystryn, M.H. (1984). Capitalism, bureaucracy and male homosexuality. *Contemporary Crises, 8,* 33–56.

Harry, J. (1982). *Gay children grown up. Gender culture and gender deviance.* New York: Praeger.

Herdt, G.H. (1981). *Guardians of the flutes.* New York: McGraw-Hill.

Herdt, G.H. (Ed.). (1984). *Ritualized homosexuality in Melanesia.* Berkeley, CA: University of California Press.

Herek, G.M. (1985). On doing, being and not being: Prejudice and the social construction of sexuality. *Journal of Homosexuality, 12*(1), 135–151.

Hooker, E. (1969). Parental relations and male homosexuality in patient and nonpatient samples. *Journal of Consulting and Clinical Psychology, 33,* 140–142.

Hoult, T.F. (1984). Human sexuality in biological perspective: Theoretical and methodological considerations. *Journal of Homosexuality, 9*(2/3), 137–155.

Hudson, W.W., & Ricketts, W.A. (1980). A strategy for the measurement of homophobia. *Journal of Homosexuality, 5*(4), 357–372.

Humphreys, L. (1975). *Tearoom trade.* Chicago: Aldine.

King, D. (1981). Gender confusions: Psychological and psychiatric conceptions of transvestism and transsexualism. In K. Plummer (Ed.), *The making of the modern homosexual* (pp. 155–184). Totowa, NJ: Barnes and Noble.

Kinsey, A.C., Pomeroy, W.B., & Martin, C.E. (1948). *Sexual behavior in the human male.* Philadelphia: W.B. Saunders.

Luria, Z. (1979). Psychosocial determinants of gender identity, role, and orientation. In H.A. Katchadourian (Ed.), *Human sexuality: A comparative and developmental perspective* (pp. 163–193). Berkeley, CA: University of California Press.

Paul, J.P. (1984). The bisexual identity: An idea without social recognition. *Journal of Homosexuality, 9*(2/3), 45–63.

Plummer, K. (1975). *Sexual stigma: An interactionist account.* London: Routledge & Kegan Paul.

Plummer, K. (Ed). (1981). *The making of the modern homosexual.* Totowa, NJ: Barnes and Noble.

Rich, A. (1980). Compulsory heterosexuality and lesbian experience. *Signs, 5,* 631–660.

Richardson, D. (1981). Theoretical perspectives of homosexuality. In J. Hart & D. Richardson (Ed.), *The theory and practice of homosexuality.* London: Routledge & Kegan Paul.

Richardson, D. (1984). The dilemma of essentiality in homosexual theory. *Journal of Homosexuality.* 9(2/3), 79–90.

Richardson, D., & Hart, J. (1981). The development and maintenance of a homosexual identity. In J. Hart & D. Richardson (Eds.). *The theory & practice of homosexuality* (pp. 73–92). London: Routledge & Kegan Paul.

Ricketts, W. (1984). Biological research on homosexuality: Ansell's cow or Occam's razor? *Journal of Homosexuality, 9* (2/3), 45–63.

Siegelman, M. (1974). Parental background of male homosexuals and heterosexuals. *Archives of Sexual Behavior, 3,* 3–18.

Sophie, J. (1986). A critical examination of stage theories of lesbian identity development. *Journal of Homosexuality, 12*(2), 39–51.

Stoller, R.J. (1980). Problems with the term "homosexuality." *The Hillside Journal of Clinical Psychiatry, 2,* 3–25.

Storms, M.D. (1980). Theories of sexual orientation. *Journal of Personality and Social Psychology, 38,* 783–792.

Troiden, R.R. (1988). *Gay and lesbian identity: A sociological analysis* Dix Hills, NY: General Hall.

Weeks, J. (1981). Discourse, desire and sexual deviance: Some problems in a history of homosexuality. In K. Plummer (Ed.), *The making of the modern homosexual* (pp. 76–111). London: Hutchinson.

Whitam, F.L., & Mathy, R.M. (1986). Male homosexuality in four societies. New York: Praeger.

READING 14

The Development of Gay, Lesbian, and Bisexual Identities

Heidi Levine
Nancy J. Evans

To understand the issues faced by gay, lesbian, and bisexual people on college campuses, we must first examine the life experiences of these individuals. What it means to be gay, lesbian, or bisexual is unique to each person; but some commonalities exist as individuals become aware of their attraction to others of the same sex and integrate these feelings into other aspects of their identity.

The research that considers timing and age factors in the gay and lesbian identity develop-

Heidi Levine is assistant professor of psychology at Radford University. Nancy J. Evans is associate professor of education at Iowa State University.

ment process suggests that many developmental issues occur during the traditional undergraduate years (Bell, Weinberg, & Hammersmith, 1981; McDonald, 1982). As student development professionals, we know that this is a key time for identity development in general (Chickering, 1969; Erikson, 1986; Moore & Upcraft, 1990). College and university students are faced with many areas in which they need to reconsider their self-perceptions, develop new skills, and master developmental tasks. The possibility or certainty that one is gay, lesbian, or bisexual complicates these developmental challenges and adds an additional set of complicated issues that must be resolved. . . .

[Before we proceed,] a distinction must be made between the terms *homosexual identity* and *gay identity.* Homosexual identity is a narrower term, referring to sexual behavior only, whereas gay identity suggests the total experience of being gay (Warren, 1974). The use of the term *homosexual identity* is often viewed negatively by the gay and lesbian community because it has been used as a diagnostic label by many clinicians and is often associated with a negative self-image. *Gay identity,* however, has a positive connotation within the gay and lesbian communities and is seen as encompassing emotional, lifestyle, and political aspects of life rather than being exclusively sexual (Beane, 1981).

Jandt and Darsey (1981) noted that all definitions of homosexual or gay identity have in common a shift in perception of self as a member of the majority to self as a member of the minority. Along with this change in perception comes adoption of a new set of values and a redefinition of acceptable behavior. As such, development of a gay, lesbian, or bisexual identity is mainly an internal, psychological process. . . .

LESBIAN IDENTITY DEVELOPMENT

Differences in Identity Development Between Gay Men and Lesbians

Largely because of differences in the way men and women are socialized in Western society, a number of variations are evident in the patterns of identity development and lifestyles of gay men and lesbians (Cass, 1979).

The timing of events associated with the process of developing a gay or lesbian identity is different for men and women. Lesbians exhibit more variation than gay men in age at which awareness of attraction to individuals of the same sex occurs (Moses & Hawkins, 1986), and evidence suggests that gay men become aware of same-sex attractions, act on those attractions, and self-identify as gay at earlier ages than do lesbians. Men also disclose their homosexual identity earlier than women (DeMonteflores & Schultz, 1978; Sohier, 1985–1986; Troiden, 1988). Henderson (1984) proposed two hypotheses in reference to these timing variations: (1) women's sexual orientation may be more variable than men's and more tied to particular relationships, or (2) women are more likely to be influenced by societal norms that expect everyone to be heterosexual and so adhere longer to heterosexual behavior patterns and a heterosexual identity. Gramick (1984) concurred with the latter point of view.

Lesbians tend to establish ongoing love relationships earlier than gay men (Troiden, 1988) and are more likely to commit to a homosexual identity within the context of an intense emotional relationship, whereas gay men do so within the context of their sexual experiences (Groves & Ventura, 1983; Sohier, 1985–1986; Troiden, 1988). In general, emotional attachment is the most significant aspect of relationship for lesbians, but sexual activity is most important for gay men (DeMonteflores & Schultz, 1978; Gramick, 1984). As a result, lesbians tend to look for and maintain more stable, long-term relationships than do gay men (Gramick, 1984).

Although this pattern may be changing because of concern arising from the spread of AIDS, historically, gay men have been involved with many more one-time-only sexual partners than have lesbians (Kimmel, 1978; Marmor, 1980). This pattern, again, can be related to differences in the manner in which men and women are socialized; men are expected to be interested in sex before love, whereas women look for love before sex (Henderson, 1984; Westfall, 1988). Men are also encouraged to experiment sexually more than women (Coleman, 1981–1982). As one might expect given these socialization patterns, "tricking" (picking up unknown individuals for brief sexual liaisons) has been much more common among gay men than among lesbians who tend to meet others and interact in more intimate, private settings (Cronin, 1974; Gramick, 1984; Nuehring, Fein, & Tyler, 1974).

DeMonteflores and Schultz (1978) suggested that lesbians often use feelings to avoid thinking of themselves as homosexual whereas men use denial of feelings as a way to avoid self-labeling as gay. Women use the rationale that they merely love one particular woman, but men view their homosexual activity as insignificant because they are not emotionally involved with their partners.

Some researchers (Bell & Weinberg, 1978; Sohier, 1985–1986) have suggested that acceptance of homosexuality is easier for women than for men since sexual relationships between women are less stigmatized than those between men (DeMonteflores & Schultz, 1978; Marmor, 1980; Paul, 1984). The women's movement may have assisted lesbians to come out; there has been no comparable movement for men (DeMonteflores & Schultz, 1978). Also, since many lesbians become aware of their identity at later ages, they may have resolved other identity issues and be more adept at handling the coming out process than gay men who generally self-identity during their teens (Paul, 1984).

A number of writers have suggested that lesbians are more likely to view their sexuality as a choice, whereas gay men see it as a discovery (Henderson, 1984; Kimmel, 1978; Westfall, 1988). This distinction is particularly true for feminist lesbians. Feminist lesbians also identify more strongly with the political-philosophical aspects of their lifestyle, whereas gay men are more concerned with the physical-social aspects (Jandt & Darsey, 1981).

With regard to relationship development, lesbians more closely resemble other women than they do gay men (Marmor, 1980). Women, in general, are more concerned with the relational aspects of their attachments to other people and focus on establishing intimate, long-term relationships. Because they fear displeasing others, they may have difficulty breaking norms and acknowledging that they cannot accept the roles family, friends, and society have identified for them. Men, however, are taught to be independent, competitive, and autonomous. These factors appear to play an important role in the differences exhibited between lesbians and gay men.

Relational Versus Political Lesbians

Great variation exists in the way lesbians describe themselves and how they come to identify themselves as lesbian (Miller & Fowlkes, 1980). And as Golden (1987) noted, feelings, behaviors, and self-identification do not always agree nor do they always remain the same over time. Two major philosophical approaches to lesbianism can be identified in the literature, however; a traditional relational viewpoint that focuses on emotional and sexual attraction to other women (Moses, 1978; Ponse, 1980) and a radical feminist perspective that views the lesbian lifestyle as a political statement (Faraday, 1981; Lewis, 1979).

A number of theorists note that a distinction must be made between women who view their lesbianism as beyond their control and those who see it as a choice (Golden, 1987; Richardson, 1981b). Generally, lesbian feminists adhere to the latter viewpoint, but relational lesbians take the former position (Richardson, 1981b; Sophie, 1987).

In a small study of 20 self-identified lesbians, Henderson (1979) distinguished three groups: (1) *ideological lesbians,* women who can be viewed as radical feminists for whom a lesbian lifestyle is politically correct; (2) *personal lesbians,* women concerned with establishing an independent identity who find homosexuality supportive of this goal and who view lesbianism as a choice; and (3) *interpersonal lesbians,* women who find themselves involved with another woman, often to their chagrin, and who experience their involvement as a discovery rather than a choice.

Development of a Lesbian Identity

Although a number of writers believe that sexual activity between women has become more acceptable as a result of the women's movement and the freeing of sexual norms (Blumstein & Schwartz, 1974; Henderson, 1979), the developmental process of identifying oneself as a lesbian is still difficult.

Many lesbians recall being "tomboys" as youngsters: a preference for "masculine" rather than "feminine" activities as a child is often the first indication that they do not fit the heterosexual pattern (Lewis, 1979). This awareness intensifies during puberty when the adolescent finds herself attracted to women rather than men. This discovery can lead to intense feelings of loneliness. Because of the difficulty young lesbians experience in finding a support group of other lesbians or identifying positive role models, this period is particularly difficult in the person's life (Sophie, 1982).

Most lesbians have a history of sexual involvement with men and, contrary to popular belief, become involved with women not because of unsatisfactory relationships with men but rather because they experience greater emotional and sexual satisfaction from women (Groves & Ventura, 1983). Indeed, women frequently identify themselves as bisexual prior to adopting a lesbian identity.

It needs to be noted that most lesbians go through a period during which they reject their identity because they are unable to deal with the stigma associated with the label *lesbian* (Groves & Ventura, 1983). Often they seek security and an escape from their feelings of isolation and anxiety in heterosexual activity or marriage (Lewis, 1979; Sophie, 1982).

Usually involvement in an intense, all-encompassing love relationship with another woman is the decisive factor in embracing a lesbian identity (Groves & Ventura, 1983; Lewis, 1979). Such an involvement often develops slowly, starting out as a friendship.

Sophie (1982) noted that it is difficult for lesbians to feel good about themselves until they reconceptualize the term *lesbian* into positive terms. This process rarely occurs in isolation. Interaction with other lesbians and other sources of information about positive aspects of a lesbian lifestyle are helpful.

Coming out, both to other lesbians and to accepting heterosexuals, is also supportive of establishment of a lesbian identity (Richardson, 1981b; Sophie, 1982). Often the individual decides to come out because it takes too much energy to maintain a heterosexual image. Usually the individual comes out first to close friends who appear trustworthy (Lewis, 1979). As the woman becomes involved in the lesbian community, pressure is often applied to come out publicly (Lewis, 1979). Doing so can be viewed as the final step in the solidification of a lesbian identity.

Identity Development Models

A number of theorists have proposed models of identity development specific for lesbians. Ponse (1980) noted three steps in lesbian identity development: becoming aware of feeling different because of sexual-emotional attraction to other women, becoming involved in a lesbian relationship, and seeking out other lesbians. This model differs from many of the gay male models in that a serious relationship is formed *before* the individual becomes involved in the lesbian community.

Gramick (1984) pointed out that in attempting to make meaning of their experiences, many lesbians reinterpret past events, feelings, and behaviors as sexual that were not perceived as such at the time they occurred. She suggested that the process of developing a lesbian identity first involves strong emotional attachment to other women leading to a feeling of "differentness" within the context of the social environment but without a recognition that this difference might be labeled as lesbian. In adolescence, heterosexual socialization patterns strongly influence all young women and often delay development of homosexual identity. Meeting other lesbians and becoming emotionally and sexually involved with another woman are usually key events in confirming and accepting a lesbian identity. In Gramick's model, supportive others, as well as sexual involvements, play a crucial role in identity development.

Lewis (1979) identified five stages in the development of a lesbian identity and focused more on the political aspects of lesbianism. Her stages include (1) experience of discomfort with the heterosexual and patriarchal nature of socialization, (2) labeling self as different from other women, (3) becoming aware of lesbianism, (4) finding and becoming involved in a lesbian community, and (5) educating self about the lesbian lifestyle.

Also writing from a feminist perspective, Faderman (1984) suggested that . . . the first step for lesbian feminists, involves rejection of societal norms concerning the role of women and acceptance of a lesbian identity. This step is followed by experiences of prejudice and discrimination resulting in feelings of aloneness outside of the community of radical feminists and, finally, by sexual experiences with other women. Faderman suggested that because lesbian feminists are exposed to and accept the movement's political philosophy prior to their first homosexual experience they may not experience the guilt and shame felt by other lesbians and gay men. . . .

BISEXUAL IDENTITY

The gay rights movement has generally ignored bisexual men and women. Although Kinsey and his colleagues (Kinsey, Pomeroy, & Martin, 1948; Kinsey, Pomeroy, Martin, & Gebhard, 1953) discovered that more individuals are bisexual than strictly homosexual, later researchers and theorists have held to a rigid dichotomization of sexual behavior as either heterosexual or homosexual (Klein, Sepekoff, & Wolf, 1985). Acknowledging and attempting to understand the variation and fluidity of sexual attraction and behavior are important if we are to advance our knowledge of human sexuality and sexual identity development (Paul, 1985). . . .

Bisexuality comes in many forms. MacDonald (1982) identified four areas of variation: (1) individuals may have a preference for one gender over the other or may have no preference; (2) they may have partners of both sexes either simultaneously or sequentially; (3) they may be monogamous or have several partners; and (4) their bisexuality may be transitory, transitional, a basis for homosexual denial, or an enduring pattern. Zinik (1985) proposed the following criteria for assuming a bisexual identity: (1) being sexually aroused by both males and females, (2) desiring sexual activity with both, and (3) adopting bisexuality as a sexual identity label.

Two contrasting theories have been offered to account for bisexuality (Zinik, 1985): The conflict model suggests that bisexuality is associated with conflict, confusion, ambivalence, and an inability to determine one's sexual preference; the flexibility model hypothesizes that bisexuality is characterized by flexibility, personal growth, and fulfillment. The media tends to adhere to the former view, presenting bisexuality as a confused or conflicted lifestyle, as retarded sexual development, or as a denial of a true heterosexual or homosexual identity (Hansen & Evans, 1985).

Because the stigma attached to bisexuality is greater in many ways than that associated with homosexuality, many people who are bisexual in behavior do not identify themselves as such (Blumstein & Schwartz, 1974; Golden, 1987; Hansen & Evans, 1985; Paul, 1984; Zinik, 1985). Although some individuals are quite open about their identity, others hide it from both the heterosexual and the homosexual communities (Blumstein & Schwartz, 1977a). MacDonald (1981) suggested that bisexuals are less willing to disclose their identity than any other group because they believe that neither gays nor heterosexuals will accept them.

Bisexuals experience the same type of oppression as gay men and lesbians because society tends to group bisexuals with homosexuals. Heterosexuals assume that individuals are trying to excuse their homosexual inclinations by labeling themselves as bisexual (Blumstein & Schwartz, 1977a).

Because they do not conform to heterosexist culture, many bisexuals tend to align themselves with the gay and lesbian communities (Shuster, 1987). However, an individual's self-identification as bisexual is frequently met with skepticism in the homosexual community as well and viewed as an attempt to avoid the stigma of, or commitment to, a gay or lesbian lifestyle (Paul, 1984). The lesbian community, in particular, seems to have difficulty accepting bisexuality (Golden, 1987). Bisexuals are faced with considerable pressure to identify as homosexual and to behave in an exclusively homosexual manner (Blumstein & Schwartz, 1974; Hansen & Evans, 1985; Paul, 1985). Frequently, bisexuals respond to this pressure by pretending to be either exclusively homosexual or heterosexual depending on the social situation (Zinik, 1985).

Results of a study of 156 bisexuals conducted in the early 1970s (Blumstein & Schwartz, 1976, 1977a, 1977b) suggested that no identifiable bisexual life script exists and that identity and partner preferences change over the life course. Sexual experience and identity are not necessarily synonymous. The researchers identified several conditions that they saw as necessary for assumption of a bisexual identity: labeling, conflicting homosexual and heterosexual experiences, and contact with other bisexuals.

Zinik (1985) suggested that bisexual identity development may occur in stages similar to those proposed by Cass (1979) for homosexual identity formation. As with gay men and lesbians, the coming out process is one of both self-acknowledgment and disclosure to others (Shuster, 1987). Wide variation exists, however, in the timing and ordering of sexual experiences leading to a bisexual identification. In addition, because bisexuality lacks societal and scientific affirmation, acceptance of such an identity requires a high tolerance for ambiguity and is even harder than acceptance of a homosexual identity (MacDonald, 1981, Richardson & Hart, 1981). In most cases, bisexuals tend to identify in terms of particular relationships in which they are involved rather than with the abstract label bisexual (Shuster, 1987).

Although gay men and lesbians have formed support groups and political organizations, few such groups of bisexuals exist (Paul, 1985). As MacDonald (1981) noted, there is no "bisexual liberation movement" (p. 21). As a result, no clear bisexual identity exists, and little scientific research has examined the life experiences of bisexual men and women.

REFERENCES

Beane, J. (1981). "I'd rather be dead than gay": Counseling gay men who are coming out. *Personnel and Guidance Journal, 60,* 222–226.

Bell, A. P., & Weinberg, M. S. (1978). *Homosexualities: A study of diversity among men and women.* New York: Simon and Schuster.

Bell, A. P., Weinberg, M. S., & Hammersmith, S. K. (1981). *Sexual preference: Its development in men and women.* Bloomington: Indiana University.

Blumstein, P. W., & Schwartz, P. (1974). Lesbianism and bisexuality. In E. Goode & R. R. Troiden (Eds.), *Sexual deviance and sexual deviants* (pp. 278–295). New York: Morrow.

Blumstein, P. W., & Schwartz, P. (1976). Bisexuality in women. *Archives of Sexual Behavior, 5,* 171–181.

Blumstein, P. W., & Schwartz, P. (1977a). Bisexuality in men. In C. A. B. Warren (Ed.), *Sexuality: Encounters, identities, and relationships* (pp. 79–98). Beverly Hills, CA: Sage.

Blumstein, P. W., & Schwartz, P. (1977a). Bisexuality: Some social psychological issues. *Journal of Social Issues, 33,* 30–45.

Cass, V. C. (1979). Homosexual identity formation: A theoretical model. *Journal of Homosexuality, 4,* 219–235.

Chickering, A. W. (1969). *Education and identity.* San Francisco: Jossey-Bass.

Coleman, E. (1981–1982). Developmental stages of the coming out process. *Journal of Homosexuality, 7,* 31–43.

Cronin, D. M. (1974). Coming out among lesbians. In E. Goode & R. R. Troiden (Eds.), *Sexual deviance and sexual deviants* (pp. 268–277). New York: Morrow.

DeMonteflores, C., & Schultz, S. (1978). Coming out: Similarities and differences for lesbians and gay men. *Journal of Social Issues, 34*(3), 59–72.

Erikson, E. H. (1968). *Identity: Youth and crisis.* New York: Norton.

Faderman, L. (1984). The "new gay" lesbians. *Journal of Homosexuality, 10*(3/4), 85–95.

Faraday, A. (1981). Liberating lesbian research. In K. Plummer (Ed.), *The making of the modern homosexual* (pp. 112–129). Totowa, NJ: Barnes & Noble.

Golden, C. (1987). Diversity and variability in women's sexual identities. In Boston Lesbian Psychologies Collective (Eds.), *Lesbian psychologies: Explorations and challenges* (pp. 19–34). Urbana, IL: University of Illinois Press.

Gramick, J. (1984). Developing a lesbian identity. In T. Darty & S. Potter (Eds.), *Women-identified women.* (pp. 31–44). Palo Alto, CA: Mayfield.

Groves, P. A., & Ventura, L. A. (1983). The lesbian coming out process: Therapeutic considerations. *Personnel and Guidance Journal, 62,* 146–149.

Hansen, C. E., & Evans, A. (1985). Bisexuality reconsidered: An idea in pursuit of a definition. In F. Klein & T. J. Wolf (Eds.), *Bisexualities: Theory and research* (pp. 1–6). New York: Haworth.

Henderson, A. F. (1979). College age lesbianism as a developmental phenomenon. *Journal of American College Health, 28*(3), 176–178.

Henderson, A. F. (1984). Homosexuality in the college years: Development differences between men and women. *Journal of American College Health, 32,* 216–219.

Jandt, F. E., & Darsey, J. (1981). Coming out as a communicative process. In J. W. Chesebro (Ed.), *Gayspeak* (pp. 12–27). New York: Pilgrim.

Kimmel, D. C. (1978). Adult development and aging: A gay perspective. *Journal of Social Issues, 34,* 113–130.

Kinsey, A. C., Pomeroy, W. B., & Martin, C. E. (1948). *Sexual behavior in the human male.* Philadelphia: Saunders.

Kinsey, A. C., Pomeroy, W. B., Martin, C. E., & Gebhard, P. H. (1953). *Sexual behavior in the human female.* Philadelphia: Saunders.

Klein, F., Sepekoff, B., & Wolf, T. J. (1985). Sexual orientation: A multivariable dynamic process. In F. Klein & T. J. Wolf (Eds.), *Bisexualities: Theory and research* (pp. 35–49). New York: Haworth.

Lewis, S. G. (1979). *Sunday's women: A report on lesbian life today.* Boston: Beacon.

MacDonald, Jr., A. P. (1981). Bisexuality: Some comments on research and theory. *Journal of Homosexuality, 6*(3), 21–35.

MacDonald, Jr., A. P. (1982). Research on sexual orientation: A bridge that touches both shores but doesn't meet in the middle. *Journal of Sex Education and Therapy, 8,* 9–13.

Marmor, J. (1980). Overview: The multiple roots of homosexual behavior. In J. Marmor (Ed.), *Homosexual behavior: A modern reappraisal* (pp. 3–22). New York: Basic Books.

McDonald, G. J. (1982). Individual differences in the coming out process for gay men: Implications for theoretical models. *Journal of Homosexuality, 8*(1), 47–90.

Miller, P. Y., & Fowlkes, M. R. (1980). Social and behavior constructions of female sexuality. *Signs, 5,* 783–800.

Moore, L. V., & Upcraft, M. L. (1990). Theory in student affairs: Evolving perspectives. In L. V. Moore (Ed.), *Evolving theoretical perspectives on students.* (pp. 3–23). *New Directions for Student Services,* No. 51. San Francisco: Jossey-Bass.

Moses, A. E. (1978). *Identity management in lesbian women.* New York: Praeger.

Moses, A. E., & Hawkins, R. O. (1986). *Counseling lesbian women and gay men: A life issues approach.* Columbus, OH: Merrill.

Nuehring, E., Fein, S. B., & Tyler, M. (1974). The gay college student: Perspectives for mental health professionals. *The Counseling Psychologist, 4,* 64–72.

Paul, J. P. (1984). The bisexual identity: An idea without social recognition. In J. P. DeCecco & M. G. Shively (Eds.), *Bisexual and homosexual identities: Critical theoretical issues* (pp. 45–63). New York: Haworth.

Paul, J. (1985). Bisexuality: Reassessing our paradigms of sexuality. In F. Klein & T. J. Wolf (Eds.), *Bisexualities: Theory and research* (pp. 21–34). New York: Haworth.

Ponse, B. (1980). Lesbians and their worlds. In J. Marmor (Ed.), *Homosexual behavior: A modern reappraisal.* (pp. 157–175). New York: Basic Books.

Richardson, D. (1981b). Lesbian identities. In J. Hart & D. Richardson (Eds.), *The theory and practice of homosexuality* (pp. 111–124). London: Routledge & Kegan Paul.

Richardson, D., & Hart, J. (1981). The development and maintenance of a homosexual identity. In J. Hart & D. Richardson (Eds.), *The theory and practice of homosexuality* (pp. 73–92). London: Routledge & Kegan Paul.

Shuster, R. (1987). Sexuality as a continuum: The bisexual identity. In Boston Lesbian Psychologies Collective (Eds.), *Lesbian psychologies: Explorations and challenges* (pp. 56–71). Urbana, IL: University of Illinois Press.

Sohier, R. (1985–1986). Homosexual mutuality: Variation on a theme by E. Erikson. *Journal of Homosexuality, 12*(2), 25–38.

Sophie, J. (1982). Counseling lesbians. *Personnel and Guidance Journal, 60*(6), 341–344.

Sophie, J. (1987). Internalized homophobia and lesbian identity. *Journal of Homosexuality, 14,* 53–65.

Troiden, R. R. (1988). Homosexual identity development. *Journal of Adolescent Health Care, 9*(2), 105–113.

Warren, C. A. B. (1974). *Identity and community in the gay world.* New York: Wiley.

Westfall, S. B. (1988). Gay and lesbian college students: Identity issues and student affairs. *Journal of the Indiana University Student Personnel Association,* 1–6.

Zinik, G. (1985). Identity conflict or adaptive flexibility? Bisexuality reconsidered. In F. Klein & T. J. Wolf (Eds.), *Bisexualities: Theory and research* (pp. 7–19). New York: Haworth.

PERSONAL ACCOUNT

An Opportunity to Get Even

When I was a freshman in high school, my parents sent me to a private school. I got harassed a lot by a few of the sophomore guys there because I wore pants with the uniform (instead of the pleated miniskirts), I didn't wear makeup, and probably most important, I would not date any of them (and couldn't give a reason for that). Most of this harassment was anti-gay slurs with specific references to me on the bathroom walls. One of the guys often yelled comments such as "Hey Dyke, I got what you need right here" while grabbing his crotch. My name was written on many of the bathroom stalls (both male and female), with my sexual orientation, and a rhyme about a gang bang.

After about six weeks of this, I confided in my soccer coach. I told her about the harassment and came out to her. I don't know what I expected, but I did not expect any positive reaction. She told me she was glad I came out to her, and she promised to keep my confidentiality. She also offered me an opportunity to get back at the three guys who were harassing me the most. She told me that this was my battle and that I was going to have to learn how to fight.

She knew that the three guys were part of the boys' soccer team, and made arrangements so that, as part of the homecoming festivities, our soccer team would play theirs. By doing this she gave me the opportunity to "show them up" and make them look bad in front of the school. I did my best to accomplish that. For example, every time any of them came near me, I would run into them or trip them. My goal was to embarrass them in front of the school. It did not look good for the guys because a "dyke" challenged and defeated the "jocks."

What my soccer coach did for me meant a lot. First, she was literally the only person I was out to at that time, so she was a source of support. Further, she went out of her way to help me get even with the harassers. Because of what she did for me, the harassment stopped.

Carol A. Mabry

EXPERIENCING DIFFERENCE

FRAMEWORK ESSAY II: KEY CONCEPTS

discredited and discreditable The discredited are those whose stigma is known or apparent to others. The discreditable are those whose stigma is unknown or invisible to others; they are not yet discredited. (See pages 175–81)

double consciousness A concept first offered by W. E. B. Du Bois to describe seeing oneself (or members of one's group) through the eyes of a critical, dominant group member. (See pages 178–79)

entitlement The belief that one has the right to respect, protection, reward, and other privileges. (See page 170)

flaming As used in this text, a flagrant display of one's stigmatized status; more often used to refer to gay men acting effeminately. (See pages 178–81)

looping or rereading Interpreting (and usually dismissing) someone's words or actions because of the status that the person occupies. (See page 173)

marked and unmarked statuses A marked status is one identified as "special" in some way, for example, a *blind* musician, or a *woman* doctor. Unmarked statuses, such as musician or doctor, do not have such qualifiers. (See pages 170–71)

passing Not revealing a stigmatized identity. (See pages 175–78)

privilege The advantages provided by some statuses. (See pages 167–75)

FRAMEWORK ESSAY

In the first framework essay, we considered the social construction of difference as master statuses were named, aggregated, dichotomized, and stigmatized. Now we turn to the experience of these statuses. Two examples illustrate what we mean.

Some years ago, a friend suggested renting the video *Willow* for her children. The eldest, a seven-year-old, had seen the opening scenes on television and was horrified at the prospect: "They kill the mom and steal the baby. There's dead bodies and blood everywhere." The man working in the video store, however, had seen the movie several times and vouched that it was not violent.

If you have seen *Willow,* you may recall that the movie opens as an evil queen rounds up all the pregnant women in the empire to slay the enchanted baby when she is born. The queen's soldiers kill the child's mother, but a midwife saves the baby and carries her into the forest. Then the midwife is attacked and killed by a pack of wild animals, and the baby floats downstream in a basket.

This is a small lesson about social status. What one notices in the world depends in large part on the statuses one occupies; in this way one may be said to *experience* one's social status. The seven-year-old noticed the violence both because of the unique person he is and because of his age, a master status. That the man in the video store did not see the movie as violent may be attributed, at least in part, to the same master status: age.

Although we do not specifically address age in this volume, age operates in ways that are analogous to race, sex, class, sexual orientation, and disability. Being young affects one's treatment in innumerable ways: at a minimum, restrictions on driving, employment, military enlistment, marriage, abortion, admission to movies, and alcohol and cigarette consumption; insurance rates; mandatory school attendance; and "status offenses" (acts that are illegal only for minors). In addition, minors are excluded from voting and other legal rights and are presumed to be untrustworthy and irresponsible.

In these ways, those defined as "young" are treated differently than those who are not so defined. Because of that treatment, the world looks different to them than to those who are older and no longer operating within these constraints. Those who are young notice things that older people need not notice, because they are not subject to the same rules. One's experience of the world is tied to the statuses one occupies.

The second example of experiencing one's status comes from the autobiography of one of the first black students in an exclusive white prep school. She recalls what it was like to hear "one [white] girl after another say, 'It doesn't matter to me if somebody's white or black or green or purple. I mean people are just people.'"

> Having castigated whites' widespread inability to see individuals [apart from] the skin in which they were wrapped, I could hardly argue with "it's the person that counts." I didn't know why they always chose green and purple to dramatize their indifference, but my ethnicity seemed diminished when the talk turned to Muppets. (Cary, 1991:83–84)

While she appreciates the girls' intentions, she also hears her own *real* experience being trivialized by a comparison with green and purple creatures. Her status helps to explain what she notices.

In all, you experience your social statuses; you live through them. They are the filters through which you see and make sense of the world, and in large measure they account for how you are treated and what you notice. In the sections that follow, we will focus on the experiences of privilege and stigma associated with master statuses.

THE EXPERIENCE OF PRIVILEGE

Just as status helps to explain what we notice, it also explains what we *don't* notice. In the following classroom discussion between a black and a white woman, the white woman argues that because she and the black woman are both female, they should be allied. The black woman responds,

> "When you wake up in the morning and look in the mirror what do you see?"
> "I see a woman," replied the white woman.
> "That's precisely the issue," replied the black woman. "I see a black woman. For me, race is visible every day, because it is how I am *not* privileged in this culture. Race is invisible to you [because it is how you are privileged]." (Kimmel and Messner, 1989:3; emphasis added)

Thus, we are likely to be fairly unaware of the statuses that *privilege* us, that is, provide us with advantage, and acutely aware of those that are the source of trouble—those that yield negative judgments and unfair treatment. The mirror metaphor used by the black woman in this conversation emerges frequently among those who are stigmatized: "I looked in the mirror and saw a gay man." These moments of suddenly realizing one's social position with all of its life-shaping ramifications are usually about recognizing how one is stigmatized and underprivileged, and rarely about how one is privileged or advantaged, by the statuses one occupies.

Examples of Privilege

This use of the term *privilege* was first developed by Peggy McIntosh (1988) from her experience teaching women's studies courses. She noticed that while many men were willing to grant that women were disadvantaged (or "underprivileged") because of sexism, it was more difficult for them to acknowledge that they were themselves advantaged (or "overprivileged") because of it. Extending the analysis to race, McIntosh generated a list of the ways in which she, as a white woman, was overprivileged by virtue of racism. Her list of over 40 white privileges included the following:

> I can turn on the television or open to the front page of the paper and see people of my race widely represented.
>
> When I am told about our national heritage or about "civilization," I am shown that people of my color made it what it is.
>
> I do not have to educate my children to be aware of systemic racism for their own daily protection.
>
> I can worry about racism without being seen as self-interested or self-seeking.
>
> I can think over many options, social, political, imaginative, or professional, without asking whether a person of my race would be accepted or allowed to do what I want to do. (McIntosh, 1988:5–8)

As she talked to people about her list, McIntosh learned about other white privileges: "A black woman said she was glad to hear me 'working on my own people,' because if she said these things about white privilege, she would be seen as a militant." Someone else noted that one privilege of being white was being able to be oblivious to those privileges. "Those in privileged groups are educated [to be oblivious] about what it is like for others, especially for others who have to be in their presence" (McIntosh, 1988).

One feature of privilege is that it makes life easier: it is easier to get around, to get what one wants, and to be treated in a way that is acceptable. This is illustrated by the experience of a white newspaper columnist traveling with an African

American colleague. Both were using complimentary airline tickets. The columnist turned in his ticket and was assigned a seat; then he watched the white ticket agent ask his companion for some identification:

> The black man handed over his ticket. The female agent glanced at it and asked, "Do you have some identification?" [The columnist had not been asked for any identification.]
>
> "Yes, I do," the black man said, and he reached for his wallet. "But just out of curiosity, do you mind telling me why you want to see it?"
>
> The agent grinned in embarrassment.
>
> She said nothing in response.
>
> "How about a credit card?" the black man said, and he pulled one out of his wallet.
>
> "Do you have a work ID?" she asked, apparently hoping to see something with the black man's photo on it.
>
> "No," he said, and whipped out another credit card.
>
> "A driver's license would be fine," she said, sounding trapped.
>
> "I don't have my driver's license with me," he said. "I'm taking the plane, not the car. . . ."
>
> "That's fine sir, thank you," the agent finally said, shrinking a bit with each successive credit card. "Enjoy the flight."
>
> The men rode the escalator up to the gate area in silence.
>
> The white man shook his head. "I've probably watched that a hundred times in my life," he said. "But that's the first time I've ever *seen* it."
>
> The black man nodded. He'd seen it more times than he cared to count. "You don't ever need to remind yourself that you're black," he said, "because every day there's somebody out there who'll remind you."
>
> They walked on for a while, and the black man started to laugh to himself. Pirouetting, he modeled his outfit, an Italian-cut, double-breasted suit with a red rose in his lapel for Mother's Day. "I really can't look any better than this," he said sardonically. Then, he looked into his friend's eyes and said, "I had my driver's license. But if I show it, we may as well be in Soweto." (Kornheiser, 1990)

In reading about this exchange, one black student was particularly angered: "Whites will stand by and watch this happen, and either be oblivious to the slight or sympathize with you afterward, but they won't go to the mat and fight for you."

The columnist noted for the first time a privilege that he has as a middle-class white: he is not assumed to be a thief. By contrast, his black colleague is presumed to have stolen the ticket no matter how upper-class or professional he may look. Similarly, many black and Latino students describe being closely monitored for shoplifting when they are in department stores, just as the students who work in department store security confirm that they are given explicit instructions to watch black and Latino customers. On hearing this, one black student realized why she had the habit of walking through stores with her hands out, palms open, in front of her: it was a way to prove she was not stealing. Thus, one of the privileges of being white is that shoplifting is easier, since the security people in stores are busy watching the black and Latino customers.

Just as whites are not assumed to be thieves, they are not presumed to be violent (at least by other whites). By contrast, over half of whites think blacks are aggressive or violent (National Opinion Research Center, 1990; Sniderman and Carmines, 1997). Whites' fear puts the lives of blacks at risk, since preemptive violence against blacks would then be warranted. D. Marvin Jones, in Reading 25, describes the cases that have captured national attention—Rodney King, Ted Goetz, and Charles Stuart—but the more mundane experience is that African Americans, especially men, must always be vigilant about becoming the targets of preemptive violence. Freedom from this kind of life-shaping concern is one privilege of being white.[1]

Another privilege likely to be invisible to those in single-race families is the privilege of being recognized as a family. The following account by a mother illustrates how the failure to perceive a family is linked to the expectation of black criminality.

> When my son was home visiting from college, we met in town one day for lunch. . . . On the way to the car, one of us thought of a game we'd often played when he was younger.
>
> "Race you to the car!"
>
> I passed my large handbag to him, thinking to more equalize the race since he was a twenty-year-old athlete. We raced the few blocks, my heart singing with delight to be talking and playing with my beloved son. As we neared the car, two young white men yelled something at us. I couldn't make it out and paid it no mind. When we arrived at the car, both of us laughing, they walked by and mumbled "Sorry" as they quickly passed, heads down.
>
> I suddenly understood. They hadn't seen a family. They had seen a young Black man with a pocketbook, fleeing a pursuing middle-aged white woman. My heart trembled as I thought of what could have happened if we'd been running by someone with a gun.
>
> Later I mentioned the incident in a three-day diversity seminar I was conducting at a Boston corporation. A participant related it that evening to his son, a police officer, and asked the son what he would have done if he'd observed the scene.
>
> The answer: "Shot out his kneecaps." (Lester, 1994:56–7)

Let us turn now from the privileges of race to the privileges of sexual orientation. The most obvious privilege enjoyed by heterosexuals is that they are free to talk to virtually anyone about their relationships and to display affection in almost any public setting. Those in same-sex relationships, however, can neither talk openly about their relationships nor display affection in public. Indeed, doing so puts them at risk for unemployment, ostracism, verbal abuse, loss of child custody, and potentially life-threatening physical assault.

Even the ability to display a picture of one's partner on a desk at work stands as an invisible privilege of heterosexuality.

> Consider, for example, an employee who keeps a photograph on her desk in which she and her husband smile for the camera and embrace affectionately. . . . [T]he photo implicitly conveys information about her private sexual behavior. [But] . . . most onlookers (if they even notice the photo) do not think of her partner primarily in sexual terms. . . .
>
> [But] if the photograph instead shows the woman in the same pose with a same-sex partner, everyone is likely to notice. As with the first example, the photograph conveys the information that she is in a relationship. But the fact that the partner is a woman overwhelms all other information about her. The *sexual* component of the relationship is not mundane and implicit as with the heterosexual spouse. . . . (Herek, 1992:95–6; emphasis added)

---

[1]Despite whites' fear of violence at the hands of African Americans, crime is predominately *intra*racial.

Because heterosexual public affection is so commonplace, it rarely conjures up images of sexual activity. But that is exactly what we may think of when we see a same-sex couple embrace. This is why gay and lesbian people are often accused of "flaunting" their sexuality: *any* display of affection between them is understood by many heterosexuals as virtually a display of the sex act.

In the realm of class privilege, several readings in this text address the considerable differences in health, lifespan, educational access, likelihood of arrest and imprisonment, and quality of life that accompany American class differences. But these are perhaps the more visible privileges of being middle- and upper-class. Less apparent is the privilege of being treated as a competent and valued member of the community. To get that treatment in his university, one of our working-class students described how he had to change out of his work clothes before going to campus; otherwise, staff and faculty treated him as though he did not belong at the university. The privilege of being assumed to be competent also follows from being able-bodied. As Michelle Fine and Adrienne Asch explain in Reading 18, "it is asumed that having a disability is synonymous with needing help and social support."

Two privileges in particular shape the experience of those in nonstigmatized statuses: entitlement and the privilege of being "unmarked." *Entitlement* is the belief that one has the right to be respected, acknowledged, protected, and rewarded. This is so much taken for granted by those in nonstigmatized statuses that they are often shocked and angered when it is denied them.

> [After the lecture, whites in the audience] shot their hands up to express how excluded they felt because [the] lecture, while broad in scope, clearly was addressed first and foremost to the women of color in the room. . . . What a remarkable sense of entitlement must drive their willingness to assert their experience of exclusion! If I wanted to raise my hand every time I felt excluded, I would have to glue my wrist to the top of my head. (Ettinger, 1994:51)

Like entitlement, the privilege of occupying an "unmarked" status is shared by most of those in nonstigmatized categories. *Doctor* is an *unmarked* status; *woman* doctor is *marked.* As Deborah Tannen writes in Reading 27, an unmarked status is "what you think of when you are not thinking of anything special." Unmarked categories convey the usual and expected distribution of individuals in social statuses—the distribution that does not require any special comment. Thus, the unmarked category tells us what a society takes for granted.

Theoretically, the unmarked category *doctor* might include anyone, but in truth it refers to white males. How do we know that? Because other occupants of that status are usually marked: woman doctor, black doctor, and so on. While the marking of a status signals infrequency—there are few female astronauts or male nurses—it may also imply inferiority. A "woman doctor" or a "black doctor" may be considered less qualified.

Thus, a privilege of those who are not stigmatized is that their master statuses are not used to discount their accomplishments or imply that they serve special interests. Someone described as "a politician" is presumed to operate from a universality that someone described as "a white male politician" is not. Because white male politicians are rarely described as such, their anchoring in the reality of their own master statuses is hidden. In this way, those in marked statuses appear to be always operating from an "agenda," or "special interest" (e.g., a black politician is often presumed to represent only black constituents), while those in unmarked statuses can appear to be agenda-free. Being white and male thus becomes invisible, since it is not regularly identified as important. For this reason, some recommend marking *everyone's* race and sex as a way to recognize that we are all grounded in our master statuses.

This use of marked statuses also applies to classroom interactions. At white-dominated universities, white students are unlikely to be asked to speak on behalf of all white people or to explain the "white experience." In this way, those who are white, male, heterosexual, and middle class appear to have no race, sex, sexual orientation, or social class, and thus have the privilege of not having to suffer through frequent classroom discussions about the problems of "their people."

Stigmatized People and Their Experience of Privilege; Privileged People and Their Experience of Stigma

We have described some of the privileges enjoyed by those in nonstigmatized statuses, but those with stigma also have some experience of privilege—it is just less frequent. For example, in 1991 the Urban Institute investigated racial discrimination in employment by sending pairs of black and white male college students (who had been coached to present virtually identical personal style, appearance, dialect, education, and job history) to apply for jobs in Washington, D.C., and Chicago.

> In 20 percent [of the 576 job applications], the white applicant advanced farther in the hiring process [from obtaining a job application, to interview, to hiring] than his black counterpart, and in 15 percent the white applicant was offered a job while his equally qualified black partner was not. Blacks were favored over comparable white applicants in a much smaller share of cases; in 7 percent of the audits the black advanced farther in the hiring process, and in 5 percent only the black received the job offer. (Turner, Fix, and Struyk, 1991:18)

Thus, black and white applicants both had some experience of preferential hiring, but the white applicant had about three times more. A similar study of job discrimination against Latino males conducted in Chicago and San Diego indicated an even larger gap between the amount of privilege experienced by Anglos and Latinos (Cross, Kenney, Mell, and Zimmermann, 1990).

Thus, concerns about "reverse discrimination" often miss the mark. While blacks, Latinos, Asian Americans, or white women are sometimes favored in hiring, they are not favored *as frequently* as white males. Discrimination continues in its historic direction as evidenced in the constancy of race and sex differences in income. In 1975, black per capita median annual income was 58.5 percent that of whites. Over 20 years later, in 1997, the figure was only 60.5 percent. In 1975, the same measure for Latinos was 56.1 percent of whites; by 1997, it was down to

52.7 percent (U.S. Department of Commerce, 1993:454; U.S. Bureau of the Census, 1997).[2]

Because the focus is so frequently on how stigma affects those who bear it, it is easy to assume that only the targets of racism, sexism, homophobia, or classism are affected by it. But that is not the case. For example,

> Think of white slaveowners and their wives: the meaning of the sexual difference between them was constructed in part by the alleged contrast between them as whites and other men and women who were Black; what was supposed to characterize their relationship was not supposed to characterize the relationship between white men and Black women, or white women and Black men. . . . So even though the white men and women were of the same race, and even though they were not the victims of racism, this does not mean that we can understand the relationship between them without reference to their race and to the racism that their lives enacted. (Spelman, 1988:104–5)

Similarly, interactions between men are affected by sexism, even though the men themselves are not subject to it.

> For example, we can't understand the racism that fueled white men's lynching of Black men without understanding its connection to the sexism that shaped their protective and possessive attitudes toward white women. The ideology according to which whites are superior and ought to dominate Blacks is nested with the ideology according to which white men must protect their wives from attack by Black men. . . . That men aren't subject to sexism doesn't mean sexism has no effect on their relationships to each other. . . . (Spelman, 1988:106)

Similar examples apply to sexual orientation, social class, and disability. Certainly, homophobia shapes heterosexual relations, knowledge of disability affects those who are "temporarily able-bodied," and the presence of poverty affects interactions among those in the middle class. Thus, the most obvious privilege of those in nonstigmatized statuses—that they are not affected by stigma—proves questionable.

Because privilege is usually invisible to those who possess it, they may think that everyone is treated as they are. When they learn otherwise, they may think that the incident was exceptional rather than routine, that the victim was overreacting or misinterpreting, or that the victim even provoked the encounter. Such responses do not necessarily deny that the incident took place; rather, they deny the meaning attributed to the event.

Through such dismissals, those operating from positions of privilege can deny the experience of those without privilege. For example, college students who are in their late teens and early twenties often describe university administrators as unresponsive until they have had their parents call and complain. If the parents later said, "I don't know why you had such a problem with those people, they were very

---

[2]Income figures exclude "money income received before payments for personal income, taxes, Social Security, union dues, Medicare deductions, food stamps, health benefits, subsidized housing, or rent-free housing and goods produced and consumed on the farm" (U.S. Department of Commerce, 1993:425).

nice to me. Did you do something to antagonize them?" that would indicate they were oblivious to their own privileged place in these university procedures as well as unaware of their child's underprivileged status in them.

Dismissals like these reduce the stigmatized person to a child inadequate to judge the world. Often such dismissals are framed in terms of the very stigma about which people are complaining. In this way, what stigmatized people say about their status is discounted precisely because they are stigmatized. The implication is that those who occupy a stigmatized status are somehow the ones *least* able to assess its consequence. The effect is to dismiss precisely those who have had the most experience with the problem.

This process, called *looping* or *rereading,* is described by many who have studied the lives of patients in psychiatric hospitals (Rosenhan, 1973; Schur, 1984; Goffman, 1961, 1963). If a patient says, "The staff here are being unfair to me," and the staff respond, "Of course he would think that—he's crazy," they have reread, or looped, his words through his status. His words have been heard through his stigma and dismissed for exactly that reason.

These dismissals serve a function. Dismissing another's experience of status-based mistreatment masks the possibility that one has escaped such treatment precisely because of one's privilege. If we do not acknowledge that *their* status affects *their* treatment, we need not acknowledge that *our* status affects *our* treatment. Thus, we avoid the larger truth that those who are treated well, those who are treated poorly, and all the rest in between are always evaluated both as individuals and as occupants of particular esteemed and disesteemed categories.

Hierarchies of Stigma and Privilege

While it may appear that people can be easily separated into two categories—privileged and stigmatized—every individual occupies several master statuses. The privilege or stigma that might be associated with one status emerges in the context of all of one's other statuses. For example, a middle-class, heterosexual Mexican American male may be privileged in terms of class, sex, and sexual orientation, but stigmatized by virtue of being Latino. Given the invisibility of privilege, he is more likely to notice the ways in which his status as Latino stigmatizes him than to notice the privileges that follow from his other statuses. Nonetheless, he is simultaneously all of his statuses; the privileges and disadvantages of each emerge in the context of all the others. An Anglo male and a Latino male may both be said to experience the privilege of sex, but they do not experience the same privilege.

While individuals may experience both privilege and stigma in the mix of their various statuses, some stigmas are so strong that they cancel out the privileges that one's other statuses might provide. For example, there is much evidence that the stigma of being black in America cancels out the privileges that might be expected to follow from being middle-class.

> The first large-scale study of treatment decisions made by primary care physicians found that, when faced with identical complaints of chest pain, doctors were much more likely to recommend further cardiac testing for their white male patients than any others. Black

> and female patients were referred to heart specialists only 60 percent as often. (Goldstein, 1999:1)
>
> Blacks also remain about half as likely as Latinos or Asians to live in the suburbs. And despite their consistent preference for residential integration, blacks in almost all central cities remain highly segregated from non-Hispanic whites. They are more racially isolated from whites than are Latinos and Asians, and high incomes or levels of education make it no easier for African Americans to move into white neighborhoods. (Hochschild, 1995:42)
>
> In 1999 the U.S. Department of Agriculture agreed to settle a class-action lawsuit filed in 1997 by black farmers who claimed they had been denied government loans or given smaller and more restrictive loans than those awarded to white farmers with similar credit histories and assets. "Discrimination by USDA officials has been cited as a major reason why the ranks of black farmers have dwindled at three times the rate of white farmers. Blacks, who were 14 percent of the nation's farmers in the 1920s, now account for less than 1 percent." (Fletcher, 1999:10)
>
> *Roberts v. Texaco,* the class action filed in June 1994, charged the company with persistent failure to hire, promote or even treat with decency its African-American staffers. It cited numbers: in 1994 only four of Texaco's top 498 executives were black. And it included stunning affidavits of abuse and insult. . . . The case languished in court until late 1996, when a downsized Texaco executive, in an act of revenge or repentance, turned over tapes that caught top officials at the company—including him—making racist remarks . . . and plotting to purge the documents in the discrimination case. Texaco agreed to pay more than $115 in racial reparations. (Solomon, 1996:48–49)

Research on the effects of other stigmatized racial statuses has not been as thorough, nor are its findings as consistent, but it is clear that for African Americans, middle-class standing provides little protection against racism.

Does the stigma of being an out-of-the-closet gay or lesbian cause one to lose the privilege that comes from being middle-class, white, or both? Sexual orientation is not covered by the civil rights protections of federal legislation. While the proportion of Americans who believe gays should have equal job opportunities has increased—from 56 percent in 1977 to 84 percent in 1996 (Berke, 1998)—there is still no federal legislation barring discrimination against gays in employment, housing, or health care. In 1998, President Clinton issued an executive order barring federal agencies from such discrimination, but the House of Representatives proposed legislation that would deny funding to carry out the order (Berke, 1998). Thus, it often looks as though gays are predominately white and at least middle-class; in the absence of employment protection, few others can afford to publicly identify themselves as gay (Lester, 1994). While some jurisdictions have enacted protections, many of those ordinances were later challenged and repealed. At present, it appears that the stigma of being gay often overwhelms the privileges that one's other statuses might afford.

But which is most important: one's race, sex, sexual orientation, or social class? For the sizable population that occupies multiple stigmatized statuses, it makes little sense to argue which status presents the greatest obstacle. Yet in the public discussion of racism, sexism, classism, and homophobia, people are often asked to make alliances on that basis—pick a single status as the most significant one.

Philosopher Elizabeth Spelman (1988) suggests a way to assess how an individual or a culture prioritizes these statuses. If each master status is imagined as a room we will enter, we can consider which sequential ordering of these rooms most accurately reflects our experience. If the first rooms we encounter are labeled black, white, or Asian, we will find ourselves in a room with those who share our "race" but are different in terms of sex, social class, ethnicity, and sexual orientation. If the second set of rooms is labeled male and female, we will find ourselves with people of the same race and sex. Other rooms might be labeled with sexual orientation or social class categorizations.

Many white feminists have presumed that the first rooms we encounter are sex categorizations, thus arguing that the statuses of female and male have priority over race or class designations; that one is discriminated against first by virtue of one's sex and then by race. Latino, black, and some white feminists have countered that the first rooms are race classifications. In this case, it is argued that racism so powerfully affects people that men and women within racial categories have more in common with one another than they do with those of the same sex but of a different race. Alliances of gay and lesbian people by implication assume that the first doors are marked gay and straight, with sex, race, and class following; disability rights activists would argue that that status takes precedence over everything else. In addition to the orderings that correspond to the historical experience of categories of people, each of us likely maintains an ordering derived from our personal experience of these statuses.

THE EXPERIENCE OF STIGMA

The previous section considered the privileges conferred by some master statuses; now we turn to stigma conferred by other master statuses.

In his classic analysis of stigma, sociologist Erving Goffman (1963) distinguished between the *discredited,* whose stigma is immediately apparent to an observer (for example, race, sex, some physical disabilities), and the *discreditable,* whose stigma can be hidden (for example, sexual orientation, social class). Since stigma plays out differently in the lives of the discredited and the discreditable, each will be examined separately.

The Discreditable: "Passing"

The discreditable are those who are *passing,* that is, not publicly acknowledging the stigmatized statuses they occupy. (Were they to acknowledge that status, they would become discredited.) The term *passing* comes from "passing as white," which emerged as a phenomenon after 1875 when southern states re-established racial segregation through hundreds of "Jim Crow"[3] laws. At that point, some African Americans passed as a way to get better jobs.

---

[3]"Jim Crow" was "a blackface, singing-dancing-comedy characterization portraying black males as childlike, irresponsible, inefficient, lazy, ridiculous in speech, pleasure-seeking, and happy, [and was] a widespread stereotype of blacks during the last decades before emancipation . . . " (Davis, 1991:51). "Jim Crow" laws were laws by which whites imposed segregation following the Civil War.

> [S]ome who passed as white on the job lived as black at home. Some lived in the North as white part of the year and as black in the South the rest of the time. More men passed than women . . . the vast majority who could have passed permanently did not do so, owing to the pain of family separation, condemnation by most blacks, their fear of whites, and the loss of the security of the black community. . . . Passing as white probably reached an all-time peak between 1880 and 1925. (Davis, 1991:56–57)

"Passing as white" is now quite rare and strongly condemned by African Americans, a reaction that "indicate[s] the resolute insistence that anyone with even the slightest trace of black ancestry is black, and a traitor to act like a white" (Davis, 1991:138). We will use the term *passing* here to refer to those who have not made their stigmatized status evident; it is similar to the phrase "being in the closet" which is usually applied to gays. Because it is among gays that passing is now most frequent—as well as most vehemently debated—many of our examples will focus on that stigmatized status.

One may come to be passing by chance as well as by choice. For example, the presumption that everyone is heterosexual can have the effect of putting gay people in the closet even when they had not intended to be. In the midst of a series of lectures on marriage and the family, one of our colleagues realized that he had been making assignments, lecturing, and encouraging discussion with the presumption that all of the students in the class had, or wanted to have, heterosexual relationships. Unless his gay and lesbian students wished to do something specific to counter his assumption, they were effectively passing. His actions forced them to choose between announcing or remaining silent about their status. Had he assumed that students would be involved only with others of the same race, he would have created a similar situation for those in interracial relationships. Thus, assumptions about others' private lives may have the effect of making them choose between silence or an announcement of something they may consider private.

Since most heterosexuals assume that everyone else is heterosexual, many social encounters either put gay people in the closet or require they announce their status.

> Every encounter with a new classful of students, to say nothing of a new boss, social worker, loan officer, landlord, doctor, erects new closets [that] . . . exact from at least gay people new surveys, new calculations, new draughts and requisitions of secrecy or disclosure. Even an *out* gay person deals daily with interlocutors about whom she doesn't know whether they know or not [or whether they would care]. . . . The gay closet is not a feature only of the lives of gay people. But for many gay people it is still the fundamental feature of social life; there can be few gay people . . . in whose lives the closet is not a shaping presence. (Sedgwick, 1990:68)

Inadvertent passing is also experienced by those whose racial status is not immediately apparent. An African American acquaintance of ours who looks white is often in settings in which others do not know that she is African American—or in which she does not know if they know. Thus, she must regularly decide how and when to convey that information. This is important to her as a way to discourage racist remarks, since whites often assume it is acceptable to make racist remarks to one another (as men often assume it is acceptable to make sexist remarks to other men, or as straights presume it acceptable to make homophobic remarks to those they think are also straight). It is also important to her that others know she is black so that they understand the meaning of her words—so that they will hear her words through her status as an African American woman. Those whose stigma is not apparent must go to some lengths to avoid being in the closet by virtue of others' assumptions. Those with relatively invisible disabilities also face the tension of inadvertent passing. One of our students arrived in class in tears following an encounter with someone she had not realized was disabled. Seeing the young woman trip, the student had asked if she could help—and was angrily rebuffed. The offer of help had been taken as a show of pity.

But passing may also be an intentional choice. For example, one of our students, who was in the process of deciding that he was gay, had worked for many years at a local library, where he became friends with several of his coworkers. Much of the banter at work, however, involved disparaging gay, or presumably gay, library patrons. As he grappled with a decision about his own sexual identity, his social environment reminded him that being gay is a stigmatized status in American society. The student did not so much face prejudice against himself (since he was not "out" to his work friends) as he faced an "unwilling acceptance of himself by individuals who are prejudiced against persons of the kind he can be revealed to be" (Goffman, 1963:42). Thus, he was not the person his friends took him to be. While survey research indicates that those who personally know a gay man hold consistently more positive feelings about the group (Herek and Glunt, 1993), the decision to reveal oneself as possessing a stigma that others have gone on record as opposing is not made lightly.

Revealing stigma changes one's interactions with "normals," even with those who are not particularly prejudiced. Such revelations are likely to alter important relationships. Parents sometimes disown gay children, just as they do children involved in interracial relationships. Thus, the decision to pass or be "out" is not taken lightly. For the discreditable, what Goffman euphemistically described as "information management" is at the core of one's life. "To tell or not to tell; to let on or not to let on; to lie or not to lie; and in each case, to whom, how, when, and where" (Goffman, 1963:42). Such choices are faced daily by those who are discreditable—not just those who are gay and lesbian, but also those who are poor, have been imprisoned, attempted suicide, terminated a pregnancy through abortion, are HIV-positive, are drug or alcohol dependent, or have been the victims of incest or rape. Returning to the discussion of privilege, note that those who do not occupy stigmatized statuses needn't invest emotional energy in monitoring information about themselves; when they choose, they can talk openly about their personal history.

Passing has both positive and negative aspects. On the positive side, passing lets the stigmatized person exert some power over the situation; the person controls the information, the flow of events, and his or her privacy. By withholding his or her identity until choosing to reveal it, the person may create a situation in which others' prejudices are challenged. In some ways, passing is an effort to be judged as an individual rather than be discounted by virtue of one's stigma. Passing also limits one's exposure to verbal and physical abuse, allows for the development of relationships outside the constraints of stigma, and improves job and income security by reducing one's exposure to discrimination.

On the negative side, passing consumes a good deal of time, energy, and emotion in the management of personal information. It introduces a significant level of deception and secrecy even into close relationships. Passing also denies others the opportunity to prove themselves unprejudiced, and it makes one vulnerable to blackmail by those who do know about one's stigma.

The Discredited: Flaming

The discreditable face problems of invisibility, but visibility is the problem for those who are discredited. As we shall see, those who are discredited suffer from a disproportionate share of attention and are subject to being stereotyped. In the face of these difficulties, it is not surprising that the discredited sometimes "flame."

Being discredited means that one's stigma is immediately apparent to others. As essayist bell hooks describes below, those who are discredited often have little patience for those who at least have the option of passing.

> Many of us have been in discussions where a non-white person—a black person—struggles to explain to white folks that while we can acknowledge that gay people of all colors are harassed and suffer exploitation and domination, we also recognize that there is a significant difference that arises because of the visibility of dark skin. . . . While it in no way lessens the severity of such suffering for gay people, or the fear that it causes, it does mean that in a given situation the apparatus of protection and survival may be simply not identifying as gay. In contrast, most people of color have no choice. No one can hide, change, or mask dark skin color. White people, gay and straight, could show greater understanding of the impact of racial oppression on people of color by not attempting to make these oppressions synonymous, but rather by showing the ways they are linked and yet differ. (hooks, 1989:125)

For the discredited, stigma is likely to be always shaping interaction with those who are not stigmatized. However, its effect does not necessarily play out in ways one can easily determine. Those whose stigma is visible must daily decide whether the world is responding to them or their stigma. Florynce Kennedy, a black activist in the civil rights and women's movements, once commented that the problem with being black in America was that you never knew whether what happened to you, good or bad, was because of your talents or because you were black (Kennedy, 1976). This situation was described in 1903 by sociologist W.E.B. Du Bois as the "double consciousness" of being black in America. The concept was key to Du Bois's classic, *The Souls of Black Folk,* for which he was rightfully judged "the father of serious black thought as we know it today" (Hare, 1982:xiii). Du Bois described double consciousness this way:

> the Negro . . . [is] gifted with a second-sight in this American world—a world which yields him no true self-consciousness, but only lets him see himself through the revelation of the other world. It is a peculiar sensation, this double consciousness, this sense of always looking at one's self through the eyes of others, of measuring one's soul by the tape of a world that looks on in amused contempt and pity. One ever feels his twoness. . . . (1982:45)

This is the sense of seeing oneself through the eyes of a harshly critical other, and it ties back to our discussion of objectification in Framework Essay I. When those who are stigmatized view themselves from the perspective of the nonstigmatized, they have reduced themselves to objects. This theme of double or "fractured" consciousness can also be found in contemporary analyses of women's experience.

The greatest effect of being visibly stigmatized is on one's life chances—literally, one's chances for living. Thus, the readings in this book detail differences in income, employment, health, lifespan, education, targeting for violence, and the likelihood of arrest and imprisonment. In this essay, however, we will consider the more mundane difficulties created by stigmatization, particularly the sense of being "on stage."

The discredited often have the feeling of being watched or on display when they are in settings dominated by nonstigmatized people. For example, when women walk through male-dominated settings, they often feel they are on display in terms of their physical appearance. Asian, black, and Latino students in white/Anglo-dominated universities often describe a feeling of being on display in campus dining facilities. In such cases, the discredited are likely to feel that others are judging them in terms of their stigma.

As sociologist Rosabeth Moss Kanter (1980, 1993) has shown, this impression is likely to be accurate. When Kanter studied corporate settings in which there was one person visibly different from the others, that person was likely to get a disproportionate share of attention. In fact, people in the setting were likely to closely monitor what the minority person did, which meant his or her mistakes were more likely to be noticed—and the mistakes of those in the rest of the group were more likely to be overlooked, since everyone was watching the minority person. Even in after-work socializing, the minority member was still subject to disproportionate attention.

Kanter also found that the minority person's behavior was likely to be interpreted in terms of the prevailing stereotypes about the members of that category. For example, when there were only a few men in a setting dominated by women, the men were subject to intense observation and their behavior was filtered through the women's stereotypes about them. Perceptions were distorted to fit the pre-existing beliefs.

Without the presence of a visibly different person, members of a setting are likely to see themselves as different from one another in various ways. Through contrast with the visibly different person, however, they notice their similarities. In this way, majority group members may construct dichotomies—"us" and "them"—out of settings in which there are a few who are different. It is not surprising that those who are visibly different sometimes isolate themselves in response.

Still, none of this is inevitable. Kanter argues strongly that once minority membership in a setting reaches 15 percent, these processes abate. Until that point, however, those who are in the minority (or visibly stigmatized) are the subject of a good deal of attention. As a consequence, they are often accused of "flaming." *Flaming* usually means acting in an effeminate manner, with the intention of letting observers know that one is gay. Most likely, the term originated as a criticism of gay men but has since been appropriated more positively by that community. We use the term here to describe an unabashed display of any stigmatized status.

Flaming is a charge those who are not stigmatized often level at those who are stigmatized. Although there are certainly occasions on which the discredited may deliberately make a show of their status, Kanter's work indicates that when their representation is low, the discredited are likely to be charged with flaming no matter what they do. Subjected to a disproportionate amount of attention and viewed through the lenses of stereotypes, almost anything the discredited do is likely to be noticed and attributed to the category to which they belong. Thus, one charge frequently leveled at those in discredited groups is that they are "so" black, Latino, gay, and so on—that is, that they make too big a show of their status.

This charge may affect those who are visibly stigmatized in various ways. Many are careful to behave in ways contrary to expectations. At other times, however, flaming may be deliberate. In the first session of one class, a student opened his remarks by saying, "Well, you all know I am a gay man, and as a gay man I think. . . ." The buzz of conversation stopped, other students stared at him, and one asked, "How would we know you were gay?" The student pointed to a button showing a pink triangle he had pinned to his book bag and explained that he thought they knew that someone wearing it would be gay. (Pink triangles were assigned to gay men during the Nazi era, black triangles to lesbians and other "unwanted" women. Both have been adopted as badges of pride among gay activists. Still, his logic was weak: Anyone supportive of gay rights might wear the button.)

This announcement—which moved the student from a discreditable to a discredited status—may have been intended to keep his classmates from making overtly anti-gay comments in his presence. His was a strategy designed to counter the problems of passing. To avoid being mistakenly identified as straight, he was required to flame.

Similarly, light-skinned African Americans are required to "flame" as black, lest they be accused of trying to pass. In adolescence, light-skinned black men are often derided by their black and white peers as not "really" black and so go to great lengths to counter that. As an instance of this, writer Itaberi Njeri offered a moving description of her cousin Jeffrey, who looked like singer Ricky Nelson, spent his brief life trying to demonstrate that he was black and tough, and died violently as a result (Njeri, 1991). While many light-skinned black men indicate that, when they are older, their skin color puts them at an advantage in both the black and white communities, in adolescence that is certainly not the case and thus they must "flame" their identity (Russell, Wilson, and Hall, 1992).

But flaming need not have this tragic side. For example, many bilingual Latino students talk about how much they enjoy a loud display of Spanish when Anglos are present; some Asian American students have described their pleasure in pursuing extended no-English-used card games in public spaces on campus. Black students and gay students sometimes entertain themselves by loudly affecting stereotypical behavior and then watching the disapproving looks that follow. Those who do not occupy stigmatized statuses may better appreciate these displays by remembering their experience of deliberate flaming as "obnoxious teenagers" in public settings. Thus, flaming may also be fun.

In all, those who are visibly stigmatized—who cannot or will not hide their identity—generate a variety of mechanisms to try to neutralize that stigma. Flaming is one of those mechanisms. It both announces one's stigmatized status and proclaims one's disregard for those who judge it negatively. Flaming neutralizes stigma by denying there is anything to be ashamed of. Thus, it functions as a statement of group pride.

European Ethnic Groups and Flaming

Whites of European ancestry sometimes envy the ethnic "flaming" of African Americans, Hispanics, and Asian Americans. As one student said, "It makes me feel like I just don't have anything." While his ancestry was a mix of Russian Jew, Italian Catholic, and Scotch-Irish Protestant, none of these identities seemed as compelling as the black, Asian, and Hispanic identities he saw around him.

This student's reaction reflects the transformed ethnic identity of the grandchildren and great-grandchildren of people who arrived in the peak immigration period of 1880 to 1920. At that time, Hungarians, Bohemians, Slovaks, Czechs, Poles, Russians, and Italians differed culturally and linguistically from one another and from the Irish, German, Scandinavian, and English immigrants who preceded them. Over the generations—and through intermarriage—this ethnic distinctiveness has been replaced by a socioeconomic "convergence" (Alba, 1990). Among non-Hispanic whites, ethnic ancestry no longer shapes occupation, residence, or political interest, nor is it the basis of the creation of communities of interest. While many enjoy ethnic food and celebrations or have strong feelings attached to stories of immigration, the attachment is not likely to be deep or have much impact on behavior. Most important, the attachment is understood in terms of the history of one's family rather than of a particular culture or nationality (Alba, 1990; Schaefer, 1990).[4]

Thus, it is possible that "European American" is emerging as a panethnic identity much like Asian American (Omi, 1996); both are identities that span a wide range of ancestries. It is also possible that as ethnic identities disappear for whites, they will be replaced by heightened attention to race. "[M]ost whites do not experience their ethnicity as a definitive aspect of their social identity. . . . The 'twilight of white ethnicity' in a racially defined, and increasingly polarized, environment means that white racial identity will grow in salience" (Omi, 1996:182).

The Expectations of Those Who Share One's Stigma

Stigma also affects interaction among those within the stigmatized category. From others in the category one learns a sense of group pride and cues about how to behave, what to expect from those in and outside the category, and how to protect oneself. For those stigmatized by color, sex, or social class, such lessons likely come

---

[4]An exception to the process of convergence among European-originated groups may be white, urban, Catholic ethnics. Throughout the 19th century, American Catholic churches were established as specifically ethnic churches (called "nationality churches"). These mostly urban churches were tailored to serve a particular ethnic group, which often included sending a priest from the home country who spoke the immigrants' native language. Thus, within a single urban area one might find separate Irish, Italian, and Polish Catholic churches, as well as effectively separate Catholic schools. The formation of ethnic churches meant that parishes also became ethnically segregated. On occasion, those parishes came to constitute stable, distinctive, working-class ethnic enclaves. In these cases ethnic identity continues as an active, viable reality.

from family members. For those who are gay or lesbian, the lessons are usually provided later in life by members of the gay community.

Particularly for those with visible stigma, there are also frequent reminders that one will be seen as a representative of all members of the category. Thus, many in stigmatized categories must factor in virtually everyone's opinion: What will others in my category think? What will those who are not stigmatized think? Indeed, one may even be criticized for failing to deal with oneself as a stigmatized person—"After all, who do you think you are?" In a sense, members of stigmatized categories may police one another much as they are policed by those outside the category, with the difference that those within one's category can at least claim to be operating for one's defense.

This point is illustrated in a story from the late tennis champion Arthur Ashe (1993). Ashe described watching his daughter play with a gift she had just received—a white doll—as they sat in the audience of a televised match in his honor. When the cameras panned his section of seats, he realized that he needed to get the doll away from his daughter or risk the anger of some black viewers who would argue that by letting his child play with a white doll, he stood as a bad role model for the black community.

A different example is provided by a Mexican American acquaintance who worked in an office that employed only a few other Hispanics, most of whom felt that the routes to upward mobility were closed to them. Together they drafted a letter to the firm's president detailing their concerns and seeking some corrective action. Although he had qualms about signing the letter, our acquaintance felt there was no alternative. Because he worked for management, he was then called in for an explanation of his behavior, which his supervisor saw as disloyal. Thus, he was put in the position of having to explain that, as a Chicano, he could not have refused to sign the letter.

Codes of conduct for those in stigmatized categories often require loyalty to the group, a fact of life that in this case the supervisor was unaware of. Indeed, the operating rule for many in stigmatized categories is to avoid public disagreement with one another or public airing of the group's "dirty laundry." Such codes are not trivial, since in their violation members of stigmatized categories risk ostracism from a critical support network. The reality of discrimination makes it foolhardy to reject those who share one's stigma. What would it have meant to Arthur Ashe to lose the support of other African Americans? To whom would our acquaintance have turned in that organization had he refused to sign the letter? When they are unaware of these pressures, those in privileged categories may make impossible demands of those who are stigmatized; when aware of these pressures, however, such requests are clear tests of loyalty.

POINTS OF CONTENTION, STAGES OF CONTENTIOUSNESS

This essay has focused on privilege and stigma and how they yield different treatment and different world views. In this final section we will examine the differing conceptions of racism. Then we will consider the stages of identity development within which privilege and stigma are experienced.

As we said earlier, flaming sometimes leaves those who are not members of the stigmatized category feeling excluded. For example, when Latino students talked about their enjoyment of using Spanish, an Anglo friend immediately responded with a description of how excluded she felt on those occasions. While aware of this, the Latino students nonetheless made it clear that they were not willing to forgo these opportunities. Their non-Spanish-speaking friends would just have to understand that it wasn't anything personal. This may well mark the bottom line: Those not part of stigmatized categorizations will sometimes feel and be excluded by their friends.

But another question is implied here: If the Hispanics exclude the Anglos, can the Anglos similarly exclude the Hispanics? As a way to approach this, consider the following two statements about gays and straights. In what ways are they similar, and in what ways different?

> A heterosexual says, "I can't stand gays. I don't want to be anywhere around them."
>
> A gay says, "I can't stand straights. I don't want to be anywhere around them."

While the statements are almost identical, they speak from very different positions of power. The heterosexual could likely structure his or her life so as to rarely interact with anyone gay, or at least anyone self-identified as gay. Most important, however, the heterosexual's attitude is consistent with major social, political, legal, and religious practices. Thus, the heterosexual in this example speaks from a position of some power, if only that derived from alignment with dominant cultural practices.

This is not the case for the gay person in this example, who is unlikely to be able to avoid contact with straights—and who would probably pay a considerable economic cost for self-segregation if that were attempted. There are no powerful institutional supports for hatred of straights. Analogously, the pleasure of exclusiveness enjoyed by bilingual Latino students exists against a backdrop of relative powerlessness, discrimination, stigmatization, and the general necessity of speaking English. The same might be said of men's disparagement of women compared to women's disparagement of men. As one student wrote, "As a male I have at times been on the receiving end of comments like, 'Oh, you're just like all men,' or 'Why can't men show more emotion?' but these comments or the sentiments behind them do not carry any power to affect my status. Even in the instance of a black who sees me as a representative of all whites, his vision of me does not change my privileged status."

Thus, the exclusiveness of those in nonstigmatized statuses has as its backdrop relative powerfulness, a sense of entitlement, infrequent discrimination based on master status, and a general ability to avoid those who might be prejudiced against people like themselves. The forms of exclusion available to minority group members are unlikely to tangibly affect the lives of those in privileged statuses. Being able to exclude someone from a dance or a club is not as significant as being able to exclude that person from employment, residence, education, professional organizations, or financing. This is what is meant when it is said that members of stigmatized categories may be prejudiced but not racist, or sexist, etc.; they do not have access to the institutional power by which to significantly affect the lives of those in nonstigmatized groups.

The term *racist* also carries different connotations for blacks and whites. As Robert Blauner describes in Reading 23, among whites being color conscious is taken as evidence of racism; those who are not color conscious are not racists. This understanding of what it means to be a racist has its base in the civil rights movement. If, as the civil rights movement taught, color should not make a difference in the way people are treated, whites who make a point of not noticing race argue that they are being polite and not racist (Frankenberg, 1993).

But given America's historical focus on race, it seems unrealistic for any of us to claim that we are oblivious to it. While many consider it impolite to mention race, differential treatment does not disappear as a consequence. Further, a refusal to notice race conveys that being black, Asian, or Latino is a "defect" that is indelicate (for whites) to mention. Thus, it can be argued that colorblindness is not really a strategy of politeness; rather, it is a strategy of power evasion. Since race clearly makes a difference in people's lives, pretending not to see it is a way to avoid noticing its effect. The alternative would be a strategy of race cognizance, that is, of systematic attention to the impact of race on oneself and others (Frankenberg, 1993).

Different conceptions of racism also emerge in the course of *racial and ethnic identity development,* which is the "understanding shared by members of ethnic groups, of what it means to be black, white, Chicano, Irish, Jewish, and so on" (White and Burke, 1987:311). We offer here a brief composite sketch of what appear to be the stages of this development (Cross, 1971, 1978; Hazen, 1992, 1994; Helms, 1990; Morton and Atkinson, 1983; Thomas, 1970; Thomas and Thomas, 1971). This framework might also be extended to the sex, class, disability, and sexual orientation identities we have focused on in this text. One important caution is necessary, however: Not everyone necessarily goes through each of these stages. For example, it is argued that African Americans are rarely found in the first of the stages we detail next (Hazen, 1992).

For those who are stigmatized, the first stage of identity development involves an internalization of the culture's negative imagery. This stage may include the disparagement of others in one's group and a strong desire to be accepted by dominant group members. For women, this might mean being highly critical of other women. For those who are low income or gay, this stage might entail feelings of shame. For people of color, it might involve efforts to lighten one's skin, straighten one's hair, or have an eye tuck.

In the second stage, anger at the dominant culture emerges, usually as the result of specific encounters with discrimination. Philosopher Sandra Bartky (1990), focusing on women's discovery of the extent of sexism, describes this as a period in which sexism appears to be everywhere. Events and objects that before had been neutral are discovered to be sexist; it becomes impossible to get through the day without becoming enraged—and the injustices one discovers are communicated to everyone within earshot. One's own behavior is also subject to scrutiny: "Am I being sexist to buy a doll for my niece?" Things that used to be straightforward become moral tests.

The third stage is sometimes called an immersion stage, because it involves immersing oneself in the culture of one's own people. In the previous stage, the individual is focused on evaluating and reacting to the dominant culture. In this stage, however, the focus shifts to one's own group. Dominant group members and the dominant group culture become less relevant to one's pursuits. This is often a period of participation in segregated activities and organizations as one seeks distance from dominant group members. Anger is somewhat lessened here, but the process of re-evaluating one's old identity continues.

The final stage is described as a period of integration as one's stigmatized status becomes integrated with the other aspects of one's life rather than taking precedence over them. Still, an opposition to prejudice and discrimination continues. At this point, one can distinguish between supportive and unsupportive dominant group members and thus is more likely to establish satisfying relations with them.

For those who do not occupy stigmatized statuses, the first stage of race or ethnic identity development is identified as an unquestioning acceptance of dominant group values. This acceptance might take shape either as an obliviousness to discrimination or as the espousing of supremacist ideologies.

In the second stage, one becomes aware of stigmatization, often through an eye-opening encounter with discrimination. Such an experience may produce a commitment to social change or a sense of powerlessness. As is the case for those in stigmatized statuses, in this stage those in privileged statuses also find themselves overwhelmed by all the forms of discrimination they see, often accompanied by a sense of personal guilt. In an attempt to affiliate and offer assistance, they are likely to seek alliances with those in stigmatized statuses. On college campuses this timing couldn't be worse, since many of those in stigmatized statuses are at their peak level of anger at those in privileged groups.

In stage three, those in privileged statuses focus less on trying to win the approval of those in stigmatized groups and instead explore the history of privileged and stigmatized statuses. Learning how privilege has affected one's own life is often a central question in this period.

The final stage involves integrating one's privileged statuses with all the other aspects of one's life, recognizing those in stigmatized categorizations as distinctive individuals rather than romanticizing them as a category ("just because oppressors are bad, doesn't mean that the oppressed are good" [Spivak, 1994]), and understanding that many with privilege have worked effectively against discrimination.

It appears that movement through the stages of ethnic or racial identity is positively related to self-esteem for all American race and ethnic groups, but the relationship is stronger for those who are Asian American, African American, and Latino than for those who are white (Hazen, 1994:55). Indeed, on various measures of self-esteem, African Americans score significantly higher than those in other race or ethnic groups (Hazen, 1992).

We once observed an African American student explain to his white classmates that he and his sister both self-identified as black, even though their mother was white. At that point a white student asked why he didn't call himself white since he looked white and that status would yield him more privilege. In response, he detailed all the qualities he prized in the black community and said he would never give up that status to be white. Much of what he said was new to the white students; many had never thought there was anything positive about being black in America.

The student's question reflected the common assumption that those who are stigmatized wish they belonged to the privileged group. Yet the woman who asked the question was clear that she never wanted to be a male, which was equally surprising to the men in the class. Thus, many men presume there is nothing positive about being female, many straights assume there is nothing positive about being gay, many able-bodied people assume that being disabled guarantees misery and loneliness (French, 1996), and many in the middle and upper classes assume there is nothing positive in life for those who are poor. But most people value and appreciate the statuses they occupy. We may wish those statuses weren't stigmatized or overprivileged, but that does not mean we would want to be other than who we are.

THE READINGS IN THIS SECTION

Our goal in this essay was to provide you with a framework by which to make sense of people's experience of privilege and stigma. Because there is a great deal of material that illustrates privilege and stigma, we have included readings that raise general issues or concepts applicable to those in various stigmatized or privileged statuses.

REFERENCES

Alba, Richard D. 1990. *Ethnic Identity: The Transformation of White America.* New Haven, CT: Yale University Press.

Ashe, Arthur. 1993. *Days of Grace.* New York: Ballantine.

Bartky, Sandra. 1990. *Femininity and Domination: Studies in the Phenomenology of Oppression.* New York: Routledge.

Berke, Richard. 1998. Chasing the Polls on Gay Rights. *New York Times,* August 2, 4:3.

Cary, Lorene. 1991. *Black Ice.* New York: Knopf.

Cross, H., G. Kenney, J. Mell, and W. Zimmerman. 1990. *Employer Practices: Differential Treatment of Hispanic and Anglo Job Seekers.* Washington, DC: The Urban Institute.

Cross, W. E., Jr. 1971. The Negro-to-Black Conversion Experience: Toward a Psychology of Black Liberation. *Black World* 20 (9):13–17.

———. 1978. The Thomas and Cross Models of Psychological Nigresence: A Review. *The Journal of Black Psychology* 5 (1):13–31.

Davis, F. James. 1991. *Who Is Black? One Nation's Definition.* University Park, PA: Pennsylvania University Press.

Du Bois, W.E.B. 1982. *The Souls of Black Folk.* New York: Penguin (Originally published in 1903.)

Ettinger, Maia. 1994. The Pocahontas Paradigm, or Will the Subaltern Please Shut Up? *Tilting the Tower,* edited by Linda Garber, 51–55. New York: Routledge.

Fletcher, Michael A. 1999. USDA Settlement Too Little, Too Late for Many Black Farmers. *Washington Post,* January 10, A:10.

Frankenberg, Ruth. 1993. *White Women, Race Matters: The Social Construction of Whiteness.* Minneapolis: University of Minnesota Press.

French, Sally. 1996. Simulation Exercises in Disability Awareness Training: A Critique. *Beyond Disability: Towards an Enabling Society,* edited by Gerald Hales, 114–23. London: Sage Publications.

Goffman, Erving. 1961. *Asylums.* New York: Doubleday Anchor.

——. 1963. *Stigma: Notes on the Management of Spoiled Identity.* Englewood Cliffs, NJ: Prentice-Hall.

Goldstein, Auram. 1999. G.U. Study Finds Disparity in Heart Care. *Washington Post,* February 25, A:1, 13.

Hare, Nathan. 1982. W.E. Burghart Du Bois: An Appreciation, pp. xiii–xxvii in *The Souls of Black Folk.* New York: Penguin (Originally published in 1969.)

Hazen, Sharlie Hogue. 1992. *The Relationship between Ethnic/Racial Identity Development and Ego Identity Development.* Ph.D. proposal, Department of Psychology, George Mason University.

——. 1994. *The Relationship between Ethnic/Racial Identity Development and Ego Identity Development.* Ph.D. dissertation, Department of Psychology, George Mason University.

Helms, J. E. 1990. An Overview of Black Racial Identity Theory. *Black and White Racial Identity: Theory, Research, and Practice,* edited by J. E. Helms, 9–33. New York: Greenwood Press.

Herek, Gregory M. 1992. The Social Context of Hate Crimes. *Hate Crimes: Confronting Violence against Lesbians and Gay Men,* edited by Gregory Herek and Kevin Berrill, 89–104. Newbury Park, CA: Sage.

——, and Eric K. Glunt. 1993. Heterosexuals Who Know Gays Personally Have More Favorable Attitudes. *The Journal of Sex Research* 30:239–244.

Hochschild, Jennifer L. 1995. *Facing Up to the American Dream.* Princeton, NJ: Princeton University Press.

hooks, bell. 1989. *Talking Back: Thinking Feminist, Thinking Black.* Boston: South End Press.

Kanter, Rosabeth Moss. 1993. *Men and Women of the Corporation.* New York: Basic Books, (Originally published in 1976.)

——, with Barry A. Stein. 1980. *A Tale of 'O': On Being Different in an Organization.* New York: Harper and Row.

Kennedy, Florynce. 1976. *Color Me Flo: My Hard Life and Good Times.* Englewood Cliffs, NJ: Prentice-Hall.

Kimmel, Michael S., and Michael A. Messner, eds. 1989. *Men's Lives.* New York: Macmillan Publishing.

Kornheiser, Tony. 1990. The Ordinary Face of Racism. *Washington Post,.* May 16, F:1, 9.

Lester, Joan. 1994. The Future of White Men and Other Diversity Dilemmas. Berkeley, CA: Conari Press.

McIntosh, Peggy. 1988. White Privilege and Male Privilege: A Personal Account of Coming to See Correspondences through Work in Women's Studies. Working Paper Number 189, Wellesley College, Center for Research on Women, Wellesley, Massachusetts.

Morton, G., and Atkinson, D. R. 1983. Minority Identity Development and Preference for Counselor Race. *Journal of Negro Education* 52(2):156–61.

National Opinion Research Center. 1990. *An American Profile: Opinions and Behavior 1972–1989.* Detroit: Gale Research.

Njeri, Itaberi. 1991. Who Is Black? *Essence,* September, 64–66, 114–16.

Omi, Michael. 1996. Racialization in the Post–Civil Rights Era. *Mapping Multiculturalism,* edited by Avery F. Gordon and Christopher Newfield, 178–86. Minneapolis: University of Minnesota Press.

Rosenhan, D. L. 1973. On Being Sane in Insane Places. *Science* 179:250–58.

Russell, Kathy, Midge Wilson, and Ronald Hall. 1992. *The Color Complex: The Politics of Skin Color among African Americans.* New York: Harcourt Brace Jovanovich.

Schaefer, Richard T. 1990. *Racial and Ethnic Groups.* 4th ed. Glenview, IL: Scott, Foresman/Little, Brown Higher Education.

Schur, Edwin. 1984. *Labeling Women Deviant: Gender, Stigma, and Social Control.* New York: Random House.

Sedgwick, Eve Kosofsky. 1990. *The Epistemology of the Closet.* Berkeley, CA: University of California Press.

Sniderman, Paul M., and Edward G. Carmines. 1997. *Reaching beyond Race.* Cambridge, MA: Harvard University Press.

Solomon, Jolie. 1996. Texaco's Troubles. *Newsweek,* November 25, 48–50.

Spelman, Elizabeth. 1988. *Inessential Woman.* Boston: Beacon Press.

Spivak, Gayatre. 1994. George Mason University Cultural Studies presentation.

Thomas, C. 1970. Different Strokes for Different Folks. *Psychology Today* 4(4):48–53, 78–80.

——, and Thomas, S. 1971. Something Borrowed, Something Black. In *Boys No More: A Black Psychologist's View of Community,* edited by C. Thomas. Beverly Hills: Glencoe Press.

Turner, Margery Austin, Michael Fix, and Raymond J. Struyk. 1991. *Opportunities Denied, Opportunities Diminished: Discrimination in Hiring.* Washington, DC: The Urban Institute.

U.S. Bureau of the Census. 1997. *Money Income in the United States.* Washington, DC: U.S. Government Printing Office.

U.S. Department of Commerce. 1993. *Statistical Abstract of the United States, 1992.* Washington, DC: U.S. Government Printing Office.

U.S. Department of Labor, Bureau of Labor Statistics. 1993. *Employment and Earnings.* Washington, DC: U.S. Government Printing Office

White, C. L., and Burke, P. J. 1987. Ethnic Role Identity among Black and White College Students: An Interactionist Approach. *Sociological Perspectives* 30(3):310–331.

READING 15

What Are You?

Joanne Nobuko Miyamoto

when I was young
kids used to ask me
what are you?
I'd tell them what my mom told me
I'm an American
chin, chin, Chinaman
you're a Jap!
flashing hot inside
I'd go home
my mom would say
don't worry
he who walks alone
walks faster

people kept asking me
what are you?
and I would always answer
I'm an American
they'd say
no, what nationality
I'm an American!
that's where I was born
flashing hot inside

and when I'd tell them what they wanted to know
Japanese
. . . Oh, I've been to Japan

I'd get it over with
me they could catalogue and file me
pigeon hole me
so they'd know just how
to think of me
priding themselves
they could guess the difference
between Japanese and Chinese

they had me wishing
I was American
just like them

they had me wishing I was what I'd
been seeing in movies and on TV
on bill boards and in magazines
and I tried

while they were making laws in California
against us owning land
we were trying to be american
and laws against us intermarrying with white people
we were trying to be american
our people volunteered to fight against
their own country
trying to be american
when they dropped the atom bomb
Hiroshima and Nagasaki
we were still trying

finally we made it
most of our parents
fiercely dedicated to give us
a good education
to give us everything they never had
we made it

now they use us as an example
to the blacks and browns
how we made it
how we overcame

but there was always
someone asking me
what are you?

Now I answer
I'm an Asian
and they say
why do you want to separate yourselves
now I say
I'm Japanese
and they say
don't you know this is the greatest country
in the world
Now I say in america
I'm part of the third world people
and they say
if you don't like it here
why don't you go back.

No biographical material available.

READING 16

Oppression

Marilyn Frye

It is a fundamental claim of feminism that women are oppressed. The word 'oppression' is a strong word. It repels and attracts. It is dangerous and dangerously fashionable and endangered. It is much misused, and sometimes not innocently.

The statement that women are oppressed is frequently met with the claim that men are oppressed too. We hear that oppressing is oppressive to those who oppress as well as to those they oppress. Some men cite as evidence of their oppression their much-advertised inability to cry. It is tough, we are told, to be masculine. When the stresses and frustrations of being a man are cited as evidence that oppressors are oppressed by their oppressing, the word 'oppression' is being stretched to meaninglessness; it is treated as though its scope includes any and all human experience of limitation or suffering, no matter the cause, degree or consequence. Once such usage has been put over on us, then if ever we deny that any person or group is oppressed, we seem to imply that we think they never suffer and have no feelings. We are accused of insensitivity; even of bigotry. For women, such accusation is particularly intimidating, since sensitivity is one of the few virtues that has been assigned to us. If we are found insensitive, we may fear we have no redeeming traits at all and perhaps are not real women. Thus are we silenced before we begin: the name of our situation drained of meaning and our guilt mechanisms tripped.

But this is nonsense. Human beings can be miserable without being oppressed, and it is perfectly consistent to deny that a person or group is oppressed without denying that they have feelings or that they suffer.

Marilyn Frye is one of the country's leading feminist philosophers and theorists.

We need to think clearly about oppression, and there is much that mitigates against this. I do not want to undertake to prove that women are oppressed (or that men are not), but I want to make clear what is being said when we say it. We need this word, this concept, and we need it to be sharp and sure.

The root of the word 'oppression' is the element 'press'. *The press of the crowd; pressed into military service; to press a pair of pants; printing press; press the button.* Presses are used to mold things or flatten them or reduce them in bulk, sometimes to reduce them by squeezing out the gasses or liquids in them. Something pressed is something caught between or among forces and barriers which are so related to each other that jointly they restrain, restrict or prevent the thing's motion or mobility. Mold. Immobilize. Reduce.

The mundane experience of the oppressed provides another clue. One of the most characteristic and ubiquitous features of the world as experienced by oppressed people is the double bind situations in which options are reduced to a very few and all of them expose one to penalty, censure or deprivation. For example, it is often a requirement upon oppressed people that we smile and be cheerful. If we comply, we signal our docility and our acquiescence in our situation. We need not, then, be taken note of. We acquiesce in being made invisible, in our occupying no space. We participate in our own erasure. On the other hand, anything but the sunniest countenance exposes us to being perceived as mean, bitter, angry or dangerous. This means, at the least, that we may be found "difficult" or unpleasant to work with, which is enough to cost one one's livelihood; at worst, being seen as mean, bitter, angry or dangerous has been known to result in rape, arrest, beating and murder. One can only choose to risk one's preferred form and rate of annihilation.

Another example: It is common in the United States that women, especially younger women, are in a bind where neither sexual activity nor sexual inactivity is all right. If she is heterosexually active, a woman is open to censure and punishment for being loose, unprincipled or a whore. The "punishment" comes in the form of criticism, snide and embarrassing remarks, being treated as an easy lay by men, scorn from her more restrained female friends. She may have to lie and hide her behavior from her parents. She must juggle the risks of unwanted pregnancy and dangerous contraceptives. On the other hand, if she refrains from heterosexual activity, she is fairly constantly harassed by men who try to persuade her into it and pressure her to "relax" and "let her hair down"; she is threatened with labels like "frigid," "uptight," "manhater," "bitch" and "cocktease." The same parents who would be disapproving of her sexual activity may be worried by her inactivity because it suggests she is not or will not be popular, or is not sexually normal. She may be charged with lesbianism. If a woman is raped, then if she has been heterosexually active she is subject to the presumption that she liked it (since her activity is presumed to show that she likes sex), and if she has not been heterosexually active, she is subject to the presumption that she liked it (since she is supposedly "repressed and frustrated"). Both heterosexual activity and heterosexual nonactivity are likely to be taken as proof that you wanted to be raped, and hence, of course, weren't *really* raped at all. You can't win. You are caught in a bind, caught between systematically related pressures.

Women are caught like this, too, by networks of forces and barriers that expose one to penalty, loss or contempt whether one works outside the home or not, is on welfare or not, bears children or not, raises children or not, marries or not, stays married or not, is heterosexual, lesbian, both or neither. Economic necessity; confinement to racial and/or sexual job ghettos; sexual harassment; sex discrimination; pressures of competing expectations and judgments about *women, wives* and *mothers* (in the society at large, in racial and ethnic subcultures and in one's own mind); dependence (full or partial) on husbands, parents or the state; commitment to political ideas; loyalties to racial or ethnic or other "minority" groups; the demands of self-respect and responsibilities to others. Each of these factors exists in complex tension with every other, penalizing or prohibiting all of the apparently available options. And nipping at one's heels, always, is the endless pack of little things. If one dresses one way, one is subject to the assumption that one is advertising one's sexual availability; if one dresses another way, one appears to "not care about oneself" or to be "unfeminine." If one uses "strong language," one invites categorization as a whore or slut; if one does not, one invites categorization as a "lady" one too delicately constituted to cope with robust speech or the realities to which it presumably refers.

The experience of oppressed people is that the living of one's life is confined and shaped by forces and barriers which are not accidental or occasional and hence avoidable, but are systematically related to each other in such a way as to catch one between and among them and restrict or penalize motion in any direction. It is the experience of being caged in: all avenues, in every direction, are blocked or booby trapped.

Cages. Consider a birdcage. If you look very closely at just one wire in the cage, you cannot see the other wires. If your conception of what is before you is determined by this myopic focus, you could look at that one wire, up and down the length of it, and be unable to see why a bird would not just fly around the wire any time it wanted to go somewhere. Furthermore, even if, one day at a time, you myopically inspected each wire, you still could not see why a bird would have trouble going past the wires to get anywhere. There is no physical property of any one wire, *nothing* that the closest scrutiny could discover, that will reveal how a bird could be inhibited or harmed by it except in the most accidental way. It is only when you step back, stop looking at the wires one by one, microscopically, and take a macroscopic view of the whole cage, that you can see why the bird does not go anywhere;

and then you will see it in a moment. It will require no great subtlety of mental powers. It is perfectly *obvious* that the bird is surrounded by a network of systematically related barriers, no one of which would be the least hindrance to its flight, but which, by their relations to each other, are as confining as the solid walls of a dungeon.

It is now possible to grasp one of the reasons why oppression can be hard to see and recognize: one can study the elements of an oppressive structure with great care and some good will without seeing the structure as a whole, and hence without seeing or being able to understand that one is looking at a cage and that there are people there who are caged, whose motion and mobility are restricted, whose lives are shaped and reduced.

The arresting of vision at a microscopic level yields such common confusion as that about the male door opening ritual. This ritual, which is remarkably widespread across classes and races, puzzles many people, some of whom do and some of whom do not find it offensive. Look at the scene of the two people approaching a door. The male steps slightly ahead and opens the door. The male holds the door open while the female glides through. Then the male goes through. The door closes after them. "Now how," one innocently asks, "can those crazy womenslibbers say that is oppressive? The guy *removed* a barrier to the lady's smooth and unruffled progress." But each repetition of this ritual has a place in a pattern, in fact in several patterns. One has to shift the level of one's perception in order to see the whole picture.

The door-opening pretends to be a helpful service, but the helpfulness is false. This can be seen by noting that it will be done whether or not it makes any practical sense. Infirm men and men burdened with packages will open doors for able bodied women who are free of physical burdens. Men will impose themselves awkwardly and jostle everyone in order to get to the door first. The act is not determined by convenience or grace. Furthermore, these very numerous acts of unneeded or even noisome "help" occur in counterpoint to a pattern of men not being helpful in many practical ways in which women might welcome help. What *women* experience is a world in which gallant princes charming commonly make a fuss about being helpful and providing small services when help and services are of little or no use, but in which there are rarely ingenious and adroit princes at hand when substantial assistance is really wanted either in mundane affairs or in situations of threat, assault or terror. There is no help with the (his) laundry; no help typing a report at 4:00 a.m.; no help in mediating disputes among relatives or children. There is nothing but advice that women should stay indoors after dark, be chaperoned by a man, or when it comes down to it, "lie back and enjoy it."

The gallant gestures have no practical meaning. Their meaning is symbolic. The door-opening and similar services provided are services which really are needed by people who are for one reason or another incapacitated—unwell, burdened with parcels, etc. So the message is that women are incapable. The detachment of the acts from the concrete realities of what women need and do not need is a vehicle for the message that women's actual needs and interests are unimportant or irrelevant. Finally, these gestures imitate the behavior of servants toward masters and thus mock women, who are in most respects the servants and caretakers of men. The message of the false helpfulness of male gallantry is female dependence, the invisibility or insignificance of women, and contempt for women.

One cannot see the meanings of these rituals if one's focus is riveted upon the individual event in all its particularity, including the particularity of the individual man's present conscious intentions and motives and the individual woman's conscious perception of the event in the moment. It seems sometimes that people take a deliberately myopic view and fill their eyes with things seen microscopically in order not to see macroscopically. At any rate, whether it is deliberate or not, people can and do fail to see the oppression of women because they fail to see macroscopically and hence fail to see the various elements of the situation as systematically related in larger schemes.

As the cageness of the birdcage is a macroscopic phenomenon, the oppressiveness of the situations in which women live our various and different lives is a macroscopic phenomenon. Neither can be *seen* from a microscopic perspective. But when you look macroscopically you can see it a network of forces and barriers which are systematically related and which conspire to the immobilization, reduction and molding of women and the lives we live. . . .

It seems to be the human condition that in one degree or another we all suffer frustration and limitation, all encounter unwelcome barriers, and all are damaged and hurt in various ways. Since we are a social species, almost all of our behavior and activities are structured by more than individual inclination and the conditions of the planet and its atmosphere. No human is free of social structures, nor (perhaps) would happiness consist in such freedom. Structure consists of boundaries, limits and barriers; in a structured whole, some motions and changes are possible, and others are not. If one is looking for an excuse to dilute the word 'oppression', one can use the fact of social structure as an excuse and say that everyone is oppressed. But if one would rather get clear about what oppression is and is not, one needs to sort out the sufferings, harms and limitations and figure out which are elements of oppression and which are not.

From what I have already said here, it is clear that if one wants to determine whether a particular suffering, harm or limitation is part of someone's being oppressed, one has to look at it *in context* in order to tell whether it is an element in an oppressive structure: one has to see if it is part of an enclosing structure of forces and barriers which tends to the immobilization and reduction of a group or category of people. One has to look at how the barrier or force fits with others and to whose benefit or detriment it works. As soon as one looks at examples, it becomes obvious that not everything which frustrates or limits a person is oppressive, and not every harm or damage is due to or contributes to oppression.

If a rich white playboy who lives off income from his investments in South African diamond mines should break a leg in a skiing accident at Aspen and wait in pain in a blizzard for hours before he is rescued, we may assume that in that period he suffers. But the suffering comes to an end; his leg is repaired by the best surgeon money can buy and he is soon recuperating in a lavish suite, sipping Chivas Regal. Nothing in this picture suggests a structure of barriers and forces. He is a member of several oppressor groups and does not suddenly become oppressed because he is injured and in pain. Even if the accident was caused by someone's malicious negligence, and hence someone can be blamed for it and morally faulted, that person still has not been an agent of oppression.

Consider also the restriction of having to drive one's vehicle on a certain side of the road. There is no doubt that this restriction is almost unbearably frustrating at times, when one's lane is not moving and the other lane is clear. There are surely times, even, when abiding by this regulation would have harmful consequences. But the restriction is obviously wholesome for most of us most of the time. The restraint is imposed for our benefit, and does benefit us; its operation tends to encourage our *continued* motion, not to immobilize us. The limits imposed by traffic regulations are limits most of us would cheerfully impose on ourselves given that we knew others would follow them too. They are part of a structure which shapes our behavior, not to our reduction and immobilization, but rather to the protection of our continued ability to move and act as we will.

Another example: The boundaries of a racial ghetto in an American city serve to some extent to keep white people from going in, as well as to keep ghetto dwellers from going out. A particular white citizen may be frustrated or feel deprived because s/he cannot stroll around there and enjoy the "exotic" aura of a "foreign" culture, or shop for bargains in the ghetto swap shops. In fact, the existence of the ghetto, of racial segregation, does deprive the white person of knowledge and harm her/his character by nurturing unwarranted feelings of superiority. But this does not make the white person in this situation a member of an oppressed race or a person oppressed because of her/his race. One must look at the barrier. It limits the activities and the access of those on both sides of it (though to different degrees). But it is a product of the intention, planning and action of whites for the benefit of whites, to secure and maintain privileges that are available to whites generally, as members of the dominant and privileged group. Though the existence of the barrier has some bad consequences for whites, the barrier does not exist in systematic relationship with other barriers and forces forming a structure oppressive to whites; quite the contrary. It is part of a structure which oppresses the ghetto dwellers and thereby (and by white intention) protects and furthers white interests as dominant white culture understands them. This barrier is not oppressive to whites, even though it is a barrier to whites.

Barriers have different meanings to those on opposite sides of them, even though they are barriers to both. The physical walls of a prison no more dissolve to let an outsider in than to let an insider out, but for the insider they are confining and limiting while to the outsider they may mean protection from what s/he takes to be threats posed by insiders—freedom from harm or anxiety. A set of social and economic barriers and forces separating two groups may be felt, even painfully, by members of both groups and yet may mean confinement to one and liberty and enlargement of opportunity to the other.

The service sector of the wives/mommas/assistants/girls is almost exclusively a woman-only sector; its boundaries not only enclose women but to a very great extent keep men out. Some men sometimes encounter this barrier and experience it as a restriction on their movements, their activities, their control or their choices of "lifestyle." Thinking they might like the simple nurturant life (which they may imagine to be quite free of stress, alienation and hard work), and feeling deprived since it seems closed to them, they thereupon announce the discovery that they are oppressed, too, by "sex roles." But that barrier is erected and maintained by men, for the benefit of men. It consists of cultural and economic forces and pressures in a culture and economy controlled by men in which, at every economic level and in all racial and ethnic subcultures, economy, tradition—and even ideologies of liberation—work to keep at least local culture and economy in male control.* . . .

*Of course this is complicated by race and class. Machismo and "Black manhood" politics seem to help keep Latin or Black men in control of more cash than Latin or Black women control; but these politics seem to me also to ultimately help keep the larger economy in *white* male control.

READING 17

"Can You See the Rainbow?" The Roots of Denial

Sally French

CHILDHOOD

Some of my earliest memories are of anxious relatives trying to get me to see things. I did not understand why it was so important that I should do so, but was acutely aware of their intense anxiety if I could not. It was aesthetic things like rainbows that bothered them most. They would posi-

Sally French is a lecturer in health and social welfare at the Open University in England.

tion me with great precision, tilting my head to precisely the right angle, and then point to the sky saying "Look, there it is; look, there, there . . . THERE!" As far as I was concerned there was nothing there, but if I said as much their anxiety grew even more intense; they would rearrange my position and the whole scenario would be repeated.

In the end, despite a near total lack of colour vision and a complete indifference to the rainbow's whereabouts, I would say I could see it. In that way I was able to release the mounting tension and escape to pursue more interesting tasks. It did not take long to learn that in order to avert episodes such as these and to protect the feelings of the people around me, I had to deny my disability.

The adults would also get very perturbed if ever I looked "abnormal." Being told to open my eyes and straighten my face, when all I was doing was trying to see, made me feel ugly and separate. Having adults pretend that I could see more than I could, and having to acquiesce in the pretence, was a theme throughout my childhood.

Adults who were not emotionally involved with the issue of whether or not I could see also led me along the path of denial. This was achieved by their tendency to disbelieve me and interpret my behaviour as "playing up" when I told them I could not see. Basically they were confused and unable to cope with the ambiguities of partial sight and were not prepared to take instruction on the matter from a mere child. One example of this occurred in the tiny country primary school that I attended. On warm, sunny days we had our lessons outdoors where, because of the strong sunlight, I could not see to read, write or draw. It was only when the two teachers realised I was having similar difficulties eating my dinner that they began to doubt their interpretation that I was a malingerer. On several occasions I was told off by opticians when I failed to discriminate between the different lenses they placed before my eyes. I am not sure whether they really disbelieved me or whether their professional pride was hurt when nothing they could offer seemed to help; whatever it was I rapidly learned to say "better" or "worse," even though all the lenses looked the same.

It was also very difficult to tell the adults, when they had scraped together the money and found the time to take me to the pantomime or wherever, that it was a frustrating and boring experience. I had a strong sense of spoiling other people's fun, just as a sober person among a group of drunken friends may have. As a child, explaining my situation without appearing disagreeable, sullen and rude was so problematic that I usually denied my disability and suffered in silence. All of this taught me from a very early age that, while the adults were working themselves up about whether or not I could see rainbows, my own anxieties must never be shared.

These anxieties were numerous and centred on getting lost, being slow, not managing and, above all, looking stupid and displaying fear. I tried very hard to be "normal," to be anonymous and to merge with the crowd. Beaches were a nightmare; finding my way back from the sea to specific people in the absence of landmarks was almost impossible, yet giving in to panic was too shameful to contemplate. Anticipation of difficulties could cause even greater anguish than the difficulties themselves and was sufficient to ruin whole days. The prospect of outings with lots of sighted children to unfamiliar places, was enough to make me physically ill, and with a bewildering mix of remorse and relief, I would stay at home.

Brownie meetings were worrying if any degree of independent movement was allowed; in the summer when we left the confines and safety of our hut to play on the nearby common, the other children would immediately disperse, leaving me alone among the trees, feeling stupid and frightened and wondering what to do next. The adults were always adamant that I should join in, that I should not miss out on the fun, but how much they or the other children noticed my difficulties I do not know; I was never teased or blamed for them, they were simply never discussed, at least not with me. This lack of communication gave me a powerful unspoken message that my disability must be denied.

By denying the reality of my disability I protected myself from the anxiety, disapproval, frustration and disappointment of the adults in my life. Like most children I wanted their acceptance, approval and warmth, and quickly learned that this could best be gained by colluding with their perceptions of my situation. I denied my disability in response to their denial, which was often motivated by a benign attempt to integrate me in a world which they perceived as fixed. My denial of disability was thus not a psychopathological reaction, but a sensible and rational response to the peculiar situation I was in.

Special School

Attending special school at the age of nine was, in many ways, a great relief. Despite the crocodile walks,[1] the bells, the long separations from home, the regimentation and the physical punishment, it was an enormous joy to be with other partially sighted children and to be in an environment where limited sight was simply not an issue. I discovered that many other children shared my world and, despite the harshness of institutional life, I felt relaxed, made lots of friends, became more confident and thrived socially. For the first time in my life I was a standard product and it felt very good. The sighted adults who looked after us were few in number with purely custodial roles, and although they seemed to be in a permanent state of anger, provided we stayed out of trouble we were basically ignored. We lived peer-orientated, confined and unchallenging lives where lack of sight rarely as much as entered our heads.

Although the reality of our disabilities was not openly denied in this situation, the only thing guaranteed to really enthuse the staff was the slightest glimmer of hope that our sight could be improved. Contact lenses were an innovation at this time, and children who had previously been virtually ignored were nurtured, encouraged and congratulated, as they learned to cope with them, and were told how good they looked without their glasses on. After I had been at the school for about a year, I was selected as one of the guinea-pigs for the experimental "telescopic lenses" which were designed, at least in part, to preserve our postures (with which there was obsessive concern) by enabling us to read and write from a greater distance. For most of us they did not work.

I remember being photographed wearing the lenses by an American man whom I perceived to be very important. First of all he made me knit while wearing them, with the knitting held right down on my lap. This was easy as I could in any case knit without looking. He was unduly excited and enthusiastic and told me how much the lenses were helping. I knew he was wrong. Then he asked me to read, but this changed his mood completely; he became tense, and before taking the photograph he pushed the book, which was a couple of inches from my face, quite roughly to my knees. Although I knew he had cheated and that what he had done was wrong, I still felt culpable for his displeasure and aware that I had failed an important test.

We were forced to use equipment like the telescopic lenses even though it did not help, and sometimes actually made things worse; the behaviour of the adults clearly conveyed the message, "You are not acceptable as you are." If we dared to reject the equipment we were reminded of the cost, and asked to reflect on the clever and dedicated people who were tirelessly working for the benefit of ungrateful creatures like ourselves. No heed was ever taken of our own suggestions; my requests to try tinted lenses were always ignored and it was not until I left school that I discovered how helpful they would be.

The only other times that lack of sight became an issue for us at the school were during the rare and clumsy attempts to integrate us with able-bodied children. The worst possible activity, netball,[2] was usually chosen for this. These occasions were invariably embarrassing and humiliating for all concerned and could lead to desperate manoeuvres on the part of the adults to deny the reality of our situation—namely that we had insufficient sight to compete. I am reminded of one netball match, with the score around 20/nil, during which we overheard the games mistress[3] of the opposing team anxiously insisting that they let us get some goals. It was a mortifying experience to see the ball fall through the net while they stood idly by. Very occasionally local Brownies would join us for activities in our extensive grounds. We would be paired off with them for a treasure hunt through the woods, searching for milk-bottle tops—the speed at which they found them was really quite amazing. They seemed to know about us, though, and would be very kind and point the "treasure" out, and even let us pick it up ourselves sometimes, but relying on their bounty spoiled the fun and we wished we could just talk to them or play a different game.

Whether the choice of these highly visual activities was a deliberate denial of our disabilities or simply a lack of imagination on the part of the adults, I do not know. Certainly we played such games successfully among ourselves, and as we were never seen in any other context, perhaps it was the latter. It was only on rare occasions such as these that our lack of sight (which had all but been forgotten) and the artificiality of our world became apparent.

As well as denying the reality of their disabilities, disabled children are frequently forced to deny painful feelings associated with their experiences because their parents and other adults simply cannot cope with them. I am reminded of a friend who, at the age of six or seven, was repeatedly promised expensive toys and new dresses provided she did not cry when taken back to school; we knew exactly how we must behave. Protecting the feelings of the adults we cared about became an arduous responsibility which we exercised with care.

Bravery and stoicism were demanded by the institution too; any outward expression of sadness was not merely ridiculed and scorned, it was simply not allowed. Any hint of dejection led to stern reminders that, unlike most children, we were highly privileged to be living in such a splendid house with such fantastic grounds—an honour which was clearly not our due. There was no one to turn to for comfort or support, and any tears which were shed were, of necessity, silent and private. In contrast to this, the institution, normally so indifferent to life outside its gates, was peculiarly concerned about our parents' states of mind. Our letters were meticulously censored to remove any trace of despondency and the initial letter of each term had a compulsory first sentence: "I have settled down at school and am well and happy." Not only were we compelled to deny our disabilities, but also the painful feelings associated with the lifestyles forced upon us because we were disabled.

Such was our isolation at this school that issues of how to behave in the "normal" world were rarely addressed, but at the next special school I attended, which offered a grammar school education and had an entirely different ethos, much attention was paid to this. The headmaster, a strong, resolute pioneer in the education of partially sighted children, appeared to have a genuine belief not only that we were as good as everyone else, but that we were almost certainly better, and he spent his life tirelessly battling with people who did not share his view.

He liked us to regard ourselves as sighted and steered us away from any connection with blindness; for example, although we were free to go out by ourselves to the nearby town and beyond, the use of white canes was never suggested although many of us use them now. He delighted in people who broke new, visually challenging ground, like acceptance at art school or reading degrees in mathematics, and "blind" occupations, like physiotherapy, were rarely encouraged. In many ways his attitudes and behaviour were refreshing, yet he placed the onus to achieve and succeed entirely on ourselves; there was never any suggestion that the world could adapt, or that our needs could or should be accommodated. The underlying message was always the same: "Be superhuman and deny your disability."

ADULTHOOD

In adulthood, most of these pressures to deny disability persist, though they become more subtle and harder to perceive. If disabled adults manage to gain control of their lives, which for many is very difficult, these pressures may be easier to resist. This is because situations which pose difficulties, create anxieties or cause boredom can be avoided, or alternatively adequate assistance can be sought; many of the situations I was placed in as a child I now avoid. As adults we are less vulnerable and less dependent on other people, we can more easily comprehend our situation, and our adult status makes the open expression of other people's disapproval, frustration and disbelief less likely. In addition, disabled adults arouse less emotion and misplaced optimism than disabled children, which serves to dilute the insatiable drive of many professionals to cure or "improve" us. Having said this, many of the problems experienced by disabled adults are similar to those experienced by disabled children.

Disabled adults frequently provoke anxiety and embarrassment in others simply by their presence. Although they become very skillful at dealing with this, it is often achieved at great cost to themselves by denying their disabilities and needs. It is not unusual for disabled people to endure boredom or distress to safeguard the feelings of others. They may, for example, sit through lectures without hearing or seeing rather than embarrass the lecturer, or endure being carried rather than demanding an accessible venue. In situations such as these reassuring phrases, such as "I'm all right" or "Don't worry about me" become almost automatic.

One of the reasons we react in this way, rather than being assertive about our disabilities, is to avoid the disapproval, rejection and adverse labelling of others, just as we did when we were children. Our reactions are viewed as resulting from our impairments rather than from the ways we have been treated. Thus being "up front" about disability and the needs which emanate from it can easily lead us to be labelled "awkward'" "selfish" or "warped." Such labelling is very difficult to endure without becoming guilty, anxious and depressed; it eats away at our confidence, undermining our courage and leading us to deny our disabilities.

Disbelief remains a common response of able-bodied people when we attempt to convey the reality of our disabilities. If, for example, I try to explain my difficulty in coping with new environments, the usual response is, "Don't worry we all get lost" or "It looks as if you're doing fine to me." Or when I try to convey the feelings of isolation associated with not recognizing people or not knowing what is going on around me, the usual response is "You will in time" or "It took me ages too." This type of response renders disabled people "just like everyone else." For those of us disabled from birth or early childhood, where there is no experience of "normality" with which to compare our situation, knowing how different we really are is problematic and it is easy to become confused and to have our confidence undermined when others insist we are just the same.

An example of denial through disbelief occurred when I was studying a statistics component as part of a course in psychology. I could see absolutely nothing of what was going on in the lectures and yet my frequent and articulate requests for help were met with the response that all students panic about statistics and that everything would work out fine in the end. As it happens it did, but only after spending many hours with a private tutor. As people are generally not too concerned about how we "got there," our successes serve to reinforce the erroneous assumption that we really are "just like everyone else." When I finally passed the examination, the lecturer concerned informed me, in a jocular and patronising way, that my worries had clearly been unfounded! When people deny our disabilities they deny who we really are.

This tendency to disbelieve is exacerbated by the ambiguous nature of impairments such as partial sight. It is very hard for people to grasp that although I appear to manage "normally" in many situations, I need considerable help in others. The knowledge of other people's perceptions of me is sufficiently powerful to alter my behaviour in ways which are detrimental to myself; for example, the knowledge that fellow passengers have seen me use a white cane to cross the road, can be enough to deter me from reading a book on the train. A more common strategy among people with limited sight is to manage roads unaided, thereby risking life and limb to avoid being labelled as frauds.

A further reaction, often associated with the belief that we are really no different, is that because our problems are no greater than anyone else's we do not deserve any special treatment or consideration. People who react in this way view us as whingeing and ungrateful complainers whenever we assert ourselves, explain our disabilities, ask that our needs be met or demand our rights. My most recent and overt experience of this reaction occurred during a visit to Whitehall to discuss the lack of transport for disabled people. Every time I mentioned a problem which disabled people encounter, such as not being able to use the underground system or the buses, I was told in no uncertain terms that many other people have transport problems too; what about old people, poor people, people who live in remote areas? What was so special about disabled people, and was not a lot being done for them anyway? I was the only disabled person present in this meeting and my confidence was undermined sufficiently to affect the quality of my argument. Reactions such as this can easily give rise to feelings of insecurity and doubt; it is, of course, the case that many people do have problems, but disabled people are among them and cannot afford to remain passive or to be passed by.

College

At the age of 19, after working for two years, I started my physiotherapy training at a special segregated college for blind and partially sighted students. For the first time in my life my disability was, at least in part, defined as blindness. Although about half the students were partially sighted, one of the criteria for entry to the college was the ability to read and write braille (which I had never used before) and to type proficiently, as, regardless of the clarity of their handwriting, the partially sighted students were not permitted to write their essays or examinations by hand, and the blind students were not permitted to write theirs in braille. No visual teaching methods were used in the college and, for those of us with sight, it was no easy matter learning subjects like anatomy, physiology and biomechanics without the use of diagrams.

The institution seemed unable to accept or respond to the fact that our impairments varied in severity and gave rise to different types of disability. We were taught to use special equipment which we did not need and were encouraged to "feel" rather than "peer" because feeling, it was thought, was aesthetically more pleasing, especially when dealing with the poor, unsuspecting public. There was great concern about the way we looked in our professional roles; white canes were not allowed inside the hospitals where we practised clinically, even by totally blind students, and guide dogs were completely banned. It appeared that the blind students were expected to be superhuman whereas the partially sighted students were expected to be blind. Any attempt to defy or challenge these rules was very firmly quashed so, in the interests of "getting through," we outwardly denied the reality of our disabilities and complied.

Employment

Deciding whether or not to deny disability probably comes most clearly to the fore in adult life when we attempt to gain employment. Until very recently it was not uncommon to be told very bluntly that, in order to be accepted, the job must be done in exactly the same way as everyone else. In many ways this was easier to deal with than the situation now, where "equal opportunity" policies have simultaneously raised expectations and pushed negative attitudes underground, and where, in reality, little has changed. Although I have no way of proving it, I am convinced that the denial of my disability has been absolutely fundamental to my success in gaining the type of employment I have had. I have never completely denied it (it is not hidden enough for that) but rather, in response to the interviewers' sceptical and probing questions, I have minimised the difficulties I face and portrayed myself in a way which would swell my headmaster's pride.

Curiously, once in the job, people have sometimes decided that certain tasks, which I can perform quite adequately, are beyond me, while at the same time refusing to relieve me of those I cannot do. At one college where I worked it was considered impossible for me to cope with taking the minutes of meetings, but my request to be relieved of invigilating large numbers of students, on the grounds that I could not see them, was not acceded to; once again the nature of my disability was being defined by other people. On the rare occasions I have been given "special" equipment or consideration at work it has been regarded as a charitable act or donation for which I should be grateful and beholden. This behaviour signals two distinct messages: first that I have failed to be "normal" (and have therefore failed), and, second that I must ask for nothing more.

In these more enlightened days of "equal opportunities," we are frequently asked and expected to educate others at work about our disabilities. "We know nothing about it, you must teach us" is the frequent cry. In some ways this is a positive development but, on the other hand, it puts great pressure on us because few formal structures have been developed in which this educative process can take place. In the absence of proactive equal opportunity policies, we are rarely taken seriously and what we say is usually forgotten or ignored. Educating others in this way can also mean that we talk of little else but disability, which, as well as becoming boring to ourselves, can lead us to be labelled adversely or viewed solely in terms of problems. Challenging disabling attitudes and structures, especially as a lone disabled person, can become frustrating and exhausting, and in reality it is often easier and (dare I say) more functional, in the short term at least, to cope with inadequate conditions rather than fight to improve them. We must beware of tokenistic gestures which do little but put pressure on us.

CONCLUSION

The reasons I have denied the reality of my disability can be summarised as follows:

1. To avoid other people's anxiety and distress.
2. To avoid other people's disappointment and frustration.
3. To avoid other people's disbelief.
4. To avoid other people's disapproval.
5. To live up to other people's ideas of "normality."
6. To avoid spoiling other people's fun.
7. To collude with other people's pretences.

I believe that from earliest childhood denial of disability is totally rational given the situations we find ourselves in, and that to regard it as a psychopathological reaction is a serious mistake. We deny our disabilities for social, economic and emotional survival and we do so at considerable cost to our sense of self and our identities; it is not something we do because of flaws in our individual psyches. For those of us disabled from birth or early childhood, denial of disability has deeply penetrating and entangled roots; we need support and encouragement to make our needs known, but this will only be achieved within the context of genuine structural and attitudinal change.

In this paper I have drawn upon my life experiences and personal reactions to elucidate the pressures placed upon disabled people to deny the reality of their experience of disability. This approach is limited inasmuch as personal experiences and responses can never be divorced from the personality and biography of the person they concern. In addition these pressures will vary according to the individual's impairment. But with these limitations in mind, I am confident that most disabled people will identify with what I have described and that only the examples are, strictly speaking, mine.

NOTES

1. Walking two-by-two in a long file.
2. Girls' basketball.
3. Physical education teacher.

READING 18

Disability beyond Stigma: Social Interaction, Discrimination, and Activism

Michelle Fine and Adrienne Asch

DEFINING THE POPULATION OF INTEREST

. . . In 1980 Bowe estimated the total population of people with disabilities in the United States to be 36 million or perhaps 15% of the nation's people. In 1986 ("Census Study"), the *New York Times* reported some 37 million people over 15 years of age with disabling conditions. As Asch (1984) has discussed elsewhere, the mere attempt to define and enumerate the population shows that disability is a social construct. The Rehabilitation Act of 1973, as amended in 1978, defines a handicapped individual as "any person who (i) has a physical or mental impairment which substantially limits one or more of such person's major life activities, (ii) has a record of such an impairment, or (iii) is regarded as having such an impairment" (Section 7B).

We can say the following with assurance: The nation's population includes some 10% of school-aged children classified as handicapped for the purposes of receipt of special educational services (Biklen, 1988); somewhere between 9 and 17% of those between 16 and 64 years of age report disabilities that influence their employment situation (Haber & McNeil, 1983); nearly half of those over 65 indicate having one or more disabilities that interfere with their life activities or are regarded by others as doing so (DeJong & Lifchez, 1983). . . .

First, different conditions cause different types of functional impairment. Deafness, mental retardation, paralysis, blindness, congenital limb deficiencies, and epilepsy may pose common social problems of stigma, marginality, and discrimination, but they also produce quite different functional difficulties. Several of these disabilities obviously interfere with functions of daily life, but the last, epilepsy, may not. Some persons with epilepsy have no inherent limitations whatever. Nevertheless, they are likely to be regarded as having an impairment.

Furthermore, people with disabilities have different degrees of impairment: Amounts of hearing and visual loss differ; some people with impairment of mobility can walk in some situations while others cannot. Mental retardation ranges from profound to mild—so mild that many out of school never get the label. In addition, some disabilities are static, while others are progressive. Multiple sclerosis, muscular dystrophy, cystic fibrosis, some vision and hearing impairments. some types of cancer and heart conditions present progressive disabilities that

Michelle Fine is a professor of psychology at the City University of New York. Adrienne Asch is a professor in the program on biology, ethics, and the politics of human Reproduction at Wellesley College.

cause ever-changing health and life situations. Some conditions are congenital, others are acquired. All of these factors that distinguish the origin, experience, and effects of disability must be kept in mind in social science research on disability. . . .

DISABLED PEOPLE AS A MINORITY

Having acknowledged differences among these more than 36 million people in terms of their diagnoses, their social contexts, and their experiences of disability, it is important to return to the analysis that informs this article and this issue as a whole: disabled people comprise a minority group and most of their problems can and must be understood in a minority-group framework. This view is neither novel nor exclusively a post–Civil Rights Era position. Roger Baker in 1948 advanced thinking about disability in minority-group terms. Lee Meyerson, in his introduction to the 1948 *Journal of Social Issues,* opened by commenting, "There is general agreement in the literature on physical disability that the problems of the handicapped are not physical, but social and psychological" (p. 2). Our own analysis owes much to the Lewinian person-in-environment thinking of the 1948 *JSI* contributors, and to the thoughtful work of Wright (1960, 1983), herself a frequent collaborator with Barker, Meyerson, and Dembo. These authors acknowledged that people with disabilities must be understood as having psychological responses to their impairments themselves, but they went on to point out the following: environmental factors posed many barriers of discrimination, marginality, and uncertain social acceptance; people with disabilities faced ambiguous, if not rejecting, social responses; and these people responded psychologically and socially to such situations.

Our analysis expands on this significant work and the 40 intervening years of social and legislative change. In the last 15 years, the movement for disability rights has embraced a minority-group perspective. Scholars of disability outside of social psychology such as Gliedman and Roth (1980), Hahn (1983, 1988), and Scotch (1984, 1988) have attempted to elaborate a minority-group analysis of disability issues and the disability experience. Unfortunately, as seen from the ensuing discussion, much of the frequently cited social-psychological work on disability has not learned all it could from the 1948 *JSI* contributors, nor from others in the emerging field of disability studies.

The minority-group perspective that frames this volume accepts Dworkin and Dworkin's (1976) definition of a minority group, applying it to people with disabilities. The criteria include "identifiability, differential power, differential and pejorative treatment, and group awareness" (p. viii).

While disabled people as a group may fit these criteria, they nevertheless face many obstacles in developing minority-group consciousness, as Hahn (1988) and Scotch (1988) discuss in some detail. Not the least of these obstacles is the inaccessibility of the built environment, rendering transportation and public facilities unusable for people with any impairment and disrupting potential efforts at organizing. While many people with disabilities have not developed a minority-group consciousness, a recent Louis Harris survey of disabled Americans reported that 74% of people with disabilities feel some common identity with one another and that 45% see themselves as a minority in the same sense as people who are black or Hispanic (Hill, Mehnert, Taylor, Kagey, Leizhenko et al., 1986). As a footnote to Dworkin and Dworkin, we begin with the premise that a lack of shared consciousness *by some* does not negate the importance of understanding the social, structural, and psychological situation of people with disabilities in minority-group terms. As Hahn (1983, 1988) argues, the consequences of any impairment cannot be understood or appreciated without giving due weight to the environment—physical, structural, social, economic, psychological, and political—

of the person with the disability. Just how disabling would deafness be if 20th-century urbanites, like Groce's (1985) rural villagers of Martha's Vineyard in the 19th century, all practice sign language? How disabling would paraplegia be if all cities were barrier free? (See Scheer & Groce, 1988). How limiting would mental retardation be if nearly all labeled children received their educations in settings with the nonlabeled, as Biklen (1988) discusses?

Barker (1948) was right when he reminded us that not all of the disabled person's situation can be explained by prejudice and discrimination. It is true that some activities are foreclosed merely because of the biological impairment itself. But the articles in this volume expand upon his thinking by demanding that we cease considering the environment—whether physical or attitudinal—as given. The *JSI* contributors of 1948 and 1988 contrast sharply with much of the social-psychological writing about disability in the intervening decades, which assumes that the issues of disability reside in the person and tends to minimize or neglect the environment.

ASSUMPTIONS ABOUT DISABILITY

Considered below are a set of common assumptions about what disability means. For each, there have been important methodological and theoretical consequences:

1. *It is often assumed that disability is located solely in biology, and thus disability is accepted uncritically as an independent variable.* The disability and the person are assumed synonymous, and the cause of others' behaviors and attitudes. Several experimental social psychologists (Katz, 1981; Kleck, Ono, & Hastorf, 1966) have simulated disability in the laboratory to verify Goffman's reports that handicapped people arouse anxiety and discomfort in others and are socially stigmatized. In these experiments, researchers have simulated disability by using a confederate who in one experimental condition appeared disabled and in another appeared nondisabled. The experiments did support the hypothesis that nondisabled people react differently to people with disabilities than they do to people without them. Nevertheless, it should be remembered that the confederate, whose only experience of having disability may have been simulating it by sitting in a wheelchair, employed none of the strategies commonly used by disabled people to ease the discomfort of strangers in first meetings (Davis, 1961; Goffman, 1963). By focusing on initial encounters with strangers and by using a confederate whose only experience with disability might be simulating it, these experiments tell us nothing about how disabled people *actually* negotiate meaningful social interactions. Reports by Davis (1961) and Goffman (1963) acknowledge that obvious disability is generally prominent in initial social encounters. However, the extent to which an experimental confederate's naivete about living with a disability can contribute to the prominence and the awkwardness of disability has not been recognized as an intervening variable. In these experiments, disability is viewed as an independent variable, much as gender had been considered prior to the early 1970's (Under & Denmark, 1975). Disability is portrayed as the variable that predicts the outcome of social interaction when, in fact, social contexts shape the meaning of a disability in a person's life.

Most social-psychological work using mobility to examine the concept of stigma takes the experience as equivalent, regardless of such factors as the disabled person's race, culture, class and gender. Scheer and Groce (1988), Becker and Arnold (1986) provide valuable correctives by viewing the situation of disabled people through the disciplines of anthropology and history.

2. *When a disabled person faces problems, it is assumed that the impairment causes them.* In a very thoughtful expansion of Goffman's notion of stigma, Jones et al. (1984) elaborate on the consequences for the "marked" person of being singled out by others. Throughout their discus-

sion of marking and its social-psychological consequences for disabled and nondisabled alike, however, these authors never question the extent to which disability per se poses difficulties in social participation, as contrasted with difficulties caused by the environment—architectural, social, economic, legal, and cultural. For example, in their discussion of changes in the life situations of people who became disabled, the authors never question that *the disability* keeps the person from continuing the employment or from going to restaurants or other recreational facilities. The entire discussion of stigma and marked relationships assumes as "natural" what Hahn aptly terms as *disabling environment;* it views obstacles as being solely the person's biological limitations rather than the human-made barriers of architecture or discriminatory work practices.

Even Barker's (1948) early work went only part way to indicting the environment as an obstacle to the disabled person's participation. Far ahead of his time, he called for antidiscrimination laws in education and employment, although he failed to challenge the architecture, the transportation, and the communication methods that confronted people with disabilities and hampered full participation. Barker's concluding comments took social arrangements as given, urging counseling and psychotherapy for people with disabilities, so that they could come to accept "the fact that the world in which [they live] presents serious restrictions and frustrations." He went on to say that education and antidiscrimination laws cannot "remove all restrictions on the physically deviant in a world constructed for the physically normal. The ultimate adjustment must involve changes in the values of the physically normal. The ultimate adjustment must involve changes in the values of the physically disabled person" (p. 37). . . .

3. *It is assumed that the disabled person is a "victim."* In a great deal of social-psychological research on attribution, the disabled person is seen as a victim who copes with suffering by self-blame (Bulman & Wortman, 1977), by reinterpreting the suffering to find positive meaning (Taylor, Wood, & Lichtman, 1983), or by denying that he or she is really suffering (Taylor et al., 1983). Bulman and Wortman studied 29 people paralysed in accidents. Lerner (1980) describes these people as "young people who had been recently condemned to spend the rest of their lives crippled" (p. 161). In order for Lerner to make sense of why Bulman and Wortman's respondents were not displaying a sense of victimization, he posits their belief in a just world and suggests that their interpretations of the disabling events are constructed so as to retain a strong belief that the world is a just place and that bad things only happen to people for reasons. The psychological experiences of the persons with disabilities are thus examined *not* on their own terms, but instead as a form of denial. Disability is used as a synonym for victimization in this theoretical analysis. . . .

There are two more problems with the interpretations of disabled-person-as-victim put forward by Bulman and Wortman (1977), Janoff-Bulman and Frieze (1983), Lerner (1980), and Taylor et al. (1983). First, in contrast to Ladieu et al.'s (1948) report on the reactions of disabled veterans after World War II, these later researchers seem to discount the experiences described by the people they interviewed. Taylor et al., for example, view their respondents as having strategies for managing or camouflaging what must be truly tragic. To the "outsider," the researcher, the "objective situation" is that a diagnosis of cancer is primarily a tragedy. That "insiders," those with cancer, overwhelmingly state that they had fared better than they would have expected is not used self-reflectively by the researchers to reframe their notions about how people think about traumatic life events (cf. Frank, 1988). Rather, the statement is interpreted to illustrate psychological defenses that disabled people mobilize in order to manage what researchers feel is not really manageable. What needs to be stated is that disability—while never wished for—may simply not be as wholly disastrous as imagined.

Second, these authors presume that the disability itself constitutes the victimizing experience. None of them emphasize the subsequent reactions or deprivations that people experience because of social responses to their disability or environmentally imposed constraints. While Janoff-Bulman and Frieze (1983) recognize discrimination based on sex or gender to be a societal injustice, disability is assumed a biological injustice and the injustices that lie in its social treatment are ignored.

4. *It is assumed that disability is central to the disabled person's self-concept, self-definition, social comparison, and reference groups.* Taylor and her colleagues (1983) describe their respondents as having to make downward social comparisons, lest they come face to face with how bad their situations really are. Jones et al. (1984), in their discussion of stigma, assume that the recently disabled paraplegic compares herself to others who are also paralysed. She may, but perhaps only when it comes to assessing her capacity to perform certain activities from a wheelchair. Gibbons (1986) claims that while such severely stigmatized people as those labeled retarded must make only downward social comparison to preserve self-esteem, more "mildly stigmatized" people such as those using wheelchairs seek out similarly disabled people with whom to compare themselves, and avoid social interactions and social comparisons with nondisabled people. Because disability is clearly salient for the nondisabled, it is assumed that the marked person incorporates the mark as central to self-definition.

The above authors forget that the woman who is paralysed may be as likely to compare herself with other women her age, others of her occupation, others of her family, class, race, or a host of other people and groups who function as reference groups and social comparison groups for her. Disability may be more salient to the researchers studying it than to the people being studied, who may define themselves as "similar to" or worthy of comparison with people without disabilities. Gurin (1984) reminds researchers in social comparison and relative deprivation to pay more attention to the conditions under which people choose particular groups with whom to compare themselves, and she stresses that social comparison may have nothing to do with gender, race, or disability. . . .

5. *It is assumed that having a disability is synonymous with needing help and social support.* People with disabilities are perceived to be examples of those ever in need of help and social support (Brickman et al., 1982; Deutsch, 1985; Dunkel-Schetter, 1984; Jones et al., 1984; Katz, 1981; Krebs, 1970; Sarason, 1986). Such an assumption is sustained both by what researchers study and write about those with disabilities and by their omission of disabled people in their discussions as providers of support.

The assumption that disability is synonymous with helplessness is not surprising when we remember that "the handicapped role" in the United States has been seen as one of helplessness, dependence, and passivity (Gliedman & Roth, 1980; Goffman, 1963). Brickman et al. (1982), in their excellent discussion of different models of helping and coping, review the essence of the medical model: The person is responsible for neither the problem encountered nor the solution required. The handicapped role, like the sick role of which it is an extension, compels the occupant to suspend other activities until recovered, to concentrate on getting expert therapy, to follow instructions, to get well, and only then to resume normal life. The nonhandicapped person equates having a disability with a *bad and eternal flu,* toothache, or broken leg. When such conditions are temporary, it may be acceptable to entrust oneself to helpers and to forgo decision making briefly; but when forced to confront a moment of weakness, unsteadiness, or limitations in the capacity to see, hear, or move, people experience grave difficulty in adjusting. However, it is erroneous to conclude that their difficulties mirror those of the person who has a long-term disability and who has learned to use alternative methods to accomplish tasks of daily living and working.

That disability is assumed tantamount to incompetence and helplessness has been investigated, and supported in laboratory research. Unfortunately, the writing that has been generated *accepts* rather than *challenges* this stereotype. Katz (1981), who found that whites gave more help to competent blacks than to ones they perceived to be less competent and enterprising, expected that the same help-giving pattern would be true for nondisabled subjects when confronting a person with a disability. Contrary to his hypothesis, however, he found that nondisabled people gave *less* help to disabled persons perceived as competent and friendly than to those perceived as incompetent and unfriendly. They also gave less help to the "disabled person" (simulated) than to the nondisabled persons. To explain this, Katz relied on Goffman (1963) and Gliedman and Roth (1980) in asserting that nondisabled persons are relatively offended or uncomfortable when confronting a person with an impairment who manages life competently. As Jones and his colleagues (1984) remind us, the able-bodied deny the reality of successful adaptation by the disabled person. They perceive it as the disabled person "making the best of a bad job," and this view supports their conviction that their own health and capacities are as important, and infallible, as they think (p. 87).

Even while we wonder whether Katz would have gotten the same finding had he used a person who actually had a disability rather than one who had simulated an impairment, it is valuable to have this experimental support for what Goffman, Gliedman and Roth, and untold numbers of people with disabilities have described. Unfortunately, Jones et al. (1984) fall prey to their own unchallenged assumptions in thinking about ongoing relationships between people with and without disabilities: Throughout their book, and especially in the chapter by French (1984), it is assumed that the person with the disability is in constant need of help and support, rather than being a victim of nondisabled persons' projections or fantasies. Thereby, three problems arise: first, that the person with a disability may need assistance with certain acts is generalized to all aspects of the relationship between a person with a disability and one without. Second, if the person does need assistance, it is assumed that a previous reciprocal relationship will change, rather than that new methods or relationships will develop to provide it. Concurrently, it is assumed that the biological condition rather than the environment and social context makes one-way assistance inevitable. Third, it perpetuates the idea that the impaired person is forever the recipient, rather than ever the provider, of help and support. If disabled people are mentioned, they are mentioned as only on the receiving end of a helping transaction.

In French's (1984) chapter on marriages between disabled and nondisabled people, the assumptions are never challenged that the disability causes marital roles to change fundamentally, that blindness or quadriplegia per se will make resuming a work role difficult or impossible, that recreation will have to be curtailed. The spouse who performs certain amounts of physical caretaking is seen not only as a physical caretaker but as a generous intellectual and emotional caretaker as well. Physical incapacities are perceived as leading inevitably to incapacities in other spheres of life. Wright's (1983) notion that disability "spreads" throughout a relationship is embedded unchallenged in this entire discussion.

Moreover, it is the disability, not the institutional, physical, or attitudinal environment, that is blamed for role changes that may occur. The person with a disability may (initially, or always) need physical caretaking, such as help in dressing, household chores, or reading. It must be asked, however, whether such assistance would be necessary if environments were adapted to the needs of people with disabilities—if, for example, more homes were built to accommodate those who used wheelchairs, if technological aids could be developed to assist in performing manual tasks, if existing technology to convert the printed word into speech or Braille were affordable to all who needed it. Thus, again, the physical environment as an obstruction remains an unchallenged given. In addition, the author is assuming that the role of human assistant for all these tasks will automatically fall to the "significant other" rather than considering whether such activities could be performed by others, including public sector employees, thus permitting the primary relationship to function in its primary spheres of intimacy, sharing, and emotional nurturance for both participants. If the partners reorganize their roles after the impairment of one member, such reorganizations may result from a variety of factors: the way they think about disability, their relational obligations, the way that health care professionals inform them about the implications of disability, or the difficulties faced in affording appropriate assistance in the United States. These are consequences of how people think about disability and of current national disability policy, not of disability per se. As with all too much of this literature, as Wright (1983) points out researchers who are outsiders make attributions to persons and thus neglect the powerful role of the environment.

The third problem mentioned above—that disabled people are always seen as recipients—may stem not only from distortions about people with disabilities but also from using disability as a metaphor to illustrate theory rather than to reveal more about the lives of people with impairments. Deutsch (1985) may be correct in speculating that, at least temporarily, resources would or should go to a sick child rather than to a well one; Dunkel-Schetter (1984) may plausibly learn about the mechanisms of social support by studying what people with cancer find valuable and supportive from others after such a diagnosis; Krebs (1970) makes an important point in discussing how assumptions of legitimacy of others' dependency influence the helping process. Nonetheless, by staying with questions about theories of distributive systems (Deutsch, 1985), social support (Dunkel-Schetter, 1984), or altruism (Krebs, 1970) and by not focusing on ongoing reciprocal transactions, the person with a disability is never imagined or shown to be a provider of support. As Schumaker and Brownell (1984) remind us, those who receive support also commonly seek to provide it, if not to those who gave it to them, then to others. It is regrettable that people with disabilities, when studied or considered at all in most social-psychological literature, are examined only in ways that reinforce and perpetuate existing stereotypes rather than in ways that question and challenge them. In this manner, the literature fails to enrich our understanding of the lives of people with handicapping conditions. . . .

THE ROLE OF THESE ASSUMPTIONS FOR SOCIETY AND FOR SOCIAL SCIENCE

It is worth speculating on how these assumptions get made, why they persist, and what functions they serve for researchers and society. It remains a task for future research to discover the plausibility of these speculations.

Jones and his colleagues (1984) contend that the thought or awareness of disability evokes feelings of vulnerability and death. They suggest that the nondisabled person almost wants the one with the disability to suffer so as to confirm that the "normal" state is as good and as important as the "normal" thinks it is. Because disability can be equated with vulnerability to the controllable, observing someone with a disability forces all of us to wonder about the consequences of what one cannot control. In a society seeking to control ever more of life, is there a leap to the assumption that one cannot live with the consequences of what one cannot control? Social researchers are in the business of expanding knowledge of the world and trying to optimize prediction and control. As researchers, we highly prize knowledge and the control it can provide. Does such a commitment to control suggest that social scientists may view disability as fearful, unacceptable, and different because the person with the disability is a reminder that we cannot control all life events?

As discussed earlier, perceptions of disability have been the repository and projection of human needs. How much do the social and psychological problems that many people associate with disability actually pervade all of human life? If one can think of a person with a disability as needy, in contrast, one can view those without impairments as strong and as not having needs. By thinking of the disabled person as dependent in a given situation, and the one without disabilities as independent and autonomous, one can avoid considering how extensively people without disabilities too are dependent and sometimes not. Rather than the world being divided into givers and receivers of help, we are all actually interdependent. Attributing neediness and lack of control to people with disabilities permits those who are not disabled to view themselves as having more control and more strength in their lives than may be the case.

Last, perceiving a person with a disability as a suffering victim, as a stimulus object, as in need, or as different and strange, all reinforce what Goffman (1963) describes as perception of the stigmatized as "not quite human" (p. 6). In discussing the scope of justice, Deutsch (1985) comments, "Justice is not involved in relations with others. . . . The narrower one's concept of community, the narrower will be the scope of situations in which one's actions will be governed by considerations of justice" (pp. 36–37). Deutsch goes on to contend that it has been a

> too-common assumption of victimizers, even those of good will, as well as of many social scientists, that the social pathology has been in the ghetto rather than in those who have built the walls to surround it, that the disadvantaged are the ones who need to be changed rather than the people and institutions who have kept the disadvantaged in a submerged position. . . . It is more important to change educational institutions and economic and political systems so that they will permit those groups who are now largely excluded from important positions of decision-making to share power than to try to inculcate new attitudes and skills in those who are excluded (p. 61).

These words apply as much to the situation of people with disabilities as to that of people with economic disadvantages whom Deutsch considered. By concentrating on cure or on psychological and physical restoration of the impaired person, society and the discipline of psychology have avoided the need to focus on essential changes in the environmental side of the "person-in-environment" situation. If the person with a disability is "not quite human," then that person can remain outside the community of those who must receive just distributions of rewards and resources (Deutsch, 1985). In contrast, if people with disabilities were perceived as having the same rights to mobility and life's opportunities as people without impairments, we would inevitably be compelled to rethink the view that transportation for people with mobility impairments, or access to treatment for infants or adults with disabilities, are gifts or charities that can be withdrawn when times are tight. Once people with disabilities are admitted inside the human and moral community, the task becomes one of creating an environment where all humans—including those with impairments—can truly flourish. . . .

REFERENCES

Asch, A. (1984). The experience of disability: A challenge for psychology. *American Psychologist, 39,* 529–536.

Barker, R. B. (1948). The social psychology of physical disability. *Journal of Social Issues, 4* (4), 28–37.

Becker, G., & Arnold, R. (1986). Stigma as a social and cultural construct. In S. Ainlay, G. Becker, & L. Coleman (Eds.), *The dilemma of difference: A multidisciplinary view of stigma* (pp. 39–58). New York: Plenum.

Bilken, D. (1988). The myth of clinical judgment. *Journal of Social Issue, 44* (1), 127–141.

Bowe, F. (1980). *Rehabilitating America.* New York:

Harper & Row.

Brickman, P., Rabinowitz, V. C., Karuza, J., Coats, D., Cohn, E., & Kidder, L. (1982). Models of helping and coping. *American Psychologist, 37,* 368–384.

Bulman, R., & Wortman, C. (1977). Attributions of blame and coping with the "real world": Severe accident victims react to their lot. *Journal of Personality and Social Psychology, 35,* 351–363.

Census study reports one in five adults suffers from disability. (1986, December 23). *New York Times,* p. 67.

Davis, F. (1961). Deviance disavowal: The management of strained interaction by the visibly handicapped. *Social Problems, 9,* 120–132.

Deutsch, M. (1985). *Distributive justice.* New Haven, CT: Yale University Press.

Disability Rag. (1984, February–March). Entire issue.

Dunkel-Schetter, C. (1984). Social support and cancer: Findings based on patient interviews and their implications. *Journal of Social Issues, 40* (4), 77–98.

Dworkin, A., & Dworkin, R. (Eds.) (1976). *The minority report.* New York: Praeger.

Editorial, *New York Times* (1983, June 17).

Frank, G. (1988). Beyond stigma: Visibility and self-empowerment of persons with congenital limb deficiencies. *Journal of Social Issues 44* (1), 95–117.

French, R. De S. (1984). The long-term relationships of marked people. In E. E. Jones et al., *Social stigma: The psychology of marked relationships* (pp. 254–295). New York: Freeman.

Gibbons, F. X. (1986). Stigma and interpersonal relations. In S. Ainlay, G. Becker, & L. Coleman (Eds.), *The dilemma of difference: A multi-disciplinary view of stigma* (pp. 123–144). New York: Plenum.

Gliedman, J., & Roth, W. (1980). *The unexpected minority: Handicapped children in America.* New York: Harcourt, Brace, Jovanovich.

Goffman, E. (1963). *Stigma: Notes on the management of spoiled identity.* Englewood Cliffs, NJ: Prentice-Hall.

Groce, N. (1985). *Everyone here spoke sign language: Hereditary deafness on Martha's Vineyard.* Cambridge, MA: Harvard University Press.

Gurin, P. (1984). Review of *Relative deprivation and working men. Contemporary Psychology, 29,* 209–210.

Hahn, H. (1983, March–April). Paternalism and public policy. *Society,* pp. 36–46.

Hahn, H. (1988). The politics of physical differences: Disability and discrimination. *Journal of Social Issues, 44* (1), 39–49.

Hill, N., Mehnert, T., Taylor, T., Kagey, M., Leizhenko, S., et al. (1986). *The ICD survey of disabled Americans: Bringing disabled Americans into the mainstream.* New York: International Center for the Disabled.

Janoff-Bulman, R., & Frieze, I. H. (1983). A theoretical perspective for understanding reactions to victimization. *Journal of Social Issues, 39* (2), 1–17.

Jones, E. E., Farina, A., Hastorf, A. H., Markus, H., Miller, D. T., Scott, R. A., & French, R. De S. (1984). *Social stigma: The psychology of marked relationships.* New York: Freeman.

Katz, I. (1981). *Stigma: A social-psychological analysis.* Hillsdale, NJ: Erlbaum.

Kleck, R., Ono, H., & Hastorf, A. (1966). The effects of physical deviance upon face-to-face interaction. *Human Relations, 19,* 425–436.

Krebs, D. L. (1970). Altruism: An examination of the concept and review of the literature. *Psychological Bulletin, 73,* 258–302.

Ladieu, G., Adler, D. L., & Dembo, T. (1948). Studies in adjustment to visible injuries: Social acceptance of the injured. *Journal of Social Issues, 4* (4) 55–61.

Lerner, M. J. (1980). *The belief in a just world: A fundamental delusion.* New York: Plenum.

Myerson, L. (1948). Physical disability as a social psychological problem. *Journal of Social Issues, 4* (4), 107–109.

Rehabilitation Act of 1973, Pub. L. No. 93-112, 87 Stat. 357 (1973).

Sampson, E. (1983). *Justice and the critique of pure psychology.* New York: Plenum.

Sarason, S. B. (1986). And what is the public interest? *American Psychologist, 41,* 899–906.

Scheer, J., & Groce, N. (1988). Impairment as a human constant: Cross-cultural and historical perspectives on variation. *Journal of Social Issues, 44* (1), 23–39.

Scotch, R. K. (1984). *From good will to civil rights: Transforming federal disability policy.* Philadelphia: Temple University Press.

Scotch, R. K. (1988). Disability as the basis for a social movement: Advocacy and the politics of definition. *Journal of Social Issues, 44* (1), 159–173.

Shumaker, S., & Brownell, A. (1984). Toward a theory of social support: Closing conceptual gaps. *Journal of Social Issues, 40* (4), 11–36.

Taylor, S. E., Wood, J. V., & Lichtman, R. R. (1983). "It could be worse": Selective evaluation as a response to victimization. *Journal of Social Issues, 39* (2), 19–40.

Unger, R. K., & Denmark, F. L. (1975). *Woman: Dependent or independent variable?* New York: Psychological Dimensions.

Wight, B. A. (1960). *Physical disability: A psychosocial approach.* New York: Harper & Row.

Wight, B. A. (1983). *Physical disability: A psycho-social approach.* New York: Harper & Row.

PERSONAL ACCOUNT

I Am Legally Blind

Like approximately 1.1 million people in the United States, I am legally blind, which means that I have some remaining vision. Therefore, I have the option to "come out" as a blind person or "pass" as someone who is fully sighted.

When I am passing, I avoid using my magnifier or my reading glasses, which have an obviously protruded lens and require me to hold items close to my face. By not asking for assistance, I avoid having to tell anyone I am blind. In restaurants, I order without consulting the menu. If I go out walking, I leave my white cane at home. I get on buses and subway trains without asking anyone to identify which line I'm boarding. I purchase items in stores without using my pocket magnifier to read labels or prices. On elevators that have not been adapted to meet ADA (Americans with Disabilities Act of 1990) guidelines of "reasonable accommodation," I take my best shot at hitting the right button. Therefore, I am never quite sure if I am exiting on the floor that I want. I wander through unfamiliar neighborhoods and buildings that are invariably marked with small print signs that are placed above doorways.

There is a price I pay for passing as a sighted person. I give away ten-dollar bills when I mean to pay one dollar. I come home from grocery stores with brands or flavors of items that I don't like or that cost too much. But, the highest cost is freedom: I relinquish my rights to life, liberty and the pursuit of happiness. Here's what happens when I don't ask for help.

When I don't solicit information about buses, trains, and elevators, I waste a lot of time trying to find specific destinations and end up feeling frustrated, angry, and exhausted. When I leave my white cane at home, I give up my right to travel freely because I can't navigate in unfamiliar places or go anywhere at all after dark: I jeopardize my own safety because I trip and fall on curbs, stairs, bumps, and potholes. I surrender my freedom of choice when, in fast food restaurants where the menus are inaccessible to me, I order the same food time and time again. I limit my choice of products when I don't use my visual aids because I have to choose by label color rather than to read the print, and I don't learn about new products, either. If I hadn't identified myself as a blind person at the university, I would have relinquished my right to pursue an education because I would have had no adaptive equipment nor would I have made use of the university's Disability Support Services. I would have failed in school, which is exactly what I did, both in high school and the first time I attended college.

So, why in the world would I ever choose to pass? Because sometimes, I get sick of people's stares, whispers, ignorant comments, and nosy questions. When I ask for directions or for someone to read something to me, I am often responded to as if I am stupid or a child. People often answer my questions in irritated or condescending tones. More times than not, they don't answer verbally, but point at the object instead, which forces me to have to ask again or to explain why I am asking. This happens a lot at checkout stands.

I have had people grab my arm and try to pull me where I don't want to go. Recently, at a concert, my companion and I, with my white cane in hand, were easing our way through the aisle to our seats when a woman jumped up, grabbed my arm, knocking me off balance, then pushed me toward my seat. She didn't even ask if I wanted help. It really was an assault. Indeed, to a mugger or rapist, my white cane identifies me as a potential victim.

When I go shopping, I behave differently than fully sighted people do. I must juggle my list, purse, magnifier, reading glasses as well as the product and shopping basket or cart. I hold items very close to my face to read product labels, tags, and prices. A surprising number of people have asked "What are you looking for?" Sometimes, I reply, "Why do you ask?" I don't like having to explain my methods of adaptation. I have been followed by security guards and even stopped once in a drug store. The guard said that I was "acting suspiciously." He felt pretty bad when I told him that I was trying to see the prices. After that, whenever I went into that store, he was right there asking me if I needed any help finding things. Even though he meant well, the end result was that he still was following me. Ever since that experience, I stay alert to the possibility that I might look suspicious and I stand in open areas when I go into my purse for my glasses. I don't like having to be concerned about this, but I like the idea of being nabbed for shoplifting even less.

These are the paradoxical consequences of passing or coming out. Both cause me trouble, although I have learned the hard way that the more I use adaptive techniques and aids, and the more often I ask for help, the more efficient and independent I become. Thus, when I am "out," I am true to my own needs and desires.

Beth Omansky Gordon

READING 19

Time to Look and Listen

Magdoline Asfahani

I love my country as many who have been here for generations cannot. Perhaps that's because I'm the child of immigrants, raised with a conscious respect for America that many people take for granted. My parents chose this country because it offered them a new life, freedom and possibilities. But I learned at a young age that the country we loved so much did not feel the same way about us.

Discrimination is not unique to America. It occurs in any country that allows immigration. Anyone who is unlike the majority is looked at a little suspiciously, dealt with a little differently. The fact that I wasn't part of the majority never occurred to me. I knew that I was an Arab and a Muslim. This meant nothing to me. At school I stood up to say the Pledge of Allegiance every day. These things did not seem incompatible at all. Then everything changed for me, suddenly and permanently, in 1985. I was only in seventh grade, but that was the beginning of my political education.

That year a TWA plane originating in Athens was diverted to Beirut. Two years earlier the U.S. Marine barracks in Beirut had been bombed. That seemed to start a chain of events that would forever link Arabs with terrorism. After the hijacking, I faced classmates who taunted me with cruel names, attacking my heritage and my religion. I became an outcast and had to apologize for myself constantly.

After a while, I tried to forget my heritage. No matter what race, religion or ethnicity, a child who is attacked often retreats. I was the only Arab I knew of in my class, so I had no one in my peer group as an ally. No matter what my parents tried to tell me about my proud cultural history, I would ignore it. My classmates told me I came from an uncivilized, brutal place, that Arabs were by nature anti-American, and I believed them. They did not know the hours my parents spent studying, working, trying to preserve part of their old lives while embracing, willingly, the new.

I tried to forget the Arabic I knew, because if I didn't I'd be forever linked to murderers. I stopped inviting friends over for dinner, because I thought the food we ate was "weird." I lied about where my parents had come from. Their accents (although they spoke English perfectly) humiliated me. Though Islam is a major monotheistic religion with many similarities to Judaism and Christianity, there were no holidays near Chanukah or Christmas, nothing to tie me to the "Judeo-Christian" tradition. I felt more excluded. I slowly began to turn into someone without a past.

Civil war was raging in Lebanon, and all that Americans saw of that country was destruction and violence. Every other movie seemed to feature Arab terrorists. The most common questions I was asked were if I had ever ridden a camel or if my family lived in tents. I felt burdened with responsibility. Why should an adolescent be asked questions like "Is it true you hate Jews and you want Israel destroyed?" I didn't hate anybody. My parents had never said anything even alluding to such sentiments. I was confused and hurt.

As I grew older and began to form my own opinions, my embarrassment lessened and my anger grew. The turning point came in high school. My grandmother had become very ill, and it was necessary for me to leave school a few days before Christmas vacation. My chemistry teacher was very sympathetic until I said I was going to the Middle East. "Don't come back in a body bag," he said cheerfully. The class laughed. Suddenly, those years of watching movies that mocked me and listening to others who knew

---

Magdoline Asfahani is a student at the University of Texas, El Paso.

nothing about Arabs and Muslims except what they saw on television seemed like a bad dream. I knew then that I would never be silent again.

I've tried to reclaim those lost years. I realize now that I come from a culture that has a rich history. The Arab world is a medley of people of different religions; not every Arab is a Muslim, and vice versa. The Arabs brought tremendous advances in the sciences and mathematics, as well as creating a literary tradition that has never been surpassed. The language itself is flexible and beautiful, with nuances and shades of meaning unparalleled in any language. Though many find it hard to believe, Islam has made progress in women's rights. There is a specific provision in the Koran that permits women to own property and ensures that their inheritance is protected—although recent events have shown that interpretation of these laws can vary.

My youngest brother, who is 12, is now at the crossroads I faced. When initial reports of the Oklahoma City bombing pointed to "Arab-looking individuals" as the culprits, he came home from school crying. "Mom, why do Muslims kill people? Why are the Arabs so bad?" She was angry and brokenhearted, but tried to handle the situation in the best way possible: through education. She went to his class, armed with Arabic music, pictures, traditional dress and cookies. She brought a chapter of the social-studies book to life, and the children asked intelligent, thoughtful questions, even after the class was over. Some even asked if she was coming back. When my brother came home, he was excited and proud instead of ashamed.

I only recently told my mother about my past experience. Maybe if I had told her then, I would have been better equipped to deal with the thoughtless teasing. But, fortunately, the world is changing. Although discrimination and stereotyping still exist, many people are trying to lessen and end it. Teachers, schools and the media are showing greater sensitivity to cultural issues. However, there is still much that needs to be done, not for the sake of any particular ethnic or cultural group but for the sake of our country.

The America that I love is one that values freedom and the differences of its people. Education is the key to understanding. As Americans we need to take a little time to look and listen carefully to what is around us and not rush to judgment without knowing all the facts. And we must never be ashamed of our pasts. It is our collective differences that unite us and make us unique as a nation. It's what determines our present and our future.

READING 20

The Accidental Asian

Eric Liu

The Asian American identity was born, as I was, roughly thirty years ago. In those three decades it has struggled to find relevance and a coherent voice. As I have. It has tried to adapt itself to the prevailing attitudes about race—namely, that one matters in this society, if one is colored, mainly to the extent that one claims a race for oneself. I, too, have tried to accommodate these forces. The Asian American identity, like me, renounces whiteness. It draws strength from the possibility of transcending the fear and blindness of the past. So do I. It is the so very American product of a rejection of history's limitations, rooted in little more than its own creation a generation ago. As I am.

What I am saying is that I can identify with the Asian American identity. I understand why it does what it does. It is as if this identity and I were twin siblings, separated at birth but en-

Eric Liu is a speech writer for President Bill Clinton and a commentator for MSNBC.

dowed with uncanny foreknowledge of each other's motives. The problem is, I disagree with it often. I become frustrated by it, even disappointed. The feeling is mutual, I suspect. We react to the same world in very different ways.

And yes, I do think of this identity as something that reacts, something almost alive, in the way that a shadow, or a mirror image—or a conscience—is almost alive. It has, if not a will of its own, then at least a highly developed habit of asserting its existence. It is like a storm, a beautiful, swirling weather pattern that moves back and forth across my mind. It draws me in, it repulses me. I am ever aware of its presence. There is always part of me that believes I will find deliverance if I merge with this identity. Yet still I hold it at a remove. For I fear that in the middle of this swirl, this great human churn, lies emptiness.

What must it be like to be told you are Asian American? Imagine that you are an immigrant, young, but old enough to get by, and you have been in America for only a few months. Imagine that you come from Korea. Imagine that you speak Korean, read Korean newspapers, eat Korean food. Imagine that you live in East Flushing or in South Central and you see only the Korean faces. There are other faces, yes, brown and black and yellow and white, but the ones you see, the ones you can read, are Korean. Imagine that time passes, and you realize now that you see the other faces. Imagine that the order of life in this city, the invisible grid, has become visible to you. More than that, it has affected you. What was Korean before is not exactly Korean anymore: your speech is interspersed now with fragments of English, Spanish; your daily paper you must find at a crowded, strange-smelling newsstand, tucked among bundles of other scripts and shades of print; your strong, salty food, supplemented now by frosted cereal and cookies, you eat while quietly absorbed by a television program you cannot understand except in mime. Imagine that you are becoming a Korean American. Is that not shock enough? To know that what was once the noun is becoming the adjective? And so perhaps you retreat, you compensate, you remind yourself every night before you pray that you are Korean so that you and your Maker will not forget. But imagine that the forgetting is relentless. That more time passes, and a knock on the door of your apartment brings you face-to-face with a Japanese, and something deep inside you, a passing sneer or a cautionary tale, a history, twinges. And imagine that this Japanese begins speaking to you in English, the kind of English the television produces, and you understand perfectly what she is saying. Imagine that what she is saying is that she needs your help. That you are invited to a rally (or is it a party?). That we—you and this Japanese and so many unseen others—must stand together against a common foe. Imagine that what she is saying is that you are Asian American. What must it be like? What do you think about when you close the door and walk to the window and realize, while peering out over a scene of so many unknowable lives but four knowable colors, how faint the aroma of your own kitchen has become, how strong the scent of the street?

I find myself in a cavernous television studio, seated beside the anchorwoman. The cameras are on us, lights are burning overhead. I am nervous, although I shouldn't be: this is my job. I do commentary for a cable news network and I come to this studio often. This day, I have been called in as a "special guest" to discuss a recent and controversial cover of the *National Review* magazine depicting the president, vice president, and first lady in yellowface—that is, in stereotypical Oriental caricature. "The Manchurian

Candidate," reads the cover text, referring, of course, to Bill Clinton and his role in the "Asian money" scandal that has been brewing since the 1996 election.

The news package leading up to my entrance describes the brouhaha that has arisen over the cover, and as the tape comes to a close a red light comes on, signaling that we are on the air. The anchor turns to me, her brow knit at the appropriate angle of concern: "What about this cover do you find offensive, Eric?"

Truth be told, I was not deeply offended when I first saw the cover. (My mother, in fact, was much angrier.) I mainly thought it was juvenile, sophomoric. And I didn't think about it again until a few days later, when my producer waved it at me and asked for a reaction. I knew what answer he was looking for; what answer any self-respecting Asian would give.

"Well," I say, turning now to the camera, "these caricatures play off a long history of demeaning anti-Asian stereotypes—the buckteeth, the slanted eyes, the bamboo hat. They are racist in their effect." And on I go. I play, in other words, the Asian spokesman, ever vigilant against affronts to my race. The anchor nods understandingly as I speak.

Soon a staff writer from the *Review* joins the discussion via satellite. He, too, is Asian American, South Asian. "We didn't think this cover would be particularly controversial," I hear this other Asian say. "Normal people aren't offended by it."

Normal people? The more this other Asian talks, the more heated I become in my responses. At first I assume it's the adrenaline rush of verbal combat. But as he goes on mouthing his disingenuous party line—something like, "We would've used leprechauns if this scandal was about Irish money"—I become more than just irked, more than angry, until suddenly I realize that I am outraged. I am sending a searing look into my own reflection in the camera as I argue. And I am shouting now: I have raised my voice to defend *my people.*

"Somehow, we have gotten to the point where those who protest bias and insensitivity are *demonized* more than those who commit it!" I boom.

"I'm not demonizing you," the other Asian offers.

The segment ends shortly afterward, the red light goes off. An Asian American employee comes over to shake my hand. I feel pleased with myself, pumped up. But even before I've removed my mike, I realize something unusual has happened. When the debate began I was playing a part, because I felt I should. Eight minutes later I had merged completely with my role. Almost by chance, it seemed, I'd become a righteous, vocal Asian American. All it had taken was a stage and a villain.

That's how it is with Asian American identity—nothing brings it out like other people's expectations and a sense of danger. Until recently, I rarely self-identified as "Asian American." I might say "Chinese American," if asked. Otherwise, pointedly, "American." But there are times when what you choose to call yourself becomes irrelevant. Ask Tiger Woods, whose insistence that he was "Cablinasian" didn't keep the media from blackening him, when he first arrived, into golf's Jackie Robinson. There are times when other people *need* to think of you as X even if you believe you are Y. This was one of those times. I was in the studio to speak *as an Asian American.*

Of course, I was complicit in this casting; I chose to take the role. What was curious to me, however, is how I managed, if even for a moment, to lose myself in it. Here is where the sense of danger came into play. I may not have started out being terribly exercised about the perils of Yellow Peril stereotyping. But once I perceived the smarmy hypocrisy of this fellow—once I heard his intransigent insistence that the fault lay only with whiny, race-peddling Asians like me—I was chilled by the sense that maybe there *is* a danger out there. Maybe it *is* true, as I was then asserting on camera, that what separates insulting caricatures from more troubling forms of anti-Asian sentiment is only a slippery slope. At that moment I began to comprehend the most basic rationale for pan-Asian solidarity: self-defense.

I still understand that rationale, and many others. I understand, that is, why so many Americans of various ethnic origins have chosen, over the last generation, to adopt a one-size-fits-all "Asian American" identity. It is an affirming counterstatement to the narrative in which yellow people are either foreigners or footnotes. It is a bulwark against bigotry. It is, perhaps most important, a community. I can recount the ways, over the years, that I've become more Asian American myself. I've learned the appropriate cultural and political references. I've become familiar with the history. And of course, I've spoken out against Asian-bashing on national television.

Nevertheless, the fact remains: I am not an Asian American activist; I just play one on TV. Even though I have a grasp of why this identity matters, I cannot escape the feeling that it is contrived and, in a more profound way, unnecessary. In a way, I envy those who choose to become wholeheartedly Asian American: those who believe. At least they have a certain order to their existence. I, on the other hand, am an accidental Asian. Someone who has stumbled onto a sense of race; who wonders now what to do with it.

We are inventors, all. We assemble our selves from fragments of story.

Every identity is a social construction, a drawing of arbitrary lines. But are all identities *equally* arbitrary—and equally necessary? It's worthwhile to compare a racial identity like "Asian American" with what might be said to exist "within" it (ethnicity) and "around" it (nation).

An ethnic identity like "Chinese" matters because it is a medium of cultural continuity and meaning. "Chineseness," to be sure, is not an easy thing to delineate. It is a simplified marker for a complex reality. But the fact is that when I speak of my heritage—or when I speak of losing my heritage—I am referring to sounds and stories and customs that are *Chinese* American.

National identity, in the American case, is more problematic. It is far-flung and often contradictory. It is more reliant on myth and paradox than many other national identities. It is not, however, empty of meaning. America matters in both a civic sense and a cultural one. As a state, it is a guarantor of unmatched freedoms. As a place, it is an unrivaled incubator of ambition. The syntheses that America generates are, for better and worse, what pushes humanity forward today.

Race matters, too, of course. The difference is, race matters mainly because race matters. It's undeniable, in other words, that society is still ordered by the random bundle of traits we call "race"—and that benefits and penalties are often assigned accordingly. But it is this persistent social fact, more than any *intrinsic* worth, that makes racial identity deserving of our moral attention.

Don't get me wrong: it's not that I wish for a society without race. At bottom, I consider myself an identity libertarian. I wish for a society that treats race as an option, the way white people today are able to enjoy ethnicity as an option. As something cost-free, neutral, fluid. And yet I know that the tendency of race is usually to solidify: into clubs, into shields.

To a great degree, then, my misgivings about racial identity flow from a fear of ethnosclerosis: the hardening of the walls between the races. But perhaps my worries, like the pageants of difference that prompted them, belong to a time that is already passing. Perhaps over the horizon, beyond multiculturalism, awaits the cosmopolitan realm that David Hollinger calls "postethnic America." And perhaps there is no way to call forth this horizon but with the stories we have at hand.

I have a friend from college who used to be a deracinated East Coast suburban ABC—someone, in other words, quite like me. When he moved to the West Coast for graduate school, though, he got religion. He was, for the first time, in a place where Asian Americans were not few and far between. He joined the Asian student union, began reading Asian American journals and literature anthologies, spent more and more of his days with Asian friends, entered into his first relationship with a girl who wasn't white (she was Japanese, to the vexation of his parents). Soon he was speaking to me in earnest about the importance of being Asian. And he seemed genuinely happy, at ease.

It's not hard to see why my friend became what I call a "born-again Asian." He had found fellowship and, with the fellowship, meaning. He had found a place where he would always fit in, always be recognized. He had found a way to fill a hole, the gnawing sense of heritage deficit that plagues many a second-generation banana. And the mortar he was using was not anything so ancient and musty as Chinese civilization; it was a new, synthetic, made-in-the-U.S.A. adhesive called "Asianness." For my friend, this was *exciting* as well as fulfilling.

My own conversion, if I can call it that, is far from complete. Having spent so much of my life up through college soft-pedaling my Asianness, I began afterward to realize how unnecessary that had been. I began, tentatively, to peel back the topmost layers of my anti-race defenses. Did I have an epiphany? No; I think I simply started to grow up. I became old enough to shed the mask of perpetual racelessness; old enough, as well, to sense in myself a yearning for affinity, for *affiliation.* So I joined a couple of Asian American organizations, began going to their meetings and conventions. And I was welcome. Nobody questioned my authenticity, my standing. Mainly I encountered people quite like me: second-generation, mainstream, in search of something else. Soon I was conversant in the patois of "the community." Soon I was calling myself, without hesitation, "Asian American."

Don't give me too much credit, though. The truth is, I was mainly exploring the public, institutional, side of Asian America. The private side, the realm of close friendships formed through race, I have entered only lately. Perhaps the most you could say of me is that I am an assimilist in recovery: once in denial, now halfway up the twelve-step to full, self-actualized Asian Americanness. I am glad to have climbed this far and to have left behind some insecurities. I am not sure, however, how much farther I should go.

Thirty-some years ago, there were no "Asian Americans." Not a single one. There were Japanese Americans, Chinese Americans, Filipino Americans, and so on: a disparate lot who shared only yellow-to-brown skin tones and the experience of bigotry that their pigmentation provoked. Though known to their countrymen, collectively, as "Orientals," and assumed to share common traits and cultures, they didn't think of themselves at all as a collective. It really wasn't until the upheavals of the late 1960s that some of them began to.

Stirred by the precedent of Black Power, a cadre of Asian student activists, mostly in California, performed an act of conceptual jujitsu: they would create a positive identity out of the unhappy fact that whites tend to lump all Asians together. Their first move was to throw off the "Oriental" label, which, to their thinking, was the cliché-ridden product of a colonial European gaze. They replaced it with "Yellow," and after protests from their darker-hued constituents, they replaced "Yellow" with "Asian American." In their campaign for semantic legitimacy, the ex-Orientals got an unlikely assist from bean-counting federal bureaucrats. Looking to make affirmative action programs easier to document, the Office of Management and Budget in 1973 christened the term *Asian and Pacific Islander* for use in government forms. In the eyes of the feds, all Asians now looked alike. But this was a *good* thing.

The greatest problem for "Asian America," at least initially, was that this place existed mostly in the arid realm of census figures. It was a statistical category more than a social reality. In the last few decades, though, Asian American activists, intellectuals, artists, and students have worked, with increasing success, to transform their label into a lifestyle and to create, by every means available, a truly pan-ethnic identity for their ten million members. They have begun to build a nation.

The scholar Benedict Anderson has aptly defined the nation as an "imagined community," a grouping that relies for cohesion on an intangible, exclusive sense of connection among its far-flung members. Sometimes a nation has a state to enforce its will, sometimes it does not. But it must *always* have a mythology, a quasi-official culture that is communicated to all who belong, wherever they may be.

The Asian American narrative is rooted deeply in threat. That is one of the main things polyglot Americans of Asian descent have had in common: the fear of being discriminated against simply on account of being, metaphorically if not genetically, Chinamen. It is no accident that an early defining skirmish for Asian American activists was the push for Asian American Studies programs at San Francisco State and Berkeley in 1968. For what these programs did, in part, was to record and transmit the history of mistreatment that so many immigrants from Asia had endured over the centuries. Today, in the same vein, one of the most powerful allegories in Asian American lore is the tale of Vincent Chin, a Chinese American beaten to death in 1982 by two laid-off white auto workers who took him to be Japanese. The Chin story tells of a lingering strain of vicious, indiscriminate racism that can erupt without warning.

Yet no race can live on threat alone. To sustain a racial identity, there must be more than other people's racism, more than a negation. There must also be an affirmative sensibility, an aesthetic that emerges through the fusing of arts and letters with politics. Benedict Anderson again, in *Imagined Communities,* points to vernacular "print-capitalism"—books, newspapers, pamphlets—as the driving force of an incipient national consciousness. On the contemporary scene, perhaps no periodical better epitomizes the emerging aesthetic than the New York–based bimonthly *A. Magazine: Inside Asian America.*

Founded eight years ago by a Harvard graduate and entrepreneurial dynamo named Jeff Yang, *A. Magazine* covers fashion, politics, film, books, and trends in a style one might call Multiculti Chic. To flip through the glossy pages of this publication is to be swept into a cosmopolitan, cutting-edge world where Asians *matter.* It is to enter a realm populated by Asian and Asian American luminaries: actors like Jackie Chan and Margaret Cho, athletes like Michael Chang and Kristi Yamaguchi. It is to see everyday spaces and objects—sporting events, television shows, workplaces, bookstores, boutiques—through the eyes of a well-educated, socially conscious, politically aware, media-savvy, left-of-center, twenty-to-thirty-something, second-generation Asian American. It is to create, and be created by, an Ideal Asian.

There is something fantastic about all this, and I mean that in every way. That the children of Chinese and Japanese immigrants, or Korean and Japanese, or Indian and Pakistani, should so heedlessly disregard the animosities of their ancestors; that they should prove it possible to reinvent themselves as one community; that they should catalog their collective contributions to society so very sincerely: what can you say, really, but "Only in America"? There is an impressive, defiant ambition at work here: an assertion of ownership, a demand for respect. But there is also, on occasion, an under-oxygenated air of fantasy, a shimmering mirage of whitelessness and Asian self-sufficiency. A *dream.*

The dream of a nation-race called Asian America makes the most sense if you believe that the long-discredited "melting pot" was basically replaced by a "quintuple melting pot." This is the multicultural method at its core: liquefy the differences *within* racial groups, solidify those *among* them. It is a method that many self-proclaimed Asian Americans, with the most meliorative of intentions, have applied to their own lives. They have thrown the *chink* and the *jap* and the *gook* and the *flip* into the same great bubbling cauldron. Now they await the emergence of a new and superior being, the *Asian American.* They wish him into existence. And what's troubling about this, frankly, is precisely what's inspiring: that it is possible.

The invention of a race testifies not only to the power of the human imagination but also to its limits. There is something awesome about the coalescence of a sprawling conglomerate identity. There is something frustrating as well, the sense that all this creativity and energy could have been harnessed to a greater end. For the challenge today is not only to announce the arrival of color. It is also to form combinations that lie beyond color. The creators of Asian America suggest that racial nationalism is the most meaningful way of claiming American life. I worry that it defers the greater task of confronting American life.

Power. Race, in the guise of whiteness, has always been about power. Now, in the masks of color, it is also about countervailing power. To call yourself a minority today is not only to acknowledge that you are seen by whites as nonwhite. It can also be to choose, as a matter of vocation, to sustain the dichotomy.

Frank Wu, a law professor and correspondent for *Asian-Week,* once wrote a candid and elegant essay in which he confessed to becoming a Professional Asian American. "Much like someone who becomes famous for being famous," he wrote, "I am making a career out of my race." He is not alone, of course, in his career choice. Over the last twenty years, there has been a proliferation of pan-Asian associations, advocacy groups, and political lobbies. These groups offer their members connections, capital, standing, protection. They do important work on behalf of those without a voice. Together, they represent the bureaucratization—the mechanization, really—of the race. The Professional Asian Americans who run these groups have learned well from their black and Hispanic counterparts that *if you build it, they will come:* if you construct the institutions that a "legitimate" race is supposed to have, then people will treat your race as legitimate.

One thing Professional Asian Americans are quick to point out is that they are not honorary whites. Fair enough: one would like to be able to do well in this country without being called white. And one should be able to address the fact that plenty of Asian Americans, unlike "real" whites, still pay a social penalty for their race. But something Professional Asian Americans sometimes overlook is that they are not honorary blacks either. African Americans created the template for minority politics in this country. That template, set in the heavy type of protest and opposition, is not always the best fit for Asian Americans. For Asian Americans haven't the moral purchase that blacks have upon our politics.

Asian Americans belong not to a race so much as to a confederation, a big yellow-and-brown tent that covers a panoply of interests. And while those interests converge usefully on some points—antidiscrimination, open immigration—they diverge on many others. This is a "community," after all, that consists of ten million people of a few dozen ethnicities, who have roots all across America and around the globe, whose families have been here anywhere from less than a week to more than a century, whose political beliefs run the ideological gamut, who are welfare mothers and multimillionaires, soldiers and doctors, believers and pagans. It would take an act of selective deafness to hear, in this cacophony, a unitary voice.

Without a unitary voice, however, there can never be maximum leverage in the bargaining for benefits. There can be no singular purpose for the Professional Asian American, no stable niche in the marketplace of identities. It will grow ever harder to speak of "the race." So be it. What will remain is the incalculable diversity of a great and growing mass of humanity. And there, in the multitudes, will lie a very different kind of power.

What maketh a race?

To people in China, the Chinese constitute a single race. Except, that is, for those Chinese who aren't Chinese; those who aren't of the dominant Han group, like the Miao or Yao or Zhuang or whatever. They belong to separate races.

To the Chinese, Indians are a single, and separate, race. But "Indian" to many Indians, is like "Asian American" to me: an artificial, monochrome label. The distinctions that matter in India are between Bengalis and Punjabis and Gujeratis and others.

To the Japanese, who certainly think of themselves as a race, the Chinese, Indians, and Koreans are all separate races. To the Koreans, the Filipinos are; to the Filipinos, the Vietnamese. And so on.

To the Anglos who founded the United States, the Irish who arrived in great waves in the early nineteenth century were a separate race. To the Germans who killed Jews in this century and the French who watched, the Jews were a separate race. To the blacks of America, the Anglos and the Irish and the Germans and French and the Jews have always ended up being part of the same, and separate, race.

To the judiciary system of the United States, Asian Indians were held to be: probably not white (1909), white (1910), white again (1913), not white (1917), white (1919 and 1920), not white (1923), still not white (1928), probably never again white (1939 and 1942).

To those who believe in race, the spaces in between are plugged tight with impurities: quadroons, octoroons, mulattoes, morenas, mutts, mongrels, half-castes, half-breeds, halfies, hapas.

To those who do not believe, there is only this faith: the mixed shall inherit the earth.

What maketh a race is not God but man. What maketh a race is only the sin of self-love.

Last May, I received in the mail a calendar of events and exhibits "celebrating Asian Pacific American Heritage Month." Here is what it included: A Celebration of APA Women's Leadership into the Twenty-first Century. An APA Spring Benefit. An APA Scholarship Dinner. An APA Performance Series. An APA Writers' Reading. A Performance of Music in the Lives of APAs. An APA Heritage Festival. (The theme this year: "One Vision, One Mission, One Voice.")

When I read the calendar the first time, I took all the information at face value, noted a few events that sounded interesting. When I read it a second time, a question pressed its way through the hazy membrane of multiculturalism in my brain and presented itself starkly, even rudely: What the heck is an "APA"?

If "Asian Pacific American" is an overbroad generalization, then what is "APA" but a soulless distillation of an overbroad generalization? I know it's a typographical and linguistic convenience, like the "USA" in *USA Today.* But the truncation and abbreviation of *experience* that the label perpetrates reflects the truncation and abbreviation of *reasoning* that you'll find in the call for celebration.

I agree that in the form of a coalition—that is, as a set of political alliances among organized groups—the Asian American identity can be quite important. But it is not a coalition that I am being asked to celebrate. It is a *race:* a discrete entity with "one vision, one mission, one voice." A race, which is supposed to be more primordial than any temporary, tactical alliance. A race, which apparently does not need justification for its existence but merely *is.* One celebrates the race as a matter of tradition, because it is there. Moreover, to celebrate the race is to nourish it, to sustain it. And that is precisely what gives me pause.

In a provocative book called *The Rise and Fall of Gay Culture,* Daniel Harris describes the way that the longtime isolation of the gay community inspired an intensely creative and pointedly oppositional gay culture. Now that intolerance and ostracism are declining, Harris says, elements of that subculture are being coopted by the mainstream: assimilated. He laments this fact, because in his view, a real cultural legacy is disappearing. But he does not lament it so much that he wishes for a return to the kind of homophobia that had yielded the subculture in the first place. Gay culture is no longer so necessary, Harris reluctantly acknowledges, and this is a triumph as much as it is a tragedy.

The case of gay culture is relevant because it raises the big questions of identity politics: After discrimination subsides, is it still necessary for a minority group to keep the cultural wagons circled? Should walls that once existed to keep a minority group *out* now be maintained to keep them *in?* Should a prison of identity be converted, upon liberation, into a home? It seems that many who cheer Asian Pacific American Heritage Month are saying "yes" to these questions.

I don't mean to suggest that Asian Americans are able to live bigotry-free lives today, or that most Asian American activists are cultural segregationists, or that the gay community provides a perfect parallel to the Asian community. What I am saying, simply, is that more than ever before, Asian Americans are only as isolated as they want to be. They—we—do not face the levels of discrimination and hatred that *demand* an enclave mentality, particularly among the second generation, which, after all, provides most of the leadership for the nation-race. The choice to invent and sustain a pan-Asian identity is just that: a choice, not an imperative.

When you think about it, though, this choice seems almost like a reflex, a compensatory reaction to a derogatory action. What troubles me about becoming Asian American is not that it entails associating with a certain kind of person who, in some respects, is like me. What troubles me is associating with a certain kind of person whose similarity to me is defined on the primary basis of pigmentation, hair color, eye shape, and so forth. On the basis, that is, of the very badge that was once the source of stigma. This progression is natural, perhaps even necessary. But it lends a fragile quality to calls for "Asian American pride." For what is such pride, in this light, but shame turned upside down?

There are, of course, many ways to be Asian American: single-mindedly, offhandedly, out of conviction, out of convention. Racial identity needn't be an all-or-none proposition. But the more I have had occasion to let out my "inner Asian," the more I have felt a tinge of insincerity. For it is as if I were applying a salve to a wound I am not even sure I have, nursing a memory of exclusion and second-class treatment that people who look like me are presumed to suffer. Is this memory of wounds, this wounded memory, really mine? Is there anything more to my "APA-ness"?

What's missing from Asian American culture is culture.

The idea seems absurd at first. No Asian American culture? What about Zen Buddhism, feng shui, karaoke bars? Well, yes. The problem, though, is that these and other forms of culture inherited by Asian Americans are *ethnic* in origin. The folkways are Chinese, for example, not "Asian." The holidays are Vietnamese, the language Korean, the dress Japanese. As far as an organically pan-Asian culture is concerned, there isn't much there. As one Asian American activist once said tellingly, "I think Asian American culture is anything that Asian Americans are doing. Just that."

Does the same logic apply to "Asian American history"? There is something undeniably powerful about a work like *Strangers from a Different Shore,* Ronald Takaki's synoptic history of Asian Americans. Chinese laborers built the railroads and challenged discriminatory laws, Japanese Americans fought for principle and for country in World War II. More people should know about these and other legacies. But herding such facts under the heading of "Asian American history" feels faintly like anachronism. In a subtle way, it ascribes to distinct ethnic communities of the past the pan-ethnic mind-set of the present. It serves to create collective memory *retroactively.*

Collective memory, like individual memory, can of course be constructed after the fact. But it has greater force in the world when it derives from a past of collective action and shared experience. And that is something that Asian Americans—*as* Asian Americans—have had for only two or three decades. That's why, compared with the black or Jewish or even Latino identity, the Asian American identity seems so awfully incoherent. Unlike blacks, Asians do not have a cultural idiom that arose from centuries of thinking of themselves as a race; unlike Jews, Asians haven't a unifying spiritual and historical legacy; unlike Latinos, another recently invented community, Asians don't have a linguistic basis for their continued apartness. While the Asian American identity shares with these other identities the bones of collective victimization, it does not have their flesh of cultural content.

It is more meaningful, I think, to celebrate Korean or Vietnamese or Chinese heritage—something with an identifiable cultural core. Something deeper than a mere label. Ultimately, though, my objection is not only to the APA label; it is to the labeling mind itself. The hunger for ethnic heritage is a hunger for classification, for the nostalgic certainty of place. "Heritage" offers us a usable past, coded easily by color. It does not tell us enough about how we—we of every color—should fashion a workable future.

Let me admit: When I read accounts of growing up Nisei in the middle of the century, when I read short stories by Indian immigrants about the struggle of life here, or when I read poems by the children of those immigrants, poems of loss and discovery, I feel connected to something. I find it easy to see in these characters and to hear in their diction the faces and voices of my own family. The scents, textures, and rhythms of my childhood come speeding into vibrant immediacy. This, the knowledge of cross-cultural connection, the possibility of pan-Asian empathy, is something to be valued.

But why, in the end, should empathy be skin-deep? Experiences like migration, generational conflict, language barriers, and ostracism are not the sole province of Asians or any other "race." I admire many Asian American writers who deal in such themes. I cannot get enough of Chang-Rae Lee's work. I quite enjoy Gish Jen. I find David Mura and Shawn Wong powerful. But at the same time, some of the most resonant scenes of youthful acculturation I ever read were to be found in Philip Roth's *Portnoy's Complaint.* Or *Colored People,* by Henry Louis Gates, Jr. Or

Richard Rodriguez's *Hunger of Memory.* Or Norman Podhoretz's *Making It.*

I define my identity, then, in the simplest way possible: according to those with whom I identify. And I identify with whoever moves me.

No identity is stable in today's wild, recombinant mix of culture, blood, and ideas. Things fall apart; they make themselves anew. Every race carries within it the seeds of its own destruction.

Today, close to 50 percent of Asian Americans under thirty-five are marrying non-Asians, which promises rather quickly to change the meaning of the race. At the same time, growing numbers are reconstituting themselves into subcommunities of ethnicity, spurred by the Indian, Filipino, Korean, and other "Asian" Americans who have at times felt like extras in this Chinese- and Japanese-dominated show. Meanwhile, mass immigration has made for an Asian American population that is now two-thirds foreign-born, and among many recent arrivals, a pan-Asian identity seems uncomfortable and unnecessary. Finally, the accelerating whirl of global capitalism now means that the most noteworthy kind of Asian American culture may be Asian/American culture: fads and fashions that arrive directly from Asia; things you don't have to be Asian American to enjoy or to claim.

To put it simply: the Asian American identity as we now know it may not last another generation. Which makes doubters like me grow more doubtful—and more hopeful. There was something about the creation of this race, after all, that embodied the spirit of the times: compensatory, reactive, consumed with what Charles Taylor calls "the politics of recognition." There is something now about the mutation of the race that reflects a change in that spirit. If whiteness was once the thesis of American life, and colored cults of origin the antithesis, what remains to be written is the synthesis. From the perspective of my children and their children, from the perspective, that is, of those who will *be* the synthesis, it may seem that "Asian American" was but a cocoon: something useful, something to outgrow. And in this way, the future of the race may reflect the future of race itself. A future beyond recognition.

I am speaking now to a group of students, mostly freshmen and sophomores, at a small midwestern college. It is Asian Pacific American Heritage Month, and the students are members of the Asian Student Association. I have come to implore them to get more involved in politics, in public life.

College is supposed to be where Americans of Asian descent become Asian Americans, where the consciousness is awakened. But not this college. The students, improbably, are looking to me for guidance. Though they haven't said it in so many words, they want to know why it is they gather. They want to know what it is, besides the fact that there are so few of them on this white prairie campus, that should bring and hold them together; what, besides great potluck dinners, there is for them to *do.*

I am tempted for a moment to preach the gospel of The Individual, of the "unencumbered self" who has transcended such trivialities as race. I consider telling them that the Asian American identity is a leaky raft and that they had better learn to swim. But I don't have the heart to say any of this. For I, too, am of two minds. Instead, I tell them they should search for meaning as Asian Americans, if they so choose, or as whatever variety of self they feel free to express. So long as they feel free.

Afterward, I join a few students for dinner at a local Japanese restaurant. It is a nice place, spare and serene. We order, and then the oldest among them thanks me formally for coming to their school. For a few minutes, their attention is focused on me; they ask questions about my work, my opinions. Pretty soon, though, they're just talking to one another, in two or three different conversations, laughing, telling tales, flirting. That's all right with me. I am a stranger to them, after all, an outsider who doesn't know their stories. I am here by accident. And so I sit back, quietly, as they share their meal.

READING 21

Can Asian-Americans Turn the Media Tide?

Helen Zia

The first week of December, and the patriotic fervor it brings, aroused by the "date which will live in infamy," serves as an annual reminder to Asian-Americans of our link in the public mind to events in Asia. This is due in no small measure to the peculiarly American way in which the media portray us as eternal foreigners, regardless of our pedigrees.

During World War II, the perceived genetics of loyalty sent 120,000 Japanese-American civilians into ten U.S. concentration camps while Italian- and German-Americans kept their homes and citizenship. Back then, journalists from such giants as the Hearst and McClatchy chains were instrumental in stirring "yellow peril" race hysteria. A relentless stream of headlines like "Caps on Japanese Tomato Plants Point to Air Base" sounded xenophobic alarms about the Japanese-Americans who farmed throughout the West Coast before they were locked away and their land sold off.

In the fifties and sixties, J. Edgar Hoover, declaring Chinese-Americans to be China's "fifth column" of domestic spies, dispatched the F.B.I. to the nation's Chinatowns. My father, an inveterate writer of letters to the editor and to politicians, was one of his targets. Our phones were tapped, our mail opened and our neighbors quizzed about his activities. Within the past decade, much of the economic war with Japan was fought in the media; in this same period, hate crimes against Asian-Americans dramatically increased.

Media coverage of Asian-Americans [in 1997 offered] little change: The image of yellow spooks at the White House, with ties to Indonesia and the post-*glasnost* Evil Empire, China, was too tempting for pundits and politicians not to exploit. *New York Times* columnist William Safire wrote that China was responsible for an infection then imported "into the American political system," as though Tammany Hall, the spoils system and the Nixon Administration in which he served weren't homespun.

On December 5 [1997] Asian-Americans [hoped] to reverse the media juggernaut at a set of fact-finding briefings conducted by the U.S. Commission on Civil Rights, which [investigated] the racial impact of the campaign finance morass on Asian-Americans. The briefings came in response to a twenty-eight-page petition filed by fourteen national Asian-American groups charging members of the media, Congress, the Democratic National Committee and the National Republican Senatorial Committee with bias. The petitioners [cited] D.N.C. policies and bills before Congress that infringe on the political rights of Asian-Americans and immigrants.

Media coverage receives special mention in the petition, which lists numerous examples of poor and racially inflammatory reporting. *Newsweek* ran dozens of photos of the notables who paid millions to sleep in the Lincoln Bedroom; not a single Asian face was among them, yet the accompanying story highlighted the "mysterious Asian-Americans." CNBC newscaster Chris Matthews referred to "all those strange characters from Asia." Ross Perot observed in a speech, "Wouldn't you like to have someone . . . named O'Reilly? . . . so far we haven't found an American name"—one of many

Helen Zia is former executive editor of *Ms.* magazine.

remarks by politicians reported widely without journalistic comment As investigative news teams joined the F.B.I., the D.N.C., the Senate, House and various subcommittees in a racialized version of guilt by association, any politically active person with an Asian surname was a target for investigation. The news media were used as a weapon by D.N.C. auditors Ernst & Young—which itself made $2 million in donations—when the accounting firm threatened on numerous occasions to release the names of Asian-Americans who refused to provide detailed personal financial information.

One might conclude from the news that the corruption in the campaign finance system is caused by Asians and Asian-Americans. Yet Asian-Americans contributed only $3.4 million out of the more than $200 million in soft money raised by both parties in a year when more than $2.2 billion was spent on national races. Few stories examined European, Canadian and Australian companies, who gave questionable soft-money donations of about $6 million. Virtually no coverage was given to the $3.2 million in soft money donated by Disney/ABC, TimeWarner/CNN, News Corp./Fox, General Electric/NBC and Westinghouse/CBS.

Most unsettling were the efforts to silence Asian-American protests. *The Boston Globe* called complaints of racial stereotyping "a shabby maneuver to avoid scrutiny," and *The Washington Post* declared that "the idea of 'Asian bashing' has been floated in [Huang's] defense." *The New York Times* laced weird logic with racial innuendo: "We can reasonably assume that *something* was going on, given the huge amounts of mysterious money . . . and the rich variety of well-connected players. . . . it seems only a matter of time before the sprinkled facts are arranged into a pattern."

While that pattern has yet to emerge, Asian-Americans are particularly galled by the media's failure to cover other significant news in their community's political empowerment. Most notably, 1996 marked a record year for Asian-American voter registration and turnout. Exit polls in several heavily Asian-American districts throughout California found that 70 to 84 percent of Asian-Americans voted against Proposition 209, the state's anti–affirmative action ballot measure. None of the networks or national newspapers reported this news, despite heavy pre-election reportage that Asian-Americans would side with *whites* against affirmative action. . . .

Asian-Americans hope their testimony before the civil rights commission will cause politicians and media to rethink their racialized excesses. The commission has no enforcement powers, but the official forum is an opportunity to educate and to change the tenor of the news. Whether the media are willing to learn from the people they have long misrepresented remains to be seen.

READING 22

Diversity and Its Discontents

Arturo Madrid

My name is Arturo Madrid. I am a citizen of the United States, as are my parents and as were my grandparents and my great-grandparents. My ancestors' presence in what is now the United States antedates Plymouth Rock, even without taking into account any American Indian heritage I might have.

I do not, however, fit those mental sets that define America and Americans. My physical appearance, my speech patterns, my name, my profession (a professor of Spanish) create a text that confuses the reader. My normal experience is to be asked, "And where are *you* from?" My response depends on my mood. Passive-aggressive, I answer, "From here." Aggressive-passive, I ask, "Do you mean where am I origi-

Arturo Madrid is the Murchison Distinguished Professor of the Humanities at Trinity University in San Antonio, Texas.

nally from?" But ultimately my answer to those follow-up questions that ask about origins will be that we have always been from here.

Overcoming my resentment I try to educate, knowing that nine times out of ten my words fall on inattentive ears. I have spent most of my adult life explaining who I am not. I am exotic, but—as Richard Rodriguez of *Hunger of Memory* fame so painfully found out—not exotic enough . . . not Peruvian, or Pakistani, or whatever. I am, however, very clearly the *other,* if only your everyday, garden-variety, domestic *other.* I will share with you another phenomenon that I have been a part of, that of being a missing person, and how I came late to that awareness. But I've always known that I was the *other,* even before I knew the vocabulary or understood the significance of otherness.

I grew up in an isolated and historically marginal part of the United States, a small mountain village in the state of New Mexico, the eldest child of parents native to that region, whose ancestors had always lived there. In those vast and empty spaces, people who look like me, speak as I do, and have names like mine predominate. But the *americanos* lived among us: the descendants of those nineteenth-century immigrants who dispossessed us of our lands; missionaries who came to convert us and stayed to live among us; artists who became enchanted with our land and humanscape and went native; refugees from unhealthy climes, crowded spaces, unpleasant circumstances; and, of course, the inhabitants of Los Alamos, whose socio-cultural distance from us was accentuated by the fact that they occupied a space removed from and proscribed to us. More importantly, however, they—*los americanos*—were omnipresent (and almost exclusively so) in newspapers, newsmagazines, books, on radio, in movies and, ultimately, on television.

Despite the operating myth of the day, school did not erase my otherness. It did try to deny it, and in doing so only accentuated it. To this day what takes place in schools is more socialization than education, but when I was in elementary school—and given where I was—socialization was everything. School was where one became an American, because there was a pervasive and systematic denial by the society that surrounded us that we were Americans. That denial was both explicit and implicit.

Quite beyond saluting the flag and pledging allegiance to it (a very intense and meaningful action, given that the United States was involved in a war and our brothers, cousins, uncles, and fathers were on the frontlines), becoming American was learning English, and its corollary: not speaking Spanish. Until very recently ours was a proscribed language, either *de jure*—(by rule, by policy, by law—or *de facto*—by practice, implicitly if not explicitly, through social and political and economic pressure. I do not argue that learning English was not appropriate. On the contrary. Like it or not, and we had no basis to make any judgments on that matter, we were Americans by virtue of having been born Americans, and English was the common language of Americans. And there was a myth, a pervasive myth, to the effect that if we only learned to speak English well—and particularly without an accent—we would be welcomed into the American fellowship.

Sam Hayakawa and the official English movement folks notwithstanding, the true text was not our speech, but rather our names and our appearance, for we would always have an accent, however perfect our pronunciation, however excellent our enunciation, however divine our diction. That accent would be heard in our pigmentation, our physiognomy, our names. We were, in short, the *other.*

Being the *other* involves a contradictory phenomenon. On the one hand being the *other* frequently means being invisible. Ralph Ellison wrote eloquently about that experience in his magisterial novel *Invisible Man.* On the other hand, being the *other* sometimes involves sticking out like a sore thumb. What is she/he doing here?

For some of us being the *other* is only annoying; for others it is debilitating; for still others it is damning. Many try to flee otherness by taking on protective colorations that provide invisibility, whether of dress or speech or manner or name. Only a fortunate few succeed. For the majority of us otherness is permanently sealed by physical appearance. For the rest, otherness is betrayed by ways of being, speaking, or doing.

The first half of my life I spent downplaying the significance and consequences of otherness. The second half has seen me wrestling to understand its complex and deeply ingrained realities; striving to fathom why otherness denies us a voice or visibility or validity in American society and its institutions; struggling to make otherness familiar, reasonable, even normal to my fellow Americans.

I spoke earlier of another phenomenon that I am part of: that of being a missing person. Growing up in northern New Mexico I had only a slight sense of us being missing persons. *Hispanos,* as we called (and call) ourselves in New Mexico, were very much a part of the fabric of the society and there were *hispano* professionals everywhere about me: doctors, lawyers, schoolteachers, and administrators. My people owned businesses, ran organizations, and were both appointed and elected public officials.

My awareness of our absence from the larger institutional life of society became sharper when I went off to college, but even then it was attenuated by the circumstances of history and geography. The demography of Albuquerque still strongly reflected its historical and cultural origins, despite the influx of Midwesterners and Easterners. Moreover, many of my classmates at the University of New Mexico were *hispanos*, and even some of my professors. I thought that would obtain at UCLA, where I began graduate studies in 1960. Los Angeles had a very large Mexican population and that population was visible even in and around Westwood and on the campus. Many of the groundskeepers and foodservice personnel at UCLA were Mexican. But Mexican-American students were few and mostly invisible, and I do not recall seeing or knowing a single Mexican-American (or, for that matter, black, Asian, or American Indian) professional on the staff or faculty of that institution during the five years I was there. Needless to say, persons like me were not present in any capacity at Dartmouth College, the site of my first teaching appointment, and of course were not even part of the institutional or individual mind-set. I knew then that we—a we that had come to encompass American Indians, Asian-Americans, African-Americans, Puerto Ricans, and women—were truly missing persons in American institutional life.

Over the past three decades, the *de jure* and *de facto* types of segregation that have historically characterized American institutions have been under assault. As a consequence, minorities and women have become part of American institutional life. Although there are still many areas where we are not to be found, the missing persons phenomenon is not as pervasive as it once was. However, the presence of the *other,* particularly minorities, in institutions and in institutional life resembles what we call in Spanish a *flor de tierra* (a surface phenomenon): we are spare plants whose roots do not go deep, vulnerable to inclemencies of an economic, or political, or social nature.

Our entrance into and our status in institutional life are not unlike a scenario set forth by my grandmother's pastor when she informed him that she and her family were leaving their mountain village to relocate to the Rio Grande Valley. When he asked her to promise that she would remain true to the faith and continue to involve herself in it, she asked why he thought she would do otherwise. "Doña Trinidad," he told her, "in the Valley there is no Spanish church. There is only an American church." "But," she protested, "I read and speak English and would be able to worship there." The pastor responded, "It is possible that they will not admit you, and even if they do, they might not accept you. And that is why I want you to promise me that you are going to go to church. Because if they don't let you in through the front door, I want you to go in through the back door. And if you can't get in through the back door, go in the side door. And if you are unable to enter through the side door I want you to go in through the window. What is important is that you enter and stay."

Some of us entered institutional life through the front door; others through the back door; and still others through side doors. Many, if not most of us, came in through windows, and continue to come in through windows. Of those who entered through the front door, some never made it past the lobby; others were ushered into corners and niches. Those who entered through back and side doors inevitably have remained in back and side rooms. And those who entered through windows found enclosures built around them. For, despite the lip service given to the goal of the integration of minorities into institutional life, what has frequently occurred instead is ghettoization, marginalization, isolation.

Not only have the entry points been limited, but in addition the dynamics have been singularly conflictive. Gaining entry and its corollary, gaining space, have frequently come as a consequence of demands made on institutions and institutional officers. Rather than entering institutions more or less passively, minorities have of necessity entered them actively, even aggressively. Rather than waiting to receive, they have demanded. Institutional relations have thus been adversarial, infused with specific and generalized tensions.

The nature of the entrance and the nature of the space occupied have greatly influenced the view and attitude of the majority population within those institutions. All of us are put into the same box; that is, no matter what the individual reality, the assessment of the individual is inevitably conditioned by a perception that is held of the class. Whatever our history, whatever our record, whatever our validations, whatever our accomplishments, by and large we are perceived unidimensionally and dealt with accordingly. I remember an experience I had in this regard, atypical only in its explicitness. A few years ago I allowed myself to be persuaded to seek the presidency of a well-known state university. I was invited for an interview and presented myself before the selection committee, which included members of the board of trustees. The opening question of that brief but memorable interview was directed at me by a member of that august body. "Dr. Madrid," he asked, "why does a one-dimensional person like you think he can be the president of a multi-dimensional institution like ours?"

Over the past four decades America's demography has undergone significant changes. Since 1965 the principal demographic growth we have experienced in the United States has been of peoples whose national origins are non-European. This population growth has occurred both through birth and through immigration. A few years ago discussion of the national birthrate had a scare dimension: the high—"inordinately high"—birthrate of the Hispanic population. The popular discourse was informed by words such as "breeding." Several years later, as a consequence of careful tracking by government agencies, we now know that what has happened is that the birthrate of the majority population has decreased. When viewed historically and comparatively, the minority populations (for the most part) have also had a decline in birthrate, but not one as great as that of the majority.

There are additional demographic changes that should give us something to think about. African-Americans are now to be found in significant numbers in every major urban center in the nation. Hispanic-Americans now number over 15 million people, and although they are a regionally concentrated (and highly urbanized) population, there is a Hispanic community in almost every major urban center of the United States. American Indians, heretofore a small and rural population, are increasingly more numerous and urban. The Asian-American population, which has historically consisted of small and concentrated communities of Chinese-, Filipino-, and Japanese-Americans, has doubled over the past decade, its complexion changed by the addition of Cambodians, Koreans, Hmongs, Vietnamese, et al.

Prior to the Immigration Act of 1965, 69 percent of immigration was from Europe. By far the largest number of immigrants to the United States since 1965 have been from the Americas and from Asia: 34 percent are from Asia; another 34 percent are from Central and South America; 16 percent are from Europe; 10 percent are from the Caribbean; the remaining 6 percent are from other continents and Canada. As was the case with previous immigration waves, the current one consists principally of young people: 60 percent are between the ages of 16 and 44. Thus, for the next few decades, we will continue to see a growth in the percentage of non-European-origin Americans as compared to European-Americans.

To sum up, we now live in one of the most demographically diverse nations in the world, and one that is increasingly more so.

During the same period social and economic change seems to have accelerated. Who would have imagined at mid-century that the prototypical middle-class family (working husband, wife as homemaker, two children) would for all intents and purposes disappear? Who could have anticipated the rise in teenage pregnancies, children in poverty, drug use? Who among us understood the implications of an aging population?

We live in an age of continuous and intense change, a world in which what held true yesterday does not today, and certainly will not tomorrow. What change does, moreover, is bring about even more change. The only constant we have at this point in our national development is change. And change is threatening. The older we get the more likely we are to be anxious about change, and the greater our desire to maintain the status quo.

Evident in our public life is a fear of change, whether economic or moral. Some who fear change are responsive to the call of economic protectionism, others to the message of moral protectionism. Parenthetically, I have referred to the movement to require more of students without in turn giving them more as academic protectionism. And the pronouncements of E. D. Hirsch and Allan Bloom are, I believe, informed by intellectual protectionism. Much more serious, however, is the dark side of the populism which underlies this evergoing protectionism—the resentment of the *other*. An excellent and fascinating example of that aspect of populism is the cry for linguistic protectionism—for making English the official language of the United States. And who among us is unaware of the tensions that underlie immigration reform, of the underside of demographic protectionism?

A matter of increasing concern is whether this new protectionism, and the mistrust of the *other* which accompanies it, is not making more significant inroads than we have supposed in higher education. Specifically, I wish to discuss the question of whether a goal (quality) and a reality (demographic diversity) have been erroneously placed in conflict, and, if so, what problems this perception of conflict might present.

As part of my scholarship I turn to dictionaries for both origins and meanings of words. Quality, according to the *Oxford English Dictionary*, has multiple meanings. One set defines quality as being an essential character, a distinctive and inherent feature. A second describes it as a degree of excellence, of conformity to standards, as superiority in kind. A third makes reference to social status, particularly to persons of high social status. A fourth talks about quality as being a special or distinguishing attribute, as being a desirable trait. Quality is highly desirable in both principle and practice. We all aspire to it in our own person, in our experiences, in our acquisitions and products, and of course we all want to be associated with people and operations of quality.

But let us move away from the various dictionary meanings of the word and to our own sense of what it represents and of how we feel about it. First of all we consider quality to be finite; that is, it is limited with respect to quantity; it has very few manifestations; it is not widely distributed. I have it and you have it, but they don't. We associate quality with homogeneity, with uniformity, with standardization, with order, regularity, neatness. All too often we equate it with smoothness, glibness, slickness, elegance. Certainly it is always expensive. We tend to identify it with those who lead, with the rich and famous. And, when you come right down to it, it's inherent. Either you've got it or you ain't.

Diversity, from the Latin *divertere*, meaning to turn aside, to go different ways, to differ, is the condition of being different or having differences, is an instance of being different. Its companion word, diverse, means differing, unlike, distinct; having or capable of having various forms; composed of unlike or distinct elements. Diversity is lack of standardization, of regularity, of orderliness, homogeneity, conformity, uniformity. Diversity introduces complications, is difficult to organize, is troublesome to manage, is problematical. Diversity is irregular, disorderly, uneven, rough. The way we use the word diversity gives us away. Something is too diverse, is extremely diverse. We want a little diversity.

When we talk about diversity, we are talking about the *other*, whatever that other might be: someone of a different gender, race, class, national origin; somebody at a greater or lesser distance from the norm; someone outside the set; someone who possesses a different set of characteristics, features, or attributes; someone who does not fall within the taxonomies we use daily and with which we are comfortable; someone who does not fit into the mental configurations that give our lives order and meaning.

In short, diversity is desirable only in principle, not in practice. Long live diversity . . . as long as it conforms to my standards, my mind set, my view of life, my sense of order. We desire, we like, we admire diversity, not unlike the way the French (and others) appreciate women; that is, *Vive la difference!*—as long as it stays in its place.

What I find paradoxical about and lacking in this debate is that diversity is the natural order of things. Evolution produces diversity. Margaret Visser, writing about food in her latest book, *Much Depends on Dinner*, makes an eloquent statement in this regard:

> Machines like, demand, and produce uniformity. But nature loathes it: her strength lies in multiplicity and in differences. Sameness in biology means fewer possibilities and therefore weakness.

The United States, by its very nature, by its very development, is the essence of diversity. It is diverse in its geography, population, institutions, technology; its social, cultural, and intellectual modes. It is a society that at its best does not consider quality to be monolithic in form or finite in quantity, or to be inherent in class. Quality in our society proceeds in large measure out of the stimulus of diverse modes of thinking and acting; out of the creativity made possible by the different ways in which we approach things; out of diversion from paths or modes hallowed by tradition.

One of the principal strengths of our society is its ability to address, on a continuing and substantive basis, the real economic, political, and social problems that have faced and continue to face us. What makes the United States so attractive to immigrants is the protections and opportunities it offers; what keeps our society together is tolerance for cultural, religious, social, political, and even linguistic difference; what makes us a unique, dynamic, and extraordinary nation is the power and creativity of our diversity.

The true history of the United States is one of struggle against intolerance, against oppression, against xenophobia, against those forces that have prohibited persons from participating in the larger life of the society on the basis of their race, their gender, their religion, their national origin, their linguistic and cultural background. These phenomena are not consigned to the past. They remain with us and frequently take on virulent dimensions.

If you believe, as I do, that the well-being of a society is directly related to the degree and extent to which all of its citizens participate in its institutions, then you will have to agree that we have a challenge before us. In view of the extraordinary changes that are taking place in our society, we need to take up the struggle again, irritating, grating, troublesome, unfashionable, unpleasant as it is. As educated and educator members of this society we have a special responsibility for ensuring that all American institutions, not just our elementary and secondary schools, our juvenile halls, or our jails, reflect the diversity of our society. Not to do so is to risk greater alienation on the part of a growing segment of our society; is to risk increased social tension in an already conflictive world; and, ultimately, is to risk the survival of a range of institutions that, for all their defects and deficiencies, provide us the opportunity and the freedom to improve our individual and collective lot.

Let me urge you to reflect on these two words—quality and diversity—and on the mental sets and behaviors that flow out of them. And let me urge you further to struggle against the notion that quality is finite in quantity, limited in its manifestations, or is restricted by considerations of class, gender, race, or national origin; or that quality manifests itself only in leaders and not in followers, in managers and not in workers, in breeders and not in drones; or that it has to be associated with verbal agility or elegance of personal style; or that it cannot by seeded, nurtured, or developed.

Because diversity—the *other*—is among us, will define and determine our lives in ways that we still do not fully appreciate, whether that other is women (no longer bound by tradition, house, and family); or Asians, African-Americans, Indians, and Hispanics (no longer invisible, regional, or marginal); or our newest immigrants (no longer distant, exotic, alien). Given the changing profile of America, will we come to terms with diversity in our personal and professional lives? Will we begin to recognize the diverse forms that quality can take? If so, we will thus initiate the process of making quality limitless in its manifestations, infinite in quantity, unrestricted with respect to its origins, and more importantly, virulently contagious.

I hope we will. And that we will further join together to expand—not to close—the circle.

PERSONAL ACCOUNT

Going Home

It was the end of July on a day when the temperature climbed, yet again, into the middle 90s. Hot, hazy, and humid. I had just finished a summer program and was moving my things out of the college dormitory. My friend gathered my belongings on the sidewalk while I stood partially in the street to flag down a cab. When an empty cab *finally* stopped, I opened the door with the intention of putting my things into the trunk of the cab. However, before I could complete a full pivot, the cab driver asked me where I was going. I gave him my home address in the African-American neighborhood. "Where's that?" was his response. "Off of Shamut Avenue and Ruggles Street," I said. "No, sorry, I don't go there."

It actually took me a few minutes to collect myself afterward. There are countless nights when I must rely on cabs to get around the city. Surprisingly, I had grown accustomed to cab drivers ignoring my attempt to catch a taxi, but I had never had a brazen refusal after stopping. In this situation, it was hard for me to politely close the cab door without doing some damage by slamming it. I wanted the cab driver to know that I didn't appreciate his refusal, but words were hard to come by at that time. Action seemed more appropriate. At the sidewalk, my friend just shook his head.

In this and similar situations, one is forced to confront the issue of privilege. Since the cab driver did stop for me, my race could not have been a negative factor, or was it? I am giving him my money, so I should call the shots. Would he have dared to ask additional questions or refused to drive a middle-class man in a business suit? Or an elderly woman? I am an inner-city, young, Black woman. It's a shame that I cannot depend on a cab to take me home safely. No, I must stand partially in front of an oncoming cab so that it must stop. Is this even a Black or White issue? If so, would it surprise you to know that the cab driver who refused to transport me was himself Black?

Keeva Haynes

READING 23

Talking Past Each Other

Black and White Languages of Race

Bob Blauner

For many African-Americans who came of age in the 1960s, the assassination of Martin Luther King, Jr. in 1968 was a defining moment in the development of their personal racial consciousness. For a slightly older group, the 1955 lynching of the fourteen-year-old Chicagoan Emmett Till in Mississippi had been a similar awakening. Now we have the protest and violence in Los Angeles and other cities in late April and early May of 1992, spurred by the jury acquittal of four policemen who beat motorist Rodney King.

The aftermath of the Rodney King verdict, unlike any other recent racial violence, will be seared into the memories of Americans of *all* colors, changing the way they see each other and their society. Spring 1992 marked the first time since the 1960s that incidents of racial injustice against an African-American—and by extension the black community—have seized the entire nation's imagination. Even highly publicized racial murders, such as those of African-American men in two New York City neighborhoods—Howard Beach (1986) and Bensonhurst (1989)—stirred the consciences of only a minority of whites. The response to the Rodney King verdict is thus a long-overdue reminder that whites still have the capacity to feel deeply about white racism—when they can see it in unambiguous terms.

The videotaped beating by four Los Angeles police officers provided this concreteness. To be sure, many whites focused their response on the subsequent black rioting, while the anger of blacks tended to remain fixed on the verdict itself. However, whites initially were almost as upset as blacks: An early poll reported that 86 percent of European-Americans disagreed with the jury's decision. The absence of any black from the jury and the trial's venue, Simi Valley, a lily-white suburban community, enabled mainstream whites to see the parallels with the Jim Crow justice of the old South. When we add to this mixture the widespread disaffection, especially of young people, with the nation's political and economic conditions, it is easier to explain the scale of white emotional involvement, unprecedented in a matter of racial protest since the 1960s.

In thirty years of teaching, I have never seen my students so overwrought, needing to talk, eager to do something. This response at the University of California at Berkeley cut across the usual fault lines of intergroup tension, as it did at high schools in Northern California. Assemblies, marches, and class discussions took place all over the nation in predominantly white as well as nonwhite and integrated high schools. Considering that there were also incidents where blacks assaulted white people, the scale of white involvement is even more impressive.

While many whites saw the precipitating events as expressions of racist conduct, they were much less likely than blacks to see them as part of some larger pattern of racism. Thus two separate polls found that only half as many whites as blacks believe that the legal system treats whites better than blacks. (In each poll, 43 percent of whites saw such a generalized double standard, in contrast to 84 percent of blacks in one survey, 89 percent in the other.)

This gap is not surprising. For twenty years European-Americans have tended to feel that systematic racial inequities marked an earlier era, not our own. Psychological denial and a kind of post-1960s exhaustion may both be factors in producing the sense among mainstream whites that civil rights laws and other changes resolved blacks' racial grievances, if not the economic basis of urban problems. But the gap in perceptions of racism also reflects a deeper difference. Whites and blacks see racial issues through different lenses and use different scales to weigh and assess injustice.

Bob Blauner is professor emeritus of sociology at the University of California, Berkeley.

I am not saying that blacks and whites have totally disparate value systems and worldviews. I think we were more polarized in the late 1960s. It was then that I began a twenty-year interview study of racial consciousness published in 1989 as *Black Lives, White Lives.* By 1979 blacks and whites had come closer together on many issues than they had been in 1968. In the late 1970s and again in the mid-to-late 1980s, both groups were feeling quite pessimistic about the nation's direction. They agreed that America had become a more violent nation and that people were more individualistic and less bound by such traditional values as hard work, personal responsibility, and respect for age and authority. But with this and other convergences, there remained a striking gap in the way European-Americans and African-Americans evaluated *racial* change. Whites were impressed by the scale of integration, the size of the black middle class, and the extent of demonstrable progress. Blacks were disillusioned with integration, concerned about the people who had been left behind, and much more negative in their overall assessment of change.

In the 1990s this difference in general outlook led to different reactions to specific racial issues. That is what makes the shared revulsion over the Rodney King verdict a significant turning point, perhaps even an opportunity to begin bridging the gap between black and white definitions of the racial situation.

I want to advance the proposition that there are two languages of race in America. I am not talking about black English and standard English, which refer to different structures of grammar and dialect. "Language" here signifies a system of implicit understandings about social reality, and a racial language encompasses a worldview.

Blacks and whites differ on their interpretations of social change from the 1960s through the 1990s because their racial languages define the central terms, especially "racism," differently. Their racial languages incorporate different views of American society itself, especially the question of how central race and racism are to America's very existence, past and present. Blacks believe in this centrality, while most whites, except for the more race-conscious extremists, see race as a peripheral reality. Even successful, middle-class black professionals experience slights and humiliations—incidents when they are stopped by police, regarded suspiciously by clerks while shopping, or mistaken for messengers, drivers, or aides at work—that remind them they have not escaped racism's reach. For whites, race becomes central on exceptional occasions: collective, public moments such as the recent events, when the veil is lifted, and private ones, such as a family's decision to escape urban problems with a move to the suburbs. But most of the time European-Americans are able to view racial issues as aberrations in American life, much as Los Angeles Police Chief Daryl Gates used the term "aberration" to explain his officers' beating of Rodney King in March 1991.

Because of these differences in language and worldview, blacks and whites often talk past one another, just as men and women sometimes do. I first noticed this in my classes, particularly during discussions of racism. Whites locate racism in color consciousness and its absence in color blindness. They regard it as a kind of racism when students of color insistently underscore their sense of difference, their affirmation of ethnic and racial membership, which minority students have increasingly asserted. Many black, and increasingly also Latino and Asian, students cannot understand this reaction. It seems to them misinformed, even ignorant. They in turn sense a kind of racism in the whites' assumption that minorities must assimilate to mainstream values and styles. Then African-Americans will posit an idea that many whites find preposterous: Black people, they argue, cannot be racist, because racism is a system of power, and black people as a group do not have power.

In this and many other arenas, a contest rages over the meaning of racism. Racism has become the central term in the language of race. From the 1940s through the 1980s new and multiple meanings of racism have been added to the social science lexicon and public discourse. The 1960s were especially critical for what the English sociologist Robert Miles has called the "inflation" of the term "racism." Blacks tended to embrace the enlarged definitions, whites to resist them. This conflict, in my view, has been at the very center of the racial struggle during the past decade.

THE WIDENING CONCEPTION OF RACISM

The term "racism" was not commonly used in social science or American public life until the 1960s. "Racism" does not appear, for example, in the Swedish economist Gunnar Myrdal's classic 1944 study of American race relations, *An American Dilemma.* But even when the term was not directly used, it is still possible to determine the prevailing understandings of racial oppression.

In the 1940s racism referred to an ideology, an explicit system of beliefs postulating the superiority of whites based on the inherent, biological inferiority of the colored races. Ideological racism was particularly associated with the belief systems of the Deep South and was originally devised as a rationale for slavery. Theories of white supremacy, particularly in their biological versions, lost much of their legitimacy after the Second World War due to their association with Nazism. In recent years cultural explanations of "inferiority" are heard more commonly than biological ones, which today are associated with such extremist "hate groups" as the Ku Klux Klan and the White Aryan Brotherhood.

By the 1950s and early 1960s, with ideological racism discredited, the focus shifted to a more discrete approach to racially invidious attitudes and behavior, expressed in the model of prejudice and discrimination. "Prejudice" referred (and still does) to hostile feelings and beliefs about racial minorities and the web of stereotypes justifying such negative attitudes. "Discrimination" referred to actions meant to harm the members of a racial minority group. The logic of this model was that racism implied a double standard, that is, treating a person of color differently—in mind or action —than one would a member of the majority group.

By the mid-1960s the terms "prejudice" and "discrimination" and the implicit model of racial causation implied by them were seen as too weak to explain the sweep of racial conflict and change, too limited in their analytical power, and for some critics too individualistic in their assumptions. Their original meanings tended to be absorbed by a new, more encompassing idea of racism. During the 1960s the referents of racial oppression moved from individual actions and beliefs to group and institutional processes, from subjective ideas to "objective" structures or results. Instead of intent, there was now an emphasis on process: those more objective social processes of exclusion, exploitation, and discrimination that led to a racially stratified society.

The most notable of these new definitions was "institutional racism." In their 1967 book *Black Power,* Stokely Carmichael and Charles Hamilton stressed how institutional racism was different and more fundamental than individual racism. Racism, in this view, was built into society and scarcely required prejudicial attitudes to maintain racial oppression.

This understanding of racism as pervasive and institutionalized spread from relatively narrow "movement" and academic circles to the larger public with the appearance in 1968 of the report of the commission on the urban riots appointed by President Lyndon Johnson and chaired by Illinois Governor Otto Kerner. The Kerner Commission identified "white racism" as a prime reality of American society and the major underlying cause of ghetto unrest. America, in this view, was moving toward two societies, one white and one black (it is not clear where other racial minorities fit in). Although its recommendations were never acted upon politically, the report legitimated the term "white racism" among politicians and opinion leaders as a key to analyzing racial inequality in America.

Another definition of racism, which I would call "racism as atmosphere," also emerged in the 1960s and 1970s. This is the idea that an organization or an environment might be racist because its implicit, unconscious structures were devised for the use and comfort of white people, with the result that people of other races will not feel at home in such settings. Acting on this understanding of racism, many schools and universities, corporations, and other institutions have changed their teaching practices or work environments to encourage a greater diversity in their clientele, students, or work force.

Perhaps the most radical definition of all was the concept of "racism as result." In this sense, an institution or an occupation is racist simply because racial minorities are underrepresented in numbers or in positions of prestige and authority.

Seizing on different conceptions of racism, the blacks and whites I talked to in the late 1970s had come to different conclusions about how far America had moved toward racial justice. Whites tended to adhere to earlier, more limited notions of racism. Blacks for the most part saw the newer meanings as more basic. Thus African-Americans did not think racism had been put to rest by civil rights laws, even by the dramatic changes in the South. They felt that it still pervaded American life, indeed, had become more insidious because the subtle forms were harder to combat than old-fashioned exclusion and persecution.

Whites saw racism largely as a thing of the past. They defined it in terms of segregation and lynching, explicit white supremacist beliefs, or double standards in hiring, promotion, and admissions to colleges or other institutions. Except for affirmative action, which seemed the most blatant expression of such double standards, they were positively impressed by racial change. Many saw the relaxed and comfortable relations between whites and blacks as the heart of the matter. More crucial to blacks, on the other hand, were the underlying structures of power and position that continued to provide them with unequal portions of economic opportunity and other possibilities for the good life.

The newer, expanded definitions of racism just do not make much sense to most whites. I have experienced their frustrations directly when I try to explain the concept of institutional racism to white students and popular audiences. The idea of racism as an "impersonal force" loses all but the most theoretically inclined. Whites are more likely than blacks to view racism as a personal issue. Both sensitive to their own possible culpability (if only unconsciously) and angry at the use of the concept of racism by angry minorities, they do not differentiate well between the racism of social structures and the accusation that they as participants in that structure are personally racist.

The new meanings make sense to blacks, who live such experiences in their bones. But by 1979 many of the African-Americans in my study, particularly the older activists, were critical of the use of racism as a blanket explanation for all manifestations of racial inequality. Long before similar ideas were voiced by the black conservatives, many blacks sensed that too heavy an emphasis on racism led to the false conclusion that blacks could only progress through a conventional civil rights strategy of fighting prejudice and discrimination. (This strategy, while necessary, had proved very limited.) Overemphasizing racism, they feared, was interfering with the black community's ability to achieve greater self-determination through the politics of self-help. In addition, they told me that the prevailing rhetoric of the 1960s had affected many young blacks. Rather than taking responsibility for their own difficulties, they were now using racism as a "cop-out."

In public life today this analysis is seen as part of the conservative discourse on race. Yet I believe that this position originally was a progressive one, developed out of self-critical reflections on the relative failure of 1960s movements. But perhaps because it did not seem to be "politically correct," the left-liberal community, black as well as white, academic as well as political, has been afraid of embracing such a critique. As a result, the neoconservatives had a clear field to pick up this grass-roots sentiment and to use it to further their view that racism is no longer significant in American life. This is the last thing that my informants and other savvy African-Americans close to the pulse of their communities believe.

By the late 1970s the main usage of racism in the mind of the white public had undoubtedly become that of "reverse racism." The primacy of "reverse racism" as "the really important racism" suggests that the conservatives and the liberal-center have, in effect, won the battle over the meaning of racism.

Perhaps this was inevitable because of the long period of backlash against all the progressive movements of the 1960s. But part of the problem may have been the inflation of the idea of racism. While institutional racism exists, such a concept loses practical utility if every thing and every place is racist. In that case, there is effectively nothing to be done about it. And without conceptual tools to distinguish what is important from what is not, we are lost in the confusion of multiple meanings.

BACK TO BASICS

While public discourse was discounting white racism as exaggerated or a thing of the past, the more traditional forms of bigotry, harassment, and violence were unfortunately making a comeback. (This upsurge actually began in the early 1980s but was not well noticed, due to some combination of media inattention and national mood.) What was striking about the Bernhard Goetz subway shootings in New York, the white on black racial violence in Howard Beach, the rise of organized hate groups, campus racism, and skinhead violence is that these are all examples of old-fashioned racism. They illustrate the power and persistence of racial prejudices and hate crimes in the tradition of classical lynchings. They are precisely the kind of phenomena that many social analysts expected to diminish as I did.

If there was one positive effect of this upsurge, it was to alert many whites to the destructive power of racial hatred and division in American life. At the same time, these events also repolarized racial attitudes in America. They have contributed to the anger and alienation of the black middle class and the rapid rise of Afrocentrism, particularly among college students.

As the gap in understanding has widened, several social scientists have proposed restricting the concept of racism to its original, more narrow meaning. However, the efforts of African-Americans to enlarge the meaning of racism is part of that group's project to make its view of the world and of American society competitive with the dominant white perspective. In addition, the "inflated" meanings of racism are already too rooted in common speech to be overturned by the advice of experts. And certainly some way is needed to convey the pervasive and systematic character of racial oppression. No other term does this as well as racism.

The question then becomes what to do about these multiple and confusing meanings of racism and their extraordinary personal and political charge. I would begin by honoring both the black and white readings of the term. Such an attitude might help facilitate the interracial dialogue so badly needed and yet so rare today.

Communication can only start from the understandings that people have. While the black understanding of racism is, in some sense, the deeper one, the white views of racism (ideology, double standard) refer to more specific and recognizable beliefs and practices. Since there is also a cross-racial consensus on the immorality of racist ideology and racial discrimination, it makes sense whenever possible to use such a concrete referent as discrimination, rather than the more global concept of racism. And reemphasizing discrimination may help remind the public that racial discrimination is not just a legacy of the past.

The intellectual power of the African-American understanding lies in its more critical and encompassing perspective. In the Rodney King events, we have an unparalleled opportunity to bridge the racial gap by pointing out that racism and racial division remain essential features of American life and that incidents such as police beatings of minority people and stacked juries are not aberrations but part of a larger pattern of racial abuse and harassment. Without resorting to the overheated rhetoric that proved counterproductive in the 1960s, it now may be possible to persuade white Americans that the most important patterns of discrimination and disadvantage are not to be found in the "reverse racism" of affirmative action but sadly still in the white racism of the dominant social system. And, when feasible, we need to try to bridge the gap by shifting from the language of race to that of ethnicity and class.

RACE OR ETHNICITY?

In the American consciousness the imagery of race—especially along the black-white dimension—tends to be more powerful than that of class or ethnicity. As a result, legitimate ethnic affiliations are often misunderstood to be racial and illegitimate.

Race itself is a confusing concept because of the variance between scientific and common sense definitions of the term. Physical anthropologists who study the distribution of those characteristics we use to classify "races" teach us that race is a fiction because all peoples are mixed to various degrees. Sociologists counter that this biological fiction unfortunately remains a sociological reality. People define one another racially, and thus divide society into racial groups. The "fiction" of race affects every aspect of peoples' lives, from living standards to landing in jail.

The consciousness of color differences, and the invidious distinctions based on them, have existed since antiquity and are not limited to any one corner of the world. And yet the peculiarly modern division of the world into a discrete number of hierarchically ranked races is a historic product of Western colonialism. In precolonial Africa the relevant group identities were national, tribal, or linguistic. There was no concept of an African or black people until this category was created by the combined effects of slavery, imperialism, and the anticolonial and Pan-African movements. The legal definitions of blackness and whiteness, which varied from one society to another in the Western hemisphere, were also crucial for the construction of modern-day races. Thus race is an essentially political construct, one that translates our tendency to see people in terms of their color or other physical attributes into structures that make it likely that people will act for or against them on such a basis.

The dynamic of ethnicity is different, even though the results at times may be similar. An ethnic group is a group that shares a belief in its common past. Members of an ethnic group hold a set of common memories that make them feel that their customs, culture, and outlook are distinctive. In short, they have a sense of peoplehood. Sharing critical experiences and sometimes a belief in their common fate, they feel an affinity for one another, a "comfort zone" that leads to congregating together, even when this is not forced by exclusionary barriers. Thus if race is associated with biology and nature, ethnicity is associated with culture. Like races, ethnic groups arise historically, transform themselves, and sometimes die out.

Much of the popular discourse about race in America today goes awry because ethnic realities get lost under the racial umbrella. The positive meanings and potential of ethnicity are overlooked, even overrun, by the more inflammatory meanings of race. Thus white students, disturbed when blacks associate with each other, justify their objections through their commitment to *racial* integration. They do not appreciate the ethnic affinities that bring this about, or see the parallels to Jewish students meeting at the campus Hillel Foundation or Italian-Americans eating lunch at the Italian house on the Berkeley campus.

When blacks are "being ethnic," whites see them as "being racial." Thus they view the identity politics of students who want to celebrate their blackness, their *chicanoismo,* their Asian heritages, and their American Indian roots as racially offensive. Part of this reaction comes from a sincere desire, almost a yearning, of white students for a color-blind society. But because the ethnicity of darker people so often gets lost in our overracialized perceptions, the white students misread the situation. When I point out to my class that whites are talking about race and its dynamics and the students of color are talking about ethnicity and its differing meaning, they can begin to appreciate each other's agendas.

Confounding race and ethnicity is not just limited to the young. The general public, including journalists and other opinion makers, does this regularly, with serious consequences for the clarity of public dialogue and sociological analysis. A clear example comes from the Chicago mayoral election of 1983. The establishment press, including leading liberal columnists, regularly chastised the black electorate for giving virtually all its votes to Harold Washington. Such racial voting was as "racist" as whites voting for the other candidate because they did not want a black mayor. Yet African-Americans were voting for ethnic representation just as Irish-Americans, Jews, and Italians have always done. Such ethnic politics is considered the American way. What is discriminatory is the double standard that does not confer the same rights on blacks, who were not voting primarily out of fear or hatred as were many whites.

Such confusions between race and ethnicity are exacerbated by the ambiguous sociological status of African-Americans. Black Americans are *both* a race and an ethnic group. Unfortunately, part of our heritage of racism has been to deny the ethnicity, the cultural heritage of black Americans. Liberal-minded whites have wanted to see blacks as essentially white people with black skins. Until the 1960s few believed that black culture was a real ethnic culture.

Because our racial language is so deepseated, the terminology of black and white just seems more "natural" and commonsensical than more ethnic labels like African-American or European-American. But the shift to the term "African-American" has been a conscious attempt to move the discourse from a language of race to a language of ethnicity. "African-American," as Jesse Jackson and others have pointed out, connects the group to its history and culture in a way that the racial designation, black, does not. The new usage parallels terms for other ethnic groups. Many whites tend to dismiss this concern about language as mere sloganeering. But "African-American" fits better into the emerging multicultural view of American ethnic and racial arrangements, one more appropriate to our growing diversity. The old race relations model was essentially a view that generalized (often inappropriately) from black-white relations. It can no longer capture—if it ever could—the complexity of a multiracial and multicultural society.

The issue is further complicated by the fact that African-Americans are not a homogeneous group. They comprise a variety of distinct ethnicities. There are the West Indians with their long histories in the U.S., the darker Puerto Ricans (some of whom identify themselves as black), the more recently arrived Dominicans, Haitians, and immigrants from various African countries, as well as the native-born African-Americans, among whom regional distinctions can also take on a quasi-ethnic flavor.

Blacks from the Caribbean are especially likely to identify with their homeland rather than taking on a generic black or even African-American identity. While they may resist the dynamic of "racialization" and even feel superior to native blacks, the dynamic is relentless. Their children are likely to see themselves as part of the larger African-American population. And yet many native-born Americans of African descent also resist the term "African-American," feeling very little connection to the original homeland. Given the diversity in origin and outlook of America's largest minority, it is inevitable that no single concept can capture its full complexity or satisfy all who fall within its bounds.

For white Americans, race does not overwhelm ethnicity. Whites see the ethnicity of other whites; it is their own whiteness they tend to overlook. But even when race is recognized, it is not conflated with ethnicity. Jews, for example, clearly distinguish their Jewishness from their whiteness. Yet the long-term dynamic still favors the development of a dominant white racial identity. Except for recent immigrants, the various European ethnic identities have been rapidly weakening. Vital ethnic communities persist in some cities, particularly on the East Coast. But many whites, especially the young, have such diverse ethnic heritages that they have no meaningful ethnic affiliation. In my classes only the Jews among European-Americans retain a strong sense of communal origin.

Instead of dampening the ethnic enthusiasms of the racial minorities, perhaps it would be better to encourage the revitalization of whites' European heritages. But a problem with this approach is that the relationship between race and ethnicity is more ambiguous for whites than for people of color. Although for many white groups ethnicity has been a stigma, it also has been used to gain advantages that have marginalized blacks and other racial minorities. Particularly for working-class whites today, ethnic community loyalties are often the prism through which they view their whiteness, their superiority.

Thus the line between ethnocentrism and racism is a thin one, easily crossed—as it was by Irish-Americans who resisted the integration of South Boston's schools in the 1970s and by many of the Jews and Italians that sociologist Jonathan Rieder describes in his 1985 book *Canarsie*.

White students today complain of a double standard. Many feel that their college administrations sanction organization and identification for people of color, but not for them. If there can be an Asian business organization and a black student union, why can't there be a white business club or a white student alliance? I'd like to explain to them that students of color are organized ethnically, not racially, that whites have Hillel and the Italian theme house. But this makes little practical sense when such loyalties are just not that salient for the vast majority.

Out of this vacuum the emerging identity of "European-American" has come into vogue. I interpret the European-American idea as part of a yearning for a usable past. Europe is associated with history and culture. "America" and "American" can no longer be used to connote white people. "White" itself is a racial term and thereby inevitably associated with our nation's legacy of social injustice.

At various California colleges and high schools, European-American clubs have begun to form, provoking debate about whether it is inherently racist for whites to organize as whites—or as European-Americans. Opponents invoke the racial analogy and see such organizations as akin to exclusive white supremacist groups. Their defenders argue from an ethnic model, saying that they are simply looking for a place where they can feel at home and discuss their distinctive personal and career problems. The jury is still out on this new and, I suspect, burgeoning phenomenon. It will take time to discover its actual social impact.

If the European-Americans forming their clubs are truly organizing on an ethnic or panethnic rather than a racial model, I would have to support these efforts. Despite all the ambiguities, it seems to me a gain in social awareness when a specific group comes to be seen in ethnic rather than racial terms. During the period of the mass immigration of the late nineteenth century and continuing through the 1920s, Jews, Italians, and other white ethnics were viewed racially. We no longer hear of the "Hebrew race," and it is rare for Jewish distinctiveness to be attributed to biological rather than cultural roots. Of course, the shift from racial to ethnic thinking did not put an end to anti-Semitism in the United States—or to genocide in Germany, where racial imagery was obviously intensified.

It is unrealistic to expect that the racial groupings of American society can be totally "deconstructed," as a number of scholars now are advocating. After all, African-Americans and native Americans, who were not immigrants, can never be exactly like other ethnic groups. Yet a shift in this direction would begin to move our society from a divisive biracialism to a more inclusive multiculturalism.

To return to the events of spring 1992, I ask what was different about these civil disturbances. Considering the malign neglect of twelve Reagan-Bush years, the almost two decades of economic stagnation, and the retreat of the public from issues of race and poverty, the violent intensity should hardly be astonishing.

More striking was the multiracial character of the response. In the San Francisco Bay area, rioters were as likely to be white as nonwhite. In Los Angeles, Latinos were prominent among both the protesters and the victims. South Central Los Angeles is now more Hispanic than black, and this group suffered perhaps 60 percent of the property damage. The media have focused on the specific grievances of African-Americans toward Koreans. But I would guess that those who trashed Korean stores were protesting something larger than even the murder of a fifteen-year-old black girl. Koreans, along with other immigrants, continue to enter the country and in a relatively short time surpass the economic and social position of the black poor. The immigrant advantage is real and deeply resented by African-Americans, who see that the two most downtrodden minorities are those that did not enter the country voluntarily.

During the 1960s the police were able to contain riots within the African-American community. This time Los Angeles police were unable to do so. Even though the South Central district suffered most, there was also much destruction in other areas including Hollywood, downtown, and the San Fernando Valley. In the San Francisco Bay area the violence occurred primarily in the white business sections, not the black neighborhoods of Oakland, San Francisco, or Berkeley. The violence that has spilled out of the inner city is a distillation of all the human misery that a white middle-class society has been trying to contain—albeit unsuccessfully (consider the homeless). As in the case of an untreated infection, the toxic substances finally break out, threatening to contaminate the entire organism.

Will this widened conflict finally lead Americans toward a recognition of our common stake in the health of the inner cities and their citizens, or toward increased fear and division? The Emmett Till lynching in 1955 set the stage for the first mass mobilization of the civil rights movement, the Montgomery bus boycott later that year. Martin Luther King's assassination provided the impetus for the institution of affirmative action and other social programs. The Rodney King verdict and its aftermath must also become not just a psychologically defining moment but an impetus to a new mobilization of political resolve.

PERSONAL ACCOUNT

Where Are You From?

As a freshman at a predominantly white private college, I was confronted with a number of unusual situations. I was extremely young for a college freshman (I was sixteen), I was African American, and I was placed in upper-division courses, because of my academic background. So being accepted and fitting in were crucial to me.

I was enrolled in a course, Political Thought, with approximately thirty other students, mostly juniors and seniors who had taken courses with this professor before. I was the only African American in the class. During introductions for the first class, he never got around to letting me speak, even though he went alphabetically on the list (my last name begins with a "C"). Later, I began to be aware of his exclusion of me from class discussion. By the third class, I guess he felt there was no longer any way he could avoid speaking to me. He asked me a few questions about myself—where was I from, what high school had I attended, and what was my major. His questions began to seem like a personal attack, and then finally he asked, "Why are you here?" "Where are you from?" I was quite taken aback by his line of questioning, when one of the upperclassmen (a white man) responded for me. "She's a freshman, Dr. B. Any more questions?" That guy became one of my closest friends. We have maintained contact ever since college. His response to Dr. B. totally changed the professor's way of treating me.

C.C.

READING 24

Driving While Black

A Statistician Proves That Prejudice Still Rules the Road

John Lamberth

In 1993, I was contacted by attorneys whose clients had been arrested on the New Jersey Turnpike for possession of drugs. They told me they had come across 25 African American defendants over a three-year period, all arrested on the same stretch of turnpike in Gloucester County, but not a single white defendant. I was asked whether, and how much, this pattern reflected unfair treatment of blacks.

They wanted to know what a professional statistician would make of these numbers. What were the probabilities that this pattern could occur naturally, that is, by chance? Since arrests for drug offenses occurred after traffic stops on the highway, was it possible that so many blacks were arrested because the police were disproportionately stopping them? I decided to try to answer their questions and embarked on one of the most intriguing statistical studies of my career: a census of traffic and traffic violators by race on Interstate 95 in New Jersey. It would require a careful design, teams of researchers with binoculars and a rolling survey.

To relieve your suspense, the answer was that the rate at which blacks were stopped was greatly disproportionate to their numbers on the road and to their propensity to violate traffic laws. Those findings were central to a March 1996 ruling by Judge Robert E. Francis of the Superior Court of New Jersey that the state police were de facto targeting blacks, in violation of their rights under the U.S. and New Jersey constitutions. The judge suppressed the evidence gathered in the stops. New Jersey is now appealing the case.

The New Jersey litigation is part of a broad attack in a number of states, including Maryland, on what has been dubbed the offense of "DWB"—driving while black. While this problem has been familiar anecdotally to African Americans and civil rights advocates for years, there is now evidence that highway patrols are singling out blacks for stops on the illegal and incorrect theory that the practice, known as racial profiling, is the most likely to yield drug arrests. Statistical techniques are proving extremely helpful in proving targeting, just as they have been in proving systemic discrimination in employment.

John Lamberth is in the psychology department of Temple University.

This was not my first contact with the disparate treatment of blacks in the criminal justice system. My academic research over the past 25 years had led me from an interest in small group decision-making to jury selection, jury composition and the application of the death penalty. I became aware that blacks were disproportionately charged with crimes, particularly serious ones; that they were underrepresented on jury panels and thus on juries; and that they were sentenced to death at a much greater rate than their numbers could justify.

As I began the New Jersey study, I knew from experience that any research that questioned police procedures was sensitive. I knew that what I did must stand the test of a court hearing in which every move I made would be challenged by experts.

First, I had to decide what I needed to know. What was the black "population" of the road—that is, how many of the people traveling on the turnpike over a given period of time were African American? This task is a far cry from determining the population of a town, city or state. There are no Census Bureau figures. The population of a roadway changes all day, every day. By sampling the population of the roadway over a given period, I could make an accurate determination of the average number of blacks on the road.

I designed and implemented two surveys. We stationed observers by the side of the road, with the assignment of counting the number of cars and the race of the occupants in randomly selected three-hour blocks of time over a two-week period. The New Jersey Turnpike has four lanes at its southern end, two in each direction. By the side of the road, we placed an observer for each lane, equipped with binoculars to observe and note the number of cars and the race of occupants, along with a person to write down what the observers said. The team observed for an hour and a half, took a 30-minute break while moving to another observation point and repeated the process.

In total, we conducted more than 21 sessions between 8 A.M. and 8 P.M. from June 11 to June 24, 1993, at four sites between Exits 1 and 3 of the turnpike, among the busiest highway segments in the nation. We counted roughly 43,000 cars, of which 13.5 percent had one or more black occupants. This was consistent with the population figures for the 11 states from which most of the vehicles observed were registered.

For the rolling survey, Fred Last, a public defender, drove at a constant 60 mph (5 mph above the speed limit at the time). He counted all cars that passed him as violators and all cars he passed as nonviolators. Speaking into a tape recorder, he also noted the race of the driver of each car. At the end of each day, he collated his results and faxed them to me.

Last counted 2,096 cars. More than 98 percent were speeding and thus subject to being stopped by police. African Americans made up about 15 percent of those drivers on the turnpike violating traffic laws. Utilizing data from the New Jersey State Police, I determined that about 35 percent of those who were stopped on this part of the turnpike were African Americans.

To summarize: African Americans made up 13.5 percent of the turnpike's population and 15 percent of the speeders. But they represented 35 percent of those pulled over. In stark numbers, blacks were 4.85 times as likely to be stopped as were others.

We did not obtain data on the race of drivers and passengers searched after being stopped or on the rate at which vehicles were searched. But we know from police records that 73.2 percent of those arrested along the turnpike over a 3½-year period by troopers from the area's Moorestown barracks were black—making them 16.5 times more likely to be arrested than others.

Attorneys for the 25 African Americans who had been arrested on the turnpike and charged with possessing drugs or guns filed motions to suppress evidence seized when they were stopped, arguing that police stopped them because of their race. Their motions were consolidated and heard by Judge Francis between November 1994 and May 1995. My statistical study, bolstered by an analysis of its validity by Joseph B. Kadane, professor of statistics at Carnegie Mellon University, was the primary exhibit in support of the motions.

But Francis also heard testimony from two former New Jersey troopers who said they had been coached to make race-based "profile" stops to increase their criminal arrests. And the judge reviewed police in-service training aids such as videos that disproportionately portrayed minorities as perpetrators.

The statistical disparities, Francis wrote, are "indeed stark. . . . Defendants have proven at least a de facto policy on the part of the State Police . . . of targeting blacks for investigation and arrest." The judge ordered that the state's evidence be suppressed.

My own work in this field continues. In 1992, Robert L. Wilkins was riding in a rented car with family members when Maryland State Police stopped them, ordered them out, and conducted a search for drugs, which were not found. Wilkins happened to be a Harvard Law School trained public defender in Washington. With the support of the Maryland ACLU, he sued the state police, who settled the case with, among other things, an agreement to provide highway-stop data to the organization.

I was asked by the ACLU to evaluate the Maryland data in 1996 and again in 1997. I conducted a rolling survey in Maryland similar to the one I had done before and found a similar result. While 17.5 percent of the traffic violators on I-95 north of Baltimore were African American, 28.8 percent of those stopped and 71.3 percent of those searched by the Maryland State Police were African American. U.S. District Judge Catherine Blake ultimately ruled in 1997 that the ACLU made a "reasonable showing" that Maryland troopers on I-95 were continuing to engage in a "pattern and practice" of racial discrimination. Other legal actions have been filed in Pennsylvania, Florida, Indiana and North Carolina. Police officials everywhere deny racial profiling.

Why, then, are so many more African American motorists stopped than would be expected by their frequency on the road and their violation of the law? It seems clear to me that drugs are the issue.

The notion that African Americans and other minorities are more likely than whites to be carrying drugs—a notion that is perpetuated by some police training films—seems to be especially prevalent among the police. They believe that if they are to interdict drugs, then it makes sense to stop minorities, especially young men. State police are rewarded and promoted at least partially on the basis of their "criminal programs," which means the number of arrests they make. Testimony in the New Jersey case pointed out that troopers would be considered deficient if they did not make enough arrests. Since, as Judge Francis found, training points to minorities as likely drug dealers, it makes a certain sort of distorted sense to stop minorities more than whites.

But there is no untainted evidence that minorities are more likely to possess or sell drugs. There is evidence to the contrary. Indirect evidence in statistics from the National Institute of Drug Abuse indicates that 12 percent to 14 percent of those who abuse drugs are African American, a percentage that is proportionate to their numbers in the general population.

More telling are the numbers of those people who are stopped and searched by the Maryland State Police who have drugs. This data, which has been unobtainable from other states, indicates that of those drivers and passengers searched in Maryland, about 28 percent have contraband, whether they are black or white. The same percentage of contraband is found no matter the race.

The Maryland data may shed some light on the tendency of some troopers to believe that blacks are somehow more likely to possess contraband. This data shows that for every 1,000 searches by the Maryland State Police, 200 blacks and only 80 non-blacks are arrested. This could lead one to believe that more blacks are breaking the law—until you know that the sample is deeply skewed. Of those searched, 713 were black and only 287 were non-black.

We do not have comparable figures on contraband possession or arrests from New Jersey. But if the traffic along I-95 there is at all similar to I-95 in Maryland—and there is a strong numerical basis to believe it is—it is possible to speculate that black travelers in New Jersey also were no more likely than non-blacks to be carrying contraband.

The fact that a black was 16.5 times more likely than a non-black to be arrested on the New Jersey Turnpike now takes on added meaning. Making only the assumption that was shown accurate in Maryland, it is possible to say even more conclusively that racial profiling is prevalent there and that there is no benefit to police in singling out blacks. More important, even if there were a benefit, it would violate fundamental rights. The constitution does not permit law enforcement authorities to target groups by race.

Fundamental fairness demands that steps be taken to prohibit profiling in theory and in practice. There is legislation pending at the federal level and in at least two states, Rhode Island and Pennsylvania, that would require authorities to keep statistics on this issue. This is crucial legislation and should be passed.

Only when the data are made available and strong steps are taken to monitor and curtail profiling, will we be able to assure minorities, and all of us who care about fundamental rights, that this practice will cease.

READING 25

Darkness Made Visible: Law, Metaphor, and the Racial Self

D. Marvin Jones

> Then it dawned upon me with a certain suddenness that I was different from the others; or like, mayhap, in heart and life and longing, but shut out from their world by a vast veil. . . . The shades of the prison-house closed round us all: walls strait and stubborn to the whitest, but relentlessly narrow, tall and unscalable to sons of night who must plod darkly on in resignation, or beat unavailing palms against stone, or steadily, half hopelessly, watch the streak of blue above.[1]

In August 1862, Abraham Lincoln called a number of "Negro" leaders to the White House. Laboring under harsh racial assumptions, which conflicted with the moral eloquence to come at Gettysburg, Lincoln told his assembled audience, "You and we are different races. . . . This physical difference is a great disadvantage to us both, as I think your race suffer very greatly, many of them by living among us, while ours suffer from your presence."[2] With these prefatory remarks, Lincoln proceeded to try to persuade his audience of the merits of his plan: To emancipate slaves and expatriate them to a colony in Central America.

For Lincoln, race signified a natural and immovable wall between communities, a wall of difference. Homogeneity, by contrast, is the basic stuff of the social bond. By invoking the notion of race, and invoking it in a strong essentialist sense,[3] Lincoln rhetorically posited that blacks and whites lacked any basic human bond upon which they could form one society. Race reverberated as a metaphor of kinship, denying that there was the requisite brotherhood between blacks and whites, and denying that blacks and whites could co-exist on the same social plane.[4]

Historically, this world view was most explicitly expressed in institutional structures such as de jure and de facto segregation. This bleak nineteenth century world view remains in our current constitutional jurisprudence. The idea of race as a natural, objective demarcation of difference between groups is the lens through which courts continue to view claims by blacks. Thus, in *City of Richmond v. J. A. Croson Co.*,[5] Justice O'Connor criticizes as fundamentally illogical the means-ends connection of a set-aside program requiring thirty percent participation by "minorities." O'Connor explains:

> [T]he 30% quota cannot be said to be narrowly tailored to any goal, except perhaps outright racial

---

D. Marvin Jones is professor of law at the University of Miami Law School in Miami, Florida.

> balancing. It rests upon the "completely unrealistic" assumption that minorities will choose a particular trade in lockstep proportion to their representation in the local populations.[6]

On the surface, this opinion represents hostility toward using groups, rather than the individual, as the unit of social inquiry, a relentlessly particularizing perspective that denies both the problem of caste and the relevance or reality of societal discrimination. Moreover, it is a denial that group disparities between the socioeconomic situations of blacks and whites are legally meaningful. The source of this denial of meaning is a conception of race as difference. O'Connor seems to say: "Blacks and whites are *different* races. . . . Why assume they would have similar interests or display statistically similar occupational patterns?"

But race, for all its rhetorical power, is an incoherent fiction. "The truth is," as Anthony Appiah notes, "there are no races."[7] Racial categories are neither objective nor natural, but ideological and constructed. In these terms race is not so much a category but a practice: *people are raced.* Yet conventional legal theory understands race as something that is already "there," freestanding.[8] As we shall see, this conventional account ultimately collides with its own lurking objectivism. From President Lincoln to Justice O'Connor, from classical to modern American law, this specious perspective has imposed false horizons on our values and discourse. This figure of race seeks to draw its line of difference in the dialogue about democracy and equality between those who fit within and those who fit without. So long as this trope of difference remains as the dark glass through which we view the world, it will distort our vision and conceptions of law, justice, and ourselves.

LAW THROUGH THE EYE/I OF THE OTHER: RACIAL IDENTITY AS A LENS

Race is a mask that grins and lies.[9] Its assumptions distort our images of ourselves and close off our vision of the world. Like the doll-wood mask of African ritual, its cramped confines become the limits of our vision. The black mask envelops us in a sealed hemisphere where we may observe only the darkness of the mask's own interiority. The white mask becomes a lens through which the eye/I may visualize itself at the center of the universe, hermetically sealed. The mask—black or white—becomes a screen between self and other.[10] The two masks represent a singular phenomenon—the radical falsification of the self. The mask of race does not merely divide between self and other; it divides internally. We become two people, inhabiting radically different worlds. One of us is a child of the enlightenment: an autonomous, individual actor with discrete tastes and values. Our other person is an undifferentiated part of a whole.[11] We live as a fragmented entity, with two faces, two lives, and two identities: one individual, one racial.[12]

The white minstrels of the nineteenth century wore a mask when they painted themselves with black greasepaint symbolic of racial identity. This racial identification prompted the acting out of fantasies, referring equally to the caricatures of blacks they sought to represent and to the inner conflict about their own powerlessness in the changing industrial order. This process of racial identification and the acting out of internal instability occurred as parody in the minstrel shows and continues as an unconscious drama in contemporary American law. By accepting the posts inscribed with the historical narrative of black and white to which we have been tied, we engage in the psychological equivalent of the putting on of greasepaint. The categories of racial identity become the mask that stands between the judge or jury and the black subject.

This problematic of racial identity accounts for a number of cases that the conventional problematic of racism does not. The conventional problematic of "racism" conceives of the difficulty as a problem of ethos—in the moral sphere.[13] The problematic of race locates it as a problem of world view, structured by historical narratives that transform our picture of experience. Racism understands the problem in terms of moral opposites: in good/bad and like/dislike distinctions. It understands the problem as a cognitive difficulty flowing from positional status in which notions of inside versus outside and center versus periphery structure both empathy and perception.

Race inscribes its meaning through the ordinary rituals of adjudication. Historically, race was an idea whose significance was worked out on the bodies of blacks, particularly black slaves. Uncannily, the significance of race is particularly apparent today in cases in which black men have been brutalized or killed. In our modern context, the body remains the medium in which the significance of race is most dramatically seen in law. I trace this to a cognitive problem—an almost systematic distortion of thinking and perception that is not random, but follows the general pattern of historical narrative. It is as though the judge or jury is looking at the record through a filter constituted by the symbols, concepts, and imagery of race. Rather than reconstruct what happened and search for truth within the welter of statements and circumstances presented in the legal record, their search is conducted among the ruins of our racial mythology. It is as if, when race is involved, we substitute the notion of an essentialistic model of truth as internal to race itself for a notion of truth as empirical. A few examples will illuminate this point.

A DARK NIGHT OF THE SOUL

When a white man faces a black man, especially if the black man is helpless, terrible things are often revealed.[14]

At 12:47 A.M., California Highway Patrol (CHP) officers are in pursuit of a white Hyundai for failing to yield. The driver is Rodney Glenn King—a black, unemployed construction worker—who will later say he fled from police because he felt the traffic infraction would interfere with his parole. After several units of the Los Angeles Police Department (LAPD) take up chase, Rodney King's vehicle is finally stopped in full view of the Mountainback apartment complex. There, he finds himself surrounded by over twenty armed LAPD officers, several of whom proceed to "beat him half to death" while he is lying defenseless on the ground. King is hit between fifty-three and fifty-six times by officers wielding their batons. The bones holding his eye in its right socket are broken, and he suffers broken bones at the base of his skull. In addition to clubbing him wildly, one officer stomps on his head.[15]

At first sight, the story of King's midnight beating sounds a familiar note. Brutality against blacks by police officers in urban areas is generally not exposed to the light of day. It generally occurs in darkness: in neighborhoods and settings where the only witness is the victim or his peers, who are also victims of socioeconomic disadvantage. Within the shadow of race and class and attendant matters such as criminal records, a black person becomes invisible. Miraculously, King found visibility through a black and white videotape that shows, in grisly detail, King—prone and unarmed—being beaten by at least three officers. King offers no resistance while ten or more officers stand around. After the beating, the following transmissions occur over police computers:

> From [Officers Laurence] Powell and [Tim] Wind to Foot Patrol Officers: *"Oops."*
> From Foot Patrol Officers to Powell and Wind: *"Oops, what?"*
> Powell and Wind to Foot Patrol Officers: *"I haven't beaten anyone this bad in a long time."*
> From Sergeant Stacey Koon to Watch Commander: *"U [Unit] just had a big-time use of force. Tased [electrically shocked] and beat the subject of a CHP pursuit big time."*
> From Watch Commander to Sergeant Stacey Koon: *"Oh well . . . I'm sure the lizard didn't deserve it."*[16]

At the hospital, Officer Powell jokes with King: "Don't you remember the hardball game? We hit quite a few home runs."[17] And before the King incident, Powell referred to a previous police encounter with blacks in which he (Powell) was involved as something straight out of *Gorillas in the Mist*.[18]

Thus far, all this fits neatly within the simple, conventional notion of racism, a problem of "sick minds." Perhaps. However, what happens at trial, I suggest, is more complex. Officers Tim Wind, Laurence Powell, Stacey Koon, and Theodore Briseno were charged, among other things, with assault with a deadly weapon. They were tried before a jury of ten whites, one Asian, and one nonblack Hispanic.

At trial, there was no claim that the officers acted in self-defense, no claim that King was armed, and no denial of participation. The video tape and all of the computer messages containing racial slurs referring to gorillas in the mist and lizards were played and entered as exhibits in the record.[19]

The officers told a story dramatically different from what appeared on the film. They began by claiming that the video did not film the entire event. They said that King, in a desperate attempt to escape the California Highway Patrol, had caused a traffic accident and that when he finally was blocked and made to stop, he got out of the car and shook his behind at the police officers.[20] The officers also characterized the scene on the tape in a way to suggest a struggle. They claimed that King refused to be handcuffed, acted oblivious to blows and tasing, charged into police officers, and swung his arms in a wild and hostile manner. They also argued that their blows were "jabs." Officer Briseno, who was observed by witnesses and was captured by the film stomping King's head, testified he was only trying to get King to stay down. The police told a story of embattled police handling an unruly suspect with statements from a defense witness that King was in a "trance-like" state, and that he was on PCP.[21]

The story of the police was contradicted—in some instances by the film itself and in other instances by eyewitnesses, including police officers:

King caused accident during chase.	CHP officer Melanie Singer said no.
King was on PCP.	Dr. Mancia, who treated King, said no.
King charged into over 20 armed policemen.	Eyewitnesses consistently said no.
King swung his arms wildly and in hostile manner.	According to *L.A. Times* reporter who saw tape, King moves his arms "feebly."

The question before the jury was simply whether the force used to subdue Rodney King, the fifty-plus baton blows (many to the head), the stomping on King's neck, the tasing while he was unarmed (most of it while he was prone on the ground), was reasonable. The jury, however, found none of the officers guilty. Three of the policemen were acquitted outright and the jury hung on the others.

For the jury to find that the force used was reasonable, the jury had to see something different from what the witnesses saw at Mountainback, different from what the reporters who viewed the film saw, different from what I saw. One juror, for example, said that he saw clearly that some of the blows did not connect. I submit that what they saw, at a deep cognitive level, was race. The story told by Sergeant Koon—of a black man who was in a trance, immune to electric shock, unfazed by blows, who kept fighting, charging unarmed into a crowd of LAPD officers—was the old story of blacks as beasts or animals. The initial corollary is that black men like Rodney King are particularly dangerous because they are semi-animals, dramatically less controlled, less rational, and less predictable than white men. Moreover, the scene of the beating—across the street from a place where drugs are sold—is, in a real sense, a jungle (albeit an urban version). This, at a cognitive level, argues for a different way of looking at things.

A second corollary, which is evident within the historical narratives about blacks as Others, is the idea of the black man as anticitizen, as the archetypal threat to law and order. Rodney King, by failing to yield, causes car accidents and endangers life instead of submitting to arrests. In this anticitizen narrative white police officers are faced with an alien "black" consciousness that does not partake of the notions of responsibility accepted by whites. Rodney King, who is perceived by all of the interpretive communities as a representation of urban blacks, became the embodiment of alien "black consciousness": the anticitizen. This image is sharpened by his status as an unemployed and uneducated parolee.

Ironically, the concept of citizenship figures prominently in another story, the "story" people of color hold concerning the Fourteenth Amendment: The Fourteenth Amendment represented a promise of "full citizenship." This promise was made during the Reconstruction Era and remade within the framework of the panoply of state and federal laws that were passed over the last thirty years guaranteeing equal treatment of blacks—the "second reconstruction." The unconscious image of black identity as anticitizenship became the counterstory to the narrative about equal citizenship that minorities and many others would have liked to tell. This same image of black identity worked as a distorting prism, powerfully filtering how the jury saw the film.

The jury simply revised what they "saw" to fit the narrative they already knew, a story that resonates deep within our social history. None of the racial slurs, none of the contradictions in the testimony, and none of the graphic brutality of the video really mattered to the jurors. It was the race story that mattered. The jury merely chose the essentialist knowledge of the story over the lived experience-as-knowledge of the film. This phenomenon has been referred to as a function of the "mythic mentality."

In the mythic mentality,

> the nuances of significance and value which knowledge creates in its concept of the object, which enable it to distinguish different spheres of objects and to draw a line between the world of truth and the world of appearance, are utterly lacking. . . . Instead of the dialectical movement of thought, in which every given particular is linked with other particulars in a series and thus ultimately subordinated to a general *law* and process, we have here a mere subjection to the impression itself and its momentary "presence."[22]

The will to knowledge, like a rushing river, is drawn down through the primitivism of racial symbols, from the experientialist conceptions of truth down a more ancient path. We leave a surface legal world of rationality and empiricism, and descend to a subterranean world of racial essentialism and mythic models of knowledge. From this perspective, the filmed experience cannot penetrate the darkness. How could the film help us to know what happens in the ghetto anyway? Like Africa, the ghetto is a place beyond the experience of whites and, hence, a place of darkness. Who knows what happened? King's blackness blended with both the blackness of the setting and the black and white of the video to become a screen upon which the image of race and racial fears could be projected.

The source of the projection would seem to be the racial self: the jurors identified with the white policemen who were "like them." An admission of racial barbarism on the part of the officers would be an admission of their own racial barbarism and, as such, self-negating. Like Joseph Conrad's Kurtz,[23] the jury flees from "the horror" into the primitive narrative fantasies of the colonial regime.

THE MANICHEAN WORLD

> Nightmare
> That's what I am
> America's Nightmare
> I am what you made me
> The hate and evil that you gave me . . .[24]

According to the Transit Authority Police, "[a] middle-aged man with a silver-colored pistol strode into a subway car rolling through lower Manhattan yesterday and shot four young men he had apparently singled out from among the passengers."[25] In this second story, life imitated film: the shootings by Bernhard Goetz—a thirty-nine year old, straitlaced white man—appeared to parallel the ritualized violence of the protagonist in *Death Wish,*[26] who walked the streets hunting for "criminals" to execute. Witnesses and police on the scene testified that Goetz pursued the men from car to car and shot each of the four "methodically"—shooting two of his victims in the back. Goetz would later confess that he calmly drew a pistol from his belt and shot at each of the four teenagers. As Goetz himself stated, he shot them while they were running away: "[T]hey trapped themselves. The two from left to right, they had nowhere to go. . . . The two on my left, they tried to run through the crowd and of course they had nowhere to run, because the crowd would stop them and I . . . got 'em. . . ." When he discovered that the fourth man, cowering on a bench, was not bleeding, he said, "You seem to be alright, here's another." In his confession, Goetz stated, "I know this sounds horrible, but my intention was to murder them, to hurt them, to make them suffer as much as possible." This gratuitous gunplay against four unarmed teenagers was referred to the morning after as "one of the worst crimes of the year." Yet, immediately after the shootings, the gunman clearly perceived himself as a hero. He helped frightened women off the floor and held a conversation with the conductor before jumping from the train and fleeing "in the dark tunnel."[27]

Goetz was later indicted and tried for attempted murder and assault. He pleaded self-defense. Legally, if the facts were as initially described by the transit police, by the witnesses on the scene, and by Bernhard Goetz himself in his confession, his defense should fail. As Police Commissioner Benjamin Ward stated: "You don't shoot two people running away from you and say it's self-defense."[28]

However clear and grotesquely culpable the actual events appeared, they were later shrouded in the minds of the jury in ambiguity and shadow. As fleshed out by the "evidence" and the opening and closing statements of the defense attorneys, the four youths got up and went over to Goetz to ask for five dollars. Three of the victims had large screwdrivers in their jacket pockets, but Goetz couldn't have known that. The victims all had criminal records, but Goetz could not have known that either. Goetz confessed that the shooting was not linked to anything they said. Rather, he based the "threat" on two things: that they were standing there and that they had "shiny" eyes.[29] The image the defense literally conjured up for the jury—less from the spotty and inconsistent record than from courtroom theatrics and lawyer oratory—was of four black men standing around Goetz, menacing him with their presence and "looks," thus prompting him to draw his revolver and shoot them out of fear.

Much was made to hinge upon whether the youths actually stood around Goetz. Although standing around conveys no objective threat, there was the notion that one with street sense would recognize a potential threat when certain types of kids gather around in certain ways. There is much in this particular flight into "common sense": this arbitrary and subjective reasoning represented the collapse of legal reasoning or legal sense into a sense of fear and the substitution of racial assumptions or fantasies for traditional factual determinations (i.e., Was there a threat? Was there a use of force?). For example, asserting that the youths were standing and "menacing" would require an explanation of how the bullets ended up in the backs of two of the teenagers. Aside from the self-contradictory and transparently speculative ruminations of "experts" paid by the defense, there was literally no evidence whatsoever to explain the position of the bullets. The only uncontroversial evidence that explains why two of the victims were shot in the back was Goetz's own statement: "[M]y intention was to murder them."[30]

Thus, how to get from the physical evidence (from the explicit, detailed confession) to a finding that Goetz was innocent of attempted murder and assault was less a matter of what happened and more a matter of who was involved. Logic and reason were overshadowed by the invocation of historical narratives of race. The story of actual events, as told by the physical evidence and by Goetz himself, was transformed by the Manichean[31] allegory of an inner story of racial symbols that appeared within the surface narrative of evidence and facts.

In this narrative, middle class people are cast as innocent victims who work hard and are preyed upon by shiftless, *dirty* criminals who come out of the alleys and dim recesses of the urban sprawl. Meanwhile, the legal system designed to protect middle class people has become so corrupted with liberalism—sympathizing with blacks and other minorities—that the system no longer works. To New Yorkers and other American urban dwellers, the legal system has become part of the darkness.

Implicit in the story is a familiar representation: the criminals are stereotyped as black and the innocent victims are stereotyped as white. The criminal is not merely black, he is the African Other constructed by the early European travelers: he is uncivilized and part beast. This African Other was explicitly invoked when Slotnick, Goetz's lead defense counsel, called the black victims "savages."[32] The imagery of a moral Great Chain of Being was also mobilized when Slotnick alternatively referred to the victims as "predators" and as a "wolf pack."[33] The moral of the story is that it is natural for whites to subdue savages who threaten social order.

Goetz was cast not merely as someone acting in self-defense, but also as the vanguard of the forces of light who comes to enforce rough justice upon the untamed, dark hordes. Through the economy of Manichean allegory, all individuality vanishes, allowing a transference of the anger (felt by Goetz and white society) to black society, as represented by four anonymous, faceless black youths. In this projection of negative personhood, Cabey, Canty, Ramseur, and Allen cease to be victims or youths or even criminals. They are quite simply black and, as such, proper targets for shooting.

The process at work here is neither the individual desire for domination or aversion, nor a problematic of ethos or morality. That would be far too simple. Rather, it is a process of a collective unconscious perception: a paradigm of cognition. The metaphor of race as embedded in historical narrative becomes a lens that polarizes and colors how we see the social world. This contemporary narrative revises and reinscribes the historical narrative. Its truths are the "truths" of racial myths: truths that do not vary over time or social contexts. The revised historical narrative transforms the experienced facts of a particular case into an invocation of racial essence, racial identity, and racial fear. Racial fear becomes the cognitively distorting medium in which Goetz's confession is silenced, in which physical evidence dissolves, and in which some of our aspiration for community disappears.

THE REBIRTH OF BIGGER THOMAS

> She was dead and he had killed her.
> He was a murderer, a *Negro* murderer, a *black* murderer. . . . [34]

> We are here in the realm of fiction, with which it is said the law has always been connected.[35]

The *Boston Globe* reported the story: "A Reading man and his pregnant wife were shot in Roxbury last night by a gunman who forced his way into their car after the couple left Brigham and Women's Hospital." The suburban couple had come into the inner city to attend childbirth classes. Carol Stuart was shot in the head and her husband, Charles, in the abdomen by a gunman who fled with Carol's purse and about one hundred dollars in jewelry. Although Carol died shortly after the incident, her seven month old fetus was delivered by cesarean section. Officers at the highest levels of the police department participated in the telling of the story. The Deputy Superintendent offered an explanation as to why the shooting occurred: "The gunman who robbed the couple apparently thought the driver was a police officer, perhaps because he saw a cellular phone in the car. . . . " Before he shot the Stuarts, the Deputy Superintendent alleged that the gunman said, "I think you're five-o," a slang term for police.[36]

In the story, the police go on to describe Charles Stuart as ignoring pain, making a desperate call for help for his wife and himself on his cellular phone. Charles reportedly blacked out, but the phone line remained open. The story of heroic intervention continued with the police dispatcher resourcefully ordering cars to take turns turning on their sirens. The couple's location is triangulated by matching sounds heard through the phone with the actual location of police cars. The murderer, who fired a thirty-eight caliber round into Carol Stuart's head, was described as a black man with a raspy voice dressed in a jogging suit.

The story combined elements of melodrama and fevered racial vision: it portrayed white heroes as the personification of innocence and a black villain as the personification of evil.[37] The police and newspapers painted a picture of a suburban white couple mercilessly gunned down when they entered the inner city for the most blameless of purposes. The narrative continued with both Charles and the police painted in bright colors as heroes, overcoming odds to snatch the lives of Charles and his young son from the jaws of death.

The story told first by Charles Stuart, then adopted almost simultaneously by the staid *Boston Globe* and the normally skeptical Boston police, is a story about indiscriminate violence in the city; it is a story about dark men in rumpled jogging clothes who come out of the fog to invade cars, abduct families, shoot helpless pregnant women, and then fade back into the fog. The story brimmed over with archetypal images of urban "savages" threatening the "innocent." The then-Mayor of Boston, Raymond Flynn, injected into the story: "I demand that the Boston Police Department continue to be extremely aggressive in cracking down on people who are using guns and killing *innocent* people. It's intolerable. We will use every lawful tool to support our police officers in cracking down on gun-wielding criminals."[38] Notice how, again, the innocents are white and the savage, real or imagined, is black.

The "crackdown" that actually occurred following the incident featured indiscriminate stops and, in some instances, strip searches of scores of black men whose only crime was being young and black. During the manhunt for the killer, a minister reported watching as "officers lined 15 black teenagers against a wall and made them empty their pockets and drop their pants and undershorts. After about 15 minutes there were 15 bare bottoms displayed on the street." The searches were not limited to gang members or even to particular places; black men were searched in frontyards, in pizza shops, on their way to work. Soon thereafter, two black teenagers overheard a relative of a black man named Bennett jokingly say he believed Mr. Bennett had committed the killing. They were repeatedly picked up and threatened with twenty years in prison unless they signed an affidavit implicating Bennett.[39]

In their zeal to find the black killer, the police failed to learn that a thirty-eight caliber revolver had been stolen from the fur store where Charles Stuart worked, or that Charles had recently taken out large amounts of insurance on his wife. Charles eventually killed himself by jumping into the Mystic River. His brother confessed that he and Charles had murdered Carol. In the end, the black man with the raspy voice who stepped out of the fog to penetrate the lives of suburban whites was imaginary. If Ellison is correct that a living black exists as an invisible man,[40] as a reified abstraction to whites who refuse to see the actual "person," then the phantom of the Stuart case was the invisible man's twin. The raspy-voiced man was a mirage, but one no less illusory than the image the jurors had of Rodney King, the image Goetz had of the Bronx teenagers he attempted to kill, or the image the police had of the black youths they searched and violated.

But I think there is something more precise than unexamined racial assumptions that would explain why only the usual suspects were rounded up, why the most obvious suspect was never questioned, why the most elementary police work was not done, and why the black robber in the jogging suit was *seen* to be so real. There is operating in this story something that is internal to the racial stereotype, something that is all-encompassing in its cognitive effect. It is our set of basic assumptions about self and other that have become intertwined in the problematic of the racial self. The omissions of the Boston police were less a problem of negligent overlooking than of outward looking. Race, the great signifier, draws a circle around the signified. It is a figure of inside/outside distinctions. Inside the circle, individuals are presumed to be good, decent, normal, and white. Outside the circle is the realm of criminals, deviants, and savages. The circle of race traces the dividing line of innocence and guilt along the dividing line between self and other, which is cognitively a difference between the within and the without. For the police to look at Charles would have required them to look within the circle, to look within *themselves* in a sense. More than that, to recognize Charles as "the savage" raises questions about the coherence of the circle altogether.

In each case, there is an opposition in which whites confront real or imagined blacks as "blacks"; that is, as blacks asserting themselves such that whites are physically threatened (Stuart), their manhood is threatened (King), or their sense of well-being is threatened by cultural alterity (Goetz). This confrontation leads to a moment of what I call "racial recognition." It takes the white observer to a mental plane at which logic and reason occur along an essentialist axis.

In adjudication, whites insist upon an interpretation of the facts that does violence to notions of equality and truth as lived experience. The illogical (seemingly impossible) results are entirely logical within the mythic zone of race. The idea of race is not to frame truth from past events, but to convert events into their own mythical structure with cognitive and cosmological distortions as the result. What emerges from cases like *People v. Powell,* the *Goetz* case, and the *Stuart* case is not justice or truth, but a picture of race as a practice and as a source of signification that still mediates between us and the world as it is.

NOTES

1. W.E.B. DuBois, *The Souls of Black Folk* 8 (John E. Wideman ed., 1990) (1903).
2. Abraham Lincoln, *Collected Works* 371 (Roy Basler ed., 1953).
3. By essentialist, I refer to the notion that there is some unchanging, immanent nature in things. See Garth L. Hallett, *Language and Truth* 7 (1988). From an essentialist perspective, race is an immutable essence and "exists" independently of what individuals might think about it.
4. This framework provided the organizing logic for Southern opposition to the Civil Rights Acts of the Reconstruction Era. Thus, in opposing the Civil Rights Act of 1871, Joshua Hill argued:

   I must confess, sir, that I cannot see the magnitude of this subject. I object to this great Government descending to the business of regulating the hotels and common taverns of this country, and the street railroads, stage-coaches, and everything of that sort. It looks to me to be petty business for the government of the United States.

   Cong. Globe, 42d Cong., 2d Sess. 242 (1871).

   And he further explained: "What he may term a right may be the right of any man that pleases to come into my parlor and to be my guest. That is not the right of any colored man upon earth, nor of any white man, unless it is agreeable to me." *Id.*
5. 488 U.S. 469 (1992).
6. 488 U.S. at 507.
7. "The truth is there are no races. . . . Talk of 'race' is particularly distressing for those of us who take

culture seriously. For, where race works . . . it does so only at the price of biologizing what is culture, or ideology." Anthony Appiah, "The Uncompleted Argument," in *Race, Writing, and Difference* 21, 35–36 (Henry Louis Gates, Jr. ed., 1985); see also Peter Figueroa, *Education and the Social Construction of "Race"* 9–10 (1991). ("'Physical and cultural differences do not of themselves create groups or categories.' Race and ethnicity are not natural or fixed categories. 'It is only when physical and cultural differences are given cultural significance . . . that social forms result.'" [quoting M. Banton, *Racial and Ethnic Competition* 105 (1983)]; Ashley Montagu, *Statement on Race* 10 (Oxford University Press, 3d ed. 1972) ("For all practical social purposes 'race' is not so much a biological phenomenon as a social myth.").

8. See Gordon W. Allport, *The Nature of Prejudice* 3–15 (1958).
9. We wear the mask that grins and lies,
   It hides our cheeks and shades our eyes,
   This debt we pay to human guile,
   With torn and bleeding heart we smile;
   And mouth with myriad subtleties.

   Fenton Johnson, "We Wear the Mask," in *American Negro Poetry* 14 (1963).
10. Racial identity mediates between the legal interpreter and the subject. Through this filter, there appears to be an inside and an outside, an us and a them. Whites perceive themselves in the inside, which is to say at the center—as an us. Blacks are outside, decentered—a them. Thus, the problem of blacks may be understood as one of positional inferiority.
11. Racial thinking is not some foreign cultural artifact somehow embedded in an "autonomous" individual subjectivity, but rather represents, at a deep level, one dimension of our subjectivity. The self that constructs and projects racial identity onto others must itself be constituted by, and defined in terms of, race. The individual awareness and the cultural framework are mutually entailed. Charles Lambi explains:

    For myself, earth-bound and fettered to the scene of my activities, I confess that I do feel the differences of mankind, national and individual. . . . I am, in plainer words, a bundle of prejudices—made up of likings and dislikings—the veriest thrall to sympathies, apathies, and antipathies.

    Allport, *supra* at 3 (quoting Charles Lambi).
12. For blacks, the self is fragmented between a subjective self (individual identity) and an objective or racial self. This line tracks the division between a self that is within society and within the language, and a self that is negated by society and language and is alienated from it.
13. For a classic expression of this conception, see Martin Luther King, Jr., *Why We Can't Wait* 28 (1964) (speaking of racial problems as moral and spiritual problems); *cf.* Anthony Appiah, *In My Father's House* (1992) (speaking of racialism or the problem of race as implicit in the claim of racism).
14. James Baldwin, *The Price of the Ticket* 355 (1985).
15. Tracy Wood & Sheryl Stolberg, "Patrol Car Log in Beating Released," *L.A. Times,* Mar. 19, 1991, at A1.
16. Richard A. Serrano, "Officers Are Heard Laughing on Tapes," *L.A. Times,* Mar. 12, 1992, at B1.
17. Michael Miller, "Police Told King He Was Used as a Baseball," *Reuters,* Mar. 13, 1992, available in Lexis, News library.
18. Richard A. Serrano & Tracy Wilkinson, "All Four in King Beating Acquitted," *L.A. Times,* Apr. 30, 1992, at A1.
19. Lois Timnick, "Judge Will Allow Race Evidence in King Case," *L.A. Times,* June 11, 1992, at B1.
20. Richard A. Serrano, "CHP Officer Describes Chase, Beating of King," *L.A. Times,* Mar. 7, 1992, at A1. The struggle between King and the police takes place on a field of pain and violence and a field of symbolic expression. That is, the violence against King is intended as a particular representation of something more specific than white supremacy. It seems to stand for something like white manhood. If King was a threat to the police officers, I suggest he became a threat at the point at which white maleness is constructed, a juncture at which race and sex intersect. Under this view, King's shaking his behind at the police officers was qualitatively the same as shaking his penis at them. As it is traditionally constructed, maleness is concerned with domination and power, and de-

pends on hierarchy for coherence. The notion of white maleness depends for its coherence not only upon domination vis-à-vis women, but also vis-à-vis blacks. King's wagging of his body represented a negation of that hierarchy and, therefore, his beating was no doubt designed to represent a restoration of the "proper order."

21. Richard A. Serrano & Leslie Berger, "Koon Quizzed on Accuracy of Report on King Beating," *L.A. Times,* May 21, 1992 at A1.
22. Ernst Cassirer, *Philosophy of Symbolic Forms* 35 (Rapid Mannheim trans. 1955).
23. Kurtz is a figure who resides at the "inner station" in the "Congo." Alone in this "dark" place Kurtz dies muttering about "the horror." Joseph Conrad, "Heart of Darkness," in *Tales of Land and Sea* 33 (1953). According to the orthodox interpretation, Kurtz represents the deterioration of the mind from solitude and isolation. However, the imagery speaks, even if only unconsciously, of fantasies of Africa not merely as a land of dark people, but as a place of darkness that is the moral antithesis of Europe. This demonizing of Africa and Africans is a projection of the evil of colonialism itself.
24. 2 Pac, "Words of Wisdom," on *2 Apocalypse Now* (Interscope Records 1991).
25. Robert D. McFadden, "A Gunman Wounds Four on IRT Train then Escapes," *N.Y. Times,* Dec. 23, 1984, at A1.
26. See generally *Death Wish* (Paramount Pictures 1974); *Death Wish II* (Paramount Pictures 1982). In the original film Charles Bronson plays an architect who becomes a self-appointed executioner of criminals after his wife is murdered and his daughter raped by New York muggers. Interestingly, the muggers who rape Bronson's daughter are cast as blacks. Bronson, who portrays in his role the growing racially adumbrated rage that would produce a Bernhard Goetz, described his role in these films not as brutal but as heroic—that of a gardener ridding his garden of snakes.
27. McFadden, *supra;* David E. Sanger, "Callers Support Subway Gunman," *N.Y. Times,* Dec. 25, 1984, at A1; Alan Finder & Albert Scardino, "Goetz Checked, Then Fired Another Round," *N.Y. Times,* Mar. 3, 1985, § 4, at E6; "You Have to Think in a Cold-Blooded Way," *N.Y. Times,* Apr. 30, 1987, at B6; Dennis Hevesi, "Goetz Confronts Victims in Court Suit Hearing" *N.Y. Times,* Sept. 27, 1990, at B2.
28. Joyce Purnick, "Ward Declares Goetz Didn't Shoot in Self-Defense," *N.Y. Times,* Feb. 22, 1985, at A1.
29. Goetz explained:

    I looked at his face, and, you know, his eyes were shiny. . . . [T]hey wanted to play with me . . . like a cat plays with a mouse before, you know, it's horrible. . . . [I]t's the confrontation, that was the threat right there. It was seeing his smile and his eyes lit up and the presence of the other four. . . .

    "You Have to Think in a Cold-Blooded Way," *supra* at B6 (quoting Bernhard Goetz).
30. *Id.*
31. Manicheanism is a syncretistic religious dualism that originated in Persia and was widely adhered to in the Roman empire during the third and fourth centuries A.D. It teaches that a cosmic conflict exists between a good realm of light and an evil realm of darkness. See *Webster's Third New International Dictionary* 1375 (Phillip Babcock ed., 1971).
32. Kirk Johnson, "Everybody Is Edgy as Goetz Trial Opens," *N.Y. Times,* May 3, 1987, § 4, at 6.
33. Margot Hornblower, "Jury Exonerates Goetz in Four Subway Shootings; New Yorker Convicted of Weapon Possession," *Wash. Post,* June 17, 1987, at A1.
34. Richard Wright, *Native Son* 75 (1940) (emphasis added).
35. H.L.A. Hart, *The Concept of Law* 11 (1961).
36. Peter S. Canellos & Irene Sege, "Couple Shot After Leaving Hospital; Baby Delivered," *Boston Globe,* Oct. 24, 1989, Metro Sec., at 1.
37. The black man who supposedly murdered the pregnant Carol Stuart and shot her apparently loving husband is characterized as the extreme instance of a depraved black criminal. He bears an uncanny resemblance to Bigger Thomas, a figure created by Richard Wright in the classic *Native Son.* See generally Wright, *supra.* Bigger is a fearful, and in a deep sense innocent, black man who in a moment of fear of being caught in a white woman's bedroom "accidentally" smothers her. He is portrayed and hunted as a sadistic murderer, a negro murderer, a black murderer, becoming the incarnation of racial fears. So is the black man

with the raspy voice equally an incarnation of the same fear, not a real person, but a figure who expresses, and allows for the expression of, shared anxiety.

38. Canellos & Sege, *supra* (emphasis added).
39. Fox Butterfield, "Massachusetts Says Police in Boston Illegally Stopped Black Youths," *N.Y. Times*, Dec. 20, 1990, at B16.
40. Ellison wrote:

I am an invisible man. No, I am not a spook like those who haunted Edgar Allen Poe. . . . I am a man of substance, of flesh and bone, fiber and liquids—and I might even be said to possess a mind. I am invisible, understand, simply because people refuse to see me. Like the bodiless heads you see sometimes in circus sideshows, it is as though I have been surrounded by mirrors of hard distorting glass. When they approach me they see only my surroundings, themselves, or figments of their imagination. . . .

Ralph Ellison, *Invisible Man* 3 (1980) (1952).

PERSONAL ACCOUNT

Play Some Rolling Stones

I left my favorite tavern late on a Friday night. On my way home I stopped to listen to the acoustic reggae of a black street musician. I threw a few dollars into a jar and he asked me what I would like to hear. He spoke with a heavy Jamaican accent and said he could only play reggae. As he began to play my request, several other white males gathered around. As my song ended, a member of the group told the street musician to stop playing that "nigger music" and play some Rolling Stones. The musician replied that he only knew the words to reggae songs. With that, the white male kicked the musician's money jar from his stool, shattering it on the sidewalk. When I objected, the white guy turned on me. Luckily he had spent several hours in the tavern, because his first punch missed its mark. Unfortunately, the other five punches were on target.

At night in the hospital and twenty-two sutures later, I wondered if it was worth it. But when I went back down to the same area the following weekend, the musician thanked me graciously. Then he began to play a classic Rolling Stones song.

Mark Donald Stockenberg

READING 26

Of Race and Risk

Patricia J. Williams

Several years ago, at a moment when I was particularly tired of the unstable lifestyle that academic careers sometimes require, I surprised myself and bought a real house. Because the house was in a state other than the one where I was living at the time, I obtained my mortgage by telephone. I am a prudent little squirrel when it comes to things financial, always tucking away stores of nuts for the winter, and so I meet the criteria of a quite good credit risk. My loan was approved almost immediately.

A little while later, the contract came in the mail. Among the papers the bank forwarded were forms documenting compliance with the Fair Housing Act, which outlaws racial discrimination in the housing market. The act monitors lending practices to prevent banks from redlining—redlining being the phenomenon whereby banks circle certain neighborhoods on the map and refuse to lend in those areas. It is a practice for which the bank with which I was dealing, unbeknownst to me, had been cited previously—as well as since. In any event, the act tracks the race of all banking customers to prevent such discrimination. Unfortunately, and with the creative variability of all illegality, some banks also use the racial information disclosed on the fair housing forms to engage in precisely the discrimination the law seeks to prevent.

I should repeat that to this point my entire mortgage transaction had been conducted by telephone. I should also note that I speak a Received Standard English, regionally marked as Northeastern perhaps, but not easily identifiable as black. With my credit history, my job as a law professor and, no doubt, with my accent, I am not only middle class but apparently match the

Patricia J. Williams is a professor of law at the Columbia University Law School in New York.

cultural stereotype of a good white person. It is thus, perhaps, that the loan officer of the bank, whom I had never met, had checked off the box on the fair housing form indicating that I *was* white.

Race shouldn't matter, I suppose, but it seemed to in this case, so I took a deep breath, crossed out "white" and sent the contract back. That will teach them to presume too much, I thought. A done deal, I assumed. But suddenly the transaction came to a screeching halt. The bank wanted more money, more points, a higher rate of interest. Suddenly I found myself facing great resistance and much more debt. To make a long story short, I threatened to sue under the act in question, the bank quickly backed down and I procured the loan on the original terms.

What was interesting about all this was that the reason the bank gave for its new-found recalcitrance was not race, heaven forbid. No, it was all about economics and increased risk: The reason they gave was that property values in that neighborhood were suddenly falling. They wanted more money to buffer themselves against the snappy winds of projected misfortune.

Initially, I was surprised, confused. The house was in a neighborhood that was extremely stable. I am an extremely careful shopper; I had uncovered absolutely nothing to indicate that prices were falling. It took my realtor to make me see the light. "Don't you get it," he sighed. "This is what always happens." And even though I suppose it was a little thick of me, I really hadn't gotten it: For of course, I was the reason the prices were in peril.

The bank's response was driven by demographic data that show that any time black people move into a neighborhood, whites are overwhelmingly likely to move out. In droves. In panic. In concert. Pulling every imaginable resource with them, from school funding to garbage collection to social workers who don't want to work in black neighborhoods. The imagery is awfully catchy, you had to admit: the neighborhood just tipping on over like a terrible accident, whoops! Like a pitcher, I suppose. All that nice fresh wholesome milk spilling out, running away . . . leaving the dark, echoing, upended urn of the inner city.

In retrospect, what has remained so fascinating to me about this experience was the way it so exemplified the problems of the new rhetoric of racism. For starters, the new rhetoric of race never mentions race. It wasn't race but risk with which the bank was so concerned.

Second, since financial risk is all about economics, my exclusion got reclassified as just a consideration of class. There's no law against class discrimination, goes the argument, because that would represent a restraint on that basic American freedom, the ability to contract or not. If schools, trains, buses, swimming pools and neighborhoods remain segregated, it's no longer a racial problem if someone who just happens to be white keeps hiking up the price for someone who accidentally and purely by the way happens to be black. Black people end up paying higher prices for the attempt to integrate, even as the integration of oneself threatens to lower the value of one's investment.

By this measure of mortgage-worthiness, the ingredient of blackness is cast not just as a social toll but as an actual tax. A fee, an extra contribution at the door, an admission charge for the high costs of handling my dangerous propensities, my inherently unsavory properties. I was not judged based on my independent attributes or financial worth; not even was I judged by statistical profiles of what my group actually does. (For in fact, anxiety-stricken, middle-class black people make grovelingly good cake-baking neighbors when not made to feel defensive by the unfortunate historical strategies of bombs, burnings or abandonment.) Rather, I was being evaluated based on what an abstraction of White Society writ large thinks we—or I—do, and that imagined "doing" was treated and thus established as a self-fulfilling prophecy. It is a dispiriting message: that some in society apparently not only devalue black people but devalue *themselves* and their homes just for having us as part of their landscape.

"I bet you'll keep your mouth shut the next time they plug you into the computer as white," laughed a friend when he heard my story. It took me aback, this postmodern pressure to "pass," even as it highlighted the intolerable logic of it all. For by these "rational" economic measures, an investment in my property suggests the selling of myself.

READING 27

Wears Jump Suit. Sensible Shoes. Uses Husband's Last Name.

Deborah Tannen

Some years ago I was at a small working conference of four women and eight men. Instead of concentrating on the discussion I found myself looking at the three other women at the table, thinking how each had a different style and how each style was coherent.

One woman had dark brown hair in a classic style, a cross between Cleopatra and Plain Jane. The severity of her straight hair was softened by wavy bangs and ends that turned under. Because she was beautiful, the effect was more Cleopatra than plain.

The second woman was older, full of dignity and composure. Her hair was cut in a fashionable style that left her with only one eye, thanks to a side part that let a curtain of hair fall across half her face. As she looked down to read her prepared paper, the hair robbed her of bifocal vision and created a barrier between her and the listeners.

Deborah Tannen is a professor of linguistics at Georgetown University in Washington, D.C.

The third woman's hair was wild, a frosted blond avalanche falling over and beyond her shoulders. When she spoke she frequently tossed her head, calling attention to her hair and away from her lecture.

Then there was makeup. The first woman wore facial cover that made her skin smooth and pale, a black line under each eye and mascara that darkened already dark lashes. The second wore only a light gloss on her lips and a hint of shadow on her eyes. The third had blue bands under her eyes, dark blue shadow, mascara, bright red lipstick and rouge; her fingernails flashed red.

I considered the clothes each woman had worn during the three days of the conference: In the first case, man-tailored suits in primary colors with solid-color blouses. In the second, casual but stylish black T-shirts, a floppy collarless jacket and baggy slacks or a skirt in neutral colors. The third wore a sexy jump suit; tight sleeveless jersey and tight yellow slacks; a dress with gaping armholes and an indulged tendency to fall off one shoulder.

Shoes? No. 1 wore string sandals with medium heels; No. 2, sensible, comfortable walking shoes; No. 3, pumps with spike heels. You can fill in the jewelry, scarves, shawls, sweaters—or lack of them.

As I amused myself finding coherence in these styles, I suddenly wondered why I was scrutinizing only the women. I scanned the eight men at the table. And then I knew why I wasn't studying them. The men's styles were unmarked.

The term "marked" is a staple of linguistic theory. It refers to the way language alters the base meaning of a word by adding a linguistic particle that has no meaning on its own. The unmarked form of a word carries the meaning that goes without saying—what you think of when you're not thinking anything special.

The unmarked tense of verbs in English is the present—for example, *visit.* To indicate past, you mark the verb by adding *ed* to yield *visited.* For future, you add a word: *will visit.* Nouns are presumed to be singular until marked for plural, typically by adding *s* or *es,* so *visit* becomes *visits* and *dish* becomes *dishes.*

The unmarked forms of most English words also convey "male." Being male is the unmarked case. Endings like *ess* and *ette* mark words as "female." Unfortunately, they also tend to mark them for frivolousness. Would you feel safe entrusting your life to a doctorette? Alfre Woodard, who was an Oscar nominee for best supporting actress, says she identifies herself as an actor because "actresses worry about eyelashes and cellulite, and women who are actors worry about the characters we are playing." Gender markers pick up extra meanings that reflect common associations with the female gender: not quite serious, often sexual.

Each of the women at the conference had to make decisions about hair, clothing, makeup and accessories, and each decision carried meaning. Every style available to us was marked. The men in our group had made decisions, too, but the range from which they chose was incomparably narrower. Men can choose styles that are marked, but they don't have to, and in this group none did. Unlike the women, they had the option of being unmarked.

Take the men's hair styles. There was no marine crew cut or oily longish hair falling into eyes, no asymmetrical, two-tiered construction to swirl over a bald top. One man was unabashedly bald; the others had hair of standard length, parted on one side, in natural shades of brown or gray or graying. Their hair obstructed no views, left little to toss or push back or run fingers through and, consequently, needed and attracted no attention. A few men had beards. In a business setting, beards might be marked. In this academic gathering, they weren't.

There could have been a cowboy shirt with string tie or a three-piece suit or a necklaced hippie in jeans. But there wasn't. All eight men wore brown or blue slacks and nondescript shirts of light colors. No man wore sandals or boots; their shoes were dark, closed, comfortable and flat. In short, unmarked.

Although no man wore makeup, you couldn't say the men didn't wear makeup in the sense that you could say a woman didn't wear makeup. For men, no makeup is unmarked.

I asked myself what style we women could have adopted that would have been unmarked, like the men's. The answer was none. There is no unmarked woman.

There is no woman's hair style that can be called standard, that says nothing about her. The range of women's hair styles is staggering, but a woman whose hair has no particular style is perceived as not caring about how she looks, which can disqualify her for many positions, and will subtly diminish her as a person in the eyes of some.

Women must choose between attractive shoes and comfortable shoes. When our group made an unexpected trek, the woman who wore flat, laced shoes arrived first. Last to arrive was the woman in spike heels, shoes in hand and a handful of men around her.

If a woman's clothing is tight or revealing (in other words, sexy), it sends a message—an intended one of wanting to be attractive, but also a possibly unintended one of availability. If her clothes are not sexy, that too sends a message, lent meaning by the knowledge that they could have been. There are thousands of cosmetic products from which women can choose and myriad ways of applying them. Yet no makeup at all is anything but unmarked. Some men see it as a hostile refusal to please them.

Women can't even fill out a form without telling stories about themselves. Most forms give four titles to choose from. "Mr." carries no meaning other than that the respondent is male. But a woman who checks "Mrs." or "Miss" communicates not only whether she has been married but also whether she has conservative tastes in forms of address—and probably other conservative values as well. Checking "Ms." declines to let on about marriage (checking "Mr." declines nothing since nothing was asked), but it also marks her as either liberated or rebellious, depending on the observer's attitudes and assumptions.

I sometimes try to duck these variously marked choices by giving my title as "Dr."—and in so doing risk marking myself as either uppity (hence sarcastic responses like "Excuse *me!*") or an overachiever (hence reactions of congratulatory surprise like "Good for you!").

All married women's surnames are marked. If a woman takes her husband's name, she announces to the world that she is married and has traditional values. To some it will indicate that she is less herself, more identified by her husband's identity. If she does not take her husband's name, this too is marked, seen as worthy of comment: she has *done* something; she has "kept her own name." A man is never said to have "kept his own name" because it never occurs to anyone that he might have given it up. For him using his own name is unmarked.

A married woman who wants to have her cake and eat it too may use her surname plus his, with or without a hyphen. But this too announces her marital status and often results in a tongue-tying string. In a list (Harvey O'Donovan, Jonathan Feldman, Stephanie Woodbury McGillicutty), the woman's multiple name stands out. It is marked.

I have never been inclined toward biological explanations of gender differences in language, but I was intrigued to see Ralph Fasold bring biological phenomena to bear on the question of linguistic marking in his book "The Sociolinguistics of Language." Fasold stresses that language and culture are particularly unfair in treating women as the marked case because biologically it is the male that is marked. While two X chromosomes make a female, two Y chromosomes make nothing. Like the linguistic markers *s, es* or *ess,* the Y chromosome doesn't "mean" anything unless it is attached to a root form—an X chromosome.

Developing this idea elsewhere, Fasold points out that girls are born with fully female bodies, while boys are born with modified female bodies. He invites men who doubt this to lift up their shirts and contemplate why they have nipples.

In his book, Fasold notes "a wide range of facts which demonstrates that female is the unmarked sex." For example, he observes that there are a few species that produce only females, like the whiptail lizard. Thanks to parthenogenesis, they have no trouble having as many daughters as they like. There are no species, however, that produce only males. This is no surprise, since any such species would become extinct in its first generation.

Fasold is also intrigued by species that produce individuals not involved in reproduction, like honeybees and leaf-cutter ants. Reproduction is handled by the queen and a relatively few males; the workers are sterile females. "Since they do not reproduce," Fasold says, "there is no reason for them to be one sex or the other, so they default, so to speak, to female."

Fasold ends his discussion of these matters by pointing out that if language reflected biology, grammar books would direct us to use "she" to include males and females and "he" only for specifically male referents. But they don't. They tell us that "he" means "he or she," and that "she" is used only if the referent is specifically female. This use of "he" as the sex-indefinite pronoun is an innovation introduced into English by grammarians in the 18th and 19th centuries, according to Peter Mühlhäusler and Rom Harré in "Pronouns and People." From at least about 1500, the correct sex-indefinite pronoun was "they," as it still is in casual spoken English. In other words, the female was declared by grammarians to be the marked case.

Writing this article may mark me not as a writer, not as a linguist, not as an analyst of human behavior, but as a feminist—which will have positive or negative, but in any case powerful, connotations for readers. Yet I doubt that anyone reading Ralph Fasold's book would put that label on him.

I discovered the markedness inherent in the very topic of gender after writing a book on differences in conversational style based on geographical region, ethnicity, class, age and gender. When I was interviewed, the vast majority of journalists wanted to talk about the differences between women and men. While I thought I was simply describing what I observed—something I had learned to do as a researcher—merely mentioning women and men marked me as a feminist for some.

When I wrote a book devoted to gender differences in ways of speaking, I sent the manuscript to five male colleagues, asking them to alert me to any interpretation, phrasing or wording that might seem unfairly negative toward men. Even so, when the book came out, I encountered responses like that of the television talk show host who, after interviewing me, turned to the audience and asked if they thought I was male-bashing.

Leaping upon a poor fellow who affably nodded in agreement, she made him stand and asked, "Did what she said accurately describe you?" "Oh, yes," he answered. "That's me exactly." "And what she said about women—does that sound like your wife?" "Oh yes," he responded. "That's her exactly." "Then why do you think she's male-bashing?" He answered, with disarming honesty, "Because she's a woman and she's saying things about men."

To say anything about women and men without marking oneself as either feminist or anti-feminist, male-basher or apologist for men seems as impossible for a woman as trying to get dressed in the morning without inviting interpretations of her character.

Sitting at the conference table musing on these matters, I felt sad to think that we women didn't have the freedom to be unmarked that the men sitting next to us had. Some days you just want to get dressed and go about your business. But if you're a woman, you can't, because there is no unmarked woman.

READING 28

Gender Bending

Judith Lorber

It is difficult to see how gender is constructed because we take it for granted that it's all biology, or hormones, or human nature. The differences between women and men seem to be self-evident, and we think they would occur no matter what society did. But in actuality, human females and males are physiologically more similar in appearance than are the two sexes of many species of animals and are more alike than different in traits and behavior (C. F. Epstein 1988). Without the deliberate use of gendered clothing, hairstyles, jewelry, and cosmetics, women and men would look far more alike.[1] Even societies that do not cover women's breasts have gender-identifying clothing, scarification, jewelry, and hairstyles.

The ease with which many transvestite women pass as men and transvestite men as women is corroborated by the common gender misidentification in Westernized societies of people in jeans, T-shirts, and sneakers. Men with long hair may be addressed as "miss," and women with short hair are often taken for men unless they offset the potential ambiguity with deliberate gender markers (Devor 1987, 1989). Jan Morris, in *Conundrum,* an autobiographical account of events just before and just after a

Judith Lorber is emeritus professor of sociology at the City University of New York Graduate Center.

sex-change operation, described how easy it was to shift back and forth from being a man to being a woman when testing how it would feel to change gender status. During this time, Morris still had a penis and wore more or less unisex clothing; the context alone made the man and the woman:

> Sometimes the arena of my ambivalence was uncomfortably small. At the Travellers' Club, for example, I was obviously known as a man of sorts—women were only allowed on the premises at all during a few hours of the day, and even then were hidden away as far as possible in lesser rooms or alcoves. But I had another club, only a few hundred yards away, where I was known only as a woman, and often I went directly from one to the other, imperceptibly changing roles on the way—"Cheerio, sir," the porter would say at one club, and "Hello, madam," the porter would greet me at the other. (1975, 132)

Gender shifts are actually a common phenomenon in public roles as well. Queen Elizabeth II of England bore children, but when she went to Saudi Arabia on a state visit, she was considered an honorary man so that she could confer and dine with the men who were heads of a state that forbids unrelated men and women to have face-to-unveiled-face contact. In contemporary Egypt, lower-class women who run restaurants or shops dress in men's clothing and engage in unfeminine aggressive behavior, and middle-class educated women of professional or managerial status can take positions of authority (Rugh 1986, 131). In these situations, there is an important status change: These women are treated by the others in the situation as if they are men. From their own point of view, they are still women. From the social perspective, however, they are men.[2]

In many cultures, gender bending is prevalent in theater or dance—the Japanese kabuki are men actors who play both women and men; in Shakespeare's theater company, there were no actresses—Juliet and Lady Macbeth were played by boys. Shakespeare's comedies are full of witty comments on gender shifts. Women characters frequently masquerade as young men, and other women characters fall in love with them; the boys playing these masquerading women, meanwhile, are acting out pining for the love of men characters.[3] In *As You Like It,* when Rosalind justifies her protective cross-dressing, Shakespeare also comments on manliness:

> Were it not better,
> Because that I am more than common tall,
> That I did suit me all points like a man:
> A gallant curtle-axe upon my thigh,
> A boar-spear in my hand, and in my heart
> Lie there what hidden women's fear there will,
> We'll have a swashing and martial outside,
> As many other mannish cowards have
> That do outface it with their semblances.
> (I, i, 115–22)

Shakespeare's audience could appreciate the double subtext: Rosalind, a woman character, was a boy dressed in girl's clothing who then dressed as a boy; like bravery, masculinity and femininity can be put on and taken off with changes of costume and role (Howard 1988, 435).[4]

M Butterfly is a modern play of gender ambiguities, which David Hwang (1989) based on a real person. Shi Peipu, a male Chinese opera singer who sang women's roles, was a spy as a man and the lover as a woman of a Frenchman, Gallimard, a diplomat (Bernstein 1986). The relationship lasted twenty years, and Shi Peipu even pretended to be the mother of a child by Gallimard. "She" also pretended to be too shy to undress completely. As "Butterfly," Shi Peipu portrayed a fantasy Oriental woman who made the lover a "real man" (Kondo 1990). In Gallimard's words, the fantasy was "of slender women in chong sams and kimonos who die for the love of unworthy foreign devils. Who are born and raised to be perfect women. Who take whatever punishment we give them, and bounce back, strengthened by love, unconditionally" (D. H. Hwang 1989, 91). When the fantasy woman betrayed him by turning out to be the more powerful "real man," Gallimard assumed the role of Butterfly and, dressed in a geisha's robes, killed himself: "because 'man' and 'woman' are oppositionally defined terms, reversals . . . are possible" (Kondo 1990, 18).[5]

But despite the ease with which gender boundaries can be traversed in work, in social relationships, and in cultural productions, gender statuses remain. Transvestites and transsexuals do not challenge the social construction of gender. Their goal is to be feminine women and masculine men (Kando 1973). Those who do not want to change their anatomy but do want to change their gender behavior fare less well in establishing their social identity. The women Holly Devor called "gender blenders" wore their hair short, dressed in unisex pants, shirts, and comfortable shoes, and did not wear jewelry or makeup. They described their everyday dress as women's clothing: One said, "I wore jeans all the time, but I didn't wear men's clothes" (Devor 1989, 100). Their gender identity was women, but because they refused to "do femininity," they were constantly taken for men (1987, 1989, 107–42). Devor said of them: "The most common area of complaint was with public washrooms. They repeatedly spoke of the humiliation of being challenged or ejected from women's washrooms. Similarly, they found public change rooms to be dangerous territory and the buying of undergarments to be a difficult feat to accomplish" (1987, 29). In an ultimate ironic twist, some of these women said "they would feel like transvestites if they were to wear dresses, and two women said that they had been called transvestites when they had done so" (1987, 31). They resolved the ambiguity of their gender status by identifying as women in private and passing as men in public to avoid harassment on the street, to get men's jobs, and, if they were lesbians, to make it easier to display affection publicly with their lovers (Devor 1989, 107–42). Sometimes they even used men's bathrooms. When they had gender-neutral names, like Leslie, they could avoid the bureaucratic hassles that arose when they had to present their passports or other proof of identity, but because most had names associated with women, their appearance and their cards of identity were not conventionally congruent, and their gender status was in constant jeopardy.[6] When they could, they found it easier to pass as men than to try to change the stereotyped notions of what women should look like.

Paradoxically, then, bending gender rules and passing between genders does not erode but rather preserves gender boundaries. . . .

NOTES

1. When unisex clothing and men wearing long hair came into vogue in the United States in the mid-1960s, beards and mustaches for men also came into style again as gender identifications.
2. For other accounts of women being treated as men in Islamic countries, as well as accounts of women and men cross-dressing in these countries, see Garber 1992, 304–52.
3. Dollimore 1986; Garber 1992, 32–40; Greenblatt 1987, 66–93; Howard 1988. For Renaissance accounts of sexual relations with women and men of ambiguous sex, see Laqueur 1990, 134–39. For modern accounts of women passing as men that other women find sexually attractive, see Devor 1989, 136–37; Wheelwright 1989, 53–59.
4. Females who passed as men soldiers had to "do masculinity," not just dress in a uniform (Wheelwright 1989, 50–78). On the triple entendres and gender resonances of Rosalind-type characters, see Garber 1992, 71–77.
5. Also see Garber 1992, 234–66.
6. Bolin describes how many documents have to be changed by transsexuals to provide a legitimizing "paper trail" (1988, 145–47). Note that only members of the same social group know which names are women's and which men's in their culture, but many documents list "sex."

REFERENCES

Bernstein, Richard. 1986. France jails 2 in odd case of espionage. *New York Times,* 11 May.

Bolin, Anne. 1988. *In search of Eve: Transsexual rites of passage.* South Hadley, Mass.: Bergin & Garvey.

Devor, Holly. 1987. Gender blending females: Women and sometimes men. *American Behavioral Scientist* 31:12–40.

———. 1989. *Gender blending: Confronting the limits of duality.* Bloomington: Indiana University Press.

Eichler, Margrit. 1989. Sex change operations: The last bulwark of the double standard.

———. 1989. Richardson, Laurel and Verta Taylor (eds.) *Feminist Frontiers II.* New York: Random House.

Epstein, Cynthia Fuchs. 1988. *Deceptive distinctions: Sex, gender and the social order.* New Haven: Yale University Press.

Garber, Marjorie. 1992. Vested interests: Cross-dressing and cultural anxiety. New York and London: Routledge.

Greenblatt, Stephen. 1987. *Shakespearean negotiations: The circulation of social energy in Renaissance England.* Berkeley: University of California Press.

Howard, Jean E. 1988. Crossdressing, the theater, and gender struggle in early modern England. *Shakespeare Quarterly* 39:418–41.

Hwang, David Henry. 1989. *M Butterfly.* New York: New American Library.

Kando, Thomas. 1973. *Sex change: The achievement of gender identity among feminized transsexuals.* Springfield, Ill.: Charles C Thomas.

Kondo, Dorinne K. 1990. *M. Butterfly:* Orientalism, gender, and a critique of essentialist identity. *Cultural Critique,* no. 16 (Fall): 5–29.

Laqueur, Thomas. 1990. *Making sex: Body and gender from the Greeks to Freud.* Cambridge, Mass.: Harvard University Press.

Morris, Jan. 1975. *Conundrum.* New York: Signet.

Rugh, Andrea B. 1986. *Reveal and conceal: Dress in contemporary Egypt.* Syracuse, N.Y.: Syracuse University Press.

Wheelwright, Julie. 1989. *Amazons and military maids: Women who cross-dressed in pursuit of life, liberty and happiness.* London: Pandora Press.

PERSONAL ACCOUNT

A White Male Rescued Me

There was one incident where a white male came to my rescue when I was being discriminated against for being a woman, a black woman, and a black-gay woman.

I was on the metro with my friends on the way to a club when two black men started making derogatory, disgusting statements about us. All of a sudden I heard this voice saying, "You need to leave those girls alone. They're college people and they're trying to experience life. This is the '90s. People have the right to express how they are no matter what you think about it." I turned around and it was a *white man.* I was shocked. Another gay person might have stood up for us, but I would never have expected a white, middle-aged man to do that. They all started to get in a fight, but when the train came to a stop the security guard got on and escorted the two harassers off. I thought it was very nice of the man to come to our rescue. I would like for people to stand up for those who are either in a minority status in society or just for those people who are in need of help. But I would also like to thank the man, regardless of his race, for coming to my rescue. Gay people are human beings too, and we also have rights. But a special thanks goes out to this gentleman for seeing me and my friends as people with feelings first, and gay women second. Thank you.

Meticia Watson

READING 29

A Question of Class

Dorothy Allison

. . . My people were not remarkable. We were ordinary, but even so we were mythical. We were the *they* everyone talks about, the ungrateful poor. I grew up trying to run away from the fate

Dorothy Allison is an award-winning writer and author of *Bastard out of Carolina.*

that destroyed so many of the people I loved, and having learned the habit of hiding, I found that I also had learned to hide from myself. I did not know who I was, only that I did not want to be *they,* the ones who are destroyed or dismissed to make the real people, the important people, feel safer. By the time I understood that I was queer, that habit of hiding was deeply set in me, so deeply that it was not a choice but an instinct. Hide, hide to survive, I thought, knowing that if I told the truth about my life, my family, my sexual desire, my real history, then I would move over into that unknown territory, the land of *they,* would never have the chance to name my own life, to understand it or claim it.

Why are you so afraid? my lovers and friends have asked me the many times when I have suddenly seemed to become a stranger, someone who would not speak to them, would not do the things they believed I should do, simple things like applying for a job, or a grant, or some award they were sure I could acquire easily. Entitlement, I have told them, is a matter of feeling like *we, not they.* But it has been hard for me to explain, to make them understand. You think you have a right to things, a place in the world, I try to say. You have a sense of entitlement I don't have, a sense of your own importance. I have explained what I know over and over again, in every possible way I can, but I have never been able to make clear the degree of my fear, the extent to which I feel myself denied, not only that I am queer in a world that hates queers but that I was born poor into a world that despises the poor. The need to explain is part of why I write fiction. I know that some things must be felt to be understood, that despair can never be adequately analyzed; it must be lived. . . .

I have known I was a lesbian since I was a teenager, and I have spent a good twenty years making peace with the effects of incest and physical abuse. But what may be the central fact of my life is that I was born in 1949 in Greenville, South Carolina, the bastard daughter of a poor white woman from a desperately poor family, a girl who had left the seventh grade the year before, who worked as a waitress and was just a month past fifteen when she had me. That fact, the inescapable impact of being born in a condition of poverty that this society finds shameful, contemptible, and somehow deserved, has dominated me to such an extent that I have spent my life trying to overcome or deny it. I have learned with great difficulty that the vast majority of people pretend that poverty is a voluntary condition, that the poor are different, less than fully human, or at least less sensitive to hopelessness, despair, and suffering.

The first time I read Melanie Kaye Kantrowitz's poems, I experienced a frisson of recognition. It was not that my people had been "burned off the map" or murdered as hers had. No, we had been erased, encouraged to destroy ourselves, made invisible because we did not fit the myths of the middle class. Even now, past forty and stubbornly proud of my family, I feel the draw of that mythology, that romanticized, edited version of the poor. I find myself looking back and wondering what was real, what true. Within my family, so much was lied about, joked about, denied or told with deliberate indirection, an undercurrent of humiliation, or a brief pursed grimace that belies everything that has been said—everything, the very nature of truth and lies, reality and myth. What was real? The poverty depicted in books and movies was romantic, a kind of backdrop for the story of how it was escaped. The reality of self-hatred and violence was either absent or caricatured. The poverty I knew was dreary, deadening, shameful. My family was ashamed of being poor, of feeling hopeless. What was there to work for, to save money for, to fight for or struggle against? We had generations before us to teach us that nothing ever changed, and that those who did try to escape failed.

My mama had eleven brothers and sisters, of whom I can name only six. No one is left alive to tell me the names of the others. It was my grandmother who told me about my real daddy, a shiftless pretty man who was supposed to have married, had six children, and sold cut-rate life insurance to colored people out in the country. My mama married when I was a year old, but her husband died just after my little sister was born a year later. When I was five, Mama married the man she lived with until she died. Within the first year of their marriage Mama miscarried, and while we waited out in the hospital parking lot, my stepfather molested me for the first time, something he continued to do until I was past thirteen. When I was eight or so, Mama took us away to a motel after my stepfather beat me so badly it caused a family scandal, but we returned after two weeks. Mama told me that she really had no choice; she could not support us alone. When I was eleven I told one of my cousins that my stepfather was molesting me. Mama packed up my sisters and me and took us away for a few days, but again, my stepfather swore he would stop, and again we went back after a few weeks. I stopped talking for a while, and I have only vague memories of the next two years.

My stepfather worked as a route salesman, my mama as a waitress, laundry worker, cook, or fruit packer. I could never understand how, since they both worked so hard and such long hours, we never had enough money, but it was a fact that was true also of my mama's brothers and sisters, who worked in the mills or the furnace industry. In fact, my parents did better than anyone else in the family, but eventually my stepfather was fired and we hit bottom—nightmarish months of marshals at the door, repossessed furniture, and rubber checks. My parents worked out a scheme so that it appeared my stepfather had abandoned us, but instead he went down to Florida, got a new job, and rented us a house. In the dead of night, he returned with a U-Haul trailer, packed us up, and moved us south.

The night we left South Carolina for Florida, my mama leaned over the back seat of her old Pontiac and promised us girls, "It'll be better there." I don't know if we believed her, but I remember crossing Georgia in the early morning, watching the red clay hills and swaying gray blankets of moss recede through the back window. I kept looking back at the trailer behind us, ridiculously small to contain everything we owned. Mama had, after all, packed nothing that wasn't fully paid off, which meant she had only two things of worth, her washing and sewing machines, both of them tied securely to the trailer walls. Through the whole trip, I fantasized an accident that would burst that trailer, scattering old clothes and cracked dishes on the tarmac.

I was only thirteen. I wanted us to start over completely, to begin again as new people with nothing of the past left over. I wanted to run away completely from who we had been seen to be, who we had been. That desire is one I have seen in other members of my family, to run away. It is the first thing I think of when trouble comes, the geographic solution. Change your name, leave town, disappear, and make yourself over. What hides behind that solution is the conviction that the life you have lived, the person you are, are valueless, better off abandoned, that running away is easier than trying to change anything, that change itself is not possible, that death is easier than this life. Sometimes I think it is that conviction—more seductive than alcoholism or violence and more subtle than sexual hatred or gender injustice—that has dominated my life, and made real change so painful and difficult.

Moving to central Florida did not fix our lives. It did not stop my stepfather's violence, heal my shame, or make my mother happy. Once there our lives became dominated by my mother's illness and medical bills. She had a hysterectomy when I was about eight and endured a series of hospitalizations for ulcers and a chronic back problem. Through most of my adolescence she superstitiously refused to allow anyone to mention the word cancer. (Years later when she called me to tell me that she was recovering from an emergency mastectomy, there was bitter fatalism in her voice. The second mastectomy followed five years after the first, and five years after that there was a brief bout with cancer of the lymph system which went into remission after prolonged chemotherapy. She died at the age of fifty-six with liver, lung, and brain cancer.) When she was not sick, Mama, and my stepfather, went on working, struggling to pay off what seemed an insurmountable load of debts.

By the time I was fourteen, my sisters and I had found ways to discourage most of our stepfather's sexual advances. We were not close but we united against our stepfather. Our efforts were helped along when he was referred to a psychotherapist after losing his temper at work, and was prescribed psychotropic drugs that made him sullen but less violent. We were growing up quickly, my sisters moving toward dropping out of school, while I got good grades and took every scholarship exam I could find. I was the first person in my family to graduate from high school, and the fact that I went on to college was nothing short of astonishing.

Everyone imagines her life is normal, and I did not know my life was not everyone's. It was not until I was an adolescent in central Florida that I began to realize just how different we were. The people we met there had not been shaped by the rigid class structure that dominated the South Carolina Piedmont. The first time I looked around my junior high classroom and realized that I did not know who those people were—not only as individuals but as categories, who their people were and how they saw themselves—I realized also that they did not know me. In Greenville, everyone knew my family, knew we were trash, and that meant we were supposed to be poor, supposed to have grim low-paid jobs, have babies in our teens, and never finish school. But central Florida in the 1960s was full of runaways and immigrants, and our mostly white working-class suburban school sorted us out, not by income and family background, but by intelligence and aptitude tests. Suddenly I was boosted into the college-bound track, and while there was plenty of contempt for my inept social skills, pitiful wardrobe, and slow drawling accent, there was also something I had never experienced before, a protective anonymity, and a kind of grudging respect and curiosity about who I might become. Because they did not see poverty and hopelessness as a foregone conclusion for my life, I could begin to imagine other futures for myself.

Moving into that new world and meeting those new people meant that I began to see my family from a new vantage point. I also experienced a new level of fear, a fear of losing what before had never been imaginable. My family's lives were not on television, not in books, not even comic books. There was a myth of the poor in this country, but it did not include us, no matter how hard I tried to squeeze us in. There was an idea of the good poor—hardworking, ragged but clean, and intrinsically noble. I understood that we were the bad poor, the ungrateful: men who drank and couldn't keep a job; women, invariably pregnant before marriage, who quickly became worn, fat, and old from working too many hours and bearing too many children; and children with runny noses, watery eyes, and bad attitudes. My cousins quit school, stole cars, used drugs, and took dead-end jobs pumping gas or waiting tables. We were not noble, not grateful, not even hopeful. We knew ourselves despised.

But in that new country, we were unknown. The myth settled over us and glamorized us. I saw it in the eyes of my teachers, the Lions' Club representative who paid for my new glasses, and the lady from the Junior League who told me about the scholarship I had won. Better, far better, to be one of the mythical poor than to be part of the *they* I had known before. *Don't let me lose this chance,* I prayed, and lived in fear that I might suddenly be seen again as what I knew I really was.

As an adolescent, I thought that the way my family escaped South Carolina was like a bad movie. We fled like runaway serfs and the sheriff who would have arrested my stepfather seemed like a border guard. Even now, I am certain that if we had remained in South Carolina, I would have been trapped by my family's heritage of poverty, jail, and illegitimate children—that even being smart, stubborn, and a lesbian would have made no difference. My grandmother died when I was twenty and after Mama went home for the funeral, I had a series of dreams in which we still lived up in Greenville, just down the road from where Granny had died. In the dreams I had two children and only one eye, lived in a trailer, and worked at the textile mill. Most of my time was taken up with deciding when I would finally kill my children and myself. The dreams were so vivid, I became convinced they were about the life I was meant to have had, and I began to work even harder to put as much distance as I could between my family and me. I copied the dress, mannerisms, attitudes, and ambitions of the girls I met in college, changing or hiding my own tastes, interests, and desires. I kept my lesbianism a secret, forming a relationship with an effeminate male friend that served to shelter and disguise us both. I explained to friends that I went home so rarely because my stepfather and I fought too much for me to be comfortable in his house. But that was only part of the reason I avoided home, the easiest reason. The truth was that I feared the person I might become in my mama's house.

It is hard to explain how deliberately and thoroughly I ran away from my own life. I did not forget where I came from, but I gritted my teeth and hid it. When I could not get enough scholarship money to pay for graduate school, I spent a year of blind rage working as a salad girl, substitute teacher, and maid. I finally managed to get a job by agreeing to take any city assignment where the Social Security Administration needed a clerk. Once I had a job and my own place far away from anyone in my family, I became sexually and politically active, joining the Women's Center support staff and falling in love with a series of middle-class women who thought my accent and stories thoroughly charming. The stories I told about my family, about South Carolina, about being poor itself, were all lies, carefully edited to seem droll or funny. I knew damn well that no one would want to hear the truth about poverty, the hopelessness and fear, the feeling that nothing you do will make any difference, and the raging resentment that burns beneath the jokes. Even when my lovers and I formed an alternative lesbian family, sharing all our resources, I kept the truth about my background and who I knew myself to be a carefully obscured mystery. I worked as hard as I could to make myself a new person, an emotionally healthy radical lesbian activist, and I believed completely that by remaking myself I was helping to remake the world.

For a decade, I did not go home for more than a few days at a time.

It is sometimes hard to make clear how much I have loved my family, that every impulse to hold them in contempt has sparked in me a counter-surge of stubborn pride. (What is equally hard to make clear is how much that impulse toward love and pride is complicated by an urge to fit us into the acceptable myths and theories of both mainstream society—Steven Spielberg movies or Taylor Caldwell novels, the one valorizing and the other caricaturing—and a lesbian feminist reinterpretation—the patriarchy as the villain and the trivialization of the choices the men and women of my family have made.) I have had to fight broad generalizations from every possible theoretical viewpoint. Traditional feminist theory has had a limited understanding of class differences or of how sexuality and self are shaped by both desire and denial. The ideology implies that we are all sisters who should turn our anger and suspicion only on the world outside the lesbian community. It is so simple to say the patriarchy did it, that poverty and social contempt are products of the world of the fathers. How often I felt a need to collapse my sexual history into what I was willing to share of my class background, to pretend that both my life as a lesbian and my life as a working-class escapee were constructed by the patriarchy. The difficulty is that I can't ascribe everything that has been problematic or difficult about my life simply and easily to the patriarchy, or even to the invisible and much-denied class structure of our society. . . .

One of the things I am trying to understand is how we internalize the myths of our society even as we hate and resist them. Perhaps this will be more understandable if I discuss specifically how some of these myths have shaped my life and how I have been able to talk about and change my own understanding of my family. I have felt a powerful temptation to write about my family as a kind of moral tale with us as the heroes and the middle and upper classes as the villains. It would be within the romantic myth, for example, to pretend that we were the kind of noble Southern whites portrayed in the movies, mill workers for generations until driven out of the mills by alcoholism and a family propensity to rebellion and union talk. But that would be a lie. The truth is that no one in my family ever joined a union. Taken as far as it can go, the myth of the poor would make my family over into union organizers or people broken by the failure of the unions. The reality of my family is far more complicated and lacks the cardboard nobility of the myth.

As far as my family was concerned, union organizers, like preachers, were of a different class, suspect and hated as much as they might be admired for what they were supposed to be trying to achieve. Serious belief in anything—any political ideology, any religious system, or any theory of life's meaning and purpose—was seen as unrealistic. It was an attitude that bothered me a lot when I started reading the socially conscious novels I found in the paperback racks when I was eleven or so. I particularly loved Sinclair Lewis's novels and wanted to imagine my own family as part of the working man's struggle. But it didn't seem to be that simple.

"We were not joiners," my Aunt Dot told me with a grin when I asked her about the union. My cousin Butch laughed at that, told me the union charged dues and said, "Hell, we can't even be persuaded to toss money in the collection plate. An't gonna give it to no fat union man." It shamed me that the only thing my family wholeheartedly believed in was luck, and the waywardness of fate. They held the dogged conviction that the admirable and wise thing to do was to try and keep a sense of humor, not to whine or cower, and to trust that luck might someday turn as good as it had been bad—and with just as much reason. Becoming a political activist with an almost religious fervor was the thing I did that most outraged my family and the Southern working-class community they were part of.

Similarly, it was not my sexuality, my lesbianism, that was seen by my family as most rebellious; for most of my life, no one but my mama took my sexual preference very seriously. It was the way I thought about work, ambition, and self-respect that seemed incomprehensible to my aunts and cousins. They were waitresses, laundry workers, and counter girls. I was the one who went to work as a maid, something I never told any of them. They would have been angry if they had known, though the fact that some work was contemptible was itself a difficult notion. They believed that work was just work, necessary, that you did what you had to do to survive. They did not believe so much in taking pride in doing your job as they did in stubbornly enduring hard work and hard times when you really didn't have much choice about what work you did. But at the same time they did believe that there were some forms of work, including maid's work, that were only for black people, not white, and while I did not share that belief, I knew how intrinsic it was to how my family saw the world. Sometimes I felt as if I straddled cultures and belonged on neither side. I would grind my teeth at what I knew was my family's unquestioning racism but still take pride in their pragmatic endurance, but more and more as I grew older what I truly felt was a deep estrangement from the way they saw the world, and gradually a sense of shame that would have been completely incomprehensible to them.

"Long as there's lunch counters, you can always find work," I was told by both my mother and my aunts, and they'd add, "I can always get me a little extra with a smile." It was obvious that there was supposed to be nothing shameful about it, that needy smile across a lunch counter, that rueful grin when you didn't have rent, or the half-provocative, half-begging way my mama could cajole the man at the store to give her a little credit. But I hated it, hated the need for it and the shame that would follow every time I did it myself. It was begging as far as I was concerned, a quasi-prostitution that I despised even while I continued to use it (after all, I needed the money). But my mother, aunts, and cousins had not been ashamed, and my shame and resentment pushed me even further away from them.

"Just use that smile," my girl cousins used to joke, and I hated what I knew they meant. After college, when I began to support myself and study feminist theory, I did not become more understanding of the women of my family but more contemptuous. I told myself that prostitution is a skilled profession and my cousins were never more than amateurs. There was a certain truth in this, though like all cruel judgments made from the outside, it ignored the conditions that made it true. The women in my family, my mother included, had sugar daddies, not johns, men who slipped them money because they needed it so badly. From their point of view they were nice to those men because the men were nice to them, and it was never so direct or crass an arrangement that they would set a price on their favors. They would never have described what they did as prostitution, and nothing made them angrier than the suggestion that the men who helped them out did it just for their favors. They worked for a living, they swore, but this was different.

I always wondered if my mother had hated her sugar daddy, or if not *him* then her need for what he offered her, but it did not seem to me in memory that she had. Her sugar daddy had been an old man, half-crippled, hesitant and needy, and he treated my mama with enormous consideration and, yes, respect. The relationship between them was painful because it was based on the fact that she and my stepfather could not make enough money to support the family. Mama could not refuse her sugar daddy's money, but at the same time he made no assumptions about that money buying anything she was not already offering. The truth was, I think, that she genuinely liked him, and only partly because he treated her so well.

Even now, I am not sure whether or not there was a sexual exchange between them. Mama was a pretty woman and she was kind to him, a kindness he obviously did not get from anyone else in his life, and he took extreme care not to cause her any problems with my stepfather. As a teenager with an adolescent's contempt for moral failings and sexual complexity of any kind, I had been convinced that Mama's relationship with that old man was contemptible and also that I would never do such a thing. The first time a lover of mine gave me money, and I took it, everything in my head shifted. The amount she gave me was not much to her but it was a lot to me and I needed it. I could not refuse it, but I hated myself for taking it and I hated her for giving it to me. Worse, she had much less grace about my need than my mama's sugar daddy had displayed toward her. All that bitter contempt I had felt for my needy cousins and aunts raged through me and burned out the love I had felt. I ended the relationship quickly, unable to forgive myself for *selling* what I believed should only be offered freely—not sex but love itself.

When the women in my family talked about how hard they worked, the men would spit to the side and shake their heads. Men took real jobs—hard, dangerous, physically daunting work. They went to jail, not just the hard-eyed, careless boys who scared me with their brutal hands and cold eyes, but their gentler, softer brothers. It was another family thing, what people expected of my mama's family, my people. "His daddy's that one was sent off to jail in Georgia, and his uncle's another. Like as not, he's just the same," you'd hear people say of boys so young they still had their milk teeth. We were always driving down to the county farm to see somebody, some uncle, cousin, or nameless male relation. Shaven-headed, sullen and stunned, they wept on Mama's shoulder or begged my aunts to help. "I didn't do nothing, Mama," they'd say and it might have been true, but if even we didn't believe them, who would? No one told the truth, not even about how their lives were destroyed.

When I was eight years old, Butch, one of my favorite cousins, went to jail for breaking into pay phones with another boy. The other boy was returned to the custody of his parents. Butch was sent to the boys' facility at the county farm and after three months, my mama took us down there to visit, carrying a big basket of fried chicken, cold cornbread, and potato salad. Along with a hundred others we sat out on the lawn with Butch and watched him eat like he hadn't had a full meal in the whole three months. I stared at his head, which had been shaved near bald, and his ears, which were newly marked with fine blue scars from the carelessly handled razor. People were laughing, music was playing, and a tall lazy man in uniform walked past us chewing on toothpicks and watching us all closely. Butch kept his head down, his face hard with hatred, only looking back at the guard when he turned away.

"Sons-a-bitches," he whispered, and my mama shushed him. We all sat still when the guard turned back to us. There was a long moment of quiet and then that man let his face relax into a big wide grin.

"Uh-huh," he said. That was all he said. Then he turned and walked away. None of us spoke. None of us ate any more. Butch went back inside soon after and we left. When we got back to the car, my mama sat there for a while crying quietly. The next week Butch was reported for fighting and had his stay extended by six months.

Butch was fifteen. He never went back to school and after jail he couldn't join the army. When he finally did come home we never talked, never had to talk. I knew without asking that the guard had had his little revenge, knew too that my cousin would break into another phone booth as soon as he could, but do it sober and not get caught. I knew without asking the source of his rage, the way he felt about clean, well-dressed, contemptuous people who looked at him like his life wasn't as important as a dog's. I knew because I felt it too. That guard had looked at me and Mama with the same expression he used on my cousin. We were trash. We were the ones they built the county farm to house and break. The boy who had been sent home had been the son of a deacon in the church, the man who managed the hardware store.

As much as I hated that man, and his boy, there was a way in which I also hated my cousin. He should have known better, I told myself, should have known the risk he ran. He should have been more careful. As I became older and started living on my own, it was a litany that I used against myself even more angrily than I used it against my cousin. I knew who I was, knew that the most important thing I had to do was protect myself and hide my despised identity, blend into the myth of both the "good" poor and the reasonable lesbian. Even when I became a feminist activist, that litany went on reverberating in my head, but by then it had become a groundnote, something so deep and omnipresent, I no longer heard it even when everything I did was set to the cadence that it established.

By 1975, I was earning a meager living as a photographer's assistant in Tallahassee, Florida, but the real work of my life was my lesbian feminist activism, the work I did with the local Women's Center and the committee to found a Feminist Studies Department at Florida State University. Part of my role as I saw it was to be a kind of evangelical lesbian feminist, and to help develop a political analysis of this woman-hating society. I did not talk about class, more than by giving lip service to how we all needed to think about it, the same way I thought we all needed to think about racism. I was a serious and determined person, living in a lesbian collective, studying each new book that purported to address feminist issues and completely driven by what I saw as a need to revolutionize the world. . . .

The idea of writing fiction or essays seemed frivolous when there was so much work to be done, but everything changed when I found myself confronting emotions and ideas that could not be explained away or postponed for a feminist holiday. The way it happened was simple and completely unexpected. One week I was asked to speak to two completely divergent groups: an Episcopalian Sunday School class and a juvenile detention center. The Episcopalians were all white, well-dressed, highly articulate, nominally polite, and obsessed with getting me to tell them (without their having to ask directly) just what it was that two women did together in bed. The delinquents were all women, eighty percent black and Hispanic, dressed in green uniform dresses or blue jeans and workshirts, profane, rude, fearless, witty, and just as determined to get me to talk about what it was that two women did together in bed.

I tried to have fun with the Episcopalians, teasing them about their fears and insecurities, and being as bluntly honest as I could about my sexual practices. The Sunday School teacher, a man who had assured me of his liberal inclinations, kept blushing and stammering as the questions about my growing up and coming out became more detailed. When the meeting was over, I stepped out into the sunshine angry at the contemptuous attitude implied by all their questions, and though I did not know why, also so deeply depressed that I couldn't even cry. The delinquents were different. Shameless, they had me blushing within the first few minutes, yelling out questions that were partly curious and partly a way of boasting about what they already knew.

"You butch or femme?" "You ever fuck boys?" "You ever want to?" "You want to have children?" "What's your girlfriend like?" I finally broke up when one very tall confident girl leaned way over and called out, "Hey girlfriend! I'm getting out of here next weekend. What you doing that night?" I laughed so hard I almost choked. I laughed until we were all howling and giggling together. Even getting frisked as I left didn't ruin my mood. I was still grinning when I climbed into the waterbed with my lover that night, grinning right up to the moment when she wrapped her arms around me and I burst into tears.

It is hard to describe the way I felt that night, the shock of recognition and the painful way my thoughts turned. That night I understood suddenly everything that happened to my cousins and me, understood it from a wholly new and agonizing perspective, one that made clear how brutal I had been to both my family and myself. I understood all over again how we had been robbed and dismissed, and why I had worked so hard not to think about it. I had learned as a child that what could not be changed had to go unspoken, and worse, that those who cannot change their own lives have every reason to be ashamed of that fact and to hide it. I had accepted that shame and believed in it, but why? What had I or my cousins really done to deserve the contempt directed at us? Why had I always believed us contemptible by nature? I wanted to talk to someone about all the things I was thinking that night, but I could not. Among the women I knew there was no one who would have understood what I was thinking, no other working-class women in the women's collective where I was living. I began to suspect that we shared no common language to speak those bitter truths.

In the days after that I found myself remembering that afternoon long ago at the county farm, that feeling of being the animal in the zoo, the thing looked at and laughed at and used by the real people who watched us. For all his liberal convictions, that Sunday School teacher had looked at me with eyes that reminded me of Butch's long-ago guard. Suddenly I felt thrown back into my childhood, into all the fears and convictions I had tried to escape. Once again I felt myself at the mercy of the important people who knew how to dress and talk, and would always be given the benefit of the doubt while I and my family would not.

I felt as if I was at the mercy of an outrage so old I could not have traced all the ways it shaped my life. I understood again that some are given no quarter, no chance, that all their courage, humor, and love for each other is just a joke to the ones who make the rules, and I hated the rule makers. Finally I also realized that part of my grief came from the fact that I no longer knew who I was or where I belonged. I had run away from my family, refused to go home to visit, and tried in every way to make myself a new person. How could I be working-class with a college degree? As a lesbian activist? I thought about the guards at the detention center, and the way they had looked at me. They had not stared at me with the same picture-window emptiness they turned on the girls who came to hear me, girls who were closer to the life I had been meant to live than I could bear to examine. The contempt in their eyes was contempt for me as a lesbian, different and the same, but still contempt. . . .

In the late 1970s, the compartmentalized life I had created burst open. It began when I started to write and work out what I really thought about my family. . . . I went home again. I went home to my mother and my sisters, to visit, talk, argue, and begin to understand.

Once home I saw that, as far as my family was concerned, lesbians were lesbians whether they wore suitcoats or leather jackets. Moreover, in all that time when I had not made peace with myself, my family had managed to make a kind of peace with me. My girlfriends were treated like slightly odd versions of my sisters' husbands, while I was simply the daughter who had always been difficult but was still a part of their lives. The result was that I started trying to confront what had made me unable to really talk to my sisters for so many years. I discovered that they no longer knew who I was either, and it took time and lots of listening to each other to rediscover my sense of family, and my love for them.

It is only as the child of my class and my unique family background that I have been able to put together what is for me a meaningful politics, gained a sense of why I believe in activism, why self-revelation is so important for lesbians, reexamining the way we are seen and the way we see ourselves. There is no all-purpose feminist analysis that explains away all the complicated ways our sexuality and core identity are shaped, the way we see ourselves as parts of both our birth families and the extended family of friends and lovers we invariably create within the lesbian community. For me the bottom line has simply become the need to resist that omnipresent fear, that urge to hide and disappear, to disguise my life, my desires, and the truth about how little any of us understand—even as we try to make the world a more just and human place for us all. Most of all I have tried to understand the politics of *they,* why human beings fear and stigmatize the different while secretly dreading that they might be one of the different themselves. Class, race, sexuality, gender, all the categories by which we categorize and dismiss each other need to be examined from the inside.

The horror of class stratification, racism, and prejudice is that some people begin to believe that the security of their families and community depends on the oppression of others, that for some to have good lives others must have lives that are mean and horrible. It is a belief that dominates this culture; it is what made the poor whites of the South so determinedly racist and the middle class so contemptuous of the poor. It is a myth that allows some to imagine that they build their lives on the ruin of others, a secret core of shame for

PERSONAL ACCOUNT

That Moment of Visibility

I never realized how much my working-class background and beliefs played a role in my education. My family, friends, and neighbors never placed much importance on college. Instead, we were strongly encouraged to find work immediately after high school so we could support ourselves financially. My sisters and I were encouraged to do secretarial work until we married. There was no particular positive status attached to obtaining a degree except maybe the chance of making a lot of money. In fact, friends who went to college were looked at somewhat suspiciously. Among my reference group, college was often seen as a way to get out of having to work.

No one in my family had ever gone to college. It was not financially feasible and a college environment was equal to the unknown. It really was scary terrain. When I decided to go to a local community college after having worked for five years in a secretarial position, family and friends could not understand my decision. Why would I choose college when I already had a job? I could pay bills, buy what I needed, and I had a savings account. So I started by taking a course a semester—and I barely got through the first course. Although I received a good grade, I felt incredibly isolated, like I was an impostor who did not belong in a classroom. I had no idea how someone in college was supposed to act. I stayed silent, scared, and consciously invisible most of the time. I was not even close to making a commitment to a college education when I signed up for a second course—but because my job payed for it (one of the benefits), I felt I had nothing to lose. I signed up for Introduction to Juvenile Delinquency and midway through, our class received an assignment to do a fifteen-page self-analysis applying some of the theories we were learning. The thought of consciously revealing myself when I was trying so hard not to look, act, or be different was not something I was willing (or, I think, able at the time) to do. When I discussed the assignment with the people close to me, they agreed that the assignment was too personal and revealing. I decided not to do it and I also decided that college was probably not for me.

I went to see my professor (who was the only woman in her department) to let her know that I was refusing to do the assignment and would not complete the course. We had spoken two or three times outside of class and she knew a little about me. I knew that she was also from a working-class background and had returned to school after working some years. I felt the least I could do was tell her I was quitting the class. When I said that I was unwilling to do the assignment, she stared at me for some time, and then asked me what I would prefer to write about. I was stunned that I was noticed and was being asked what I would like to do. When I had no reply, she asked if I would write a paper on the importance of dissent. All I could think to say was yes. I completed the course successfully and found an ally in my department. I can't overstate the importance of that moment of acknowledgement. It was the first time I felt listened to. It was the moment when you feel safe enough to reveal who you are, the deep breath you can finally take when you figure out that the person you're talking to understands, appreciates, and may even share your identity.

I think of this experience as a turning point for me—when I realized that despite all my conscious efforts to be invisible and to "pass," it was that moment of visibility and acknowledgement that kept me in school.

Rose B. Pascarell

the middle class, a goad and a spur to the marginal working class, and cause enough for the homeless and poor to feel no constraints on hatred or violence. The power of the myth is made even more apparent when we examine how within the lesbian and feminist communities, where so much attention has been paid to the politics of marginalization, there is still so much exclusion and fear, so many of us who do not feel safe even within our chosen communities.

I grew up poor, hated, the victim of physical, emotional, and sexual violence, and I know that suffering does not ennoble. It destroys. To resist destruction, self-hatred, or lifelong hopelessness, we have to throw off the conditioning of being despised, the fear of becoming that *they* that is talked about so dismissively, to refuse lying myths and easy moralities, to see ourselves as human, flawed and extraordinary. All of us—extraordinary.

READING 30

Why Are Droves of Unqualified, Unprepared Kids Getting into Our Top Colleges? Because Their Dads Are Alumni.

John Larew

Growing up, she heard a hundred Harvard stories. In high school, she put the college squarely in her sights. But when judgment day came in the winter of 1988, the Harvard admissions guys were frankly unimpressed. Her academic record was solid—not special. Extracurriculars, interview, recommendations? Above average, but not by much. "Nothing really stands out," one admissions officer scribbled on her application folder. Wrote another, "Harvard not really the right place."

At the hyperselective Harvard, where high school valedictorians, National Merit Scholarship finalists, musical prodigies—11,000 ambitious kids in all—are rejected annually, this young woman didn't seem to have much of a chance. Thanks to Harvard's largest affirmative action program, she got in anyway. No, she wasn't poor, black, disabled, Hispanic, native American, or even Aleutian. She got in because her mom went to Harvard.

Folk wisdom at Harvard holds that "Mother Harvard does not coddle her young." She sure treats her grandkids right, though. For more than 40 years, an astounding one-fifth of Harvard's students have received admissions preference because their parents attended the school. Today, these overwhelmingly affluent, white children of alumni—"legacies"—are three times more likely to be accepted to Harvard than high school kids who lack that handsome lineage.

Yalies, don't feel smug: Offspring of the Old Blue are two-and-a-half times more likely to be accepted than their unconnected peers. Dartmouth this year admitted 57 percent of its legacy applicants, compared to 27 percent of nonlegacies. At the University of Pennsylvania, 66 percent of legacies were admitted last year—thanks in part to an autonomous "office of alumni admissions" that actively lobbies for alumni children before the admissions committee. "One can argue that it's an accident, but it sure doesn't look like an accident," admits Yale Dean of Admissions Worth David.

If the legacies' big edge seems unfair to the tens of thousands who get turned away every year, Ivy League administrators have long defended the innocence of the legacy stat. Children of alumni are just smarter; they come from privileged backgrounds and tend to grow up in homes where parents encourage learning. That's what Harvard Dean of Admissions William Fitzsimmons told the campus newspaper, the *Harvard Crimson,* when it first reported on the legacy preference last year. Departing Harvard President Derek Bok patiently explained that the legacy preference worked only as a "tie-breaking factor" between otherwise equally qualified candidates.

Since Ivy League admissions data is a notoriously classified commodity, when Harvard officials said in previous years that alumni kids were just better, you had to take them at their word. But then federal investigators came along and pried open those top-secret files. The Harvard guys were lying.

This past fall, after two years of study, the U.S. Department of Education's Office for Civil Rights (OCR) found that, far from being more qualified or even equally qualified, the average admitted legacy at Harvard between 1981 and 1988 was significantly *less* qualified than the average admitted nonlegacy. Examining admissions office ratings on academics, extracurriculars, personal qualities, recommendations, and

---

No biographical information available.

other categories, the OCR concluded that "with the exception of the athletic rating, [admitted] nonlegacies scored better than legacies in *all* areas of comparison."

Exceptionally high admit rates, lowered academic standards, preferential treatment . . . hmmm. These sound like the cries heard in the growing fury over affirmative action for racial minorities in America's elite universities. Only no one is outraged about legacies.

- In his recent book, *Preferential Policies,* Thomas Sowell argues that doling out special treatment encourages lackluster performance by the favored and resentment from the spurned. His far-ranging study flits from Malaysia to South Africa to American college campuses. Legacies don't merit a word.
- Dinesh D'Souza, in his celebrated jeremiad *Illiberal Education,* blames affirmative action in college admissions for declining academic standards and increasing racial tensions. Lowered standards for minority applicants, he hints, may soon destroy the university as we know it. Lowered standards for legacies? The subject doesn't come up.
- For all his polysyllabic complaints against preferential admissions, William F. Buckley Jr. (Yale '50) has never bothered to note that son Chris (Yale '75) got the benefit of a policy that more than doubled his chance of admission.

With so much silence on the subject, you'd be excused for thinking that in these enlightened times hereditary preferences are few and far between. But you'd be wrong. At most elite universities during the eighties, the legacy was by far the biggest piece of the preferential pie. At Harvard, a legacy is about twice as likely to be admitted as a black or Hispanic student. As sociologists Jerome Karabel and David Karen point out, if alumni children were admitted to Harvard at the same rate as other applicants, their numbers in the class of 1992 would have been reduced by about 200. Instead, those 200 marginally qualified legacies outnumbered all black, Mexican-American, native American, and Puerto Rican enrollees put together. If a few marginally qualified minorities are undermining Harvard's academic standards as much as conservatives charge, think about the damage all those legacies must be doing.

Mind you, colleges have the right to give the occasional preference—to bend the rules for the brilliant oboist or the world-class curler or the guy whose remarkable decency can't be measured by the SAT. (I happened to benefit from a geographical edge: It's easier to get into Harvard from West Virginia than from New England.) And until standardized tests and grade point average perfectly reflect the character, judgment, and drive of a student, tips like these aren't just nice, they're fair. Unfortunately, the extent of the legacy privilege in elite American colleges suggests something more than the occasional tie-breaking tip. Forget meritocracy. When 20 percent of Harvard's student body gets a legacy preference, aristocracy is the word that comes to mind.

A CASTE OF THOUSANDS

If complaining about minority preferences is fashionable in the world of competitive colleges, bitching about legacies is just plain gauche, suggesting an unhealthy resentment of the privileged. But the effects of the legacy trickle down. For every legacy that wins, someone—usually someone less privileged—loses. And higher education is a high-stakes game.

High school graduates earn 59 percent of the income of four-year college graduates. Between high school graduates and alumni of prestigious colleges, the disparity is far greater. A *Fortune* study of American CEOs shows the usual suspects—graduates of Yale, Princeton, and Harvard—leading the list. A recent survey of the Harvard Class of 1940 found that 43 percent were worth more than $1 million. With some understatement, the report concludes, "A picture of highly advantageous circumstances emerges here, does it not, compared with American society as a whole?"

An Ivy League diploma doesn't necessarily mean a fine education. Nor does it guarantee future success. What it *does* represent is a big head start in the rat race—a fact Harvard will be the first to tell you. When I was a freshman, a counselor at the Office of Career Services instructed a group of us to make the Harvard name stand out on our resumes: "Underline it, boldface it, put it in capital letters."

Of course, the existence of the legacy preference in this fierce career competition isn't exactly news. According to historians, it was a direct result of the influx of Jews into the Ivy League during the twenties. Until then, Harvard, Princeton, and Yale had admitted anyone who could pass their entrance exams, but suddenly Jewish kids were outscoring the WASPs. So the schools began to use nonacademic criteria—"character," "solidity," and, eventually, lineage—to justify accepting low-scoring blue bloods over their peers. Yale implemented its legacy preference first, in 1925—spelling it out in a memo four years later: The school would admit "Yale sons of good character and reasonably good record . . . regardless of the number of applicants and the superiority of outside competitors." Harvard and Princeton followed shortly thereafter.

Despite its ignoble origins, the legacy preference has only sporadically come under fire, most notably in 1978's affirmative action decision, *University of California Board of Regents v. Bakke.* In his concurrence, Justice Harry Blackmun observed, "It is somewhat ironic to have us so deeply disturbed over a program where race is an element of consciousness, and yet to be aware of the fact, as we are, that institutions of higher learning . . . have given conceded preferences to the children of alumni."

If people are, in fact, aware of the legacy preference, why has it been spared the scrutiny given other preferential policies? One reason is public ignorance of the scope and scale of those preferences—an ignorance carefully cultivated by America's elite institutions. It's easy to maintain the fiction that your legacies get in strictly on merit as long as your admissions bureaucracy controls all access to student data. Information on Harvard's legacies became publicly available not because of any fit of disclosure by the university, but because a few civil rights types noted that the school had a suspiciously low rate of admission for Asian-Americans, who are statistically stronger than other racial groups in academics.

While the ensuing OCR inquiry found no evidence of illegal racial discrimination by Harvard, it did turn up some embarrassing information about how much weight the "legacy" label gives an otherwise flimsy file. Take these comments scrawled by admissions officers on applicant folders:

- "Double lineage who chose the right parents."
- "Dad's [deleted] connections signify lineage of more than usual weight. That counted into the equation makes this a case which (assuming positive TRs [teacher recommendations] and Alum IV [alumnus interview]) is well worth doing."
- "Lineage is main thing."
- "Not quite strong enough to get the clean tip."
- "Classical case that would be hard to explain to dad."
- "Double lineage but lots of problems."
- "Not a great profile, but just strong enough #'s and grades to get the tip from lineage."
- "Without lineage, there would be little case. With it, we'll keep looking."

In every one of these cases, the applicant was admitted.

Of course, Harvard's not doing anything other schools aren't. The practice of playing favorites with alumni children is nearly universal among private colleges and isn't unheard of at public institutions, either. The rate of admission for Stanford's alumni children is "almost twice the general population," according to a spokesman for the admissions office. Notre Dame reserves 25 percent of each freshman class for legacies. At the University of Virginia, where native Virginians make up two-thirds of each class, alumni children are automatically treated as Virginians even if they live out of state—giving them a whopping competitive edge. The same is true of the University of California at Berkeley. At many schools, Harvard included, all legacy applications are guaranteed a read by the dean of admissions himself—a privilege nonlegacies don't get.

LITTLE WHITE ELIS

Like the Harvard deans, officials at other universities dismiss the statistical disparities by pointing to the superior environmental influences found in the homes of their alums. "I bet that, statistically, [legacy qualifications are] a little above average, but not by much," says Paul Killebrew, associate director of admissions at Dartmouth. "The admitted group [of legacies] would look exactly like the profile of the class."

James Wickenden, a former dean of admissions at Princeton who now runs a college consulting firm, suspects otherwise. Wickenden wrote of "one Ivy League university" where the average combined SAT score of the freshman class was 1,350 out of a possible 1,600, compared to 1,280 for legacies. "At most selective schools, [legacy status] doubles, even trebles the chances of admission," he says. Many colleges even place admitted legacies in a special "Not in Profile" file (along with recruited athletes and some minority students), so that when the school's SAT scores are published, alumni kids won't pull down the average.

How do those kids fare once they're enrolled? No one's telling. Harvard, for one, refuses to keep any records of how alumni children stack up academically against their nonlegacy classmates—perhaps because the last such study, in 1956, showed Harvard sons hogging the bottom of the grade curve.

If the test scores of admitted legacies are a mystery, the reason colleges accept so many is not. They're afraid the alumni parents of rejected children will stop giving to the colleges' unending fundraising campaigns. "Our survival as an institution depends on having support from alumni," says Richard Steele, director of undergraduate admissions at Duke University, "so according advantages to alumni kids is just a given."

In fact, the OCR exonerated Harvard's legacy preference precisely because legacies bring in money. (OCR cited a federal district court ruling that a state university could favor the children of out-of-state alumni because "defendants showed that the alumni provide monetary support for the university.") And there's no question that alumni provide significant support to Harvard: Last year, they raised $20 million for the scholarship fund alone.

In a letter to OCR defending his legacies, Harvard's Fitzsimmons painted a grim picture of a school where the preference did not exist—a place peeved alumni turned their backs on when their kids failed to make the cut. "Without the fundraising activities of alumni," Fitzsimmons warned darkly, "Harvard could not maintain many of its programs, including needs-blind admissions."

Ignoring, for the moment, the question of how "needs-blind" a system is that admits one-fifth of each class on the assumption that, hey, their parents might give us money, Fitzsimmons's defense doesn't quite ring true. The "Save the Scholarship Fund" line is a variation on the principle of "Firemen First," whereby bureaucrats threatened with a budget cut insist that essential programs rather than executive perks and junkets will be the first to be slashed. Truth be told, there is just about nothing that Harvard, the richest university in the world, could do to jeopardize needs-blind admissions, provided that it placed a high enough priority on them.

But even more unclear is how closely alumni giving is related to the acceptance of alumni kids. "People whose children are denied admission are initially upset," says Wickenden, "and maybe for a year or two their interest in the university wanes. But typically they come back around when they see that what happened was best for the kids." Wickenden has put his money where his mouth is: He rejected two sons of a Princeton trustee involved in a $420 million fundraising project, not to mention the child of a board member who managed the school's $2 billion endowment, all with no apparent ill effect.

Most university administrators would be loathe to take such a chance, despite a surprising lack of evidence of the legacy/largess connection. Fitzsimmons admits Harvard knows of no empirical research to support the claim that diminishing legacies would decrease alumni contributions, relying instead on "hundreds, perhaps thousands of conversations with alumni whose sons and daughters applied."

No doubt some of Fitzsimmons's anxiety is founded: It's only natural for alumni to want their kids to have the same privileges they did. But the historical record suggests that alumni are far more tolerant than administrators realize. Admit women and blacks? *Well, we would,* said administrators earlier this century—*but the alumni just won't have it.* Fortunately for American universities, the bulk of those alumni turned out to be less craven than administrators thought they'd be. As more blacks and women enrolled over the past two decades, the funds kept pouring in, reaching an all-time high in the eighties.

Another significant historical lesson can be drawn from the late fifties, when Harvard's selectiveness increased dramatically. As the number of applications soared, the rate of admission for legacies began declining from about 90 percent to its current 43 percent. Administration anxiety rose inversely, but Harvard's fundraising machine has somehow survived. That doesn't mean there's *no* correlation between alumni giving and the legacy preference, obviously; rather, it means that the people who would withhold their money at the loss of the legacy privilege were far outnumbered by other givers. "It takes time to get the message out," explains Fitzsimmons, "but eventually people start responding. We've had to make the case [for democratization] to alumni, and I think that they generally feel good about that."

HEIR CUT

When justice dictates that ordinary kids should have as fair a shot as the children of America's elite, couldn't Harvard and its sister institutions trouble themselves to "get the message out" again? Of course they could. But virtually no one—liberal or conservative—is pushing them to do so.

"There must be no goals or quotas for any special group or category of applicants," reads an advertisement in the right-wing *Dartmouth Review.* "Equal opportunity must be the guiding policy. Males, females, blacks, whites, Native Americans, Hispanics . . . can all be given equal chance to matriculate, survive, and prosper based solely on individual performance."

Noble sentiments from the Ernest Martin Hopkins Institute, an organization of conservative Dartmouth alumni. Reading on, though, we find these "concerned alumni" aren't sacrificing *their* young to the cause. "Alumni sons and daughters," notes the ad further down, "should receive some special consideration."

Similarly, Harvard's conservative *Salient* has twice in recent years decried the treatment of Asian-Americans in admissions, but it attributes their misfortune to favoritism for blacks and Hispanics. What about legacy university favoritism—a much bigger factor? *Salient* writers have twice endorsed it.

What's most surprising is the indifference of minority activists. With the notable exception of a few vocal Asian-Americans, most have made peace with the preference for well-off whites.

Mecca Nelson, the president of Harvard's Black Students Association, leads rallies for the hiring of more minority faculty. She participated in an illegal sit-in at an administration building in support of Afro-American studies. But when it comes to the policy that Asian-American activist Arthur Hu calls "a 20-percent-white quota," Nelson says, "I don't have any really strong opinions about it. I'm not very clear on the whole legacy issue at all."

Joshua Li, former co-chair of Harvard's Asian-American Association, explains his complacency differently: "We understand that in the future Asian-American students will receive these tips as well."

At America's elite universities, you'd expect a somewhat higher standard of fairness than that—especially when money is the driving force behind the concept. And many Ivy League types *do* advocate for more just and lofty ideals. One of them, as it happens, is Derek Bok. In one of Harvard's annual reports, he warned that the modern university is slowly turning from a truth-seeking enterprise into a money-grubbing corporation—at the expense of the loyalty of its alums. "Such an institution may still evoke pride and respect because of its intellectual achievements," he said rightly. "But the feelings it engenders will not be quite the same as those produced by an institution that is prepared to forgo income, if need be, to preserve values of a nobler kind."

Forgo income to preserve values of a nobler kind—it's an excellent idea. Embrace the preferences for the poor and disadvantaged. Wean alumni from the idea of the legacy edge. And above all, stop the hypocrisy that begrudges the great unwashed a place at Harvard while happily making room for the less qualified sons and daughters of alums.

After 70 years, it won't be easy to wrest the legacy preference away from the alums. But the long-term payoff is as much a matter of message as money. When the sons and daughters of today's college kids fill out *their* applications, the legacy preference should seem not a birthright, but a long-gone relic from the Ivy League's inequitable past.

SECTION III

THE MEANING OF DIFFERENCE

FRAMEWORK ESSAY III: KEY CONCEPTS

hegemonic Dominating or ruling. A **hegemonic ideology** is a belief that is pervasive in a culture. (See page 281)

ideology A belief that primarily reflects the experiences of those with power, but is presented as universally valid. (See pages 280–81)

natural-law language Language that treats human behavior as bound by natural law. (See pages 281–83)

social Darwinism The belief that those who dominate a society are necessarily the fittest. (See pages 286–91)

stereotype A characterization of a category of people as all alike, possessing the same set of characteristics, and likely to behave in the same ways. (See pages 282–86)

FRAMEWORK ESSAY

The first framework essay in this text considered how contemporary American master statuses are named, dichotomized, and stigmatized. The second essay focused on the experience of privilege and stigma that accompanies those master statuses. In this final section, we will look at the *meaning* that is attributed to difference. What significance are differences of race, sex, class, disability, and sexual orientation presumed to have? What difference does difference make?

The meaning that is attributed to difference comes in large part from the operation of social institutions. Thus, the readings in this section are organized around law and politics, the economy, science, and popular culture. In this framework essay, however, we will focus on the concept of ideology because being able to see and understand its operation goes a long way toward breaking out of constructions of difference. First, we will define *ideology* and consider how it is conveyed through stereotypes and "natural-law" language. We will then examine the ideologies about difference conveyed by science and popular culture.

Ideology

The concept of *ideology* originated in the work of Marx and Engels, particularly *The German Ideology* (1846). It is now a concept used throughout the social sciences and humanities. In general, an ideology can be defined as a widely shared belief or idea that has been constructed and disseminated by the powerful, primarily reflects their experiences, and functions for their benefit.

Ideologies are anchored in the experiences of their creators; thus, they offer only a partial view of the world. "Ideologies are not simply false, they can be 'partly true,' and yet also incomplete [or] distorted. . . . [They are not] consciously crafted by the ruling class and then injected into the minds of the majority; [they are] instead *produced* by specifiable, complex, social conditions" (Brantlinger, 1990:80). While ideologies primarily reflect the experiences of their creators, they nonetheless become the pervasive ideas of a society. Ideologies have the power to supplant, distort, or silence the experiences of those outside their production. Because those who control the means of disseminating ideas have a better chance of having their ideas become the ones that prevail, Marx and Engels concluded that "the ideas of the ruling class are in every epoch the ruling ideas."

The idea that people are rewarded on the basis of their merit is an example of an ideology. It is an idea promoted by those with power—for example, teachers and employers—and many opportunities are created for the expression of the belief. Report cards, award banquets, and merit raises are all occasions for the expression of the belief that people are rewarded on the basis of their merit.

But certainly, most know this idea is not really true: People are not rewarded only or even primarily on the basis of their merit. The idea that merit is rewarded is only partly true and reflects only *some* people's experiences. The frequent repetition of the idea, however, has the potential to overwhelm contrary experience. Even those whose experience has not generally been that people are rewarded based on merit are likely to subscribe to this philosophy, because they hear it reproduced so often. In any event, we have few safe opportunities to describe beliefs to the contrary and little chance of getting those beliefs widely disseminated.

Thus, the idea that people are rewarded on the basis of merit is an ideology. It is a belief that reflects primarily the experiences of those with power, but is presented as universally valid. The idea overwhelms and silences the voices of those who are outside its production. In effect, ideologies ask us to discount our own experience.

This conflict between one's own experience and the ideas conveyed by an ideology is implied in W.E.B. Du Bois's description of the "double consciousness" experienced by African Americans discussed in Framework Essay II. It is also what many feminists refer to as the double or fractured consciousness experienced by women. In both cases, the dominant ideas fail to reflect the real-life experiences of people in these categories. For example, the actual experience of poverty, discrimination, motherhood, disability, sexual assault, life in a black neighborhood, or in a gay relationship rarely coincides with the public discussion on these topics. Because those in stigmatized categories do not control the production or distribution of the prevailing ideas, *their* experience is not likely to be reflected in them. The ideology not only silences their experience; it may invalidate it even in their own minds: "*I* must be the one who's crazy!" In this way, the dominant discourse can invade and overwhelm our own experience, since what we know doesn't fit with it (Kasper, 1986; Smith, 1978, 1990).

Ideas which so dominate a culture as to become the prevailing and unquestioned beliefs were described in the 1920s by Italian political theorist Antonio Gramsci as the *hegemonic,* or ruling, ideology. Gramsci argued that social control was primarily accomplished by the control of ideas, especially whatever was considered to be "common sense" (Omi and Winant, 1994:67). Commonsense beliefs are likely to embody widely shared ideas primarily reflective of the interests and experience of those who are powerful. We are all encouraged to express such notions even when that requires discounting our own experience.

Conveying Ideologies: Natural-Law Language and Stereotypes

Hegemonic, or ruling, ideologies often take the form of commonsense beliefs and are especially embodied in stereotypes and what is called *natural-law language.*

Natural-Law Language When people use the word *natural,* they usually mean that something is inevitable, predetermined, or outside human control (Pierce, 1971). *Human nature* and *instinct* (in reference to humans) are often used in the same way. For example, "It's only natural to care about what others think," "It's human nature to want to get ahead," or "It's just instinctive to be afraid of someone different" all convey the sense that something is inevitable, automatic, and independent of one's will.

Thus, it is not surprising when, in discussions about discrimination, someone says, "It's only natural for people to be prejudiced" or "It's human nature to want to be with your own kind." Such phrasings convey a belief in the inevitability of discrimination and prejudice, as if such processes emerged independently of anyone's will.

Even regarding an issue of which we disapprove, the word *natural* can convey this sense of inevitability. For example, "I am against racism, but it's only natural" puts nature on the side of prejudice. Arguing that something is natural because it happens frequently has the same consequence. "All societies have discriminated against women, so there is little we can do about it" implies (illogically) that something that happens frequently is therefore inevitable. But something that happens frequently as likely argues for the presence of an extensive set of social controls ensuring the outcome.

At least three consequences follow from using natural-law language. First, it ends discussion, as if having described something as natural makes any further exploration of the topic unnecessary. This makes sense given that the word *natural* is equated with inevitability: If something is inevitable, there is little sense in questioning it.

Second, because natural-law language treats behavior as predetermined, it overlooks the actual cultural and historical variability of human societies. If something is natural, it should always happen. Yet there is virtually no human behavior that emerges everywhere and always; all social life is susceptible to change. Thus, natural-law language ignores the variability of social life.

Third, natural-law language treats individuals as passive, lacking an interest in or control over social life. If it is "natural" to dislike those who are different, then there is really nothing we can do about that feeling. It is no one's responsibility; it is just natural. If there is nothing I can do about my own behavior, there is little I could expect to do about the behavior of others. Human nature thus is depicted as a limitation beyond which people cannot expect to move (Gould, 1981). Describing certain behavior as "only natural" implies that personal and social change is impossible.

In all these ways—by closing off discussion, masking variability and change, and treating humans as passive—natural-law language tells us not to question the world that surrounds us. Natural-law language has this effect no matter what context it emerges in: "It's only natural to discriminate," "It's only natural to want to have children," "It's only natural to marry and settle down," "Inequality is only natural; the poor will always be with us," "Aggression and war are just human nature," "Greed is instinctive." In each case, natural-law language not only discourages questions, it carries a covert recommendation about what one *ought* to do. If something is "just natural," you cannot prevent others from doing it, and you are well advised to do it yourself. Thus, natural-law language serves as a forceful mechanism of social control (Pierce, 1971).

Natural-law language is used to convey ruling ideologies. It reduces the complexity and historic variability of the social world to a claim for universal processes, offering a partial and distorted truth that silences those with contrary experience. Natural-law language can make discrimination appear to be natural, normal, and inevitable. Thus, natural-law language itself contributes to the creation of difference.

Stereotypes In stereotyping, all the individuals in a category are assumed to possess the same set of characteristics. Thus, a *stereotype* is a prediction that "members of a group will behave in certain ways" (Andre, 1988:259)—that black men will have athletic ability or that Asian American students will excel in the sciences. Stereotypes persist despite evidence to the contrary because they are not formulated in a way that is testable or falsifiable (Andre, 1988). In this way stereotypes differ from descriptions. Descriptions offer no prediction; they can be tested for accuracy and rejected when they are wrong; they encourage explanation and a consideration of historical variability.

For example, "Most great American athletes are African American" is a description. First, there is no prediction that a particular African American can be expected to be a good athlete, or that someone who is white will be a poor one. Second, the claim is falsifiable; that is, it can be tested for accuracy and proven wrong (e.g., by asking what proportion of the last two decades' Olympic medal winners were African American). Third, the statement turns our attention to explanation and historical variation: Why might this be the case? Has this always been the case?

In contrast, "African Americans are good athletes" is a stereotype. It attempts to characterize a whole population, thus denying the inevitable variation among the people in the category. It predicts that members of a group will behave in a particular way. It cannot be falsified since there is no direct way to test the claim. Further, the stereotype denies the reality of historical and cultural variation by suggesting that this has always been the case. Thus, stereotypes essentialize: they assume that if you know something about the physical package someone comes in, you can predict that person's behavior.

Both stereotypes and natural-law language offer broad-based predictions about behavior. Stereotypes predict that members of a particular category will possess particular attributes; natural-law language predicts that certain behavior is inevitable. Neither stereotypes nor natural-law language is anchored in any social or historical context and, for that reason, both are frequently wrong. Basketball great Bill Russell's reaction when asked if he thought African Americans were "natural" athletes makes clear the similarity of natural-law language and stereotyping. As Russell said, this was a stereotypic image of African American athletes that deprecated the skill and effort he brought to his craft—as if he were great because he was black rather than because of the talent he cultivated in hours of work.

Stereotyping and Asian Americans As we have said, stereotypes explain life outcomes by attributing some essential, shared quality to all those in a particular category. The current depiction of Asian Americans as a "model minority" is a good example of this. This stereotype masks the considerable economic, educational, and occupational heterogeneity among Asian Americans. The model-minority stereotype is itself a fairly recent invention: Among those now called "model minority" are categories of people previously barred as unworthy to immigrate, denied citizenship through naturalization, and placed in internment camps as potential traitors.

In American culture, the production of stereotypes is often driven by the necessity to explain why some categories of people succeed more than others (Steinberg, 1989). Thus, the model-minority stereotype is often used to claim that if racism has not hurt Asian Americans' success, it could not have hurt African Americans'.

> The myth of the Asian-American "model minority" has been challenged, yet it continues to be widely believed. One reason for this is its instructional value. For whom are Asian Americans supposed to be a "model"? Shortly after the Civil War, southern planters recruited Chinese immigrants in order to pit them against the newly freed blacks as "examples" of laborers willing to work hard for low wages. Today, Asian Americans are again being used to discipline blacks. . . . Our society needs an Asian-American "model minority" in an era anxious about a growing black underclass. (Takaki, 1993:416)

A brief review of American immigration policy explains the misguided nature of the comparison between African and Asian Americans. From 1921 until 1965, U.S. immigration was restricted by national-origin quotas that set limits on the number of immigrants from each nation based on the percentage of people from that country residing in the United States at the time of the 1920 census. This had the obvious and intended effect of severely restricting immigration from Asia, as well as from Southern and Eastern Europe and Africa. The civil rights movement of the 1960s raised national embarrassment about this quota system such that in 1965 Congress replaced national-origin quotas with an annual 20,000-person limit for every nation regardless of its size. Within that quota, preference went first to those who were relatives of American citizens and then to those with occupational skills needed in America.

The result was an increase in the total volume of immigration and a change in its composition. Because few individuals from non-European countries could immigrate on the grounds of having family in America—previous restrictions would have made that almost impossible—the quotas were filled with people meeting designated *occupational* needs. Thus, those immigrating to the United States since 1965 have had high educational and occupational profiles. These high occupational and educational profiles have characterized immigrants from African as well as Asian countries.[1]

In all, selective immigration goes a long way toward explaining the success of some recent immigrants from Asian countries. The middle- and upper-class professionals and entrepreneurs who have immigrated to the United States did not suddenly become successful here; rather, they continued their home-country success here.

However, it is important not to confuse the situation of people who are immigrants with those who are refugees. The circumstances of arrival and resettlement for those who have fled their home countries make the refugee population exceedingly heterogeneous and quite different from those who have immigrated to the United States (Haines, 1989). Thus, Vietnamese, Laotian, Cambodian, and Hmong refugees are unlikely to have the high occupational or educational profiles of other Asian immigrants.

The misguided contemporary formulation—if Asian Americans can make it, why can't African Americans?—echoes an earlier question: If European immigrants can make it, why can't African Americans? The answer to that question is summarized as follows:

> Conditions within the cities to which they had migrated [beginning in the 1920s], not slavery, strained blacks' ability to retain two-parent families. Within those cities, blacks faced circumstances that differed fundamentally from those found earlier by European immigrants. They entered cities in large numbers as unskilled and semiskilled manufacturing jobs were leaving, not growing. The discrimination they encountered kept them out of the manufacturing jobs into which earlier immigrants had been recruited. One important goal of public schools had been the assimilation and "Americanization" of immigrant children; by contrast, they excluded and segregated blacks. Racism enforced housing segregation, and residential concentration among blacks increased at the same time it less-

[1]Those with high educational profiles do not always realize high incomes, however. For example, while Nigerian and Iranian immigrants have high educational profiles, their household incomes have been low, a situation most likely explained by the recency of their arrival in the United States. Similarly, although Asian immigrants may have a high household income (as a result of income pooling), their average individual income is lower than that for European immigrants and U.S. natives (Portes and Rimbaut, 1990). Note that the figures above are lower if U.S.-born Asian, Indians, and Taiwanese are included.

ened among immigrants and their children. Political machines had embraced earlier immigrants and incorporated them into the system of "city trenches" by which American cities were governed; they excluded blacks from effective political power until cities had been so abandoned by industry and deserted by whites that resistance to black political participation no longer mattered. All the processes that had opened opportunities for immigrants and their children broke down for blacks. . . . (Katz, 1989:51)

Stereotyping and African Americans Despite the significance of prejudice against blacks in American history, large-scale survey research on racial prejudice has been pursued only since the beginning of the 1990s (Sniderman and Carmines, 1997). That research shows a mixed picture.

While prejudice has decreased significantly over the last decades, negative stereotypes about African Americans still prevail among whites across all educational levels. "With the exception of citizens who are uncommonly well educated and uncommonly liberal, what is striking is the sheer pervasiveness throughout contemporary American society of negative characterizations of blacks" (Sniderman and Piazza, 1993:50). When whites are asked to select adjectives that describe "most blacks," few pick positive ones. Seventy-five percent are willing to describe African Americans as "friendly," but only "50–60 percent are prepared to describe blacks as 'smart at everyday things,' 'good neighbors,' 'hard-working,' 'intelligent at school,' 'dependable,' 'law-abiding,' or 'determined to succeed'" (Sniderman and Carmines, 1997:62–63). For negative characterizations, 20 percent of whites describe blacks as "irresponsible" and 50 percent say blacks are "aggressive or violent" (Sniderman and Carmines, 1997).

However, when presented with real-life scenarios containing hidden tests of racial attitudes, whites who *said* they felt positively about African Americans appear to have actually *meant* it (Sniderman and Carmines, 1997). In addition, whites were less discriminatory when responding to scenarios about *individual* African Americans than they were when considering African Americans as a group.

> Claims for government assistance made on behalf of blacks as *individuals* are treated [by white survey respondents] as those made on behalf of individual whites, and indeed, insofar as race makes a difference, a black who has lost his or her job meets with a more sympathetic and generous response [in the survey] than a white who has lost his or her job. On the other hand, when it comes to judgments about what blacks as a group are entitled to, a racial double standard manifestly persists. . . .
>
> The evenhandedness characteristic of reactions to blacks as individuals is not characteristic of reactions to blacks as a group. We found significantly more support for government guarantees of equal opportunity for women than for blacks. (Sniderman and Piazza, 1993:13 and 169)

Well-educated whites did not operate from this double standard, but other whites—irrespective of their political orientation—did. "Thus, conservatives with a high school education or less are almost three times as likely to approve of government assurances of equal opportunity for women as for blacks—plainly a double standard. But the same is true on the left" (Sniderman and Piazza, 1993:83).

(Sniderman and Piazza argue that education lessens this double standard because it encourages consistency in thinking.) "Given this duality of response, it is easier to understand why whites see themselves as living in a world where the meaning of race has changed, while blacks see themselves as living in a world where its meaning has remained much the same" (Sniderman and Piazza, 1993:68).

Social Institutions and the Support of Ideologies

The specific messages carried by natural-law language and stereotypes are often echoed by the workings of social institutions. In the sections that follow, we will consider how late-19th-and early-20th-century science and popular culture constructed the meaning of race, class, sex, and sexual orientation differences. Throughout, there is a striking congruence among scientific pronouncements, popular culture messages, and the prejudices of the day.

Science The need to explain the meaning of human difference forcefully emerged with Europeans' 15th-century encounters with previously unknown regions and peoples. "Three centuries of exploration brought home as never before the tremendous diversity of human behavior and life patterns within environments and under circumstances dramatically different from those of Europe. . . . Out of that large laboratory of human experience was born the [idea of the] conflict between nature and nurture" (Degler, 1991:4–5).

The "nature-nurture" conflict offered two ways to explain human variation. Explanations from the nature side stressed that the diversity of human societies—and the ability of some to conquer and dominate others—reflected significant biological differences among populations. Explanations from the nurture side argued that human diversity resulted from historical, environmental, and cultural difference. From the nature side, humans were understood to act out behaviors that are biologically driven. From the nurture side, humans were something of a *tabula rasa,* a blank slate, on which particular cultural expectations were inscribed.

Whether nature or nurture was understood to dominate, however, the discussion of the meaning of human difference always assumed that people could be ranked as to their worth (Gould, 1981). Thus, the real question was whether the rankings reflected in social hierarchies were the result of nature, and thus inevitable and fixed, or could be affected by human action and were thus subject to social change.

The question was not merely theoretical. In the 1800s in America, the historical backdrop was the appropriation of Native American territories and the forced relocation of vast numbers of people beginning with the Indian Removal Act of 1830; the 1848 signing of the Treaty of Guadalupe Hidalgo ending the Mexican-American War and ceding what is now Texas, New Mexico, California, Utah, Nevada, and Arizona to the United States with the 75,000 Mexican nationals residing in those territories becoming U.S. citizens; passage of the Chinese Exclusion Act; a prolonged national debate about slavery and women's suffrage; the unprecedented immigration of poor and working-class people from Southern and Eastern Europe; and, at the close of the century, the internationally publicized trial of

English playwright Oscar Wilde, resulting in a sentence of two years' hard labor for homosexuality.

Thus, whether social hierarchy reflected natural, permanent, and inherent differences in capability (the nature side) or was the product of specific social and historical circumstances and therefore was susceptible to change (the nurture side) raised a profound question. Because Africans were held by whites in slavery, did that mean Africans were by their nature inferior to whites? Were Native Americans literally "savages" occupying some middle ground between animals and civilized humans, and did they therefore benefit from domination by those who supposedly were more advanced? Did the dissimilarity of Chinese immigrants from American whites mean they were not "human" in the way whites were? If homosexuality was congenital, did that mean homosexuals were profoundly different from heterosexuals? Were women closer to plants and animals than to civilized men, as some social scientists asserted (Degler, 1991:28)? Were the poor and working classes composed of those who not only lacked the talents by which to rise in society but also passed their defects on to their children? In all, were individuals and categories of people located in the statuses for which they were best suited? If one believed that the social order simply reflected immutable biological differences, the answer to the question would likely be affirmative. That would not have been the case, however, for those who believed these differences were the outcome of specific social and historical processes overlaying a shared humanity. In all, the question behind the nature-nurture debate was about the *meaning* of what appeared to be *natural* difference.

In this debate, Charles Darwin's publication of *The Origin of the Species* (1859) and *The Descent of Man* (1871) shifted the weight of popular and scholarly opinion toward the nature side of the equation (Degler, 1991). In its broadest terms, Darwin's conclusions challenged head on the two central beliefs of the time (Darwin himself was quite distressed to have arrived at these conclusions [Shipman, 1994]). First, the idea of evolutionary change challenged "traditional, Christian belief in a single episode of creation of a static, perfect, and unchanging world." The significance of evolutionary change was clear: "If the world were not created perfect, then there was no implicit justification for the way things were . . ." (Shipman, 1994:18).

Second, his work implied that all humans share a common ancestry. If differences among birds were the result of their adaptation to distinctive environments, then their differences existed within an overall framework of similarity and common ancestry. By analogy, the distinctiveness of human populations might also be understood as "variability within overall similarity" (Shipman, 1994:22)—a shocking possibility at the time. "It was the age of imperialism and most non-Europeans were regarded, even by Darwin, as 'barbarians'; he was astonished and taken aback by their wildness and animality. The differences among humans seemed so extreme that the humanity . . . of some living groups was scarcely credible" (Shipman, 1994:19).

The idea that change in the physical environment resulted in the success of some species and demise of others (the idea of natural selection) bolstered the pre-existent concept of "survival of the fittest." This phrase had been authored by English sociologist Herbert Spencer, who had been applying evolutionary principles to human societies several years before Darwin published *The Origin of the Species.*

Spencer's position, eventually called *social Darwinism,* was extremely popular in America. Spencer strongly believed that modern societies are inevitably improvements over earlier forms of social organization and that progress would necessarily follow from unimpeded competition for social resources. In all, social Darwinism argued that those who are more advanced naturally rise to the top of any stratification ladder.

Through social Darwinism, the prevailing hierarchies—slave owner over people held in slavery, white over Mexican and Native American, native-born over immigrant, upper-class over poor, male over female—could be attributed to natural processes and justified as a reflection of inherent differences among categories of people. As one sociologist at the turn of the century framed it, "under the tutelage of Darwinism the world returns again to the idea that *might* as evidence of fitness has something to do with *right*" (Degler, 1991:13).

Social Darwinism has since been discredited, since it attributes the supremacy of certain groups to biology and evolution rather than to the exercise of power within specific historical and economic contexts. Social Darwinism lacked a socially or historically grounded explanation for social stratification. Instead, it treated those hierarchies as a reflection of the biological merit of categories of people. Thus, social Darwinism was used to justify slavery, colonialism, immigration quotas, the criminalization of homosexuality, the forced relocation of Native Americans, and the legal subordination of women.

For example, social Darwinism justified keeping women subordinate. Spencer argued that the specialization of tasks, also called the *division of labor,* was the outcome of a biologically mandated evolution. The sexual division of labor "was a product of the organic law of progress," thus making equal treatment of men and women impossible and even potentially dangerous.

The social Darwinist position was used by those opposed to equal education for women. Just as American institutions of higher education yielded to the logic of the women's movement that women should have access to the same level of education as men—Vassar College was founded in 1865, Smith and Wellesley 10 years later, and by 1870 many state universities had become coeducational—biologist Edward Clarke published a book (1873) that argued that the physical energy education required would endanger women's reproductive abilities (an idea first put forward by Spencer). Clarke's case was based on meager and questionable empirical evidence, citing seven clinical cases, only one of which actually supported his position (Sayers, 1982:14). His work was a response to social rather than scientific developments, since it was prompted by no new discoveries in biology. Nonetheless, the book was an immediate and enduring success. For the next 30 years it was used in the argument against women's education despite the accumulation of evidence refuting its claims. While Clarke's research should have been suspect, it instead became influential in policymaking. In part, "the reason why Clarke's argument seemed so serviceable to those opposed to women's higher education was that it was couched in biological terms and thus appeared to offer a legitimate scientific basis for conservative opposition to equal education" (Sayers, 1982:11).

In a similar fashion, science shaped ideas about the meaning of same-sex relationships. By the turn of the century in Europe, a gay rights movement had arisen in Germany and gay themes had emerged in French literature (Adam, 1987). At the same time, however, an international move to criminalize sexual relations between men gathered momentum: a revision of the German criminal code increased the penalties for male homosexuality, the British imprisoned Oscar Wilde, and Europe and the United States experienced a social reform movement directed against prostitution and male homosexuality. (The possibility of sexual relations between women was not considered until later.)

The move to criminalize homosexuality was countered by physicians arguing, from a social Darwinist position, that homosexuality is the product of "hereditary weakness" and is thus beyond individual control. Though their hope was for increased tolerance, scientists who took this position offered the idea of "homosexuality as a medical entity and the homosexual as a distinctive kind of person" (Conrad and Schneider, 1980:184). Thus, they contributed to the idea that heterosexual and homosexual people were profoundly different from each other.

Science also supported the argument that people of different skin colors are different in significant, immutable ways. Certainly Spencer's idea of the survival of the fittest was understood to support the belief that whites are superior to all people of color: "The most prevalent form of social Darwinism at the turn of the century was actually racism, that is, the idea that one people might be superior to another because of differences in their biological nature" (Degler, 1991:15).

The scientific defense of American slavery first emerged with the work of two eminent scientists, Swiss naturalist Louis Agassiz and Philadelphia physician Samuel Morton. Agassiz immigrated to America in 1840 and became a professor at Harvard. There he garnered immense popularity by countering the biblically based theory of the unity of all people (which attributed racial differences to "degeneration" from a shared origin) with a "scientific" theory that different races had descended from different moments of creation—"different Adams" as it was called (Gould, 1981:39).

Morton tested Agassiz's theories by weighing the amount of metal shot that could be fit into skulls from people of different races. His idea was that the size of the skull would correlate with the intelligence of the race. His results "matched every good Yankee's prejudices—whites on top, Indians in the middle, and blacks on the bottom; and among whites, Teutons and Anglo-Saxons on top, Jews in the middle, and Hindus on the bottom" (Gould, 1981:53).

As we now know, Morton's findings were simply wrong. Others who replicated his measurements did not arrive at the same conclusions about skull capacity: There were "*no* significant differences among races for Morton's own data" (Gould, 1981:67). Morton's research was inadequate even to the less rigorous scientific standards of his time. There is no evidence that Morton intended to deceive. Rather, his assumptions of white superiority were so firm that he was oblivious to his own errors and illogic, errors that yielded the conclusion of white superiority only because of his miscalculations.

The use of questionable research to support prevailing beliefs (Gould, 1981) was also evident in the development of intelligence testing. In 1904, Alfred Binet, director of the psychology lab at the Sorbonne, was commissioned by the French minister of public education to develop a test to identify children whose poor performance in school might indicate a need for special education. Binet developed a test with a series of tasks that children of "normal" intelligence were expected to have mastered. Binet's own claims for the test were fairly limited. He did not equate intelligence with the score produced by his test, arguing that intelligence was too complex a factor to be reduced to a simple number. Nor did he construe his test as measuring inborn, permanent, or inherited limitations (Gould, 1981).

Binet's hesitations regarding the significance of the test, however, were ignored by the emerging field of American psychology, which used intelligence as a way to explain social hierarchies. "The people who are doing the drudgery are, as a rule, in their proper places," wrote H. H. Goddard, who introduced the Binet test to America. Stanford psychologist Lewis M. Termin (author of the Stanford-Binet IQ test) argued that "the children of successful and cultured parents test higher than children from wretched and ignorant homes for the simple reason that their heredity is better" (Degler, 1991:50). Indeed, "Terman believed that class boundaries had been set by innate intelligence" (Gould, 1981:183). In all, systems of stratification were defended by social science as simply reflecting the distribution of ability.

Such conclusions were used to shape decisions about the distribution of resources. For example, intelligence was described as a capacity like the capacity of a jug for a certain amount of milk. A pint jug could not be expected to hold a quart of milk; similarly, it was pointless to waste "too much" education on someone whose capacity was supposedly limited. The findings of intelligence testers were thus used to advocate particular social policies such as restrictions on immigration. While it is not clear that the work of intelligence testers *directly* affected the Immigration Restriction Act of 1924 (Degler, 1991), the ultimate shape of the legislation limited immigration from Southern and Eastern Europe, which was consistent with intelligence testers' claims about the relative intelligence of the "races" in Europe. These quotas barred the admission of European Jews fleeing the impending holocaust (Gould, 1981).

Still, by about 1930 a considerable body of research showed that social environment more than biology accounts for differing IQ scores and that the tests themselves measured not innate intelligence but familiarity with the culture of those who wrote the tests. In the end, the psychologists who had promoted intelligence testing were forced to repudiate the idea that intelligence is inherited or that it can be separated from cultural knowledge.[2]

---

[2]"...There is also a lot of evidence for the whole American population, for American ethnic groups, and for populations wherever tests are given that IQ is changing in ways that can't possibly be genetic because they happen too fast. It is widely recognized that average IQs are increasing fairly rapidly. These changes in IQ clearly must have more to say about relationships between testing and real performance, or about social patterns of learning, than about biologically rooted 'intelligence.' The genes of a large population don't change that fast unless there is a very dramatic episode of natural selection such as an epidemic. It is also widely recognized that African Americans are slowly but steadily gaining on white Americans in IQ" (Cohen, 1998:210).

Whether measuring cranial capacity, developing paper-and-pencil intelligence tests, positing the effect of education on women, or arguing for hereditary weakness as an explanation of homosexuality, the work of these scientists supported the prevailing ideologies about the merit and appropriate social location of people of different sexes, races, ethnic groups, sexual orientations, and social classes. Most of these scientists do not appear to have been ideologically motivated; indeed they were sometimes troubled by their own findings. Still, their research was riddled with technical errors and questionable findings. Their research proved "the surprising malleability of 'objective,' quantitative data in the interest of a preconceived idea" (Gould, 1981:147). Precisely because their research confirmed prevailing beliefs, it was more likely to be celebrated than scrutinized.

Why were these findings eventually repudiated? Since they offered a defense of the status quo and confirmed the prevailing ideology, who would have criticized them?

First, the scientific defense of immutable hierarchy was eroded by the steady accumulation of evidence about the "intellectual equality and therefore the equal cultural capacity of all peoples" (Degler, 1991:61). A good deal of the research that made that point was produced by the many "prominent or soon to be prominent" scholars of African American, Chinese, and European immigrant ancestry who, after finally being admitted to institutions of higher education, were pursuing scientific research. Black scholars such as W.E.B. Du Bois and E. Franklin Frazier, and those of recent European immigrant ancestry such as anthropologists Franz Boas, Alfred Kroeber, and Edward Sapir, trenchantly criticized the social science of the day and by their very presence challenged the prevailing expectations about the "inherent inferiority" of people like themselves (Degler, 1991).

The presumptions about the meaning of race were also challenged by increased interracial contact. The 1920s began the Great Migration, in which hundreds of thousands of African Americans from the rural South moved to northern cities. This movement continued through two world wars as black, Latino, Asian, and Native American men joined the armed forces and women followed wartime employment opportunities. The 1920s also brought the Harlem Renaissance, an outpouring of creativity from black writers, scholars, and artists in celebration of African and African American culture. Overall, white social scientists "gained an unprecedented opportunity to observe blacks in a fresh and often transforming way" (Degler, 1991:197). Their attitudes and expectations changed as a result of this increased contact.

In sum, the scientific argument for the inherent inferiority of some groups of people was advanced by upper-class, native-born, white male faculty of prestigious universities. Few others would have had the means with which to disseminate their ideas or the prestige to make those ideas influential. These theories of essential difference were not written by Native Americans, Mexicans, women, gays, African Americans, or immigrants from Asia or Southern and Eastern Europe. Most of these people lacked access to the public forums by which to make their experience known until the rise of the antislavery, suffrage, labor, and gay rights movements. Insofar as the people in these categories could be silenced, it was easier to depict them as essentially and profoundly different.

Popular Culture Like the sciences, popular culture (the forms of entertainment available for mass consumption such as popular music, theater, film, literature, and television) may convey ideologies about difference and social stratification. At virtually the same time that social Darwinism gained popularity in America—indeed within two years of Louis Agassiz's arrival in the States—America's first minstrel show was organized. Like social Darwinism, minstrel shows offered a defense of slavery.

Minstrel shows, which became an enormously popular form of entertainment, were musical variety shows in which white males in "blackface" ridiculed blacks, abolitionism, and women's suffrage. Their impact can be seen in the movies and cartoons of the 1930s and 1940s and in current American stereotypes. The shows built on strongly negative stereotypes about blacks. As they traveled the country, their images were impressed on whites who themselves had no direct contact with blacks and thus no information by which to counter the minstrel images.

The three primary characters of the minstrel show were the happy slave, Zip Coon, and the mammy (Riggs, 1987). The image of the happy slave—singing and dancing, naive and childlike, taken care of through old age by the master, a virtual member of the family—asserted that blacks held in slavery were both content and cared for. Zip Coon was a northern, free black man characterized by a ridiculous use of language and laughable attempts to emulate whites; the caricature was used to show that blacks lacked the intelligence to handle freedom. The mammy was depicted as a large and presumably unattractive black woman fully devoted to the white family she served. Like the happy slave, the mammy was unthreatening and content—no sexual competition to the white mistress of the house, no children of her own needing attention, committed to and fulfilled by her work with her white family. Thus, the characters of the minstrel show hid the reality of slavery. The happy slave and mammy denied the brutality of the slave system. Zip Coon denied the reality of blacks' organization of the underground railroad, their production of slave narratives in books and lectures, and their undertaking of slave rebellions and escapes.

In all, minstrel shows offered an ideology about slavery constructed by and in the interests of those with power. They ridiculed antislavery activists and legitimatized the status quo. Minstrel shows asserted that blacks did not mind being held as slaves and that they did not suffer loss and pain in the same way whites did. The minstrel show was not the only source of this ideology, but as a form of popular entertainment it was a very effective means of disseminating such beliefs. The shows traveled to all parts of the country, their message masked as mere entertainment. The fact that they were part of popular culture made it easier to ignore their serious message—after all, they were "just" entertainment.

But within popular culture, an effective counter to the ideology of the minstrel show emerged in the speakers of the antislavery lecture circuit and in the publication of numerous slave narratives. Appearing as early as 1760, these narratives achieved an enormous and enduring popularity among northern white readers. Frederick Douglass, former slave and the renowned antislavery activist, was the most famous public lecturer in the history of the movement and wrote its best-selling slave narrative. Whether as book or lecture, slave narratives provided an image of blacks as human beings. Access to these life histories provided the first opportunity for most whites to see a shared humanity between themselves and those held in slavery (Bodziock, 1990). Thus, slave narratives directly countered the images of the minstrel show. While popular culture may offer a variety of messages, all parties do not meet equally on its terrain. Those with power have better access and more legitimacy, but popular culture cannot be so tightly controlled as to entirely exclude the voice of the less powerful.

Conclusion

As Karl Marx first considered it, ideology was "the mechanism whereby there can occur a difference between how things really are in the economy and the wider society and how people think they are" (Marshall, 1994:234). In this framework essay, we have examined how science and popular culture sometimes support the pervasive ideologies about the meanings of color, class, sexual orientation, and sex. The readings that follow focus on law and politics, the economy, science, and popular culture as social institutions that interpret and construct what difference means.

REFERENCES

Adam, Barry D. 1987. *The Rise of a Gay and Lesbian Movement.* Boston: G. K. Hall & Co.

Andre, Judith. 1988. Stereotypes: Conceptual and Normative Considerations. *Racism and Sexism: An Integrated Study.* Ed. Paula S. Rothenberg, 257–62. New York: St. Martin's Press.

Bodziock, Joseph. 1990. The Weight of Sambo's Woes. *Perspectives on Black Popular Culture.* Ed. Harry B. Shaw, 166–79. Bowling Green, OH: Bowling Green State University Popular Press.

Brantlinger, Patrick. 1990. *Crusoe's Footprints: Cultural Studies in Britain and America.* New York: Routledge.

Cherry, Robert. 1989. *Discrimination: Its Economic Impact on Blacks, Women, and Jews.* Lexington, MA: Lexington Books.

Cohen, Mark Nathan. 1998. *Culture of Intolerance: Chauvinism, Class, and Race in the United States.* New Haven, CT: Yale University Press.

Conrad, Peter, and Joseph W. Schneider. 1980. *Deviance and Medicalization.* Philadelphia: Temple University Press.

Degler, Carl N. 1991. *In Search of Human Nature: The Decline and Revival of Darwinism in American Social Thought.* New York: Oxford University Press.

Garber, Marjorie. 1992. *Vested Interests: Cross Dressing and Cultural Anxiety.* New York: Harper.

Gould, Stephen Jay. 1981. *The Mismeasure of Man.* New York: W. W. Norton.

Haines, David W. 1989. *Refugees as Immigrants.* Totowa, NJ: Rowman and Littlefield.

Kasper, Anne. 1986. Consciousness Re-evaluated: Interpretive Theory and Feminist Scholarship. *Sociological Inquiry* 56(1).

Katz, Michael B. 1989. *The Undeserving Poor.* New York: Pantheon Books.

Marshall, Gordon. 1994. *The Concise Oxford Dictionary of Sociology.* Oxford, UK: Oxford University Press.

Omi, Michael, and Howard Winant. 1994. *Racial Formation in the United States.* New York: Routledge.

Pierce, Christine. 1971. Natural Law Language and Women. *Woman in Sexist Society.* Ed. Vivian Gornick and Barbara K. Moran, 242–58. New York: New American Library.

Portes, Alejandro, and Ruben G. Rumbaut. 1990. *Immigrant America: A Portrait.* Berkeley, CA: University of California Press.

Riggs, Marlon. 1987. *Ethnic Notions.* California Newsreel (video).

Sayers, Janet. 1982. *Biological Politics: Feminist and Anti-feminist Perspectives.* London: Tavistock Publications.

Shipman, Pat. 1994. *The Evolution of Racism: Human Differences and the Use and Abuse of Science.* New York: Simon and Schuster.

Smith, Dorothy. 1978. A Peculiar Eclipsing: Women's Exclusion from Men's Culture. *Women's Studies International Quarterly* 1:281–95.

——. 1990. *The Conceptual Practices of Power: A Feminist Sociology of Knowledge.* Boston: Northeastern University Press.

Sniderman, Paul M., and Thomas Piazza. 1993. *The Scar of Race.* Cambridge, MA: Harvard University Press.

——, and Edward G. Carmines. 1997. *Reaching Beyond Race.* Cambridge, MA: Harvard University Press.

Steinberg, Steven. 1989. *The Ethnic Myth: Race, Ethnicity, and Class in America.* Boston: Beacon Press.

Takaki, Ronald. 1993. *A Different Mirror: A History of Multicultural America.* Boston: Little, Brown.

Law, Politics, and Policy

READING 31

Twelve Key Supreme Court Cases

Individuals' lives are affected not only by social practices but also by law as interpreted in the courts. Under U.S. federalism Congress makes laws, the president swears to uphold the law, and the Supreme Court interprets the law. When state laws appear to be in conflict with the United States Constitution or when the terminology of the Constitution is vague, the Supreme Court interprets such laws. We will focus here on Supreme Court rulings that have defined the roles individuals are allowed to assume in American society.

As the supreme law above laws enacted by Congress, the U.S. Constitution determines individual and group status. A brief document, the Constitution describes the division of power between the federal and state governments, as well as the rights of individuals. Only 16 amendments to the Constitution have been added since the ratification of the Bill of Rights (the first ten amendments). Although the Constitution appears to be sweeping in scope—relying on the principle that all men are created equal—in reality the Constitution is an exclusionary document. It omitted women, Native Americans, and African Americans except for the purpose of determining a population count. In instances where the Constitution was vague on the rights of each of these groups, clarification was later sought through court cases.

Federalism provides four primary methods by which citizens may influence the political process. First, the Constitution grants citizens the right to petition the government, that is, the right to lobby. Second, as a civic duty, citizens are expected to vote and seek office. Once in office citizens can change conditions by writing new legislation, known as *statutory law.* Third, changes can be achieved through the lengthy procedure of passing constitutional amendments, which affect all citizens. Controversial amendments have often become law after social movement activists advocated passage for several years or after a major national upheaval, such as the Civil War.

Last, the Constitution provides that citizens can sue to settle disputes. Through this method, sweeping social changes can take place when Supreme Court decisions affect all the individuals in a class. Thus, the assertion of individual rights has become a key tool of those who were not privileged by the Constitution to clarify their status in American society.

An examination of landmark cases reveals the continuous difficulties some groups have had in securing their rights through legal remedy. The Court has often taken a narrow perspective on what classes of people were to receive equal protection of the law, or were covered under the privileges and immunities clause.[1] Each group had to bring suit in every area where barriers existed. For example, white women who were citizens had to sue to establish that they had the right to inherit property, to serve on juries, to enter various professions, and in general to be treated as a class apart from their husband and family. Blacks sued to attend southern state universities and law schools, to participate in the all-white Democratic Party primary election,[2] to attend public schools which had been ordered to desegregate by the Supreme Court, and to vote without having to pay a poll tax. When these landmark cases were decided, they were perceived to herald sweeping changes in policy. Yet they proved to be only a guide to determining the rights of individuals.

I. *DRED SCOTT V. SANFORD* (1857)

Prior to the Civil War the Constitution was not precise on whether one was simultaneously a citizen of a given state and of the entire United

States. Slavery further complicated the matter because the status of slaves and free persons of color was not specified in the Constitution, nor were members of either group considered citizens. Each state had the option of determining the status and rights of these nonwhites.

A federal form of government permitted flexibility by allowing states to differ on matters such as rights for its citizens. Yet as a newly invented form of government, a number of issues that were clear under British law were not settled until the Thirteenth, Fourteenth, and Fifteenth Amendments were added to the United States Constitution. Federalism raised questions about rights and privileges because a citizen was simultaneously living under the laws of a state and of the United States. Who had rights and privileges guaranteed by the Constitution? Did all citizens have all rights and privileges?

For example, what was the status of women? The Constitution provided for citizenship, but did not specify which rights and privileges were granted to female citizens. State laws considered white men and white women citizens, yet white women were often not allowed to own property, sue in court, or vote. Under federalism, each state enacted laws determining the rights and status of free blacks, slaves, white men, and white women so long as the laws did not conflict with the United States Constitution.

The *Dred Scott* case of 1846 considered the issues of slavery, property, citizenship, and the supremacy of the United States over individual states when a slave was taken to a free territory. The Court's holding primarily affected blacks, now called African Americans,[3] who sought the benefits of citizenship. Broadly, the case addressed American citizenship, a matter not clearly defined until passage of the Fourteenth Amendment in 1868.

Dred Scott was an enslaved man owned by Dr. John Emerson, a U.S. Army surgeon stationed in Missouri. When Emerson was transferred to Rock Island, Illinois, where slavery was forbidden, he took Dred Scott with him. Emerson was subsequently transferred to Fort Snelling, a territory (now Minnesota) where slavery was forbidden by the Missouri Compromise of 1820. In 1838, he returned to Missouri with Dred Scott.

In 1846 Scott brought suit in a Missouri circuit court to obtain his freedom on the grounds he had resided in free territory for periods of time. Scott won the case and his freedom. However, the judgment was reversed by the Missouri Supreme Court. Later, when John Sanford, a citizen of New York and the brother of Mrs. Emerson, arranged for the sale of Scott, the grounds were established for Scott to take his case to the federal circuit court in Missouri. The federal court ruled that Scott and his family were slaves and therefore the "lawful property" of Sanford. With the financial assistance of abolitionists, Scott appealed his case to the Supreme Court.

The Court's decision addressed these key questions:

1. Are blacks citizens?
2. Are blacks entitled to sue in court?
3. Can one have all the privileges and immunities of citizenship in a state, but not the United States?
4. Can one be a citizen of the United States and not be qualified to vote or hold office?

Excerpts from the Supreme Court Decision in *Dred Scott v. Sanford*[4]

Mr. Chief Justice Taney delivered the opinion of the Court:

. . . The question is simply this: Can a Negro, whose ancestors were imported into this country and sold as slaves, become a member of the political community formed and brought into existence by the Constitution of the United States, and as such become entitled to all the rights, and privileges and immunities, guaranteed by that instrument to the citizen? One of which rights is the privilege of suing in a court of the United States. . . .

The question before us is whether the class of persons described are constituent members of this sovereignty? We think they are not, and that they are not included, and were not intended to be included, under the word "citizens" in the Constitution, and can therefore claim none of the rights and privileges which that instrument provides for and secures to citizens of the United States.

In discussing this question, we must not confound the rights of citizenship which a State may confer within its own limits and the rights of citizenship as a member of the Union. It does not by any means follow, because he has all the rights and privileges of a citizen of a State, that he must be a citizen of the United States. He may have all of the rights and privileges of a citizen of a State, and yet not be entitled to the rights and privileges of a citizen in any other State. . . .

Undoubtedly a person may be a citizen . . . although he exercises no share of the political power, and is incapacitated from holding particular office. Those who have not the necessary qualifications cannot vote or hold the office, yet they are citizens.

The court is of the opinion, that . . . Dred Scott was not a citizen of Missouri within the meaning of the Constitution of the United States, and not entitled as such to sue in its courts: and, consequently, that the Circuit Court had no jurisdiction. . . .

II. THE CIVIL WAR AMENDMENTS

The Civil War (1861–1865) was fought over slavery, as well as the issue of supremacy of the national government over the individual states.

After the Civil War, members of Congress known as the Radical Republicans sought to protect the freedom of the former slaves by passing the Thirteenth, Fourteenth, and Fifteenth Amendments. These amendments, especially the Fourteenth, have provided the foundation for African Americans, as well as women, gays, Native Americans, immigrants, and those who are disabled to bring suit for equal treatment under the law.

Amendment XIII, 1865

(Slavery)

This amendment prohibited slavery and involuntary servitude in the United States. The entire amendment follows:

Section 1. Neither slavery nor involuntary servitude, except as a punishment whereof the party shall have been duly convicted, shall exist within the United States, or any place subject to their jurisdiction.

Section 2. Congress shall have power to enforce this article by appropriate legislation.

Amendment XIV, 1868

(Citizenship, Due Process, and Equal Protection of the Laws)

This amendment defined citizenship; prohibited the states from making or enforcing laws that abridged the privileges or immunities of citizenship; forbade states to deprive persons of life, liberty, or property without due process of law; and forbade states to deny equal protection of the law to any person. Over time the Fourteenth Amendment became the most important of the Reconstruction amendments. Key phrases such as "privileges and immunities," "deprive any person of life, liberty, or the pursuit of justice," and "deny to any person within its jurisdiction equal protection of the law" have caused this amendment to be the subject of more Supreme Court cases than any other provision of the Constitution. The entire amendment follows:

Section 1. All persons born or naturalized in the United States, and subject to the jurisdiction thereof, are citizens of the United States and of the State wherein they reside. No State shall make or enforce any law which shall abridge the privileges or immunities of citizens of the United States; nor shall any State deprive any person of life, liberty, or property, without due process of law; nor deny to any person within its jurisdiction the equal protection of the laws.

Section 2. Representatives shall be apportioned among the several States according to their respective numbers, counting the whole number of persons in each State, excluding Indians not taxed. But when the right to vote at any election for the choice of electors for President and Vice President of the United States, Representatives in Congress, the Executive and Judicial officers of a State, or the members of the Legislature thereof, is denied to any of the male inhabitants of such State, being twenty-one years of age, and citizens of the United States, or in any way abridged, except for participation in rebellion, or other crime, the basis of representation therein shall be reduced in proportion which the number of such male citizens shall bear to the whole number of male citizens twenty-one years of age in such State.

Section 3. No person shall be a Senator or Representative in Congress, or elector or President and Vice President, or hold any office, civil or military, under the United States, or under any State, who, having previously taken an oath, as a member of Congress, or as an officer of the United States, or as a member of any State legislature, or as an executive or judicial officer of any State, to support the Constitution of the United States, shall have engaged in insurrection or rebellion against the same, or given aid or comfort to the enemies thereof. But Congress may by a vote of two-thirds of each House, remove such disability.

Section 4. The validity of the public debt of the United States, authorized by law, including debts incurred for payments of pensions and bounties for services in suppressing insurrection or rebellion, shall not be questioned. But neither the United States nor any State shall assume or pay any debt or obligation incurred in aid of insurrection or rebellion against the United States, or any claim for the loss or emancipation of any slave, but all such debts, obligations and claims shall be held illegal and void.

Section 5. The Congress shall have power to enforce, by appropriate legislation, the provisions of this article.

Amendment XV, 1870

(The Right to Vote)

The entire amendment follows:

Section 1. The right of citizens of the United States to vote shall not be denied or abridged by the United States or by any State on account of race, color, or previous condition of servitude.

Section 2. The Congress shall have power to enforce this article by appropriate legislation.

As we have seen, the Thirteenth, Fourteenth, and Fifteenth Amendments were added to the Constitution expressly with former slaves in mind. In Section 1 of the Fourteenth Amendment, the definition of *citizenship* was clarified and granted to blacks. In the Fifteenth Amendment black males, former slaves, were granted the right to vote. For women, however, the situation was different.

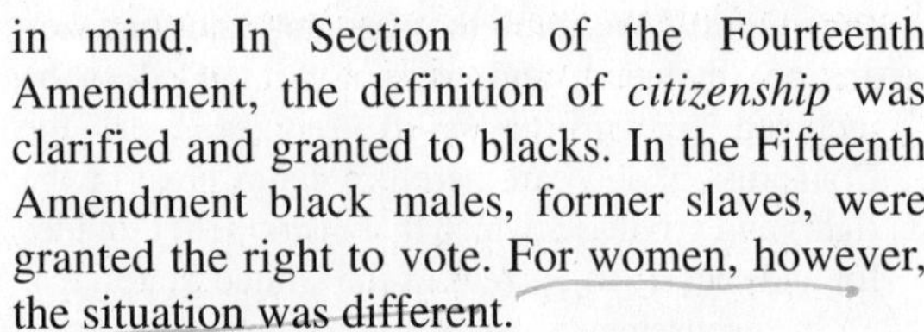

During the 19th century there was no doubt that white females were U.S. citizens, but their rights as citizens were unclear. For example, although they were citizens, women were not automatically enfranchised. Depending on state laws, they were barred from owning property, holding office, or voting. The 1872 case of *Bradwell v. The State of Illinois* specifically tested whether women as United States citizens had the right to become members of the bar. More generally, it addressed whether the rights of female citizens included the right to pursue any employment.

III. *BRADWELL V. THE STATE OF ILLINOIS* (1872)

Mrs. Myra Bradwell applied to the Supreme Court of Illinois for a license to practice law. Her petition included certification that she was of good character and met other qualifications through examination. She also filed an affidavit stating that she was a U.S. citizen who was born in Vermont, although she was currently residing in Chicago, Illinois. She petitioned the court for a license under the Fourteenth Amendment.

The Court's decision addressed these key questions:

1. Is Bradwell a citizen?
2. Is the right to practice law a privilege or an immunity of a U.S. citizen?
3. Can a married woman practice law?
4. Did the legislators of Illinois intend to exclude females from the practice of law?
5. What is the proper role and status of women?

This case hinges on an interpretation of the "privileges and immunities" clause (Section 1) of the Fourteenth Amendment, which was defined over time through cases that came to the

Supreme Court. (Specific privileges and immunities are not enumerated in the Constitution.) Justice Bradley's opinion is of particular importance because it goes beyond a review of the scope of the Fourteenth Amendment, analyzing which privileges and immunities Bradwell possessed or lacked as a woman.

Excerpts From the Supreme Court Decision in *Bradwell v. The State of Illinois*[5]

Mr. Justice Miller delivered the opinion of the Court:

> We agree with him [Bradwell's counsel] that there are privileges and immunities belonging to citizens of the United States. . . . But the right to admission to practice in the courts of a State is not one of them. This right in no sense depends on citizenship of the United States. . . .
>
> The right to control and regulate the granting of a license to practice law in the courts of a State is one of those powers which are not transferred for its protection to the Federal government, or controlled by citizenship of the United States. . . .

Mr. Justice Bradley:

> . . . The civil law, as well as nature herself, has always recognized a wide difference in the respective spheres and destinies of man and woman. Man is, or should be, woman's protector and defender. The natural and proper timidity and delicacy which belongs to the female sex is evidently unfit for many of the occupations of civil life. The constitution of the family organization, which is founded in the divine ordinance, as well as in the nature of things, indicates the domestic sphere as that which properly belongs to the domain and functions of womanhood. The harmony, not to say identity, of interests and views which belong, should belong, to the family institution is repugnant to the idea of a woman adopting a distinct and independent career from that of her husband. So firmly fixed was this sentiment in the founders of the common law that it became a maxim of that system of jurisprudence that a woman had no legal existence separate from her husband, who was regarded as her head and representative in the social state. . . . Many of the special rules of law flowing from and dependent upon this cardinal principle still exist in full force in most States. One of these is, that a married woman is incapable, without her husband's consent, of making contracts which shall be binding on her or him. This very incapacity was one circumstance which the Supreme Court of Illinois deemed important in rendering a married woman incompetent fully to perform the duties and trusts that belong to the office of attorney and counsellor.
>
> . . . The paramount destiny and mission of women are to fulfill the noble and benign offices of wife and mother. This is the law of the Creator.
>
> . . . I am not prepared to say that it is one of her fundamental rights and privileges to be admitted into every office and position, including those which require highly special qualifications and demanding special responsibilities. In the nature of things it is not every citizen of every age, sex, and condition that is qualified for every calling and position. It is the prerogative of the legislator to prescribe regulations founded on nature, reason, and experience for the due admission of qualified persons to professions and callings demanding special skill and confidence. This fairly belongs to the police power of the State. . . . It is within the province of the legislature to ordain what offices, positions, and callings shall be filled and discharged by men. . . .

IV. *MINOR V. HAPPERSETT* (1875)

The Fifteenth Amendment was not viewed as a triumph for women because it specifically denied them the vote. Section 2 of the Fourteenth Amendment for the first time made reference to males as citizens. Since black men were included but women of all races were omitted, women were left to continue to seek changes through the courts. This was a difficult route because in subsequent cases, judges often held a narrow view that the legislators wrote the amendment only with black males in mind. Thus, a pattern was soon established in which white women followed black men and women in asserting their rights as citizens as seen in the 1875 case of *Minor v. Happersett.* In *Dred Scott* the question was whether Scott was a citizen; in *Minor* the question was whether *Minor* as a citizen had the right to vote. In both cases the Supreme Court said no.

Virginia Minor, a native-born, free, white citizen of the United States and the state of Missouri, and over the age of 21 wished to vote for president, vice president, and members of Congress in the election of November 1872. She applied to the registrar of voters but was not allowed to vote because she was not a "male citizen of the United States." As a citizen of the United States, Minor sued under the privileges and immunities clause of the Fourteenth Amendment.

The Court's decision addressed these key questions:

1. Who is covered under the term *citizen?*
2. Is suffrage one of the privileges and immunities of citizenship?
3. Did the Constitution, as originally written, make all citizens voters?
4. Did the Fifteenth Amendment make all citizens voters?
5. Can a state confine voting to only male citizens without violating the Constitution?

While women were citizens of the United States and the state where they resided, they did not automatically possess all the privileges granted to male citizens, such as suffrage. This landmark case was not overturned until the passage of the Nineteenth Amendment, which enfranchised women, in 1920.[6]

Excerpts from the Supreme Court Decision in *Minor v. Happersett*[7]

Mr. Chief Justice Waite delivered the opinion of the Court:

> . . . It is contended [by Minor's counsel] that the provisions of the Constitution and laws of the State of Missouri which confine the right of suffrage and registration therefore to men, are in violation of the Constitution of the United States, and therefore void. The argument is, that as a woman, born or naturalized in the United States is a citizen of the United States and of the State in which she resides, she has the right of suffrage as one of the privileges and immunities of her citizenship, which the State cannot by its laws or Constitution abridge.
>
> There is no doubt that women may be citizens. . . .
>
> . . . From this it is apparent that from the commencement of the legislation upon this subject alien women and alien minors could be made citizens by naturalization, and we think it will not be contended that native women and native minors were already citizens by birth.
>
> . . . More cannot be necessary to establish the fact that sex has never been made one of the elements of citizenship in the United States. In this respect men have never had an advantage over women. The same laws precisely apply to both. The Fourteenth amendment did not affect the citizenship of women any more than it did of men . . . therefore, the rights of Mrs. Minor do not depend upon the amendment. She has always been a citizen from her birth, and entitled to all the privileges and immunities of citizenship. The amendment prohibited the State, of which she is a citizen, from abridging any of her privileges and immunities as a citizen of the United States.
>
> . . . The direct question is, therefore, presented whether all citizens are necessarily voters.
>
> The Constitution does not define the privileges and immunities of citizens. For that definition we must look elsewhere.
>
> . . . The [Fourteenth] amendment did not add to the privileges and immunities of a citizen. It simply furnished an additional guarantee for the protection of such as he already had. No new voters were necessarily made by it.
>
> . . . No new State has ever been admitted to the Union which has conferred the right of suffrage upon women, and this has never been considered a valid objection to her admission.
>
> . . . Certainly, if the courts can consider any question settled, this is one. For nearly ninety years the people have acted upon the idea that the Constitution, when it conferred citizenship, did not necessarily confer the right of suffrage. . . . Our province is to decide what the law is, not to declare what it should be.

The *Dred Scott, Bradwell,* and *Minor* cases point to the similarity in the status of black men and women of all races in 19th-century America. As one judicial scholar noted, race and sex were comparable classes, distinct from all others. Historically, these "natural classes" were considered permanent and unchangeable.[8] Thus, both slavery and the subjugation of women have been described as a caste system where one's status is fixed from birth and not alterable based on wealth or talent.[9]

Indeed, the connection between the enslavement of black people and the legal and social standing of women was often traced to the Old Testament. Historically slavery was justified on the grounds that one should look to Abraham; the Bible refers to Abraham's wives, children, men servants, maid servants, camels, and cattle as his property. A man's wife and children were considered his slaves. By the logic of the 19th century, if women were slaves, why shouldn't blacks be also?

Thus, the concepts of race and sex have been historically linked. Since "the doctrines were developed by the same people for the same purpose it is not surprising to find anti-feminism to be an echo of racism, and vice versa."[10]

Additional constitutional amendments were necessary for women and African Americans to exercise the privileges of citizenship that were automatically granted to white males. Nonetheless, even after amendments were enacted, African Americans still had to fight for enforcement of the law.

V. *PLESSY V. FERGUSON* (1896)

After the Civil War the northern victors imposed military rule on the South.[11] White landowners and former slave holders often found themselves with unproductive farmland and no free laborers. Aside from the economic loss of power, white males were in a totally new political environment: Black men had been elevated to citizens; former slaves were now eligible to vote, run for office, and hold seats in the state or national legislature. To ensure the rights of former slaves, the U.S. Congress passed the Civil War Amendments and provided federal troops to oversee federal elections.

However, when federal troops were withdrawn from the southern states in 1877, enfranchised black men became vulnerable to former masters who immediately seized political control of the state legislatures. In order to solidify political power, whites rewrote state constitutions to disenfranchise black men. To ensure that all blacks were restricted to a subordinate status, southern states systematically enacted "Jim Crow" laws, rigidly segregating society into black and white communities. These laws barred blacks from using the same public facilities as whites, including schools, hospitals, restaurants, hotels, and recreation areas. With the cooperation of southern elected officials, the Ku Klux Klan, a white supremacist, terrorist organization, grew in membership. The return of political power to whites without any federal presence to protect the black community set the stage for "separate but equal" legislation to become a constitutionally valid racial doctrine.

Under slavery, interracial sexual contact was forbidden but white masters nonetheless had the power to sexually exploit the black women who worked for them. The children of these relationships, especially if they looked white, posed potential inheritance problems because whites feared that such children might seek to exercise the privileges accorded to their white fathers. In order to keep all children of such relationships subordinate in the two-tiered racial system, descent was based on the race of the mother. Consequently, regardless of color, all the children of black women were defined as black.

This resulted in a rigid biracial structure where all persons with "one drop" of black blood were labeled black. Consequently, the "black" community consisted of a wide range of skin color based on this one-drop rule. Therefore, at times individuals with known black ancestry might look phenotypically white. This situation created a group of African Americans who had one-eighth or less African ancestry.

Louisiana was one of the few states to modify the one-drop rule of racial categorization because it considered mulattoes a valid racial category. A term derived from Spanish, *mulatto* refers to the offspring of a "pure African Negro" and a "pure white." Over time, *mulatto* came to encompass children of whites and "mixed Negroes."

These were the social conditions in 1896, when Homer Adolph Plessy, a mulatto, sought to test Louisiana laws that imposed racial segregation. Plessy and other mulattoes decided to test the applicability of the law requiring racial separation on railroad cars traveling in interstate transportation.

In 1890, Louisiana had followed other southern states in enacting Jim Crow laws that were written in compliance with the Equal Protection Clause of Section 1 of the Fourteenth Amendment. These laws required separate accommodations for white and black railroad passengers. In this case, Plessy, a U.S. citizen and a resident of Louisiana who was one-eighth black, paid for a first-class ticket on the East Louisiana Railway traveling from New Orleans to Covington, Louisiana. When he entered the passenger train, Plessy took a vacant seat in a coach designated for white passengers. He claimed that he was entitled to every "recognition, right, privilege, and immunity" granted to white citizens of the United States by the Constitution. Under Louisiana law, the conductor, who knew Plessy, was required to ask him to sit in a coach specifically assigned to nonwhite persons. By law, passengers who sat in the inappropriate coach were fined or imprisoned. When Plessy refused to comply with the order, he was removed from the train and imprisoned.

Plessy v. Ferguson is the one case that solidified the power of whites over blacks in southern states. Through state laws, and with the additional federal weight in the *Plessy* decision, whites began to enforce rigid separation of the races in every aspect of life.

In *Plessy,* Justice John Marshall Harlan wrote the only dissenting opinion. Usually in Supreme Court cases, attention is focused on the majority, rather than the dissenting opinion. However, in this case Justice Harlan's dissent is noteworthy because his views on race and citizenship pointed out a line of reasoning that eventually broke down segregation and second-class citizenship for blacks.

Justice Harlan's background as a Kentucky slaveholder who later joined the Union side during the Civil War is cited as an explanation of his views. Some scholars speculate that his shift from slaveholder to a defender of the rights of blacks was caused by his observation of beatings, lynchings, and the use of intimidation tactics against blacks in Kentucky after the Civil War. In a quirk of history, when *Plessy v. Ferguson* was overturned in 1954 by a unanimous opinion in *Brown v. Board of Education,* Justice Harlan's grandson was a member of the Supreme Court.

The Court's decision addressed these key questions:

1. How is a black person defined?
2. Who determines when an individual is black or white?
3. Does providing separate but equal facilities violate the Thirteenth Amendment?
4. Does providing separate but equal facilities violate the Fourteenth Amendment?
5. Does a separate but equal doctrine imply inferiority of either race?
6. Can state laws require the separation of the two races in schools, theaters, and railway cars?
7. Does the separation of the races when applied to commerce within the state of Louisiana abridge the privileges and immunities of the "colored man,"[12] deprive him of equal protection of the law, or deprive him of his property without due process of law under the Fourteenth Amendment?

Excerpts from the Supreme Court Decision in *Plessy v. Ferguson*[13]

Mr. Justice Brown delivered the opinion of the Court:

> . . . An [1890] act of the General Assembly of the State of Louisiana, provid[ed] for separate railway carriages for the white and colored races.

. . . No person or persons, shall be admitted to occupy seats in coaches, other than the ones assigned to them on account of the race they belong to.

. . . The constitutionality of this act is attacked upon the ground that it conflicts both with the Thirteenth Amendment of the Constitution, abolishing slavery, and the Fourteenth Amendment, which prohibits certain restrictive legislation.

. . . A statute which implied merely a legal distinction between the white and colored races . . . has no tendency to destroy the legal equality of the two races, or reestablish a state of servitude.

. . . The object of the amendment [the Fourteenth Amendment] was undoubtedly to enforce the absolute equality of the two races before the law, but in the nature of things it could not have been intended to abolish distinctions based upon color, or a commingling of the two races upon terms unsatisfactory to either.

Laws permitting and even requiring their separation in places where they are liable to be brought into contact do not necessarily imply the inferiority of either race to the other, and have been generally, if not universally recognized as within the competency of the state legislatures in the exercise of their police power. The most common instance of this is connected with the establishment of separate schools for white and colored children, which has been held to be a valid exercise of the legislative power even by courts of States where the political rights of the colored race have been longest and most earnestly enforced. One of the earliest of these cases is that of *Roberts v. City of Boston,* 5 Cush. 198, in which the Supreme Judicial Court of Massachusetts held that the general school committee of Boston had power to make provision for the instruction of colored children in separate schools established exclusively for them, and to prohibit their attendance upon the other schools.

. . . We are not prepared to say that the conductor, in assigning passengers to the coaches according to their race, does not act at his peril. . . . The power to assign to a particular coach obviously implies the power to determine to which race the passenger belongs, as well as the power to determine who, under the laws of the particular State, is to be deemed a white, and who is a colored person.

. . . We consider the underlying fallacy of the plaintiff's argument to consist in the assumption that the enforced separation of the two races stamps the colored race with a badge of inferiority. If this be so, it is not by reason of anything found in the act, but solely because the colored race chooses to put that construction upon it. . . . The argument also assumes that social prejudices may be overcome by legislation, and that equal rights cannot be secured to the negro except by an enforced commingling of the two races. We cannot accept this proposition. If the two races are to meet upon terms of social equality, it must be the result of natural affinities, a mutual appreciation of each other's merits and a voluntary consent of individuals.

. . . If the civil and political rights of both races be equal one cannot be inferior to the other civilly or politically. If one race be inferior to the other socially, the Constitution of the United States cannot put them upon the same plane.

It is true that the question for the proportion of colored blood necessary to constitute a colored person, as distinguished from a white person, is one upon which there is a difference of opinion in the different States, some holding that any visible admixture of black blood stamps the persons as belonging to the colored races, others that it depends upon the preponderance of blood . . . still others that the predominance of white blood must only be in the proportion of three fourths. . . . But these are questions to be determined under the laws of each State. . . .

Mr. Justice Harlan in the dissenting opinion:

. . . It was said in argument that the statute of Louisiana does not discriminate against either race, but prescribes a rule applicable alike to white and colored citizens. . . . [But] everyone knows that the statute in question had its origin in the purpose, not so much to exclude white persons from railroad cars occupied by blacks, as to exclude colored people from coaches occupied by or assigned to white persons.

. . . It is one thing for railroad carriers to furnish, or to be required by law to furnish, equal accommodations for all whom they are under a legal duty to carry. It is quite another thing for government to forbid citizens of the white and black races from travelling in the same public conveyance, and to punish officers of railroad companies for permitting persons of the two races to occupy the same

> passenger coach. If a State can prescribe, as a rule of civil conduct, that whites and blacks shall not travel as passengers in the same railroad coach, why may it not so regulate the use of the streets of its cities and towns as to compel white citizens to keep on one side of a street and black citizens to keep on the other? Why may it not, upon like grounds, punish whites and blacks who ride together in street cars or in open vehicles on a public road or street? Why may it not require sheriffs to assign whites to one side of a court-room and blacks to the other? And why may it not also prohibit the commingling of the two races in the galleries of legislative halls or in public assemblages convened for the consideration of the political questions of the day? Further, if this statute of Louisiana is consistent with the personal liberty of citizens, why may not the State require the separation in railroad coaches of native and naturalized citizens of the United States, or of Protestants and Roman Catholics?
>
> . . . In my opinion, the judgment this day rendered will, in time, prove to be quite pernicious as the decision made by this tribunal in the Dred Scott case.
>
> . . . The thin disguise of "equal" accommodations for passengers in railroad coaches will not mislead anyone, nor atone for the wrong this day done.

Thus, the *Plessy v. Ferguson* decision firmly established the separate but equal doctrine in the South until the National Association for the Advancement of Colored Persons (NAACP) began to systematically attack Jim Crow laws. It is ironic that in *Plessy* the systematic social, political, and economic suppression of blacks in the South through Jim Crow laws was justified in terms of a case decided in the northern city of Boston, where the segregation of schools occurred in practice *(de facto),* but not by force of law *(de jure).* In that 1849 case (*Roberts v. City of Boston,* 5 Cush. 198), a parent had unsuccessfully sued on behalf of his daughter to attend a public school. Thus, educational access became both the first and last chapter—in the 1954 case of *Brown v. Board of Education*—of the doctrine of separate but equal.

VI. *BROWN V. BOARD OF EDUCATION* (1954)

Unlike many of the earlier cases brought by individual women, blacks, or Native Americans, *Brown v. Board of Education* was the result of a concerted campaign against racial segregation led by Howard University School of Law graduates and the NAACP. In the 1930s, the NAACP Legal Defense Fund began to systematically fight for fair employment, fair housing, and desegregation of public education. Key lawyers in the campaign against segregation were Charles Houston, Thurgood Marshall, James Nabrit, and William Hastie. Marshall later became a Supreme Court justice, Nabrit became president of Howard University, and Hastie became a federal judge.

By using the Fourteenth Amendment, *Brown* became the key case in an attempt to topple the 1896 separate but equal doctrine. Legal strategists knew that educational opportunity and better housing conditions were essential if black Americans were to achieve upward mobility. While one group of lawyers focused on restrictive covenant cases,[14] which prevented blacks from buying housing in white neighborhoods, another spearheaded the drive for blacks to enter state-run professional schools.

In 1954, suits were brought in Kansas, South Carolina, Virginia, and Delaware on behalf of black Americans seeking to attend nonsegregated public schools. However, the case is commonly referred to as *Brown v. Board of Education.* The plaintiffs in the suit contended that segregation in the public schools denied them equal protection of the laws under the Fourteenth Amendment. The contention was that since segregated public schools were not and could not be made equal, black American children were deprived of equal protection of the laws.

The Court's unanimous decision addressed these key questions:

1. Are public schools segregated by race detrimental to black children?

2. Does segregation result in an inferior education for black children?
3. Does the maintenance of segregated public schools violate the Equal Protection Clause of the Fourteenth Amendment?
4. Is the maintenance of segregated public school facilities *inherently* unequal?
5. What was the intent of the framers of the Fourteenth Amendment regarding distinctions between whites and blacks?
6. Is the holding in *Plessy v. Ferguson* applicable to public education?
7. Does segregation of children in public schools *solely on the basis of race,* even though the physical facilities and other "tangible" factors may be equal, deprive the children of the minority group of equal educational opportunities?

Excerpts from the Supreme Court Decision in *Brown v. Board of Education*[15]

Mr. Chief Justice Warren delivered the opinion of the Court:

> . . . In each of these cases [NAACP suits in Kansas, South Carolina, Virginia, and Delaware] minors of the Negro race, through their legal representatives, seek the aid of the courts in obtaining admission to the public schools of their community on a nonsegregated basis. . . . This segregation was alleged to deprive the plaintiffs of the equal protection of the laws under the Fourteenth Amendment. In each of the cases other than the Delaware case, a three-judge federal district court denied relief to the plaintiffs on the so-called "separate but equal" doctrine announced by this Court in *Plessy v. Ferguson,* 163 U.S. 537. Under that doctrine, equality of treatment is accorded when the races are provided substantially equal facilities, even though these facilities be separated. . . .
>
> The plaintiffs contend that segregated schools are not "equal" and cannot be made "equal," and that hence they are deprived of the equal protection of the laws.
>
> . . . The most avid proponents of the post–[Civil] War amendments undoubtedly intended them to remove all legal distinctions among "all persons born or naturalized in the United States."
>
> In the first cases in this Court construing the Fourteenth Amendment, decided shortly after its adoption, the Court interpreted it as prescribing all state imposed discriminations against the Negro race. The doctrine of "separate but equal" did not make its appearance in this Court until 1896 in the *Plessy v. Ferguson, supra,* involving not education but transportation.
>
> In these days, it is doubtful that any child may reasonably be expected to succeed in life if he is denied the opportunity of an education. Such an opportunity where the state has undertaken to provide it, is a right which must be made available to all on equal terms.
>
> We come then to the question presented: Does segregation of children in public schools solely on the basis of race, even though the physical facilities and other "tangible" factors may be equal, deprive the children of the minority group of equal educational opportunities? We believe that it does.
>
> To separate them [the children] from others of similar age and qualifications solely because of their race generates a feeling of inferiority as to their status in the community that may affect their hearts and minds in a way unlikely ever to be undone.
>
> 
>
> We conclude that in the field of public education the doctrine of "separate but equal" has no place. Separate educational facilities are inherently unequal. Therefore, we hold that the plaintiffs and others similarly situated for whom the actions have been brought are, by reason of the segregation complained of, deprived of the equal protection of the laws guaranteed by the Fourteenth Amendment.
>
> . . . We have now announced that such segregation is a denial of the equal protection of the laws.

VII. *YICK WO V. HOPKINS* (1886)

In the 1880s, the questions of citizenship and the rights of citizens were raised again by Native Americans and Asian immigrants. While the status of citizenship for African Americans was settled by the Thirteenth and Fourteenth

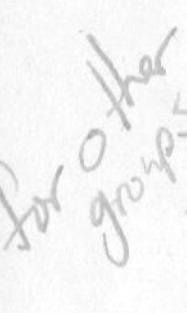

Amendments, the extent of the privileges and immunities clause still needed clarification. Yick Wo, a Chinese immigrant living in San Francisco, brought suit under the Fourteenth Amendment to see if it covered all persons in the territorial United States regardless of race, color, or nationality.

The Chinese were different than European immigrants because they came to the United States under contract to work as laborers building the transcontinental railroad. When Chinese workers remained, primarily in California, after the completion of the railroad in 1869, Congress became anxious about this "foreign element" that was non-Christian and non-European. Chinese immigrants were seen as an economic threat because they would work for less than white males. To address the issue of economic competition, the Chinese Exclusion Act was passed in 1882 to prohibit further immigration to the United States. This gave the Chinese the unique status among immigrants of being the only group barred from entry into the United States and barred from becoming naturalized U.S. citizens.

Yick Wo, a subject of the Emperor of China, went to San Francisco in 1861, where he operated a laundry at the same premise for 22 years with consent from the Board of Fire Wardens. When the consent decree expired on October 1, 1885, Yick Wo routinely reapplied to continue to operate a laundry. He was, however, denied a license. Of the over 300 laundries in the city and county of San Francisco, about 240 were owned by Chinese immigrants. Most of these laundries were wooden, the most common construction material used at that time, although it posed a fire hazard. Yick Wo and more than 150 of his countrymen were arrested and charged with carrying on business without having special consent, while those who were not subjects of China and were operating some 80 laundries under similar conditions, were allowed to conduct business.

Yick Wo stated that he and 200 of his countrymen with similar situations petitioned the Board of Supervisors for permission to continue to conduct business in the same buildings they had occupied for more than 20 years. The petitions of all the Chinese were denied, while all petitions of those who were not Chinese were granted (with one exception).

Did this prohibition of the occupation and destruction of the business and property of the Chinese laundrymen in San Francisco constitute the proper regulation of business, or was it discrimination and a violation of important rights secured by the Fourteenth Amendment?

The Court's decision addressed these key questions:

1. Does this municipal ordinance regulating public laundries within the municipality of San Francisco violate the United States Constitution?
2. Does carrying out this municipal ordinance violate the Fourteenth Amendment?
3. Does the guarantee of protection of the Fourteenth Amendment extend to all persons within the territorial jurisdiction of the United States regardless of race, color, or nationality?
4. Are the subjects of the Emperor of China who, temporarily or permanently, reside in the United States entitled to enjoy the protection guaranteed by the Fourteenth Amendment?

Excerpts from the Supreme Court Decision in *Yick Wo v. Hopkins*[16]

Mr. Justice Matthews delivered the opinion of the Court:

> . . . In both of these cases [*Yick Wo v. Hopkins* and *Wo Lee v. Hopkins*] the ordinance involved was simply a prohibition to carry on the washing and ironing of clothes in public laundries and wash-houses, within the city and county of San Francisco, from ten o'clock p.m. until six o'clock a.m. of the following day. This provision was held to be purely a police regulation, within the competency of any municipality.
>
> . . . The rights of the petitioners are not less because they are aliens and subjects of the Emperor of China.

> The Fourteenth amendment to the Constitution is not confined to the protection of citizens. It says: "Nor shall any State deprive any person of life, liberty, or property without due process of law; nor deny to any person within its jurisdiction the equal protection of the laws." These provisions are universal in their application, to all persons within the territorial jurisdiction, without regard to any differences of race, or color, or of nationality; and the equal protection from the laws is a pledge of the protection of equal laws. . . .
>
> Though the law itself be fair on its face and impartial in appearance, yet, it is applied and administered by public authority with an evil eye and unequal hand, so as practically to make unjust and illegal discriminations between persons in similar circumstances. . . .
>
> . . . No reason whatever, except the will of the supervisors, is assigned why they should not be permitted to carry on, in the accustomed manner, their harmless and useful occupation, on which they depend for a livelihood. And while this consent of the supervisors is withheld from them and from two hundred others who have also petitioned, all of whom happened to be Chinese subjects, eighty others, not Chinese subjects, are permitted to carry on similar business under similar conditions. The fact of this discrimination is admitted. No reason for it is shown, . . . no reason for it exists except hostility to the race and nationality to which the petitioners belong, and which in the eye of the law is not justified. The discrimination is, therefore, illegal, and the public administration which enforces it is a denial of the equal protection of the laws and a violation of the Fourteenth amendment of the Constitution. The imprisonment of the petitioners is, therefore illegal, and they must be discharged.

The decision in *Yick Wo* demonstrated the Court's perspective that the Fourteenth Amendment applied to all persons, citizens and noncitizens.

VIII. *ELK V. WILKINS* (1884)

In the late 19th century, Native Americans constituted a problematic class when the Supreme Court considered citizenship. Although Native Americans were the original inhabitants of the territory that became the United States, they were considered outside the concept of citizenship. They were viewed as a separate nation, and described as uncivilized, alien people who were not worthy of citizenship in the political community. As Native Americans were driven from their homeland and pushed farther west, the United States government developed a policy of containment by establishing reservations. Native Americans who lived with their tribes on such reservations were presumed to be members of "not strictly speaking, foreign states, but alien nations." The Constitution made no provisions for naturalizing Native Americans or defining the status of those who chose to live in the territorial United States rather than be assigned to reservations. It was presumed that Native Americans would remain on the reservations. The framers of the Constitution had not given any thought as to when or how a Native American might become a U.S. citizen. When the Naturalization Law of 1790 was written, only Europeans were anticipated as future citizens. The citizenship of Native Americans was not settled until 1924, when a statutory law, not a constitutional amendment, granted citizenship.

Elk v. Wilkins raised the question of citizenship and voting behavior as a privilege of citizenship. In 1857, the Court had easily dismissed Dred Scott's suit on the grounds that he was not a citizen. Since he did not hold citizenship, he could not sue. *Minor v. Happersett* in 1872 considered the citizenship and voting issue with a female plaintiff. In that case, citizenship was not in doubt but the court stated that citizenship did not automatically confer the right to suffrage. In *Elk,* a Native American claimed citizenship and the right to vote. Before considering the right to vote, the Court first examined whether Elk was a citizen and the process by which one becomes a citizen.

As midwestern cities emerged from westward expansion in the 1880s, a few Native Americans left their reservations to live and work in those cities. John Elk left his tribe and moved to Omaha, Nebraska, under the jurisdiction of the United States. In April 1880, he attempted to vote for members of the city council. Elk met the residency requirements in Nebraska and Douglas County for voting. Claiming that he complied with all of the statutory provisions, Elk asserted that under the Fourteenth and Fifteenth Amendments, he was a citizen of the United States who was entitled to exercise the franchise, regardless of race or color. He further claimed that Wilkins, the voter registrar, "designedly, corruptly, willfully, and maliciously" refused to register him for the sole reason that he was a Native American.

The Court's decision addressed these key questions:

1. Is a Native American still a member of an Indian tribe when he voluntarily separates himself from his tribe and seeks residence among the white citizens of the state?
2. What was the intent of the Fourteenth Amendment regarding who could become a citizen?
3. Can Native Americans become naturalized citizens?
4. Can Native Americans become citizens of the United States without the consent of the U.S. government?
5. Must Native Americans adopt the habits of a "civilized" life before they become U.S. citizens?
6. Is a Native American who is taxed a citizen?

Excerpts from the Supreme Court Decision in *Elk v. Wilkins*[17]

Mr. Justice Gray delivered the opinion of the Court.

> . . . The plaintiff . . . relies on the first clause of the first section of the Fourteenth amendment of the Constitution of the United States, by which "all persons born or naturalized in the United States, and subject to the jurisdiction thereof, are citizens of the United States and of the State wherein they reside"; and on the Fifteenth amendment, which provides that "the right of citizens of the United States to vote shall not be denied or abridged by the United States or by any State on account of race, color, or previous condition of servitude."
>
> . . . The question then is, whether an Indian, born a member of the Indian tribes within the United States, is, merely by reason of his birth within the United States, and of his afterwards voluntarily separating himself from his tribe and taking up his residence among white citizens, a citizen of the United States, within the meaning of the first section of the Fourteenth amendment of the Constitution.
>
> . . . The Indian tribes, being within the territorial limits of the United States, were not, strictly speaking, foreign States; but they were alien nations, distinct political communities, with whom the United States might and habitually did deal, as they thought fit, either through treaties made by the President and Senate, or through acts of Congress in the ordinary forms of legislation. The members of those tribes owed immediate allegiance to their several tribes, and were not a part of the United States. They were in a dependent condition, a state of pupilage, resembling that of a ward to his guardian.
>
> . . . They were never deemed citizens of the United States, except under explicit provisions of treaty or statute to that effect, either declaring a certain tribe, or such members of it as chose to remain behind on the removal of the tribe westward, to be citizens, or authorizing individuals of particular tribes to become citizens. . . .
>
> This [opening] section of the Fourteenth amendment contemplates two sources of citizenship, and two sources only: birth and naturalization.
>
> . . . Slavery having been abolished, and the persons formerly held as slaves made citizens. . . . But Indians not taxed are still excluded from the count [U.S. Census count for apportioning seats in the U.S. House of Representatives],[18] for the reason that they are not citizens. Their absolute exclusion from the basis of representation, in which all other persons are now included, is wholly inconsistent with their being considered citizens.
>
> . . . Such Indians, then, not being citizens by birth, can only become so in the second way men-

tioned in the Fourteenth amendment, by being "naturalized in the United States," by or under some treaty or statute.

. . . The treaty of 1867 with the Kansas Indians strikingly illustrates the principle that no one can become a citizen of a nation without its consent, and directly contradicts the supposition that a member of an Indian tribe can at will be alternately a citizen of the United States and a member of the tribe.

. . . But the question whether any Indian tribes, or any members thereof, have become so far advanced in civilization, that they should be let out of the state of pupilage, and admitted to the privileges and responsibilities of citizenship, is a question to be decided by the nation whose wards they are and whose citizens they seek to become, and not by each Indian for himself.

. . . And in a later case [Judge Deady in the District Court of the United States for the District of Oregon] said: "But an Indian cannot make himself a citizen of the United States without the consent and co-operation of the government. The fact that he has abandoned his nomadic life or tribal relations, and adopted the habits and manners of civilized people, may be a good reason why he should be made a citizen of the United States, but does not of itself make him one. To be a citizen of the United States is a political privilege which no one, not born to, can assume without its consent in some form.

Mr. Justice Harlan in the dissenting opinion:

. . . We submit that the petition does sufficiently show that the plaintiff is taxed, that is, belongs to the class which, by the laws of Nebraska, are subject to taxation.

. . . The plaintiff is a citizen and *bona fide* resident of Nebraska. . . . He is subject to taxation, and is taxed, in that State. Further: The plaintiff has become so far incorporated with the mass of the people of Nebraska that . . . he constitutes a part of her militia.

By the act of April 9, 1866, entitled "An Act to protect all persons in the United States in their civil rights, and furnish means for their vindication" (14 Stat. 27), it is provided that "all persons born in the United States and not subject to any foreign power, excluding Indians not taxed, are hereby declared to be citizens of the United States". . . . Beyond question, by that act, national citizenship was conferred directly upon all persons in this country, of whatever race (excluding only "Indians not taxed"), who were born within the territorial limits of the United States, and were not subject to any foreign power. Surely every one must admit that an Indian, residing in one of the States, and subject to taxation there, became by force alone of the act of 1866, a citizen of the United States, although he may have been, when born, a member of a tribe.

. . . If he did not acquire national citizenship on abandoning his tribe [moving from the reservation] and . . . by residence in one of the States, subject to the complete jurisdiction of the United States, then the Fourteenth amendment has wholly failed to accomplish, in respect of the Indian race, what, we think, was intended by it, and there is still in this country a despised and rejected class of persons, with no nationality; who born in our territory, owing no allegiance to foreign power, and subject, as residents of the States, to all the burdens of government, are yet not members of any political community nor entitled to any of the rights, privileges, or immunities of citizens of the United States.

In all, the Court never addressed Elk's right to vote because the primary question involved Elk's citizenship. By excluding him from citizenship because he had not been naturalized and because there was no provision for naturalization, John Elk was left outside of the political community as was Dred Scott.

IX. *LAU V. NICHOLS* (1974)

In the 19th century, Native Americans and Asian immigrants sought to exercise rights under the Fourteenth Amendment although it had been designed explicitly to protect blacks. In the 20th century, issues first raised by African Americans, such as equality in public education, again presented other minority groups with an opportunity to test their rights under the Constitution.

Brown v. Board of Education forced the Court to consider the narrow question of the distribution of resources between black and white school systems. The *Brown* decision addressed only education. It did not extend to the other areas of segregation in American society, such as the segregation of public transportation (e.g., buses) or public accommodations (e.g., restaurants and hotels). Indeed, *Brown* had not even specified how the integration of the school system was to take place. All of these questions were taken up by the Civil Rights movement that followed the *Brown* decision.

Once the separate but equal doctrine was nullified in education, immigrants raised other issues of equality. In the 1970s, suits were brought on behalf of the children of illegal immigrants, non-English-speaking children of Chinese ancestry, and children of low-income parents.

In *Lau v. Nichols,* a non-English-speaking minority group questioned equality in public education. The case was similar to *Brown* because it concerned public education, the Equal Protection Clause of the Fourteenth Amendment, and the suit was brought on behalf of minors; but the two cases also differed in many respects. The 1954 decision in *Brown* was part of a series of court cases attacking segregated facilities primarily in southern states. It addressed only the issues of black/white interaction.

In *Lau v. Nichols,* a suit was brought on behalf of children of Chinese ancestry who attended public schools in San Francisco. Although the children did not speak English, their classes in school were taught entirely in that language. (Some of the children received special instruction in the English language; others did not.) The suit did not specifically ask for bilingual education, nor did the Court require it, but *Lau* led to the development of such programs. In bilingual education, the curriculum is taught in children's native language, but they are also given separate instruction in the English language, and over time they are moved into English throughout their courses.

The *Lau* decision hinged in part on Department of Health, Education, and Welfare guidelines that prohibited discrimination in federally assisted programs. The decision was narrow because it instructed only the lower court to provide appropriate relief. The Court's ruling did not guarantee minority language rights, nor did it require bilingual education.

The Court's decision addressed these key questions:

1. Does a public school system that provides for instruction only in English violate the equal protection clause of the Fourteenth Amendment?
2. Does a public school system that provides for instruction only in English violate section 601 of the Civil Rights Act of 1964?
3. Do Chinese-speaking students who are in the minority receive fewer benefits from the school system than the English-speaking majority?
4. Must a school system that has a minority of students who do not speak English provide bilingual instruction?

Excerpts from the Supreme Court Decision in *Lau v. Nichols*[19]

Mr. Justice Douglas delivered the opinion of the Court:

> The San Francisco, California, school system was integrated in 1971 as a result of a federal court decree. The District Court found that there are 2,856 students of Chinese ancestry in the school system who do not speak English. Of those who have that language deficiency, about 1,000 are given supplemental courses in the English language. About 1,800 however, do not receive that instruction.
>
> This class suit brought by non-English-speaking Chinese students against officials responsible for the operation of the San Francisco Unified School District seeks relief against the unequal educational opportunities, which are alleged to violate, *inter alia,* the Fourteenth Amendment. No specific remedy is urged upon us. . . .
>
> The Court of Appeals [holding that there was no violation of the Equal Protection Clause of the Fourteenth Amendment or of section 601 of the Civil Rights Act of 1964] reasoned that "[e]very student brings to the starting line of his educational career different advantages and disadvantages

caused in part by social, economic and cultural background, created and continued completely apart from any contribution by the school system." . . . Section 71 of the California Education Code states that "English shall be the basic language of instruction in all schools." That section permits a school district to determine "when and under what circumstances instruction may be given bilingually". . . .

Under these state-imposed standards there is no equality of treatment merely by providing students with the same facilities, textbooks, teachers, and curriculum; for students who do not understand English are effectively foreclosed from any meaningful education.

. . . We know that those who do not understand English are certain to find their classroom experiences wholly incomprehensible and in no way meaningful.

We do not reach the Equal Protection Clause argument which has been advanced but rely solely on section 601 of the Civil Rights Act of 1964, 42 U.S.C. section 2000d. to reverse the Court of Appeals.

That section bans discrimination based "on the ground of race, color, or national origin, in any program or activity receiving Federal financial assistance." The school district involved in this litigation receives large amounts of federal financial assistance. The Department of Health, Education, and Welfare (HEW), which has authority to promulgate regulations prohibiting discrimination in federally assisted school systems, in 1968 issued one guideline that "[s]chool systems are responsible for assuring that students of a particular race, color, or national origin are not denied the opportunity to obtain the education generally obtained by other students in the system." In 1970 HEW made the guidelines more specific, requiring school districts that were federally funded "to rectify the language deficiency in order to open" the instruction to students who had "linguistic deficiencies". . . .

It seems obvious that the Chinese-speaking minority receive fewer benefits than the English-speaking majority from respondents' school system which denies them a meaningful opportunity to participate in the educational program—all earmarks of the discrimination banned by the regulations. . . .

Lau differed from *Brown* because it was decided not on the basis of the Fourteenth Amendment but on the Civil Rights Act of 1964. In reference to *Brown,* the justices noted that equality of treatment was not achieved by providing students with the same facilities, textbooks, teachers, or curriculum. *Lau* underscores the idea that equality may not be achieved by treating different categories of people in the same way.

X. *SAN ANTONIO SCHOOL DISTRICT V. RODRIGUEZ* (1973)

The 1973 case of *San Antonio School District v. Rodriguez* raised the question of equality in public education from another perspective. As was the case in *Brown* and *Lau,* the Fourteenth Amendment required interpretation. However, unlike the earlier cases, the issue was the financing of local public schools.

Education is not a right specified in the Constitution. Under a federal system, education is a local matter in each state. This allows for the possibility of vast differences among states and even within states on the quality of instruction, methods of financing, and treatment of nonwhite students. Whereas the *Brown* decision examined inequality between races, *San Antonio* considered inequality based on financial resources through local property taxes. *San Antonio* raised the question of the consequence of the unequal distribution of wealth among Texas school districts. As with *Brown* and *Lau,* minors were involved; however, the issue was not race or language instruction but social class. Did the Texas school system discriminate against the poor?

Traditionally, the states have financed schools based on property tax assessments. Since wealth is not evenly distributed, some communities are able to spend more on education and provide greater resources to children. This is the basis of the *San Antonio* case, where the charge was that children in less affluent communities necessarily received an inferior education because those communities had fewer resources to draw on. The Rodriguez family contended that the Texas school system of financing public schools through local property taxes denied them equal protection of the laws in violation of the Fourteenth Amendment.

Financing public schools in Texas entailed state and local contributions. About half of the revenues were derived from a state-funded program that provided a minimal educational base; each district then supplemented state aid with a property tax. The Rodriguez family brought a class action suit on behalf of school children who claimed to be members of poor families who resided in school districts with a low property tax base. The contention was that the Texas system's reliance on local property taxation favored the more affluent and violated equal protection requirements because of disparities between districts in per-pupil expenditures.

The Court's decision addressed these key questions:

1. Does Texas's system of financing public school education by use of a property tax violate the Equal Protection Clause (Section 1) of the Fourteenth Amendment?
2. Does the Equal Protection Clause apply to wealth?
3. Is education a fundamental right?
4. Does this state law impinge on a fundamental right?
5. Is a state system for financing public education by a property tax that results in interdistrict disparities in per-pupil expenditures unconstitutionally arbitrary under the Equal Protection Clause?

Excerpts from the Supreme Court Decision in *San Antonio School District v. Rodriguez*[20]

Mr. Justice Powell delivered the opinion of the Court:

. . . The District Court held that the Texas system [of financing public education] discriminates on the basis of wealth in the manner in which education is provided for its people. Finding that wealth is a "suspect" classification and that education is a "fundamental" interest, the District Court held that the Texas system could be sustained only if the State could show that it was premised upon some compelling state interest.

. . . We must decide, first, whether the Texas system of financing public education operates to the disadvantage of some suspect class or impinges upon a fundamental right explicitly or implicitly protected by the Constitution, thereby requiring strict judicial scrutiny. If so, the Texas scheme must still be examined to determine whether it rationally furthers some legitimate, articulated state purpose and therefore does not constitute an invidious discrimination in violation of the Equal Protection Clause of the Fourteenth Amendment.

. . . In concluding that strict judicial scrutiny was required, the [District] court relied on decisions dealing with the rights of indigents to equal treatment in the criminal trial and appellate processes, and on cases disapproving wealth restrictions on the right to vote. Those cases, the District Court concluded, established wealth as a suspect classification. Finding that a local property tax system discriminated on the basis of wealth, it regarded those precedents as controlling. It then reasoned, based on decisions of this Court affirming the undeniable importance of education, that there is a fundamental right to education and that, absent some compelling state justification, the Texas system could not stand.

We are unable to agree that this case, which in significant aspects is *sui generis,* may be so neatly fitted under the Equal Protection Clause. Indeed, we find neither the suspect-classification nor the fundamental-interest analysis persuasive.

The wealth discrimination discovered by the District Court in this case, and by several other courts that have recently struck down school financing in other States, is quite unlike any of the forms of wealth discrimination heretofore reviewed by this Court.

. . . First, in support of their charge that the system discriminates against the "poor," appellees have made no effort to demonstrate that it operates to the peculiar disadvantage of any class fairly definable as indigent, or as composed of persons whose incomes are beneath any designated poverty level. Indeed, there is reason to believe that the poorest families are not necessarily clustered in the poorest property districts. . . .

Second, neither appellees nor the District Court addressed the fact that . . . lack of personal resources has not occasioned an absolute deprivation of the desired benefit. The argument here is not that the children in districts having relatively low assessable property values are receiving no public education; rather, it is that they are receiving a poorer quality education than that available to children in districts having more assessable wealth. Apart from the unsettled and disputed question whether the quality of education may be determined by the amount of money expended for it, a sufficient answer to appellee's argument is that, at least where wealth is involved, the Equal Protection Clause does not require absolute equality or precisely equal advantages. . . .

For these two reasons . . . the disadvantaged class is not susceptible of identification in traditional terms. . . .

. . . [I]t is clear that appellee's suit asks this Court to extend its most exacting scrutiny to review a system that allegedly discriminates against a large, diverse, and amorphous class, unified only by the common factor of residence in districts that happen to have less taxable wealth than other districts. The system of alleged discrimination and the class it defines have none of the traditional indicia of suspectness: the class is not saddled with such disabilities, or subjected to such a history of purposeful unequal treatment, or relegated to such a position of political powerlessness as to command extraordinary protection from the majoritarian political process.

We thus conclude that the Texas system does not operate to the peculiar disadvantage of any suspect class. . . .

Education, of course, is not among the rights afforded explicit protection under our Federal Constitution. Nor do we find any basis for saying it is implicitly so protected. . . .

In sum, to the extent that the Texas system of school financing results in unequal expenditures between children who happen to reside in different districts, we cannot say that such disparities are the product of a system that is so irrational as to be invidiously discriminatory. . . .

Mr. Justice White, with whom Mr. Justice Douglas and Mr. Justice Brennan join, dissenting:

. . . In my view, the parents and children in Edgewood, and in like districts, suffer from an invidious discrimination violative of the Equal Protection Clause. . . .

There is no difficulty in identifying the class that is subject to the alleged discrimination and that is entitled to the benefits of the Equal Protection Clause. I need go no further than the parents and children in the Edgewood district, who are plaintiffs here and who assert that they are entitled to the same choice as Alamo Heights to augment local expenditures for schools but are denied that choice by state law. This group constitutes a class sufficiently definite to invoke the protection of the Constitution. . . .

In San Antonio v. Rodriguez, the Court did not find that the differences between school districts constituted invidious discrimination. A majority of the justices felt that Texas satisfied constitutional standards under the Equal Protection Clause. On the other hand, four justices in dissenting opinions saw a class (the poor) that was subject to discrimination and that lacked the protection of the Constitution.

XI. *BOWERS V. HARDWICK* (1986)

In most of the cases we have considered, plaintiffs have sued on the basis that their rights under the Fourteenth Amendment were violated. However, cases can reach the Supreme Court by several routes, one of which is a *writ of certiorari,* which is directed at an inferior court to bring the record of a case into a superior court for re-examination and review. This was the case in *Bowers v. Hardwick,* in which the constitutionality of a Georgia sodomy statute was challenged. This became a key case in the battle for constitutional rights for gay women and men.

The case of *Bowers v. Hardwick* began on the issue of privacy because the behavior in question took place in Michael Hardwick's home. In deciding the case, however, the justices shifted from the issue of privacy to question whether gays have a fundamental right to engage in consensual sex.

Michael Hardwick's suit was based on the following facts. On August 3, 1982, a police officer went to Hardwick's home to serve Hardwick a warrant for failure to pay a fine. Hardwick's roommate answered the door, but was not sure if Hardwick was at home. The roommate allowed the officer to enter and approach Hardwick's bedroom. The officer found the bedroom door partly open and observed Hardwick engaged in oral sex with another man. The officer arrested both men, charged them with sodomy, and held them in the local jail for 10 hours.

The Georgia sodomy statute under which the men were charged made "any sexual act involving the sex organs of one person and the mouth or anus of another" a felony punishable by imprisonment for up to 20 years. When the district attorney decided not to submit the case to a grand jury, Hardwick brought suit attacking the constitutionality of the Georgia statute. Later, a divided court of appeals held that the Georgia statute violated Hardwick's fundamental rights. The attorney general of Georgia appealed that judgment to the Supreme Court.

The Court's decision on the case was split. Five justices ruled that the constitutional right of privacy did not apply to Hardwick's case; four argued that it did. While the Georgia statute did not specify that only homosexual sodomy was prohibited, the Court's majority opinion was framed in those terms. (Most legal prohibitions are directed at nonprocreative acts irrespective of the sex of the participants.) The majority opinion also equated consensual sex within the home to criminal conduct within the home, an equation criticized by both gay rights activists and the dissenting justices.

> [The majority opinion] emphasized that the home does not confer immunity for criminal conduct, comparing gay sex first to drugs, firearms, and stolen goods and then to adultery, incest, and bigamy. In so doing, the Court evoked images of dissolution, fear, seizure, and instability. . . . [and] the stereotypical fear of gay men as predators and child molestors. . . . The majority [opinion] advances, mostly by implication, its view of gay sexuality as unrelated to recognized forms of sexual activity or intimate relationships, and as exploitative, predatory, threatening to personal and social stability. [Writing for the dissent] Justice Blackmun excoriates the majority's choice of analogies and its failure to explain why it did not use nonthreatening analogies such as private, consensual heterosexual activity or even sodomy within marriage for comparison[21]

While the majority argued that the past criminalization of sodomy argued for its continued criminalization, critics responded that "Whereas the task of the Court was to decide whether the criminalization of sodomy is consistent with the Constitution, the majority treated the fact of past criminalization as determinative. . . . It had no answer to Justice Blackmun's contention 'that by such lights, the Court should have no authority to invalidate miscegenation laws.'"[22]

The Court's decision addressed these key questions:

1. Does Georgia's sodomy law violate the fundamental rights of gays?
2. Does the Constitution confer the fundamental right to engage in homosexual sodomy?
3. Is Georgia's sodomy law selectively being enforced against gays?

Excerpts from the Supreme Court Decision in *Bowers v. Hardwick*[23]

Mr. Justice White delivered the opinion of the Court:

> This case does not require a judgment on whether laws against sodomy between consenting adults in general, or between homosexuals in particular, are wise or desirable. . . . The issue presented is whether the Federal Constitution confers a fundamental right upon homosexuals to engage in sodomy and hence invalidates the laws of the many States that still makes such contact illegal and have done so for a very long time.
>
> We first register our disagreement with the Court of Appeals and with respondent that the Court's prior cases have construed the Constitution

to confer a right of privacy that extends to homosexual sodomy. . . .

Precedent aside, however, respondent would have us announce, as the Court of Appeals did, a fundamental right to engage in homosexual sodomy. This we are quite unwilling to do. . . .

It is obvious to us that neither of these formulations [*Palko v. Connecticut,* 302 U.S. 319 (1937) and *Moore v. East Cleveland,* 431 U.S. 494 (1977)] would extend a fundamental right to homosexuals to engage in acts of consensual sodomy. Proscriptions against that conduct have ancient roots. . . . Sodomy was a criminal offense at common law and was forbidden by the laws of the original thirteen States when they ratified the Bill of Rights. In 1868, when the Fourteenth Amendment was ratified, all but 5 of the 37 States in the Union had criminal sodomy laws. In fact, until 1961, all 50 States outlawed sodomy, and today 24 States and the District of Columbia continue to provide criminal penalties for sodomy performed in private and between consenting adults. . . . Against this background, to claim that a right to engage in such conduct is "deeply rooted in this Nation's history and tradition" or "implicit in the concept of ordered liberty" is, at best, facetious. . . .

Respondent . . . asserts that the result should be different where the homosexual conduct occurs in the privacy of the home. He relies on *Stanley v. Georgia,* 394 U.S. 557, (1969) . . . where the Court held that the First Amendment prevents conviction for possessing and reading obscene material in the privacy of one's home: "If the First Amendment means anything, it means that a State has no business telling a man, sitting alone in his house, what books he may read or what films he may watch . . .".

Stanley did protect conduct that would not have been protected outside the home, and it partially prevented the enforcement of state obscenity laws; but the decision was firmly grounded in the First Amendment. The right pressed upon us here has no similar support in the text of the Constitution, and it does not qualify for recognition under the prevailing principles for construing the Fourteenth Amendment. Its limits are also difficult to discern. Plainly enough, otherwise illegal conduct is not always immunized whenever it occurs in the home. Victimless crimes, such as the possession and use of illegal drugs, do not escape the law where they are committed at home. *Stanley* itself recognized that its holding offered no protection for the possession in the home of drugs, firearms, or stolen goods. . . . And if respondent's submission is limited to the voluntary sexual conduct between consenting adults, it would be difficult, except by fiat, to limit the claimed right to homosexual conduct while leaving exposed to prosecution adultery, incest, and other sexual crimes even though they are committed in the home. We are unwilling to start down that road. . . .

Justice Blackmun, with whom Justice Brennan, Justice Marshall, and Justice Stevens join, dissenting:

This case is no more about "a fundamental right to engage in homosexual sodomy," as the Court purports to declare, . . . than *Stanley v. Georgia,* 394 U.S. 557 (1969), . . . was about a fundamental right to watch obscene movies. . . . Rather, this case is about "the most comprehensive of rights and the right most valued by civilized men," namely, "the right to be let alone." *Olmstead v. United States,* 277 U.S. 438, (1928) (Brandeis, J., dissenting).

The statute at issue, Ga. Code Ann. section 16-6-2 (1984), denies individuals the right to decide for themselves whether to engage in particular forms of private, consensual sexual activity. The Court concludes that section 16-6-2 is valid essentially because "the laws of . . . many States . . . still make such conduct illegal and have done so for a very long time . . ." (Holmes, J., dissenting). Like Justice Holmes [dissenting in *Lochner v. New York,* 198 U.S. 45 (1905)], I believe that "[i]t is revolting to have no better reason for a rule of law than that it was laid down in the time of Henry IV. It is still more revolting if the grounds upon which it was laid down have vanished long since, and the rule simply persists from blind imitation of the past." Holmes, The Path of Law, 10 *Harvard Law Review* 457, 469 (1897). I believe we must analyze Hardwick's claim in the light of the values that underlie the constitutional right to privacy. If that right means anything, it means that, before Georgia can prosecute its citizens for making choices about the most intimate aspects of their lives, it must do more than assert that the choice they have made is an "'abominable crime not fit to be named among Christians'."

Like the statute that is challenged in this case, the rationale of the Court's opinion applies equally to the prohibited conduct regardless of whether the parties who engage in it are married or unmarried, or are of the same or different sexes. Sodomy was condemned as an odious and sinful type of behavior during the formative period of the common law. That condemnation was equally damning for heterosexual and homosexual sodomy. Moreover, it provided no special exemption for married couples. The license to cohabit and to produce legitimate offspring simply did not include any permission to engage in sexual conduct that was considered a "crime against nature."

The Court's decision did not uphold Michael Hardwick's contention that his sexual conduct in the privacy of his own home was constitutionally protected. While the decision was seen as a blow to the assertion of gay rights, the majority's narrow one-vote margin also indicated the Court's shifting opinion on this issue.

XII. *REGENTS OF THE UNIVERSITY OF CALIFORNIA V. BAKKE* (1978)

The Supreme Court has reviewed several cases concerning equitable treatment in public education. Key cases include racially separate public schools (*Brown v. Board of Education,* 1954); the practice of English-only instruction for Chinese students in public schools (*Lau v. Nichols,* 1974); and the practice of operating public schools based solely on revenue from local property taxes (*San Antonio School District v. Rodriguez,* 1973).

African Americans not only had to fight for equity in public schools but also had to sue to gain admission to law and medical schools in state universities. See *Sipuel v. Oklahoma,* 1948; *Missouri ex rel Gaines,* 1938; and *Sweatt v. Painter,* 1950.

In 1978, race-based admissions became an issue again when a *white* person sued for admission to the medical school at the University of California at Davis. The case of *The Regents of the University of California v. Bakke,* however, must be seen in light of the policy of affirmative action, which sought to redress historic injustices against racial minorities and other specified groups by providing educational and employment opportunities to members of these groups.

In 1968, the University of California at Davis opened a medical school with a track admission policy for a 100-seat class. In 1974, applicants who identified themselves as economically and/or educationally disadvantaged or a member of a minority group (blacks, Chicanos, Asians, American Indians) were reviewed by a special committee. They could also compete for the remaining 84 seats. However, no disadvantaged white was ever admitted to the school through the special admissions program, although some applied. Bakke, a white male, applied to the medical school in 1973 and 1974 under the general admissions program. He was rejected both times because he did not meet the requisite cutoff score. In both years, special applicants with significantly lower scores than Bakke were admitted. After his second rejection Bakke sued for admission to the medical school, alleging that the special admissions program excluded him on the basis of his race in violation of the Equal Protection Clause of the Fourteenth Amendment, a provision of the California Constitution, and section 601 of Title VI of the Civil Rights Act of 1964, which provides that no person shall, on the ground of race or color, be excluded from participating in any program receiving federal financial assistance. The California Supreme Court applied a strict-scrutiny standard. It concluded that the special admissions program was not the least intrusive means of achieving the goals of the admittedly compelling state interests of integrating the medical profession and increasing the number of doctors willing to serve minority patients. The California court held that Davis's special admissions program violated the Equal Protection Clause of the U.S. Constitution. The

Davis Medical School was ordered to admit Bakke.

The Court's divided opinion addressed these key questions:

1. Does the University of California, Davis Medical School's admission policy violate the Fourteenth Amendment?
2. Does giving preference to a group of non-white applicants constitute discrimination?
3. Does the University of California, Davis Medical School use a racial classification that is suspect?
4. Was Bakke denied admission to the University of California, Davis Medical School on the basis of race?
5. Can race be used as a criterion for admission to a university?

Excerpts from the Supreme Court Decision in *The Regents of the University of California v. Bakke*[24]

Mr. Justice Powell delivered the opinion of the Court:

> The guarantees of the Fourteenth Amendment extend to all persons. Its language is explicit: "No State shall . . . deny to any person within its jurisdiction the equal protection of the laws." . . . The guarantee of equal protection cannot mean one thing when applied to one individual and something else when applied to a person of another color. . . .
>
> . . . the [Fourteenth] Amendment itself was framed in universal terms, without reference to color, ethnic origin, or condition of prior servitude.
>
> Petitioner [University of California, Davis] urges us to adopt for the first time a more restrictive view of the Equal Protection Clause and hold that discrimination against members of the white "majority" cannot be suspect if its purpose can be characterized as "benign."
>
> . . . Moreover, there are serious problems of justice connected with the idea of preference itself. First, it may not always be clear that a so-called preference is in fact benign. . . . Second, preferential programs may only reinforce common stereotypes holding that certain groups are unable to achieve success without special protection based on a factor having no relationship to individual worth. Third, there is a measure of inequity in forcing innocent persons in respondent's position to bear the burdens of redressing grievances not of their making.
>
> . . . When a classification denies an individual opportunities or benefits enjoyed by others solely because of his race or ethnic background, it must be regarded as suspect.
>
> If petitioner's purpose is to assure within its student body some specified percentage of a particular group merely because of its race or ethnic origin, such a preferential purpose must be rejected. . . . Preferring members of any one group for no reason other than race or ethnic origin is discrimination for its own sake. This the Constitution forbids.
>
> . . . [A] goal asserted by petitioner is the attainment of a diverse student body. This clearly is a constitutionally permissible goal for an institution of higher education. Academic freedom, though not a specifically enumerated constitutional right, long has been viewed as a special concern of the First Amendment. . . .
>
> Ethnic diversity, however, is only one element in a range of factors a university properly may consider in attaining the goal of a heterogeneous student body.
>
> It may be assumed that the reservation of a specified number of seats in each class for individuals from the preferred ethnic groups would contribute to the attainment of considerable ethnic diversity in the student body. But petitioner's argument that this is the only effective means of serving the interest of diversity is seriously flawed. . . . Petitioner's special admissions program, focused *solely* on ethnic diversity, would hinder rather than further attainment of genuine diversity.
>
> . . . In summary, it is evident that the Davis special admissions program involves the use of an explicit racial classification never before countenanced by this Court. It tells applicants who are not Negro, Asian, or Chicano that they are totally excluded from a specific percentage of the seats in the class.
>
> The fatal flaw in petitioner's preferential program is its disregard of individual rights as

guaranteed by the Fourteenth Amendment. Such rights are not absolute.

Mr. Justice Brennan, Mr. Justice White, Mr. Justice Marshall, and Mr. Justice Blackmun, concurring in part and dissenting in part:

We conclude . . . that racial classifications are not *per se* invalid under the Fourteenth Amendment.

Unquestionably we have held that a government practice or statute which restricts "fundamental rights" or which contains "suspect classifications" is to be subjected to "strict scrutiny" and can be justified only if it furthers a compelling government purpose. . . . But no fundamental right is involved here. Nor do whites as a class have any of the "traditional indicia of suspectness; the class is not saddled with such disabilities, or subjected to such a history of purposeful unequal treatment, or relegated to such a history of purposeful unequal treatment, or relegated to such position of political powerlessness as to command extraordinary protection from the majoritarian political process." . . .

Certainly . . . Davis had a sound basis for believing that the problem of under-representation of minorities was substantial and chronic. . . . Until at least 1973, the practice of medicine in this country was, in fact, if not in law, largely the prerogative of whites. In 1950, for example, while Negroes constituted 10% of the total population, Negro physicians constituted only 2.2% of the total number of physicians. The overwhelming majority of these . . . were educated in two predominantly Negro medical schools, Howard and Meharry. By 1970, the gap between the proportion of Negroes in medicine and their proportion in the population had widened: The number of Negroes employed in medicine remained frozen at 2.2% while the Negro population had increased to 11.1%. The number of Negro admittees to predominantly white medical schools, moreover, had declined in absolute numbers during the years 1955 to 1964.

Moreover, Davis had very good reason to believe that the national pattern of under-representation of minorities in medicine would be perpetuated if it retained a single admissions standard. . . .

Davis clearly could conclude that the serious and persistent under-representation of minorities in medicine depicted by these statistics is the result of handicaps under which minority applicants labor as a consequence of . . . deliberate, purposeful discrimination against minorities in education and in society generally, as well as in the medical profession. . . .

It is not even claimed that Davis' program in any way operates to stigmatize or single out any discrete . . . or even any identifiable, nonminority group. Nor will harm comparable to that imposed upon racial minorities by exclusion or separation on grounds of race be the likely result of the program. . . .

Nor was Bakke in any sense stamped as inferior by the Medical School's rejection of him. Indeed, it is conceded by all that he satisfied those criteria regarded by the school as generally relevant to academic performance better than most of the minority members who were admitted. Moreover, there is absolutely no basis for concluding that Bakke's rejection that was a result of Davis' use of racial preference will affect him throughout his life in the same way as the segregation of the Negro schoolchildren in *Brown I* would have affected them. Unlike discrimination against racial minorities, the use of racial preferences for remedial purposes does not inflict a pervasive injury upon individual whites in the sense that wherever they go or whatever they do there is a significant likelihood that they will be treated as second-class citizens because of their color. . . .

In addition, there is simply no evidence that the Davis program discriminated intentionally or unintentionally against any minority group which it purports to benefit. The program does not establish a quota in the invidious sense of a ceiling on the number of minority applicants to be admitted. . . .

Finally, Davis' special admissions program cannot be said to violate the Constitution. . . .

. . . we would reverse the judgment of the Supreme Court of California holding the Medical School's special admissions program unconstitutional and directing respondent's admission.

Justices Stevens and Stewart, along with Chief Justice Rehnquist, concurred and dissented in part. They found that the university's special admissions program violated Title VI of the Civil Rights Act of 1964, which prohibits discrimination under any program or activity receiving federal funding assistance. This dissent found that Bakke was not admitted to the Davis Medical School because of his race.

Race-based admissions were again considered in *Hopwood v. Texas,* a 1994 case in the Western District of Texas. The suit, brought by four white Texas residents, claimed that the affirmative action admissions program of the University of Texas School of Law violated the Equal Protection Clause of the Fourteenth Amendment and Title VI of the Civil Rights Act of 1964. The district court agreed that the plaintiffs' equal protection rights had been violated, but refused to direct the school to cease making admission decisions based on race. The case was subsequently appealed in the Court of Appeals for the Fifth Circuit, which held that the University of Texas School of Law could not use race as an admissions factor in order to achieve a diverse student body. The holding of the circuit court stands because the Supreme Court refused to hear the case.

This decision in effect overruled Justice Powell's opinion in *Bakke,* which held that universities can take account of an applicant's race in some circumstances. He asserted that the goal of achieving a diverse student body was permissible under the Constitution.

NOTES

1. *Privileges and immunities* refer to the ability of one state to discriminate against the citizens of another state. A resident of one state cannot be denied legal protection, access to the courts, or property rights in another state.
2. In *Smith v. Allwright,* 321 U.S. 649 (1944), the Supreme Court held that a 1927 Texas law that authorized political parties to establish criteria for membership in the state Democratic party violated the Fifteenth Amendment. In effect, the criteria excluded nonwhites from the Democratic party. Since only party members could vote in the primary election, the result was a whites-only primary. The Democratic party so dominated politics in the southern states after the Civil War that winning the primary was equivalent to winning the general election.
3. Americans of African descent have been called *blacks, Negroes, colored,* or *African Americans,* depending on the historical period.
4. 19 Howard 393 (1857).
5. 16 Wallace 130 (1872).
6. The Nineteenth Amendment that was ratified on August 18, 1920, stated, "The right of citizens of the United States to vote shall not be denied or abridged by the United States or by any state on account of sex. Congress shall have the power to enforce this article by appropriate legislation."
7. 21 Wallace 162 (1875).
8. Crozier, "Constitutionality of Discrimination Based on Sex," 15 *B.U.L. Review,* 723, 727–28 (1935) as quoted in William Hodes, "Women and the Constitution: Some Legal History and a New Approach to the Nineteenth Amendment" *Rutgers Law Review,* Vol. 25, 1970, p. 27.
9. Hodes, p. 45.
10. Gunnar Myrdal, *An American Dilemma: The Negro Problem and Modern Democracy.* New York: Harper and Row (2nd ed. 1962 [1944]), pp. 1073–74, as quoted in Hode, p. 29. This same biblical ground has yielded the idea that a woman is an extension of her husband and his status.
11. The states under military rule were Virginia, North Carolina, South Carolina, Georgia, Florida, Tennessee, Alabama, Mississippi, Texas, Louisiana, and Arkansas.
12. The term *colored* was used in Louisiana to describe persons of mixed race who had some African ancestry.
13. 163 U.S. 537 (1896).
14. Restrictive covenants were written in deeds restricting the use of the land. Covenants could prohibit the sale of land to nonwhites or non-Christians.
15. 347 U.S. 483 (1954).
16. 118 U.S. 356 (1886).
17. 112 U.S. 94 (1884).

18. Native Americans and slaves posed a problem when taking the census count, which was the basis for apportioning seats in the U.S. House of Representatives. Some states stood to lose representation if some of their slave or Native American population was not counted. Blacks were counted as three-fifths of a white man, and only those Native Americans who were taxed were counted.
19. 414 U.S. 563 (1974).
20. 411 U.S. 1 (1973).
21. Rhonda Copelon, "A Crime Not Fit to Be Named: Sex, Lies, and the Constitution," p. 182. In David Kairys (ed.), *The Politics of Law,* pp. 177–94, New York: Pantheon.
22. Copelon, p. 184.
23. 478 U.S. 186 (1986).
24. 438 U.S. 265 (1978).

READING 32

The Rise and Fall of Affirmative Action

James E. Jones, Jr.

INTRODUCTION

Twenty years ago as a novice in the academic arena I wrote an article entitled "The Bugaboo of Employment Quotas."[1] It began: "It is a tribute to the power of persuasive public relations that new terms or slogans can be created, or old terms imbued with new meanings which become code words triggering mindless support of, or opposition to, the concept symbolized by the magic slogan. . . . The term 'quota' [seems to] stimulate lurid fantasies in the minds of otherwise sober and conservative citizens. . . . Undefined, laden with old prejudices, one need only label the opposed activity to evoke the desired opposition. In the current flap over the Government's halting efforts to require affirmative action to ensure equality of employment opportunity in government assisted construction, we can see a classic example of the 'lurid fantasies' reaction to a program."[2]

There followed an article exploring the development, theory, design, and argument for the legality and constitutionality of the revised Philadelphia Plan. That plan, as we shall see below, was pivotal to the modern affirmative action concept. Little did I realize that 20 years later I would still be writing and speaking on the same issues addressed in that publication.

I am bitterly disappointed that affirmative action is still a current events topic in the 1990s. However, the Supreme Court's decision in *City of Richmond v. J. A. Croson Co.,*[3] a case invalidating the city of Richmond's program requiring a percentage of city contracts or subcontracts set aside for minorities or women, enunciated such stringent standards for approval of such programs as to put their continued legality in grave jeopardy. The lack of clarity which has typified recent Supreme Court cases ensures that the debates on affirmative action, both in and out of the Court, will continue for some time to come. . . .

Although the title I have used here is "The Rise and Fall of Affirmative Action," I shall endeavor to convey my conviction that, like the mythical Phoenix, affirmative action shall rise again.

AFFIRMATIVE ACTION DEFINED

The modern debate over affirmative action has occupied us for over 20 years without achieving resolution of the underlying issues or contributing to clarification of what divides the nation. . . .

As a working definition of affirmative action I have adopted the following formulation: "Public or private actions or programs which provide or seek to provide opportunities or other benefits to

James E. Jones, Jr., is emeritus professor of law and industrial relations at the University of Wisconsin, Madison.

persons on the basis of, among other things, their membership in a specified group or groups."[4] This definition permits us to direct attention to earlier efforts of the country to deal with the nagging problem of racism before the modern emergence, in 1961, of the presidential effort to utilize the affirmative action concept to secure equality of *employment opportunity* in government service and in government contracting.

Most of the cases today which directly address the issue of affirmative action have involved one of the following: (1) programs or plans for the enrollment of minorities or women in schools, primarily professional schools; (2) the set-aside of a percentage of subcontracts for minority or female subcontractors; or (3) the imposition of targets or goals for minority or female participation in employment.

It is worth noting that in the school desegregation cases involving busing to ensure desegregation, percentages of black or white students were required to be transferred between schools to achieve some semblance of proportionate representation. Busing has incurred inordinate attention and resistance over time; however, the cases were rarely if ever identified as involving affirmative action as the terminology has been used in modern debate. The Supreme Court has finally begun to recognize that the underlying principles are the same.[5]

SOME HISTORICAL BACKGROUND

In 1987 we celebrated the bicentennial of the American Constitution. I am certain that countless schoolchildren from grades K through 6 and beyond were treated to the glorious phrases which we celebrate in that memorable document. I am equally sure, however, that few if any were told that the Constitution was never conceived of as a color-blind document. Whatever "original intent" may mean, on this point the intent of the founding fathers is certainly clear. From the Declaration of Independence to the signing of the Articles of Confederation they did not intend that the brave statement "All men are created equal" include blacks. Moreover, blacks, slave or free, were not included in the word "citizens." The Supreme Court in *Dred Scott v. Sanford*[6] in 1857, concluding that at the time of the adoption of the Constitution, blacks were considered a "subordinate and inferior class of beings" who had no rights except those which whites might choose to grant them, made these limitations in our fundamental documents clear. I believe all students should be required to read that case as a peek into our dim, dark past. It is a well-documented statement of the status of black people in America. Moreover, it is irrefutable constitutional history that the Constitution of the United States was not color-blind.[7]

It took the Civil War and two constitutional amendments to affect the conditions described in the *Dred Scott* case as a matter of law. However, even with the Thirteenth and Fourteenth amendments on the books, the translation of the new *freedmen* from the condition of servitude to the condition of freedom and socioeconomic independence required more than brave words on yellowing parchment. While the Thirteenth Amendment abolished slavery, it did nothing to provide protection for the ex-slaves in their efforts to use the newly won freedom.

Whatever else the Fourteenth Amendment was intended to accomplish, there is compelling documentation to indicate that it was designed to place beyond constitutional doubt the early efforts of the federal government to aid the former slaves. Congress had adopted a series of social welfare laws expressly delineating the racial groups entitled to participate in the benefits of each program. These race-specific measures were adopted over the objections of critics who opposed giving special assistance to a single racial group. The most far-reaching of these programs was the 1866 Freedmen's Bureau Act, which was passed less than a month after Congress approved the Fourteenth Amendment.

The evidence is overwhelming that one reason for the adoption of the amendment was to provide a clear constitutional basis for such race-conscious programs.[8]

What was striking about the Reconstruction Era legislation was the range and diversity of the measures designed to provide race-related relief. Included were programs providing land, education, special monies for colored military personnel, charters to organizations to support the aged or indigent and destitute colored women and children, federal charters for banks, and even the establishment of a special hospital in the District of Columbia for freedmen. Few if any of these programs were restricted to identified victims of specific acts of discrimination. All were race-specific. "Affirmative action" (i.e., racial preference) was the law and policy of the United States. Yet, more than 120 years later we are still litigating the legality and constitutionality of the principle.

One might question why Congress was concerned with the enactment of the Fourteenth Amendment to authorize the Freedmen's Bureau acts and related legislation. The language of the amendment makes it clear that it applies only to states. However, much of the legislation of that era (such as the Civil Rights Act of 1866, 42 U.S.C. 1983) was directed specifically at states, and it seems that Congress merely failed to recognize that there was anything in the Constitution which might have barred its actions at the federal level. It was not until much later in the development of our constitutional law that the loophole was closed, when the Fifth Amendment's due process clause was interpreted to prohibit conduct of the federal government which, if engaged in by a state, would violate the Fourteenth Amendment's equal protection clause. This incorporation of the Fourteenth Amendment equal protection standards into the Fifth was not fully accomplished until the 1950s.[9]

In the balance of my discussion in this essay I have adopted a perverse approach. Usually, one declares a proposition in the affirmative. Instead, I purport to declare a series of negatives. Why? Most people have learned whatever they know about affirmative action from the media. Most media presentations have been unsympathetic to affirmative action and frequently contain misconceptions and misinformation. In an effort to respond, I shall concentrate on what affirmative action is not.

NOT A NOVEL CONCEPT

The legal and conceptual underpinnings of the term "affirmative action" are rooted in ancient history of Anglo-American law. The basic concept comes from equity, which was originally a separate body of law administered in England by the court of chancery. Legal rules were unduly rigid and legal remedies were often inadequate. To do equity was to attempt to make things right, an attempt at fundamental fairness, if you will. When we became a separate country we retained the English system of common law, including the concept of equity.

More modern adaptations of the flexibility and equitable responses to novel problems where the law has proved inadequate are most readily illustrated by the New Deal's proliferation of administrative agencies during the Depression of the 1930s. Much of the social legislation of that era empowered the courts or the agencies to require such affirmative action as would effectuate the purposes of the law.

The "preferential treatment" or "reverse discrimination" aspects of modern affirmative action are also not novel. As noted earlier, as far back as 1866 in the congressional debates over the enactment of the Freedmen's Bureau acts, Congress explored both the constitutionality and the desirability of race-conscious remedies for the freedmen and other refugees of war. The reading of those debates impresses me with two things: (1) except for differences in terminology the concepts discussed were the same as modern debates over affirmative action; (2) it was clear that one of the purposes of that Congress was to resolve any doubt that such race-conscious programs were legal.

NOT ONE CONCEPT BUT TWO

The first and older notion of affirmative action is as remedy postadjudication, or as part of the adjudication process. It was called into being only after parties had adjudicated the issue before the court; the court had determined that a wrong had been done by the defendant to the plaintiff and exercised its power to fashion relief. This remedial power involves two aspects: (1) the power of the court to grant *make-whole relief* to the identified victims of the defendant's misconduct, *and* (2) the power, and the duty, of the court to issue such orders as would ensure compliance with the law in the future. The second aspect is *prospective* relief that focuses on the bad deeds of the defendant and not upon entitlement of identified victims of discrimination.

The second concept is affirmative action as legislative or executive program. Both approaches are directed to remedying a situation considered to be socially undesirable. In the first instance it has been determined by a court to be a violation of existing law. In the second instance, a legislative or administrative agency determines that some problem needs specific attention. A private entity, without benefit of adjudication or pressure by a public body, may also decide that a situation in which it has responsibility or authority needs attention. It could establish a program to deal with such a problem. Charitable institutions abound that are devoted to addressing particular problems.

Since at least 1969, beginning with the first case arising under Title VII of the Civil Rights Act of 1964 to reach the court of appeals, federal courts in designing remedies to deal with employment discrimination have imposed affirmative action plans upon defendants as part of their prospective relief after adjudication. This practice has tended to blur the distinction in modern debates between the two contexts in which affirmative action arises.

The principal modern application of the second concept was first embodied in an executive order issued by President Kennedy in 1961 and carried forward to the present day by an executive order issued by Lyndon Johnson in 1965.[10]

It should be noted that those executive orders required government contractors to refrain from discrimination *and* to take affirmative action to ensure equality of employment opportunity. They were not concerned with either the guilt of any defendants or the entitlements of any victims. They were concerned with addressing an existing social problem that had been unresponsive to other efforts.[11]

NOT A RESULT BUT A PROCESS

The federal government's affirmative action programs in employment require every good-faith effort to reach objectives or goals. They do not require that any particular goal be reached. Failure to reach the goal does not require the employer to lose his status as a contractor but may result in an investigation to determine what good-faith efforts he made to achieve the objectives. The federal government first embarked upon this approach in 1969 when the Department of Labor issued the revised Philadelphia Plan. After analyzing the relevant labor market and determining the availability of both qualified minorities and jobs subject to the federal government's contracting program, the Secretary of Labor mandated that contractors participating in such programs make every good-faith effort to achieve a range of minority participation. The goals were well within the availability of minorities in the *qualified* labor pool. The requirement was to make every good-faith effort to reach the targets; it did not call for the impossible. Legal challenges to the program were successfully met.[12]

What we learn from Supreme Court cases is that a quota is a system which restricts or requires participation of a fixed and inflexible number or ratio of minorities, which includes sanctions to enforce compliance with the requirements, and in which the relevance of the requirements to the class affected and to the evil perceived is questionable or unestablished.[13] These "quota" elements are *not* those which are present in plans and programs which have met with approval in the courts.

NOT A MANDATE TO HIRE THE UNQUALIFIED

I have been unable to discover any affirmative action program, or any case imposing affirmative action as remedy, or after a consent decree, that requires the hiring of the unqualified. Affirmative action *methodology* excludes from the goals those people in the protected class in the labor market who are unqualified. The assertions of people who would mislead us regarding affirmative action when faced with these legal points are, "Well, you know how people behave. The employers will hire anybody just so they reach their quotas."

The logic of that argument would seem to be that since some people will continue to violate the law we ought to repeal the laws.

NOT CONCEIVED BY "LIBERALS"

. . . The modern affirmative action obligation which we have traced to John F. Kennedy's 1961 executive order had *its* "roots" in the prior administration.

In 1959, then Vice President Nixon was in charge of the president's executive order program prohibiting discrimination by government contractors. In his final report to President Eisenhower, Nixon identified the problem. It was not that evil people, with bad motives, intentionally harmed victims, but rather that *systems* operated in a business-as-usual fashion and kept re-creating the patterns of the past. I have paraphrased it here, but this is a "textbook" formulation of what we now call institutional racism or institutional sexism.

In 1961, John F. Kennedy responded by issuing an executive order which required federal contractors, and subcontractors, to take affirmative action to ensure equality of opportunity. He also *separately* prohibited intentional discrimination on the basis of race, color, religion, national origin, and so forth.

The implementation of goals and timetables occurred under the Nixon-Ford administration. The revised Philadelphia Plan was issued when George Schultz, the secretary of state under President Reagan, was secretary of labor serving under President Nixon. As indicated above, the Philadelphia Plan was unsuccessfully challenged in court, was unsuccessfully challenged in Congress, and ultimately the Department of Labor issued general rules and regulations requiring affirmative action for all government contractors.[14]

Every president since Roosevelt . . . has either issued his own executive order or continued the order in effect when he was elected. While there was much "sound and fury" from the Reagan administration regarding the demise of the affirmative action rules, and even a proposal that the executive order be revised, the fact is that these rules stand on the books as the existing requirements. Documentation of failure to enforce them would subject the government to legal action in the court.[15] Reagan signed into law bills requiring affirmative action. It would be difficult to sustain a charge that Eisenhower, Nixon, and Reagan were "liberals."

We heard little from the Bush administration regarding its intentions except first vetoing legislative efforts to address civil rights cases which threatened affirmative action and other equal employment gains. Bush finally signed the Civil Rights Act of 1991 which Congress passed with some minor compromise language addressing the quota issue. Efforts by some in his administration to water down the affirmative action requirements under the existing executive order were quickly rejected by the president.

NOT REJECTED BY MAJOR PRIVATE EMPLOYERS

Under the Reagan administration the United States Department of Justice aggressively attacked affirmative action, appearing in the Supreme Court in opposition to existing programs and counseling cities and other local entities to revoke or modify their affirmative action requirements. During that era representatives of large employers particularly indicated that they not only considered goals and timetables good business but believed them to be right as well. More significantly, both they and their lawyers concluded that it was legally prudent to maintain affirmative action programs. So long as programs are not declared illegal, and all efforts of the Justice Department during the earlier period failed to establish that the programs violated Title VII, then employers are able to use them defensively when they are accused of individual or class-action discrimination in Title VII cases.

The burden of the so-called reverse-discrimination plaintiff who would challenge the employer's affirmative action plan requires proof of intent to discriminate. The official rules and regulations of the Equal Employment Opportunity Commission accord to an employer operating under a bona fide affirmative action plan a good-faith defense against litigation. Although that defense might not be considered operative against the unconsenting plaintiff, it would certainly seem reasonable that the Supreme Court would conclude that the employer's good-faith compliance with such an affirmative action plan is a legitimate business justification for his action. Answers to these questions await future litigation. . . .

NOT A BOON TO THE UNDERCLASS

It is not likely that any of the affirmative action programs have measurably helped the underclass of America, which seems to be growing. I should limit this assertion to affirmative action in employment, since training and educational programs certainly would and should target members of our society who lack the education and skills to be beneficiaries of other affirmative action programs.

This is not a minority problem alone. Most of the unemployed poor, most of the people in this country who are below the poverty level, are not minorities. Minorities are disproportionately represented in this group, to be sure, but it is mostly white. Women, single heads of households, are disproportionately represented in the group, and a disproportionate number of those are also black.

It is obvious on its face that affirmative action goals and timetables in employment, which focus upon qualified protected-class members, could have no appreciable impact on the plight of the people who are unqualified. The reason is clear. For persons without education or skills, without some qualification that is in demand, affirmative action in employment is of little benefit.

If anti-affirmative action forces are victorious in attacks on contract setasides, then efforts in employment, in education and training, in housing and health and all other social activities wherein special efforts have been undertaken to include minorities, will also cease.

NEITHER UNCONSTITUTIONAL NOR ILLEGAL

In the last 20 years, the Supreme Court has addressed the constitutionality and the legality of affirmative action in a multiplicity of settings. It has been confronted with the programs of private parties, of states, and of Congress itself. It has looked at admission to educational institutions, at government subcontracting, and at employment in hiring and in layoffs. Most of these cases have been decided by a divided Court, often with a plurality opinion not supported by a majority of the Court, and with "opinion salad" of three or four concurrences and dissents. What often gets lost in all this confusion is the basic posture of affirmative action programs. The Supreme Court has never held that the principle of affirmative action is impermissible. Even when the Justices have found a particular program to be over the line, they have stuck to the position that the Constitution of the United States and the civil rights laws do allow for some affirmative action programs. The Court has articulated factors that should be considered and conditions that must be met for a particular plan to be upheld, but the basic concept is still considered constitutional and legal. As a practical matter, however, it may well be that what the Court has given with one hand it has taken away with the other.

Except to deny review of numerous employment cases, the United States Supreme Court did not enter the affirmative action debate until *DeFunis v. Odegaard,*[16] a law school admissions case that the Supreme Court accepted for review and then dismissed as moot. Then Justice Douglas in dissent spawned a host of commentary and the debate raged on until the Court addressed the issue again in *Regents of the University of California v. Bakke.*[17] In these two cases, at issue were affirmative action programs established for minority students by a law school in the first instance and a medical school in the second. In both cases the universities had sought to reserve a set number of seats in the entering classes for minorities. Due to the limited number of places in the entering class, and the differential performance rates of minorities generally as compared to majority candidates on admissions examinations, it was unlikely that sufficient minorities would be admitted into those classes if acceptance for admission were determined by rank-ordering applicants by grade point and test scores.

Both these cases involved two American myths: (1) "distinctions between citizens solely because of their ancestry are by their nature odious to a free people whose institutions are founded upon the doctrine of equality",[18] (2) the myth of merit.

As far as the first myth—classification by race or ancestry being odious to a free people—is concerned, we might well contemplate the lessons learned from a brief examination of the status of America circa 1857 as illustrated by the Supreme Court's decision in *Dred Scott v. Sanford.*

Even more paradoxical, at the moment when the Supreme Court in 1943 intoned this principle of equality, racial segregation was the law of the land and constitutionally valid. Indeed, how can racial separation exist without classification by race in the first instance? In 1943 we were engaged with our allies in World War II, a war to make the world free for democracy. The military forces of the United States were segregated by race. Merit was irrelevant to the classification. Blacks who scored above the 90th percentile on the navy's exams were still ineligible for officers' training. In the army and air force, they were relegated to segregated units. The war effort was color-coded.

Granted, since this country's inception we have been chasing something called a meritocracy. Divorced from England, where positions of aristocracy were determined primarily by birthright, a principle we rejected, the new America believed that positions of leadership were to be determined on the basis of merit. Somewhere along the line we got the notion that we could discover superior intellectual ability by a series of tests, could rank people in order of their performance thereon, and could thus determine comparative merit. A score of 100 demonstrated merit superior to 99, 99 to 98, 98 to 97, and so on. In our pursuit of meritocracy, we have imbued test performance with the halo of superior merit, at least in theory. Those who achieve high test scores perceive themselves as having a right to the best opportunities. The fact of the matter is that virtually no system operates in such a stilted fashion. I suspect the use of tests in jobs has its roots in educational testing. The first affirmative action cases to reach the Supreme Court were school admission cases.[19] Schools that claim that merit controls admission have always had a multiplicity of exceptions, ranging from the size of the contribution of alumni and the relationship of the applicants to such benefactors, to the determination that no matter what the merit of the applicants, certain ones would not be admissible. Even when the exclusions were modified, frequently a quota limiting the number of applicants from certain classes of people was imposed.*

Similarly, in almost all civil service systems where merit allegedly controls, actual practice deviates from the principle. What usually happens is that the top three candidates or the top five (or some other number) on the eligibility list are referred to the selecting officer, who may, without explanation, choose anyone from that group. Moreover, in most instances veterans are given points to add to their scores, not because of any test performance but as entitlement for service to the country.

It is important to note also that in neither *DeFunis* nor *Bakke* was there an assertion that the minority applicants were unqualified. The issues were that the majority plaintiff scored higher on the tests and had better grades than some minority candidates accepted and therefore was entitled to a position, which but for the affirmative action program he would have received, or so the argument goes.

The pivotal opinion in the *Bakke* case was that of Justice Powell. He and four of his colleagues found that it was not *per se* unconstitutional to use race in affirmative action programs when the programs were appropriately crafted. However, Powell concluded that the particular program offended the law. Four other colleagues of his agreed that it offended the law and thought that the discussion of the constitutionality of the programs was inappropriate. In that case, with the welter of opinions, everybody won and everybody lost.

The next significant case on affirmative action in the Supreme Court was *United Steelworkers of America v. Weber.*[20] The Court there approved an affirmative action program over the protests of a white male employee who alleged reverse discrimination. The company and its union voluntarily entered into a program to deal with what they perceived to be a problem of minority workers' entry into skilled crafts. Noting the widespread exclusion of blacks by construction industry unions, the Court approved a voluntary program which provided in-house training for the skilled jobs, with participation in the program divided equally between black and white employees on the basis of seniority. The narrow issue the Court decided in the *Weber* case was that voluntary adoption of such a program under the circumstances did not violate Title VII of the Civil Rights Act of 1964, which prohibited employment discrimination. Again, the Court was divided, with dissenting opinions contending that the majority misread the statute.

In *Fullilove v. Klutznick*[21] the Court examined a program in which Congress had established a 10 percent set-aside of certain federal contracts for minority contractors. By a 6–3 vote the Court sustained the constitutionality of the program, although several opinions were written taking different approaches. Thus, the theory upon which the Court sustained the program is somewhat uncertain. Significantly, then Chief Justice Warren Burger determined that the judiciary was not the exclusive branch to address the effects of past discrimination; rather, elected officials, such as chief executives and appropriate legislative bodies, are the more appropriate governmental entities to establish affirmative action programs to deal with the legacy of our past.[22] A major issue dividing the Supreme Court in these affirmative action cases was by what standard courts should evaluate programs which admittedly used race classification as a significant ingredient. . . .

*An interesting aside on the myth of merit from the past: No matter how bright and agile a woman was, prior to affirmative action, she would not be acceptable as an appointment to West Point, to the naval academy, or to other military schools. After affirmative action, however, a woman cadet was chosen to lead the entire corps at West Point in 1989. The football teams of all the academies were disproportionately black.

In *United States v. Paradise,*[23] a case which had been in litigation in one form or another since 1971, the federal district court finally ordered the state of Alabama to hire one black for every white state trooper and to adopt a promotion plan based on numerical goals as well as on the availability of qualified applicants from the pool of black state troopers eligible for promotion. The Court again debated its fundamental differences. However, a plurality suggested that "In determining whether race conscious remedies are appropriate we look to several factors, including the necessity for the relief and the efficacy of alternative remedies, the flexibility and duration of the relief, including the availability of waiver provisions; the relationship of the numerical goals to the relevant labor markets; and the impact of the relief on the rights of third parties."[24] . . .

In *City of Richmond v. J. A. Croson,* there is finally a majority on the issue of which standard shall be applicable to race-based remedial programs. The Supreme Court struck down a provision enacted by the Richmond city council whereby prime contractors awarded city construction contracts were required to subcontract at least 30 percent of the dollar amount to one or more minority-owned business enterprises. The Court cleared up the confusion which had been spawned by the plurality in [a previous case] regarding whether the state actor must itself be implicated in prior discrimination as a predicate for establishing an affirmative action program. If a local subdivision of a state has the delegated authority to do so, the Supreme Court concluded it may act to eradicate the effects of private discrimination within its own jurisdiction. It was not necessary to implicate the state or local entity in the discrimination. It would be enough if the city demonstrated that it was a passive participant in a system of racial exclusion practiced by other elements of the industry.

Significantly, the majority of the Court concluded that strict scrutiny was the required standard of analysis. To institute a program requiring classification based on race (1) any racial classification must be justified by a compelling government interest; (2) the means chosen by the state to effectuate its purpose must be narrowly tailored to the achievement of that goal. The Court found neither prong of the strict-scrutiny test satisfied in the *Croson* case. The case directs our attention to the *details* upon which these programs rest as well as the *details* upon which the plans themselves, in a remedial sense, rest. It seems that the factor analysis set forth in the plurality opinion in *Paradise* is endorsed by a majority. The difficulty is that one is unable to conclude with certainty the specificity to which compliance with these programs will be held. . . .

NO PARTICULAR LEVEL OF SCRUTINY CONSTITUTIONALLY REQUIRED

The Supreme Court debate over the applicability of the strict-scrutiny standard versus some intermediate level of review is an internal debate between competing "academic" theories of analysis neither of which is compelled by the Constitution. I hasten to add that neither is prohibited by the Constitution, nor is there any apparent reason why both might not operate, as indeed they do. By a 5–4 majority in *Croson,* the strict-scrutiny standard is applied to state classifications by race even where affirmative action programs are involved and the action of the state is "benign" with regard to the race so classified. Where the classification is based on sex, on the other hand, the Supreme Court has utilized a different, so-called sliding, scale of scrutiny.

The strict-scrutiny standard did not come etched in articles of the Constitution in its original or its amended form. It is a doctrine of rather recent vintage, suggested in a footnote in *United States v. Carolene Products Co.* in 1938.[25] It has been said that Justice Harlan Stone, a former law professor at Columbia University, was probably using the footnote to spark debate over ideas he had not fully developed.[26] As nearly as I can tell, this "strict-scrutiny analysis" was not again referred to until Stone's concurring opinion in 1942 in *Skinner v. State of Oklahoma.*[27] . . .

It should be noted that the issue of the applicability of the strict-scrutiny standard to efforts by a state, or the federal government, to classify by race in order to do something beneficial to the group so classified did not arise until the affirmative action cases. The earliest one of which I am aware is the *Regents of the University of California v. Bakke,* which we have examined above.[28]

To summarize the commentary on the choice of level of scrutiny which the Court adopted, I submit that there is no compelling rationale for using the strict-scrutiny standard to evaluate affirmative action programs designed to address the persistent national problem of underutilization. Lack of equitable participation by minorities in the largess of a democratic system is an adequate basis for concluding that those programs deserve a treatment different from classification by race that serves to perpetuate the disadvantaged position of minority persons. Making the distinction between the level of scrutiny applied when classification by sex is at issue and that utilized when race or other ethnicity is at issue is not particularly persuasive. Just as the Court decided in the forties that strict scrutiny was necessary to protect discrete and insular minorities from deprivation, it could as easily have decided that the intermediate level of scrutiny was appropriate when the purpose of the program was to benefit the race so classified.[29] . . .

NEITHER MORAL ISSUE NOR MATTER OF REPARATIONS

The survival of affirmative action programs for the future is not a moral issue, nor a matter of reparations; it is a matter of the survival of this nation. In 1987 the Hudson Institute compiled *Workforce 2000, Work and Workers for the 21st Century.* Subsidized by a grant from the Labor Department, this study contains a host of scenarios, assumptions, and projections for the year 2000. . . .

Workforce 2000, chapter 3, suggests that *demographics* are *destiny.* I think that probably is a safe assertion. The conclusions the report draws are the following:

1. The average age of the population of the workforce will rise and the pool of young workers entering the labor market will shrink;
2. More women will enter the workforce, although the rate of increase will taper off;
3. Minorities will be a larger share of new entrants into the labor force;
4. Immigrants will represent the largest share of the increase in the population in the workforce since World War I.[30]

The only fact enunciated above that would be subject to manipulation by external forces, it seems to me, is the fourth one, regarding the size of the immigrant pool.

By the year 2000 it is projected that approximately 47 percent of the workforce will be women, with 61 percent of the women in the country at work. Additionally, women will constitute about three-fifths of the new entrants into the labor force between 1985 and the year 2000.[31] Minorities—blacks, Hispanics, and others—will constitute 29 percent of the net additions to the workforce between 1985 and the year 2000 and will account for more than 15 percent of the workforce in the year 2000.[32]

The report projects that by the year 2000 white males, thought a generation ago to be the mainstays of the economy, will constitute only 15 percent of the net additions to the labor force.[33]

If minorities and women continue to join the workforce at such disproportionate rates, it will not be too long before they are the majority.

If we assume a work life of 30 years, by the time the 18–24-year-old entries into the workforce in 1990 get to retirement age, the workforce upon which the health of their retirement fund and of our America will depend will be overwhelmingly minority and female. Those people are the targets of today's affirmative action programs which are threatened with discontinuance.

Let me suggest that while in my generation the argument for affirmative action was based on a moral imperative—an argument not too persuasive in some sectors of our society—the issue now is a matter of the national economic health. Indeed, health and happiness in the "golden years" of today's "me" generation may well depend upon the vigor of affirmative action.

Prognosticators assure us, and point to evidence readily available, that the jobs of the future will be predominantly high-tech ones requiring a greater degree of skill and education. Moreover, as our world of work becomes more complicated, frequent training and retraining are likely to be necessary. If there is not a sufficient educational base to begin with, keeping up with changing technical needs and absorbing new training will be impossible. We cannot afford to have minorities and women excluded from mainstream education and job activities. We cannot risk increasing percentages of dropouts of minority males, black males in particular, from the labor market. We cannot afford the increasing rate of incarceration of larger and larger proportions of the minority population, particularly the males.

It costs from a low figure of $20,000 to a high one of $40,000 a year to keep an inmate in prison. That is more money than the cost of maintaining a student for one year in our most expensive private colleges. There certainly must be some other way we can utilize our resources.

If these projections, which have come principally from government-subsidized research, are close to accurate, we must stop thinking, if we do, of affirmative action as a program that shows a preference for minorities or women or grants them a privilege. We must consider it an obligation to reach out and include them in the mainstream of our society, and an obligation on their part to participate to the fullest of their potential.

Now one might argue, as some of the optimistic prognostications do, that a combination of an ageing workforce, a declining percentage of young people going into that workforce, and an increase in high-tech jobs equals tight labor markets, and therefore the job demand will take care of the utilization of all of our human capital. That rosy view ignores history. The modern push of blacks for antidiscrimination measures occurred in 1941 when Asa Philip Randolph threatened President Roosevelt with a March on Washington if the president didn't do something about discrimination by war contractors. At the point of implementation of Executive Order 8802 there was a *tight labor market,* at least for skilled craftsmen. And yet, fully qualified black craftsmen, graduates from the industrial arts departments of a myriad of segregated colleges, were denied employment on the basis of race.

It was only as the job market tightened during the war that women were heavily recruited for light assembly work in the war industries. Despite the glamorization of the role of women workers in the war effort—epitomized in the popular song "Rosie the Riveter"—even into the midfifties women were still considered the "secondary workforce."

We must maintain the momentum which has been achieved in the last 15 or 20 years in opening up employment opportunities. Even more imperative is the mounting of new initiatives to ensure that women, minorities, and all of our society referred to by the sociologists as the "underclass" be drawn into the educational process.

We should realize that it takes at least a generation—that is, 20 years—to develop a potentially competent worker. For various high-tech activities it will take somewhat longer than that. If we let affirmative action fall by the wayside now, and if old patterns of underutilization of women and minorities reassert themselves—as I believe they would—by the time the cumulative impact of the neglect manifested itself we would have lost an entire generation of progress.

Although the leadership cohorts of today—that is, persons aged 45 to 65—may have less reason to feel threatened by these projections, for those who are on the threshold of their careers, *the crisis is now.*

CONCLUSION

All of us in this country are the ultimate victims of invidious discrimination. The fraud of racism, which has infected our society since its inception, has tarnished our Constitution, our laws, our education, our science, our morals, and our religions. It has been the most persistent and devisive element in this society and one that has limited our growth and happiness as a nation. The only way to put racism behind us is to be race conscious in our remedies. Affirmative action alone cannot solve all of our problems, but it can continue to make a contribution. If sustained sufficiently over time it could help to cleanse our country of the effects of its sordid history.

If we do not continue to address this issue, racism will continue to be a strain and a drain upon our corporate resources. If there is such a thing as human capital, our society cannot afford to continue to underutilize what is likely to become an ever-increasing share of its human resources.[34]

NOTES

An earlier version of this paper was delivered as a Distinguished Lecture at Northeastern University, Boston, Massachusetts, October 18, 1989.

1. *Wisconsin Law Review* (1970): 341–403.
2. Ibid., p. 341.
3. 488 U.S. 469 (1989).
4. James E. Jones, Jr., "The Origins of Affirmative Action," *University of California-Davis Law Review* 21 (1988): 383–419; quotation, p. 389.
5. See *United States v. Paradise,* 480 U.S. 149 (1987), concurring opinion of Justice Stevens at 189–90; *City of Richmond v. J. A. Croson Co.,* 488 U.S. 469 (1989), concurring opinion of Justice Scalia at 521–23, 525–26; dissenting opinion of Justice Marshall at 535–40.
6. 60 U.S. 393 (1857).
7. The Chief Justice of the Court wrote that "[T]here are two clauses in the Constitution which point directly and specifically to the negro race as a separate class of persons, and show clearly that they were not regarded as a portion of the people or citizens of the government then formed." Ibid. at 411. . . . "[T]he language of the Declaration of Independence and of the Articles of Confederation, in addition to the plain words of the Constitution itself; the legislation of the different states, before, about the time, and since the Constitution was adopted; . . . the legislation of the Congress from the time of its adoption to a recent period; and we have the constant and uniform action of the Executive Department, all concurring together and leading to the same result [that is, that blacks were not a portion of the people or citizens of the government]." Ibid. at 426.
8. See Eric Schnapper, "Affirmative Action and the Legislative History of the Fourteenth Amendment," *Virginia Law Review* 71 (1985): 753–98, esp. pp. 780–85; see also Judith Baer, *Equality Under the Constitution: Reclaiming the Fourteenth Amendment* (Ithaca, N.Y.: Cornell University Press, 1983) (particularly ch. 4 and the references cited therein).
9. See *Bolling v. Sharpe,* 347 U.S. 497 (1954); see also Kenneth L. Karst, "The Fifth Amendment's Guarantee of Equal Protection," *North Carolina Law Review* 55 (1977): 541–62; and Schnapper, "Affirmative Action," p. 787.
10. Executive Order 11246, *Code of Federal Regulations* (1964–65 comp.): 339.
11. The best judicial discussion of the two contexts in which affirmative action arises is found in *Associated Contractors of Massachusetts v. Altshuler,* 490 F.2d 9 (1st Cir. 1973), *cert. denied,* 416 U.S. 957 (1974).
12. *Contractors Association of Eastern Pennsylvania v. Secretary of Labor,* 442 F.2d 159 (3d Cir. 1971), *cert. denied,* 404 U.S. 854 (1971).
13. See Jones, "The Bugaboo of Employment Quotas," pp. 373–78.
14. Affirmative Action Rules are in *Code of Federal Regulations* 41 (rev. 1991): part 60–2.

15. See, e.g., *Legal Aid Society of Almeda County v. Brennan,* 608 F.2d 1319 (9th Cir. 1979), *cert. denied,* 447 U.S. 921 (1980).
16. 416 U.S. 312 (1974).
17. 438 U.S. 265 (1978).
18. *Hirabayshi v. United States,* 320 U.S. 81, 100 (1943); *Loving v. Commonwealth of Virginia,* 388 U.S. 1, 11 (1967).
19. *DeFunis v. Odegaard,* 416 U.S. 312 (1974), and *Regents of the University of California v. Bakke,* 438 U.S. 265 (1978).
20. 443 U.S. 193 (1979).
21. 448 U.S. 448 (1980).
22. Ibid. at 483.
23. 480 U.S. 149 (1987).
24. Ibid. at 171.
25. 304 U.S. 144, 152 n. 4 (1938); see also Lewis F. Powell, Jr., "*Carolene Products* Revisited," *Columbia Law Review* 82 (1982): 1087–92.
26. See Alpheus Thomas Mason, *Harlan Fisk Stone: Pillar of the Law* (New York: Viking Press, 1956), p. 513.
27. 316 U.S. 535 (1942).
28. The substantive issue was not joined in *DeFunis v. Odegaard,* 416 U.S. 312 (1974).
29. See, e.g., Herman Schwartz, "The 1986 and 1987 Affirmative Action Cases: It's All Over but the Shouting," *Michigan Law Review* 86 (1987): 524–76, esp. pp. 524, 545–76; see also Mary C. Daly, "Some Runs, Some Hits, Some Errors—Keeping Score in the Affirmative Action Ball-park from Weber to Johnson," *Boston College Law Review* 30 (1988): 1–97; George Rutherglen and Daniel R. Ortiz, "Affirmative Action under the Constitution and Title VII: From Confusion to Convergence," *UCLA Law Review* 35 (1988): 467–518.
30. William B. Johnston and Arnold E. Packer, *Workforce 2000: Work and Workers for the 21st Century* (Indianapolis: Hudson Institute, and Washington, D.C.: U.S. Department of Labor, 1987), pp. 15–16.
31. Ibid., p. 85.
32. Ibid., p. 89.
33. Ibid., p. 95.
34. Jones, "Origins of Affirmative Action," p. 418.

READING 33

The Shape of the River

Long-Term Consequences of Considering Race in College and University Admissions

William G. Bowen and Derek Bok

"You've got to know the shape of the river perfectly. It is all there is left to steer by on a very dark night. . . . "

"Do you mean to say that I've got to know all the million trifling variations of shape in the banks of this interminable river as well as I know the shape of the front hall at home?"

"On my honor, you've got to know them better."

—Mark Twain, *Life on the Mississippi*

The "river" that is the subject of this [study] can never be "learned" once and for all. The larger society changes, graduates of colleges and universities move from one stage of life to another, and educational institutions themselves evolve. Similarly, there is much yet to be learned about the future lives of those who have attended selective colleges and professional schools over the last thirty years. This study, then, does not purport to provide final answers to questions about race-sensitive admissions in higher education. No piece of this river can ever be considered to be "all down" in anyone's book. But we are persuaded of the value of examining each piece "*both* ways"—when "coming upstream," as students enroll in college, and "when it was behind me," as graduates go on to pursue their careers and live their lives.

So much of the current debate relies on anecdotes, assumptions about "facts," and conjectures that it is easy for those who have worked hard to

William G. Bowen is president of the Andrew W. Mellon Foundation and former president of Princeton University. Derek Bok is a university professor at Harvard University. He is a former president of Harvard University and former dean of the Harvard Law School.

increase minority enrollments to become defensive or disillusioned. It is easy, too, for black and Hispanic graduates, as well as current minority students, to be offended by what they could well regard as unjustified assaults on their competence and even their character. Some of the critics of affirmative action may also feel aggrieved, sensing that they are unjustly dismissed as Neanderthals or regarded as heartless. In short, the nature of the debate has imposed real costs on both individuals and institutions just as it has raised profound questions of educational and social policy that deserve the most careful consideration. In the face of what seems like a veritable torrent of claims and counterclaims, there is much to be said for stepping back and thinking carefully about the implications of the record to date before coming to settled conclusions.

On inspection, many of the arguments against considering race in admissions—such as allegations of unintended harm to the intended beneficiaries and enhanced racial tensions on campus—seem to us to lack substance. More generally, our data show that the overall record of accomplishment by black students after graduation has been impressive. But what more does this detailed examination of one sizable stretch of the river suggest about its future course? What wide-angle view emerges?

THE MEANING OF "MERIT"

One conclusion we have reached is that the meaning of "merit" in the admissions process must be articulated more clearly. "Merit," like "preference" and "discrimination," is a word that has taken on so much baggage we may have to re-invent it or find a substitute.

Still, it is an important and potentially valuable concept because it reminds us that we certainly do not want institutions to admit candidates who *lack* merit, however the term is defined. Most people would agree that rank favoritism (admitting a personal friend of the admissions officer, say) is inconsistent with admission "on the merits," that no one should be admitted who cannot take advantage of the educational opportunities being offered, and that using a lottery or some similar random numbers scheme to choose among applicants who are over the academic threshold is too crude an approach.

One reason why we care so much about who gets admitted "on the merits" is because, as this study confirms, admission to the kinds of selective schools included in the College and Beyond [C&B]* universe pays off handsomely for individuals of all races, from all backgrounds. But it is not individuals alone who gain. Substantial additional benefits accrue to society at large through the leadership and civic participation of the graduates and through the broad contributions that the schools themselves make to the goals of a democratic society. These societal benefits are a major justification for the favored tax treatment that colleges and universities enjoy and for the subsidies provided by public and private donors. The presence of these benefits also explains why these institutions do not allocate scarce places in their entering classes by the simple expedient of auctioning them off to the highest bidders. The limited number of places is an exceedingly valuable resource—valuable both to the students admitted and to the society at large—which is why admissions need to be based "on the merits."

Unfortunately, however, to say that considerations of merit should drive the admissions process is to pose questions, not answer them. There are no magical ways of automatically identifying those who merit admission on the basis of intrinsic qualities that distinguish them from all others. Test scores and grades are useful measures of the ability to do good work, but they are no more than that. They are far from infallible indicators of other qualities some might regard as intrinsic, such as a deep love of learning

**Editors' note:* The College and Beyond study surveyed the 1976 and 1989 entering cohorts of 28 selective institutions.

or a capacity for high academic achievement. Taken together, grades and scores predict only 15–20 percent of the variance among all students in academic performance and a smaller percentage among black students. . . . Moreover, such quantitative measures are even less useful in answering other questions relevant to the admissions process, such as predicting which applicants will contribute most in later life to their professions and their communities.[1]

Some critics believe, nevertheless, that applicants with higher grades and test scores are more deserving of admission because they presumably worked harder than those with less auspicious academic records. According to this argument, it is only "fair" to admit the students who have displayed the greatest effort. We disagree on several grounds.

To begin with, it is not clear that students who receive higher grades and test scores have necessarily worked harder in school. Grades and test scores are a reflection not only of effort but of intelligence, which in turn derives from a number of factors, such as inherited ability, family circumstances, and early upbringing, that have nothing to do with how many hours students have labored over their homework. Test scores may also be affected by the quality of teaching that applicants have received or even by knowing the best strategies for taking standardized tests, as coaching schools regularly remind students and their parents. For these reasons, it is quite likely that many applicants with good but not outstanding scores and B+ averages in high school will have worked more diligently than many other applicants with superior academic records.

More generally, selecting a class has much broader purposes than simply rewarding students who are thought to have worked especially hard. The job of the admissions staff is not, in any case, to decide who has earned a "right" to a place in the class, since we do not think that admission to a selective university is a right possessed by anyone. What admissions officers must decide is which set of applicants, *considered individually and collectively,* will take fullest advantage of what the college has to offer, contribute most to the educational process in college, and be most successful in using what they have learned for the benefit of the larger society. Admissions processes should, of course, be "fair," but "fairness" has to be understood to mean only that each individual is to be judged according to a consistent set of criteria that reflect the objectives of the college or university. Fairness should not be misinterpreted to mean that a particular criterion has to apply—that, for example, grades and test scores must always be considered more important than other qualities and characteristics so that no student with a B average can be accepted as long as some students with As are being turned down.

Nor does fairness imply that each candidate should be judged in isolation from all others. It may be perfectly "fair" to reject an applicant because the college has already enrolled many other students very much like him or her. There are numerous analogies. When making a stew, adding an extra carrot rather than one more potato may make excellent sense—and be eminently "fair"—if there are already lots of potatoes in the pot. Similarly, good basketball teams include both excellent shooters and sturdy defenders, both point guards and centers. Diversified investment portfolios usually include some mix of stocks and bonds, and so on.

To admit "on the merits," then, is to admit by following complex rules derived from the institution's own mission and based on its own experiences educating students with different talents and backgrounds. These "rules" should not be thought of as abstract propositions to be deduced through contemplation in a Platonic cave. Nor are they rigid formulas that can be applied in a mechanical fashion. Rather, they should have the status of rough guidelines established in large part through empirical examination of the actual results achieved as a result of long experience. How many students with characteristic "x" have done well in college, contributed to the education of their fellow students, and gone on to make major contributions to society? Since different institutions operate at very different places along our metaphorical river (some placing more emphasis on research, some with deeper pools of applicants than others), the specifics of these rules should be expected to differ from one institution to another. They should also be expected to change over time as circumstances change and as institutions learn from their mistakes.

Above all, merit must be defined in light of what educational institutions are trying to accomplish. In our view, race is relevant in determining which candidates "merit" admission because taking account of race helps institutions achieve three objectives central to their mission—identifying individuals of high potential, permitting students to benefit educationally from diversity on campus, and addressing long-term societal needs.

Identifying Individuals of High Potential

An individual's race may reveal something about how that person arrived at where he or she is today—what barriers were overcome, and what the individual's prospects are for further growth. Not every member of a minority group will have had to surmount substantial obstacles. Moreover, other circumstances besides race can cause "disadvantage." Thus colleges and universities should and do give special consideration to the hardworking son of a family in Appalachia or the daughter of a recent immigrant from Russia who, while obviously bright, is still struggling with the English language. But race is an important factor in its own right, given this nation's history and the evidence presented in many studies of the continuing effects of discrimination and prejudice.[2] Wishing it were otherwise does not make it otherwise. It would seem to us to be ironic indeed—and wrong—if admissions officers were permitted to consider all other factors that help them identify individuals of high potential who have had to overcome obstacles, but were proscribed from looking at an applicant's race.

Benefiting Educationally from Diversity on the Campus

Race almost always affects an individual's life experiences and perspectives, and thus the person's capacity to contribute to the kinds of learning through diversity that occur on campuses. This form of learning will be even more important going forward than it has been in the past. Both the growing diversity of American society and the increasing interaction with other cultures worldwide make it evident that going to school only with "the likes of oneself" will be increasingly anachronistic. The advantages of being able to understand how others think and function, to cope across racial divides, and to lead groups composed of diverse individuals are certain to increase.

To be sure, not all members of a minority group may succeed in expanding the racial understanding of other students, any more than all those who grew up on a farm or came from a remote region of the United States can be expected to convey a special rural perspective. What does seem clear, however, is that a student body containing many different backgrounds, talents, and experiences will be a richer environment in which to develop. In this respect, minority students of all kinds can have something to offer their classmates. The black student with high grades from Andover may challenge the stereotypes of many classmates just as much as the black student from the South Bronx.

Until now, there has been little hard evidence to confirm the belief of educators in the value of diversity. Our survey data throw new light on the extent of interaction occurring on campuses today and of how positively the great majority of students regard opportunities to learn from those with different points of view, backgrounds, and experiences. Admission "on the merits" would be short-sighted if admissions officers were precluded from crediting this potential contribution to the education of all students.

Imposition of a race-neutral standard would produce very troubling results from this perspective: such a policy would reduce dramatically the proportion of black students on campus—probably shrinking their number to less than 2 percent of all matriculants at the most selective colleges and professional schools. Moreover, our examination of the application and admissions files indicates that such substantial reductions in the number of black matriculants, with attendant losses in educational opportunity for all students, would occur without leading to any appreciable improvement in the academic credentials of the remaining black students and would lead to only a modest change in the overall academic profile of the institutions.[3] . . .

HOW FAST ARE WE HEADING DOWNSTREAM?

Final questions to ponder concern a longer sweep of the river. What is our ultimate objective? How much progress has been made? How far do we still have to go? Along with many others, we look forward to a day when arguments in favor of race-sensitive admissions policies will have become unnecessary. Almost everyone, on all sides of this debate, would agree that in an ideal world race would be an irrelevant consideration. As a black friend said almost thirty years ago: "Our ultimate objective should be a situation in which every individual, from every background, feels *unselfconsciously included.*"

Many who agree with Justice Blackmun's aphorism, "To get beyond racism, we must first take account of race," would be comforted if it were possible to predict, with some confidence, when that will no longer be necessary. But we do not know how to make such a prediction, and we would caution against adopting arbitrary timetables that fail to take into account how deep-rooted are the problems associated with race in America.

At the same time, it is reassuring to see, even within the C&B set of institutions, the changes that have occurred between the admission of the '76 and '89 cohorts. Over that short span of time, the average SAT scores of black matriculants at the C&B schools went up 68 points—a larger gain than that of white matriculants. The overall black graduation rate, which was already more than respectable in the '76 cohort (71 percent), rose to 79 percent. Enrollment in the most highly regarded graduate and professional schools has continued to increase. The '89 black matriculants are even more active in civic affairs (relative to their white classmates) than were the '76 black matriculants. Appreciation for the education they received and for what they learned from diversity is voiced even more strongly by the '89 cohort than by their '76 predecessors.

Whatever weight one attaches to such indicators, and to others drawn from national data, the trajectory is clear. To be sure, there have been mistakes and disappointments. There is certainly much work for colleges and universities to do in finding more effective ways to improve the academic performance of minority students. But, overall, we conclude that academically selective colleges and universities have been highly successful in using race-sensitive admissions policies to advance educational goals important to them and societal goals important to everyone. Indeed, we regard these admissions policies as an impressive example of how venerable institutions with established ways of operating can adapt to serve newly perceived needs. Progress has been made and continues to be made. We are headed downstream, even though there may still be miles to go before the river empties, finally, into the sea.

NOTES

1. Martin Luther King, Jr., now regarded as one of the great orators of this century, scored in the bot-

tom half of all test-takers on the verbal GRE (Cross and Slater, 1997, p. 12).

2. One of the most compelling findings of this study is that racial gaps of all kinds remain after we have tried to control for the influences of other variables that might be expected to account for "surface" differences associated with race. We have described and discussed black-white gaps in SAT scores, socioeconomic status, high school grades, college graduation rates, college rank in class, attainment of graduate and professional degrees, labor force participation, average earnings, job satisfaction, marital status, household income, civic participation, life satisfaction, and attitudes toward the importance of diversity itself. In short, on an "other things equal" basis, race is a statistically significant predictor of a wide variety of attributes, attitudes, and outcomes. People will debate long and hard, as they should, whether particular gaps reflect unmeasured differences in preparation and previous opportunity, patterns of continuing discrimination, failures of one kind or another in the educational system itself, aspects of the culture of campuses and universities, individual strengths and weaknesses, and so on. But no one can deny that race continues to matter.
3. While it is, of course, possible for an institution to be so committed to enrolling a diverse student population that it enrolls unprepared candidates who can be predicted to do poorly, we do not believe that this is a consequential problem today in most academically selective institutions. Three pieces of evidence are relevant: (1) the close correspondence between the academic credentials of those students who would be retrospectively rejected under a race-neutral standard and those who would be retained; (2) the modest associations (within this carefully selected population) of the test scores and high school grades of black matriculants at the C&B schools with their in-college and after-college performance; and (3) the remarkably high graduation rates of black C&B students—judged by any national standard.

REFERENCE

Cross, Theodore, and Robert Bruce Slater. 1997. "Why the End of Affirmative Action Would Exclude All but a Very Few Blacks from America's Leading Universities and Graduate Schools." *Journal of Blacks in Higher Education* 17 (Autumn): 8–17.

READING 34

Social Movements and the Politics of Difference

Cheryl Zarlenga Kerchis and Iris Marion Young

There was once a time of caste and class when tradition held that each group had its place in the social hierarchy—that some were born to rule and others to be ruled. In this time of darkness, rights, privileges, and obligations were different for people of different sexes, races, religions, classes, and occupations. Inequality between groups was justified by both the state and the church on the grounds that some kinds of people were better than others.

Then one day, a period in the history of ideas known as the Enlightenment dawned, and revolutionary ideas about the equality of people emerged. During the Enlightenment, which reached its zenith in Europe in the eighteenth century, philosophers called into question traditional ideas and values that justified political inequality between groups. They declared that all people are created equal because all people are able to reason and to think about morality. They also argued that because all people are created equal, all people should have equal political and civil rights.

The ideas of Enlightenment thinkers have marked the battle lines of political struggle in the United States for the past two hundred years. The Revolutionary War was fought on Enlightenment

---

Cheryl Zarlenga Kerchis is a doctoral student in public policy at the University of Pittsburgh. Iris Marion Young is a professor of public and international affairs at the University of Pittsburgh.

principles, and our Constitution was based on the principles of liberty and equality. In the beginning, however, the vision of liberty and equality of our founders (as well as most Enlightenment philosophers) excluded certain groups. Women did not have equal political and civil rights, and African Americans were enslaved. Inspired by the ideals of liberty and equality, women and African Americans engaged in a long and bitter struggle for political equality. By the 1960s, the battle for legal equal political and civil rights was won, though the struggle for equality in all walks of life continues.

Today in our society, prejudice and discrimination remain, but in many respects we have realized the vision that the Enlightenment thinkers set out. Our laws express rights in universal terms, that is, applied equally to everyone. We strive for a society in which differences of race, sex, religion, and ethnicity do not affect people's opportunities to participate in all aspects of social life. We believe that people should be treated as individuals, not as members of groups, and that their rewards in life should be based on their individual achievement—not on their race, sex, or any other purely accidental characteristic.

Though there is much to admire in this vision of a society that eliminates group differences, it has its own limitations, which contemporary social movements have called into question. Just as Enlightenment social movements challenged widely held traditional ideas and values that justified oppression in their time, today's social movements are challenging widely held ideas about justice that justify oppression in our time. These social movements criticize the idea that a just society is one that eliminates group differences under the law and guarantees equal treatment for all individuals. The central question they wish to ask is this: is it possible that the ideal of equal treatment of all persons under the law and the attempt to eliminate group differences under the law in fact perpetuates oppression of certain groups?

. . . We will argue that the answer to this question is yes. In our argument we will first discuss the ideal of justice that defines liberation as the transcendence of group difference. We call this the *ideal of assimilation.* This ideal usually promotes the equal treatment of all groups as the primary way to achieve justice. In this discussion, we will show how recent social movements of oppressed groups in the United States have challenged this ideal of assimilation. These movements believe that by organizing themselves and defining their own positive group cultural identity they will be more likely to achieve power and increase their participation in public institutions. We call this positive recognition of difference the politics of difference, and explain how it is more likely to aid in the liberation of oppressed groups.

. . . We will [also] discuss the need to change the way we think about group differences in order to have a politics of difference that leads to the liberation of oppressed groups. We will explore the risks associated with a politics of difference, in particular, the risk of recreating the harmful stigma that group difference has had in the past. To avoid this restigmatizing of groups, we will argue for a new and positive understanding of difference that rejects past exclusionary understandings of difference.

. . . [Finally,] we will consider practical issues of policy and representation in relation to a politics of difference. First, we will discuss the issue of group-neutral versus group-conscious policies. By this we mean policies that treat all groups in the same way (group-neutral) versus policies that treat different groups differently (group-conscious). We will discuss two specific cases in which group-conscious policies are needed to ensure fairness to disadvantaged groups. Lastly, we will argue for group representation in American social institutions including governmental and non-governmental institutions. We will explain how group representation promotes justice, suggest the kinds of groups that should be represented, and give some examples of group representation within some already-existing organizations and movements in the United States.

LIBERATION FOR OPPRESSED GROUPS THROUGH THE IDEAL OF ASSIMILATION

The Ideal of Assimilation and Equal Treatment of Social Groups

What strategy of reform is most effective for achieving the liberation of oppressed groups? If we desire a non-racist, non-sexist society, how can we get there? One strategy for achieving this society is to pursue what we call an ideal of assimilation. The ideal of assimilation as a strategy for the liberation of oppressed groups involves the elimination of group-based differences under the law. Thus, in a truly non-racist, non-sexist society, a person's race or sex would be no more significant in the eyes of the law than eye color or any other accidental characteristic. People would have different physical characteristics (such as skin color), but these would play no part in determining how people treated each other or how they were treated under the law. Over time, people would see no reason to consider race or sex in policies or in everyday activities, and group-based differences by and large would no longer matter.

Many contemporary thinkers argue for this ideal of assimilation and against the ideal of diversity that we will argue for later in this chapter. And there are many convincing reasons to support such an ideal. Perhaps the most convincing reason is that the principle of equal treatment of groups provides a clear and easily applied standard of equality and justice for use by courts and government institutions that deal with issues of race and sex discrimination. Under a standard of equal treatment, any discrimination whatsoever on the basis of group differences is considered illegal. Any law, regulation, employment practice, or government policy that treats persons differently on the basis of the race or sex is labeled unjust. The simplicity of this principle of equal treatment makes it a very attractive standard of justice.

There are two other convincing reasons to support the ideal of assimilation and the principle of justice as equal treatment. First, the ideal of assimilation may help to change the way people think about group differences. It treats classifications of people according to accidental characteristics like skin color or gender as arbitrary, not natural or necessary. Some people happen to be Black. Some are female or Hispanic or Jewish or Italian. But these differences do not mean that these people have different moral worth or that they necessarily aspire to anything different than anyone else in political life, in the workplace, or in the family. By suggesting that these categories are not important, the ideal of assimilation helps us realize how often we limit people's opportunities in society (because they are Black, female, and so on) for arbitrary reasons. Second, the ideal of assimilation gives individuals a great deal of choice in their lives. When group differences have no social importance, people are free to develop themselves as individuals, without feeling the pressures of group expectations. If I am a woman, I can aspire to anything I wish to and not feel any special pressure to pursue or settle for, for instance, one occupation versus another.

The ideal of assimilation, which calls for equal treatment of groups and the elimination of group difference in social life, has been extremely important in the history of oppressed groups. Its assertion of the equal moral worth of all persons (regardless of their group characteristics) and the right of all to participate in the institutions of society inspired many movements against discrimination. There is no question that it continues to have considerable value in our nation today, where many forms of discrimination against groups persist.

Contemporary Challenges to the Ideal of Assimilation

Since the 1960s, a number of groups have questioned the value of this ideal of assimilation and equal treatment. Is it possible, they have asked, that this ideal is not truly liberating for some oppressed groups? Instead of seeking to eliminate group difference, they wonder, would it not be more liberating for groups to organize themselves and assert their own positive group cultural identity? These groups see a politics of difference as opposed to a politics without difference as a better strategy for achieving power and participation in the institutions of social and political life. In the next section, we will discuss the efforts of four contemporary social movements to redefine the importance of group difference and cultural identity in social and political life in a way that they find more liberating.

The African American Movement In the 1960s, with the enactment of the Civil Rights Act of 1964, the Voting Rights Act of 1965, and numerous lawsuits spawned by these new laws, African Americans won major victories that declared racial discrimination in politics and the workplace illegal. Despite these successes, however, criticisms of the civil rights strategy emerged from within the African American community in the form of the Black Power movement. Black Power leaders criticized the civil rights movement for three reasons: they were unhappy with the civil rights movement's goal of integration of African Americans into a society dominated by whites; they criticized the movement's alliance with white liberals and instead called upon African Americans to confidently affirm their cultural identity; and they criticized the movement for not encouraging African Americans to organize themselves on their own terms and to determine their political goals within their own organizations.

Instead of supporting integration with whites, Black Power leaders called on African Americans to strengthen their own separate and culturally distinct neighborhoods as a better means of obtaining economic and political power. In sum, they rejected the ideal of assimilation and the suppression of group difference in political and economic life. In its place, they advocated self-organization and a strengthening of cultural identity as a better strategy for achieving power and participation in dominant institutions.

In recent years, many of the ideas of the Black Power movement have resurfaced among African Americans. Despite the legal protections won during the civil rights era, African American economic and political oppression persists. In economic life today, African Americans experience unemployment rates more than twice those of whites and poverty rates more than three times those of whites. And they still face substantial discrimination in educational opportunities, business opportunities, and the housing market.

What has happened since the 1960s? Why the persistence of inequalities almost forty years after *Brown v. Board of Education,* and almost thirty years after the Civil Rights and Voting Rights acts? Many African Americans argue that the push toward integration by the civil rights movement had unintended negative effects on the African American community. While civil rights protections opened the doors of opportunity for some African Americans, those left behind were made worse off. Many African Americans have been assimilated into the middle class and no longer associate as closely with poor and working class African Americans. As a consequence, African American solidarity has been weakened, and in many neighborhoods African American businesses, schools, and churches have been hurt by the exodus of middle-class African American families. Hence, once again, many African American leaders are calling for a rejection of the goal of integration and assimilation and are calling upon African Americans to organize themselves and seek economic and political empowerment within their own neighborhoods.

Another legacy of the Black Power movement that lives on today is the assertion of a positive Black cultural identity. The "Black is beautiful" movement that emerged in the 1960s celebrated a distinct African American culture and struggled against the assimilation of that culture into the dominant culture of American society. In their clothing and hairstyles, members confidently asserted their own cultural styles and rejected the narrow definition of style and beauty of the predominantly white culture. Since that time, African American historians and educators have sought to recover the rich history of African America and have retold the stories of African American writers, artists, musicians, inventors, and political figures, who received little attention in the history textbooks of white America. And they have subsequently fought with school boards across the nation to ensure that respect for African American history and culture is integral to the history curricula under which every student in this country is educated.

All of these examples reflect a rejection of the idea that assimilation of African Americans into the dominant culture of America is a desirable goal. They instead reflect a desire for an alternative politics of difference through which African Americans can gain their fair share of power and increase their participation in social, political, and economic life in America without shedding their own self-determined group cultural identity.

The American Indian Movement Not long after the Black Power movement emerged in the 1960s, a movement with similar ideals arose among Native Americans. American Indian Movement leaders called for Red Power, which, like Black Power, rejected the assimilation of Native American peoples that had been the goal of government policies toward Indians throughout the nineteenth and twentieth centuries. In many ways, their rejection of the dominant culture and its values was even stronger than that of Black Power.

The American Indian Movement claimed a right to self-government on Indian lands and struggled to gain a powerful Indian voice in the federal government branch responsible for policy making toward Native American peoples—the Bureau of Indian Affairs. They went to the courts to fight for land taken away from them. They also used the court system to fight for Indian control of natural resources on reservations that were being exploited by mining companies and other corporations.

Like Black Power, Red Power also extended its struggle beyond political and economic issues. Red Power advocates wanted to restore and strengthen cultural pride among Native Americans. In the last twenty years, Native Americans have struggled to recover and preserve elements of their traditional culture such as religious rituals, crafts, and languages that have been ravaged by the government's policy of Indian assimilation.

The Gay and Lesbian Movement The gay and lesbian movement that emerged in the 1960s began, much like the African American movement of that period, as a struggle for equality and civil rights. Gay-rights advocates wanted to protect gay men and lesbians from discrimination in government institutions and in employment. The movement strived for the ideal of assimilation and equal treatment that we have talked about throughout this [article]. They asked society to recognize that gay people are no different from anyone else in their aspirations or moral worth, and that they too deserve the same protections under the law extended to all other U.S. citizens.

Over time, however, many members of the gay and lesbian movement came to believe that the achievement of civil rights alone would not liberate gay men and lesbians from the discrimination they faced in society. Though they had achieved some legal victories, gay men and lesbians were still often harassed, beaten up, and intimidated by heterosexuals who disapproved of their gay "lifestyle." It seemed the dominant culture could tolerate gays and even extend limited legal protection to gay people as long as they kept their sexuality a *private* matter. But *public* displays of gay lifestyles were (and still are) often met with hostility and violence. For many gay men and lesbians, concealing their sexuality and lifestyles in a private world is just as oppressive as the public and explicit discrimination they often face in institutions.

Today, most gay and lesbian liberation groups seek not only equal protection under the law but also group solidarity and a positive affirmation of gay men and lesbians as social groups with shared experiences and cultures. They reject the ideal of assimilation that suppresses group differences in political and social life and makes these differences a purely private matter. They refuse to accept the dominant heterosexual culture's definition of healthy sexuality and respectable family life, and instead have insisted on the right to proudly display their gay or lesbian identity. Like the other groups mentioned above, they have engaged in a politics of difference that they find more liberating than the politics of assimilation.

The Women's Movement Until the late 1970s, the aims of the contemporary women's movement were for the most part those of the ideal of assimilation. Women's movement members fought for women's civil rights and the equal treatment of and equal opportunity for women in political institutions and the workplace. The movement strived to eliminate the significance of gender differences in social life. Women and men were to be measured by the same standards and treated in the same way in social institutions. Women's rights advocates saw any attempt to define men and women as fundamentally different in their aspirations for successful careers outside the home as just another means of oppressing women and limiting their opportunity to participate in the male-dominated spheres of government and business. This strategy of assimilation was extremely successful in undermining traditional ways of thinking about sex differences and women's roles. The idea that women naturally aspired to less in terms of participation in politics and the workplace was finally overturned.

Despite these successes, however, many in the women's movement grew uncomfortable with this strategy of assimilation, which defined equality as the elimination of sex differences in social life. Since the late seventies, a politics of difference has emerged from within the women's movement that rejects the goals of gender assimilation. The first signs of this rejection were seen among women who advocated feminist separatism.

Feminist separatists believed that women should aspire to more than formal equality in a male-dominated world. They argued that entering the male-dominated world meant playing according to rules and standards that men had set up and had used against women for centuries and across cultures. Instead of trying to measure up to male-defined standards, they called for the empowerment of women through self-organization and the creation of separate and safe places where women could share their experiences and devise their own rules of the game. In such separate and safe places, women could decide for themselves what was socially valuable activity instead of uncritically accepting the values and activities of a male-dominated society. One of the outcomes of this separatism was the creation of women's organizations and services to address the needs of women that have historically received little attention from male-dominated society. The organizations formed in this period include women's health clinics, battered women's shelters, and rape crisis centers, all of which today continue to improve the lives of many women.

Some of the ideas of this separatist movement are reflected in the recent work of feminist philosophers and political thinkers. Unlike earlier feminist thinkers, these women question the idea that women's liberation means equal participation of women in male-dominated political institutions and workplaces. While they do not suggest that women withdraw from such institutions, they suggest that society ought to rethink the value of femininity and women's ways of approaching human relations. These theorists suggest that women tend to be socialized in a way that, in comparison with men, makes them more sensitive to others' feelings, more empathetic, more nurturing of others and the world, and better at smoothing over tensions between people.

They argue that this more caring, nurturing, and cooperative approach to relations with other people should not be rejected out of hand by feminists as limiting women's human potential or their ability to contribute to the world. They suggest that women's attitudes toward others and toward nature constitute a healthier way to think about the world than the competitive and individualistic attitudes that characterize male-dominated culture in the Western world. By holding on to these values, women can help to transform institutions, human relations, and the interaction of people with nature in ways that may better promote people's self-development within institutions and better protect the environment.

Thus, a political strategy that asks women to give up the values of caring or nurturing in order to succeed in the workplace or in politics not only undervalues what women have to contribute to those spheres, but undermines the possibility of transforming male-dominated institutions in a way that will result in a healthier society as a whole. To resolve this dilemma, then, the politics of assimilation needs to be replaced by a politics of difference that makes it possible for women to participate fully in social and political institutions without suppressing or undervaluing gender differences.

WHY IS THE POLITICS OF DIFFERENCE LIBERATING?

The Importance of Group Difference in Social Life

All of the social movements discussed above have offered an alternative view of liberation that rejects the ideal of assimilation. In their assertion of a positive sense of group difference, these social movements have put forth an ideal of liberation that we will call the politics of difference. In their view, a just society does not try to eliminate or ignore the importance of group differences. Rather, society seeks equality among social groups, requiring each to recognize and respect the value of the experiences and perspectives of all other groups. No group asks another to give up or hide its distinct experiences and perspectives as a condition of participation in social institutions.

Is a politics of difference really necessary? Are group differences really that important? Many political philosophers deny the importance of social groups. To them, the notion of group difference was created and kept alive by people who sought to justify their own privilege and the oppression of specific groups. Some theorists agree that there are important differences among groups that affect the way people see themselves and others, but they see these differences as undesirable. The ideal of assimilation either denies the importance of social groups or sees them as undesirable.

In contrast, we doubt that a society without social groups is possible *or* desirable. Today, whether we like it or not, our society is structured by social groups that have important consequences for people's lives. Social groups do affect the way people see themselves and others in both positive and negative ways. People form their identities—their sense of who they are—in part through their membership in social or cultural groups. There is nothing inherently bad about people identifying with certain groups. Attachment to an ethnic tradition, language, culture, or set of common experiences has always been a feature of social life. The problem for a democratic nation occurs when group membership affects people's capacities to participate fully in our social institutions. In the United States today, some groups are privileged while others are oppressed. The politics of difference offers a way of retaining the positive, identity-affirming aspect of group difference while eliminating the negative aspect—the privileging of some groups over others.

The Oppressive Consequences of Ignoring Group Difference

None of the social movements that we have discussed deny the claim that the strategy of eliminating group difference and treating all groups the same has helped improve the situation of oppressed social groups. On the contrary, each of these social movements at one time pursued such a strategy. But why did they eventually begin to question its effectiveness in eliminating group oppression? Why was assimilation called into question?

Many of these social movements of oppressed groups found that the achievement of formal equality under the law did not put an end to their disadvantaged position. Even though in many resects the law is now blind to group differences like sex and race, certain groups continue to be oppressed while other groups are privileged. Many forms of oppression, such as racial slurs, are more subtle, yet they are just as corrosive than the more easily identifiable forms of overt and intentional discrimination. They persist in the structure of institutions that make it difficult for members of disadvantaged groups to develop their capacities. Oppression also exists in forms of everyday interaction and decision making in which people make assumptions about the aspirations and needs of women, African Americans, Hispanics, gay men and lesbians, and other groups that continue to be oppressed. The idea that equality and liberation can only be achieved by ignoring group differences has three oppressive consequences for disadvantaged social groups.

First, ignoring group difference disadvantages groups whose experience and culture differ from those of privileged groups. The strategy of assimilation aims to bring excluded groups into the mainstream of social life. But assimilation always implies coming into the game after it has already begun, after the rules and standards have already been set. Therefore, disadvantaged groups play no part in making up the rules and standards that they must prove themselves by—those rules and standards are defined by privileged groups. The rules and standards may appear to be neutral since they are applied equally to all groups. In actuality though, their formation was based only upon the experiences of privileged groups—oppressed groups being excluded from the rule-making process.

If such standards are applied equally to all groups, why do they then place some groups at a disadvantage? The real differences between oppressed groups and dominant groups often make it difficult for oppressed groups to measure up to the standards of the privileged. These real differences may have to do with cultural styles and values or with certain distinct capacities (for example, women's capacity to bear children). But quite often these differences are themselves the result of group oppression. For example, the long history of exclusion and marginalization of African American people from the economic and educational systems of this country has made it very difficult for many of them to gain the levels of educational attainment and technical skills that whites have. Yet, despite this history of oppression, they must compete for jobs on the basis of qualifications that are the same for all groups, including historically privileged groups.

The second oppressive consequence of ignoring group difference is that it allows privileged groups in society to see their own culture, values, norms, and experiences as universal (shared by all groups) rather than group specific. In other words, ignoring group differences allows the norms and values that express the point of view and experience of privileged groups to appear neutral and uncontroversial. When the norms and values of particular privileged groups are held as normal, neutral, and universal, those groups that do not adhere to those norms and values are viewed by society as deviant or abnormal. . . .

When groups that do not share the supposedly neutral values and norms of privileged groups are viewed as deviant or abnormal, a third oppressive consequence of ignoring difference is produced. Members of those groups that are viewed as deviant often internalize society's view of them as abnormal or deviant. The internalization of the negative attitudes of others by members of oppressed groups often produces feelings of self-hatred and ambivalence toward their own culture. The ideal of assimilation asks members of oppressed groups to fit in and be like everyone else, yet society continues to see them as different, making it impossible for them to fit in comfortably. Thus, members of groups marked as different or deviant in comparison to privileged groups are caught in a dilemma they cannot resolve. On one hand, participating in mainstream society means accepting and adopting an identity that is not their own. And on the other, when they do try to participate, they are reminded by society and by themselves that they do not fit in.

The Liberating Consequences of the Politics of Difference

We have given three reasons why a strategy of assimilation that attempts to ignore, transcend, or devalue group differences is oppressive. We would now like to turn to the politics of difference and to explain the ways in which it is liberating and empowering for members of oppressed groups. The key difference between the politics of difference and the politics of assimilation lies in the definition of group difference itself. The politics of assimilation defines group difference in a negative way, as a liability or disadvantage to be overcome in the process of assimilating into mainstream society. In contrast, the politics of difference defines group difference in a positive way, as a social and cultural condition that can be liberating and empowering for oppressed groups. There are four ways in which this positive view of difference is liberating for oppressed groups.

First, a politics of difference that defines group difference in a positive way makes it easier for members of oppressed groups to celebrate and be proud of their identity, which the dominant culture has taught them to despise. In a politics of difference, members of oppressed groups are not asked to assimilate, to try to be something they are not. They are not asked to reject or hide their own culture as a condition of full participation in the social life of the nation. Instead, the politics of difference recognizes that oppressed groups have their own cultures, experiences, and points of view that have positive value for themselves *and* society as a whole. Some of their values and norms may even be superior to those of more privileged groups in society.

Second, by recognizing the value of the cultures and experiences of oppressed groups, the politics of difference exposes the values and norms of privileged groups as group specific, not neutral or universal. The politics of difference recognizes that the values and norms of privileged groups are expressions of their own experience and may conflict with those of other groups. In the politics of difference, oppressed groups insist on the positive value of their own cultures and experiences. When they insist on this, it becomes more and more difficult for dominant groups to parade their norms and values as neutral, universal, or uncontroversial. It also becomes more difficult for dominant groups to point to oppressed groups as deviant, abnormal, or inferior.

Thus, for example, when feminists assert the positive value of a caring and nurturing approach to the world, they call into question the competitive and individualistic norms of white male society. When African Americans proudly affirm the culture and history of Afro-America, they expose the culture and history of white society as expressing a particular experience—only *one* part of America's story. When Native Americans assert the value of a culture tied to and respectful of the land, they call into question the dominant culture's materialism, which promotes pollution and environmental destruction. All of these questions posed by oppressed groups suggest that the values and norms of dominant groups comprise one perspective, one way of looking at the world, that is neither neutral, shared, nor necessarily superior to the ways of oppressed groups.

When we realize that the norms and values of privileged groups are not universal, it becomes possible to think about the relation between groups in a more liberating way. Oppressed groups are not deviant with respect to privileged groups. They simply differ from privileged groups in their values, norms, and experiences, just as privileged groups are different from them. Difference is a two-way street; each group differs from the other; each earns the label "different." When the relations among groups are defined this way, we eliminate the assumption of the inferiority of oppressed groups and the superiority of privileged groups and replace it with a recognition and respect for the value of the particular experiences and perspectives of all groups.

Third, by asserting the positive value of different groups' experiences, the politics of difference makes it possible to look critically at dominant institutions and values from the perspective of oppressed groups. In other words, the experiences and perspectives of oppressed groups provide critical insights into mainstream social institutions and values that can serve as a starting point for reform of those institutions and values. For example, by referring to their members as "brother" or "sister," African Americans engender in their traditional neighborhoods a sense of community and solidarity not found in the highly individualistic mainstream society. As mentioned earlier, feminists find in the human values of nurturing and caring a more superior way of approaching social and ecological relations than the competitive, militarist, and environmentally destructive approach of male-dominated society. The politics of difference takes these critiques by oppressed groups seriously, as a basis for reform of dominant institutions. Such critiques shed light on the ways that dominant institutions should be changed so that they no longer reinforce patterns of privilege and oppression.

Fourth, the politics of difference promotes the value of group solidarity amidst the pervasive individualism of contemporary social life and the politics of assimilation. Assimilationist politics treats each person as an individual, ignoring differences of race, sex, religion, and ethnicity; everyone should be treated equally and evaluated according to his or her individual effort and achievement. It is true that under this politics of assimilation many members of oppressed groups have achieved individual success, even by the standards of privileged groups. However, as we have already learned, many groups continue to be oppressed despite the individual success of some group members. For example, over the last thirty years, Blacks have increased their representation in well-paying occupations such as law, medicine, and engineering. Yet they are still very much underrepresented in these fields and overrepresented in less well-paying occupations like orderlies, taxicab drivers, and janitors. That is why oppressed groups refuse to see these individual successes as evidence that group oppression has been eliminated. Instead of celebrating the success of some of their members, they insist that the celebration wait until their whole group is liberated. In the politics of difference, oppressed groups, in solidarity, struggle for the fundamental institutional changes that will make this liberation possible.

By now, the distinctions between the politics of assimilation and the politics of difference should be clear. Some people might object to the way we have made these distinctions. We anticipate that the strongest objection will be that we have not presented fairly the advantages of a politics of assimilation that strives to transcend or get beyond group differences. Many who support the politics of assimilation do recognize the value of a pluralistic society in which a variety of lifestyles, cultures, and associations can flourish. We do not, however, take issue with this vision of a pluralistic society. What we emphasize is that this vision does not deal with fundamental issues that suggest the need for the politics of difference.

As we have repeated throughout this [article], we think it is counterproductive and dishonest to try to eliminate the public and political significance of group difference in a society in which some groups are more privileged than others. The danger in this approach is that group differences get pushed out of the sphere of public discussion and action and come to be seen as a purely private or non-political matter. When this happens, the problem of oppression of some groups tends to go unaddressed in our public institutions, and patterns of privilege and oppression among groups are reinforced. The politics of difference that we advocate recognizes and takes seriously the public and political importance of group differences, and takes the experiences of oppressed groups as a starting point for reform of our public institutions. The goal of this politics of difference is to change our institutions so that no group is disadvantaged or advantaged due to its distinct culture or capacities, thus ensuring that all groups have the opportunity to participate fully in the nation's social and political institutions.

REDEFINING THE MEANING OF DIFFERENCE IN CONTEMPORARY LIFE

The Risk of Restigmatizing Oppressed Groups

Many people inside and outside the liberation movements we have discussed in this chapter are fearful of the politics of difference and its rejection of the politics of assimilation. The fear of many is that any public admission of the fact that groups are different will be used to justify once again the exclusion and separation of certain kinds of people from mainstream society. Feminists fear that the affirmation of values of caring and nurturing that are associated with motherhood will lead to a call for women to return to the kitchen and the home, places where it is claimed those values can best be utilized.

African Americans fear that an affirmation of their different values and experiences will lead again to a call for separate schools and communities, "where they can be with their own kind." Many in these groups are willing to accept the fact that formal equality (treating everyone the same under the law) reinforces current patterns of advantage. This, they say, is preferable to a politics of difference that risks the restigmatization of certain groups and the reestablishment of separate and unequal spheres for such groups.

We are sympathetic to these fears. It certainly is not unusual in political life for one's ideas, actions, or policies to have unintended negative effects because others have used them to justify ends different from those intended. Nevertheless, we believe that this risk is warranted since the strategy of ignoring group differences in public policy has failed to eliminate the problem of group oppression; the same patterns of privilege and oppression continue to be reproduced. All of which begs the question, Is there a way to avoid this risk of restigmatizing groups and rejustifying their exclusion? We believe there is a solution and it depends on redefining the meaning of difference itself.

Rejecting the Oppressive Meaning of Difference

In order to avoid the risk of recreating the stigma that oppressed groups have faced in the past, the meaning of difference itself must be redefined. In other words, we must change the way people think about differences among groups. In the politics of difference, the meaning of difference itself becomes an issue for political struggle.

There is an oppressive way of understanding difference that has dominated Western thinking about social groups for many centuries. This meaning of difference, which we will call the essentialist meaning, defines social groups in opposition to a normative group—typically the dominant social group. The culture, values, and standards of one social group provide the standards against which all other groups are measured.

The attempt to measure all groups against some universal standard or norm generates a meaning of difference as dichotomy, a relation of two opposites. Thus we have paired categories of groups—men/women, white/Black, healthy/disabled, rich/poor, young/old, civilized/uncivilized, to name a few. Very often, the second term in the pair is defined negatively in relation to the first. Those in the second category are defined as lacking valued qualities of those in the first.

There are rational men, and there are irrational women. There are productive, active young people, and there are feeble old people. There is a superior standard of humanity, and there is an inferior one.

This way of thinking about difference as a good/bad opposition in which groups are defined in relation to a supposedly universal norm has oppressive consequences. Some groups are marked out as having different natures, which leads quickly to the assumption that they therefore must have different aspirations and dispositions that fit them for some activities and not others. It also leads to the argument that because nature is static, change is impossible. Women are defined as lacking men's rationality, which justifies their exclusion from high-ranking positions in business and government. People with disabilities are seen as unhealthy or helpless, which justifies isolating them in institutions.

The essentialist meaning of difference just described lies at the heart of racism, sexism, anti-Semitism, homophobia, and other negative attitudes toward specific groups. In these ideologies only the oppressed groups are defined as different. When oppressed groups are thought of as having fundamentally different natures from the "normal" group, it becomes easier for the "normal" group to justify excluding those groups from mainstream institutions and communities. On the other hand, once it is admitted that all groups have some things in common and that no group represents a universal or "normal" standard, it becomes more difficult to justify any group's exclusion from political and social life.

Redefining Difference as Variation

The politics of difference rejects the essentialist definition of difference, which defines it as deviance from a neutral norm and holds that some groups have essentially different natures and aspirations. In the politics of difference, however, group difference is seen as ambiguous and shifting, without clear categories of opposites that narrowly define people. Difference represents variation among groups that have similarities and dissimilarities. Groups are neither completely the same nor complete opposites. In the politics of difference, the meaning of group difference encompasses six key principles:

1. *Group difference is relational.* We can only understand groups in relation to each other. Group differences can be identified when we compare different groups, but no group can be held up as the standard of comparison. Thus, whites are just as specific a group as African Americans or Hispanics, men just as specific as women, able-bodied people just as specific as people with disabilities. Difference does not mean a clear and specific set of attributes that a group shares, but means variation and heterogeneity. It appears as a relationship between groups and the interaction of groups with social institutions.
2. *Group difference is contextual.* That difference is contextual simply means that group differences may be more or less relevant depending on the context or situation in which they come up. In any context, the importance of group difference will depend on the groups being compared and the reasons for the comparison. For example, in the context of athletics, health care, or social service support, wheel chair–bound people are different from others in terms of the special needs they might have. But in many other contexts, these differences would be unimportant. In the past, people with disabilities were often excluded and segregated in institutions because their physical difference was seen as extending to all their capacities and all facets of their lives. Understanding difference as contextual eliminates this oppressive way of thinking about difference as all-encompassing.
3. *Group difference does not mean exclusion.* An understanding of difference as relational and contextual rejects the possibility of exclusion. No two groups lie exclusively outside each other in their experiences, perspectives, or

goals. All groups have overlapping experiences and therefore are always similar in some respects.

4. *Members within a group share affinity for each other, not a fixed set of attributes.* Groups are not defined by a fixed set of characteristics or attributes that all group members share. What makes a group a group is the fact that they have a particular affinity for each other. The people I have an affinity for are simply those who are familiar to me and with whom I feel the most comfortable. Feelings of affinity develop through a social process of interaction and shared experience. People in an affinity group often share common values, norms, and meanings that express their shared experience. No person's affinities are fixed: a person's affinities may shift with changes in his or her life. Likewise, group identities may shift over time with changes in social realities. . . .
5. *Groups define themselves.* Once we reject the idea that groups are defined by a set of common, essential attributes, groups are left to define for themselves what makes their particular group a group. This process of *self*-definition is emancipating in that it allows groups to reclaim a positive meaning for their difference and to decide collectively what they wish to affirm as their culture. Thus, the culture of oppressed groups is no longer defined by dominant groups in negative relation to mainstream culture. Many social movements of oppressed groups have begun this process of redefining their group identity for themselves. Both African American and Native American social movements have sought to redefine and reaffirm their cultural distinctiveness, often reclaiming from the past traditional values and norms that have meaning for them today. Some gays and lesbians are reappropriating the term "queer" and redefining it themselves.
6. *All groups have differences within them.* Our society is highly complex and differentiated, and no group is free of intragroup difference. For instance, a woman who is African American and a lesbian might identify with a variety of social groups—women, African Americans, lesbians. A woman who is Hispanic and heterosexual might have different affinities. Within the context of a social movement such as the women's movement, these differences between women are potential sources of wisdom and enrichment as well as conflict and misunderstanding. Because there is a potential for conflict within groups among persons who identify with more than one group, groups, like society as a whole, must also be attentive to difference. . . .

CONCLUSION

This [article] relies on a handful of clear principles, which we will summarize here. Social justice requires democracy. People should be involved in collective discussion and decision making in all the settings that ask for their obedience to rules—workplaces, schools, neighborhoods, and so on. Unfortunately, these social and political institutions privilege some groups over others. When some groups are more disadvantaged than others, ensuring democracy requires group representation for the disadvantaged. Group representation gives oppressed groups a voice in setting the public agenda and discussing matters on it. It also helps to ensure just outcomes of the democratic process by making sure that the needs and interests of all groups are expressed.

. . . We have asserted that the ideal of a society that eliminates, transcends, or ignores group difference is both unrealistic and undesirable. Justice in a society with groups requires the social equality of all groups, and mutual and explicit recognition and affirmation of the value of group differences. The politics of difference promotes social equality and undermines group oppression by affirming the value of group difference, attending to group-specific needs,

PERSONAL ACCOUNT

Memories of Summer Camp

I first set foot on Camp Sunrise as a timid eight-year-old camper along the beautiful shores of a New England lake. Summers at Sunrise became a tradition for the next eight years. Following my sophomore year in high school, I was overjoyed to learn I had been accepted as a counselor in training (CIT). What could be better? I considered the camp, along the shore of a New England lake, my home away from home. Eight weeks at the place I loved most, a place where I could be myself—or so I thought. Camp Sunrise is a Lutheran camp. And my religion? Well, I am a Catholic. I had never encountered a problem because of my religion. As I recall, there were always several nonpracticing Lutheran campers. However, when you are paying hundreds of dollars a week to attend, the camp makes sure every child feels welcome.

Every Sunday the camp held a church service. My Irish Catholic parents, however, had asked that I not receive communion. It was their only request of their Catholic daughter, so I agreed to obey their wishes. The majority of my CIT group was Lutheran, although there were a few Catholics whose parents allowed them to receive communion. On the first Sunday service, I was the only one from my CIT group not to receive communion. I thought nothing of it.

As the CITs were walking back to their tents, however, a bunkmate asked, "How come you didn't take communion?" "Well, my parents asked that I not receive because I am a baptized Catholic," I replied. "Well, do you want to?" she asked. "I don't really know. I just feel that this is the least I can do for them after all they have done for me," I answered, while thinking that the only time the camp focused on Lutheranism was during the Sunday services. At other times Christianity was discussed in general, and I certainly joined the discussion. Her response cut through my stomach like a knife. "Then why do you come here?" she asked before walking away.

I could not believe what I had just heard. I was in shock. It didn't make sense. How could this be happening? I could never imagine being treated this way. Why did she think she belonged here more than I did? This camp was like my second home. I was just as good a counselor as she was whether or not I received communion. I had never been looked down on because of my religious beliefs. I wanted to go home then and there, but I knew better.

I told my CIT trainer about this confrontation. She helped me to understand that no matter where you go in life, if you are not part of the majority, you may be resented for your differences. This, unfortunately, also held true at Sunrise. Nevertheless, I went on to have one of the best summers of my life. I have continued as a counselor, while following my religious beliefs, which do not interfere with my counseling abilities. My peers now understand that my Catholicism is as important to me as Lutheranism is to them, and respect me for my beliefs. However, I will never forget that Sunday of my CIT summer. It still hurts. But I have learned that you can't please everyone and you must hold strong to what is important to you.

Patricia Kelley

and providing for group representation in social institutions.

The challenges faced by such a politics are formidable. While many public and private institutions have begun to recognize the value of diversity, demands for a real voice for oppressed groups in decision-making processes are often met with fear and hostility. Still, we are hopeful that a politics of difference may be on the horizon. The United States is becoming more diverse, not less. Women and minorities comprise increasing proportions of the labor force and their needs are more and more difficult for employers and public officials to ignore.

However, demographic changes alone are unlikely to induce substantive policy change. Politics matters. While oppressed groups are increasing their representation in political institutions, social movements of oppressed groups will continue to play a critical role in shaping attitudes and dialogues about change and mobilizing the public to act. It is our hope that the ideas [presented here] provide a source of inspiration to social movements. The politics of difference is an alternative vision of politics that challenges the assumption that the present system is the only or best system. It is not meant as a blueprint for change, but as a starting point for dialogue. It provides a standpoint from which we can identify forms of injustice in our current institutions and explore different strategies to remedy them.

The Economy

READING 35

The Possessive Investment in Whiteness: How White People Profit from Identity Politics

George Lipsitz

Whiteness is everywhere in U.S. culture, but it is very hard to see. As Richard Dyer suggests, "[W]hite power secures its dominance by seeming not to be anything in particular."[1] As the unmarked category against which difference is constructed, whiteness never has to speak its name, never has to acknowledge its role as an organizing principle in social and cultural relations.[2] To identify, analyze, and oppose the destructive consequences of whiteness, we need what Walter Benjamin called "presence of mind." Benjamin wrote that people visit fortune-tellers less out of a desire to know the future than out of a fear of not noticing some important aspect of the present. "Presence of mind," he suggested, "is an abstract of the future, and precise awareness of the present moment more decisive than foreknowledge of the most distant events."[3] In U.S. society at this time, precise awareness of the present moment requires an understanding of the existence and the destructive consequences of the possessive investment in whiteness that surreptitiously shapes so much of our public and private lives." . . .

. . . The possessive investment is not simply the residue of conquest and colonialism, of slavery and segregation, of immigrant exclusion and "Indian" extermination. Contemporary whiteness and its rewards have been created and recreated by policies adopted long after the emancipation of slaves in the 1860s and even after the outlawing of *de jure* segregation in the 1960s. There has always been racism in the United States, but it has not always been the same racism. Political and cultural struggles over power have shaped the contours and dimensions of racism differently in different eras. Antiracist mobilizations during the Civil War and civil rights eras meaningfully curtailed the reach and scope of white supremacy, but in each case reactionary forces engineered a renewal of racism, albeit in new forms, during succeeding decades. Racism has changed over time, taking on different forms and serving different social purposes in each time period.

Contemporary racism has been created anew in many ways over the past five decades, but most dramatically by the putatively race-neutral, liberal, social democratic reforms of the New Deal Era and by the more overtly race-conscious neoconservative reactions against liberalism since the Nixon years. It is a mistake to posit a gradual and inevitable trajectory of evolutionary progress in race relations; on the contrary, our history shows that battles won at one moment can later be lost. Despite hard-fought battles for change that secured important concessions during the 1960s in the form of civil rights legislation, the racialized nature of social policy in the United States since the Great Depression has actually increased the possessive investment in whiteness among European Americans over the past half century.

During the New Deal Era of the 1930s and 1940s, both the Wagner Act and the Social Security Act excluded farm workers and domestics from coverage, effectively denying those

George Lipsitz is a professor of ethnic studies at the University of California, San Diego.

disproportionately minority sectors of the work force protections and benefits routinely afforded whites. The Federal Housing Act of 1934 brought home ownership within reach of millions of citizens by placing the credit of the federal government behind private lending to home buyers, but overtly racist categories in the Federal Housing Agency's (FHA) "confidential" city surveys and appraisers' manuals channeled almost all of the loan money toward whites and away from communities of color.[4] In the post–World War II era, trade unions negotiated contract provisions giving private medical insurance, pensions, and job security largely to the white workers who formed the overwhelming majority of the unionized work force in mass production industries, rather than fighting for full employment, medical care, and old-age pensions for all, or even for an end to discriminatory hiring and promotion practices by employers in those industries.[5]

Each of these policies widened the gap between the resources available to whites and those available to aggrieved racial communities. Federal housing policy offers an important illustration of the broader principles at work in the possessive investment in whiteness. By channeling loans away from older inner-city neighborhoods and toward white home buyers moving into segregated suburbs, the FHA and private lenders after World War II aided and abetted segregation in U.S. residential neighborhoods. FHA appraisers denied federally supported loans to prospective home buyers in the racially mixed Boyle Heights neighborhood of Los Angeles in 1939, for example, because the area struck them as a "'melting pot' area literally honeycombed with diverse and subversive racial elements."[6] Similarly, mostly white St. Louis County secured five times as many FHA mortgages as the more racially mixed city of St. Louis between 1943 and 1960. Home buyers in the county received six times as much loan money and enjoyed per capita mortgage spending 6.3 times greater than those in the city.[7]

The federal government has played a major role in augmenting the possessive investment in whiteness. For years, the General Services Administration routinely channeled the government's own rental and leasing business to realtors who engaged in racial discrimination, while federally subsidized urban renewal plans reduced the already limited supply of housing for communities of color through "slum clearance" programs. In concert with FHA support for segregation in the suburbs, federal and state tax monies routinely funded the construction of water supplies and sewage facilities for racially exclusive suburban communities in the 1940s and 1950s. By the 1960s, these areas often incorporated themselves as independent municipalities in order to gain greater access to federal funds allocated for "urban aid."[8]

At the same time that FHA loans and federal highway building projects subsidized the growth of segregated suburbs, urban renewal programs in cities throughout the country devastated minority neighborhoods. During the 1950s and 1960s, federally assisted urban renewal projects destroyed 20 percent of the central-city housing units occupied by blacks, as opposed to only 10 percent of those inhabited by whites.[9] More than 60 percent of those displaced by urban renewal were African Americans, Puerto Ricans, Mexican Americans, or members of other minority racial groups.[10] The Federal Housing Administration and the Veterans Administration financed more than $120 billion worth of new housing between 1934 and 1962, but less than 2 percent of this real estate was available to nonwhite families—and most of that small amount was located in segregated areas.[11]

Even in the 1970s, after most major urban renewal programs had been completed, black central-city residents continued to lose housing units at a rate equal to 80 percent of what had been lost in the 1960s. Yet white displacement declined to the relatively low levels of the 1950s.[12] In addition, the refusal first to pass, then to enforce, fair housing laws has enabled realtors, buyers, and sellers to profit from racist collusion against minorities largely without fear of legal retribution. During the decades following World War II, urban renewal helped construct a new "white" identity in the suburbs by helping to destroy ethnically specific European American urban inner-city neighborhoods. Wrecking balls and bulldozers eliminated some of these sites, while others were transformed by an influx of minority residents desperately competing for a declining supply of affordable housing units. As increasing numbers of racial minorities moved into cities, increasing numbers of European American ethnics moved out. Consequently, ethnic differences among whites became a less important dividing line in U.S. culture, while race became more important. The suburbs helped turn Euro-Americans into "whites" who could live near each other and intermarry with relatively little difficulty. But this "white" unity rested on residential segregation, on shared access to housing and life chances largely unavailable to communities of color.[13]

During the 1950s and 1960s, local "pro-growth" coalitions led by liberal mayors often justified urban renewal as a program designed to build more housing for poor people, but it actually destroyed more housing than it created. Ninety percent of the low-income units removed for urban renewal during the entire history of the program were never replaced. Commercial, industrial, and municipal projects occupied more than 80 percent of the land cleared for these projects, with less than 20 percent allocated for replacement housing. In addition, the loss of taxable properties and the tax abatements granted to new enterprises in urban renewal zones often meant serious tax increases for poor, working-class, and middle-class home owners and renters.[14] Although the percentage of black suburban dwellers also increased during this period, no significant desegregation of the suburbs took place. From 1960 to 1977, 4 million whites moved out of central cities, while the number of whites living in suburbs increased by 22 million; during the same years, the inner-city black population grew by 6 million, but the number of blacks living in suburbs increased by only 500,000.[15] By 1993, 86 percent of suburban whites still lived in places with a black population below 1 percent. At the same time, cities with large numbers of minority residents found themselves cut off from loans by the FHA. For example, because of their growing black and Puerto Rican populations, neither Camden nor Paterson, New Jersey, in 1966 received one FHA-sponsored mortgage.[16]

In 1968, lobbyists for the banking industry helped draft the Housing and Urban Development Act, which allowed private lenders to shift the risks of financing low-income housing to the government, creating a lucrative and thoroughly unregulated market for themselves. One section of the 1968 bill authorized FHA mortgages for inner-city areas that did not meet the usual eligibility criteria, and another section subsidized interest payments by low-income families. If administered wisely, these provisions might have promoted fair housing goals, but FHA administrators deployed them in ways that actually promoted segregation in order to provide banks, brokers, lenders, developers, realtors, and speculators with windfall profits. As a U.S. Commission on Civil Rights investigation later revealed, FHA officials collaborated with blockbusters in financing the flight of low-income whites out of inner city neighborhoods, and then aided unscrupulous realtors and speculators by arranging purchases of substandard housing by minorities desperate to own their own homes. The resulting sales and mortgage foreclosures brought great profits to lenders (almost all of them white), but their actions led to price fixing and a subsequent inflation of housing costs in the inner city by more than 200 percent between 1968 and 1972. Bankers then foreclosed on the mortgages of thousands of these uninspected and substandard homes, ruining many inner-city neighborhoods. In response, the Department of Housing and Urban Development essentially red-lined inner cities, making them ineligible for future loans, a decision that destroyed the value of inner-city housing for generations to come.[17]

Federally funded highways designed to connect suburban commuters with downtown places of employment also destroyed already scarce housing in minority communities and often disrupted neighborhood life as well. Construction of the Harbor Freeway in Los Angeles, the Gulf Freeway in Houston, and the Mark Twain Freeway in St. Louis displaced thousands of residents and bisected neighborhoods, shopping districts, and political precincts. The processes of urban renewal and highway construction set in motion a vicious cycle: population loss led to decreased political power, which made minority neighborhoods more vulnerable to further urban renewal and freeway construction, not to mention more susceptible to the placement of prisons, incinerators, toxic waste dumps, and other projects that further depopulated these areas.

In Houston, Texas—where blacks make up slightly more than one quarter of the local population—more than 75 percent of municipal garbage incinerators and 100 percent of the city-owned garbage dumps are located in black neighborhoods.[18] A 1992 study by staff writers for the *National Law Journal* examined the Environmental Protection Agency's response to 1,177 toxic waste cases and found that polluters of sites near the greatest white population received penalties 500 percent higher than penalties imposed on polluters in minority areas—an average of $335,566 for white areas contrasted with $55,318 for minority areas. Income did not account for these differences—penalties for low-income areas on average actually exceeded those for areas with the highest median incomes by about 3 percent. The penalties for violating all federal environmental laws regulating air, water, and waste pollution were 46 percent lower in minority communities than in white communities. In addition, superfund remedies left minority communities waiting longer than white communities to be placed on the national priority list, cleanups that began from 12 to 42 percent later than at white sites, and with a 7 percent greater likelihood of "containment" (walling off a hazardous site) than cleanup, while white sites experienced treatment and cleanup 22 percent more often than containment.[19]

The federal Agency for Toxic Substances and Disease Registry's 1988 survey of children suffering from lead poisoning showed that among families with incomes under $6,000 per year, 36 percent of white children but 68 percent of black children suffered from excess lead in their bloodstreams. Among families with incomes above $15,000 per year, only 12 percent of white children but 38 percent of black children suffered from toxic levels of lead.[20] In the Los Angeles area, only 34 percent of whites inhabit areas with the most polluted air, but 71 percent of African Americans and 50 percent of Latinos live in neighborhoods with the highest levels of air pollution.[21] Nationwide, 60 percent of African Americans and Latinos live in communities with uncontrolled toxic waste sites.[22]

Scholarly studies reveal that even when adjusted for income, education, and occupational status, aggrieved racial minorities encounter higher levels of exposure to toxic substances than white people experience.[23] In 1987, the Commission for Racial Justice of the United Church of Christ found race to be the most significant variable in determining the location of commercial hazard facilities.[24] In a review of sixty-four studies examining environmental disparities, the National Wildlife Federation found that racial disparities outnumbered disparities by income, and in cases where disparities in race and income were both present, race proved to be more important in twenty-two out of thirty tests.[25] As Robert D. Bullard demonstrates, "race has been found to be an independent factor, not reducible to class" in predicting exposure to a broad range of environmental hazards, including polluted air, contaminated fish, lead poisoning, municipal landfills, incinerators, and toxic waste dumps.[26] The combination of exposure to environmental hazards and employment discrimination establishes a sinister correlation between race and health. One recent government study revealed that the likelihood of dying from nutritional deficiencies was two and a half times greater among African Americans than among European Americans.[27] Another demonstrated that Asian and Pacific Islander recipients of aid for at-risk families exhibited alarming rates of stunted growth and underweight among children under the age of five.[28] Corporations systematically target Native American reservations when looking for locations for hazardous waste incinerators, solid waste landfills, and nuclear waste storage facilities; Navajo teenagers develop reproductive organ cancer at seventeen times the national average because of their exposure to radiation from uranium mines.[29] Latinos in East Los Angeles encounter some of the worst smog and the highest concentrations of air toxins in southern California because of prevailing wind patterns and the concentration of polluting industries, freeways, and toxic waste dumps.[30] Environmental racism makes the possessive investment in whiteness literally a matter of life and death; if African Americans had access to the nutrition, wealth, health care, and protection against environmental hazards offered routinely to whites, seventy-five thousand fewer of them would die each year.[31]

Minorities are less likely than whites to receive preventive medical care or costly operations from Medicare. Eligible members of minority communities are also less likely than European Americans to apply for food stamps.[32] The labor of migrant farm workers from aggrieved racialized groups plays a vital role in providing adequate nutrition for others, but the farm workers and their children suffer disproportionately from health disorders caused by malnutrition.[33] In her important research on health policy and ethnic diversity, Linda Wray concludes that "the lower life expectancies for many ethnic minority groups and subgroups stem largely from their disproportionately higher rates of poverty, malnutrition, and poor health care."[34]

Just as residential segregation and urban renewal make minority communities disproportionately susceptible to health hazards, their physical and social location gives these communities a different relationship to the criminal justice system. A 1990 study by the National Institute on Drug Abuse revealed that while only 15 percent of the thirteen million habitual drug users in the United States were black and 77 percent were white, African Americans were four times more likely to be arrested on drug charges than whites in the nation as a whole, and seven to nine times more likely in Pennsylvania, Michigan, Illinois, Florida, Massachusetts, and New Jersey. A 1989 study by the Parents' Resource Institute for Drug Education discovered that African American high school students consistently showed lower levels of drug and alcohol use than their European American counterparts, even in high schools populated by residents of low-income housing projects. Yet, while comprising about 12 percent of the U.S. population, blacks accounted for 10 percent of drug arrests in 1984, 40 percent in 1988, and 42 percent in 1990. In addition, white drug defendants receive considerably shorter average prison terms than African Americans convicted of comparable crimes. A U.S. Sentencing Commission study found in 1992 that half of the federal court districts that handled cases involving crack cocaine prosecuted minority defendants *exclusively.* A *Los Angeles Times* article in 1995 revealed that "black and Latino crack dealers are hammered with 10-year mandatory federal sentences while whites prosecuted in state court face a minimum of five years and often receive no more than a year in jail." Alexander Lichtenstein and Michael A. Kroll point out that sentences for African Americans in the federal prison system are 20 percent longer than those given to whites who commit the same crimes. They observe that if blacks received the same sentences as whites for these offenses, the federal prison system would require three thousand fewer prison cells, enough to close completely six of the new five-hundred bed institutions.[35]

Racial animus on the part of police officers, prosecutors, and judges accounts for only a small portion of the distinctive experience that racial minorities have with the criminal justice system. Economic devastation makes the drug trade appealing to some people in the inner city, while the dearth of capital in minority neighborhoods curtails opportunities for other kinds of employment. Deindustrialization, unemployment, and lack of intergenerational transfers of wealth undermine parental and adult authority in many neighborhoods. The complex factors that cause people to turn to drugs are no more prevalent in minority communities than elsewhere, but these communities and their inhabitants face more stress while having fewer opportunities to receive private counseling and treatment for their problems.

The structural weaknesses of minority neighborhoods caused by discrimination in housing, education, and hiring also play a crucial role in relations between inner-city residents and the criminal justice system. Cocaine dealing, which initially skyrocketed among white suburban residents, was driven into the inner city by escalating enforcement pressures in wealthy white communities. Ghettos and barrios became distribution centers for the sale of drugs to white suburbanites. Former New York and Houston police commissioner Lee Brown, head of the federal government's antidrug efforts during the early years of the Clinton presidency and later mayor of Houston, noted, "There are those who bring drugs into the country. That's not the black community. Then you have wholesalers, those who distribute them once they get here, and as a rule that's not the black community. Where you find the blacks is in the street dealing."[36]

You also find blacks and other minorities in prison. Police officers in large cities, pressured to show results in the drive against drugs, lack the resources to effectively enforce the law everywhere (in part because of the social costs of deindustrialization and the tax limitation initiatives designed to shrink the size of government). These officers know that it is easier to make arrests and to secure convictions by confronting drug users in areas that have conspicuous street corner sales, that have more people out on the street with no place to go, and that have residents more likely to plead guilty and less likely to secure the services of attorneys who can get the charges against them dropped, reduced, or wiped off the books with subsequent successful counseling and rehabilitation. In addition, politicians supported by the public relations efforts of neoconservative foundations often portray themselves to suburban voters as opponents of the "dangerous classes" in the inner cities.

Minority disadvantages craft advantages for others. Urban renewal failed to provide new housing for the poor, but it played an important role in transforming the U.S. urban economy from one that relied on factory production to one driven by producer services. Urban renewal projects subsidized the development of downtown office centers on previously residential land, and they frequently created buffer zones of empty blocks dividing poor neighborhoods from new shopping centers designed for affluent commuters. To help cities compete for corporate investment by making them appealing to high-level executives, federal urban aid favored construction of luxury housing units and cultural centers like symphony halls and art museums over affordable housing for workers. Tax abatements granted to these producer services centers further aggravated the fiscal crisis that cities faced, leading to tax increases on existing industries, businesses, and residences.

Workers from aggrieved racial minorities bore the brunt of this transformation. Because the 1964 Civil Rights Act came so late, minority workers who received jobs because of it found themselves more vulnerable to seniority-based layoffs when businesses automated or transferred operations overseas. Although the act initially made real progress in reducing employment discrimination, lessened the gaps between rich and poor and between black and white workers, and helped bring minority poverty to its lowest level in history in 1973, that year's recession, initiated a reversal of minority progress and a reassertion of white privilege.[37] In 1977, the U.S. Civil Rights Commission reported on the disproportionate impact of layoffs on minority workers. In cases where minority workers made up only 10 to 12 percent of the work force in their area, they accounted for from 60 to 70 percent of those laid off in 1974. The principle of seniority, a trade union triumph designed to protect workers from age discrimination, in this case guaranteed that minority workers would suffer most from technological changes, because the legacy of past discrimination by their employers left them with less seniority than white workers.[38]

When housing prices increased dramatically during the 1970s, white home owners who had been able to take advantage of discriminatory FHA financing policies in the past realized increased equity in their homes, while those excluded from the housing market by earlier policies found themselves facing even higher costs of entry into the market in addition to the traditional obstacles presented by the discriminatory practices of sellers, realtors, and lenders. The contrast between European Americans and African Americans is instructive in this regard. Because whites have access to broader housing choices than blacks, whites pay 15 percent less than blacks for similar housing in the same neighborhood. White neighborhoods typically experience housing costs 25 percent lower than would be the case if the residents were black.[39]

A recent Federal Reserve Bank of Boston study revealed that Boston bankers made 2.9 times as many mortgage loans per 1,000 housing units in neighborhoods inhabited by low-income whites than in neighborhoods populated by low-income blacks.[40] In addition, loan officers were far more likely to overlook flaws in the credit records of white applicants or to arrange creative financing for them than they were with black applicants.[41] A Los Angeles study found that loan officers more frequently used dividend income and underlying assets as criteria for judging black applicants than for whites.[42] In Houston, the NCNB Bank of Texas disqualified 13 percent of middle-income white loan applicants but 36 percent of middle-income black applicants.[43] Atlanta's home loan institutions gave five times as many home loans to whites as to blacks in the late 1980s. An analysis of sixteen Atlanta neighborhoods found that home buyers in white neighborhoods received conventional financing four times as often as those in black sections of the city.[44] Nationwide, financial institutions receive more money in deposits from black neighborhoods than they invest in them in the form of home mortgage loans, making home lending a vehicle for the transfer of capital away from black savers toward white investors.[45] In many locations high-income blacks were denied loans more often than low-income whites.[46]

When confronted with evidence of systematic racial bias in home lending, defenders of the possessive investment in whiteness argue that the disproportionate share of loan denials to members of minority groups stems not from discrimination, but from the low net worth of minority applicants, even those who have high incomes. This might seem a reasonable position, but net worth is almost totally determined by past opportunities for asset accumulation, and therefore is the one figure most likely to reflect the history of discrimination. Minorities are told, in essence, "We can't give you a loan today because we've discriminated against members of your race so effectively in the past that you have not been able to accumulate any equity from housing and to pass it down through the generations."

Most white families have acquired their net worth from the appreciation of property that they secured under conditions of special privilege in a discriminatory housing market. In their prize-winning book *Black Wealth/White Wealth,* Melvin Oliver and Thomas Shapiro demonstrate how the history of housing discrimination makes white parents more able to borrow funds for their children's college education or to loan money to their children to enter the housing market. In addition, much discrimination in home lending is not based on considerations of net worth; it stems from decisions made by white banking officials based on their stereotypes about minority communities. The Federal Reserve Bank of Boston study showed that black and Latino mortgage applicants are 60 percent more likely to be turned down for loans than whites, even after controlling for employment, financial, and neighborhood characteristics.[47] Ellis Cose reports on a white bank official confronted with evidence at a board of directors' meeting that his bank denied loans to blacks who had credit histories and earnings equal to those of white applicants who received loans. The banker replied that the information indicated that the bank needed to do a better job of "affirmative action," but one of his colleagues pointed out that the problem had nothing to do with affirmative action—the bank was simply letting prejudice stand in the way of its own best interests by rejecting loans that should be approved.[48]

Yet bankers also make money from the ways in which discrimination creates artificial scarcities in the market. Minorities have to pay more for housing because much of the market is off limits to them. Blockbusters profit from exploiting white fears and provoking them into panic selling. Minority home owners denied loans in mainstream banks often turn to exploitative lenders who make "low end" loans at enormously high interest rates. If they fail to pay back these loans, regular banks can acquire the property cheaply and charge someone else exorbitant interest for a loan on the same property.

Federal home loan policies have put the power of the federal government at the service of private discrimination. Urban renewal and highway construction programs have enhanced the possessive investment in whiteness directly through government initiatives. In addition, decisions about where to locate federal jobs have also systematically subsidized whiteness. Federal civilian employment dropped by 41,419 in central cities between 1966 and 1973, but total federal employment in metropolitan areas grew by 26,558.[49] While one might naturally expect the location of government buildings that serve the public to follow population trends, the federal government's policy of locating offices and records centers in suburbs aggravated the flight of jobs to suburban locations less accessible to inner-city residents. Because racial discrimination in the private sector forces minority workers to seek government positions disproportionate to their numbers, these moves exact particular hardships on them. In addition, minorities who follow their jobs to the suburbs must generally allocate more for commuter costs, because housing discrimination makes it harder and more expensive for them than for whites to relocate. . . .

. . . Even seemingly race-neutral policies supported by both neoconservatives and liberals in the 1980s and 1990s have increased the absolute value of being white. In the 1980s, changes in federal tax laws decreased the value of wage income and increased the value of investment income—a move harmful to minorities, who suffer from a gap between their total wealth and that of whites even greater than the disparity between their income and white income. The failure to raise the minimum wage between 1981 and 1989 and the decline of more than one-third in the value of Aid to Families with Dependent Children (AFDC) payments injured all poor people, but they exacted special costs on nonwhites, who faced even more constructed markets for employment, housing, and education than poor whites.[50]

Similarly, the "tax reforms" of the 1980s made the effective rate of taxation higher on investment in actual goods and services than on profits from speculative enterprises. This change encouraged the flight of capital from industrial production with its many employment opportunities toward investments that can be turned over quickly to allow the greatest possible tax write-offs. Government policies thus discouraged investments that might produce high-paying jobs and encouraged investors to strip companies of their assets to make rapid short-term profits.

These policies hurt almost all workers, but they fell particularly heavily on minority workers, who because of employment discrimination in the retail and small business sectors were overrepresented in blue-collar industrial jobs.

On the other hand, while neoconservative tax policies created incentives for employers to move their enterprises elsewhere, they created disincentives for home owners to move. Measures like California's Proposition 13 (passed in 1978) granting tax relief to property owners badly misallocate housing resources, because they make it financially unwise for the elderly to move out of large houses, further reducing the supply of housing available to young families. While one can well understand the necessity for protecting senior citizens on fixed incomes from tax increases that would make them lose their homes, the rewards and punishments provided by Proposition 13 are so extreme that they prevent the kinds of generational succession that have routinely opened up housing to young families in the past. This reduction works particular hardships on those who also face discrimination by sellers, realtors, and lending institutions. . . .

Because they are ignorant of even the recent history of the possessive investment in whiteness—generated by slavery and segregation, immigrant exclusion and Native American policy, conquest and colonialism, but augmented by liberal and conservative social policies as well—Americans produce largely cultural explanations for structural social problems. The increased possessive investment in whiteness generated by disinvestment in U.S. cities, factories, and schools since the 1970s disguises as *racial* problems the general social problems posed by deindustrialization, economic restructuring, and neoconservative attacks on the welfare state. It fuels a discourse that demonizes people of color for being victimized by these changes, while hiding the privileges of whiteness by attributing the economic advantages enjoyed by whites to their family values, faith in fatherhood, and foresight—rather than to the favoritism they enjoy through their possessive investment in whiteness.

The demonization of black families in public discourse since the 1970s is particularly instructive in this regard. During the 1970s, the share of low-income households headed by blacks increased by one-third, while black family income fell from 60 percent of white family income in 1971 to 58 percent in 1980. Even adjusting for unemployment and for African American disadvantages in life-cycle employment (more injuries, more frequently interrupted work histories, confinement to jobs most susceptible to layoffs), the wages of full-time year-round black workers fell from 77 percent of white workers' income to 73 percent by 1986. In 1986, white workers with high school diplomas earned $3,000 per year more than African Americans with the same education.[51] Even when they had the same family structure as white workers, blacks found themselves more likely to be poor.

Recent economic gains by blacks brighten the picture somewhat, but the deindustrialization and economic restructuring of the 1970s and 1980s imposes yet another racial penalty on wage earners from minority communities, who suffered setbacks while members of other groups accumulated equity-producing assets. And even when some minority groups show improvement, others do not. In 1995, for example, every U.S. ethnic and racial group experienced an increase in income except the twenty-seven million Hispanics, who experienced a 5.1 percent drop in income during that year alone.[52]

Forty-six percent of black workers between the ages of twenty and twenty-four held blue-collar jobs in 1976, but only 20 percent by 1984. Earnings by young black families that had reached 60 percent of white families' income in 1973, fell to 46 percent by 1986. Younger African American families experienced a 50 percent drop in real earnings between 1973 and 1986, with the decline in black male wages particularly steep.[53] . . .

Group interests are not monolithic, and aggregate figures can obscure serious differences within racial groups. All whites do not benefit from the possessive investment in whiteness in precisely the same ways; the experiences of members of minority groups are not interchangeable. But the possessive investment in whiteness always affects individual and group life chances and opportunities. Even in cases where minority groups secure political and economic power through collective mobilization, the terms and conditions of their collectivity and the logic of group solidarity are always influenced and intensified by the absolute value of whiteness in U.S. politics, economics, and culture.[54] . . .

Walter Benjamin's praise for "presence of mind" came from his understanding of how difficult it may be to see the present. But more important, he called for presence of mind as the means for implementing what he named "the only true telepathic miracle"—turning the forbidding future into the fulfilled present.[55] Failure to acknowledge our society's possessive investment in whiteness prevents us from facing the present openly and honestly. It hides from us the devastating costs of disinvestment in America's infrastructure over the past two decades and keeps us from facing our responsibility to reinvest in human resources by channeling resources toward education, health, and housing—and away from subsidies for speculation and luxury. After two decades of disinvestment, the only further disinvestment we need is from the ruinous pathology of whiteness, which has always undermined our own best instincts and interests. In a society suffering so badly from an absence of mutuality, an absence of responsibility and an absence of justice, presence of mind might be just what we need.

NOTES

1. Richard Dyer, "White," *Screen* 29, 4 (Fall 1998): 44.
2. I thank Michael Schudson for pointing out to me that since the passage of civil rights legislation in the 1960s whiteness dares not speak its name, cannot speak in its own behalf, but rather advances through a color-blind language radically at odds with the distinctly racialized distribution of resources and life chances in U.S. society.
3. Walter Benjamin, "Madame Ariane: Second Courtyard on the Left," in *One-Way Street* (London: New Left Books, 1969), 98–99.
4. See Kenneth Jackson, *Crabgrass Frontier: The Suburbanization of the United States* (New York: Oxford University Press, 1985), and Douglas S. Massey and Nancy A. Denton, *American Apartheid: Segregation and the Making of the Underclass* (Cambridge: Harvard University Press, 1993).
5. I thank Phil Ethington for pointing out to me that these aspects of New Deal policies emerged out of political negotiations between the segregationist Dixiecrats and liberals from the North and West. My perspective is that white supremacy was not a gnawing aberration within the New Deal coalition but rather an essential point of unity between southern whites and northern white ethnics.
6. Records of the Federal Home Loan Bank Board of the Home Owners Loan Corporation, City Survey File, Los Angeles, 1939, Neighborhood D-53, National Archives, Box 74, RG 195.
7. Massey and Denton, *American Apartheid,* 54.
8. John R. Logan and Harvey Molotch, *Urban Fortunes: The Political Economy of Place* (Berkeley and Los Angeles: University of California Press, 1987), 182.
9. Ibid., 114.
10. Arlene Zarembka, *The Urban Housing Crisis: Social, Economic, and Legal Issues and Proposals* (Westport, Conn.: Greenwood, 1990), 104.
11. Jill Quadagno, *The Color of Welfare: How Racism Undermined the War on Poverty* (New York: Oxford University Press, 1994), 92, 91.
12. Logan and Molotch, *Urban Fortunes,* 130.
13. See Gary Gerstle, "Working-Class Racism: Broaden the Focus," *International Labor and Working Class History* 44 (Fall 1993): 36.
14. Logan and Molotch, *Urban Fortunes,* 168–69.
15. Troy Duster, "Crime, Youth Unemployment, and the Underclass," *Crime and Delinquency* 33, 2 (April 1987): 308, 309.
16. Massey and Denton, *American Apartheid,* 55.
17. Quadagno, *The Color of Welfare,* 105, 113; Massey and Denton, *American Apartheid,* 204–5.

18. Logan and Molotch, *Urban Fortunes,* 113.
19. Robert D. Bullard, "Environmental Justice for All," in *Unequal Protection: Environmental Justice and Communities of Color,* ed. Robert Bullard (San Francisco: Sierra Club, 1994), 9–10.
20. Robert D. Bullard, "Anatomy of Environmental Racism and the Environmental Justice Movement," in *Confronting Environmental Racism: Voices from the Grass Roots,* ed. Robert D. Bullard (Boston: South End, 1993), 21.
21. Bullard, "Environmental Justice for All," 13.
22. Charles Lee, "Beyond Toxic Wastes and Race," in *Confronting Environmental Racism: Voices from the Grass Roots,* ed. Robert D. Bullard (Boston: South End, 1993), 49. Two corporate-sponsored research institutes challenged claims of racial bias in the location and operation of toxic and hazardous waste systems. Andy B. Anderson, Douglas L Anderton, and John Michael Oakes made the corporate case in "Environmental Equity: Evaluating TSDF Siting over the Past Two Decades," *Waste Age,* July 1994. These results were trumpeted in a report by the Washington University Center for the Study of American Business, funded by the John M. Olin Foundation. But the study by Anderson, Anderton, and Oakes was sponsored by the Institute of Chemical Waste Management, an industry trade group. The researchers claimed that their results were not influenced by corporate sponsorship, but they limited their inquiry to urban areas with toxic storage, disposal, and treatment facilities, conveniently excluding seventy facilities, 15 percent of TSDFs, and 20 percent of the population. The world's largest waste company, WMX Company, contributed $250,000 to the study, and the study's research plan excluded from scrutiny two landfills owned by WMX: the nation's largest commercial landfill, located in the predominately African American city of Emelle, Alabama, and the nation's fifth largest landfill, in Kettelman City Hills, California, a predominately Latino community.
23. Bunyan Bryant and Paul Mohai, *Race and the Incidence of Environmental Hazards* (Boulder, Colo.: Westview, 1992).
24. Lee, "Beyond Toxic Wastes and Race," 48.
25. Robert D. Bullard, "Decision Making," in Laura Westra and Peter S. Wenz, eds., *Faces of Environmental Racism: Confronting Issues of Global Justice* (Lanham, MD: Rowman and Littlefield, 1995), 4.
26. Bullard, "Anatomy of Environmental Racism," 21.
27. David L.L. Shields, "What Color is Hunger?" in David L.L. Shields, ed., *The Color of Hunger: Race and Hunger in National and International Perspective* (Lanham, MD: Rowman and Littlefield, 1996), 4.
28. Centers for Disease Control, "Nutritional Status of Minority Children: United States, 1986," *Morbidity and Mortality Weekly Reports* (*MMWR*) 36, 23 (June, 19, 1987): 366–69.
29. Peter S. Wenz, "Just Garbage," in Laura Westra and Peter S. Wenz, eds., *Faces of Environmental Racism: Confronting Issues of Global Justice* (Lanham, MD: Rowman and Littlefield, 1996), 66; Robert D. Bullard, "Decision Making," in Laura Westra and Peter S. Wenz, eds., *Faces of Environmental Racism,* 8.
30. Laura Pulido, "Multiracial Organizing Among Environmental Justice Activists in Los Angeles," in Michael J. Dear, H. Eric Shockman, and Greg Hise, eds., *Rethinking Los Angeles* (Thousand Oaks, CA, London, New Delhi: Sage, 1996): 175.
31. Charles Trueheart, "The Bias Most Deadly," *Washington Post,* October 30, 1990, sec. 7, cited in Shields, *The Color of Hunger,* 3.
32. George Anders, "Disparities in Medicare Access Found Among Poor, Black or Disabled Patients," *Wall Street Journal,* November 2, 1994; Lina R. Godfrey, "Institutional Discrimination and Satisfaction with Specific Government Services by Heads of Households in Ten Southern States," paper presented at the Rural Sociological Society annual meeting, 1984, cited in Shields, *The Color of Hunger,* 6, 13.
33. Jeffrey Shotland, *Full Fields, Empty Cupboards: The Nutritional Status of Migrant Farmworkers in America* (Washington: Public Voice for Food and Health: 1989), cited in Shields, *The Color of Hunger,* 3.
34. Linda A. Wray, "Health Policy and Ethnic Diversity in Older Americans: Dissonance or Harmony," *Western Journal of Medicine* 157, 3 (September 1992): 357–61.
35. Eva Bertram, Morris Blachman, Kenneth Sharpe, and Peter Andreas, *Drug War Politics: The Price of Denial* (Berkeley and Los Angeles: University of California Press, 1996), 38–42; Alexander C.

Lichtenstein and Michael A. Kroll, "The Fortress Economy: The Economic Role of the U.S. Prison System," in Elihu Rosenblatt, ed., *Criminal Injustice: Confronting the Prison Crisis* (Boston: South End, 1996), 21, 25–26.
36. Ibid., 41.
37. Massey and Denton, *American Apartheid,* 61.
38. Gertrude Ezorsky, *Racism and Justice: The Case for Affirmative Action* (Ithaca, N.Y.: Cornell University Press, 1991), 25.
39. Logan and Molotch, *Urban Fortunes,* 116.
40. Jim Campen, "Lending Insights: Hard Proof That Banks Discriminate," *Dollars and Sense,* January–February 1991, 17.
41. Mitchell Zuckoff, "Study Shows Racial Bias in Lending," *Boston Globe,* October 9, 1992.
42. Paul Ong and J. Eugene Grigsby III, "Race and Life-Cycle Effects on Home Ownership in Los Angeles, 1970 to 1980," *Urban Affairs Quarterly* 23, 4 (June 1988): 605.
43. Massey and Denton, *American Apartheid,* 108.
44. Gary Orfield and Carol Ashkinaze, *The Closing Door: Conservative Policy and Black Opportunity* (Chicago: University of Chicago Press, 1991), 58, 78.
45. Logan and Molotch, *Urban Fortunes,* 129.
46. Campen, "Lending Insights," 18.
47. Alicia H. Munnell, Lyn E. Browne, James McEneany, and Geoffrey M. B. Tootel, "Mortgage Lending in Boston: Interpreting HMDA Data" (Boston: Federal Reserve Bank of Boston, 1993); Kimberly Blanton, "Fed Blocks Shawmut's Bid to Gain N.H. Bank," *Boston Globe,* November 16, 1993.
48. Ellis Cose, *Rage of a Privileged Class* (New York: HarperCollins, 1993), 191.
49. Gregory Squires, "'Runaway Plants,' Capital Mobility, and Black Economic Rights," in *Community and Capital in Conflict: Plant Closings and Job Loss,* ed. John C. Raines, Lenora E. Berson, and David McI. Gracie (Philadelphia: Temple University Press, 1983), 70.
50. Orfield and Ashkinaze, *The Closing Door,* 225–26.
51. William Chafe, *The Unfinished Journey* (New York: Oxford University Press, 1986), 442; Noel J. Kent, "A Stacked Deck: Racial Minorities and the New American Political Economy," *Explorations in Ethnic Studies* 14, 1 (January 1991): 11.
52. Carey Goldberg, "Hispanic Households Struggle as Poorest of the Poor in the U.S.," *New York Times,* January 30, 1997, sec. A.
53. Kent, "A Stacked Deck," 13.
54. The rise of a black middle class and the setbacks suffered by white workers during deindustrialization may seem to subvert the analysis presented here. Yet the black middle class remains fragile, far less able than other middle-class groups to translate advances in income into advances in wealth and power. Similarly, the success of neoconservatism since the 1970s has rested on securing support from white workers for economic policies that do them objective harm by mobilizing countersubversive electoral coalitions against busing and affirmative action, while carrying out attacks on public institutions and resources by representing "public" space as black space. See Oliver and Shapiro, "Wealth of a Nation." See also Logan and Molotch, *Urban Fortunes.*
55. Benjamin, "Madame Ariane," 98, 99.

READING 36

Strangers Among Us

How Latino Immigration Is Transforming America

Roberto Suro

On Imelda's fifteenth birthday[1], her parents were celebrating everything they had accomplished by coming north to make a new life in the United States. Two short people in brand-new clothes, they stood in the driveway of their home in Houston and greeted relatives, friends, and neighbors, among them a few people who had come from the same village in central Mexico and who would surely carry gossip of the party back home. A disc jockey with a portable stereo presided over the backyard as if it were a cabaret instead of a patch of grass behind an overcrowded bungalow where five people shared two

Roberto Suro, the American-born son of a Puerto Rican Father and an Ecuadorean mother, is a staff writer for *The Washington Post.*

bedrooms. A folding table sagged with platters of tacos and fajitas. An aluminum keg of beer sat in a wheelbarrow atop a bed of half-melted ice cubes. For Imelda's parents, the festivities that night served as a triumphant display of everything they had earned by working two jobs each. Like most of the other adults at the party, they had come north to labor in restaurants, factories, warehouses, or construction sites by day and to clean offices at night. They had come to work and to raise children in the United States.

Imelda, who had been smuggled across the Rio Grande as a toddler, wore a frilly dress ordered by catalog from Guadalajara, as befits a proper Mexican celebrating her *quinceañera,* which is the traditional coming-out party for fifteen-year-old Latin girls. Her two younger sisters and a little brother, all U.S. citizens by birth, wore new white shirts from a discount store. Their hair had been combed down with sharp, straight parts and dabs of pomade.

When it came time for Imelda to dance her first dance, her father took her in his arms for one of the old-fashioned polkas that had been his favorite when a band played in the town square back home. By tradition, boys could begin courting her after that dance. Imelda's parents went to bed that night content they had raised their children according to proper Mexican custom.

The next morning at breakfast, Imelda announced that she was pregnant, that she was dropping out of school, and that she was moving in with her boyfriend, a Mexican-American who did not speak Spanish and who did not know his father. That night, she ate a meal purchased with food stamps and cooked on a hot plate by her boyfriend's mother. She remembers the dinner well. "That night, man, I felt like an American. I was free."

This is the promise and the peril of Latino immigration. Imelda's parents had traveled to Texas on a wave of expectations that carried them from the diminishing life of peasant farmers on a dusty *rancho* to quiet contentment as low-wage workers in an American city. These two industrious immigrants had produced a teenage welfare mother, who in turn was to have an American baby. In the United States, Imelda had learned the language and the ways. In the end, what she learned best was how to be poor in an American inner city.

Latino immigration delivers short-term gains and has long-term costs. For decades now, the United States has engaged in a form of deficit spending that can be measured in human lives. Through their hard work at low wages, Latinos have produced immediate benefits for their families, employers, and consumers, but American society has never defined a permanent place for these immigrants or their children and it has repeatedly put off considering their future. That future, however, is now arriving, and it will produce a reckoning. The United States will need new immigration policies to decide who gets into the country. More importantly, the nation will need new means of assuring political equality and freedom of economic opportunity. Soon Americans will learn once again that in an era of immigration, the newcomers not only demand change; they create change.[2]

When I last met Imelda, she was just a few weeks short of her due date, but she didn't have anything very nice to say about her baby or her boyfriend. Growing up in Houston as the child of Mexican immigrants had filled her with resentment, especially toward her parents, and that was what she wanted to talk about.

"We'd get into a lot of yelling and stuff at home because my parents, they'd say, 'You're Mexican. Speak Spanish. Act like a Mexican girl,' and I'd say, 'I'm here now and I'm going to be like the other kids.' They didn't care."

Imelda is short and plump, with wide brown eyes and badly dyed yellow hair. She wore a denim shirt with the sleeves ripped off, and her expression was a studied pout. Getting pregnant was just one more way of expressing anger and disdain. She is a dime-store Madonna.

Imelda is also a child of the Latino migration. She is a product of that great movement of people from Latin America into the United States that is older than any borders but took on a startling new meaning when it gradually gained momentum after the 1960s and then turned into something huge in the 1980s. Latino immigrants were drawn north when America needed their services, and they built communities known as barrios in every major city. But then in the 1990s, as these newcomers began to define their permanent place here, the ground shifted on them. They and their children—many of them native-born Americans—found themselves struggling with an economy that offered few opportunities to people trying to get off the bottom. They also faced a populace sometimes disconcerted by the growing number of foreigners in its midst. Immigration is a transaction between the newcomers and the hosts. It will be decades before there is a final tally for this great wave of immigration, but the terms of the deal have now become apparent.

Imelda's story does not represent the best or the worst of the Latino migration, but it does suggest some of the challenges posed by the influx. Those challenges are defined first of all by demography. No other democracy has ever experienced an uninterrupted wave of migration that has lasted as long and that has involved as many people as the recent movement of Spanish-speaking people to the United States. Twelve million foreign-born Latinos live here. If immigration and birth rates remain at current levels, the total Hispanic population will grow at least three times faster than the population as a whole for several decades, and Latinos will become the nation's largest minority group, surpassing the size of the black population a few years after the turn of the century. Despite some differences among them, Latinos constitute a distinctive linguistic and cultural group, and no single group has ever dominated a prolonged wave of immigration the way Latinos have for thirty years. By contrast, Asians, the other large category of immigrants, come from nations as diverse as India and Korea, and although the Latino migration is hardly monolithic, the Asian influx represents a much greater variety of cultures, languages, and economic experiences. Moreover, not since the Irish potato famine migration of the 1840s has any single nationality accounted for such a large share of an immigrant wave as the Mexicans have in recent decades. The 6.7 million Mexican immigrants living in the United States in 1996 made up 27 percent of the entire foreign-born population, and they outnumbered the entire Asian immigrant population by more than 2 million people. Latinos are hardly the only immigrants coming to the United States in the 1990s, but they will define this era of immigration, and this country's response to them will shape its response to all immigrants.

Latinos, like most other immigrants, tend to cluster together. Their enclaves are the barrios, a Spanish word for neighborhoods that has become part of English usage because barrios have become such a common part of every American city. Most barrios, however, remain a place apart, where Latinos live separated from others by custom, language, and preference. They are surrounded by a city but are not part of it. Imelda lived in a barrio named Magnolia Park, after the trees that once grew along the banks of the bayou there. Like other barrios, Magnolia is populated primarily by poor and working-class Latinos, and many newly arrived immigrants start out there. Magnolia was first settled nearly a hundred years ago by Mexicans who fled revolution in their homeland and found jobs dredging the ship channel and port that allowed Houston to become a great city. Latinos continued to arrive off and on, especially when Houston was growing. Since the 1980s, when the great wave of new arrivals began pouring into Magnolia, it hasn't mattered whether the oil city was in boom or bust—Latinos always find jobs, even when they lack skills and education. Most of Magnolia is poor, but it is also a neighborhood where people go to work before dawn and work into the night.

Like other barrios, Magnolia serves as an efficient port of entry for Latino immigrants because it is an easy place to find cheap housing, learn about jobs, and keep connected to home. Some newcomers and their children pass through Magnolia and find a way out to more prosperous neighborhoods where they can leave the barrio life behind. But for millions like Imelda who came of age in the 1990s, the barrios have become a dead end of unfulfilled expectations.

"We could never get stuff like pizza at home," Imelda went on, "just Mexican foods. My mother would give me these silly dresses to wear to school. No jeans. No jewelry. No makeup. And they'd always say, 'Stick with the Mexican kids. Don't talk to the Anglos; they'll boss you. Don't run around with the Chicanos [Mexican-Americans]; they take drugs. And just don't go near the *morenos* [blacks] for any reason.'"

Imelda's parents live in a world circumscribed by the barrio. Except for the places where they work, the rest of the city, the rest of America, seems to them as remote as the downtown skyline visible off in the distance on clear days. After more than a dozen years, they speak all the English they need, which isn't much. What they know best is how to find and keep work.

Imelda learned English from the television that was her constant childhood companion. Outside, as Magnolia became a venue for gangs and drug sales, she learned to be streetwise and sassy. Growing up fast in Magnolia, Imelda learned how to want things but not how to get them. . . .

Latinos are different from all other immigrants past and present because they come from close by and because many come illegally. No industrialized nation has ever faced such a vast migration across a land border with the virtual certainty that it will continue to challenge the government's ability to control that border for years to come. No immigrant group has carried the stigma of illegality that now attaches itself to many Latinos. Unlike most immigrants, Latinos arrive already deeply connected to the United States. Latinos come as relations, distant relations perhaps, but familiar and connected nonetheless. They seem to know us. We seem to know them, and almost as soon as they are in the house, they become part of our bedroom arguments. They are newcomers, and yet they find their culture imbedded in the landscape of cities that have always had Spanish names, such as Los Angeles and San Antonio, or that have become largely Spanish-speaking, such as Miami and New York. They do not consider themselves strangers here because they arrive to something familiar.

They come from many different nations, many different races, yet once here they are treated like a pack of blood brothers. In the United States, they live among folk who share their names but have forgotten their language, ethnic kinsmen who are Latinos by ancestry but U.S. citizens by generations of birthright. The newcomers and the natives may share little else, but for the most part they share neighborhoods, the Magnolias, where their fates become intertwined. Mexican-Americans and Puerto Ricans account for most of the native-born Latino population. They are the U.S.-made vessel into which the new immigration flows. They have been Americans long enough to have histories, and these are sad histories of exploitation and segregation abetted by public authorities. As a result, a unique designation was born. "Hispanics" became a minority group. This identity is an inescapable aspect of the Latino immigrant experience because newcomers are automatically counted as members of the group for purposes of public policy and because the discrimination that shaped that identity persists in some segments of the American public. However, it is an awkward fit for several reasons. The historical grievances that led to minority group designation for Latinos are significant, but compared to slavery or Jim Crow segregation they are neither as well known nor as horrible. As a result, many Americans simply do not accept the idea that Latinos have special standing, and not every native Latino embraces this history as an inescapable element of self-concept. Moreover, Latinos do not carry a single immutable marker, like skin color, that reinforces group identity. Minority group status can be an important element of a Latino's identity in the United States, but it is not such a clear and powerful element of American life that it automatically carries over to Latino immigrants.

"Hispanic" has always been a sweeping designation attached to people of diverse cultures and economic conditions, different races and nationalities, and the sweep has vastly increased by the arrival of immigrants who now make up about 40 percent of the group. The designation applies equally to a Mexican-American whose family has been in Texas since before the Alamo and a Mexican who just crossed the Rio Grande for the first time. Minority group status was meant to be as expansive as the discrimination it had to confront. But now for the first time, this concept is being stretched to embrace both a large native Latino population with a long undeniable history of discrimination and immigrants who are just starting out here. The same is occurring with some Asian groups, but the Latino phenomenon has a far greater impact because of the numbers involved. Latino immigrants are players in the old and unresolved dilemma of race in America, and because they do not fit any of the available roles, they are a force of change.

Like all other newcomers, Latino immigrants arrive as blank slates on which their future course has yet to be written. They are moving toward that future in many directions at once, not en masse as a single cohesive group. Some remain very Latino; others become very American. Their skin comes in many different colors and shades. Some are black, and some of them can pass very readily as white. Most Latinos arrive poor, but they bring new energy to the labor force even as they multiply the ranks of the chronically poor. Latino immigrants challenge the whole structure of social science, politics, and jurisprudence that categorizes people in terms of lifetime membership in racial or ethnic groups. The barrios do not fit into an urban landscape segregated between rich and poor, between the dependent and the taxed.

Latino immigrants come in large numbers. They come from nearby. They join fellow Latinos who are a native minority group. Many arrive poor, illegally, and with little education. Those are the major ingredients of a challenge unlike any other. . . .

More than a third of all Latinos are younger than eighteen years old. This vast generation is growing faster than any other segment of the population. It is also failing faster. While dropout rates among Anglos and African-Americans steadily decline, they continue to rise among Latino immigrants, and mounting evidence suggests that many who arrive in their teens simply never enter American schools at all. A 1996 Rand study of census data found that high school participation rates were similarly high—better than 90 percent—for whites, blacks, and Asians, native and immigrant alike, and for native Latinos, as well. Latino immigrants, especially from Mexico, were the only group lagging far behind, with less than 75 percent of the school-age teens getting any education. Only 62 percent of the Mexican immigrant seventeen-year-olds were in school, and these young people are the fuel of U.S. population growth into the twenty-first century.[3]

Dropout rates are only one symptom. This massive generation of young people is adapting to an America characterized by the interaction of plagues. Their new identities are being shaped by the social epidemics of youth homicides, pregnancy, and drug use, the medical epidemic of AIDS, and a political epidemic of disinvestment in social services. These young Latinos need knowledge to survive in the workforce, but the only education available to them comes from public school systems that are on the brink of collapse. They are learning to become Americans in urban neighborhoods that most Americans see only in their nightmares. Imelda and a vast generation of Latino young people like her are the victims of a vicious bait and switch. The United States offered their parents opportunities. So many of the children get the plagues.

For the parents, movement to the United States almost always brings tangible success. They may be poor by U.S. standards, but they measure their accomplishments in terms of what they have left behind. By coming north, they overcome barriers of race and class that have been insuperable for centuries in Latin America. Meanwhile, the children are left on the wrong side of the barriers of race and class that are becoming ever more insuperable in the United States. With no memory of the *rancho,* they have no reason to be thankful for escaping it. They look at their parents and all they see is toil and poverty. They watch American TV, and all they see is affluence. Immigrant children learning to live in this dark new world face painful challenges but get little help. Now, on top of everything else, they are cursed by people who want to close the nation's doors against them. The effects are visible on their faces.

"I can tell by looking in their eyes how long they've been here," said the Reverend Virgil Elizondo, rector of San Fernando Cathedral in San Antonio, Texas. "They come sparkling with hope, and the first generation finds that hope rewarded. Their children's eyes no longer sparkle. They have learned only to want jobs and money they can't have and thus to be frustrated."

The United States may not have much use now for Imelda's son, but he will be eighteen and ready to join the labor force in the second decade of the next century, just as the bulk of the baby-boom generation hits retirement age. Then, when the proportion of elderly to young workers is going out of whack, this country will have a great need for him and the other children born in the barrios, who will contribute financial sustenance in the form of their payroll deductions and other taxes. This is already an inescapable fact because of the relatively low birth rates among U.S.'s whites and African-Americans for the past several decades. Women of Mexican ancestry had fertility rates three times higher than non-Hispanic women in the 1990s (and they were the least educated mothers of any group). Mexican immigrant women account for more than a quarter of all the births in California and nearly a third of the births to teenage mothers. The United States may not care about the children of the barrios, but it must start to address their problems now. If it lets them fail, there will be a great price to pay.

Not all immigrants are in such straits. Social scientists have taken to describing an "hourglass effect" in the distribution of income, education, and skills among recent immigrants because they are bunched at the extremes. At the top, an extraordinary two-thirds of all immigrants from India arrive with at least four years of college. Newcomers from Korea, the Philippines, China, and several other Asian nations also arrive with more education than the average native-born American. At the bottom of the hourglass are most of the Latino nationalities that have recently produced large inflows. Less than 8 percent of the immigrants from the Dominican Republic or El Salvador and less than 4 percent of the Mexicans have four years of college. Many Latino immigrants lack not only the credentials to prosper but also the minimum education necessary to survive in the U.S. economy. Less than a quarter of all Mexican immigrants have a high school degree.[4]

The immigrants at the top—mostly Asians—generate a few policy controversies that generally fall under the heading "embarrassment of riches," such as when they contribute to a glut of medical specialists. A considerable number of Latino immigrants have achieved middle-class stability and are unlikely to cause much concern. However, the real social, political, and economic challenges arising from immigration today are posed by those at the bottom, and they are overwhelmingly Latinos. Again demography defines the challenge because the top and the bottom of the hourglass are not the same size. At the top, 760,000 Indian immigrants contribute exceptional skills. At the bottom, 6.7 million Mexicans represent extraordinary needs.

About a third of all recent Latino immigrants live below the official poverty line. More than a million and a half Mexicans who entered the country legally and illegally since 1980—43 percent of the total—were officially designated as poor in 1994. With little education and few skills, they have nowhere to start but low on the economic ladder, and in America today, people who start low tend to stay low and their children stay low as well unless they get an education. For two decades now, immigration has quietly added to the size of that perennially poor population and it has changed the nature of poverty in the United States. Twenty years ago there were nearly three times more poor African-Americans in this country than poor Latinos, but those numbers have been converging during the economic expansion of the 1990s with the African-American poverty figures trending down and the Latino numbers rising so that they are now nearly equal. However, they represent strikingly different forms of poverty.[5] In 1996 the workforce participation rate for Latinos was higher than for blacks, indeed it was even higher than for whites, but Latinos also had the highest poverty rate of any group. Latinos suffer the poverty of the working poor. While that is not unusual in the immigrant experience, it marks a historic departure from the kind of poverty that has plagued American cities for the past several decades. William Julius Wilson, the Harvard sociologist who invented the concept of the underclass, argues that "the disappearance of work and the consequences of that disappearance for both social and cultural life are the central problems in the inner-city ghetto." That diagnosis from Wilson's 1996 book, *When Work Disappears,* applies to urban African-American communities, but not to the barrios. As Wilson himself notes, nearly a decade of detailed research in Chicago showed that poor Mexican immigrants can share the same kind of dilapidated neighborhoods as poor blacks, but the Mexicans will be surrounded by small businesses owned by fellow immigrants and will benefit from tightly knit social networks that help them find jobs.[6]

Latino poverty will not be remedied by the welfare-to-work programs that are now virtually the sole focus of U.S. social policy, and it will not be fixed by trying to close the nation to further immigration. The Latino poor are here and they are not going to go away. Unless new avenues of upward mobility open up for Latino immigrants and their children, the size of America's underclass will quickly double and in the course of a generation it will double again. That second generation will be different than the first. It will not only suffer the economic and political disenfranchisement that plagues poor blacks today but it will also be cut off from the American mainstream in even more profound and dangerous ways. . . .

Latino immigrants present more of a mixed picture than their native coethnics. Historically, immigrants start out earning less than native-born workers of a similar age and similar skills because the newcomer usually is facing a language barrier and lacks familiarity with the labor market, but over time that wage gap shrinks. The conventional benchmark is that immigrants who arrive when they are twenty-five or younger will close the gap and earn wages equivalent to those of a native worker after twenty years in the labor force. It is a long pull, but for many millions of people it has proved fruitful. Considerable evidence now shows that Latino immigrants, especially Mexicans, are not closing the gap. In the most extensive nationwide study of immigration's economic, fiscal, and demographic impacts on the United States, the National Research Council concluded in 1997 that Mexicans start out with the lowest wage levels of any immigrant nationality and that their wage gap actually widens substantially over time.[7] Meanwhile, European and Asian immigrants are closing the wage gap at something like the traditional pace. A 1997 UCLA study found that Mexicans who had been in the United States for thirty years had achieved modest economic gains, while recent arrivals suffered actual declines in their earnings.[8] Nearly three-quarters of the recent arrivals went to work in "low-skill occupations out of which there are few avenues of escape," writes the study's author, Vilma Ortiz, a UCLA sociologist. "Clearly, the traditional ethnic saga of hard labor followed by rewards does not apply to Latino immigrants."

The latest wave of immigrants has come to the United States only to find the ladder broken. Their arrival has coincided with changes in the structure of the U.S. economy that make the old three-generation formula obsolete. The middle rungs of the ladder, which allowed for a gradual transition into American life, are more precarious because so many jobs disappeared along with the industrial economy of smokestacks and assembly lines. In addition, the wages paid at the bottom of the labor force have declined in value steadily since the early 1980s.

The old blue-collar jobs are not the only rungs of the ladder that are now wobbly. The United States greatly expanded its system of public education in order to prepare the children and the grandchildren of the European immigrants for the workforce, extending it first to high schools and then to universities. Latino immigrants have arrived, only to find this education system dangerously in disrepair. As with the demise of the industrial economy, this reflects a fundamental change in the structure of American society. Government's priorities have shifted in ways that alter the nature of opportunity. The results have quickly become apparent. The State of California now pays better salaries to experienced prison guards than to tenured Cal State professors. The guards are more in demand. Labor unions, big-city political machines, and other institutions that helped the European immigrants are also less vigorous and far less interested in the immigrants' cause than in the early decades of this century. The Roman Catholic church gave vital help to the Europeans in establishing enclaves, gaining education, and developing ethnic solidarity, but it moved to the suburbs with the second and third generations and has played a minor institutional role—primarily as a lobbyist for liberal immigration policies—in helping the new Latinos gain a foothold in the United States.

Starting at the bottom has usually been an immigrant's fate, but this takes on a new meaning in an increasingly immobile and stratified society. Skills and education have come to mark a great divide in the U.S. workforce, and the gap is growing ever broader. The entire population is being divided into a two-tier workforce, with a college education as the price of admission to the upper tier. In the new knowledge-based economy, people with knowledge prosper. People without it remain poor. These divisions have the makings of a new class system because this kind of economic status is virtually hereditary. Very few Latino immigrants arrive with enough education to make it into the upper tier of the workforce. Their children, like the children of all poor people, face the greatest economic pressures to drop out and find work. When they do stay in school, the education they receive is, for the most part, poor.

Like Latinos today, the European ethnics built enclaves, and some were places of exceptional misery and rejection. But the Europeans' enclaves became places to make a gradual transition into American life. As they built their communities, they could nurture ethnic identity and cohesion until it evolved into a source of political strength. The Europeans established their economic claims over long periods of time, slowly moving into the mainstream as they did so.

Blacks also built enclaves when they moved north, although their separation was forced on them. A blue-collar class developed and in another generation a middle class and a professional class of blacks emerged. This upward mobility resulted from employment in the industrial economy, antipoverty programs, and a concerted effort to grant African-Americans at least minimal access to good schools and universities.

Even with these vehicles of upward mobility, it took a long time to achieve limited success.

Today, Latinos do not have the luxury of time. Immigrants and their children are no longer allowed missteps or setbacks. And there are fewer programs to ensure that at least a few of the worthy move up. Newcomers today either make it or they don't. Instead of a gradual evolution, the process of finding a place in America has become a sudden-death game.

The United States sits atop the Western Hemisphere like a beacon atop a lighthouse, a sole source, powerfully distorting everything it illuminates even as it points the way. For a hundred years, it has exercised a powerful influence over Latin America, and whether the medium was the Marine Corps or the Peace Corps, the message has always been that Americans knew better, did better, lived better. Whenever the United States became scared of Nazis or Communists, it expended huge resources to portray itself as the paragon of civic virtue and a land of boundless economic opportunity. Meanwhile, the American consumer culture penetrated deep into the Latin psyche, informing every appetite and defining new desires. With TV shows, soldiers, and political ideals, the United States has reached out and touched people across an entire hemisphere. It has gotten back immigrants in return.

America beckons, but massive human flows occur only after migrant channels have evolved into highly efficient conduits for human aspirations. In Mexico's case, emigration to the United States developed out of proximity, shared history, and encouraging U.S. business practices and government policies. When the Mexican revolution displaced millions of peasants after 1910, railroad foremen greeted them at the border and recruited them into track gangs. Dispersed by the Southern Pacific and the Santa Fe railroads, they remained in hundreds of farm towns and built the first urban barrios. Aside from these permanent settlements, a kind of circular traffic developed. Many thousands of Mexicans came to the United States for sojourns of work often lasting no more than a harvesting season but sometimes stretching to years. This migration was expanded and legalized by an agricultural guest-worker program launched in 1942 to help with wartime labor shortages. American farmers liked the cheap, disposable labor so much that that program survived until 1964. By that time, 4.5 million *braceros,* as the workers were known, had learned the way north. The *bracero* program ended, but the traffic continued even as the United States started trying to control the flow. Many Mexicans had acquired some kind of legal status here, including those born in the United States to migrant-worker parents. Others came illegally and found shelter in such barrios as Magnolia and East L.A., which had become permanent Spanish-speaking enclaves. Major changes in U.S. immigration law enacted in 1965 raised the overall ceilings for legal immigration and removed biases that favored Northern and Western Europeans. The most important change in the long run, however, gave preference to immigrants who were reuniting with kin. Having a relative here became the key qualification for a visa, rather than a prospective employer or marketable skills, and immigrant flows became self-duplicating as every new legal immigrant eventually became a potential sponsor for others. . . .

Once efficient linkages had developed, a variety of economic circumstances in the United States generated the demand for immigrant labor, which encouraged the continuation of migrant flows. Just as the rise of the industrial era created jobs for the great wave of European immigrants, the end of that era created opportunities for Latinos. Some manufacturers in old industries such as garments, furniture, and auto parts turned to low-cost immigrant labor as a way of remaining competitive with foreign producers. As the U.S. population shifted south to the Sun Belt, Latinos arrived to build the new cities. Immigrants filled hundreds of new job niches as the United States developed a postindustrial service economy that saw booms in light manufacturing and all manner of consumer and financial services.

In addition to economic demand, changes in U.S. immigration law have also promoted continued movement from Latin America. The Immigration Reform and Control Act of 1986 was meant to halt illegal immigration, but it actually encouraged its growth. It created amnesties that allowed nearly 3 million former illegal aliens—nearly 90 percent of them Latinos—to acquire legal residence and eventually become eligible for citizenship. They, in turn, have become hosts to about a million relatives, who have lived in the United States illegally while applying for legal status, and to uncounted others who have no claim on residency. The 1986 reform also imposed sanctions for the first time—mostly civil fines—on employers who hire illegal aliens. No mechanism was ever created to enforce the law, and so it eventually became a meaningless prohibition. Then in 1990, Congress raised the limits on several forms of legal immigration, thus ensuring a protracted influx.

. . . The Irish came across the Atlantic as early as the seventeenth century and kept coming steadily for nearly two hundred years in response to demand for low-wage workers. This well-established linkage allowed for a massive, explosive migration during the potato famine in the middle of the nineteenth century and another huge wave in the 1880s during a period of rapid industrialization. Although the U.S. government now tries to regulate immigration, Mexico resembles the Irish case. As with the Irish in the nineteenth century, the migrant channels are abundant and efficient—there are large receiving communities here and the native-born descendants of immigrants have begun to penetrate the mainstream of American society. When Mexico suffered a devastating economic crisis in the 1980s and the U.S. economy boomed, the number of Mexican immigrants living in the United States doubled in a decade. That explosion continues so forcefully that the numbers might nearly double again in the 1990s. And the explosion does not involve just Mexicans now. The flows from the Dominican Republic and El Salvador are also running at a rate headed for a doubling by the end of the decade.

Americans are only just waking up to the size of this immigrant wave, and yet the foreign-born already account for 9 percent of the total population—the highest proportion since World War II. For fifty years after the end of the European wave in the 1920s, there was no steady immigration, and then the long lull was followed by a demographic storm. Some 7 million more immigrants, counting the estimates of the illegal flow, came to the United States between 1975 and 1995 than during the preceding half-century hiatus. Now, like Rip van Winkle aroused from his slumber, the United States is trying to understand something that is at once familiar but changed. The nation's reference points for large-scale immigration are set in an era of steamships and telegraphs, yet the United States needs to manage a massive influx at a time of jet travel and global television. Moreover, the Latino immigration is not just unexpected and unfamiliar; many Americans consider it unwanted. No national policy debate and no clear process of decision making led to formal action opening the doors to a level of immigration unfamiliar in living memory.

When the counterreaction hit, it hit hard. In the early 1990s an extraordinary variety of events combined to present immigration as a menacing force. It began quietly during the recession at the start of the decade and grabbed the public's attention with the nanny problems of Zoë Baird, President Clinton's first nominee for attorney general. Then came the World Trade Center bombing, perpetrated by evildoers who slipped through the immigration system. Chinese smuggling ships, Haitian boat people, Cuban rafters, and swarms of Tijuana border jumpers all fueled anxieties about a chaotic world infringing on America. Even though the United States remained more open to foreigners than any other nation, immigrants had come to represent mysterious and uncontrollable dangers. . . .

NOTES

1. Imelda's story: Author's account of his first encounters with Imelda appeared in the *New York Times,* January 20, 1992.
2. Twelve million foreign-born Latinos: U.S. Census Bureau, *The Foreign Born Population: 1994* (Current Population Reports P20-486, 1995), Current Population Survey, March 1996, FB96CPS.

   Latinos will become the nation's largest minority group: U.S. Census Bureau, *Population Projections of the United States by Age, Sex, Race and Hispanic Origin: 1995 to 2050* (Current Population Reports P25-1130, 1996).

   No single group has ever dominated a prolonged wave of immigration: In the 1890s, for example, Italy, Russia, Austria-Hungary, and Germany had almost equal shares of the influx (around 15 percent each), with Scandinavia, Ireland, and Great Britain not far behind (around 10 percent each).

   The 6.7 million Mexican immigrants: U.S. Census Bureau, *The Foreign Born Population: 1994.*
3. More than a third of all Latinos are younger than eighteen years old: Georges Vernez, Allan Abrahamse, *How Immigrants Fare in U.S. Education* (Rand, 1996).
4. Fertility rates: U.S. Census Bureau, *Fertility of American Women: June 1994* (Current Population Reports P20 482, 1995). B. Meredith Burke, "Mexican Immigrants Shape California's Future," *Population Today,* September 1995 (Population Reference Bureau Inc., Washington, D.C.).

   The hourglass effect: Philip L. Martin, "The United States: Benign Neglect Towards Immigration," in *Controlling Immigration: A Global Perspective,* eds. Wayne A. Cornelius, Philip L. Martin, and James F. Hollifeld (Stanford University Press, 1995). And for statistics on the distribution of education among immigrants: Alejandro Portes and Rubén G. Rumbaut, *Immigrant America: A Portrait,* 2d ed. (University of California Press, 1996).

   About a third of all recent Latino immigrants live below the official poverty line: U.S. Census Bureau, *The Foreign Born Population: 1994.*
5. Twenty years ago there were: U.S. Census Bureau, *Poverty Income in the United States: 1996* (Current Population Reports P60-198, 1996).
6. In 1996 the workforce participation: U.S. Census Bureau, *Money Income in the United States: 1996* (Current Population Reports P60-197, 1996).

   William Julius Wilson: William Julius Wilson, *When Work Disappears* (Knopf, 1996), pp. 52, 65.
7. In the most extensive nationwide study: James P. Smith and Barry Edmonston, eds., *The New Americans: Economic, Demographic and Fiscal Effects of Immigration* (National Academy Press, 1997), chapter 5.
8. Mexicans who had been in the United States for thirty years had achieved modest economic gains: Vilma Ortiz, "The Mexican Origin Population: Permanent Working Class or Emerging Middle Class?" in *Ethnic L.A.,* eds. Roger Waldinger and Mehdi Bozogrmehr (Russell Sage Foundation, 1996).

   Prison guards and professors: Barry Munitz, "Never Make Predictions, Particularly about the Future" (American Association of State Colleges and Universities, 1995).

READING 37

The Gender Gap: Contours and Causes[1]

Andrew Hacker

American women are still far from economic parity. In some spheres progress has been made, and those gains will be documented here. There can be no denying that these advances are long overdue and far from sufficient. Yet the story is not wholly one of improvement. An unhappy fact

Andrew Hacker teaches political science at Queens College in New York City.

of our times is that in some ways women are worse off than they were in the past.

While the typical woman's wallet is fuller than ever before, it is still measurably thinner than the typical American man's. And while it is now true that when men and women hold the same jobs, they tend to be paid the same wage, women still have less chance of reaching the highest earnings levels. What's more, even though more women are entering occupations traditionally held by men, once they get there, the positions start to decline in prestige and pay.

But the world of work offers only a partial view of the economic disparities between the sexes. So it makes sense to look at the population as a whole. In 1995, the median income for the 92.1 million adult men was $22,562, while the midpoint for the 96.0 million women was $12,130. This means women receive $538 for every $1,000 going to the men. This is not an auspicious ratio. Indeed, it could be construed as society's verdict that women's needs and contributions amount to half of those of men. But even that figure can be viewed as evidence of progress: as recently as 1975, American women received a paltry $382 for each $1,000 received by men.

However, this aggregate comparison has limited meaning, because most men hold full-time jobs, whereas the majority of women have no earnings from employment or work only part-time. Indeed, almost 10 million women told the Census Bureau in 1995 that they had no incomes at all, or at least none that came to them in their own names. Most of these women are nonworking wives, ranging from blue-collar homemakers to the spouses of top executives. Their lack of a personal income pulls down the gender ratio. And when we examine marriages where both partners work, the typical wife emerges earning only $418 for each $1,000 made by her husband. (Few wives have investments of their own that yield them comfortable independent incomes.)

So marriage is the chief cause of the income gap and will remain so as long as it relegates more women than men to tending to the home and caring for the children. In fact, over 40 percent of at-home wives either have no children or all of their youngsters are grown. . . . Most of these women never developed careers, and few have shown much interest in entering the workforce. There are still husbands who declare that they do not want their wives to work, and not all are affluent executives who want their mates available to pack their suitcases and entertain business clients. In the households where only the husband brings home a paycheck, his earnings are often quite modest. Over a third of these breadwinners make less than $30,000 a year. Thus many families still rank what they see as domestic values ahead of whatever material benefits additional earnings would produce.

Far fewer Americans are married today than at any other time in our nation's history. This social change has an upside as well as a downside when spreads in income are computed. More people are postponing marriage until they are older, and more marriages are breaking up. Even after allowing for remarriages, a larger portion of the population is now single at any given time. Among women in their early to mid-thirties, almost 20 percent have not yet been married, three times the proportion of thirty years ago. Virtually all of these nonmarried women work; more of them than ever before have serious careers. This cohort comes closest to parity with men. Indeed, a 1993 Census study found that "never married" women who work at full-time jobs earn $1,005 for every $1,000 made by comparable men.

Some of these women live alone, and others have live-in roommates or partners. Indeed, this is a major reason why there are fewer intact marriages today; many people now spend several years—or more than several—in what is essentially its equivalent. They are part of a growing group of people whom sociologists have dubbed DINKs: Double Incomes with No Kids. Composed sometimes of married couples and many who are not, most of whom are straight but many of whom are gay, this stratum is notable for its discretionary spending, which is indispensable to a high-consumption economy.

But the downside of the decline in marriage is that while most Americans eventually give it a try, about half of these unions end in divorce or permanent separation. And not everyone has the opportunity or the desire to undertake it again. As it happens, men are more apt to remarry, partly because they are not adept at living alone and also because they have a wider choice of possible mates. In addition, more women now have higher expectations for a partner and have not yet found a man—or at least one who is available—who meets their standards. This has become especially evident among black women, who are now only half as likely to marry as white women. As a result, more single women than ever before are deciding to have children. Indeed, they now give birth to over 30 percent of all babies. True, many are becoming mothers while in their teens and without giving much thought to the future. However, one in six is over the age of thirty and has presumably deliberated about the decision. For these and other reasons, each year finds more women supporting offspring on their own. In most cases, their living standards will be lower than they would have been had the women been married or kept their marriages going.

So while the fact that more women are working has increased their income relative to men, the fact that more are on their own has had a countervailing effect. Today, over one-fifth of all families are headed by single women. And in more than a third of these households, the mother has never been married. Some of the single women heading families receive public assistance, which is intended to keep them alive but below the poverty line. And while over half find work, their median income is only $17,170, and fewer than a third have incomes that exceed $25,000 a year.

PROGRESS TOWARD PARITY?

Interestingly enough, the first signs of progress toward economic parity between men and women came during the still traditional 1950s. This was supposed to be a period when women eschewed paid employment and instead opted for early marriage and a procession of children. Yet as Table 1 shows, the pay ratio of women who were working rose by 25 percent, from $486 to $607, the largest increase of any postwar decade. Several reasons for this stand out. To start, women were abandoning what had been one of their principal occupations, and an ill-paid one at that: domestic service. Back in 1940, 2.4 million women cleaned and cooked and cared for children in other people's homes; by 1970, only half that number were so employed. It appears that the women who chose to work were expecting more from their jobs, including better pay. Even if many women were still secretaries, the corporate world was remaking its own image. The sassy gum chewers of Hollywood such as Joan Blondell would not fit in with the new carpeted corridors. At this time, also, two other major occupations for women began to pay more, for the classic economic reasons. Nurses and schoolteachers were in short supply because so many women were staying at home. In the suburbs, the future-oriented middle class was willing to pay for quality education and health care. Starting in the world of "women's" work, a ripple effect caused women's expectations to rise even in the domesticated Eisenhower era.

TABLE 1

CAUSE FOR APPLAUSE?

Year	Percent Working	Pay Ratio to Men
1950	31.4%	$486
1960	34.8%	$607
1970	42.6%	$594
1980	51.5%	$602
1990	57.5%	$716
1995	58.7%	$714

But progress came to a halt. The pay ratio reached by 1960 remained essentially the same in 1970 and 1980. Hence, the slogan "59 Cents!" that was emblazoned on protest placards in the early days of the women's movement, often accompanied by a popular ballad of the time: "Fifty-nine cents for every man's dollar; fifty-nine cents, it's a low-down deal!" These laments were not unavailing, since during the 1980s the ratio rose from $602 to $716. One stimulus was that lawyers and judges began applying the hitherto somnolent Equal Pay Act of 1963, which said that at jobs that called for "equal skill, effort, and responsibility," there could be no gap in "wages to employees of the opposite sex." Also significant was that fewer women were becoming secretaries and nurses or teachers, just as an earlier generation had abandoned domestic service. If we total up these traditionally "female" occupations, in 1970 they had absorbed 28 percent of all employed women, but by 1995, only 18 percent. Indeed, in 1995, the workforce had 700,000 fewer secretaries than in 1980. An obvious reason is the advent of word-processing equipment, which facilitates copying and correcting. Also, in many organizations the position has been retitled "assistant." And, as a further sign of our times, just as women were less willing to do routine typing, men were adapting to the keyboard as it was the only way to communicate with a computer. And in a reverse twist, the number of household workers began to rise in the 1980s, reflecting a demand for nannies in two-career families.

Statistics also indicate that women have been investing their time and effort in ways that augment their economic value. Postponing marriage and children is one route to a higher income; additional education is another. In 1994, the most recent figures at this writing, women accounted for well over half—54 percent—of those awarded bachelor's degrees, compared to 43 percent in 1970 and 35 percent in 1960. Even more graphic has been their entry into professional programs. As Table 2 shows, in 1964 they were barely visible in engineering, dentistry, and business administration, and received well under 10 percent of degrees awarded in architecture, law, and medicine. Today, apart from engineering, women have made substantial strides in most professional programs. In the 1995 entering classes at Yale, Stanford, and Johns Hopkins medical schools, they outnumbered men.

TABLE 2

PROPORTION OF DEGREES AWARDED TO WOMEN

Professional Programs	1964	1994
Architecture	4.0%	36.6%
Engineering	0.4%	16.4%
Business (MBA level)	2.7%	36.5%
Dentistry	0.7%	38.5%
Medicine	6.5%	37.9%
Law	3.1%	43.0%
Pharmacy	13.9%	66.8%
Academic doctorates	10.6%	44.1%*

*American citizens only.

But an increased presence in many occupations and professions does not necessarily lead to greater equity in earnings for women. Table 3 presents a mixed picture. The Bureau of Labor

TABLE 3

WOMEN'S EARNINGS (PER $1,000 RECEIVED BY MEN)

Occupation	1983	1995
More Than 10 Percent Improvement		
Chefs and cooks	$711	$885
Realtors	$683	$794
Production inspectors	$563	$649
Waiters and waitresses	$721	$822
Public administrators	$701	$786
Computer analysts	$773	$860
Less Than 10 Percent		
Journalists	$782	$855
Retail sales	$636	$693
Insurance adjustors	$651	$691
Financial managers	$638	$674
Education administrators	$671	$708
Janitors and cleaners	$810	$844
Engineers	$828	$862
Accountants	$706	$734
College faculty	$773	$781
Deterioration		
High school teachers	$886	$881
Health technicians	$839	$813
Electronic assemblers	$857	$808
Lawyers	$890	$818
Physicians	$816	$649

Statistics only began releasing pay differentials in 1983, but that at least allows comparisons across a twelve-year period. While some occupations have witnessed modest progress, in none have women's earnings breached the 90 percent mark, and in many they are still below 70 percent. Even more disturbing is the finding that in some fields women's remuneration has actually dropped relative to men's. Among salaried lawyers and physicians and high school teachers, women comprise a large share of those recently entering those professions, which may account for their lower wages. But among health technicians and electronic assemblers, the proportion of women has actually been dropping, which means another explanation is needed. . . .

SEXUAL SEGREGATION

By most measures, the last quarter century has seen steady moves by women into positions traditionally reserved for men. As Table 4 shows, the advances have been real in fields as varied as medicine and meat cutting and bartending. But in some cases, progress may be less than it first appears. In 1970, insurance adjustors were mainly men, and in their well-paid work they examined burnt-out buildings and wrecked cars. Today, insurance adjustors are mainly women, who sit at computer terminals entering insurance claims. Many are part-time employees, with few or no benefits. And some . . . even do their jobs from their homes. Or, to cite another example, in 1970, the typical typesetter was a well-paid union worker who set hot lead for a newspaper in a printing plant. Today, type is generally keyed in electronically by women who are paid a fraction of what their male forerunners received. Many of the new women pharmacists count out pills for mail-order services and never see a customer. Few of the incoming female physicians will have practices of their own, but will be employed—or subject to scrutiny—by health-maintenance organizations.

Indeed, it has been argued that occupations start to admit women just when a field is beginning to decline in prestige and economic standing. That happened many years ago, when men ceased being bank tellers. Sometimes, as with typesetting, new technologies reconfigure the

TABLE 4

WOMEN'S SHARES WITHIN OCCUPATIONS

	1970	1995
Total workforce	38.0%	46.1%
Considerable Change		
Insurance adjustors	29.6%	73.9%
Typesetters	16.8%	67.3%
Educational administrators	27.8%	58.7%
Publicists	26.6%	57.9%
Bartenders	21.0%	53.5%
Government administrators	21.7%	49.8%
College faculty	29.1%	45.2%
Insurance agents	12.9%	37.1%
Pharmacists	12.1%	36.2%
Photographers	14.8%	27.1%
Lawyers	4.9%	26.4%
Physicians	9.7%	24.4%
Butchers and meat cutters	11.4%	21.6%
Architects	4.0%	19.8%
Telephone installers	2.8%	16.0%
Dentists	3.5%	13.4%
Police officers	3.7%	12.9%
Clergy	2.9%	11.1%
Engineers	1.7%	8.4%
Sheet-metal workers	1.9%	7.5%
Modest Change		
Hotel receptionists	51.4%	75.2%
Social workers	63.3%	67.9%
High school teachers	49.6%	57.0%
Journalists	41.6%	53.2%
Realtors	31.2%	50.7%
Computer programmers	24.2%	29.5%
Essentially No Change		
Dental hygienists	94.0%	99.4%
Secretaries	97.8%	98.5%
Registered nurses	97.3%	93.1%
Elementary school teachers	83.9%	84.1%
Librarians	82.1%	83.2%
Men Replacing Women		
Telephone operators	94.0%	88.4%
Data entry keyers	93.7%	82.9%
Waiters and waitresses	90.8%	77.7%
Cooks and chefs	67.2%	44.5%

job. Moreover, women entering law and university teaching are finding the ground rules have been changed. Until recently most law partners and college professors enjoyed lifetime tenure. But now fewer attorneys can expect to become partners; and those that do can now be dismissed. Colleges, after years of being overstaffed in their top ranks, are tending to replace more of their retiring faculty members with discardable adjuncts. What may be added, though it hardly provides solace, is that young men who are also entering these and other professions will encounter the same barriers and rebuffs.

A smaller but still discernible pattern of change within the workforce has been the decision by some men to enter fields traditionally associated with women. The development began with flight attendants and then extended to nursing. By and large, these tend to be younger men who feel comfortable working with women. One has only to observe a plane's cabin crew to appreciate the symbiosis. And we are now accustomed to a male voice answering our requests for telephone numbers. The country has more restaurants with stylish pretensions than ever before, and one validation of that status is to have male waiters. Of course, many of these men view what they are doing as temporary or transitional. They may be deferring career decisions or waiting for openings in their chosen fields. Indeed, much of our service economy is predicated on the inclination of young people to remain single, to manage on modest pay, and to live and share expenses with other persons of their age.

Does the arrival of women really spell economic decline for an occupation or a profession? The task is to find if gender is the operative factor or whether other forces are at work. Between 1970 and 1995, for example, women rose from being 4.9 percent of the country's lawyers to an impressive 26.4 percent. Yet what also happened was that the head count of lawyers more than tripled, rising from 288,000 to 894,000. So a growing glut of lawyers was the principal reason for the overall decline in pay for that profession. Moreover, of some 600,000 new lawyers, only about a third were women; so they should not be blamed for a falling wage scale.

Still, because so many of them are newcomers, relatively more women will be in an occupation's lower levels. In fact, earnings for younger people of both genders have become quite comparable. Among full-time workers under the age of twenty-five, women make $950 for every $1,000 paid to men. This approach to parity is even more revealing since she is still more likely to be starting out as a teacher while he is more apt to be a better paid engineer. And if they are both beginning engineers, today their pay will usually be identical. In fact, the *National Law Journal* found that among law school students graduating in 1994, for men the median starting salary was $48,000, while the typical woman graduate began at $50,000.

It is certainly true that more women take part-time jobs, frequently because they must be—or want to be—available for family obligations. Yet it is hard to find figures to support the presumption that women give less of themselves. We do have a few measures that fill in parts of the story. For example, it might be assumed that women will choose jobs which are closer to their homes so they can attend to domestic duties or because they are less disposed to look farther afield for a better job. As it happens, the Census can provide an answer, since it collates the "travel time to work" for all employed Americans. Its most recent published study showed that the one-way journey for men averaged 23.7 minutes, while the jobs that women chose called for a 20.3 minute trip. A difference of 3.4 minutes does not suggest that women are markedly less adventuresome.

One way to hold homelife factors constant is to confine the comparison to workers who have never been married. Of course, most of these workers are younger people. It is still assumed that some single women are marking time at their jobs and have no aspirations for lifetime careers. Yet we all know older women who never married, and almost all of them have made their jobs a major part of their lives. Indeed, as was noted at the start of this [article], the Census analysis of "never married" workers on full-time schedules found that women ended up earning $1,005 for every $1,000 made by men. So when it comes to dedication, the women are actually ahead. Moreover, current demographic data suggest that in the years ahead, more women will be foregoing marriage, which will expand the pool of women who will be able to compete with men on an equal footing.

Ascending an occupation's ladder generally requires years of experience, either within a single organization or in the field as a whole. No one will be surprised to learn that women as a group do not have as many years on their résumés. Lester Thurow stressed this point several years ago, when he said that ages twenty-five to thirty-five are the takeoff years for careers, when one gets seasoned on the job and noticed for promotion. "But the decade between twenty-five and thirty-five," he said, "is precisely the decade when women are most apt to leave the labor force or become part-time workers." Thurow is about half right. In the time period he says is crucial, 73 percent of the men are fully employed, compared with only 51 percent of the women. But there is another way to look at work experience. By focusing on age distributions within the workforce, we find that women who are twenty-five to thirty-five account for 29 percent of all fully employed women, which turns out to be exactly the proportion for men in the same age range. As Thurow says, some men may be slated for success in this "takeoff" decade. The question is why so many fewer women are put on the promotion lists.

EQUAL PAY FOR EQUAL WORK?

Of course, two people doing the same job should receive the same wage. But it isn't always easy to agree on whether identical work is being done. Nor is it easy to find statistics that assess the relative competence of men and women workers. But one way to start might be by limiting ourselves to all full-time workers who are in their early thirties, from thirty to thirty-four, a group that currently contains about 8 million men and 5 million women. The women in this cohort deserve to be taken seriously. Fully 20 percent have not yet been married, in most cases by their own decision, which suggests they have other aspirations. Another 17 percent are divorced or separated or widowed, which in most cases means they must now support themselves. And the remaining 63 percent who are married are combining full-time employment with domestic obligations. Also, at this age, about the same proportions of women and men have completed college, so the two genders look quite similar in their commitment to careers and their investments in education.

Of course, Table 5 cannot tell us if the men and women are performing "equal" tasks. What we do see is that the women's median earnings stand at $825 per $1,000 for the men, a relatively high ratio as current comparisons go, but still far from parity. This age group is important because it contains what should be the most promising echelon of women. Yet they are not even half as likely to have $50,000 jobs, and they are a third less apt to be in the $35,000 to $50,000 tier. In contrast, men are a third less likely to be found in the bottom bracket. The bottom line is that employers have shown much less inclination to promote accomplished women to $50,000 positions, while they seem to feel that as few men as possible should be made to take jobs paying less than $20,000. Another factor is that, thus far, women

TABLE 5

EARNINGS OF FULL-TIME WORKERS, AGE 30 TO 34

	7,905,000 Men	5,013,000 Women
Over $50,000	15.7%	6.7%
$35,000 to $50,000	20.1%	14.6%
$20,000 to $35,000	39.4%	41.4%
Under $20,000	24.8%	37.3%
Median earnings (ratio)	$28,449 ($1,000)	$23,479 ($825)

have been more likely than men to choose lower-paying professions. For example, in museums and galleries (average earnings: $18,928) or book publishing ($35,204), rather than, say, petroleum refining ($57,616) or as security and commodity brokers ($81,796).

A double standard for incomes persists not only on earth, but in the galaxies of stars. Over the years, the top moneymakers in the music industry have been all-male groups such as the Beatles, the Rolling Stones, the Eagles, Pink Floyd, and the Grateful Dead. Individual performers such as Michael Jackson, Garth Brooks, Billy Joel, and Elton John have made measurably more than the top female performers. Among authors, Stephen King, John Grisham, Tom Clancy, and Michael Crichton command larger advances than do such blockbusting novelists as Judith Krantz, Jackie Collins, and Patricia Cornwell. The men's books are then made into big-budget movies, while the women must settle for seeing theirs prepared as four-part specials for the small screen.

There is no shortage of theories to explain why this is the case. One certainly is that men have always put their stamp on art and entertainment, at the same time making sure that enough of what they produce will appeal to women. Many more women bought novels by Anthony Trollope and Charles Dickens compared with the number of men attracted to Jane Austen and the Brontës. True, women have contributed their movie dollars and television watching to Barbra Streisand and Roseanne and Oprah Winfrey. Yet while these performers have become extremely rich, they still comprise a relatively short list. Of course, plays and movies and television series all have women stars, and most men do like seeing female faces and figures. But not always for their acting abilities. Indeed, men tend to shy away from entertainment in which women have too dominant a role. Recall how every episode of Mary Tyler Moore's long-running program had her surrounded by men with strongly written scripts. And with Roseanne, one suspects that insofar as men were watching her show, it was mainly because the women in their lives insisted on having the program on.

TABLE 6

THE TOP TEN: HOLLYWOOD'S BEST-PAID STARS THEN AND NOW

Rank	1934	1994
1	Will Rogers	Harrison Ford
2	Clark Gable	Sylvester Stallone
3	Janet Gaynor	Bruce Willis
4	Wallace Beery	Tom Hanks
5	Mae West	Kevin Costner
6	Joan Crawford	Clint Eastwood
7	Bing Crosby	Arnold Schwarzenegger
8	Shirley Temple	Michael Douglas
9	Marie Dressler	Jim Carrey
10	Norma Shearer	Robin Williams

It was not always this way. [Table 6 shows] two sets of rankings: on the left, Hollywood's best-paid stars in 1934, and on the right, the biggest moneymakers sixty years later in 1994. Most apparent, of course, is that a majority of the 1934 group were women.

It is interesting to ponder why female movie stars were popular and highly paid in the 1930s. There may be lessons that are worth resurrecting from that distant era of Janet Gaynor and Norma Shearer.

NOTE

1. The information and interpretations contained in *Money* are based on hundreds of books, articles, and documents, the most important of which will be cited below. However, two sources—one public, one private—warrant special recognition. The first is the Housing and Household Economic Statistics Division of the U.S. Bureau of the Census. Each year, this office releases hundreds of pages, thousands of columns, and literally millions of figures on the incomes and earnings of Americans. These tables, which are based primarily on responses to the Bureau's annual Current Population Survey, leave it to the reader to choose and collate and then form conclusions from this Everest of data.

For a view of who has how much money at America's higher echelons, *Forbes* magazine is the preeminent source. Its reports are not only reliable, but are also notable for their sagacity and imagination. Its roster of the four hundred richest Americans, published each fall since 1982, has become a national institution. Nor is it simply a list: *Forbes* details how old and new fortunes were made, separating self-made millionaires from silver-spoon heirs. The magazine also provides annual guides to the best-paid athletes, entertainers, and attorneys. And each spring it records the latest pay for eight hundred corporate chairmen, along with their salaries and benefits over the previous five years. And here too, *Forbes* goes the extra mile, by including information like how long the CEOs have been with their companies and where they went to college.

PERIODICALS

Academe, March–April 1996.

American Lawyer, July–August 1996.

BusinessWeek, April 25, 1994; April 22, 1996.

Chronicle of Higher Education, October 4 and October 18, 1996.

Chronicle of Philanthropy, September 19, 1996.

Crain's New York Business, November 25–December 1, 1996.

Entertainment Weekly, April 12, 1996.

Financial World, July 6, 1993; July 5, 1994; July 4, 1995; October 21, 1996.

Forbes, June 9,1980; September 13, 1982; September 12,1983; May 27,1991; November 6 and December 18, 1995; May 20, September 26, and October 14, 1996.

Fortune, May 1974; May and July 1993; April 18 and May 30,1994; April 29,1996.

Journal of the American Medical Association, July 20, 1994.

Medical Economics, September 9, 1996.

National Law Journal, July 15, 1996.

Parade, June 23, 1996.

People, November 4, 1996.

USA Today, January 18 and December 12, 1995.

U.S. GOVERNMENT DOCUMENTS

Bureau of Labor Statistics, *Employment and Earnings,* January 1996.

Bureau of the Census, *Detailed Characteristics,* 1970; *Historical Statistics of the United States,* 1975; *Studies in the Distribution of Income,* 1992; *Ancestry of the Population in the United States,* 1993; *Social and Economic Characteristics,* 1993; *Income and Poverty,* 1993; *Household Wealth and Asset Ownership,* 1994; *Educational Attainment in the United States,* 1995; *Marital Status and Living Arrangements,* 1995; *Money Income in the United States,* 1995; *Poverty in the United States,* 1995.

Committee on Ways and Means, U.S. House of Representatives, *Green Book,* 1996.

Department of Health and Human Services, *Characteristics and Financial Circumstances of AFDC Recipients,* 1995.

Internal Revenue Service, *Individual Income Tax Returns,* 1979; *Statistics of Income Bulletin,* 1993–96.

National Center for Health Statistics, *Natality,* 1995.

Office of Personnel Management, *Occupations of Federal White-Collar and Blue-Collar Workers,* 1993.

Social Security Administration, *Annual Statistical Supplement,* 1995.

OTHER DOCUMENTS, REPORTS, AND BOOKS

Altman Weil Pensa, *Law Firm Salary Survey,* 1995.

American Medical Association, *Physician Marketplace Statistics,* 1995.

Association of American Medical Colleges, *Medical School Faculty Salaries,* 1994–95.

Executive Leadership Council, *1996 Membership Roster.*

McGraw-Hill Relative Value Studies, 1996.

Organization for Economic Cooperation and Development, *Income Distribution in OECD Countries,* 1995.

Roper Reports, 1995.

World Bank Atlas, 1996.

Graef Crystal, *In Search of Excess: The Overcompensation of American Executives,* 1991.

Robert H. Frank and Philip J. Cook, *The Winner-Take-All Society,* 1995.

John Kenneth Galbraith, *American Capitalism: The Concept of Countervailing Power,* 1952.

Robert Reich, *The Next American Frontier,* 1983.

Lester Thurow, *The Zero-Sum Society,* 1986.

COURT CASES AND STATUTES

American Federation of State, County, and Municipal Employees v. State of Washington, 578 F.Supp. 846.
California Federal Savings & Loan v. Guerra, 758 F.2d 390.
Educational Amendments of 1972, Public Law 92–381, title 9.
Equal Employment Opportunity Act of 1964, Public Law 88–354.
Equal Employment Opportunity Commission v. Sears, Roebuck & Co., 628 F.Supp. 1286.
Equal Pay Act of 1963, title 29, sec. 206(d).

Science

READING 38

The DNA Mystique

Dorothy Nelkin
M. Susan Lindee

Biological explanations have long been used to justify social inequalities by casting the differential treatment and status of particular groups as a natural consequence of essential, immutable traits. In the 1990s the language of genetic essentialism has given new legitimacy to such explanations. Group differences are appearing in popular culture as genetically driven, encouraging stereotyped images of the nurturing female, the violent African American male, and the promiscuous homosexual. But the images of pathology have moved from gross to hidden body systems. Once blacks were portrayed with large genitalia and women with small brains: today the differences lie in their genes.

The belief in essential differences has been reinforced by scientific studies of body parts such as genes or neurons that seem to explain behavior, as well as by scientific theories about evolution that seem to biologically ground social practices. Molecular genetics, behavioral genetics, neurobiology, and sociobiology have provided a language through which group differences can be interpreted as biologically determined. These sciences have encouraged the increasing acceptability of genetic explanations and their strategic role in the continuing debates over gender, race, and sexual orientation.

Current interest in the genetic basis of group differences coincides with extraordinary concern about gender roles, ethnic identity, and sexual orientation. Genetic explanations can be used to marginalize groups or—as in the case of some feminists, African Americans, and homosexuals—to celebrate group differences. Some who have traditionally suffered from prevailing biological theories are now embracing biological difference as a source of legitimacy and as evidence of their own superiority.

They shrewdly exploit the discursive power of biological boundaries to promote reformist agendas. Some feminists have celebrated biological difference as a source of special identity or a rationale for equal protection, citing the "creative power that is associated with female biology" and the "native talent and superiority of women."[1] Controversial Afrocentrist Leonard Jeffries, a professor at City College in New York, has claimed that melanin is "responsible for brain development, the neurosystem and the spinal column"; since African Americans have more of it, they are more creative.[2] Meanwhile gay activist

Dorothy Nelkin is a university professor at New York University.
M. Susan Lindee is an associate professor of history and sociology of science at the University of Pennsylvania.

Simon LeVay has promoted the idea that homosexuality is inborn and unchangeable, for such a claim seems to transform nonconformist sexual behavior from a "lifestyle choice" to a natural imperative.[3] These individuals, despite radically different perspectives and conflicting social policy agendas, seem to agree about one thing: In contests over social worth, biology matters. Whoever can successfully argue that biology—and more specifically DNA—supports their particular political viewpoint has a tactical advantage in the public debate.

GENES AND GENDER

The January 20, 1992, cover of *Time* featured a photograph of two small children, a girl and a boy. The girl looked admiringly and flirtatiously at the boy, who was flexing his muscles. The caption read: "Why are men and women different? It isn't just upbringing. New studies show they are born that way." The cover story, called "Sizing Up the Sexes," reported that recent scientific research showed that "gender differences have as much to do with the biology of the brain as with the way we are raised."[4] The article focused on an experiment in which the responses of young children playing with a variety of toys were videotaped. The researcher found that the boys systematically favored sports cars and fire trucks, while the girls were drawn to kitchen toys and dolls. Those girls who defied these expectations, researchers concluded, had higher levels of testosterone, suggesting the importance of hormone levels in shaping the behavior of children.

Time went on to report a general public conversion to the idea that differences between men and women are genetically determined. Even skeptics in the professions, the article said, had come to see that nature dictated social place and behavior. It quoted psychologist Jerre Levy to illustrate a typical intellectual shift: "When I was younger, I believed that 100% of sex differences were due to the environment." But now, observing her fifteen-month-old daughter, she believed that skill in flirting must be inborn. The *Time* writer editorialized: "During the feminist revolution of the 1970s, talk of inborn differences in the behavior of men and women was distinctly unfashionable, even taboo. Men dominated fields like architecture and engineering, it was argued, because of social, not hormonal, pressures. Women did the vast majority of society's child-rearing because few other options were available to them." Feminists, said the author, expect that the "end of sexism" will change all this: "But biology has a funny way of confounding expectations. . . . Perhaps nature is more important than nurture after all."[5]

The 1992 *Time* story differed in striking ways from a *Newsweek* cover story on the same subject a decade earlier. Its title ("Just How the Sexes Differ"[6]) was similar, and like the story in *Time,* it attempted to convey prevailing scientific wisdom about the relative role of nature and nurture in shaping differences in the behavior of men and women. It even drew on some of the same authorities and referred to some of the same scientific data. The 1981 article, however, stressed the overriding importance of different social experiences and expectations on behavior. The author cited several experts on the effect of culture on behavior, including anthropologist Sarah Blaffer Hrdy, who said gender differences were the product of culture, and Michael Lewis of the Institute for the Study of Exceptional Children, who said: "As early as you can show me a sex difference, I can show you culture at work." And it cited psychologist Eleanor Maccoby: "Sex typing and the different set of expectations that society thrusts on men and women have far more to do with any differences that exist . . . than do genes or blood chemistry."

The *Newsweek* journalist pointed to the broad variation among individuals of each sex: "Not all males in a given group are more aggressive or better at math than all females. . . . women and men both fall along the whole continuum of test results." This 1981 article concluded with a statement on the nature-nurture debate: "It is clear that sex differences are not set in stone. . . . By processes still not understood, biology seems susceptible to social stimuli." Ten years later, *Time* conveyed the opposite message: sex differences are innate and unchangeable, and it is just a matter of time until scientists will be able to prove it.

These two approaches to the same subject matter, over such a short period, suggest shifts in the social meaning of science. Neither popular article was about scientific data per se. Rather, both captured popular expectations. By 1992 the consensus that had dominated public policy since the 1950s—that "nurture" was more important than "nature"—was changing.

Neither biological nor environmental explanations of human behavior have an inherent social meaning. Both forms of explanation can be used to justify liberal or conservative causes; both can be applied oppressively, and each can be used to promote greater human freedom. In the last two decades biological determinism has been the focus of several well-publicized attacks by leading academic biologists and philosophers. But environmental determinism, too, can be used to limit human rights and constrict groups identified as inferior. In the 1950s and 1960s, for instance, popular interest in the power of the environment reinforced women's traditional roles as caregivers. It justified the 1950s "back to the home" movement for mothers who had been employed during the war years; if the achievements of children were finely calibrated to their training and environment, then mothers were needed at home and entirely responsible for their children's behavior.

So too, evolutionary stories serve different social agendas. Some feminists have presented evolutionary narratives in an attempt to demonstrate the superiority of women, while sociobiologists have interpreted evolutionary history as legitimating inequalities. Elaine Morgan's 1972 account of "sexual evolution" was a popular and colorful story in which *Homo sapiens* spent a few million years as a marine mammal, during which the species lost its body hair, developed a layer of adipose fat, and invented tools and weapons. Women were important players in the development of these new technologies, Morgan said, for they needed tools to fish in the surf (babies clinging to the long hair on their heads) and to pry open shellfish. Morgan used this imagined evolutionary past to legitimate the sexual revolution of the 1960s and its promise for the "liberation" of women.[7]

Three years later entomologist and sociobiologist E. O. Wilson reached different conclusions about the meaning of the species' evolutionary past for current social stratification.[8] Drawing on his extensive work with social insects, Wilson extrapolated from the ant to the human to suggest that women will naturally seek monogamous unions and that they are biologically best suited to childrearing. Women are responsible for child care and home life in most societies because, Wilson argued, "the genetic bias is intense enough to cause a substantial division of labor even in the most free and most egalitarian of future societies." . . .

In the 1980s and 1990s, it has become increasingly fashionable to presume the existence of innate and intrinsic differences between the sexes. Even books in the self-help genre (by definition less deterministic, concerned as they are with issues of personal control) use biological ideas to enhance the confidence of their women readers and to instill group pride. Elizabeth Davis, in *Women's Intuition* (1989), proclaimed that "intuition is a natural function, and that all of us [women] have inherent intuitive abilities. . . . Women are more sensitive to context, more receptive."[9] And in their 1990 popular advice book *Why Women Worry,* Jane and Robert Handly cited scientific findings about differences in brain size that they claim confirm women's natural role as protectors of children and men's role as hunters.[10]

Purported differences in the brain were also the focus of Ann Moir and David Jessel's 1991 *Brain Sex: The Real Differences Between Men and Women,* a popular book and television program. Citing research on nonhuman primates, its authors claimed that society should accept biological differences and build them into early childhood education.[11] An article in *Mirabella* magazine, describing this book, featured a photograph of a nude woman. The writer asked: "Are women genetically programmed to enjoy pleasure? A new book . . . argues, yes, . . . Women hear better, are more tactile, even see better in the dark."[12] The women's magazine *Elle,* describing the book in an article called "Mind Over Gender," concluded that: "It just isn't the case that child rearing practices are the only influence on how we grow up. . . . The primary determinant of what and who we will turn out to be is to be found in our bodies. In other words, the old nature-versus-nurture quibble has finally been settled—and nature now appears to be the winner."[13] . . .

Biological explanations may reassure threatened groups that they possess special skills and advantages, thereby demonstrating their inherent superiority or worth. When feminist texts promote caring or intuition as unique feminine skills, they are effectively depicting their readers as advantaged. When men's movement texts celebrate male aggression as a biological strength, they are elevating a presumed necessary evil to the status of a positive social good. Both groups are engaged in setting boundaries of identity and delineating criteria of social worth. Here as in other forums, genes have become a way to establish the legitimacy of social groupings. This function is even more overt in the public debate over the meaning of race.

GENES AND RACE

At the 1990 annual meeting of the American Psychological Association, psychologist J. Phillipe Rushton presented a paper arguing that blacks have smaller brains than whites and that this explained differences in their educational performance. Apparently oblivious to the "elephant problem" (if brain size is all, why are not elephants the most intelligent creatures on earth?), Rushton suggested that racial variation in brain size was a consequence of evolutionary pressures.[14] So, too, according to his gene-based theory of racial patterns, genital size and fertility rates vary, as an evolutionary adaptation. As humans entered the colder climates of Europe, the environment favored those who had genes for "increased social organizational skill and sexual and personal restraint, with a trade-off occurring between brain size and reproductive potency."[15]

Rushton's thesis is one variant of the longstanding hypothesis that differences in social, political, and economic status between racial groups are a consequence of biological differences—in brain size, intelligence genes, or other bodily characteristics. The body's supposed differences can be used to explain the social status of oppressed groups in ways that make inequalities appear natural and appropriate. Much of this debate has focused on intelligence and, increasingly in the 1990s, on intelligence genes. But the modern debate on race, genetics, and IQ began in 1969, when Harvard psychologist Arthur Jensen published a famous essay, "How Much Can We Boost IQ and Scholastic Achievement?"[16]

Jensen argued that there was a significant average difference in IQ between blacks and whites of fifteen points on the conventional IQ test. He acknowledged that environment played some role in creating this difference, particularly since the scores of poor, white, urban children were similar to those of poor, black, urban children. But he decided that between one half to one fourth of the mean difference (7.5 points to 3.8 points) in IQ scores between blacks and whites could be attributed to genes. Jensen even used the fact that prosperous blacks tend to have lighter skin than poor blacks as evidence of their genetic superiority (rather than, for example, their greater social acceptability in mainstream white culture). He concluded, as he put it in an interview with *Newsweek,* that the school system needed to learn to accommodate "large numbers of children who have limited aptitudes for traditional academic achievement." . . . [17]

Genetic language about race appears in a more positive, but no less stereotyped, form in the context of sports. Racial differences in aptitude for sports was a prominent theme throughout the history of the eugenics movement and an integral part of Nazi sports medicine. The theme persists today, though sportscasters have been cautious since CBS commentator Jimmy the Greek was reprimanded for saying on the air that blacks were better athletes than whites because they were bred that way. Their bigger thighs, he said, developed in slave trading days "when the slave owner would breed his big black to his big woman so that he would have a big black kid."[18] References to genetic characteristics appear in a less direct form when television commentators describe African American athletes as having "natural grace," "gifted bodies," or "genetic talent."[19] To black baseball player Reggie Jackson, such flattering images, all referring to traits that are not learned, are also comments about the intellectual abilities of African Americans. The subtle message, he says, is that "we have genetic talent but we're just not intelligent."[20] But the message from Al Campanis, former general manager of the LA Dodgers, was far from subtle. Explaining the lack of minorities in upper management in sports, he said: "Blacks lack the necessities to take part in the organizational aspects to run a sports team."[21]

In the 1990s, race theorists are more and more willing to publicly express their views about genetic differences between ethnic groups and to suggest the significance of such differences for social policy. Physical anthropologist Vincent Sarich at the University of California at Berkeley lectured to hundreds of undergraduates on the genetic basis of racial differences.[22] Michael Levin of City College in New York has not only argued that blacks are less intelligent than whites but also used his theories to oppose affirmative action. He has asserted that differences in average test scores (which unquestionably exist) are self-evident proof of genetic difference as though the SAT provided direct access to DNA.[23] By 1994, the extravagant publicity launching Herrnstein and Murray's *The Bell Curve*—an immediate best seller—moved the debate over genetic differences to center stage.

For African Americans, such public statements can be both discouraging and damaging. As one minority student put it in a *New York Times* interview, African Americans are undermined by assumptions that they are not smart enough to make it, that "we don't have that thought gene."[24] To protest such constructions, some African Americans have proposed a counternarrative drawn from a long history of Pan-African ideology, in which black skin is a sign of superiority. In public lectures, Leonard Jeffries, the professor at City College in New York quoted at the beginning of this [article], presents a view of world history and race biology that celebrates biological differences. "Black Africans of the Nile Valley," he claims, are the source of all science, mathematics and religion. And melanin, the pigment that makes skin dark, is a crucial biological need. "You have to have melanin to be human. Whites are deficient in it. . . . It appears that the creative instinct is affected."[25] Distinguishing sun people (blacks) from ice people (whites), he is interested in promoting collective identity on the basis of a biological construction of "race."[26] . . .

Afrocentrists are effectively attempting to transform their differences into positive biological strengths. But they share an assumption with racist critics: that race is a biological reality with some meaning for this debate. For gay rights activists, the problems are different; they face the daunting task of redefining a "sin" or a "lifestyle choice" as a biological imperative. In the debates over the "homosexual brain" or the "gay gene," nature and nurture have even more complicated meanings.

THE HOMOSEXUAL BRAIN

In August 1991, Simon LeVay, a neuroscientist at the Salk Institute, published a paper in *Science* that linked homosexual behavior to brain structure. LeVay said that homosexual males, like all women, had a smaller hypothalamus than heterosexual males. The hypothalamus is a part of the brain between the brain stem and the cerebral hemispheres, believed to play some role in emotions. It is too small to be effectively examined through contemporary brain imaging techniques such as Positron Emission Tomography (PET scans). LeVay needed, therefore, to study the brains of cadavers. His conclusions were based primarily on the post-mortem examination of the brains of 41 persons, 19 of them homosexual males who had died of AIDS. He has acknowledged that his findings were open to several interpretations. The size differences in the hypothalamus could indicate a genetic basis of sexual orientation, but they could also be a consequence of behavior, or they could be coincidental, reflecting neither cause nor effect but the presence of some other condition (such as AIDS).

LeVay preferred the genetic explanation, describing his "belief," his "faith" in the biological basis of behavior. Indeed, LeVay's research followed from his personal conviction that "I was born gay." He has stated that virtually all human variation, including detailed personality differences and such cultural preferences as musical taste (Mahler over Bruckner, for example), are biological. LeVay is convinced that children are entirely genetic products. Some children are, from the moment of conception, fated to become gay; if parents have any influence at all, LeVay argues, it is only in the way they respond to the inevitable.

LeVay's claims were later supported by the findings of a team of geneticists led by Dean Hamer at the National Cancer Institute. In 1993 they claimed to locate genes on the X chromosome that predisposed some men toward homosexuality—the X chromosome is inherited in boys, of course, only from the mother.[27] This report and Hamer's popular book on the subject received extensive media coverage and attracted significant public interest.

The response to these claims reflected the long public debate over the social meaning of homosexuality. Homosexuals have at various times been labeled as criminals, sinners, physiologically degenerate or psychologically disturbed; in some societies they have been assigned ritual significance. In a sociology of homosexuality, David Greenberg has traced the notion, recurrent from the Renaissance to the late-eighteenth and early-nineteenth-century phrenology movement, that homosexuality is a biological and innate condition.[28] This remained a minority view, however, overwhelmed by moralizing ideas about sexuality and free will. For most of the Christian era, homosexual desire and behavior have been culturally defined as sins, moral failings, and individual choices that could be changed through prayer, repentance, and will power. Since the late nineteenth century, many physicians have also identified homoerotic attraction as a medical condition to be cured through psychoanalysis, aversive conditioning such as electric shock, and drug therapy. Yet despite its medicalization, homosexuality was (and remains) in many places a crime against the state, defined by anti-sodomy statutes.

In the 1960s and 1970s, gay rights activists began to challenge prevailing ideas about the legal, moral, and psychological meaning of homosexuality. They met with some success, convincing the American Psychiatric Association in 1973 to remove homosexuality from its listing of recognized mental illnesses, the *Diagnostic and Statistical Manual.*[29] Gay activists were convinced that medicalization promoted homophobia by constructing homosexuals as diseased. Hoping that demedicalization would precipitate social change, they fought to define homosexuality as an innate and therefore normal variation. The changing social beliefs exemplified in demedicalization did have some impact. Some states ceased enforcing anti-sodomy laws. And some religious congregations began to accept homosexuals as active parishioners, even as ministers. At the same time, however, the AIDS epidemic contributed to increased public fear of homosexuality as an emblem of death. The homosexual community was itself transformed by AIDS, and homosexual males faced new forms of discrimination as the "gay plague" invested their activities with new moral and medical meanings.[30]

In this context, the research constructing homosexuality as biological had a tactical advantage; it shifted responsibility from the person to the genes. Individual homosexuals had no choice but to behave as they did. It would therefore be unjust for society to discriminate against them, for the Constitution, demanding equal protection, prohibits discrimination on the basis of immutable characteristics.

LeVay thus sought publicity for his research, and his conclusions became a media event, discussed in popular magazines, major newspapers, and on television talk shows. The hypothalamus, a little-known organ deep within the brain, became a popular symbol of virility. A Calvin Klein advertising campaign referred to a "hypothalamus-numbing host of imitators." A *Newsweek* article called "Born or Bred?" explored the implications of the "new research that suggests that homosexuality may be a matter of genetics not parenting." The magazine's cover photo featured the face of an infant, with the headline "Is This Child Gay?"[31] "Is lesbianism a matter of genetics?" asked the headline of another 1993 article. "Little girls are made of sugar and spice and everything nice, and some of them may have a dollop of genetic frosting that increases the likelihood they'll grow up gay."[32] Vice President Dan Quayle publicly disagreed, however, insisting that homosexuality "is more of a choice than a natural situation. . . . It is a wrong choice. . . ."[33]

The media also speculated on the potential effect of genetic research on homophobia. On a segment of the prime-time news show "20/20," Barbara Walters asked: "I wonder if it were proven that homosexuality was biological if there would be less prejudice?"[34] *Newsweek* presented the views of homosexuals who welcomed the research, anticipating that it could reduce animosity. "It would reduce being gay to something like being left-handed, which in fact is all that it is," said Randy Shilts.

But the gay community has been divided about the consequences of genetic identification. Some anticipate abortion of "gay fetuses," increased discrimination empowered by genetic information, or the use of biotechnology to control homosexuality, for example with excision of the "gay gene" from embryos before implantation.[35] Janet Halley, a law professor, has predicted that essentialist arguments of biological causation will work against constitutional rights and encourage "the development of anti-gay eugenics."[36] The *National Inquirer* responded to research on the "gay gene" with the headline: "Simple injection will let gay men turn straight, doctors report."[37] And a spokesman for the National Gay and Lesbian Task Force suggested that genetic thinking would give rise to the idea that "by tweaking or zapping our chromosomes and rearranging our cells, presto, we'd no longer be gay."[38]

There is some historical justification for these concerns, since Nazi extermination of homosexuals was grounded in their presumed biological status. And other campaigns by gay activists have had unexpected consequences: The 1973 American Psychiatric Association decision to change the DSM classification failed to produce the social legitimation anticipated by those who had advocated the change. LeVay himself dismisses such historical precedents: "Those who look to history are condemned to repeat it."[39] . . .

BIOLOGICAL DIFFERENCE AND SOCIAL MEANING

. . . Biological differences in themselves have no intrinsic social meaning. Skin color is genetic—it is a real biological property—but it became a sign of political and economic difference for specific historical reasons, including the European colonization and exploitation of Africa. Due to the vagaries of evolution and population genetics, African populations happened to have skin that was uniformly darker than that of European populations. If both Africans and Europeans had instead manifested equivalent variation in skin color (displaying skin tones within each group ranging from very light to very dark), skin color would not have been a reliable sign of Continental origin and therefore could not have served as a visible mark of social or economic status. (Perhaps some other biological trait, such as eye color, would have come to stand for racial difference.) Certainly racial classifications vary across culture. For example, Brazilian ideas about race, the anthropologist Marvin Harris has observed, would be "inconceivable in the cognitive frame of descent rule" that guides American ideas. Full siblings in Brazil can be assigned to different racial categories if they differ in physical appearance.[40]

Sex, too, has a complicated history as a social category. Thomas Laqueur's work has demonstrated that for much of human history, from classical antiquity to the end of the seventeenth century, men and women functioned in two different social roles but were seen as variations on essentially one biological sex. The boundaries between male and female were understood to be "of degree and not of kind." To Galen, for example, the sex organs of both men and women were basically "the same," the uterus seen as a form of the penis, the ovaries a form of the testicles.[41] The biological story of difference was rewritten in the midst of the scientific revolution, Laqueur has argued, and two distinct biological sexes became a political necessity by the late eighteenth century on account of economic and social changes.[42] From another perspective, the biologist Anne Fausto-Sterling has noted that people do, biologically, come in more than two sexual forms—some experts estimate that hermaphrodites (individuals who have some combination of both male and female genitalia) account for one in every twenty-five births, or 4 percent of the human population. These intersex individuals are socially invisible because of medical management: Such infants are promptly designated male or female and their genitals surgically transformed.[43]

The existence of the homosexual body, too, depends on culture. In Greece in the fourth and fifth centuries B.C. there was no culturally recognized distinction between heterosexuality and homosexuality. Greek thinkers found nothing surprising in the coexistence of desire for both male and female sexual partners. They were, however, concerned about the control of desire and the uses of pleasure, and Greek texts devote significant attention to questions of control and power, though virtually none to sexual orientation.[44]

The biological groupings that appear in the contemporary debate, then, are specific historical products, not necessary biological categories. The meaning of these groups as genetically constructed is likewise flexible. Biological differences can become a source of stigmatization or of group pride. They can justify remedial socialization (extra math study for girls) or regressive social policy (expecting all mothers to stay home with their children). They can also be a source of political power (legal recognition of homosexual marriage with all attendant benefits, for example). When defined as an unchangeable and fundamental biological attribute, race, sex, or sexual preference can become a source of social support and authenticity that may be particularly valued by groups that have been the focus of past discrimination.

Biological narratives do not inherently oppress. But we argue that they are dangerous precisely because of the cultural importance attached to DNA. These narratives, attributing social differences to genetic differences, are especially problematic in a society that tends to overstate the powers of the gene. Charged with cultural meaning as the essence of the person, the gene appears to be a powerful, deterministic, and fundamental entity. And genetic explanations—of gender, race, or sexual orientation—construct difference as central to identity, definitive of the self. Such explanations thereby amplify the differences that divide society.

It is especially ironic that DNA has become a cultural resource for the construction of differences, for one of the insights of contemporary genomics research is the profound similarity, at the level of the DNA, among human beings and, indeed, between humans and other species. We differ from the chimpanzee by only one base pair out of a hundred—1 percent—and from each other by less than 0.1 percent. The cultural lesson of the Human Genome Project could be that we are all very much alike, but instead contemporary molecular genetics has been folded into enduring debates about group inferiority. Scientists have participated in these debates by seeking genes for homosexuality and alcoholism, genes for caring and genes for criminality. This research and the ideological narratives that undergird it have significant social meaning and policy implications.

. . . What is the appeal of genetic essentialism in contemporary American society? In part, the power of this concept reflects the close relationship between prevailing theories of nature and cultural conceptions of social order. Perceptions of the natural order have often reproduced, and later justified, social arrangements. Conceptions of nature, as David Bloor put it, serve as "a code for talking about society, a language in which justifications and challenges can be expressed."[45] The claims of contemporary molecular genetics have recast long-standing beliefs about the importance of heredity in defining kinship relationships, individual behavior, and group characteristics. The "germplasm" or "blood" of the early twentieth century has become DNA—and as a highly precise molecular text, the hereditary material has gained new status without losing older connotations.

The gene is a malleable concept, and its plasticity also plays an important role in its widespread and frequent appropriation. Feminists invoke genetics in debates about motherhood and reproduction; conservatives in their efforts to promote the importance of family values; the disabled in their battles against stigmatization; antiabortionists in their arguments about when life begins; parents in their legal claims for custody of children; African Americans in expressing fears of genocide; homosexuals in their claims for civil rights.

Just as the idea of genetic essentialism can serve many different social agendas, so it intersects with important American values. Genetic explanations of behavior and disease appear to locate social problems within the individual rather than in society, conforming to the ideology of individualism. They also provide the equivalent of moral redemption or absolution, exonerating individuals by attributing acts that violate the social contract to the DNA, an independent force beyond the influence of volition. And genetic explanations appear to provide a rational, neutral justification of existing social categories. Conforming to the value placed on both personal responsibility and individual exoneration, consistent with the faith in scientific and technological progress, genetic explanations have considerable rhetorical force.

They are thus a convenient way to address troubling social issues: the threats implied by the changing roles of women, the perceived decline of the family, the problems of crime, the changes in the ethnic and racial structure of American society, and the failure of social welfare programs. The status of the gene—as a deterministic agent, a blueprint, a basis for social relations, and a source of good and evil—promises a reassuring certainty, order, predictability, and control.

The new molecular genetics is also appealing for its promise of medical "breakthroughs" and wonder therapies—of biological rather than behavioral or environmental controls of disease. Genetics, claimed a journalist in a 1992 article, is "the medical story of the century, [which] will dramatically cure cancer, heart disease, aging, and much more."[46] But consider also the implications for individual, professional, and social control. In popular narratives, controlling the body depends on understanding and manipulating DNA. Health depends on biological intervention rather than diet, exercise, emotional resiliency, or other environmental or behavioral attributes. The future of medicine seems to lie in more aggressive biological manipulation, rather than in social intervention to change behaviors that promote disease. Increased authority and power are therefore vested in scientists and physicians, who become the managers of the medicalized society.[47]

At the same time, the individual—formerly responsible as the source of social problems—is helpless before the powers of DNA. In the 1990s, the popular rhetoric of DNA is as much about loss of control and acceptance of biological fate as it is about cure and the control of our future. Traits that are "genetic" appear as immutable, deeply resistant to change initiated through individual action or external intervention. This clearly bears on both personal choices and social policies. A new kind of advice book (known informally as the "don't help yourself" book) has emerged in the 1990s, presenting the individual as profoundly limited by genetic destiny. Unlike the traditional self-help book, which encourages the reader to overcome personal weaknesses in pursuit of a higher goal, these texts advise the reader to accept personal limitations, for his or her own good. As a guide to personal behavior, moreover, the idea of genetic destiny also suggests that we can "eat, drink and be merry," forgetting self-denying quests for fitness and health, since "certain things are genetic and inalterable."[48]

On a larger scale, as a guide to social policy the idea of the passive and helpless individual seems to suggest the limits of human agency and intervention. The ideology of genetic essentialism encourages submission to nature and to constraints on the possibilities for social change.

This rhetoric—this conceit of a DNA destiny—is neither a necessary nor coherent way of understanding what it means for human culture that we are biological organisms. In a trivial sense every human trait is biological; whatever our other qualities, we are indisputably bodies. At the same time every human trait is environmental, for if we are not (as embryo, infant, child, adult) nurtured in a proper environment (with sufficient air, reasonable temperature, and adequate food) we do not become anything at all. The fact that we are particular biological organisms dictates a great deal about our culture and social behavior, although not necessarily in the ways generally expected. Our biological status has a profound impact on our most fundamental conceptions of morality and civic order: If we were predatory insects who consumed our young, would not our literature, law, and religion be very different?

It is also important to recognize that many traits that are clearly genetic are also malleable, influenced by culture and environment. Height is both genetically determined and dependent on nutrition. Similarly, such common conditions as myopia and allergic rhinitis are genetic, but can be corrected with eyeglasses and behavior modification (avoidance of allergens). We routinely manipulate genetic traits, changing them for fashion (hair color), health (crooked teeth), or social success (facial features).

Our purpose in this book has not been to argue that biology is irrelevant to culture—such a claim would draw a dichotomy as problematic as that of genetic essentialism. Rather, we are suggesting that genetic essentialism, for all its grandiose claims, is a narrow way of understanding the cultural meaning of the body. By elevating DNA and granting it extraordinary powers of agency and control, genetic essentialism erases complexity and ambiguity. Problems and opportunities both disappear behind the double helix that has loomed out of proportion in the social imagination.

The forces that encourage this ideology, promoting and legitimating its use, will also shape the future implications of genomics research. In a 1993 editorial, *Nature* urged scientific temperance in the promotion of this research, cautioning that the "triumphalism" surrounding genetic discoveries was leading to a "growing belief in a kind of genetic predestination." For the editors of

Nature, the problem raised by this belief was one of public confidence: a too-zealous promotion of genomics, they warned, might lead to "disbelief, distrust, and resentment."[49] They called geneticists to task for raising public expectations too high.

We suggest a rather different construction of the problem. The findings of scientific genetics—about human behavior, disease, personality, and intelligence—have become a popular resource precisely because they conform to and complement existing cultural beliefs about identity, family, gender, and race. The promises made by scientists reflect these beliefs. Such promises express the desire for prediction, the need for social boundaries, and the hope for control of the human future. At the same time, scientists' claims about the powers of the gene meet many social needs and expectations. Whether or not such claims are sustained in fact may be irrelevant; their public appeal and popular appropriation reflect their social, not their scientific, power.

The danger, then, is not that inflated promises threaten to backfire on the scientific community, but that such promises will long outlive their scientific utility. Designed to appeal to popular interests, they quickly acquire a life of their own. With its emphasis on the natural origins of human difference, genetic essentialism can threaten marginal groups; with its focus on individual pathology, it seems to absolve society of responsibility for social problems; and with its emphasis on reproductive controls, it opens the door to oppressive state or social practices. Today the futuristic fantasies of biological management encoded in genetic essentialism take on a sinister cast, since the new biomedical technologies of the fertility clinic or the doctor's office can so readily make them come true.

While many scientists are aware of these possibilities, they see the value of genomics research in its promise for a better future—a future free of devastating disability and disease. Geneticist James Crow, in a 1988 essay, described his hopes for a "compassionate eugenics," wisely administered, protective of individual rights.[50] James Watson, in a 1993 interview, foresaw the "humane" use of genetic information, which he expected would expand individual choice and enhance personal control.[51]

Yet our study of popular culture suggests another construction of the future impact of genomics research. We find that, for the individual, greater access to genetic information may have the effect of *limiting* options as these data intersect with institutional prerogatives, economic constraints, and, especially, public attitudes toward those who make dysgenic (and therefore costly) reproductive choices.

The narratives of mass culture give shape to what is seen in the world. They define what seems to be a problem, and what promises solutions; what we take for granted, and what we question. In the 1990s, these narratives present the gene as robust and the environment as irrelevant; they devalue emotional bonds and elevate genetic ties; they promote biological solutions and debunk social interventions. Such notions are already affecting the institutional and social uses of genetic information as popular images encourage consumers to accept policies and decisions grounded in assumptions about genetic essentialism.

As the science of genetics has moved from the laboratory to mass culture, from professional journals to the television screen, the gene has been transformed. Instead of a piece of hereditary information, it has become the key to human relationships and the basis of family cohesion. Instead of a string of purines and pyramidines, it has become the essence of identity and the source of social difference. Instead of an important molecule, it has become the secular equivalent of the human soul. Narratives of genetic essentialism are omnipresent in popular culture, here explaining evil and predicting destiny, there justifying institutional decisions. They reverberate in public debates about sexuality and race, in court decisions about child custody and criminal responsibility, and in ruminations about the meaning of life. The powers of the gene in popular culture—expansive, malleable, sometimes fantastic—derive not from evolutionary forces or biological mandates, but rather from social or political expectations. Infused with cultural meanings, the gene has become a resource that is too readily appropriated, too seldom criticized, and too frequently misused in the service of narrow or socially destructive ends.

NOTES

1. Alison Jagger, *Feminist Politics and Human Nature* (Sussex: Harvester Press, 1983). See also Deborah L. Rhodes, "The No-Problem Problem: Feminist Challenges and Cultural Change," *Yale Law Journal* 100:1 (1991), 1–62.
2. Jeffries, who has published little scholarly work, is well known because of his work with the New York City Board of Education on curricular reform and his public speeches in the late 1980s and early 1990s. See Eric Pooley, "Doctor J: The Rise of Afrocentric Conspiracy Theories. Leonard Jeffries and His Odd Ideas about Blacks and Whites," *New York Magazine,* 2 September 1991.
3. Simon LeVay, *The Sexual Brain* (Cambridge: MIT Press, 1993).
4. Christine Gorman, "Sizing Up the Sexes," *Time,* 20 January 1992, 42.
5. Ibid.
6. Daniel Gelman, "Just How the Sexes Differ," *Newsweek,* 18 May 1981, 2–28.
7. Elaine Morgan, *The Descent of Woman* (New York: Stein and Day, 1972).
8. E. O. Wilson, *Sociobiology* (New York: Cambridge University Press, 1975), and E. O. Wilson, "Human Decency Is Animal," *New York Times Magazine,* 12 October 1975.
9. Elizabeth Davies, *Women's Intuition* (Berkeley: Celestial Arts, 1989), 15.
10. Jane and Robert Handly, *Why Women Worry* (New York: Fawcett Crest, 1990). Popular books on the brain have often focused on sex differences. Psychiatrist Richard Restak, who wrote the script for the 1992 television program "The Brain," wrote in 1979 that sex differences are "innate, biologically determined, and relatively resistant to change." The two sexes, he said, have distinct thought processes and use their brains in different ways. *The Brain: The Last Frontier* (New York: Doubleday, 1979).
11. Anne Moir and David Jessel, *Brain Sex: The Real Difference Between Men and Women* (New York: Carol Publishing Group, 1991).
12. Advertisement, *Mirabella,* April 1991.
13. Meme Black and Jed Springarn, "Mind Over Gender," *Elle,* March 1992, 158–162.
14. J. Phillipe Rushton expanded his ideas in *Race, Evolution and Behavior* (Newark: Transaction Books, 1994). Also see Stephen Jay Gould, *The Mismeasure of Man* (New York: W. W. Norton, 1981). Gould explores earlier efforts to measure brain size, either by weighing brains after death or by filling skulls with lead shot. He shows that attempts to find measures by which brain size was the crucial variable have always failed.
15. P. S., "Is Vincent Sarich Part of a National Trend?" *Science* 251 (25 January 1991), 369.
16. Arthur Jensen, "How Much Can We Boost IQ and Scholastic Achievement?" *Harvard Educational Review,* Winter 1969, 1–23. (The *Harvard Educational Review,* a student-edited publication, reaches about 12,000 readers.) See also Jensen, *Bias in Mental Testing* (New York: Free Press, 1979).
17. Jensen, cited in *Newsweek,* May 10, 1971.
18. Gay Floodedited and Sarah Ballard, "An Oddsmaker's Odd Views," *Sports Illustrated,* 25 January 1988, 7.
19. Tim Kurkjian, "West Al," *Sports Illustrated,* 16 April 1990, 66.
20. Reggie Jackson, "We Have a Serious Problem That Isn't Going Away," *Sports Illustrated,* 11 May 1987, 40.
21. "Nightline," 15 April 1987.
22. Paul Selvin, "The Raging Bull at Berkeley," *Science* 251 (25 January 1991), 368–371.
23. David Layzer, "Affirmative Action Is at Least on the Right Track," *New York Times,* 23 June 1990.
24. Susan Chira, "Minority Student Bias in Higher Education Quest," *New York Times,* 4 August 1992.
25. Pooley, "Dr. J," 34.
26. James Traub, "Professor Whiff," *Village Voice,* 1 October 1991.
27. D. Hamer et al., "Androgen Involvement in Homosexuality," *American Journal of Human Genetics* 53 (1993), 844–852. Also see Robert

Pool, "Evidence for a Homosexuality Gene," *Science* 261 (16 July 1993), 221–291.
28. David F. Greenberg, *The Construction of Homosexuality* (Chicago: University of Chicago Press, 1988), 1–3, 14, 18.
29. Ron Bayer, *Homosexuality in American Psychiatry* (New York: Basic Books, 1981).
30. Randy Shilts, *And the Band Played On* (New York: St. Martin's Press, 1987).
31. David Gelman, "Born or Bred," *Newsweek,* 24 February 1992, 48–53.
32. This was based on a report of a study published in the *Archives of General Psychiatry* that focused on 108 lesbians with identical and nonidentical twin sisters, plus 32 lesbians with adoptive sisters. The study results suggested that sexual preference depended on biology. Identical twins were much more likely to both be lesbians than were fraternal twins or sisters with no genetic relationship. "Most lesbians feel they were born gay," the report said. *Newsweek,* 22 March 1993, 53.
33. Quoted in Karen De Witt, "Quayle Contends Homosexuality Is a Matter of Choice, not Biology," *New York Times,* 14 September 1992.
34. "20/20," 24 April 1992.
35. See letters to the editor, *New York Times,* 27 July 1993.
36. Janet E. Hally, "Biological Causation of Homosexuality and Constitutional Rights," public lecture, New York University Law School, 11 October 1993.
37. *National Enquirer,* 10 August 1993.
38. Ron Wilson, "Study Raises Issue of Biological Basis for Homosexuality," *Wall Street Journal,* 30 August 1991.
39. Speech at a symposium on "The Homosexual Brain," City College, New York, 9 December 1991.
40. Marvin Harris, "Referential Ambiguity in the Calculus of Brazilian Racial Identity," in Norman Whitten Jr. and John Szwed, eds., *Africo-American Anthropology* (New York: Free Press, 1970), 75–86.
41. Thomas Laqueur, *Making Sex: Body and Gender from the Greeks to Freud* (Cambridge: Harvard University Press, 1990), 25–27.
42. Ibid., 201–227.
43. Anne Fausto-Sterling, "The Five Sexes: Why Male and Female Are Not Enough," *The Sciences,* March/April 1993, 20–25.
44. We are indebted to Sheila Murnaghan, who in her talk "Was Sex Different in the Ancient World?" (University of Pennsylvania, 17 February 1994) brought to our attention the extensive recent literature on sex and sexuality in ancient Greece. See also David M. Halperin, John J. Winkler, and Froma Zeitlin, eds., *Before Sexuality* (Princeton: Princeton University Press, 1990).
45. David Bloor, "Twenty Industrial Scientists," in Mary Douglas, ed., *Essays in the Sociology of Perception* (London: Routledge and Kegan Paul, 1982), 83.
46. Albert Rosenfeld, "The Medical Story of the Century," *Longevity,* May 1992, 42–53.
47. For discussion of this construct, see Jonathan Simon, "The Emergence of a Risk Society: Insurance Law and the State," *Socialist Review* 95 (September/October 1987), 63–89.
48. Dr. Martin E. P. Seligman, quoted in Molly O'Neil, "Eat, Drink and Be Merry May Be the Next Trend," *New York Times,* 2 January 1993. Some examples of recent advice books with this theme are Seligman's *What You Can Change and What You Can't Change* (New York: Knopf, 1993); and Jeffrey Harris, *Deadly Choices* (New York: Basic Books, 1993).
49. "Has Nature Overwhelmed Nurture?" *Nature* 366 (11 November 1993).
50. James Crow, "Eugenics: Must It Be a Dirty Word?" *Contemporary Psychology* 33 (January 1988), 9–12.
51. James Watson, interviewed in *Issues in Science and Technology,* Fall 1993, 44–45.

READING 39

The Health of Black Folk: Disease, Class, and Ideology in Science

Nancy Krieger and Mary Bassett

Since the first crude tabulations of vital statistics in colonial America, one stark fact has stood out:

No biographical information available.

black Americans are sicker and die younger than whites. As the epidemic infectious diseases of the nineteenth century were vanquished, the black burden of ill health shifted to the modern killers: heart disease, stroke, and cancer. Today black men under age 45 are ten times more likely to die from the effects of high blood pressure than white men. Black women suffer twice as many heart attacks as white women. A variety of common cancers are more frequent among blacks—and of cancer victims, blacks succumb sooner after diagnosis than whites. Black infant mortality is twice that of whites. All told, if the mortality rates for blacks and other minorities today were the same in the United States as for whites, more than 60,000 deaths in minority communities could be avoided each year.

What is it about being black that causes such miserable odds? One answer is the patently racist view that blacks are inherently more susceptible to disease—the genetic model. In contrast, environmental models depict blacks as victims of factors ranging from poor nutrition and germs to lack of education and crowded housing. Initially formulated as an alternative to the genetic model by liberals and much of the left, the environmental view has now gained new support from the right. . . . Instead of blaming the victims' genes, these conservatives blame black lifestyle choices as the source of the racial gap in health.

We will argue that these analytic models are seriously flawed, in essence as well as application. They are not the product of a racist use of allegedly "neutral" science, but reflect the ways in which ideology and politics penetrate scientific theory and research. Typically, they deny or obscure that the primary source of black/white health disparities is the social production of disease under conditions of capitalism and racial oppression. The "facts of being black" are not, as these models suggest, a genetically determined shade of skin color, or individual deprived living conditions, or ill-informed lifestyle choices. The facts of being black derive from the joint social relations of race and class: racism disproportionately concentrates blacks into the lower strata of the working class and further causes blacks in all class strata to be racially oppressed. It is the left's challenge to incorporate this political reality into how we approach racial differences in health.

THE GENETIC MODEL

Despite overwhelming evidence to the contrary, the theory that "race" is primarily a biological category and that black-white differences in health are genetically determined continues to exert profound influence on both medical thinking and popular ideology. For example, an editorial on racial differences in birth weight (an important determinant of infant mortality) in the January 1986 *Journal of the American Medical Association* concluded: "Finally, what are the biologic or genetic differences among racial or ethnic groups? Should we shrink from the possibility of a biologic/genetic influence?" Similarly, a 1983 handbook prepared by the International Epidemiologic Association defined "race" as "persons who are relatively homogeneous with respect to biological inheritance." Public health texts continue to enshrine "race" in the demographic triad of "age, race, and sex," implying that "race" is as biologically fundamental a predictor of health as aging or sex, while the medical literature remains replete with studies that examine racial differences in health without regard to class.

The genetic model rests on three basic assumptions, all of which are flawed: that "race" is a valid biological category; that the genes which determine "race" are linked to the genes which affect health; and that the health of any community is mainly the consequence of the genetic constitution of the individuals of which it is composed. In contrast, we will argue that the health of the black community is not simply the sum of the health of individuals who are "genetically black" but instead chiefly reflects the social forces which create racially oppressed communities in the first place.

It is of course true that skin color, hair texture, and other visible features used to identify "race" are genetically encoded—there *is* a biologic aspect to "race." The importance of these particular physical traits in the spectrum of human variation, however, has been determined historically and politically. People also differ in terms of stature and eye color, but these attributes are rarely accorded significance. Categories based primarily on skin color correlate with health because race is a powerful determinant of the location and life-destinies of individuals within the class structure of U.S. society. Ever since plantation owners realized that differences in skin color could serve as a readily identifiable and permanent marker for socially determined divisions of labor (black runaway slaves were easier to identify than escaped white indentured servants and convicts, the initial workforce of colonial America), race and class have been inextricably intertwined. "Race" is not a neutral descriptive category, but a social category born of the antagonistic relation of white supremacy and black oppression. The basis of the relative health advantage of whites is not to be found in their genes but in the relative material advantage whites enjoy as a consequence of political perogative and state power. As Richard Lewontin has pointed out, "If, after a great cataclysm, only Africans were left alive, the human species would have retained 93 percent of its total genetic variation, although the species as a whole would be darker skinned." The fact that we all know which race we belong to says more about our society than about our biology.

Nevertheless, the paradigm of a genetic basis for black ill health remains strong. In its defense, researchers repeatedly trot out the few diseases for which a clear-cut link of race is established: sickle cell anemia, G&PD deficiency, and lactose intolerance. These diseases, however, have a tiny impact on the health of the black population as a whole—if anything, even less than those few diseases linked to "whiteness," such as some forms of skin cancer. Richard Cooper has shown that of the tens of thousands of excess black deaths in 1977, only 277 (0.3 percent) could be attributed to diseases such as sickle cell anemia. Such uncommon genetic maladies have become important strictly because of their metaphorical value: they are used to support genetic explanations of racial differences in the "big diseases" of the twentieth century—heart disease, stroke, and cancer. Yet no current evidence exists to justify such an extrapolation.

Determined nonetheless to demonstrate the genetic basis of racial health differences, investigators today—like their peers in the past—use the latest techniques. Where once physicians compared cranial capacity to explain black/white inequalities, now they scrutinize surface markers of cells. The case of hypertension is particularly illustrative. High blood pressure is an important cause of strokes and heart attacks, contributing to about 30 percent of all deaths in the United States. At present, the black rate of hypertension in the United States is about twice that of whites. Of over five hundred recent medical journal articles on the topic, fewer than a dozen studies explored social factors. The rest instead unsuccessfully sought biochemical/genetic explanations—and of these, virtually none even attempted to "define" genetically who was "white" and who was "black," despite the alleged genetic nature of their enquiry. As a consequence of the wrong questions being asked, the causes of hypertension remain unknown. Nonetheless, numerous clues point to social factors. Hypertension does not exist in several undisrupted hunter/gatherer tribes of different "races" but rapidly emerges in these tribes after contact with industrial society; in the United States, lower social class begets higher blood pressure.

Turning to cancer, the authors of a recent major government report surmised that blacks have poorer survival rates than whites because they do not "exhibit the same immunologic reactions to cancerous processes." It is noteworthy, however, that the comparably poor survival rates of British breast cancer patients have never elicited such speculation. In our own work on breast cancer in Washington state, we found that the striking "racial" difference in survival evaporated when we took class into account: working-class women, whether black or white, die sooner than women of higher social class standing.

To account for the persistence of the genetic model, we must look to its political significance rather than its scientific content. First used to buttress biblical arguments for slavery in a period when science was beginning to replace religion as sanction for the status quo, the genetic model of racial differences in health emerged toward the end of the eighteenth century, long before any precise theory of heredity existed. In well-respected medical journals, doctors debated whether blacks and whites were even the same species (let alone race), and proclaimed that blacks were intrinsically suited to slavery, thrived in hot climates, succumbed less to the epidemic fevers which ravaged the South, and suffered extraordinary rates of insanity if allowed to live free. After the Civil War effectively settled the argument about whether blacks belonged to the human species, physicians and scientists began elaborating hereditarian theories to explain the disparate health profiles not only of blacks and whites, but of the different white "races"—as defined by national origin and immigrant status. Virtually every scourge, from TB to rickets, was postulated to be inherited. Rheumatic fever, now known to be due to strep bacteria combined with the poverty which permits its expression in immunocompromised malnourished people, was long believed to be linked with the red hair and pale complexions of its Irish working-class victims. Overall, genetic explanations of differences in disease rates have politically served to justify existing class relations and excuse socially created afflictions as a result of immutable biology.

Nowadays the genetic model—newly dressed in the language of molecular genetics—continues to divert attention from the class origin of disease. Genetic explanations absolve the state of responsibility for the health profile of black America by declaring racial disparities (regrettably) inevitable and normal. Intervention efforts based on this model founder for obvious reasons: short of recombinant DNA therapies, genetic screening and selective reproduction stand as supposed tools to reduce the racial gap in health.

Unfortunately, the genetic model wields influence even within the progressive health movement, as illustrated by the surge of interest in sickle cell anemia in the early 1970s. For decades after its initial description in 1925, sickle cell anemia was relegated to clinical obscurity. It occurs as often in blacks as does cystic fibrosis in whites. By linking genetic uniqueness to racial pride, such groups as the Black Panther Party championed sickle cell anemia as the number one health issue among blacks, despite the fact that other health problems—such as infant mortality—took a much greater toll. Because the sickle cell gene provides some protection against malaria, sickle cell seemed to link blacks to their African past, now three centuries removed. It raised the issue of racist neglect of black health in a setting where the victims were truly blameless: the fault lay in their genes. From the point of view of the federal government, sickle cell anemia was a uniquely black disease which did not raise the troubling issues of the ongoing oppression of the black population. In a period of political turmoil, what more could the government ask for? Small wonder that President Nixon jumped on the bandwagon and called for a national crusade.

THE ENVIRONMENTAL MODEL

The genetic model's long history and foundations in the joint race and class divisions of our society assure its continued prominence in discussions on the racial gap in health. To rebut this model, many liberals and progressives have relied upon environmental models of disease causation—only to encounter the right on this turf as well.

Whereas the rise of slavery called forth genetic models of diseases, environmental models were born of the antagonistic social relations of industrial capitalism. In the appalling filth of nineteenth-century cities, tuberculosis, typhus, and infant diarrhea were endemic in the newly forming working class; periodically, epidemics of yellow fever and cholera would attack the entire populace. A sanitary reform movement arose, advocating cleaner cities (with sewer systems and pure water) to protect the wellbeing of the wealthy as well as the poor, and also to engender a healthier, more productive workforce.

In the United States, most of the reformers were highly moralistic and staunchly procapitalist, seeing poverty and squalor as consequences of individual intemperance and ignorance rather than as necessary correlates of capital accumulation. In Europe, where the working-class movement was stronger, a class-conscious wing of the sanitary reform movement emerged. Radicals such as Frederick Engels and Rudolph Virchow (later the founder of modern pathology) argued that poverty and ill health could only be eliminated by resolving the antagonistic class relations of capitalism.

The early sanitary reform movement in the United States rarely addressed the question of racial differences in health per se. In fact, environmental models to explain black/white disparities emerged only during the mid-twentieth century, a consequence of the urban migration of blacks from the rural South to the industrial North and the rise of the civil-rights movement.

Today's liberal version of the environmental model blames poverty for black ill health. The noxious features of the "poverty environment" are catalogued and decried—lead paint from tenement walls, toxins from work, even social features like discrimination. But as in most liberal analyses, the unifying cause of this litany of woes remains unstated. We are left with an apparently unconnected laundry list of problems and no explanation of why blacks as a group encounter similar sickening conditions.

The liberal view fetishizes the environment: individuals are harmed by inanimate objects, physical forces, or unfortunate social conditions (like poverty)—by *things* rather than by people. That these objects or social circumstances are the *creations* of society is hidden by the veil of "natural science." Consequently, the "environment" is viewed as a natural and neutral category, defined as all that is external to individuals. What is not seen is the ways in which the underlying structure of racial oppression and class exploitation—which are relationships among people, not between people and things—shape the "environments" of the groups created by these relations.

The debilitating disease pellagra serves as a concrete example. Once a major health problem of poor southern farm and mill laborers in the United States, pellagra was believed to be a genetic disease. By the early 1920s, however, Joseph Goldberger had proved that the disease stemmed from a dietary deficiency in niacin and had also demonstrated that pellagra's familial nature existed because of the inheritance of nutritional options, not genes. Beyond this, Goldberger argued that pellagra, in essence, was a *social* disease caused by the single cash-crop economy of the South: reliance on cotton ensured seasonal starvation as food ran out between harvests, as well as periodic epidemics when the cotton market collapsed. Southern workers contracted pellagra because they had limited diets—and they had limited diets *because* they were southern workers. Yet governmental response was simply to supplement food with niacin: according to this view, vitamin deficiency—not socially determined malnutrition—was the chief cause of pellagra.

The liberal version of the environmental model also fails to see the causes of disease and the environment in which they exist as a historical product, a nature filtered through, even constructed by, society. What organisms and chemicals people are exposed to is determined by both the social relations and types of production which characterize their society. The same virus may cause pneumonia in blacks and whites alike, just as lead may cause the same physiologic damage—but *why* the death rate for flu and pneumonia and *why* blood lead levels are consistently higher in black as compared to white communities is not addressed. While the liberal conception of the environment can generate an exhaustive *list* of its components, it cannot *comprehend* the all-important assemblage of features of black life. What explains why a greater proportion of black mothers are single, young, malnourished, high-school dropouts, and so on?

Here the right is ready with a "lifestyle" response as a unifying theme: blacks, not racism, are the source of their own health woes. . . . The Reagan administration [was a] chief promoter of this view—made evident by the 1985 publication of the Report of the Secretary's Task Force on Black and Minority Health. Just one weapon among many in the government's vicious ideological war to justify its savage gutting of health and social service programs, the report shifts responsibility for the burden of disease to the minority communities themselves. Promoting "health education" as a panacea, the government hopes to counsel minorities to eat better, exercise more, smoke and drink less, be less violent, seek health care earlier for symptoms, and in general be better health-care consumers. This "lifestyle" version of the environmental model accordingly is fully compatible with the genetic model (i.e., genetic disadvantage can be exaggerated by lifestyle choices) and echoes its ideological messages that individual shortcomings are at the root of ill health.

In focusing on individual health habits, the task force report ironically echoes the language of many "health radicals," ranging from iconoclasts such as Ivan Illich to counterculture advocates of individually oriented self-help strategies. United in practice, if not in spirit, these apparently disparate camps all take a "holistic" view, arguing that disease comes not just from germs or chemicals but from lifestyle choices about food, exercise, smoking, and stress. Their conflation of lifestyle choices and life circumstance can reach absurd proportions. Editorializing on the task force report, the *New York Times* agreed that: "Disparities may be due to cultural or lifestyle differences. For example, a higher proportion of blacks and hispanics live in cities, with greater exposure to hazards like pollution, poor housing, and crime." But what kind of "lifestyle" causes pollution, and who chooses to live in high-crime neighborhoods? Both the conservative and alternative "lifestyle" versions of the environmental model deliberately ignore or distort the fact that economic coercion and political disenfranchisement, not free choice, locate minority communities in the most hazardous regions of cities. What qualitatively constrains the option of blacks to "live right" is the reality of being black and poor in the United States.

But liberals have had little response when the right points out that even the most oppressed and impoverished people make choices affecting their health: it may be hard to eat right if the neighborhood grocer doesn't sell fresh vegetables, but teenage girls do not have to become pregnant. For liberals, it has been easier to portray blacks as passive, blameless victims and in this way avoid the highly charged issue of health behaviors altogether. The end result is usually just proposals for more health services *for* blacks, bandaids for the gaping wounds of oppression. Yet while adequate health services certainly are needed, they can do little to stem the social forces which cause disease.

Too often the left has been content merely to trail behind the liberals in campaigns for health services, or to call only for social control of environmental and occupational exposures. The right, however, has shifted the terrain of battle to the issue of individual behavior, and we must respond. It is for the left to point out that society does not consist of abstract individuals, but rather of people whose life options are shaped by their intrinsic membership in groups defined by the social relations of their society. Race and class broadly determine not only the conditions under which blacks and whites live, but also the ways in which they can respond to these conditions and the political power they have to alter them. The material limits produced by oppression create and constrain not only the type of housing you live in, but even the most intimate choices about what you do inside your home. . . .

READING 40

Media, Science, and Sexual Ideology: The Promotion of Sexual Stability

Gilbert Zicklin

In March 1994, the Gay and Lesbian Association of the Cornell University Medical College organized a conference boldly called "The Biological Nature of Homosexuality." Among the guest speakers were Laura Allen, Dean Hamer, and Simon LeVay, all of whom have published research reports contributing to the proposition that homosexuality has a biological basis. No one on the panel argued that there is no biological basis to homosexuality, or that whatever biological factors are associated with homosexuality, they are of minimal significance in the material development of homosexual desire. No one on the panel commented critically on the biological position or on the research that has been deemed to support it.

I begin by mentioning this conference, which followed upon wide media dissemination of the reports of biologically oriented research into the origins of homosexuality, because its bias is illustrative of the currency recently gained for discussing homosexuality as a biological phenomenon. I intend to argue the following:

1. that the relationship between the data and the conclusions about a biological basis to homosexuality that some researchers assert, and the media have highlighted, is largely without scientific merit;
2. that the media's treatment of the research as "discoveries" offers the public a distorted view of the state of scientific knowledge on this subject;
3. that the narrative about sexuality underlying both the media's and the scientific community's interest in biological explanations for erotic attraction ignores the socially constructed, highly symbolic codes that make sexual desire and desirability meaningful.

To show this I will first describe a sample of studies published since 1990 that assume a biological perspective on sexual desire. I will present a critical analysis of the methodological problems of each of these studies, contrasting my critique with the print media's portrayal of the research findings. I will then focus on an exemplary journalist's coverage of the issue for the *New York Times.* I conclude with an analysis of what lies behind both the researchers' and the media's tendency to see homosexuality as a fixed condition that is set at birth or very shortly thereafter, rather than viewing it more sociologically, the way we do kinship or religious ties.

The biologically oriented research I will examine flows from two streams: (1) neuroanatomical studies of the structural similarities and differences in the brains of male and female laboratory animals, and in humans, among samples that differ by gender and by sexual orientation; and (2) studies that purport to show a chromosomal basis for homosexual desire, or from whose data such a chromosomal basis can logically be inferred. In the interests of space, I will not consider the line of study looking at brain-mediated

Gilbert Zicklin is on the faculty at Montclair State University, where he teaches the sociology of sexuality.

neuroendocrine effects on sexual behavior, though I believe the logic works the same.

I will sample this research by considering the reports of Simon LeVay, Michael Bailey and Richard Pillard, Roger Gorski and Laura Allen, and Dean Hamer et al.[1] First, a snapshot of these studies.

Simon LeVay, a biologist formerly at the Salk Institute in La Jolla, reported that he found a difference in the size of the INAH-3 region of the hypothalamus in brains identified as belonging to gay males compared with those of nongay males. The size of the gay males' region was similar to that of the females in the study (who were not identified with respect to sexual orientation).

Michael Bailey, a psychologist at Northwestern University, and Richard Pillard, a professor of psychiatry at Boston University School of Medicine, compared concordance rates for homosexuality in a sample of male identical co-twins, nonidentical co-twins, and adoptive brothers. They found that about half of the identical, or monozygotic, twins in their sample shared the trait of homosexuality, while for the dizygotic twins the concordance figure was between one-fourth and one-fifth. This translates into the highest concordance rates for the closest genetic relationship, that of monozygotic twins. Bailey and Pillard carried out a comparable study of females and reported similar results.[2]

Roger Gorski and Laura Allen, researchers at UCLA, reported a difference between homosexually and heterosexually identified males, and between males and females, in the size of the anterior commissure, an area that binds the two hemispheres of the brain. They reported that homosexual males had the largest commissures, heterosexual males the smallest.

Dean Hamer et al., of the National Cancer Institute, studied the distribution of homosexual relatives among a sample of homosexual subjects, and examined DNA samples of forty pairs of self-identified gay brothers. Subjects reported more homosexuals among their maternal relatives, and the researchers found similar DNA sequences in thirty-three out of the forty pairs of gay brothers in a region of the X chromosome known as Xq25. These findings led Hamer et al. to hypothesize the genetic transmission of homosexuality through the maternal line.

In the LeVay study, three problems stand out.[3] First, and most important, LeVay relies on hospital records for the measure of a key variable, the sexual orientation of the subjects whose brains he is dissecting. The [study of] record keeping tells us that these official designations are liable to be off the mark. What one decides to reveal to a record keeper, what the record keeper surmises one does not want to reveal but thinks should be included, what the record keeper decides is meant by certain signs the person exhibits—all these may go into the act of fixing a label on a person. The designation of a sexual orientation that is made in a hospital setting in situations of extremis may bear only a tangential relationship to the truth of a person's sexual life. LeVay relied *solely* on such hospital designations for the determination of a principal variable in his study. It is therefore unclear that sexual orientation differentiated LeVay's subjects, whatever other factors may have been involved.

The second problem with the LeVay study involves a likely confounding of independent variables. There was a disproportionate number of deaths from HIV infection among his homosexual subjects. HIV infection is known to damage brain cells directly, as well as through the lowering of testosterone levels in males, which in turn affects brain tissue. This, in itself, may account for an observed correlation between homosexual orientation and the smaller size of the INAH-3 region. . . .

LeVay engaged in the unusual practice of measuring the size of the INAH-3 area himself; scientists more commonly use additional or other researchers for this task. The absence of blind raters, coupled with his well-known desire to find a biological basis for homosexuality, leaves his work open to the charge of experimenter bias.[4] Since his findings have not been replicated, and given the methodological problems with his research, the reliability of his data as well as his interpretation of them can be questioned.

The other anatomical study, that of Gorski and Allen, also suffers from the designation of research subjects' brains as belonging to "homosexuals" or "heterosexuals," without clear operational definitions for these terms. But even if this were not so, there is a larger problem with the research. Gorski and Allen found a larger anterior commissure in the brains of "gay" males than in those of "straight" males, those of the former being comparable to that found in females' brains. But the anterior commissure has not been shown to have any relationship to sexuality; rather, it is thought to aid communication between the two brain hemispheres. Why compare this particular structure among samples with different sexual orientations, if you have no theoretical reason for looking for this difference? It is on a par with recent research reporting that the finger whorls, testicular laterality, and so forth of gay males differ in direction from those of straight males. Since we are given no theoretical basis for these associations, they have little meaning for a study of sexual orientation. In fact, this pig-in-a-poke way of searching for neuroanatomical correlates of behavior increases the risk of false positives, since five times out of one hundred, observed correlations will occur by chance and mean nothing.

Bailey and Pillard's research method included asking male monozygotic (MZ) and dizygotic (DZ) twins and biological and nonbiological nontwin siblings about their sexual orientation. They acquired their subjects through advertisements placed in gay publications in several cities in the Midwest and Southwest. The authors conclude from their data that there is a genetic basis to sexual orientation. They base their claim on the significantly higher percentage of MZ twins concordant for sexual orientation than the other, less genetically connected siblings.

But the method of subject selection undermines the study's validity. Self-selection of subjects, that is, using volunteers, introduces the possibility of a very particular bias in the case of a disapproved behavior: if more homosexual monozygotic twins with homosexual co-twins volunteered for the study than a random sample would find, or as Bailey and Pillard recognize, "if discordant MZ twins were less likely to participate than discordant DZ twins," then the difference in concordance rates for these two types of relatives could not be attributed to genetic differences but rather to the peculiarity of the sample. The overrepresentation of concordant MZ twins is quite possible, since gay MZ twins are likely to be more interested in studies that highlight the special meaning of close biological connections, and they might also have less trepidation about participating since there is a greater likelihood that they would be "out" with one another than would any other pair of male siblings. Conversely, some twins who perceive themselves as discordant on sexual orientation may be motivated to avoid studies wherein this difference may be revealed. Thus, Bailey and Pillard have a double problem: they attract the kind of twins who fit their hypothesis and deter the ones who might weaken it. . . .

The authors do not take into account the possibility that MZ twin relationships create a unique psychosocial environment that in itself can account for higher rates of concordance. The intensely shared life of identical twins including the phenomena of identification, mirroring, and imitation, might plausibly constitute fertile ground for the development of same-sex erotics.

Parenthetically, while there has been no report of a reliable replication of the Bailey and Pillard study, it is worth noting that King and McDonald recently reported far less concordance for identical twin pairs than did Bailey and Pillard.[5]

The study reported by Hamer et al. has been presented as making the most convincing case for the role of heredity. Its problems of methodology are different, but quite serious. Hamer and his colleagues recruited seventy-six homosexual men for a pedigree study to determine which other members of the families of these men were also homosexual. They reported homosexuality to be significantly more common among the maternal relatives and concluded that a putative gene for homosexuality is passed through female family members. Yet the sociology of family life in the United States suggests that women are more likely than men to keep in touch with relatives, so a son might well know more about his mother's side of the family than his father's. Moreover, in this culture as a function of gender politics, a homosexual son might be closer to his mother than to his father and might therefore be more identified with and knowledgeable about his mother's relatives, including the question of their sexual preferences. American gender and family patterns, not genes, may account for the data.

Postulating genetic transmission of homosexuality through the maternal line, Hamer et al. examined the X chromosome in forty pairs of gay brothers recruited through advertisements in homophile publications. They report finding a region of the X chromosome that was shared in thirty-three of the forty pairs. They took this to mean that a linkage was established between a region of the X chromosome and homosexuality, that is, that the gay concordant brothers received the same X chromosome from the mother significantly more often than by chance. But we do not know whether it was more often than their straight siblings, for they did not examine the X chromosome of any heterosexual brothers of the homosexual sib-pair subjects. . . .

Why didn't Hamer et al. look at these brothers' DNA? Hamer says it was because of a supposed difficulty in being sure that a heterosexually identified brother was not a secret homosexual, since if such "faux heterosexuals" were in the sample it would distort—that is, weaken—the anticipated results of the study. He suggests that since homosexual desire is morally questionable in our culture, a heterosexual would be loath to confess his homosexual desires, while someone who already experiences the opprobrium of being known as a homosexual would be unlikely to be hiding significant heterosexual desires. This *may* be true, but surely skilled researchers could have elicited the existence of homosexual desire and practice from heterosexually identified brothers with appropriate open-ended interviews. Eliminating these brothers from the study did more to undermine its validity than including them would have, even with the possible concealment of their homosexual desires. . . .

Finally, and most tellingly for the direct genetic transmission hypothesis, Hamer et al. cannot . . . state that the presence of a certain DNA pattern or gene in the Xq28 region of the X chromosome actually influences sexual desire. (This is the same logical problem encountered in the work of Bailey and Pillard.) . . .

Research that appears to accept the direct biological basis of sexual orientation has drawn criticism from many quarters in the biological and social sciences. R. Hubbard, D. Nelkin, E. Balaban, W. Byne, T. McGuire, R. Lewontin, H. Fingarette, and J. N. Katz, among others, have expressed serious reservations about the claims of biological causation of what are seen as complex social behaviors. Yet when the research of LeVay, Gorski and Allen, Bailey and Pillard, and Hamer et al. has been reported in the popular press, it is almost always represented as contributing to "*mounting evidence*" that homosexuality is biologically based.

These scientific reports have generated a great deal of attention from the popular media. From front-page stories in the *New York Times* to feature articles in *Time, Newsweek,* and *U.S. News and World Report,* from a lead article in the *Atlantic Monthly* to pieces in the *Chronicle of Higher Education, Mother Jones, Discover, National Review,* and the *Nation,* the coverage of purported anatomical and genetic findings with respect to homosexuality has been robust. I searched a select group of newspapers, news magazines, journals of opinion, and monthlies for the years 1990–93 and found dozens of articles, feature stories, personal essays, and editorial page commentaries about this work. The periodicals I searched included only the most prestigious newspapers such as the *New York Times,* the *Washington Post,* the *Los Angeles Times,* the *Houston Post,* and so on; they did not include the thousands of local newspapers, unindexed in library catalogues, that may have carried stories about this research as well.

Overwhelmingly, the articles reporting on this research tend to stress the likely validity of asserted biological bases to sexual orientation. The titles of some of these newspaper and magazine articles suggest the tilt: "Brain Differences Linked to Sexual Preferences," "Are Some Men Born to Be Gay?" "Brain Feature Linked to Sexual Orientation," "Are Some Men Born to Be Homosexual?" "Are Gay Men Born That Way?" "Study Ties Part of Brain to Men's Sexual Orientation," "Exploring the Brain for Secrets of Sexuality," "Study Shows Homosexuality Is Innate," "Report Suggests Homosexuality Is Linked to Genes," "X Marks the Spot: Male Homosexuality May Be Linked to a Gene," "Study of Gay Men and Their Brothers Links Homosexuality to Genetics," "Study Suggests Genes Sway Lesbians' Sexual Orientation," "Genes Tied to Sexual Orientation," "The Search for Sexual Identity: Genes vs. Hormones," "Study Links Genes to Homosexuality," "Research Points toward a 'Gay' Gene," "Born or Bred: The Origins of Homosexuality," "Born Gay? Studies of Family Trees and DNA Make the Case that Male Homosexuality Is in the Genes," "Opening a Window: Genes May Play a Role in Homosexuality," "The Gay Science of Genes and Brains," "Evidence for Homosexuality Gene," and finally, "Genetic Clue to Male Homosexuality Emerges." For these journalists, the mystery of homosexuality is thus solved.

While one reads the occasional dubious headline, such as "Media Hype about the 'Gay Gene,'" and "The Search for Sexual Identity: False Genetic Markers," the media tend mainly to follow a pattern in reporting on this subject. The pattern is (1) repeat claims made by the researchers about the findings; (2) quote them or a couple of friendly experts about the *import* of their findings; (3) quote one or two sources who issue a caveat about the validity of the study; and (4) imply that, caveats notwithstanding, a biological basis for sexual orientation is likely, if not yet proved. This sequence, lacking as it does any developed critical viewpoint, is seen often. While there appear to be systematic differences between the newsmagazines and newspapers, with the former even less likely to pay serious attention to any critique of these studies, on the whole, media representation of this research depicts it as a cumulative body of scientific work. It accepts the assumption of a fixed, unchanging "sexual orientation" that is biologically rooted.

Let us move beyond the headlines for a moment and see *how* the reporting of a *New York Times* journalist uses this structure in her reportage. The *Times* reporter, Natalie Angier, is . . . one of the most sophisticated covering this story. Her work is untypically inclusive of criticism from expert sources about both the methods and the claims of the biological research. Yet her work still illustrates the distorting media paradigm described above.

An article that illustrates her approach comes from the July 16, 1993, edition of the *Times.* It begins with an attempt to characterize the significance of the Hamer study: "Ushering the politically explosive study of the origins of sexual orientation into a new and *perhaps* more scientifically rigorous phase, researchers report that they have linked male homosexuality to a small region of one human chromosome" (my italics). Then the caveat: this is "just a single chapter in the intricate story of sexual orientation and behavior," followed by a repeat of the "importance" of the findings. The "findings" are then further elaborated, followed by another caveat: "But researchers warn against overinterpreting the work, or in taking it to mean anything as simplistic as that the 'gay gene' had been found"

(Angier's quotation marks around *gay gene*). Are we then to think that the idea of a "gay gene" is a function of simplistic thinking? Or is it that believing a *single* gene could control sexual orientation is simplistic? Or is it rather that concluding from the Hamer study, alone, that the gay gene has already been found is simplistic? In her very *next* sentence Angier writes, "The researchers emphasized that they do not yet have a gene isolated, but merely know the rough location of where the gene or genes may sit." The air is cleared: there *are* gay genes. Only where they are is a mystery.

Angier continues in a cautionary style, reporting that even if they do pinpoint this gene there are probably other genes on other chromosomes involved in sexual orientation. She then speculates about how "the gene" could work, using that term now without any quotation marks that might convey doubt. It could work either by directly influencing "sexual proclivity" or by doing so indirectly, through affecting temperament. Thus, Angier has now fully envisioned the existence and operation of a "gay gene," when only some paragraphs before she had signaled the wrongheadedness of such a concept.

When toward the very end of the article Angier turns to some of the methodological problems of the study, for example the lack of a control, she says, "So far the study has been limited to men who said they were gay, eliminating the ambiguity that would come from considering the genes of men who called themselves heterosexual." Instead of actually clarifying why the heterosexual brothers were not part of the DNA study—a very serious problem, as I indicated—Angier has merely restated the researchers' unconvincing explanation, which she now treats as self-explanatory. She concludes her article with the prospect of the work ahead for these scientists, who must sort out "which gene or genes is relevant." Her apparent caveat about the complex nature of sexual desire and whether it could be accounted for by a "gay gene" has now vanished; she has adopted the researchers' account of their work and their perspective on sexual orientation, namely, that it is biologically given.

Though I focus on Angier, her method is an instance of what is actually a widespread tendency in the reportage on this research. It is the use of a rhetoric that subtly inserts the belief that sexual orientation is caused by a biological condition, in gradual steps, amid all-too-stillable doubts. Despite the ambiguous, often equivocal findings that result from the studies' methodologically faulty designs, we have seen dozens of news articles proclaiming supposedly valid, reliable findings.

Questions naturally arise: (1) How is it that this bandwagon has gotten rolling, in the media and even in the lesbian/gay community, for a biological explanation of sexual desire, with so little evidence? (2) What in the scientists' perspective accounts for their persistence in pursuing the biological basis of homosexuality, despite both the experimental impossibility of showing that it is *directly* biologically caused, and the pile of equivocal findings? and (3) What are the ramifications of promoting such a perspective?

To amplify the first question, especially for this audience, we might ask why no such media attention has been showered on scholarly work in the *social sciences* that conceptualizes in a sociocultural framework: the sociological analyses of Bell and Weinberg, of Klassen, Williams, and Levitt, or of Ira Reiss; the work in history of Trumbach, Bray, or Faderman; in social psychology, Herek; in anthropology, Herdt and Williams—just to name a few of the scholars doing notable research bearing on issues related to the nature of homosexuality. Among many other things, this research has examined what sociological factors, if any, a homosexual preference is related to; what are the prevalent beliefs of the U.S. population about what causes homosexuality, what should be done about it, what is its current moral status, how prevalent is it; historically, when did our current ideas and practices first appear and why; what factors are associated with homophobic attitudes; how do other cultures organize sexual practices, and how do they explain these arrangements; how does gender intersect with homosexual preference, both in this culture and in non-Western cultures; and so forth.

An answer to why the media play up the biological studies as opposed to the sociocultural is that the former are appealing because they present themselves as having solved "the riddle of sexual desire," that is, they offer something akin to certainty. Moreover, researchers themselves have encouraged this attitude toward their studies by making grandiose claims for their findings. For example, in a *New York Times* article of December 17, 1991, one scientist, asked to comment on the first Bailey and Pillard study, asserted that "Some of the earlier evidence suggested there was a genetic effect, but the studies were not well done. This is something that really sort of clinches it." Bailey and Pillard themselves write in a *New York Times* op-ed piece, "Our own research *has shown* [my italics] that male sexual orientation is substantially genetic."[6] A reporter for the *Chronicle of Higher Education,* referring to an unnamed scientist, writes, "He found the results [of the Bailey and Pillard study] so compelling that he has decided to start a search for the gene or genes that may cause homosexuality."[7] Natalie Angier reports that Gorski and Allen "believe the[ir] finding supports the idea that brains of homosexuals differ in many subtle ways from those of heterosexuals, and that sexual orientation has *a deep biological basis*" (my italics).[8] Reporters are able to hype these studies in good conscience, since in this enterprise they apparently have the assistance of some scientists.

Interestingly, some of the researchers themselves quite consciously want the public to subscribe to a biological model of sexual orientation. LeVay talks of how he hoped to get the results he did because he thought it would be good for the gay population, both in terms of legal outcomes in civil rights cases and with respect to reducing prejudice should biological explanations come to replace moral ones in the public's understanding of homosexuality. Like LeVay, Bailey and Pillard also believe that if sexual orientation is innate, "it is," in their words "good news for homosexuals and their advocates."[9] Richard Green, another sex researcher with a biological model of homosexuality, commented to a *New York Times* reporter that "if sexual orientation were demonstrated to be essentially inborn, most laws that discriminate against gays and lesbians, including sodomy laws, housing and employment discrimination laws, all would fall."[10] Thus, there is a politics at play in this scientific quest. It is a *liberal* politics, based on the impulse to normalize and include. . . .

I will make that argument by offering another answer to the question of why the media have given this story so much play. I suggest that the assumptions behind the biological research are part of a particular politico/cultural framework for understanding erotic life. It is a framework that seeks to allay the fear of the "normals" by allowing them to believe that one is given an essential sexual orientation at birth. This can reduce some of a heterosexually identified person's fears about whether he or she is sufficiently masculine or feminine, with which fear the modern erotic is so bound up. For if sexuality is in one's genetic makeup, then in a heterosexually identified person, any erotic interest in one's *own* sex can be dismissed as small potatoes, clearly not adding up to the main thing, the *real* thing, biological homosexuality. Dichotomizing the erotic into two biologically based identities reduces the anxiety of those who might worry about being "possibly homosexual" because they experience some sexual interest in and desire for the same sex: "After all," they can reason, "to be a homosexual you've got to be born one, and if I were born one, I probably wouldn't have any heterosexual desire; I would only be attracted to my own sex, and I'm not." Klassen, Williams, and Levitt found that a fairly large minority of Americans (about 40 percent in their sample) agree "strongly" or "somewhat" with the statement that "there is some homosexuality in everyone." At the same time, large majorities believe homosexuality is morally wrong. A sizable group, then, is precariously positioned with respect to the meaning of whatever homosexual desire they experience.[11]

As such, the situation represents a classic instance of cognitive dissonance. The dissonance may be reducible if we accept the model of erotic life that says that if you are strongly disposed, in your brain, to the same sex and not much, if at all, disposed to the opposite sex, are you *really,* that is, *bodily* queer. By advancing the cut-and-dried biological model of sexual orientation, the media fulfill the hidden wishes of the public (and here I would include some of the gay public) to be free from the taint of possible perversity with respect to their sexual desires and, *within each group,* free from the deviant status to which these desires might consign them. Gays are always and only erotically interested in their own gender; the same goes in reverse for straights. In this way, identities are formed that anchor individuals in subcommunities of like-desiring persons, and a culture and politics are built around those identities that function as part of their reification. This, in turn, protects those who hold to the reified identity from the uncomfortable oscillation of erotic interest and desire. For hitherto scorned, isolated, and therefore individually often defenseless persons, the opportunity to now identify with a large and significant community that claims normal social and psychological status has strong appeal, an appeal understood early on by sociologists.

Thus genetic explanations of the gender we are sexually attracted to appeal to us and make prima facie sense in part because they do provide certain and unchanging identities (gay, straight, even bisexual) on which a supportive community can be built. We learn not to pay attention to discrepant feelings that might jeopardize our hard-won identities. And we feel under attack by those who would destabilize sexual orientations, who would see them as a complex but socially learned praxis rather than a biologically given destiny.

But our sexuality is not genetically coded. Human sexual desire long ago became unloosed from the reproductive cycle. For us, sexual contact is a richly textured experience suffused, as are all signifying acts, with culturally created meanings. We see this clearly when we look at the cross-cultural and historical studies of sexuality, but it is equally the case with the mundane heterosexual and homosexual practice of our own day. It is elementary sociology to state that far more is at stake in sexual interplay than the accomplishment of a genetically coded act, though it may be more comfortable for people to think of themselves as infra-human sexual animals, and unsociologically place responsibility for their sexual attractions on their genes, than to imagine and claim the freedom humans actually enjoy in the sexual realm.

In this sense, the biological approach to sexual orientation is a conservative one. By imagining sexual desire as akin to a biological trait like eye color or left-handedness, we neutralize the spontaneous and inventive in sexual relations, and create an essential grid of strictly coded sexual identities. Handedness is a genetically coded trait, and while it can be modified by sociocultural prescription, the underlying organization of right and left hemispheres will not be rearranged, nor will it shift apparently without warning, the way desire does. This is the framework imagined by the biologist model. It is an approach grounded in the view that "gays" are biologically, in effect categorically, different from "straights," a difference sealed by nature in hormone and brain, and ultimately, in DNA. . . .

The choice scientists make in looking for *the biological causes* of homosexuality reflects both sociopolitical and epistemological pressures. Historically, it is associated with a number of sociologically relevant conditions: the decline of the psychoanalytic model of homosexuality as an illness; the chance for medically oriented researchers to obtain research funds; the initiative and momentum created by massive spending of money and human capital on the Human Genome Project; a significant weakening of older sexual values and norms, and the consequent anxiety attendant on normlessness. Epistemologically, the conviction that the best understanding of numerous human behavioral and experiential phenomena is one that reduces them to biological, physiological, tissue-bound, and cellular etiologies is obviously pre-sociological. Such a reductionist and anti-sociological tack accounts for the persistent pursuit of biological causes for many behaviors that are politically and interpersonally quite complex—madness of various sorts, repeated violations of law, heavy drinking, individual and group differences on IQ and achievement tests, all sorts of gender-coded behaviors, and now, sexual attraction.

The biological model functions conservatively to restore stability in sexual life: it fixes sex in an ahistorical order, resolves certain tensions and ambiguities of desire, and reinforces the gender system (males do not desire other males; females do not desire other females, unless they are born that way [in which case they are forgivable]: heterosexuals have no homosexual desire; homosexuals have no heterosexual interests). It makes for a neater view of the erotic universe. But it is a retrograde choice from the point of view of a sociological model of sexuality and gender. It would be far more consonant with a sociological view of self and identity for the gay community to proclaim the message of the early gay liberation movement, that "we must free the homosexual (and the heterosexual) in all of us." . . .

NOTES

I thank David Schwartz for his inestimable help in the preparation of this essay. I would also like to thank Bill Byne for starting me thinking about the shortcomings of the new biological research into sexuality. Of course, neither one bears responsibility for the final product.

1. S. LeVay. A difference in hypothalamic structure between heterosexual and homosexual men, *Science* 253 (1991): 1034—37; M. J. Bailey and R. C. Pillard, A genetic study of male sexual orientation, *Archives of General Psychiatry* 48 (1991): 1089–96; L. S. Allen and R. Gorski. Sexual orientation and the size of the anterior commissure in the human brain, *Proceedings of the National Academy of Science* 89 (1992): 7199–7202; D. H. Hamer, S. Hu, V. L. Magnuson, N. Hu, and A. M. L. Pattatucci, A linkage between DNA markers on the X chromosome and male sexual orientation, *Science* 261 (1993): 321–27.
2. J. M. Bailey and D. S. Benishay, Familial aggregation of female sexual orientation, *American Journal of Psychiatry* 150 (1993): 272; J. M. Bailey, R. C. Pillard, M. C. Nealem, and Y. Agyei, Heritable factors influence sexual orientation in women, *Archives of General Psychiatry* 50 (1993): 217.
3. Others have noted some of these as well. See W. Byne and B. Parsons, Human sexual orientation: The biologic theories reappraised, *Archives of General Psychiatry* 50 (1993): 228–39 for an excellent review article.
4. See E. Marshall, *Science* 257 (1992): 620–21. It makes LeVay's rejection of an offer from a reputable neuroanatomist to undertake a reexamination of his brain samples, as reported by Marshall, somewhat questionable.
5. M. King and E. McDonald, Homosexuals who are twins: A study of 46 probands, *British Journal of Psychiatry* 160 (1992): 407–9.
6. *New York Times,* December 17, 1991.
7. *Chronicle of Higher Education,* December 18, 1991.
8. *New York Times,* August 1, 1992.
9. *New York Times,* December 17, 1991.
10. *New York Times,* July 18, 1993.
11. A. D. Klassen, C. J. Williams, and E. E. Levitt, *Sex and Morality in the U.S.* (Middletown: Wesleyan University Press, 1989).

PERSONAL ACCOUNT

You Can't Forget Humiliation

People who are considered minorities hardly ever forget times when they encounter a bigot. You can't forget being humiliated by the look in their eyes. Instead, you grow long, bitter memories and a defensive stance spurred by anger and fear that someone, someday, will say or do something, and you won't be able to protect yourself. So you are always on guard.

I'll never forget when I was fourteen and my mother shook and screamed at me in a 7–11 parking lot for giving a flower to my best friend because everyone would think I was a lesbian. Or the time that I watched my baby niece, Katie, one afternoon weeks after I told her mom that I was gay.

I had accidently dropped my car keys on the bed when I laid the baby down for a nap. When she woke up, it was time to take her back to my sister. My roommate (who is also gay) and I searched furiously for my keys with no luck. We were locked out of the car, so my sister had to come to our apartment to pick up the baby. My roommate found the keys on the bed when he went to make a phone call, and said "Oh! Here they are. They were on the bed. They must have dropped when you put Katie down for her nap." And my sister said, "What were you doing in bed with my child!" At first, I was stunned that she would say that, but then I started to protest and so did my roommate. She told me she was "just kidding." I told her she was gross. After she left with Katie I cried.

I guess I'm angry now because I'm no longer ashamed to be gay. And when things happen to you, you just get angry because it is not fair. And anger stems from something else—something I never had my entire life until now. And that's pride. I didn't grow up with the same pride as an African American or Jewish kid does, hearing stories of how their ancestors survived. My pride was given to me. I got it much later in life than those kids because I didn't have proud parents who had the same "blood" as me or any role models to emulate. I was raised straight, and worse than that, I was raised with hate for the people I now call family. I earned my pride slowly and gently after I came out to myself. I paid for it with many years of self-denial, and many tears, until I found decent and wonderful gay friends that I could love and know that they went through the same trials I did. Now that pride I can share with my "family" and pass it on to some kid who needs it right now as much as I did when I didn't even know it existed.

Amy L. Helm

READING 41

Disability Definitions: the Politics of Meaning

Michael Oliver

THE IMPORTANCE OF DEFINITIONS

The social world differs from the natural world in (at least) one fundamental respect; that is, human beings give meanings to objects in the social world and subsequently orientate their behaviour towards these objects in terms of the meanings given to them. W. I. Thomas (1966) succinctly puts it thus: "if men define situations as real, they are real in their consequences." As far as disability is concerned, if it is seen as a tragedy, then disabled people will be treated as if they are the victims of some tragic happening or circumstance. This treatment will occur not just in everyday interactions but will also be translated into social policies which will attempt to compensate these victims for the tragedies that have befallen them.

Alternatively, it logically follows that if disability is defined as social oppression, then disabled people will be seen as the collective victims of an uncaring or unknowing society rather than as individual victims of circumstance. Such a view will be translated into social policies geared towards alleviating oppression rather than compensating individuals. It almost goes without saying that at present, the individual and tragic view of disability dominates both social interactions and social policies.

A second reason why definitions are important historically centres on the need to identify and classify the growing numbers of the urban poor in modern industrial societies. In this process of identification and classification, disability has always been an important category, in

Michael Oliver is professor of disability studies at the University of Greenwich in the United Kingdom.

that it offers a legitimate social status to those who can be defined as unable to work as opposed to those who may be classified as unwilling to do so (Stone, 1985). Throughout the twentieth century this process has become ever more sophisticated, requiring access to expert knowledge, usually residing in the ever-burgeoning medical and paramedical professions. Hence the simple dichotomy of the nineteenth century has given way to a whole new range of definitions based upon clinical criteria or functional limitation.

A third reason why definitions are important stems from what might be called "the politics of minority groups." From the 1950s onwards, though earlier in the case of alcoholics, there was a growing realisation that if particular social problems were to be resolved, or at least ameliorated, then nothing more or less than a fundamental redefinition of the problem was necessary. Thus a number of groups including women, black people and homosexuals, set about challenging the prevailing definitions of what constituted these problems by attacking the sexist and racist biases in the language used to underpin these dominant definitions. They did this by creating, substituting or taking over terminology to provide more positive imagery (e.g., gay is good, black is beautiful, etc.). Disabled people too have realised that dominant definitions of disability pose problems for individual and group identity and have begun to challenge the use of disablist language. Whether it be offensive (cripple, spastic, mongol, etc.) or merely depersonalising (the handicapped, the blind, the deaf, and so on), such terminology has been attacked, and organisations of disabled people have fostered a growing group consciousness and identity.

There is one final reason why this issue of definitions is important. From the late fifties onwards there was an upswing in the economy and an increasing concern to provide more services for disabled people out of an ever-growing national cake. But clearly, no government (of whatever persuasion) was going to commit itself to a whole range of services without some idea of what the financial consequences of such a commitment might be. Thus, after some pilot work, the Office of Population Censuses and Surveys (OPCS) was commissioned in the late sixties to carry out a national survey in Britain which was published in 1971 (Harris, 1971). Subsequent work in the international context (Wood, 1981) and more recently a further survey in this country, which has recently been published (Martin, Meltzer and Elliot, 1988), built on and extended this work. However, this work has proceeded isolated from the direct experience of disability as experienced by disabled people themselves, and this has led to a number of wide-ranging and fundamental criticisms of it. . . .

THE POLITICS OF MEANING

It could be argued that in polarising the tragic and oppressive views of disability, a conflict is being created where none necessarily exists. Disability has both individual and social dimensions and that is what official definitions from Harris (1971) through to WHO [World Health Organization] (Wood, 1981) have sought to recognise and to operationalise. The problem with this, is that these schemes, while acknowledging that there are social dimensions to disability, do not see disability as arising from social causes. . . .

This view of disability can and does have oppressive consequences for disabled people and can be quite clearly shown in the methodology adopted by the OPCS survey in Britain (Martin *et al.,* 1988). [Table 1 presents] a list of questions drawn from the face-to-face interview schedule of this survey.

These questions clearly ultimately reduce the problems that disabled people face to their own personal inadequacies or functional limitations. It would have been perfectly possible to reformulate these questions to locate the ultimate causes of disability as within the physical and social environments [as they are in Table 2].

TABLE 1

SURVEY OF DISABLED ADULTS—OPCS, 1986

Can you tell me what is wrong with you?
What complaint causes your difficulty in holding, gripping or turning things?
Are your difficulties in understanding people mainly due to a hearing problem?
Do you have a scar, blemish or deformity which limits your daily activities?
Have you attended a special school because of a long-term health problem or disability?
Does your health problem/disability mean that you need to live with relatives or someone else who can help look after you?
Did you move here because of your health problem/disability?
How difficult is it for you to get about your immediate neighbourhood on your own?
Does your health problem/disability prevent you from going out as often or as far as you would like?
Does your health problem/disability make it difficult for you to travel by bus?
Does your health problem/disability affect your work in any way at present?

TABLE 2

ALTERNATIVE QUESTIONS

Can you tell me what is wrong with society?
What defects in the design of everyday equipment like jars, bottles and tins causes you difficulty in holding, gripping or turning them?
Are your difficulties in understanding people mainly due to their inabilities to communicate with you?
Do other people's reactions to any scar, blemish or deformity you may have, limit your daily activities?
Have you attended a special school because of your education authority's policy of sending people with your health problem or disability to such places?
Are community services so poor that you need to rely on relatives or someone else to provide you with the right level of personal assistance?
What inadequacies in your housing caused you to move here?
What are the environmental constraints which make it difficult for you to get about in your immediate neighbourhood?
Are there any transport or financial problems which prevent you from going out as often or as far as you would like?
Do poorly-designed buses make it difficult for someone with your health problem/disability to use them?
Do you have problems at work because of the physical environment or the attitudes of others?

This reformulation is not only about methodology or semantics, it is also about oppression. In order to understand this, it is necessary to understand that, according to OPCS's own figures, 2231 disabled people were given face-to-face interviews (Martin *et al.,* 1988, Table 5.2). In these interviews, the interviewer visits the disabled person at home and asks many structured questions in a structured way. It is in the nature of the interview process that the interviewer presents as expert and the disabled person as an isolated individual inexperienced in research, and thus unable to reformulate the questions in a more appropriate way. It is hardly surprising that, given the nature of the questions and their direction that, by the end of the interview, the disabled person has come to believe that his or her problems are caused by their own health/disability problems rather than by the organisation of society. It is in this sense that the process of the interview is oppressive, reinforcing on to isolated, individual disabled people the idea that the problems they experience in everyday living are a direct result of their own personal inadequacies or functional limitations. . . .

IMPAIRMENT: A STRUCTURED ACCOUNT

Recently it has been estimated that there are some 500 million severely impaired people in the world today, approximately one in ten of the population (Shirley, 1983). These impairments are not randomly distributed throughout the world but are culturally produced.

> The societies men live in determine their chances of health, sickness and death. To the extent that they have the means to master their economic and social environments, they have the means to deter-

> mine their life chances. (Susser and Watson, 1971, p. 45)

Hence in some countries impairments are likely to stem from infectious diseases, poverty, ignorance and the failure to ensure that existing medical treatments reach the population at risk (Shirley, 1983). In others, impairments resulting from infectious diseases are declining, only to be replaced by those stemming from the ageing of the population, accidents at work, on the road or in the home, the very success of some medical technologies in ensuring the survival of some severely impaired children and adults and so on (Taylor, 1977). To put the matter simply, impairments such as blindness and deafness are likely to be more common in the Third World, whereas heart conditions, spina bifida, spinal injuries and so on, are likely to be more common in industrial societies.

Again, the distribution of these impairments is not a matter of chance, either across different societies or within a single society, for

> Social and economic forces cause disorder directly; they redistribute the proportion of people at high or low risk of being affected; and they create new pathways for the transmission of disorders of all kinds through travel, migration and the rapid diffusion of information and behaviour by the mass communication media. Finally, social forces effect the conceptualisation, recognition and visibility of disorders. A disorder in one place and at one time is not seen as such in another; these social perceptions and definitions influence both the provision of care, the demands of those being cared for, and the size of any count of health needs. (Susser and Watson, 1971, p. 35)

Social class is an important factor here both in terms of the causes of impairments or what Doyal (1979) calls degenerative diseases, and in terms of outcomes, what Le Grand (1978) refers to as longstanding illnesses.

Just as we know that poverty is not randomly distributed internationally or nationally (Cole and Miles, 1984; Townsend, 1979), neither is impairment, for in the Third World at least

> Not only does disability usually guarantee the poverty of the victim but, most importantly, poverty is itself a major cause of disability. (Doyal, 1983, p. 7)

There is a similar relation in the industrial countries. . . . Hence, if poverty is not randomly distributed and there is an intrinsic link between poverty and impairment, then neither is impairment randomly distributed.

Even a structured account of impairment cannot, however, be reduced to counting the numbers of impaired people in any one country, locality, class or social group, for

> Beliefs about sickness, the behaviours exhibited by sick persons, and the ways in which sick persons are responded to by family and practitioners are all aspects of social reality. They, like the health care system itself, are cultural constructions, shaped distinctly in different societies and in different social structural settings within those societies. (Kleinman, 1980, p. 38)

The discovery of an isolated tribe in West Africa where many of the population were born with only two toes illustrates this point, for this made no difference to those with only two toes or indeed the rest of the population (Barrett and McCann, 1979). Such differences would be regarded as pathological in our society, and the people so afflicted subjected to medical intervention.

In discussing impairment, it was not intended to provide a comprehensive discussion of the nature of impairment but to show that it occurs in a structured way. However

> such a view does not deny the significance of germs, genes and trauma, but rather points out that their effects are only ever apparent in a real social and historical context, whose nature is determined by a complex interaction of material and non-material factors. (Abberley, 1987, p. 12)

This account of impairment challenges the notion underpinning personal tragedy theory, that impairments are events happening to unfortunate individuals. . . .

REFERENCES

Abberley, P. (1987). "The Concept of Oppression and the Development of a Social Theory of Disability," *Disability, Handicap and Society,* Vol. 2, no. 1, 5–19.

Barrett, D., and McCann, E. (1979). "Discovered: Two Toed Man," *Sunday Times Colour Supplement,* n.d.

Cole, S., and Miles, I. (1984). *Worlds Apart* (Brighton: Wheatsheaf).

Doyal, L. (1979). *The Political Economy of Health* (London: Pluto Press).

Doyal L. (1983). "The Crippling Effects of Underdevelopment" in Shirley, O. (ed.).

Harris, A. (1971). *Handicapped and Impaired in Great Britain* (London: HMSO).

Le Grand, J. (1978). "The Distribution of Public Expenditure: the Case of Health Care," *Economica,* Vol. 45.

Le Grand, J., and Robinson, R. (ed.) (1984). *Privatisation and the Welfare State* (London: Allen & Unwin).

Martin, J., Meltzer, H., and Elliot, D. (1988). *The Prevalence of Disability Amongst Adults* (London: HMSO).

Shirley, O. (ed.) (1983). *A Cry for Health: Poverty and Disability in the Third World* (Frome: Third World Group and ARHTAG).

Stone, D. (1985). *The Disabled State* (London: Macmillan).

Susser, M., and Watson, W. (2nd edn) (1971). *Sociology in Medicine* (London: Oxford University Press).

Taylor, D. (1977). *Physical Impairment—Social Handicap* (London: Office of Health Economics).

Thomas, W. I. (1966). In Janowitz, M. (ed.), *Organization and Social Personality: Selected Papers* (Chicago: University of Chicago Press).

Townsend, P. (1979). *Poverty in the United Kingdom* (Harmondsworth: Penguin).

Wood, P. (1981). *International Classification of Impairments, Disabilities and Handicaps* (Geneva: World Health Organization).

PERSONAL ACCOUNT

Seeing Race, Seeing Disability

I am an international student who hails from Guyana, a country located on the coast of South America. Although called South American by a few, I am identified by most others as a West Indian (native of the Caribbean) because our culture and way of life is so similar to that of the little islands that comprise the West Indies.

I have experienced culture shock in America, from aspects of food and clothing to language and weather, but my most complex adjustment pertained to the issue of race. It is still less than one year since I have taken up residence in the "Land of the Free," but I have already begun to loose the gift of being colorblind.

America and Guyana have many cultural differences; yet, at the same time, there are many noteworthy similarities. One of these similarities would be the ethnic/racial diversity evident in both societies. Guyana is a blend of six races—Indian, Portuguese, Chinese, Caucasian, Amerindian (the indigenous people), and African. In Guyana, the color of one's skin or the texture of one's hair does not generally serve as a means of dichotomization, as seems to be common in America.

I was given the opportunity to work with a disabled student in a particular course. This young man's disability had been the result of an accident as a child. I had neither seen nor met him when I decided to peruse his web page, which was conveniently divided into areas that gave helpful information about his experience, hobbies, achievements, disability history, and career goals. It also provided a section with photographs. Without a moment's thought, I opened this photographic collection and later realized that I had done so only to satisfy my curiosity as to his race. In retrospect, I found this frightening because this behavior is foreign to me. I knew that it would have made no difference what race he represented because I would still have been enthusiastic about working with him.

Being as diverse as we are in Guyana, I would not have been immediately interested in his phenotypic identity, but possibly more concerned with (the extent of) his disability because there is a greater stigma attached to disabled persons in the Third World than there is in America. In comparison, diversity in my country is generally looked upon like the colors of a rainbow . . . all different but creating a thing of beauty when combined. In this part of the world, it seems as though diversity has created division.

R. B.

Popular Culture

READING 42

Backlash

Susan Faludi

The first action of the new women's liberation movement to receive national front-page coverage was a protest of the Miss America pageant.[1] Many feminist marches for jobs, pay equity, and coeducation had preceded it, but they didn't attract anywhere near the media attention. The reason this event got so much ink: a few women tossed some padded brassieres in a trash can. No one actually burned a bra that day—as a journalist erroneously reported. In fact, there's no evidence that any undergarment was ever so much as singed at any women's rights demonstration in the decade. (The only two such displays that came close were both organized by *men,* a disc jockey and an architect, who tried to get women to fling their bras into a barrel and the Chicago River as "media events." Only three women cooperated in the river stunt—all models hired by the architect.[2]) Yet, to read the press accounts of the time, the bonfires of feminism nearly cremated the lingerie industry.

Mostly, editors at the nation's reigning publications in the late '60s and early '70s preferred not to cover the women's movement at all. The "grand press blitz," as some feminists jokingly called the media's coverage of the movement, lasted three months; by 1971, the press was already declaring this latest "fad" a "bore" or "dead."[3] All that "bra burning," the media perversely said of its own created myth, had alienated middle-American women. And publications where editors were forced to recognize the women's movement—they were under internal pressure as women on staff filed sex discrimination suits—often deployed reporters to discredit it. At *Newsday,* a male editor assigned reporter Marilyn Goldstein a story on the women's movement with these instructions: "Get out there and find an authority who'll say this is all a crock of shit."[4] At *Newsweek,* Lynn Young's 1970 story on the women's movement, the magazine's first, was rewritten every week for two months, then killed.[5] Finally, *Newsweek* commissioned a freelancer for the job, the wife of a senior editor and a self-professed antifeminist. (This tactic backfired when she changed her mind after "my first interview" and embraced the movement.[6])

By the mid-'70s, the media and advertisers had settled on a line that served to neutralize and commercialize feminism at the same time. Women, the mass media seemed to have decided, were now equal and no longer seeking new rights—just new lifestyles. Women wanted self-gratification, not self-determination—the sort of fulfillment best serviced at a shopping mall. Soon periodicals and, of course, their ad pages, were bristling with images of "liberated single girls" stocking up on designer swimsuits for their Club Med vacations, perky MBA "Superwomen" flashing credit cards at the slightest provocation. "She's Free. She's Career. She's Confident," a Tandem jewelry ad enthused, in an advertorial tribute to the gilded Tandem girl. Hanes issued its "latest liberating product"—a new variety of pantyhose—and hired a former NOW officer to peddle it.[7] The subsequent fashion show, entitled "From Revolution to Revolution: The Undercover Story," merited feature treatment in the *New York Times.* SUCCESS! was the stock headline on magazine articles about women's status—as if all barriers to women's opportunity had suddenly been swept aside. UP THE LADDER, FINALLY! *Business Week* proclaimed, in a 1975 special issue on "the Corporate Woman"—illustrated with a lone General Electric female vice president enthroned in her executive chair, her

---

Susan Faludi is a former *Wall Street Journal* reporter. She won the Pulitzer Prize in 1991 for *Backlash.*

arms raised in triumph.[8] "More women than ever are within striking distance of the top," the magazine asserted—though, it admitted, it had "no hard facts" to substantiate that claim.

The media's pseudofeminist cheerleading stopped suddenly in the early '80s—and the press soon struck up a dirge. Feminism is "dead," the banner headlines announced, all over again.[9] "The women's movement is over," began a cover story in the *New York Times Magazine.*[10] In case readers missed that issue, the magazine soon ran a second obituary, in which Ivy League students recanted their support for the women's movement and assured readers that they were "not feminists" because those were just women who "let themselves go physically" and had "no sense of style."[11]

This time around, the media did more than order up a quiet burial for the feminist corpse. They went on a rampage, smashing their own commercial icons of "liberated" womanhood, tearing down the slick portraits that they themselves had mounted. Like graffiti artists, they defaced the two favorite poster girls of the '70s press—spray-painting a downturned mouth and shriveled ovaries on the Single Girl, and adding a wrinkled brow and ulcerated stomach to the Superwoman. These new images were, of course, no more realistic than the last decade's output. But their effect on live women would be quite real and damaging.

* * *

The press first introduced the backlash to a national audience—and made it palatable. Journalism replaced the "pro-family" diatribes of fundamentalist preachers with sympathetic and even progressive-sounding rhetoric. It cosmeticized the scowling face of antifeminism while blackening the feminist eye. In the process, it popularized the backlash beyond the New Right's wildest dreams.

The press didn't set out with this, or any other, intention; like any large institution, its movements aren't premeditated or programmatic, just grossly susceptible to the prevailing political currents. Even so, the press, carried by tides it rarely fathomed, acted as a force that swept the general public, powerfully shaping the way people would think and talk about the feminist legacy and the ailments it supposedly inflicted on women. It coined the terms that everyone used: "the man shortage," "the biological clock," "the mommy track" and postfeminism." Most important, the press was the first to set forth and solve for a mainstream audience the paradox in women's lives, the paradox that would become so central to the backlash: women have achieved so much yet feel so dissatisfied; it must be feminism's achievements, not society's resistance to these partial achievements, that is causing women all this pain. In the '70s, the press had held up its own glossy picture of a successful woman and said, "See, she's happy. That must be because she's liberated." Now, under the reverse logic of the backlash, the press airbrushed a frown into its picture of the successful woman and announced, "See, she's miserable. That must be because women are too liberated."

"What has happened to American women?" ABC asked with much consternation in its 1986 special report.[12] The show's host Peter Jennings promptly answered, "The gains for women sometimes come at a formidable cost to them." *Newsweek* raised the same question in its 1986 story on the "new problem with no name."[13] And it offered the same diagnosis: "The emotional fallout of feminism" was damaging women; an "emphasis on equality" had robbed them of their romantic and maternal rights and forced them to make "sacrifices." The magazine advised: "'When the gods wish to punish us, they answer our prayers,' Oscar Wilde wrote. So it would seem to many of the women who looked forward to 'having it all.'" (This happens to be the same verdict *Newsweek* reached when it last investigated female discontent—at the height of the feminine-mystique backlash. "American women's unhappiness is merely the most recently won of women's rights," the magazine reported then.[14])

The press might have looked for the source of women's unhappiness in other places. It could have investigated and exposed the buried roots of the backlash in the New Right and a misogynistic White House, in a chilly business community and intransigent social and religious institutions. But the press chose to peddle the backlash rather than probe it.

The media's role as backlash collaborator and publicist is a familiar one in American history. The first article sneering at a "Superwoman" appeared not in the 1980s press but in an American newspaper headline at the turn of the century.[15] Feminists, according to the late Victorian press, were "a herd of hysterical and irrational she-revolutionaries," "fussy, interfering, faddists, fanatics," "shrieking cockatoos," and "unpardonably ridiculous."[16] Feminists had laid waste to the American female population; any sign of female distress was surely another "fatal symptom" of the feminist disease, the periodicals reported. "Why Are We Women Not Happy?" the male-edited *Ladies' Home Journal* asked in 1901—and answered that the women's rights movement was debilitating its beneficiaries.

As American studies scholar Cynthia Kinnard observed in her bibliography of American antifeminist literature, journalistic broadsides against women's rights "grew in intensity during the late 19th century and reached regular peaks with each new suffrage campaign." The arguments were always the same: equal education would make women spinsters, equal employment would make women sterile, equal rights would make women bad mothers. With each new historical cycle, the threats were simply updated and sanitized, and new "experts" enlisted. The Victorian periodical press turned to clergymen to support its brief against feminism; in the '80s, the press relied on therapists.

The 1986 *Newsweek* backlash article, "Feminism's Identity Crisis," quoted many experts on women's condition—sociologists, political scientists, psychologists—but none of the many women supposedly suffering from this crisis. The closest the magazine came was two drawings of a mythical feminist victim: a dour executive with cropped hair is pictured first at her desk, grimly pondering an empty family-picture frame, and then at home, clutching a clock and studying the hands—poised at five minutes to midnight.

The absence of real women in a news account that is allegedly about real women is a hallmark of '80s backlash journalism. The press delivered the backlash to the public through a series of "trend stories," articles that claimed to divine sweeping shifts in female social behavior while providing little in the way of evidence to support their generalizations. The trend story, which may go down as late-20th-century journalism's prime contribution to its craft, professes to offer "news" of changing mores, yet prescribes more than it observes. Claiming to mirror public sentiment, its reflections of the human landscapes are strangely depopulated. Pretending to take the public's pulse, it monitors only its own heartbeat—and its advertisers'.

Trend journalism attains authority not through actual reporting but through the power of repetition. Said enough times, anything can be made to seem true. A trend declared in one publication sets off a chain reaction, as the rest of the media scramble to get the story, too. The lightning speed at which these messages spread has less to do with the accuracy of the trend than with journalists' propensity to repeat one another. And repetition became especially hard to avoid in the '80s, as the "independent" press fell into a very few corporate hands.[17]

Fear was also driving the media's need to dictate trends and determine social attitudes in the '80s, as print and broadcast audiences, especially female audiences, turned to other news sources and advertising plunged—eventually falling to its lowest level in twenty years.[18] Anxiety-ridden media managements became preoccupied with conducting market research studies and "managing" the fleeing reader, now renamed "the customer" by such news corporations as Knight-

Ridder.[19] And their preoccupations eventually turned up in the way the media covered the news. "News organizations are moving on to the same ground as political institutions that mold public opinion and seek to direct it," Bill Kovach, former editor of the *Atlanta Journal-Constitution* and the Nieman Foundation's curator, observed.[20] "Such a powerful tool for shaping public opinion in the hands of journalists accustomed to handling fact is like a scalpel in a child's hands: it is capable of great damage."

Journalists first applied this scalpel to American women. While '80s trend stories occasionally considered the changing habits of men, these articles tended to involve men's latest hobbies and whimsies—fly fishing, beepers, and the return of the white shirt. The '80s female trends, by contrast, were the failure to find husbands, get pregnant, or properly bond with their children. NBC, for instance, devoted an entire evening news special to the pseudotrend of "bad girls," yet ignored the real trend of bad boys: the crime rate among boys was climbing twice as fast as for girls.[21] (In New York City, right in the network's backyard, rape arrests of young boys had jumped 200 percent in two years.) Female trends with a more flattering veneer surfaced in women's magazines and newspaper "Style" pages in the decade, each bearing, beneath new-and-improved packaging, the return-to-gender trademark: "the New Abstinence," "the New Femininity," "the New High Monogamy," "the New Morality," "the New Madonnas," "the Return of the Good Girl." While anxiety over AIDS has surely helped fuel promotion of these "new" trends, that's not the whole story. While in the '80s AIDS remained largely a male affliction, these media directives were aimed almost exclusively at women. In each case, women were reminded to reembrace "traditional" sex roles—or suffer the consequences. For women, the trend story was no news report; it was a moral reproach.

The trends for women always came in instructional pairs—the trend that women were advised to flee and the trend that they were pushed to join. For this reason, the paired trends tended to contradict each other. As one woman writer observed wryly in an *Advertising Age* column, "The media are having a swell time telling us, on the one hand, that marriage is 'in' and, on the other hand, that women's chances of marrying are slim. So maybe marriage is 'in' because it's so hard to do, like coal-walking was 'in' a year ago."[22] Three contradictory trend pairs, concerning work, marriage, and motherhood, formed the backlash media's triptych: Superwomen "burnout" versus New Traditionalist "cocooning"; "the spinster boom" versus "the return of marriage"; and "the infertility epidemic" versus "the baby boomlet."

Finally, in female trend stories fact and forecast traded places. These articles weren't chronicling a retreat among women that was already taking place; they were compelling one to happen. The "marriage panic" . . . didn't show up in the polls until after the press's promotion of the Harvard-Yale study.[23] In the mid-'80s, the press deluged readers with stories about how mothers were afraid to leave their children in "dangerous" day care centers. In 1988, this "trend" surfaced in the national polls: suddenly, almost 40 percent of mothers reported feeling fearful about leaving their children in day care; their confidence in day care fell to 64 percent, from 76 percent just a year earlier—the first time the figure had fallen below 70 percent since the survey began asking that question four years earlier.[24] Again, in 1986 the press declared a "new celibacy" trend—and by 1987 the polls showed that the proportion of single women who believed that premarital sex was acceptable had suddenly dropped six percentage points in a year; for the first time in four years, fewer than half of all women said they felt premarital sex was okay.[25]

Finally, throughout the '80s the media insisted that women were fleeing the work force to devote themselves to "better" motherhood. But it wasn't until 1990 that this alleged development made a dent—a very small one—in the labor charts, as the percentage of women in the work force between twenty and forty-four dropped a tiny 0.5 percent, the first dip since the early '60s.[26] Mostly, the media's advocacy of such a female exodus created more guilt than flight: in 1990, a poll of working women by Yankelovich Clancy Shulman found almost 30 percent of them believed that "wanting to put more energy into being a good homemaker and mother" was cause to consider quitting work altogether—an 11 percent increase from just a year earlier and the highest proportion in two decades.

The trend story is not always labeled as such, but certain characteristics give it away: an absence of factual evidence or hard numbers; a tendency to cite only three or four women, typically anonymously, to establish the trend; the use of vague qualifiers like "there is a sense that" or "more and more"; a reliance on the predictive future tense ("Increasingly, mothers will stay home to spend more time with their families"); and the invocation of "authorities" such as consumer researchers and psychologists, who often support their assertions by citing other media trend stories.

Just as the decade's trend stories on women pretended to be about facts while offering none, they served a political agenda while telling women that what was happening to them had nothing to do with political events or social pressures. In the '80s trend analysis, women's conflict was no longer with her society and culture but only with herself. Single women were simply struggling with personal problems; they were "consistently self-destructive" or "overly selective."

The only external combat the press recognized was woman on woman. THE UNDECLARED WAR, a banner headline announced on the front page of the *San Francisco Examiner*'s Style section[27]: "To Work or Not Divides Mothers in the Suburbs." *Child* magazine offered THE MOMMY WARS and *Savvy*'s WOMEN AT ODDS informed readers that "the world is soon to be divided into two enemy camps and one day they may not be civil toward each other."[28] Media accounts encouraged married and single women to view each other as opponents—and even confront each other in the ring on "Geraldo" and "Oprah." IS HE SEPARABLE? was the title of a 1988 *Newsday* article that warned married women to beware the husband-poaching trend; the man shortage had driven single women into "brazen" overtures and wives were advised to take steps to keep "the hussy" at bay.[29]

Trend journalists in the '80s were not required to present facts for the same reason that ministers aren't expected to support sermons with data. The reporters were scripting morality plays, not news stories, in which the middle-class woman played the Christian innocent, led astray by a feminist serpent. In the final scene, the woman had to pay—repenting of her ambitions and "selfish" pursuit of equality—before she could reclaim her honor and her happiness. The trend stories were strewn with judgmental language about the wages of feminist sin. The ABC report on the ill effects of women's liberation, for example, referred to the "costs" and "price" of equality thirteen times.[30] Like any cautionary tale, the trend story offered a "choice" that implied only one correct answer: Take the rocky road to selfish and lonely independence or the well-paved path to home and flickering hearth. No middle route was visible on the trend story's map of the moral feminine universe. . . .

NEW LABELS, OLD STORY

[In one celebrated trend story a] 1986 *Fortune* cover story entitled "Why Women Are Bailing Out"[31] [concluded that A third of all the female MBAs of 1976 have already returned home]. The article, about businesswomen trained at elite schools fleeing the corporate suite, inspired similar "bailing out" articles in *Forbes, USA Today,* and *U.S. News & World Report,* among others.[32]

The *Fortune* story left an especially deep and troubling impression on young women aspiring to business and management careers; after all, it seemed to have hard data. A year later at Stanford University's Graduate School of Business, women were still talking about the article and the effect it had had on them.[33] Phyllis

Strong, a Stanford MBA candidate, said she now planned to look for a less demanding career, after reading how "you give up too much" and "you lose that sense of bonding and family ties" when you take on a challenging business job. Marcia Walley, another MBA candidate, said that she now understood "how impossible it is to have a successful career and a good family life. You can't have it all and you have to choose." . . . The year after *Fortune* launched the "bailing out" trend, the proportion of women applying to business schools suddenly began to shrink—for the first time in a decade.[34]

Fortune's 1986 cover photo featured Janie Witham, former IBM systems engineer, seated in her kitchen with her two-year-old daughter on her lap. Witham is "happier at home," *Fortune*'s cover announced.[35] She has time now to "bake bread." She is one of "many women, including some of the best educated and most highly motivated," wrote the article's author, *Fortune* senior writer Alex Taylor III, who are making "a similar choice" to quit work. "These women were supposed to lead the charge into the corridors of corporate power," he wrote. "If the MBAs cannot find gratification there [in the work force], can *any* [his italics] women?"

The *Fortune* story originated from some cocktail chatter at a *Fortune* editor's class reunion. While mingling with Harvard Business School classmates, Taylor's editor heard a couple of alumnae say they were staying home with their newborns. Suspecting a trend, he assigned the story to Taylor. "He had this anecdotal evidence but no statistics," Taylor recalls.[36] So the reporter went hunting for numbers.

Taylor called Mary Anne Devanna, research coordinator at Columbia Business School's Center for Research in Career Development. She had been monitoring MBA women's progress for years—and she saw no such trend. "I told him, 'I don't believe your anecdotes are right,'" she recalls. "'We have no evidence that women are dropping out in larger numbers.' And he said, 'Well, what would convince you?'" She suggested he ask *Fortune* to commission a study of its own. "Well, *Fortune* apparently said a study would cost $36,000 so they didn't want to do one," she says, "but they ended up running the story anyway."[37]

Instead of a study, Taylor took a look at alumni records for the Class of '70 from seventeen top business schools. But these numbers did not support the trend either: in 1976, the same proportion of women as men went to work for large corporations or professional firms, and ten years later virtually the same proportion of women and men were still working for these employers.

Nonetheless, the story that Taylor wrote stated, "After ten years, significantly more women than men dropped off the management track." As evidence, Taylor cited this figure: "Fully 30 percent of the 1,039 women from the class of '70 reported they are either self-employed or unemployed, or they listed no occupation." That would seem newsworthy but for one inconvenient fact: 21 percent of the *men* from the same class also were self-employed or unemployed. So the "trend" boiled down to a 9 percentage-point difference. Given that working women still bear primary responsibility for child care and still face job discrimination, the real news was that the gap was so *small*.

"The evidence is rather narrow," Taylor concedes later. "The drop-out rates of men and women are roughly the same."[38] Why then did he claim that women were fleeing the work force in "disquieting" numbers? Taylor did not actually talk to any of the women in the story. "A [female] researcher did all the interviews," Taylor says. "I just went out and talked to the deep thinkers, like the corporate heads and social scientists." One woman whom Taylor presumably did talk to, but whose example he did not include, is his own wife. She is a director of corporate communications and, although the Taylors have two children, three years old and six months old at the time of the interview, she's still working. "She didn't quit, it's true," Taylor says. "But I'm struck by the strength of her maternal ties."

The *Fortune* article passed lightly over political forces discouraging businesswomen in the '80s and concluded that women flee the work force because they simply would "rather" stay home. Taylor says he personally subscribes to this view: "I think motherhood, not discrimination, is the overwhelming reason women are dropping out." Yet, even the ex-IBM manager featured on the cover didn't quit because she wanted to stay home. She left because IBM refused to give her the flexible schedule she needed to care for her infant. "I wish things had worked out," Witham told the magazine's interviewer. "I would like to go back."

Three months later, *Fortune* was back with more of the same. "A woman who wants marriage and children," the magazine warned, "realizes that her Salomon Brothers job probably represents a choice to forgo both."[39] But *Fortune* editors still couldn't find any numbers to support their retreat-of-the-businesswoman trend. In fact, in 1987, when they finally did conduct a survey on business managers who seek to scale back career for family life, they found an even smaller 6 percent gender gap, and 4 percent *more* men than women said they had refused a job or transfer because it would mean less family time.[40] The national pollsters were no help either: they couldn't find a gap at all; while 30 percent of working women said they might quit if they could afford it, 30 percent of the men said that too.[41] And contrary to the press about "the best and brightest" burning out, the women who were well educated and well paid were the least likely to say they yearned to go home. In fact, a 1989 survey of 1,200 Stanford business-school graduates found that among couples who both hold MBAs and work, the husbands "display more anxiety."[42] . . .

THE SPINSTER BOOM: THE SORROW AND THE PITY

"In all respects, young single American women hold themselves in higher regard now than a year ago," the *New York Times* noted in 1974.[43] Single women are more "self-assured, confident, secure." The article concluded, "The [women's] movement, apparently, is catching on."

Such media views of single women were certainly catching on in the '70s. *Newsweek* quickly elevated the news of the happy single woman to trend status. "Within just eight years, singlehood has emerged as an intensely ritualized—and newly respectable—style of American life," the magazine ruled in a 1973 cover story.[44] "It is finally becoming possible to be both single and whole." In fact, according to *Newsweek,* the single lifestyle for women was more than "respectable"; it was a thrill a minute. The cover photo featured a grinning blonde in a bikini, toasting her good fortune poolside. Inside, more singles beamed as they sashayed from sun decks to moonlit dances. "I may get married or I just may not," a flight attendant, who described her single status as "pretty groovy," told the magazine. "But if I do, it will be in my own time and on my own terms. . . . I see nothing wrong with staying single for as long as you please." And even *Newsweek*'s writers, though betraying some queasiness at such declarations, ultimately gave a round of applause to these spunky new singles who weren't "settling for just any old match."

The many features about giddy single women in the early '70s left the impression that these unwed revelers rarely left their beach towels. The stereotype got so bad that one bachelor grumbled in a 1974 *New York Times* article, "From reading the press, you'd think that every girl is 36-24-36 . . . and every guy lounges by a poolside and waits for the beautiful blondes to admire his rippling muscles."[45]

Married life, on the other hand, acquired a sour and claustrophobic reputation in the early '70s press. "Dropout Wives—Their Number Is Growing," a 1973 *New York Times* trend story advised, asserting that droves of miserable housewives were fleeing empty marriages in search of more "fulfilled" lives.[46] The *Times*'s portrait of the wedded state was bleak: it featured husbands who cheat, criticize and offer "no communication," and wives who obsessively drink and pop pills. According to *Newsweek,* married couples were worse than troubled—they were untrendy: "One sociologist has gone so far as to predict that 'eventually married people could find themselves living in a totally singles-oriented society.'"[47]

A dozen years later, these same publications were sending out the opposite signals. *Newsweek* was now busy scolding single women for refusing to "settle" for lesser mates, and the *New York Times* was reporting that single women are "too rigid to connect" and suffer from "a sickness almost."[48] Single women were no longer the press's party girls; with a touch of the media's wand, they were turned back into the scowling scullery maids who couldn't go to the ball. TOO LATE FOR PRINCE CHARMING? the *Newsweek* headline inquired sneeringly, over a drawing of a single woman sprawled on a lonely mattress, a teddy bear her only companion.[49] The magazine now offered only mocking and insincere pity for women shut out of the marital bedroom, which '80s press accounts enveloped in a heavenly, and tastefully erotic, glow. On the front page of the *New York Times,* the unwed woman stalked the empty streets like Typhoid Mary; though "bright and accomplished," she "dreads nightfall, when darkness hugs the city and lights go on in warm kitchens."[50] It's clear enough why she fears the dark: according to the '80s press, nightmares are a single girl's only bedmate. *New York* magazine's 1984 cover story on single women began with this testimony from "Mary Rodgers," which the magazine noted in small print was not her real name: "Last night, I had a terrible dream. The weight of the world was on my shoulders, and it was pressing me into the ground. I screamed for help, but nobody came. When I woke up, I wanted somebody to hold me. But it was just like the dream. There was no husband. No children. Only me."[51]

"Mary" was an executive in a garment firm. Like most of the ailing single women that the '80s media chose to pillory, she was one of the success stories from the women's movement now awakening to the error of her independent ways. She was single because, as the story's own headline put it, she was one of those women who "expect too much."

The campaign for women's rights was, once more, identified as the culprit; liberation had depressed single women. "Loveless, Manless: The High Cost of Independence," read one women's magazine headline.[52] "Feminism became a new form of defensiveness" that drove men away, explained a 1987 *Harper's Bazaar* article, entitled "Are You Turning Men Off?; Desperate and Demanding."[53] *New York*'s story on grim-faced single women summoned an expert, psychotherapist Ava Siegler, who said the women's movement should be blamed for "failing to help women order their priorities."[54] Siegler charged, "It [the women's movement] didn't outline the consequences. We were never told, 'While you're climbing up the corporate ladder, don't forget to pick up a husband and child.'"

ABC's 1986 special, "After the Sexual Revolution," also told single women to hold feminism responsible for their marital status.[55] Women's success has come "at the cost of relationships," co-host Richard Threlkeld said. Even married women are in danger, he advised: "The more women achieve in their careers, the higher their chances for divorce." Co-host Betsy Aaron concurred: Feminists never "calculated *that* as a price of the revolution, freedom and independence turning to loneliness and depression." It wasn't a trade-off Aaron could have deduced from her own life: she had a successful career and a husband—co-host Threlkeld.

The media's preoccupation with single women's miseries reared up suddenly in the mid-1980s. Between 1980 and 1982, as one study has noted, national magazines ran only five feature articles about single women; between 1983 and 1986, they ran fifty-three—and almost all were critical or pitying.[56] (Only seven articles about single men ran in this same period.) The headlines spoke bleakly of THE SAD PLIGHT OF SINGLE WOMEN, THE TERMINALLY SINGLE WOMAN, and SINGLE SHOCK.[57] To be unwed and female was to succumb to an illness with only one known cure: marriage.

The press contributed to single women's woes as much as it reported on them, by redefining single women's low social status as a personal defect. The media spoke ominously of single women's "growing isolation"—but it was an isolation that trend journalism helped create and enforce. In the '70s, the media's accounts featured photos and stories of real single women, generally in groups. In the '80s, the press offered drawings of fictional single women and tales of "composite" or "anonymous" single women—almost always depicted alone, hugging a tear-stained pillow, or gazing forlornly from a garret window. *McCall's* described the prototype this way: "She's the workaholic, who may enjoy an occasional dinner with friends but more likely spends most of her time alone in her apartment, where she nightly retreats as her own best friend."[58]

Just as the press had ignored the social inequalities that cause career women to "burn out," it depoliticized the situation of single women. While '70s press reports had chipped away at the social stigma that hurt single women, the '80s media maintained, with the aid of pop psychologists, that single women's troubles were all self-generated. As a therapist maintained in the *New York Times* story on single women, "Women are in this situation because of neurotic conflicts." This therapist was even saying it about herself; she told the *Times* she had entered "intensive analysis" to cure herself of this singular distaff disorder.

The media's presentation of single women as mental patients is a well-worn backlash tradition. In the late Victorian press, single women were declared victims of "andromania" and "marriage dread."[59] After briefly rehabilitating single women as sprightly "bachelor girls" in the early 1900s, the press condemned them to the mental ward once more for the duration of the Depression. In the '30s, *Good Housekeeping* conducted a poll of single career women that looked for signs of psychic distress. When the single women all said they were quite satisfied with their lives, the magazine inquired hopefully, "May not some of them have hidden a longing that hurt like a wound . . . as they bent above some crib and listened to the heavy sleeping breath that rhythmed from rosy lips?"[60] And yet again in the '50s, a parade of psychoanalysts led by Marynia Farnham and Ferdinand Lundberg, authors of the 1947 leading manual, *Modern Woman: The Lost Sex,* marched through the women's magazines, declaring single women "defeminized" and "deeply ill."

When the backlash press wasn't labeling single women mental misfits, it was busy counting the bodies. Not only were single women sick, the media pundits warned, they were outnumbered—a message that only helped to elevate anxiety levels. The late Victorian press was obsessed with calculating the exact number of "excess" or "redundant" single women; national periodicals printed graphs and tables listing the overabundance of unaccounted-for women. "Why Is Single Life Becoming More General?" *The Nation* pondered in 1868, noting that the issue "is fast getting into the category of topics of universal discussion."[61] The ratio was so bad, *Harper's Bazaar* exclaimed in 1874, that men could get "wives at discount," and "eight melancholy maids" clung to the same bachelor's arm at parties.[62] "The universal cry is 'No husbands! No husbands!'" (Feminist ideas, the magazine was quick to add, were to blame for this "dreadful" situation: "Many 'advanced women' forgot that there can be no true progress for them save in the company of, not in opposition to, men.")

By the mid-1980s, the media was busy once more counting heads in the single-woman pool and issuing charts that supposedly proved a surplus of unattached women, which the press now called "the spinster boom" and "hypermaidenism."[63] The most legendary tally sheet appeared in *Newsweek.* "If You're a Single Woman, Here Are Your Chances of Getting Married," the headline on *Newsweek*'s June 2, 1986 cover helpfully announced. The accompanying graph plunged like the north face of the Matterhorn, its color scheme changing from hot red to frigid blue as it slid past thirty—and into Old Maid free-fall. "The traumatic news came buried in an arid demographic study," *Newsweek*'s story began, "titled innocently enough, 'Marriage Patterns in the United States.'[64] But the dire statistics confirmed what everybody suspected all along: that many women who seem to have it all—good looks and good jobs, advanced degrees and high salaries—will never have mates."

Newsweek took the flawed and unpublished Harvard-Yale marriage study and promoted it to cover-story celebrity status. A few months later, the magazine received the more comprehensive U.S. Census Bureau marriage study and shrank it to a two-paragraph item buried in the "Update" column.[65] Why? Eloise Salholz, *Newsweek*'s lead writer on the marriage study story, later explains the showcasing of the Harvard-Yale study in this way: "We all knew this was happening before that study came out. The study summarized impressions we already had."[66]

The *New York Times* assigned a staff writer to the Harvard-Yale study and produced a lengthy story.[67] But when it came time to cover the Census Bureau study, the *Times* didn't even waste a staff writer's time; it just used a brief wire story and buried it.[68] And almost a year after demographers had discredited the Harvard-Yale study, the *New York Times* ran a front-page story on how women were suffering from this putative man shortage, citing the Harvard-Yale study as proof.[69] Asked to explain this later, the story's author, Jane Gross, says, "It was untimely, I agree."[70] But the story was assigned to her, so she made the best of it. The article dealt with the fact that the study had been invalidated by dismissing the entire critique as "rabid reaction from feminists."[71]

Some of the press's computations on the marriage crunch were at remedial levels. The *Newsweek* story declared that single women "are more likely to be killed by a terrorist" than marry.[72] Maybe *Newsweek* was only trying to be metaphorical, but the terrorist line got repeated with somber literalness in many women's magazines, talk shows, and advice books. "Do you know that . . . forty-year-olds are more likely to be killed by a terrorist than find a husband?"[73] gasped the press release that came with Tracy Cabot's *How to Make a Man Fall in Love with You.* A former *Newsweek* bureau intern who was involved in the story's preparation later explains how the terrorist analogy wound up in the magazine: "What happened is, one of the bureau reporters was going around saying it as a joke—like, 'Yeah, a woman's more likely to get bumped off by a terrorist'—and next thing we knew, one of the writers in New York took it seriously and it ended up in print."[74]

Newsweek's "marriage crunch" story, like its story on a "mother's choice," was a parable masquerading as a numbers report. It presented the "man shortage" as a moral comeuppance for independent-minded women who expected too much. *Newsweek*'s preachers found single women guilty of at least three deadly sins: Greed—they put their high-paying careers before the quest for a husband.[75] Pride—they acted "as though it were not worth giving up space in their closets for anything less than Mr. Perfect." And sloth—they weren't really out there beating the bushes; "even though they say they want to marry, they may not want it enough."

Now came judgment day. "For many economically independent women, the consequences of their actions have begun to set in," *Newsweek* intoned.[76] "For years bright young women single-mindedly pursued their careers, assuming that when it was time for a husband they could pencil one in. They were wrong." *Newsweek* urged young women to learn from the mistakes of their feminist elders: "Chastened by the news that delaying equals forgoing, they just may want to give thought to the question [of marriage] sooner than later."

For the further edification of the young, *Newsweek* lined up errant aging spinsters like sinners before the confessional grate and piously recorded their regrets: "Susan Cohen wishes she had been able to see her way clear to the altar.[77] 'Not being of sound mind,' she refused several marriage proposals when she was younger." Pediatrician Catherine Casey told the magazine's inquisitors, "I never doubted I would marry, but I wasn't ready at twenty-two. I was more interested in going to school. . . . Now my time clock is striking midnight."

Parading the penitent unwed became a regular media tearjerker, and it was on the network news programs that the melodrama enjoyed its longest run. "CBS Morning News" devoted a *five*-day special in 1987 to the regrets of single women.[78] Just like the timing of the *Newsweek* story, the show was graciously aired in the wedding month of June. "We thought we were going to be dating for twenty-five years," one woman moaned. "We'll be sitting here in our forties and our biological clocks will have stopped," wailed another. The relentless CBS newscaster behaved as if she were directing an on-air group therapy session. "Have you always been this way?" she pressed her patients. "What are you scared of?" "Do you all have strong relationships with your dads?" "Did you learn to talk as kids?"

ABC took television psychiatry one step further in its three-hour special in 1986.[79] Not only did the network hire a psychiatrist to serve as a behind-the-scenes consultant, the newscaster managed to badger one of the program's subjects into an on-camera breakdown. Laura Slutsky, thirty-seven and single, the president of her own company, tried to explain that while living alone could be a "difficult challenge," she was determined to "make my life work." "I'll do it," she said, "I'll be classy about it, at times." But the interviewer would have none of it and kept at her. Finally:

> *Interviewer:* Face that fear a minute for me.
>
> *Slutsky:* Wait a second, this is not easy stuff. [starts to cry] The fear of being alone is not—I don't like it. I'll do it though. Why am I crying? I don't know why I'm crying. . . . These are hard questions. . . . But I'll do it. I'll do it. I don't want to do it. I don't want to do it.

Apparently still not sated, ABC aired another special the following year, this one the four-day "Single in America."[80] Co-anchor Kathleen Sullivan set the tone in the opening segment: "Well, when I first heard that we were going to do this," she announced on the air, "I said, so what? I mean, who cares about singles? They don't have responsibilities of family. They're only career-motivated." But, she added generously, she's learned to pity them: "I at first wasn't compassionate, but now I am." . . .

Despite the title "Single in America," the network program never addressed the status of single men. The omission was typical. The promotional literature for ABC's "After the Sexual Revolution" actually promised to discuss the impact on men. But it never did. Asked to explain the omission later, co-host Richard Threlkeld says, "There wasn't any time. We only had three hours."[81]

When the press did manage to fit the single man into its busy schedule, it was not to extend condolences. On the cover of the *New York Times* Sunday magazine, a single man luxuriated in his well-appointed bachelor pad. Reclining on his parquet floor, his electric guitar by his side, he was casually reading a book and enjoying (much to the joy of the magazine's cigarette advertisers, no doubt) a smoke. WHY WED? was the headline.[82] Inside, the story's author Trip Gabriel clucked patronizingly about the "worries" of "the army of single women in their thirties." Of single men, however, he had this to say: "I was impressed by the men I talked with" and "I came away thinking bachelorhood a viable choice." Even the men who seemed to be avoiding women altogether earned his praise. He saw nothing wrong, for example, with a thirty-year-old man who recoiled from Saturday night dates because "Sunday's my game day." Nor did he wonder about a thirty-five-year-old single sports photographer who told him, "To me, relationships always seemed very stifling." Instead,

Gabriel praised his bachelorhood as a "mature decision."

Having whipped single women into high marital panic—or "nuptialitis," as one columnist called it—the press hastened to soothe fretted brows with conjugal tonic.[83] In what amounted to an enormous dose of free publicity for the matchmaking and bridal industries, the media helped peddle exorbitant miracle cures for the mentally, and statistically, handicapped single women—with scores of stories on $1,000 "How to Marry the Man of Your Choice" workshops, $4,600 dating service memberships that guaranteed marriage within three years, and $25,000 matchmaking consultations.[84] "Time is running out for single people," a *San Francisco Chronicle* columnist (himself an aging bachelor) advised, and then turned his column over to a dating service owner who was anxious to promote her new business: "There's a terrific scramble going on now," she alerted single women, "and in two years there just isn't going to be anyone left out there. There aren't going to be all these great surplus older guys."[85] The media even offered their own coaching and counseling assistance. *New York* trotted out inspirational role models—single women who managed to marry after forty. "When they really decided to set their sights on a marriageable man," the article, entitled "Brides at Last," declared, "they found one."[86] *USA Today* even played doctor, offering a special hot line for troubled singles—with psychologists working the phones.[87] The telephone monitors confessed to being "startled" at the results: lovelorn male callers outnumbered women—by two to one.

Women's magazines rose most grandly to the occasion. Nuptialitis was, after all, their specialty. *Cosmopolitan*'s February 1989 issue offered an eleven-page guide to oiling the husband trap, under the businesslike title "How to Close the Deal."[88] The magazine lectured, "You've read the statistics: More women than men practically everywhere but San Quentin. . . . You have to tidy up your act. *Starting right now.*" Its get-married-quick pointers were all on loan from the last backlash's advice books. Among them: pretend to be less sexually experienced than you are, play up your knitting and cooking skills, let him do most of the talking, and be "extremely accepting." At *Mademoiselle,* similar 1950s-style words of wisdom were on tap: the magazine promoted "The Return of Hard-to-Get," advised women to guard their "dating reputation," and reminded them, "Smart Cookies Don't Phone First."[89] And a *New Woman* cover story by Dr. Joyce Brothers offered some old advice for gold-band hunters: "Why You Shouldn't Move In With Your Lover."[90]

While the press was busy pressing single women into marriage, it was simultaneously ordering already married women to stay put. One effective holding action: spreading fear about life after divorce. In 1986, NBC ran a special report that focused exclusively on "the negative consequences of divorce." *Cosmopolitan* offered a four-page feature wholly devoted to divorce's drawbacks. "Singlehood seems so tempting when you're wrangling bitterly," it instructed.[91] "But be forewarned: More and more marital veterans and experts in the field are cautioning potential divorcées to be wary—extremely wary—of eight common, dangerous delusions [about divorce]." For women, the press reported over and over again, broken wedding vows lead to severe depression, a life of loneliness, and an empty bank account.

To stave off divorce, the media once more came to the rescue with friendly advice and stern moral lectures. CBS revived "Can This Marriage Be Saved?"—the old *Ladies' Home Journal* feature—as a nationwide talk show in 1989, offering on-air reconciliation for couples with rocky relations.[92] "How to Stay Married" was *Newsweek*'s offering—a 1987 cover story replete with uplifting case studies of born-again couples who had gone "right to the edge" before finding "salvation," usually through a therapist's divine intervention.[93] Several marital counselors made promotional appearances in these pages, one hawking a sixteen-week marital improvement program—for newlyweds.

"How times have changed!" *Newsweek* wrote.[94] "Americans are taking marriage more seriously." The magazine had no evidence that a marital boom was in progress. All it could produce was this flimsy statistic: an insignificant 0.2 percent drop in the divorce rate.

INFERTILITY ILLNESS AND BABY FEVERS

"Is this surge in infertility the yuppie disease of the '80s?" NBC correspondent Maria Shriver asked in a 1987 special report.[95] Could it be, she worried, turning to her lineup of experts, that barren wombs have become "The Curse of the Career Woman"? Her experts, infertility doctors hawking costly experimental cures, were only too happy to agree.

By now, the trend journalists had it down; they barely needed an expert to point out the enemy. If it was a woman's problem, then they knew women's quest for independence and equality must be to blame. In the case of the "curse of the career woman," the witch casting the spell must be carrying her own wallet—with, doubtless, a NOW membership card inside. The headlines made it clear why women's wombs were drying up: "Having It All: Postponing Parenthood Exacts a Price"[96] and "The Quiet Pain of Infertility: For the Success-Oriented, It's a Bitter Pill."[97] As a *New York Times* columnist asserted, the infertile woman today is "a walking cliché" of the feminist generation, "a woman on the cusp of forty who put work ahead of motherhood."[98]

Newsweek devoted two cover stories to the "trend of childlessness."[99] Between shots of lone career women in corner offices and lone teddy bears in empty cribs, *Newsweek* warned that as many as 20 percent of women in their early to mid-thirties will end up with no babies of their own—and "those numbers will be even higher for women with high-powered careers, the experts say."[100] The expert that *Newsweek* used to support this point was none other than Harvard economist David Bloom, co-author of the infamous Harvard-Yale marriage study.[101] Now he was saying that 30 percent of all female managers will wind up childless.

Not to be upstaged in the motherhood department, *Life* issued its own special report, "Baby Craving," which said that "millions" of career women will "pay a price for waiting."[102] *Life* produced photographic evidence: Mary Chase, a forty-two-year-old writer and producer, who stared contritely at an empty bassinet. In subsequent snapshots, Mary was examined by an infertility specialist, bared her back to an acupuncturist attempting to "stimulate the energy," sought counsel from a male psychic claiming to have inspired one pregnancy, stood on her head in her underwear after having sex, and opened her mouth wide for husband Bill, who peered in and tried "to uncover early traumas that might block Mary's ability to conceive." The couple didn't know the cause of their fertility troubles, so it was just as likely that Bill's "early traumas" were the problem. (Infertility odds are the same for both sexes.) But the *Life* story never dealt with that possibility.

As in all trend stories, the data supporting the infertility epidemic were nonexistent, so the magazines had to fudge. "It's hard to tell, but infertility may be on the rise," *Newsweek* said.[103] "There are few good statistical measures of how infertility has overtaken our lives," *Life* said.[104] Of course, plenty of good statistical measures existed; they just didn't uphold the story of the "curse of the career woman." Some magazine articles got around the lack of proof by simply shifting to the future tense. *Mademoiselle,* for example, offered this prediction—in upper-case type: THE INFERTILITY EPIDEMIC IS COMING.[105] And a 1982 feature in the *New York Times* just cast aspersions on all skeptics.[106] Women in their thirties who don't believe their infertility odds are high must be suffering "on an emotional level" from "a need to deny the findings."

The week that this *New York Times* feature ran, women who subscribed to both the *Times* and *Time* magazine must have been bewildered. While the *Times* was busy bemoaning the empty wombs of thirty-plus professional women—it ran, in fact, two such stories that week—*Time* was burbling about all the inhabited ones. The newsweekly was pushing the other half of the trend pair: a baby boomlet. "Career women are opting for pregnancy and they are doing it in style," the magazine cheered in its cover story entitled "The New Baby Bloom."[107] Once again, federal Census numbers didn't bear *Time* out; the birthrate had not changed for more than a decade. But that was beside the point. The baby-boomlet trend was only a carrot for the infertility epidemic's stick. *Time* made that clear when it complemented its boomlet story with this cautionary sidebar article: "The Medical Risks of Waiting."[108]

To get around the lack of data, *Time* resorted to the familiar trend euphemisms: "More and more career women," it asserted, "are choosing pregnancy before the clock strikes twelve."[109] Then it quickly directed readers' attention to a handful of pregnant movie stars and media celebrities. Former "Charlie's Angels" actress Jaclyn Smith and Princess Diana were expecting, so it must be a national phenomenon.

Time wasn't the only publication to substitute a few starlets for many numbers. *McCall's* gushed over "Hollywood's Late-Blooming Moms."[110] *Vogue*'s story on "baby fever" exulted over still another mom from the "Charlie's Angels" set: "Motherhood is consuming Farrah Fawcett. All she wants to talk about is breast-feeding."[111] Reaching even farther afield for evidence of baby mania, the press made much of this bulletin from a zoo official claiming to communicate with a primate: "Koko the Gorilla Tells Keeper She Would Like to Have a Baby."[112] And, just as it had done with single women, the media sought to induce pregnancy with counseling and even prizes. Radio stations in Iowa and Florida sponsored "Breeder's Cup" contests—a $1,000 savings bond, six months' diaper service, and a crib to the first couple to conceive.[113]

The mythical "baby bloom" inspired even more florid tributes on the press's editorial pages. The *San Francisco Chronicle* waxed eloquent:

> In our personal life, we must observe, we have noted an absolute blossoming of both marriages and of births to many women who seemed, not all that long ago, singlemindedly devoted to the pursuit of personal careers. It's nice to hear again the sound of wedding bells and the gurgles of contented babies in the arms of their mothers.[114]

In less purply prose, the *New York Times* conveyed the same sentiments:

> Some college alumnae answered 25th reunion questionnaires with the almost-guilty admission that they were "only" wives and mothers. But before long, other women found that success at jobs traditionally held by men doesn't infallibly produce a fulfilling life. Motherhood started to come back in style.[115]

If the articles didn't increase the birthrate, it did increase women's anxiety and guilt. "You can't pick up a magazine without reading about another would-be-mom with a fertility problem that might have been less complicated if she had just started at an earlier age," a young woman wrote in an op-ed essay in the *New York Times,* entitled "Motherhood's Better Before Thirty."[116] She was upset, but not with the media for terrorizing women. She was mad at the older women who seemed to think it was safe to wait. "I believe it is my birthright to follow a more biologically sound reproductive schedule," she sniffed, sounding suspiciously MBA-ish under those maternity clothes.

Simply being able to recognize the media onslaught put that young writer ahead of a lot of other women readers who, wondering why they suddenly felt desperate, unworthy, and shameful for failing to reproduce on the media's schedule, decided the signals were coming exclusively from their bodies, not their newspapers. "I wasn't even thinking about having a child, and suddenly, when I was about thirty-four, it gripped

me like a claw," a woman confided in *Vogue.*[117] "It was as if I had nothing to do with it, and these raging hormones were saying, 'Do what you are supposed to do, which is reproduce.' It was a physical feeling more than a mental feeling."

In the end, this would be the press's greatest contribution to the backlash: not only dictating to women how they should feel, but persuading them that the voice barking orders was only their uterus talking. . . .

NOTES

1. The first action of the . . . : Klein, *Gender Politics,* pp. 23–24.
2. (The only two such . . .): Joanna Foley Martin. "Confessions of a Non-Bra Burner," *Chicago Journalism Review,* July 1971, 4:11.
3. The "grand press blitz" . . . : Jo Freeman, *The Politics of Women's Liberation: A Case Study of an Emerging Social Movement and Its Relation to the Policy Process* (New York: David McKay, 1975) p. 148; Edith Hoshino Altbach, *Women in America* (Lexington, Mass.: D.C. Heath and Co., 1974) pp. 157–58. For an example of the media using the "bra-burning" myth to invalidate the women's movement, see Judy Klemesrud, "In Small Town USA, Women's Liberation Is Either a Joke or a Bore," *New York Times,* March 22, 1972, p. 54.
4. At *Newsday,* a male . . . : Sandie North, "Reporting the Movement," *The Atlantic,* March 1970, p. 105.
5. At *Newsweek,* Lynn . . . : *Ibid.*
6. (This tactic backfired . . .): "Women in Revolt," *Newsweek,* March 23, 1970, p. 78. Helen Dudar, the *Newsweek* editor's wife, confessed that after having "spent years rejecting feminists without bothering to look too closely at their charges," she had become a convert and wrote that she now felt a "sense of pride and kinship with all those women who have been asking all the hard questions. I thank them and so, I think, will a lot of other women."
7. Hanes issued its . . . : Veronica Geng, "Requiem for the Women's Movement," *Harper's,* Nov. 1976, p. 49.
8. UP THE LADDER . . . : "Up the Ladder, Finally," *Business Week,* Nov. 24, 1975, p. 58.
9. Feminism is "dead" . . . : See, for example, Sally Ogle Davis, "Is Feminism Dead?" *Los Angeles,* Feb. 1989, p. 114.
10. "The women's movement is over . . .": Betty Friedan, "Feminism's Next Step," *The New York Times Magazine,* July 5, 1981, p. 14.
11. In case readers . . . : Susan Bolotin, "Voices from the Post-Feminist Generation," *The New York Times Magazine,* Oct. 17, 1982, p. 29.
12. "What has happened to . . .": "After the Sexual Revolution," *ABC News Closeup,* July 30, 1986.
13. *Newsweek* raised . . . : Eloise Salholz, "Feminism's Identity Crisis," *Newsweek,* March 31, 1986, p. 58.
14. (This happens to be . . .): *Newsweek,* March 7, 1960, cited in Friedan, *Feminine Mystique,* pp. 19–20.
15. The first article sneering . . . : "Superwoman," *Independent,* Feb. 21, 1907, cited in Kinnard, *Antifeminism,* p. 214.
16. Feminists, according to the . . . : *Ibid.,* pp. 55–61, xiii–ix.
17. And repetition . . . : In 1982, fifty corporations controlled over half the media business; by the end of 1987, the number was down to twenty-six. See Ben H. Bagdikian, *The Media Monopoly* (Boston: Beacon Press, 1990), pp. xix, 3–4; *Media Report to Women,* Sept. 1987, p. 4.
18. Fear was also driving . . . : After 1985, profit margins fell steadily at papers owned by publicly traded communications companies. Women, who make up the majority of newspaper readers and network news viewers, were turning to specialty publications and cable news programs in mass numbers, taking mass advertising dollars with them. See Alex S. Jones, "Rethinking Newspapers," *New York Times,* Jan. 6, 1991, III, p. 1; "Marketing Newspapers to Women," *Women Scope Surveys of Women,* 2, no. 7 (April 1989): 1–2.
19. Anxiety-ridden . . . : In a typical media strategy of the decade, Knight-Ridder Newspapers launched a "customer-obsession" campaign to give readers what management imagined they wanted, rather than what was simply news.
20. "News organizations are . . .": Bill Kovach, "Too Much Opinion, at the Expense of Fact," *New York Times,* Sept. 13, 1989, p. A31.

21. NBC, for instance . . . : "Bad Girls," *NBC News,* August 30, 1989.
22. "The media are having . . .": "The Next Trend: Here Comes the Bribe," *Advertising Age,* June 16, 1986, p. 40.
23. The "marriage panic" . . . : "Women's Views Survey: Women's Changing Hopes, Fears, Loves," *Glamour,* Jan. 1988, p. 142.
24. In 1988, this "trend" . . . : Mark Clements Research, Women's Views Survey, 1988.
25. Again, in 1986 . . . : *Ibid.*
26. But it wasn't until . . . : Amy Saltzman, "Trouble at the Top," *U.S. News & World Report,* June 17, 1991, p. 40.
27. THE UNDECLARED WAR . . . : Carol Pogash, "The Undeclared War," *San Francisco Examiner,* Feb. 5, 1989, p. E1.
28. *Child* magazine offered . . . : Sue Woodman, "The Mommy Wars," *Child,* Sept.–Oct. 1989, p. 139; Barbara J. Berg, "Women at Odds," *Savvy,* Dec. 1985, p. 24.
29. IS HE SEPARABLE?" . . . : Kate White, "Is He Separable?" *Newsday,* May 15, 1988, p. 25.
30. The ABC report . . . : Transcript, "After the Sexual Revolution."
31. Popcorn borrowed . . . : Alex Taylor III, "Why Women Are Bailing Out," *Fortune,* August 18, 1986, p. 16.
32. The article about . . . : *USA Today's* story was, in fact, a report on the *Fortune* "findings": "1 in 3 Management Women Drop Out," *USA Today,* July 31, 1986, p. 1.
33. A year later at Stanford . . . : Personal interviews with a group of female Stanford MBA students, Summer 1988.
34. The year after *Fortune* . . . : Laurie Baum, "For Women, the Bloom Might Be Off the MBA," *Business Week,* March 14, 1988, p. 30.
35. Witham is "happier . . .": Taylor, "Bailing Out," pp. 16–23.
36. "He had this anecdotal evidence . . .": Personal interview with Alex Taylor III, 1988.
37. "I told him . . .": Personal interview with Mary Anne Devanna, 1988.
38. "The evidence is . . .": Personal interview with Taylor, 1988. (Subsequent quotes are from personal interview with Taylor unless otherwise noted.)
39. "A woman who wants marriage . . .": Stratford P. Sherman, "The Party May Be Ending," *Fortune,* Nov. 24, 1986, p. 29.
40. In fact, in 1987, . . . : F. S. Chapman, "Executive Guilt: Who's Taking Care of the Children?" *Fortune,* Feb. 16, 1987. A later review of the alumni records at Columbia University's Graduate School of Business for the class of '70 (the same class that Taylor's story focused on) found no significant female defection from the corporate world and no differences in the proportion of men and women leaving to start their own businesses. See Mary Anne Devanna, "Women in Management: Progress and Promise," *Human Resource Management,* 26, no. 4 (Winter 1987): 469.
41. "The national pollsters were . . . : The 1986 Virginia Slims Opinion Poll; Walsh, "What Women Want," p. 60. A survey conducted jointly by *Working Woman* and *Success* magazines also found that men were more concerned about family life than women and less concerned about career success than women. See Carol Sonenklar, "Women and Their Magazines," *American Demographics,* June 1986, p. 44.
42. In fact, a 1989 survey . . . : Margaret King, "An Alumni Survey Dispels Some Popular Myths About MBA Graduates," *Stanford Business School Magazine,* March 1989, p. 23.
43. "In all respects, young . . .": Philip H. Dougherty, "Women's Self Esteem Up," *New York Times,* May 15, 1974, p. 71.
44. "Within just . . .": "Games Singles Play," *Newsweek,* July 16, 1973, p. 52.
45. The stereotype got so bad . . . : Susan Jacoby, "49 Million Singles Can't All Be Right," *The New York Times Magazine,* Feb. 17, 1974, p. 12.
46. "Dropout Wives . . .": Enid Nemy, "Dropout Wives—Their Number Is Growing," *New York Times,* Feb. 16, 1973, p. 44.
47. According to *Newsweek* . . . : "Games Singles Play," p. 52.
48. *Newsweek* was now . . . : Eloise Salholz, "The Marriage Crunch: If You're a Single Woman, Here Are Your Chances of Getting Married," *Newsweek,* p. 54; Jane Gross, "Single Women: Coping With a Void," *New York Times,* April 28, 1987, p. 1.
49. "TOO LATE FOR . . .": Salholz, "Marriage Crunch," p. 54.

50. On the front page . . . : Gross, “Single Women,” p. 1.
51. *New York* magazine’s . . . : Patricia Morrisroe, “Born Too Late? Expect Too Much? You May Be Forever Single,” *New York,* Aug. 20, 1984, p. 24.
52. “Loveless, Manless . . .”: “Loveless, Manless: The High Cost of Independence,” *Chatelaine,* Sept. 1984, p. 60.
53. “Feminism became a new form . . .”: Tricia Crane, “Are You Turning Men Off? Desperate and Demanding,” *Harper’s Bazaar,* Sept. 1987, p. 300.
54. *New York*’s story . . . : Morrisroe, “Born Too Late?” p. 30.
55. ABC’s 1986 special . . . : ABC News, “After the Sexual Revolution.”
56. Between 1980 and 1982 . . . : Trimberger, “Single Women and Feminism in the 1980s.”
57. The headlines spoke . . . : “The Sad Plight of Single Women,” *Philadelphia Inquirer,* Nov. 30, 1980; Kiki Olson, “Sex and the Terminally Single Woman (There Just Aren’t Any Good Men Around),” *Philadelphia Magazine,* April 1984, p. 122.
58. *McCall’s* described . . . : Peter Filichia, “The Lois Lane Syndrome: Waiting for Superman,” *McCall’s,* Aug. 1985, p. 55.
59. In the late Victorian . . . : Kinnard, *Antifeminism,* p. 202.
60. “May not some . . .”: Kessler-Harris, *Out to Work,* p. 255.
61. “Why Is Single Life . . .”: “Why Is Single Life Becoming More General?” *The Nation,* March 5, 1868, pp. 190–91.
62. The ratio was so bad . . . . “Wives at Discount,” *Harper’s Bazaar,* Jan. 31, 1874, p. 74.
63. By the mid-1980s . . . : Billie Samkoff, “How to Attract Men Like Crazy,” *Cosmopolitan,* Feb. 1989, p. 168.
64. “The traumatic news . . .”: Salholz, “Marriage Crunch,” p. 25.
65. A few months later . . . : David Gates, “Second Opinion,” Update, *Newsweek,* Oct. 13, 1986, p. 10.
66. “We all knew . . .”: Personal interview with Eloise Salholz, July 1986.
67. The *New York Times* . . . : William R. Greer, “The Changing Women’s Marriage Market,” *New York Times,* Feb. 22, 1986, p. 48.
68. But when it came time . . . : AP, “More Women Postponing Marriage,” *New York Times,* Dec. 10, 1986, p. A22.
69. And almost a year after . . . : Gross, “Single Women,” p. 1.
70. “It was untimely . . .”: Personal interview with Jane Gross, 1988.
71. The article dealt with . . . : Gross, “Single Women,” p. 1.
72. The *Newsweek* story . . . : Salholz, “Marriage Crunch,” p. 55.
73. “Do you know that . . .”: Promotional letter from Dell Publishing Co., from Carol Tavoularis, Dell publicist, Dec. 5, 1986.
74. A former *Newsweek* bureau . . . : Personal interview, Oct. 1986.
75. *Newsweek*’s preachers . . . : Salholz, “Marriage Crunch,” pp. 61, 57.
76. “For many economically . . .”: *Ibid.,* pp. 61, 55.
77. “Susan Cohen wishes . . .”: *Ibid.,* p. 57.
78. “CBS Morning News” devoted . . . : “CBS Morning News,” “What Do Single Women Want,” Nov. 2–6, 1987.
79. ABC took television . . . : ABC News, “After the Sexual Revolution.”
80. Apparently still not . . . : ABC, “Good Morning America,” “Single in America,” May 4–7, 1987.
81. “There wasn’t any time . . .”: Personal interview with Richard Threlkeld, 1988.
82. “WHY WED?” . . . : Trip Gabriel, “Why Wed?: The Ambivalent American Bachelor,” *The New York Times Magazine,* Nov. 15, 1987, p. 24.
83. Having whipped . . . : Brenda Lane Richardson, “Dreaming Someone Else’s Dreams,” *The New York Times Magazine,* Jan. 28, 1990, p. 14.
84. In what amounted to . . . : See, for example, Barbara Kantrowitz, “The New Mating Games,” *Newsweek,* June 2, 1986, p. 58; James Hirsch, “Modern Matchmaking: Money’s Allure in Marketing Mates and Marriage,” *New York Times,* Sept. 19, 1988, p. B4, Ruthe Stein, “New Strategies for Singles,” *San Francisco Chronicle,* March 29, 1988, p. B1.
85. “Time is running out . . .”: Gerald Nachman, “Going Out of Business Sale on Singles,” *San Francisco Chronicle,* Dec. 1, 1987, p. B3.
86. “When they really decided . . .”: Barbara Lovenheim, “Brides at Last: Women Over 40 Who Beat the Odds,” *New York,* Aug. 3, 1987, p. 20.

87. *USA Today* even . . . : Marlene J. Perrin, "What Do Women Today Really Want?" *USA Today,* July 10, 1986, pp. D1, D5; Karen S. Peterson, "Men Bare Their Souls, Air Their Gripes," *USA Today,* July 14, 1986, p. D1. And the women who called weren't all pleading for a man: "How do you get people to stop asking why I'm not married yet?" was the question posed by one thirty-two-year-old woman from Virginia. See Peterson, "Stop Asking Why I'm Not Married," p. D4.
88. *Cosmopolitan*'s February . . . : Samkoff, "How To Attract Men," pp. 163–73.
89. At *Mademoiselle* . . . : Personal interview with *Mademoiselle* editors, 1988; Cathryn Jakobson, "The Return of Hard-to-Get," March 1987, p. 220.
90. And a *New Woman* . . . : Dr. Joyce Brothers, "Why You Shouldn't Move in With Your Lover," *New Woman,* March 1985, p. 54.
91. "Singlehood seems so . . .": Jeffrey Kluger, "Dangerous Delusions About Divorce," *Cosmopolitan,* Sept. 1984, p. 291.
92. CBS revived . . . : Sue Adolphson, "Marriage Encounter, Tube Style," *San Francisco Chronicle,* Datebook, Jan. 22, 1989, p. 47.
93. "How to Stay Married" . . . : Barbara Kantrowitz, "How To Stay Married," *Newsweek,* August 24, 1987, p. 52.
94. "How times have . . .": *Ibid.*
95. "Is this surge . . .": NBC News Special, "The Baby Business," April 4, 1987.
96. "Having It All . . .": "Having It All: Postponing Parenthood Exacts a Price," *Boston* magazine, May 1987, p. 116.
97. "The Quiet Pain . . .": Mary C. Hickey, "The Quiet Pain of Infertility: For the Success-Oriented, It's a Bitter Pill," *Washington Post,* April 28, 1987, p. DO5.
98. As a *New York Times* . . . : Fleming, "The Infertile Sisterhood," p. B1.
99. *Newsweek* devoted two . . . : Matt Clark, "Infertility," *Newsweek,* Dec. 6, 1982, p. 102; Barbara Kantrowitz, "No Baby on Board," *Newsweek,* Sept. 1, 1986, p. 68.
100. *Newsweek* warned . . . : Kantrowitz, "No Baby," p. 74.
101. The expert that *Newsweek* . . . : *Ibid.*
102. Not to be upstaged . . . : Anna Quindlen, "Special

PERSONAL ACCOUNT

Just Something You Did as a Man

In a class we had discussed the ways men stratify themselves in terms of masculinity. I decided I would put that discussion to the test at work.

As I sat at a table, one of my coworkers approached me with a copy of a popular men's magazine, which portrays nude women. He said, "Frank, there is this bitch in here with the most beautiful big tits I have ever seen in my life." I told him that I wasn't interested in looking at the magazine because I had decided I did not agree with the objectification of women. His reply was, "What's the matter, are you getting soft on us?" I joked that it was not a matter of getting soft, it was simply a decision I had made due to a "new and improved consciousness."

At my job, talk about homosexuals, the women who walk by, and graphic (verbal) depictions of sexual aggression toward women abound, but on this occasion I either rejected the conversation or said nothing at all. By the end of the day I was being called, sometimes jokingly and sometimes not, every derogatory homosexual slur in the English language. I was no longer "one of the boys." I did not engage in the "manly" discourse of the day so therefore I was labeled (at best) a "sissy."

My coworkers assumed that I had had or was about to have a change of sexual orientation simply because I did not engage in their conversations about women and homosexuals. Since men decide how masculine another man is by how much he is willing to put down women and gays, I was no longer considered masculine.

This experience affected me as much as it did because it opened my eyes to a system of stratification in which I have been immersed but still had no idea existed. Demeaning women and homosexuals, to me, was just something you did as a man. But to tell you the truth, I don't think I could go back to talking like that. I am sure that my coworkers will get used to my new thinking, but even if they don't I believe that it is worth being rejected for a cause such as this. I had not thought about it, but I would not want men talking about my sisters and mother in such a demeaning way.

Francisco Hernandez

Report: Baby Craving: Facing Widespread Infertility, A Generation Presses the Limits of Medicine and Morality," *Life,* June 1987, p. 23.

103. "It's hard to tell, but . . .": Clark, "Infertility," p. 102.
104. "There are few . . .": Quindlen, "Baby Craving," p. 23.
105. *Mademoiselle,* for example . . . : Laura Flynn McCarthy, "Caution: You Are Now Entering the Age of Infertility," *Mademoiselle,* May 1988, p. 230.
106. And a 1982 . . . : Georgia Dullea, "Women Reconsider Childbearing Over 30," *New York Times,* Feb. 25, 1982, p. C1.
107. "Career women are opting . . .": J. D. Reed, "The New Baby Bloom," *Time,* Feb. 22, 1982, p. 52.
108. *Time* made that . . . : Claudia Wallis, "The Medical Risks of Waiting," *Time,* Feb. 22, 1982, p. 58.
109. "More and more . . .": Reed, "New Baby Bloom," p. 52.
110. *McCall's* gushed . . . : "Hollywood's Late-Blooming Moms," *McCall's,* Oct. 1988, p. 41.
111. "Motherhood is consuming . . .": Leslie Bennetts, "Baby Fever," *Vogue,* Aug. 1985, p. 325.
112. Reaching even farther afield . . . : AP, "Koko the Gorilla Tells Keeper She Would Like to Have a Baby," *San Francisco Chronicle,* March 12, 1988, p. A3.
113. And, just as it had done . . . : Roger Munns, "Couples Race to Get Pregnant," *San Francisco Examiner,* Nov. 19, 1990, p. B5.
114. "In our personal life . . .": "The Marriage Odds Improve," *San Francisco Chronicle,* May 1, 1987, p. 38.
115. "Some college alumnae . . .": "Mothers a la Mode," *New York Times,* May 8, 1988, p. E28. The *Times* editorial writers appeared to have forgotten their own words. Only two months earlier, they had noted that there was no change in the birth rate: "New Baby Boom? No, Just a Dim Echo," *New York Times,* March 30, 1988, p. A26.
116. "You can't pick up a magazine . . .": Kim C. Flodin, "Motherhood's Better Before 30," *New York Times,* Nov. 2, 1989, p. A31.
117. "I wasn't even thinking . . .": Bennetts, "Baby Fever," p. 326.

PERSONAL ACCOUNT

Basketball

I frequently watch my boyfriend play basketball at an outdoor court with many other males in pick-up games. One time when I was there, there was a new face among the others waiting to play—a female face, and she was not sitting with the rest of the women who were watching. She was dressed and ready to play. I had never seen her in all the time I'd been there before, nor had I ever seen another women there try to play.

For several games, she did not play. The guys formed teams and she was not asked to join. It was almost like there was a purposeful avoidance of her, with no one even acknowledging that she was there. Finally, she made a noticeable effort and with some reluctance she was included in the next team waiting to play the winner of the current game. There were whispers and snickers among the guys, and I think it had a lot to do with the perception that she was challenging their masculinity. A "girl" was intruding into their area. My guess is that they were also somewhat nervous about the fact that she really might be good and embarrass some of them.

Anyway, the first couple of times up and down the court she was not given the ball despite the fact that she was wide open. The other guys on the team forced bad shots and tried super hard in what seemed like an effort to prove that she was not needed. The guy who was supposed to guard her on defense really didn't pay her much attention and that same guy who she was guarding at the other end made sure he drove around her and scored on two occasions.

Finally, one time down the court she called for the ball and sank a shot from at least 16 feet. A huge feeling of relief and satisfaction came over me. Being a basketball player myself, I figured she was probably good or would not be there in the first place, but being a woman I was also happy to see her *first* shot go in. I found out later she had played basketball for a university and she had a great outside shot.

Even after she made one more shot off a rebound that ended up in her hands, she was not given the ball again. I suppose after some of the loud comments from some of the guys on the sidelines, that she was beating the male players out there, she wasn't going to get the ball again. I was kind of shocked that she wasn't *more* accepted even after she showed she was talented. I haven't seen her there since.

Andrea M. Busch

READING 43

Ideological Racism and Cultural Resistance

Constructing Our Own Images

Yen Le Espiritu

> The slit-eyed, bucktooth Jap thrusting his bayonet, thirsty for blood. The inscrutable, wily Chinese detective with his taped eyelids and wispy moustache. The childlike, indolent Filipino houseboy. Always giggling. Bowing and scraping. Eager to please, but untrustworthy. The sexless, hairless Asian male. The servile, oversexed Asian female. The Geisha. The sultry, sarong-clad, South Seas maiden. The serpentine, cunning Dragon Lady. Mysterious and evil, eager to please. Effeminate. Untrustworthy. Yellow Peril. Fortune Cookie Psychic. Savage. Dogeater. Invisible. Mute. Faceless peasants breeding too many children. Gooks. Passive Japanese Americans obediently marching off to "relocation camps" during the Second World War.
>
> *Jessica Hagedorn (1993, p. xxii)*

. . . As is evident from the stereotypes listed above, besides structural discrimination, Asian American men and women have been subject to ideological assaults. Focusing on the ideological dimension of Asian American oppression, this [discussion] examines the cultural symbols—or what Patricia Hill Collins (1991) called "controlling images" (pp. 67–68)—generated by the dominant group to help justify the economic exploitation and social oppression of Asian American men and women over time. Writing on the objectification of black women, Collins (1991) observed that the exercise of political-economic domination by racial elites "always involves attempts to objectify the subordinate group" (p. 69). Transmitted through cultural institutions owned, controlled, or supported by various elites, these "controlling images" naturalize racism, sexism, and poverty by branding subordinate groups as alternatively inferior, threatening, or praiseworthy. These controlling images form part of a larger system of what Donald G. Baker (1983) referred to as "psychosocial dominance" (p. 37). Along with the threat and occasional use of violence, the psychosocial form of control conditions the subject minority to become the stereotype, to "live it, talk it, embrace it, measure group and individual worth in its terms, and believe it" (Chin & Chan, 1972, pp. 66–67). In so doing, minority members reject their own individual and group identity and accept in its stead "a white supremacist complex that establishes the primacy of Euro-American cultural practices and social institutions" (Hamamoto, 1994, p. 2). But the objectification of Asian Americans as the exotic and inferior "other" has never been absolute. Asian Americans have always, but particularly since the 1960s, resisted race, class, and gender exploitation not only through political and economic struggles but also through cultural activism. This [article] surveys the range of oppositional projects in which Asian American cultural workers have engaged to deconstruct the conceptual apparatus of the dominant group and to defend Asian American manhood and womanhood. My goal is to understand how the internalization and renunciation of these stereotypes have shaped sexual and gender politics within Asian America. In particular, I explore the conflicting politics of gender between Asian American men and women as they negotiate the difficult terrain of cultural nationalism—the construction of an antiassimilationist, native Asian American subject—and gender identities. . . .

YELLOW PERIL, CHARLIE CHAN, AND SUZIE WONG

A central aspect of racial exploitation centers on defining people of color as "the other" (Said, 1979). The social construction of Asian American "otherness"—through such controlling

---

Author's Note: The excerpt from Cao Tan's poem, "Tomorrow I Will Be Home," appeared in *War and exile: A Vietnamese anthology,* edited by N. N. Bich, 1989, Springfield, VA: Vietnam PEN Abroad.

Yen Le Espiritu is professor of ethnic studies at the University of California, San Diego.

images as the Yellow Peril, the model minority, the Dragon Lady, and the China Doll—is "the precondition for their cultural marginalization, political impotence, and psychic alienation from mainstream American society" (Hamamoto, 1994, p. 5). As indicated by these stereotypes, representations of gender and sexuality figure strongly in the articulation of racism. These racist stereotypes collapse gender and sexuality: Asian men have been constructed as hypermasculine, in the image of the "Yellow Peril," but also as effeminate, in the image of the "model minority," and Asian women have been depicted as superfeminine, in the image of the "China Doll," but also as castrating, in the image of the "Dragon Lady" (Mullings, 1994, pp. 279–280; Okihiro, 1995). As Mary Ann Doane (1991) suggested, sexuality is "indissociable from the effects of polarization and differentiation, often linking them to structures of power and domination" (p. 217). In the Asian American case, the gendering of ethnicity—the process whereby white ideology assigns selected gender characteristics to various ethnic "others"—cast Asian American men and women as simultaneously masculine and feminine but also as neither masculine nor feminine. On the one hand, as part of the Yellow Peril, Asian American men and women have been depicted as a *masculine* threat that needs to be contained. On the other hand, both sexes have been skewed toward the female side: an indication of the group's marginalization in U.S. society and its role as the compliant "model minority" in contemporary U.S. cultural ideology. Although an apparent disjunction, both the feminization and masculinization of Asian men and women exist to define and confirm the white man's superiority (Kim, 1990).

The Yellow Peril

In the United States, Asia and America—East and West—are viewed as mutually exclusive binaries (Kim, 1993, p. viii). Within this exclusive binary system, Asian Americans, even as citizens, are designated Asians, not Americans. Characterizing Asian Americans as "permanent houseguests in the house of America," Sau-Ling Cynthia Wong (1993) stated that "Asian Americans are put in the niche of the 'unassimilable alien': . . . they are alleged to be self-disqualified from full American membership by materialistic motives, questionable political allegiance, and, above all, outlandish, overripe, 'Oriental' cultures" (p. 6). Sonia Shah (1994) defined this form of "cultural discrimination" as a "peculiar blend of cultural and sexist oppression based on our accents, our clothes, our foods, our values and our commitments" (p. 182). This cultural discrimination brands Asians as perpetual foreigners and thus perpetuates the notion of their alleged racial unassimilability. For example, although Japanese Americans have lived in the United States since the turn of the century, many television programs, such as *Happy Days* (1974–1984) and *Gung Ho* (1986–1987), have continued to portray them as newly arrived foreigners (Hamamoto, 1994, p. 13).

As the unassimilable alien, Asian Americans embody for many other Americans the "Yellow Peril"—the threat that Asians will one day unite and conquer the world. This threat includes military invasion and foreign trade from Asia, competition to white labor from Asian labor, the alleged moral degeneracy of Asian people, and potential miscegenation between whites and Asians (Wu, 1982, p. 1). Between 1850 and 1940, U.S. popular media consistently portrayed Asian men as a military threat to the security and welfare of the United States *and* as a sexual danger to innocent white women (Wu, 1982). In numerous dime novels, movies, and comic strips, Asians appeared as feral, rat-faced men lusting after virginal white women. Arguing for racial purity, these popular media depicted Asian-white sexual union as "at best, a form of beastly sodomy, and, at worst, a Satanic marriage" (Hoppenstand, 1983, p. 174). In these popular depictions, the white man was the desirable sexual partner and the hero who rescued the white woman from "a fate worse than death" (Hoppenstand, 1983, pp. 174–175). By the mid-1880s, hundreds of garishly illustrated and garishly written dime novels were being disseminated among a wide audience, sporting such sensational titles as *The Bradys and the Yellow Crooks, The Chase for the Chinese Diamonds, The Opium Den Detective,* and *The Stranglers of New York.* As portrayed in these dime novels, the Yellow Peril was the Chinatown district of a big city "in which decent, honest white folk never ventured" (Hoppenstand, 1983, p. 177).

In 20th-century U.S. popular media, the Japanese joined the Chinese as a perceived threat to Europe and the United States (Wu, 1982, p. 2). In 1916, William Randolph Hearst produced and distributed *Petria,* a movie about a group of fanatical Japanese who invade the United States and attempt to rape a white woman (Quinsaat, 1976, p. 265). After the Japanese bombing of Pearl Harbor on December 7, 1941, the entire Yellow Peril stereotype became incorporated in the nation's war propaganda, quickly whipping white Americans into a war fever. Along with the print media, Hollywood cranked up its anti-Japanese propaganda and produced dozens of war films that centered on the Japanese menace. The fiction of the Yellow Peril stereotype became intertwined with the fact of the United States' war with Japan, and the two became one in the mind-set of the American public (Hoppenstand, 1983, pp. 182–183). It was fear of the Yellow Peril—fear of the rise of nonwhite people and their contestation of white supremacy—that led to the declaration of martial law in Hawaii on December 7, 1941, and to the internment of over 110,000 Japanese on the mainland in concentration camps (Okihiro, 1994, p. 137). In subsequent decades, reflecting changing geopolitical concerns, U.S. popular media featured a host of new yellow peril stereotypes. During the 1950s Cold War years, in television programs as well as in movies, the Communist Chinese evildoers replaced the Japanese monster; during the Vietnam war of the 1970s, the Vietnamese Communists emerged as the new Oriental villains.

Today, Yellow Perilism takes the forms of the greedy, calculating, and clever Japanese businessman aggressively buying up U.S. real estate and cultural institutions *and* the superachieving but nonassimilating Asian Americans (Hagedorn, 1993, p. xxii). In a time of rising economic powers in Asia, declining economic opportunities in the United States, and growing diversity among America's people, this new Yellow Perilism—the depiction of Asia and Asian Americans as economic and cultural threats to mainstream United States—supplies white Americans with a united identity and provides ideological justification for U.S. isolationist policy toward Asia, increasing restrictions against Asian (and Latino) immigration,[1] and the invisible institutional racism and visible violence against Asians in the United States (Okihiro, 1994, pp. 138–139).

The Racial Construction of Asian American Manhood

Like other men of color, Asian American men have been excluded from white-based cultural notions of the masculine. Whereas white men are depicted both as virile and as protectors of women, Asian men have been characterized both as asexual *and* as threats to white women. It is important to note the historical contexts of these seemingly divergent representations of Asian American manhood. The racist depictions of Asian men as "lascivious and predatory" were especially pronounced during the nativist movement against Asians at the turn of the century (Frankenberg, 1993, pp. 75–76). The exclusion of Asian women from the United States and the subsequent establishment of bachelor societies eventually reversed the construction of Asian masculinity from "hypersexual" to "asexual" and even "homosexual." The contemporary model-minority stereotype further emasculates Asian American men as passive and malleable. Disseminated and perpetuated through the popular media, these stereotypes of the emasculated Asian male construct a reality in which social and economic discrimination against these men appears defensible. As an example, the desexualization of Asian men naturalized their inability to establish conjugal families in pre–World War II

United States. Gliding over race-based exclusion laws that banned the immigration of most Asian women and antimiscegenation laws that prohibited men of color from marrying white women, these dual images of the eunuch and the rapist attributed the "womanless households" characteristic of pre-war Asian America to Asian men's lack of sexual prowess and desirability.

A popular controlling image applied to Asian American men is that of the sinister Oriental—a brilliant, powerful villain who plots the destruction of Western civilization. Personified by the movie character of Dr. Fu Manchu, this Oriental mastermind combines Western science with Eastern magic and commands an army of devoted assassins (Hoppenstand, 1983, p. 178). Though ruthless, Fu Manchu lacks masculine heterosexual prowess (Wang, 1988, p. 19), thus privileging heterosexuality. Frank Chin and Jeffrey Chan (1972), in a critique of the desexualization of Asian men in Western culture, described how the Fu Manchu character undermines Chinese American virility:

> Dr. Fu, a man wearing a long dress, batting his eyelashes, surrounded by muscular black servants in loin cloths, and with his habit of caressingly touching white men on the leg, wrist, and face with his long fingernails is not so much a threat as he is a frivolous offense to white manhood. (p. 60)

In another critique that glorifies male aggression, Frank Chin (1972) contrasted the neuterlike characteristics assigned to Asian men to the sexually aggressive images associated with other men of color: "Unlike the white stereotype of the evil black stud, Indian rapist, Mexican macho, the evil of the evil Dr. Fu Manchu was not sexual, but homosexual" (p. 66). However, Chin failed to note that as a homosexual, Dr. Fu (and by extension, Asian men) threatens and offends white masculinity—and therefore needs to be contained ideologically and destroyed physically.[2]

Whereas the evil Oriental stereotype marks Asian American men as the white man's enemy, the stereotype of the sexless Asian sidekick—Charlie Chan, the Chinese laundryman, the Filipino houseboy—depicts Asian men as devoted and impotent, eager to please. William Wu (1982) reported that the Chinese servant "is the most important single image of the Chinese immigrants" in American fiction about Chinese Americans between 1850 and 1940 (p. 60). More recently, such diverse television programs as *Bachelor Father* (1957–1962), *Bonanza* (1959–1973), *Star Trek* (1966–1969), and *Falcon Crest* (1981–1990) all featured the stock Chinese bachelor domestic who dispenses sage advice to his superiors in addition to performing traditional female functions within the household (Hamamoto, 1994, p. 7). By trapping Chinese men (and by extension, Asian men) in the stereotypical "feminine" tasks of serving white men, American society erases the figure of the Asian "masculine" plantation worker in Hawaii or railroad construction worker in the western United States, thus perpetuating the myth of the androgynous and effeminate Asian man (Goellnicht, 1992, p. 198). This feminization, in turn, confines Asian immigrant men to the segment of the labor force that performs women's work.

The motion picture industry has been key in the construction of Asian men as sexual deviants. In a study of Asians in the U.S. motion pictures, Eugene Franklin Wong (1978) maintained that the movie industry filmically castrates Asian males to magnify the superior sexual status of white males (p. 27). As on-screen sexual rivals of whites, Asian males are neutralized, unable to sexually engage Asian women and prohibited from sexually engaging white women. By saving the white woman from sexual contact with the racial "other," the motion picture industry protects the Anglo-American, bourgeois male establishment from any challenges to its hegemony (Marchetti, 1993, p. 218). At the other extreme, the industry has exploited one of the most potent aspects of the Yellow Peril discourses—the sexual danger of contact between the races—by concocting a sexually threatening portrayal of the licentious and aggressive Yellow Man lusting after the White Woman (Marchetti, 1993, p. 3). Heedful of the larger society's taboos against

Asian male–white female sexual union, white male actors donning "yellowface"—instead of Asian male actors—are used in these "love scenes." Nevertheless, the message of the perverse and animalistic Asian male attacking helpless white women is clear (Wong, 1978). Though depicting sexual aggression, this image of the rapist, like that of the eunuch, casts Asian men as sexually undesirable. As Wong (1978) succinctly stated, in Asian male–white female relations, "There can be rape, but there cannot be romance" (p. 25). Thus, Asian males yield to the sexual superiority of the white males who are permitted filmically to maintain their sexual dominance over both white women and women of color. A young Vietnamese American man describes the damaging effect of these stereotypes on his self-image:

> Every day I was forced to look into a mirror created by white society and its media. As a young Asian man, I shrank before white eyes. I wasn't tall, I wasn't fair, I wasn't muscular, and so on. Combine that with the enormous insecurities any pubescent teenager feels, and I have no difficulty in knowing now why I felt naked before a mass of white people. (Nguyen, 1990, p. 23)

White cultural and institutional racism against Asian males is also reflected in the motion picture industry's preoccupation with the death of Asians—a filmic solution to the threats of the Yellow Peril. In a perceptive analysis of Hollywood's view of Asians in films made from the 1930s to the 1960s, Tom Engelhardt (1976) described how Asians, like Native Americans, are seen by the movie industry as inhuman invaders, ripe for extermination. He argued that the theme of the nonhumanness of Asians prepares the audience to accept, without flinching, "the levelling and near-obliteration of three Asian areas in the course of three decades" (Engelhardt, 1976, p. 273). The industry's death theme, though applying to all Asians, is mainly focused on Asian males, with Asian females reserved for sexual purposes (Wong, 1978, p. 35). Especially in war films, Asian males, however advantageous their initial position, inevitably perish at the hands of the superior white males (Wong, 1978, p. 34).

The Racial Construction of Asian American Womanhood

Like Asian men, Asian women have been reduced to one-dimensional caricatures in Western representation. The condensation of Asian women's multiple differences into gross character types—mysterious, feminine, and nonwhite—obscures the social injustice of racial, class, and gender oppression (Marchetti, 1993, p. 71). Both Western film and literature promote dichotomous stereotypes of the Asian woman: Either she is the cunning Dragon Lady or the servile Lotus Blossom Baby (Tong, 1994, p. 197). Though connoting two extremes, these stereotypes are interrelated: Both eroticize Asian women as exotic "others"—sensuous, promiscuous, but untrustworthy. Whereas American popular culture denies "manhood" to Asian men, it endows Asian women with an excess of "womanhood," sexualizing them but also impugning their sexuality. In this process, both sexism and racism have been blended together to produce the sexualization of white racism (Wong, 1978, p. 260). Linking the controlling images of Asian men and women, Elaine Kim (1990) suggested that Asian women are portrayed as sexual for the same reason that men are asexual: "Both exist to define the white man's virility and the white man's superiority" (p. 70).

As the racialized exotic "others," Asian American women do not fit the white-constructed notions of the feminine. Whereas white women have been depicted as chaste and dependable, Asian women have been represented as promiscuous and untrustworthy. In a mirror image of the evil Fu Manchu, the Asian woman was portrayed as the castrating Dragon Lady who, while puffing on her foot-long cigarette holder, could poison a man as easily as she could seduce him. "With her talon-like six-inch fingernails, her skin-tight satin dress slit to the thigh," the Dragon Lady is desirable, deceitful, and dangerous (Ling, 1990, p. 11). In the 1924 film *The Thief of Baghdad,* Anna May Wong, a pioneer Chinese American actress, played a handmaid who employed treachery to help an evil Mongol prince attempt to win the hand of the Princess of Baghdad (Tajima, 1989, p. 309). In so doing, Wong unwittingly popularized a common Dragon Lady social type: treacherous women who are partners in crime with men of their own kind. The publication of *Daughter of Fu Manchu* (1931) firmly entrenched the Dragon Lady image in white consciousness. Carrying on her father's work as the champion of Asian hegemony over the white race, Fah Lo Sue exhibited, in the words of American studies scholar William F. Wu, "exotic sensuality, sexual availability to a white man, and a treacherous nature" (cited in Tong, 1994, p. 197). A few years later, in 1934, Milton Caniff inserted into his adventure comic strip *Terry and the Pirates* another version of the Dragon Lady who "combines all the best features of past moustache twirlers with the lure of the handsome wench" (Hoppenstand, 1983, p. 178). As such, Caniff's Dragon Lady fuses the image of the evil male Oriental master-mind with that of the Oriental prostitute first introduced some 50 years earlier in the dime novels.

At the opposite end of the spectrum is the Lotus Blossom stereotype, reincarnated throughout the years as the China Doll, the Geisha Girl, the War Bride, or the Vietnamese prostitute—many of whom are the spoils of the last three wars fought in Asia (Tajima, 1989, p. 309). Demure, diminutive, and deferential, the Lotus Blossom Baby is "modest, tittering behind her delicate ivory hand, eyes downcast, always walking ten steps behind her man, and, best of all, devot[ing] body and soul to serving him" (Ling, 1990, p. 11). Interchangeable in appearance and name, these women have no voice; their "nonlanguage" includes uninterpretable chattering, pidgin English, giggling, or silence (Tajima, 1989). These stereotypes of Asian women as submissive and dainty sex objects not only have impeded women's economic mobility but also have fostered an enormous demand for X-rated films and pornographic materials featuring Asian women in bondage, for "Oriental" bathhouse workers in U.S. cities, and for Asian mail-order brides (Kim, 1984, p. 64).

Sexism, Racism, and Love

The racialization of Asian manhood and womanhood upholds white masculine hegemony. Cast as sexually available, Asian women become yet another possession of the white man. In motion pictures and network television programs, interracial sexuality, though rare, occurs principally between a white male and an Asian female. A combination of sexism and racism makes this form of miscegenation more acceptable: Race mixing between an Asian male and a white female would upset not only racial taboos but those that attend patriarchal authority as well (Hamamoto, 1994, p. 39). Whereas Asian men are depicted as either the threatening rapist or the impotent eunuch, white men are endowed with the masculine attributes with which to sexually attract the Asian woman. Such popular television shows as *Gunsmoke* (1955–1975) and *How the West Was Won* (1978–1979) clearly articulate the theme of Asian female sexual possession by the white male. In these shows, only white males have the prerogative to cross racial boundaries and to choose freely from among women of color as sex partners. Within a system of racial and gender oppression, the sexual possession of women and men of color by white men becomes yet another means of enforcing unequal power relations (Hamamoto, 1994, p. 46).

The preference for white male–Asian female is also prevalent in contemporary television news broadcasting, most recently in the 1993–1995 pairing of Dan Rather and Connie Chung as coanchors of the *CBS Evening News.* Today, virtually every major metropolitan market across the United States has at least one Asian American female newscaster (Hamamoto, 1994, p. 245).

While female Asian American anchorpersons—Connie Chung, Tritia Toyota, Wendy Tokuda, and Emerald Yeh—are popular television news figures, there is a nearly total absence of Asian American men. Critics argue that this is so because the white male hiring establishment, and presumably the larger American public, feels more comfortable (i.e., less threatened) seeing a white male sitting next to a minority female at the anchor desk than the reverse. Stephen Tschida of WDBJ-TV (Roanoke, Virginia), one of only a handful of male Asian American television news anchors, was informed early in his career that he did not have the proper "look" to qualify for the anchorperson position. Other male broadcast news veterans have reported being passed over for younger, more beauteous, female Asian Americans (Hamamoto, 1994, p. 245). This gender imbalance sustains the construction of Asian American women as more successful, assimilated, attractive, and desirable than their male counterparts.

To win the love of white men, Asian women must reject not only Asian men but their entire culture. Many Hollywood narratives featuring romances between Anglo American men and Asian women follow the popular Pocahontas mythos: The Asian woman, out of devotion for her white American lover, betrays her own people and commits herself to the dominant white culture by dying, longing for, or going to live with her white husband in his country. For example, in the various versions of *Miss Saigon,* the contemporary version of *Madame Butterfly,* the tragic Vietnamese prostitute eternally longs for the white boy soldier who has long abandoned her and their son (Hagedorn, 1993, p. xxii). These tales of interracial romance inevitably have a tragic ending. The Asian partner usually dies, thus providing a cinematic resolution to the moral lapse of the Westerner. The Pocahontas paradigm can be read as a narrative of salvation; the Asian woman is saved either spiritually or morally from the excesses of her own culture, just as she physically saves her Western lover from the moral degeneracy of her own people (Marchetti, 1993, p. 218). For Asian women, who are marginalized not only by gender but also by class, race, or ethnicity, the interracial romance narratives promise "the American Dream of abundance, protection, individual choice, and freedom from the strictures of a traditional society in the paternalistic name of heterosexual romance" (Marchetti, 1993, p. 91). These narratives also carry a covert political message, legitimizing a masculinized Anglo American rule over a submissive, feminized Asia. The motion picture *China Gate* (1957) by Samuel Fuller and the network television program *The Lady From Yesterday* (1985), for example, promote an image of Vietnam that legitimizes American rule. Seduced by images of U.S. abundance, a feminized Vietnam sacrifices herself for the possibility of future incorporation into America, the land of individual freedom and economic opportunities. Thus, the interracial tales function not only as a romantic defense of traditional female roles within the patriarchy but also as a political justification of American hegemony in Asia (Marchetti, 1993, p. 108).

Fetishized as the embodiment of perfect womanhood and genuine exotic femininity, Asian women are pitted against their more modern, emancipated Western sisters (Tajima, 1989). In two popular motion pictures, *Love Is a Many-Splendored Thing* (1955) and *The World of Suzie Wong* (1960), the white women remain independent and potentially threatening, whereas both Suyin and Suzie give up their independence in the name of love. Thus, the white female characters are cast as calculating, suffocating, and thoroughly undesirable, whereas the Asian female characters are depicted as truly "feminine"—passive, subservient, dependent, and domestic. Implicitly, these films warn white women to embrace the socially constructed passive Asian beauty as the feminine ideal if they want to attract and keep a man. In pitting white women against Asian women, Hollywood affirms white male identity against the threat of emerging feminism and the concomitant changes in gender relations (Marchetti, 1993, pp. 115–116). As Robyn Wiegman (1991) observed, the absorption of women of color into gender categories traditionally reserved for white women is "part of a broader program of hegemonic recuperation, a program that has at its main focus the reconstruction of white masculine power" (p. 320). It is also important to note that as the racialized exotic "other," Asian women do not replace but merely substitute for white women, and thus will be readily dismissed once the "real" mistress returns.

The controlling images of Asian men and Asian women, exaggerated out of all proportion in Western representation, have created resentment and tension between Asian American men and women. Given this cultural milieu, many American-born Asians do not think of other Asians in sexual terms (Fung, 1994, p. 163). In particular, due to the persistent desexualization of the Asian male, many Asian females do not perceive their ethnic counterparts as desirable marriage partners (Hamamoto, 1992, p. 42). In so doing, these women unwittingly enforce the Eurocentric gender ideology that objectifies both sexes and racializes all Asians (see Collins, 1990, pp. 185–186). In a column in *Asian Week,* a weekly Asian American newspaper, Daniel Yoon (1993) reported that at a recent dinner discussion hosted by the Asian American Students Association at his college, the Asian American women in the room proceeded, one after another, to describe how "Asian American men were too passive, too weak, too boring, too traditional, too abusive, too domineering, too ugly, too greasy, too short, too . . . Asian. Several described how they preferred white men, and how they never had and never would date an Asian man" (p. 16). Partly as a result of the racist constructions of Asian American womanhood and manhood and their acceptance by Asian Americans, intermarriage patterns are high, with Asian American women intermarrying at a much higher rate than Asian American men.[3] Moreover, Asian women involved in intermarriage have usually married white partners (Agbayani-Siewert & Revilla, 1995, p. 156; Min, 1995, p. 22; Nishi, 1995, p. 128). In part, these intermarriage patterns reflect the sexualization of white racism that constructs white men as the most desirable sexual partners, frowns on Asian male–white women relations, and fetishizes Asian women as the embodiment of perfect womanhood. Viewed in this light, the high rate of outmarriage for Asian American women is the "material outcome of an interlocking system of sexism and racism" (Hamamoto, 1992, p. 42).[4] . . .

CONCLUSION

Ideological representations of gender and sexuality are central in the exercise and maintenance of racial, patriarchal, and class domination. In the Asian American case, this ideological racism has taken seemingly contrasting forms: Asian men have been cast as both hypersexual and asexual, and Asian women have been rendered both superfeminine and masculine. Although in apparent disjunction, both forms exist to define, maintain, and justify white male supremacy. The racialization of Asian American manhood and womanhood underscores the interconnections of race, gender, and class. As categories of difference, race and gender relations do not parallel but intersect and confirm each other, and it is the complicity among these categories of difference that enables U.S. elites to justify and maintain their cultural, social, and economic power. Responding to the ideological assaults on their gender identities, Asian American cultural workers have engaged in a wide range of oppositional projects to defend Asian American manhood and womanhood. In the process, some have embraced a masculinist cultural nationalism, a stance that marginalizes Asian American women and their needs. Though sensitive to the emasculation of Asian American men, Asian American feminists have pointed out that Asian American nationalism insists on a fixed masculinist identity, thus obscuring gender differences. Though divergent, both the nationalist and feminist positions advance the dichotomous stance of man or woman, gender or race or class, without recognizing the complex relationality of these categories of oppression. It is only when Asian Americans recognize the intersections of race, gender, and class that we can transform the existing hierarchical structure.

NOTES

1. In 1996, the U.S. Congress deliberated on but did not pass two bills (S. 1394/269 and H.R. 2202) that would have sharply cut legal immigration by removing the family preferences from the existing immigration laws.
2. I thank Mary Romero for pointing this out to me.
3. Filipino Americans provide an exception in that Filipino American men tend to intermarry as frequently as Filipina American women. This is partly so because they are more Americanized and have a relatively more egalitarian gender-role orientation than other Asian American men (Agbayani-Siewert & Revilla, 1995, p. 156).
4. In recent years, Asian Americans' rising consciousness, coupled with their phenomenal growth in certain regions of the United States, has led to a significant increase in inter-Asian marriages (e.g., Chinese Americans to Korean Americans). In a comparative analysis of the 1980 and 1990 Decennial Census, Larry Hajimi Shinigawa and Gin Young Pang (forthcoming) found a dramatic decrease of interracial marriages and a significant rise of inter-Asian marriages. In California (where 39% of all Asian Pacific Americans reside), inter-Asian marriages increased from 21.1% in 1980 to 64% in 1990 of all intermarriages for Asian American husbands, and from 10.8% to 45% for Asian American wives during the same time period.

REFERENCES

Agbayani-Siewert, P., & Revilla, L. (1995). Filipino Americans. In P. G. Min (Ed.), *Asian Americans: Contemporary trends and issues* (pp. 134–168). Thousand Oaks, CA: Sage.

Baker, D. G. (1983). *Race, ethnicity, and power: A comparative study.* New York: Routledge.

Chin, F., & Chan, J. P. (1972). Racist love. In R. Kostelanetz (Ed.), *Seeing through shuck* (pp. 65–79). New York: Ballantine.

Collins, P. H. (1990). *Black feminist thought: Knowledge, consciousness, and the politics of empowerment.* New York: Routledge.

Doane, M. A. (1991). *Femme fatales: Feminism, film theory, psychoanalysis.* New York: Routledge.

Engelhardt, T. (1976). Ambush at Kamikaze Pass. In E. Gee (Ed.), *Counterpoint: Perspectives on Asian America* (pp. 270–279). Los Angeles: University of California at Los Angeles, Asian American Studies Center.

Frankenberg, R. (1993). *White women, race matters: The social construction of whiteness.* Minneapolis: University of Minnesota Press.

Fung, R. (1994). Seeing yellow: Asian identities in film and video. In K. Aguilar-San Juan (Ed.), *The state of Asian America* (pp. 161–171). Boston: South End.

Goellnicht, D. C. (1992). Tang Ao in America: Male subject positions in *China Men.* In S. G. Lim & A. Ling (Eds.), *Reading the literatures of Asian America* (pp. 191–212). Philadelphia: Temple University Press.

Hagedorn, J. (1993). Introduction: "Role of dead man require very little acting." In J. Hagedorn (Ed.), *Charlie Chan is dead: An anthology of contemporary Asian American fiction* (pp. xxi–xxx). New York: Penguin.

Hamamoto, D. Y. (1994). *Monitored peril: Asian Americans and the politics of representation.* Minneapolis: University of Minnesota Press.

Hoppenstand, G. (1983). Yellow devil doctors and opium dens: A survey of the yellow peril stereotypes in mass media entertainment. In C. D. Geist & J. Nachbar (Eds.), *The popular culture reader* (3rd ed., pp. 171–185). Bowling Green, OH: Bowling Green University Press.

Kim, E. (1990). "Such opposite creatures": Men and women in Asian American literature. *Michigan Quarterly Review,* 29, 68–93.

Ling, A. (1990). *Between worlds: Women writers of Chinese ancestry.* New York: Pergamon.

Marchetti, G. (1993). *Romance and the "Yellow Peril": Race, sex, and discursive strategies in Hollywood fiction.* Berkeley: University of California Press.

Min, P. G. (1995). Korean Americans. In P. G. Min (Ed.), *Asian Americans: Contemporary trends and issues* (pp. 199–231). Thousand Oaks, CA: Sage.

Mullings, L. (1994). Images, ideology, and women of color. In M. Baca Zinn & B. T. Dill (Eds.), *Women of color in U.S. society* (pp. 265–289). Philadelphia: Temple University Press.

Nguyen, V. (1990, December 7). Growing up in white America. *Asian Week,* p. 23.

Nishi, S. M. (1995). Japanese Americans. In P. G. Min (Ed.), *Asian Americans: Contemporary trends and issues* (pp. 95–133). Thousand Oaks, CA: Sage.

Okihiro, G. Y. (1994). *Margins and mainstreams: Asians in American history and culture.* Seattle: University of Washington Press.

Okihiro, G. Y. (1995, November). *Reading Asian bodies, reading anxieties.* Paper presented at the University of California, San Diego Ethnic Studies Colloquium, La Jolla.

Quinsaat, J. (1976). Asians in the media: The shadows in the spotlight. In E. Gee (Ed.), *Counterpoint: Perspectives on Asian America* (pp. 264–269). Los Angeles: University of California at Los Angeles, Asian American Studies Center.

Said, E. (1979). *Orientalism.* New York: Random House.

Shah, S. (1994). Presenting the Blue Goddess: Toward a national, Pan-Asian feminist agenda. In K. Aguilar-San Juan (Ed.), *The state of Asian America: Activism and resistance in the 1990s* (pp. 147–158). Boston: South End.

Tajima, R. (1991). Moving the image: Asian American independent filmmaking 1970–1990. In R. Leong (Ed.), *Moving the image: Independent Asian Pacific American media arts* (pp. 10–33). Los Angeles: University of California at Los Angeles, Asian American Studies Center, and Visual Communications, Southern California Asian American Studies Central.

Tong, B. (1994). *Unsubmissive women: Chinese prostitutes in nineteenth-century San Francisco.* Norman: University of Oklahoma Press.

Wang, A. (1988). Maxine Hong Kingston's reclaiming of America: The birthright of the Chinese American male. *South Dakota Review,* 26, 18–29.

Wiegman, R. (1991). Black bodies/American commodities: Gender, race, and the bourgeois ideal in contemporary film. In L. D. Friedman (Ed.), *Unspeakable images: Ethnicity and the American cinema* (pp. 208–328). Urbana: University of Illinois Press.

Wong, E. F. (1978). *On visual media racism: Asians in the American motion pictures.* New York: Arno.

Wong, S.-L. C. (1993). *Reading Asian American literature: From necessity to extravagance.* Princeton, NJ: Princeton University Press.

Wu, W. F. (1982). *The Yellow Peril: Chinese Americans in American fiction 1850–1940.* Hamden, CT: Archon.

Yoon, D. D. (1993, November 26). Asian American male: Wimp or what? *Asian Week,* p. 16.

READING 44

What Americans Don't Know about Indians

Jerry Mander

In 1981, when my sons Yari and Kai were attending San Francisco's Lowell High School, they complained to me that their American History class began with the arrival of whites on this continent and omitted any mention of the people who were already here. The class was taught that Columbus "discovered" America and that American "history" was what came afterward.

That same year, Ronald Reagan gave his first inaugural speech, in which he praised the "brave pioneers who tamed the empty wilderness." Still, I was surprised to hear that the wilderness was also empty for the faculty at Lowell High, a school usually considered among the top public high schools in this country.

The American History teacher asked my kids why they were so keen on the subject of Indians, leading them to mention the book I was planning

---

Jerry Mander is senior fellow at the Public Media Center in San Francisco and director of the Berkeley ecological think tank, the Elmwood Institute.

to write. This in turn led to an invitation for me to speak to the class. As a result, I got some insight about the level of Indian awareness among a group of high-school kids.

The youngsters I met had never been offered one course, or even an extended segment of a course, about the Indian nations of this continent, about Indian-Anglo interactions (except for references to the Pilgrims and the Indian wars), or about contemporary Indian problems in the U.S. or elsewhere. These teenagers knew as little as I did at their age, and as little as their teacher knew at their age—or now, as he regretfully acknowledged to me. The American educational curriculum is almost bereft of information about Indians, making it difficult for young non-Indian Americans to understand or care about present-day Indian issues. European schools actually teach more about American Indians. In Germany, for example, every child reads a set of books that sensitizes them to Indian values and causes. It is not surprising, therefore, that the European press carries many more stories about American Indians than does the American press. . . .

THE MEDIA: INDIANS ARE NON-NEWS

That the Lowell High students should know nothing about Indians is not their fault. It is one of many indicators that this country's institutions do not inform people about Indians of either present or past. Indians are non-history, which also makes them non-news. Not taught in schools, not part of American consciousness, their present-day activities and struggles are rarely reported in newspapers or on television.

On the rare occasions when the media do relate to Indians, the reports tend to follow very narrow guidelines based on pre-existing stereotypes of Indians; they become what is known in the trade as "formula stories."

My friend Dagmar Thorpe, a Sac-and-Fox Indian who, until 1990, was Executive Director of the Seventh Generation Fund, once asked a network producer known to be friendly to the Indian cause about the reasons for the lack of in-depth, accurate reporting on Indian stories. According to Dagmar, the producer gave three reasons. The first reason was guilt. It is not considered good programming to make your audience feel bad. Americans don't want to see shows that remind them of historical events that American institutions have systematically avoided discussing.

Secondly, there is the "what's-in-it-for-me?" factor. Americans in general do not see how anything to do with Indians has anything to do with them. As a culture, we are now so trained to "look out for number one" that there has been a near total loss of altruism. (Of course American life itself—so speedy and so removed from nature—makes identifying with the Indians terribly difficult; and we don't see that we might have something to learn from them.)

The third factor is that Indian demands seem preposterous to Americans. What most Indians want is simply that their land should be returned, and that treaties should be honored. Americans tend to view the treaties as "ancient," though many were made less than a century ago—more recently, for example, than many well-established laws and land deals among whites. Americans, like their government and the media, view treaties with Indian nations differently than treaties with anyone else.

In fairness to the media, there are some mitigating factors. Just like the rest of us, reporters and producers have been raised without knowledge of Indian history or Indian struggles. Perhaps most important, media people have had little personal contact with Indians, since Indians live mostly in parts of the country, and the world, where the media isn't. Indians live in non-urban regions, in the deserts and mountains and tundras that have been impacted least by Western society, at least until recently. They live in the places that we didn't want. They are not part of the mainstream and have not tried to become part.

When our society *does* extend its tentacles to make contact—usually when corporations are seeking land or minerals, or military forces are seeking control—there is little media present to observe and report on what transpires. Even in the United States, virtually all Indian struggles take place far away from media: in the central Arizona desert, in the rugged Black Hills, the mountains of the Northwest, or else on tiny Pacific islands, or in the icy vastness of the far north of Alaska. The *New York Times* has no bureau in those places; neither does CBS. Nor do they have bureaus in the Australian desert or the jungles of Brazil, Guatemala, or Borneo.

As a result, some of the most terrible assaults upon native peoples today never get reported. If reports do emerge, the sources are the corporate or military public relations arms of the Western intruders, which present biased perspectives.

When reporters are flown in to someplace where Indians are making news, they are usually ill prepared and unknowledgeable about the local situation. They do not speak the language and are hard pressed to grasp the Indian perception, even if they can find Indians to speak with. In addition, these reporters often grew up in that same bubble of no contact/no education/no news about Indians.

To make matters even more difficult, as I explained at length in my TV book, it is also in the nature of modern media to distort the Indian message, which is far too subtle, sensory, complex, spiritual, and ephemeral to fit the gross guidelines of mass-media reporting, which emphasizes conflict and easily grasped imagery. A reporter would have to spend a great deal of time with the Indians to understand why digging up the earth for minerals is a sacrilege, or why diverting a stream can destroy a culture, or why cutting a forest deprives people of their religious and human rights, or why moving Indians off desert land to a wonderful new community of private homes will effectively kill them. Even if the reporter does understand, to successfully translate that understanding through the medium, and through the editors and the commercial sponsor—all of whom are looking for action—is nearly impossible.

So most reporters have little alternative but to accept official handouts, or else to patch together, from scanty reports, stories that are designed for a world predisposed to view Indian struggles as anomalies in today's technological world: formula stories, using stereotyped imagery.

PREVALENT STEREOTYPES AND FORMULAS

The dominant image of Indians in the media used to be of savages, of John Wayne leading the U.S. Cavalry against the Indians. Today the stereotype has shifted to *noble savage,* which portrays Indians as part of a once-great but now-dying culture; a culture that could talk to the trees and the animals and that protected nature. But sadly, a losing culture, which has not kept up with our dynamic times.

We see this stereotype now in many commercials. The Indian is on a horse, gazing nobly over the land he protects. Then there's a quick cut to today: to oil company workers walking alongside the hot-oil pipeline in Alaska. The company workers are there to protect against leaks and to preserve the environment for the animals. We see quick cuts of caribou and wolves, which imply that the oil company accepts the responsibility that the Indians once had.

The problem here is that the corporate sponsor is lying. It does not feel much responsibility toward nature; if it did, it would not need expensive commercials to say so, because the truth would be apparent from its behavior. More important, however, is that treating Indians this way in commercials does terrible harm to their cause. It makes Indians into conceptual relics; artifacts. Worse, they are confirmed as existing only in the past, which hurts their present efforts.

Another stereotype we see in commercials these days is the *Indian-as-guru.* A recent TV spot depicted a shaman making rain for his people. He is then hired by some corporate farmers to make rain for them. He is shown with his power objects, saying prayers, holding his hands toward the heavens. The rains come. Handshakes from the businessmen. Finally the wise old Indian is shown with a satisfied smile on his flight home via United Airlines.

Among the more insidious formula stories is the one about how Indians are always fighting each other over disputed lands. This formula fits the Western paradigm about non-industrial peoples' inability to govern themselves; that they live in some kind of despotism or anarchy. For example, in the Hopi-Navajo "dispute," . . . the truth of the matter is that U.S. intervention in the activities and governments of both tribes eventually led to American-style puppet governments battling each other for development rights that the traditional leadership of each tribe does not want. But the historical reality of that case, and most Indian cases, is unknown to the mass media and therefore left unreported.

Another very popular formula story is the one with the headline INDIANS STAND IN THE WAY OF DEVELOPMENT, as, for example, in New Guinea or Borneo or in the Amazon Basin. These stories concern Indian resistance to roads, or dams, or the cutting of forests, and their desire for their lands to be left inviolate.

The problem with these formula stories is not that they are inaccurate—Indian peoples around the world most certainly are resisting on hundreds of fronts and do indeed stand in the way of development—but that the style of reporting carries a sense of foregone conclusion. The reporters tend to emphasize the poignancy of the situation: "stone-age" peoples fighting in vain to forestall the inevitable march of progress. In their view, it is only a matter of time before the Indians lose, and the forests *are* cut down, and the land *is* settled by outsiders. However tragic the invasion, however righteous the cause of the Indians, however illegal the acts being perpetrated against them, however admirable the Indian ways, reporters will invariably adopt the stance that the cause is lost, and that no reversal is possible. This attitude surely harms the Indians more than if the story had not been reported at all.

Finally, and perhaps most outrageous, is the *rich Indian* formula story. Despite the fact that the average per-capita income of Indians is lower than any other racial or ethnic group in the United States, and that they suffer the highest disease rates in many categories, and have the least access to health care, the press loves to focus on the rare instance where some Indian hits it big. Sometimes the story is about an oil well found on some Indian's land, or someone getting rich on bingo, but often the stories emphasize someone's corruption, e.g., Peter MacDonald, the former chairman of the Navajo Nation. This formula story has a twofold purpose: it manages to confirm the greatness of America—where *anyone* can get rich, even an Indian—and at the same time manages to confirm Indian leaders as corrupt and despotic.

A corollary to this story is how certain Indian tribes have gotten wealthy through land claims cases, as, for example, the Alaska natives via the Alaska Native Claims Settlement Act. As we will see, a little digging into the story—if reporters only would—exposes that settlement as a fraud that actually deprived the Alaska natives of land *and* money.

The press's failure to pursue and report the full picture of American Indian poverty, while splashing occasional stories about how some are hitting it big, creates a public impression that is the opposite of the truth. The situation is exacerbated when national leaders repeat the misconceptions. Ronald Reagan told the Moscow press in 1987 that there was no discrimination against Indians in this country and the proof of that was that so many Indians, like those outside Palm Springs (oil wells), have become wealthy.

INDIANS AND THE NEW AGE

While most of our society manages to avoid Indians, there is one group that does not, though its interest is very measured.

I was reminded of this recently during my first visit to a dentist in Marin County, an affluent area north of San Francisco. The dentist, a friendly, trendy young man wearing a moustache, looked as if he'd stepped out of a Michelob ad. While poking my gums, he made pleasant conversation, inquiring about my work. When he pulled his tools from my mouth, I told him I was writing about Indians, which got him very excited. "Indians! Great! I love Indians. Indians are my hobby. I have Indian posters all over the house, and Indian rugs. And hey, I've lately been taking lessons in 'tracking' from this really neat Indian guide. I've learned how to read the tiniest changes in the terrain, details I'd never even noticed before."

In this expression of enthusiasm, this young man was like thousands of other people, particularly in places like Marin or Beverly Hills, or wherever there is sufficient leisure to engage in inner explorations. Among this group, which tends to identify with the "New Age," or the "human potential movement," there has been a renaissance of awareness about Indian practices that aid inner spiritual awakening.

A typical expression of this interest may be that a well-off young professional couple will invite friends to a lawn party to meet the couple's personal Indian medicine person. The shaman will lead the guests through a series of rituals designed to awaken aspects of themselves. These events may culminate in a sweat ceremony, or even a "firewalk." There was a period in the seventies when you could scarcely show up at a friend's house without having to decide whether or not to walk on hot coals, guided by a medicine man from the South Pacific.

Those who graduate from sweat ceremonies or firewalks, as my dentist had, might proceed to the now popular "vision quests." You may feel as you read this that I am ridiculing these "human potential" explorers. Actually, I find something admirable in them. Breaking out of the strictures of our contemporary lifestyles is clearly beneficial, in my opinion, but there is also a serious problem. For although the New Age gleans the ancient wisdoms and practices, it has assiduously avoided directly engaging in the actual lives and political struggles of the millions of descendants who carry on those ancient traditions, who are still alive on the planet today, and who want to continue living in a traditional manner. . . .

Language

READING 45

English in a Multicultural America

Dennis Baron

> The protection of the Constitution extends to all,—to those who speak other languages as well as to those born with English on the tongue. Perhaps it would be highly advantageous if all had ready understanding of our ordinary speech, but this cannot be coerced by methods which conflict with the Constitution,—a desirable end cannot be promoted by prohibited means.
>
> —*Associate Supreme Court Justice James Clark McReynolds Meyer v. Nebraska, 1923*

In the United States today there is a growing fear that the English language may be on its way out as the American lingua franca, that English is losing ground to Spanish, Chinese, Vietnamese, Korean, and the other languages used by newcomers to our shores.

However, while the United States has always been a multilingual as well as a multicultural nation, English has always been its unofficial

---

No biographical information available.

official language. Today, a greater percentage of Americans speak English than ever before, and the descendants of nonanglophones or bilingual speakers still tend to learn English—and become monolingual English speakers—as quickly as their German, Jewish, Irish, or Italian predecessors did in the past.

Assimilated immigrants, those who after several generations no longer consider themselves "hyphenated Americans," look upon more recent waves of newcomers with suspicion. Similarly, each generation tends to see the language crisis as new in its time. But reactions to language and ethnicity are cyclical, and the new immigrants from Asia and Latin America have had essentially the same experience as their European predecessors, with similar results.

ENGLISH VS. GERMAN

As early as the 18th century, British colonists in Pennsylvania, remarking that as many as one-third of the area's residents spoke German, attacked Germans in terms strikingly similar to those heard nowadays against newer immigrants. Benjamin Franklin considered the Pennsylvania Germans to be a "swarthy" racial group distinct from the English majority in the colony. In 1751 he complained,

> Why should the Palatine Boors be suffered to swarm into our Settlements, and by herding together establish their Language and Manners to the exclusion of ours? Why should Pennsylvania, founded by the English, become a Colony of Aliens, who will shortly be so numerous as to Germanize us instead of our Anglifying them, and will never adopt our Language or Customs, any more than they can acquire our Complexion?

The Germans were accused by other 18th-century Anglos of laziness, illiteracy, clannishness, a reluctance to assimilate, excessive fertility, and Catholicism (although a significant number of them were Protestant). In some instances they were even blamed for the severe Pennsylvania winters.

Resistance to German, long the major minority language in the country, continued throughout the 19th century, although it was long since clear that, despite community efforts to preserve their language, young Germans were adopting English and abandoning German at a rate that should have impressed the rest of the English-speaking population.

After the US entered World War I, most states quickly banned German—and, in some extreme cases, all foreign languages—from school curricula in a wave of jingoistic patriotism. In 1918, for example, Iowa Gov. William Harding forbade the use of foreign languages in schools, on trains, in public places, and over the telephone (a more public instrument then than it is now), even going so far as to recommend that those who insisted on conducting religious services in a language other than English do so not in churches or synagogues but in the privacy of their own homes.

Similarly, in 1919 the state of Nebraska passed a broad English-only law prohibiting the use of foreign languages at public meetings and proscribing the teaching of foreign languages to any student below the ninth grade. Robert T. Meyer, a teacher in the Lutheran-run Zion Parochial School, was fined twenty-five dollars because, as the complaint read, "between the hour of 1 and 1:30 on May 25, 1920," he taught German to ten-year-old Raymond Papart, who had not yet passed the eighth grade.

Upholding Meyer's conviction, the Nebraska Supreme Court found that most parents "have never deemed it of importance to teach their children foreign languages." It agreed as well that the teaching of a foreign language was harmful to the health of the young child, whose "daily capacity for learning is comparatively small." Such an argument was consistent with the educational theory of the day, which held as late as the 1950s that bilingualism led to confusion and academic failure, and was harmful to the psychological well-being of the child. Indeed, one psychologist claimed in 1926 that the use of a foreign language in the home was a leading cause of mental retardation. . . .

The US Supreme Court reversed Meyer's conviction in a landmark decision in 1923. But the decision in *Meyer v. Nebraska* was to some extent an empty victory for language teachers: while their calling could no longer be restricted, the ranks of German classes had been devastated by the instant linguistic assimilation that World War I forced on German Americans. In 1915 close to 25 percent of the student population studied German in American high schools. Seven years later only 0.6 percent—fewer than 14,000 high school students—were taking German.

ENGLISH VS. SPANISH

Like German in the Midwest, Spanish was the object of vilification in the American Southwest. This negative attitude toward Spanish delayed statehood for New Mexico for over 60 years. In 1902, in one of New Mexico's many tries for statehood, a congressional subcommittee held hearings in the territory, led by Indiana Senator Albert Jeremiah Beveridge, a "progressive" Republican who believed in "America first! Not only America first, but America only." Witness after witness before the Beveridge subcommittee was forced to admit that in New Mexico, ballots and political speeches were either bilingual or entirely in Spanish; that census takers conducted their surveys in Spanish; that justices of the peace kept records in Spanish; that the courts required translators so that judges and lawyers could understand the many Hispanic witnesses; that juries deliberated in Spanish as much as in English; and that children, who might or might not learn English in schools, as required by law, "relapsed" into Spanish on the playground, at home, and after graduation.

One committee witness suggested that the minority language situation in New Mexico resembled that in Senator Beveridge's home state of Indiana: "Spanish is taught as a side issue, as German would be in any State in the Union. . . . This younger generation understands English as well as I do." And a sympathetic senator reminded his audience, "These people who speak the Spanish language are not foreigners; they are natives, are they not?"

As Franklin did the Germans in Pennsylvania, Senator Beveridge categorized the "Mexicans" of the American Southwest as non-natives, "unlike us in race, language, and social customs," and concluded that statehood must be contingent on assimilation. He recommended that admission to the Union be delayed until a time "when the mass of the people, or even a majority of them, shall, in the usages and employment of their daily life, have become identical in language and customs with the great body of the American people; when the immigration of English-speaking people who have been citizens of other States does its modifying work with the 'Mexican' element." Although New Mexico finally achieved its goal of statehood, and managed to write protection of Spanish into its constitution, schools throughout the Southwest forbade the use of Spanish among students. Well into the present century, children were routinely ridiculed and punished for using Spanish both in class and on the playground.

LANGUAGE AND POWER

As the New Mexican experience suggests, the insistence on English has never been benign. The notion of a national language sometimes wears the guise of inclusion: we must all speak English to participate meaningfully in the democratic process. Sometimes it argues unity: we must speak one language to understand one another and share both culture and country. Those who insist on English often equate bilingualism with lack of patriotism. Their intention to legislate official English often masks racism and certainly fails to appreciate cultural difference: it is a thinly-veiled measure to disenfranchise anyone not like "us" (with notions of "us," the real Americans, changing over the years from those of English ancestry to northwestern European to "white" monolingual English speakers).

American culture assumes monolingual competence in English. The ability to speak another language is more generally regarded as a liability than a refinement, a curse of ethnicity and a bar to advancement rather than an economic or educational advantage.

In another response to non-English speaking American citizens, during the nineteenth century, states began instituting English literacy requirements for voting to replace older property requirements. These literacy laws generally pretended to democratize the voting process, though their hidden goal was often to prevent specific groups from voting. The first such statutes in Connecticut and Massachusetts were aimed at the Irish population of those states. Southern literacy tests instituted after the Civil War were anti-Black. California's test (1892) was aimed at Hispanics and Asians. Alaska's, in 1926, sought to disenfranchise its Native Americans. Wyoming's (1897) was anti-Finn and Washington state's (1889), anti-Chinese.

The literacy law proposed for New York State in 1915, whose surface aim was to ensure a well-informed electorate, targeted a number of the state's minorities. It was seen both as a calculated attempt to prevent New York's one million Yiddish speakers from voting and as a means of stopping the state's German Americans from furthering their nefarious war aims. When it was finally enacted in 1921, supporters of the literacy test saw it as a tool to enforce Americanization, while opponents charged the test would keep large numbers of the state's newly enfranchised immigrant women from voting. Later, the law, which was not repealed until the Voting Rights Act of 1965, effectively disenfranchised New York's Puerto Rican community.

AN OFFICIAL LANGUAGE?

Although many Americans simply assume English is the official language of the United States, it is not. Nowhere in the US Constitution is English privileged over other languages, and while a few subsequent federal laws require the use of English for special, limited purposes—air traffic control, product labels, service on federal juries—no law establishes English as the language of the land.

In the xenophobic period following World War I, several moves were made to establish English at the federal level, but none succeeded. On the other hand, many states at that time adopted some form of English-only legislation. This included regulations designating English the language of state legislatures, courts, and schools, making English a requirement for entrance into such professions as attorney, barber, physician, private detective, or undertaker, and in some states even preventing nonanglophones from obtaining hunting and fishing licenses.

More recently, official language questions have been the subject of state and local debate once again. An English Language Amendment to the US Constitution (the ELA) has been before the Congress every year since 1981. In 1987, the year in which more than 74 percent of California's voters indicated their support for English as the state's official language, thirty-seven states discussed the official English issue. The next year, official language laws were passed in Colorado, Florida, and Arizona. New Mexico and Michigan have taken a stand in favor of English Plus, recommending that everyone have a knowledge of English plus another language. . . .

Official American policy has swung wildly between toleration of languages other than English and their complete eradication. But neither legal protection nor community-based efforts has been able to prevent the decline of minority languages or to slow the adoption of English, particularly among the young. Conversely, neither legislation making English the official language of a state nor the efforts of the schools has done much to enforce the use of English: Americans exhibit a high degree of linguistic anxiety but continue to resist interference with their language use on the part of legislators or teachers.

A number of states have adopted official English. Illinois, for example, in the rush of post-war isolationism and anti-British sentiment, made *American* its official language in 1923; this was quietly changed to English in 1969. Official English in Illinois has been purely symbolic; it is a statute with no teeth and no discernible range or effect. In contrast, Arizona's law, which became part of the state constitution, was the most detailed and the most restrictive of any of the sixteen state official language laws currently on the books. It required all government officials and employees—from the governor down to the municipal dog catcher—to use English and only English during the performance of government business.

[In 1990] Arizona's law was ruled unconstitutional by the US District Court for the District of Arizona. Arizona's law was challenged by Maria-Kelley Yniguez, a state insurance claims administrator fluent in Spanish and English, who had often used Spanish with clients. Yniguez feared that, since she was sworn to uphold the state constitution, speaking Spanish to clients of her agency who knew no other language might put her in legal jeopardy.

Judge Paul G. Rosenblatt, of the US District Court for the District of Arizona, found that the English-only article 28 of the Arizona constitution violated the First Amendment of the US Constitution protecting free speech. The ruling voiding the Arizona law will not affect the status of other state official English laws. However, it is clear that other courts may take the Arizona decision into consideration.

TEACHING OUR CHILDREN

Perhaps the most sensitive area of minority-language use in the US has been in the schools. Minority-language schools have existed in North America since the 18th century. In the 19th century bilingual education was common in the Midwest—St. Louis and a number of Ohio cities had active English-German public schools—as well as in parochial schools in other areas with large nonanglophone populations. More commonly, though, the schools ignored non-English speaking children altogether, making no curricular or pedagogical concessions to their presence in class. Indeed, newly instituted classroom speech requirements in the early part of this century ensured that anglophone students with foreign accents would be sent to pathologists for corrective action. And professional licensing requirements that included speech certification tests were used to keep Chinese in California and Jews in New York out of the teaching corps.

The great American school myth has us believe that the schools Americanized generations of immigrants, giving them English and, in consequence, the ability to succeed. In fact, in allowing nonanglophone children to sink or swim, the schools ensured that most of them would fail: dropout rates for non-English speakers were extraordinarily high and English was more commonly acquired on the streets and playgrounds or on the job than in the classroom.

We tend to think past generations of immigrants succeeded at assimilation while the present generation has (for reasons liberals are willing to explain away) failed. In fact, today's Hispanics are acquiring English and assimilating in much the same way and at the same pace as Germans or Jews or Italians of earlier generations did.

California presented an extreme model for excluding children with no English: it segregated Chinese students into separate "oriental" English-only schools until well into the 20th century. The ending of segregation did little to improve the linguistic fortunes of California's Chinese-speakers, who continued to be ignored by the schools. They were eventually forced to appeal to the Supreme Court to force state authorities to provide for their educational needs. The decision that resulted in the landmark case of *Lau v. Nichols* (1974) did not, however, guarantee minority-language rights, nor did it require bilingual education, as many opponents of bilingual education commonly argue. Instead the Supreme Court ordered schools to provide education for all students whether or not they spoke English, a task our schools are still struggling to carry out.

Confusion over language in the schools seems a major factor behind official language concerns. Bilingual education is a prime target of English-only lobbying groups, who fear it is a device for minority language maintenance rather than for an orderly transition to English. Troubling to teachers as well is the fact that bilingual programs are often poorly defined, underfunded, and inadequately staffed, while parents and students frequently regard bilingual as a euphemism for remedial. In its defense, we can say that second language education did not come into its own in this country until after World War II. Bilingual education, along with other programs designed to teach English as a second language, are really the first attempts by American schools in more than two centuries to deal directly with the problem of non-English speaking children. They represent the first attempts to revise language education in an effort to keep children in school; to keep them from repeating the depressing and wasteful pattern of failure experienced by earlier generations of immigrants and nonanglophone natives; to get them to respect rather than revile both English, frequently perceived as the language of oppression, and their native tongue, all too often rejected as the language of poverty and failure.

Despite resistance to bilingual education and problems with its implementation, the theory behind it remains sound. Children who learn reading, arithmetic, and other subjects in their native language while they are being taught English will not be as likely to fall behind their anglophone peers, and will have little difficulty transferring their subject-matter knowledge to English as their English proficiency increases. On the other hand, when nonanglophone children or those with very limited English are immersed in English-only classrooms and left to sink or swim, as they were for generations, they will continue to fail at unacceptable rates.

ENGLISH IS HERE TO STAY

Those Americans who fear that unless English is made the official language of the United States by means of federal and state constitutional amendments they are about to be swamped by new waves of non-English-speakers should realize that even without restrictive legislation, minority languages in the US have always been marginal. Research shows that Hispanics, who now constitute the nation's largest minority-language group, are adopting English in the second and third generation in the same way that speakers of German, Italian, Yiddish, Russian, Polish, Chinese or Japanese have done in the past. However, as the experience of Hispanics in southern California suggests, simply acquiring English is not bringing the educational and economic successes promised by the melting-pot myth. Linguistic assimilation may simply not be enough to overcome more deep-seated prejudices against Hispanics.

Nonetheless, there are many minority-language speakers in the US, and with continued immigration they will continue to make their presence felt. The 1980 Census showed that one in seven Americans speaks a language other than English, or lives with someone who does. Even if the courts do not strike down English-only laws, it would be difficult to legislate minority languages out of existence because we simply have no mechanisms in this country to carry out language policy of any kind (schools, which are under local and state control, have been remarkably erratic in the area of language education). On the other hand, even in the absence of restrictive language legislation, American society enforces its own irresistible pressure to keep the United States an English-speaking nation. The Census also reports that 97 percent of Americans identify themselves as speaking English well or very well. English may not be official, but it is definitely here to stay.

. . . The issue of minority languages will not soon go away, and a constitutional amendment cannot force people to adopt English if they are unwilling or unable to do so. Nor will English cease to function as the nation's official language even if it does not have a constitutional amendment to establish it.

English-only legislation, past and present, no matter how idealistic or patriotic its claims, is supported by a long history of nativism, racism, and religious bigotry. While an English Language Amendment to the US Constitution might ultimately prove no more symbolic than the selection of an official bird or flower or fossil, it is possible that the ELA could become a tool for linguistic repression. Those who point to Canada or Belgium or India or the Soviet Union as instances where multilingualism produces civil strife would do well to remember that such strife invariably occurs when minority-language rights are suppressed. In any case, such examples have little in common with the situation in the United States.

The main danger of an ELA, as I see it, would be to alienate minority-language speakers, sabotaging their chances for education and distancing them further from the American mainstream, at the same time hindering rather than facilitating the linguistic assimilation that has occurred so efficiently up to now in the absence of legal prodding.

READING 46

Racism in the English Language

Robert B. Moore

LANGUAGE AND CULTURE

An integral part of any culture is its language. Language not only develops in conjunction with a society's historical, economic and political evolution; it also reflects that society's attitudes and thinking. Language not only *expresses* ideas and concepts but actually *shapes* thought.[1] If one accepts that our dominant white culture is racist, then one would expect our language—an indispensable transmitter of culture—to be racist as well. Whites, as the dominant group, are not subjected to the same abusive characterization by our language that people of color receive. Aspects of racism in the English language that will be discussed in this essay include terminology, symbolism, politics, ethnocentrism, and context.

Before beginning our analysis of racism in language we would like to quote part of a TV film review which shows the connection between language and culture.[2]

> Depending on one's culture, one interacts with time in a very distinct fashion. One example which gives some cross-cultural insights into the concept of time is language. In Spanish, a watch is said to "walk." In English, the watch "runs." In German, the watch "functions." And in French, the watch "marches." In the Indian culture of the Southwest, people do not refer to time in this way. The value of the watch is displaced with the value of "what time it's getting to be." Viewing these five cultural perspectives of time, one can see some definite emphasis and values that each culture places on time. For example, a cultural perspective may provide a clue to why the negative stereotype of the

---

No biographical information available.

> slow and lazy Mexican who lives in the "Land of Manana" exists in the Anglo value system, where time "flies," the watch "runs" and "time is money."

A SHORT PLAY ON "BLACK" AND "WHITE" WORDS

Some may blackly (angrily) accuse me of trying to blacken (defame) the English language, to give it a black eye (a mark of shame) by writing such black words (hostile). They may denigrate (to cast aspersions; to darken) me by accusing me of being blackhearted (malevolent), of having a black outlook (pessimistic, dismal) on life, of being a blackguard (scoundrel)—which would certainly be a black mark (detrimental fact) against me. Some may black-brow (scowl at) me and hope that a black cat crosses in front of me because of this black deed. I may become a black sheep (one who causes shame or embarrassment because of deviation from the accepted standards), who will be blackballed (ostracized) by being placed on a blacklist (list of undesirables) in an attempt to blackmail (to force or coerce into a particular action) me to retract my words. But attempts to blackjack (to compel by threat) me will have a Chinaman's chance of success, for I am not a yellow-bellied Indian-giver of words, who will whitewash (cover up or gloss over vices or crimes) a black lie (harmful, inexcusable). I challenge the purity and innocence (white) of the English language. I don't see things in black and white (entirely bad or entirely good) terms, for I am a white man (marked by upright firmness) if there ever was one. However, it would be a black day when I would not "call a spade a spade," even though some will suggest a white man calling the English language racist is like the pot calling the kettle black. While many may be niggardly (grudging, scanty) in their support, others will be honest and decent—and to them I say, that's very white of you (honest, decent).

The preceding is of course a white lie (not intended to cause harm), meant only to illustrate some examples of racist terminology in the English language.

OBVIOUS BIGOTRY

Perhaps the most obvious aspect of racism in language would be terms like "nigger," "spook," "chink," "spic," etc. While these may be facing increasing social disdain, they certainly are not dead. Large numbers of white Americans continue to utilize these terms. "Chink," "gook," and "slant-eyes" were in common usage among U.S. troops in Vietnam. An NBC nightly news broadcast, in February 1972, reported that the basketball team in Pekin, Illinois, was called the "Pekin Chinks" and noted that even though this had been protested by Chinese Americans, the term continued to be used because it was easy, and meant no harm. Spiro Agnew's widely reported "fat Jap" remark and the "little Jap" comment of lawyer John Wilson during the Watergate hearings, are surface indicators of a deep-rooted Archie Bunkerism.

Many white people continue to refer to Black people as "colored," as for instance in a July 30, 1975 *Boston Globe* article on a racist attack by whites on a group of Black people using a public beach in Boston. One white person was quoted as follows:

> We've always welcomed good colored people in South Boston but we will not tolerate radical blacks or Communists. . . . Good colored people are welcome in South Boston, black militants are not.

Many white people may still be unaware of the disdain many African Americans have for the term "colored," but it often appears that whether used intentionally or unintentionally, "colored" people are "good" and "know their place," while "Black" people are perceived as "uppity" and "threatening" to many whites. Similarly, the term "boy" to refer to African American men is now acknowledged to be a demeaning term, though still in common use. Other terms such as "the pot calling the kettle black" and "calling a spade a spade" have negative racial connotations but are still frequently used, as for example when President Ford was quoted in February 1976 saying that even though Daniel Moynihan had left the U.N., the U.S. would continue "calling a spade a spade."

COLOR SYMBOLISM

The symbolism of white as positive and black as negative is pervasive in our culture, with the black/white words used in the beginning of this essay only one of many aspects. "Good guys" wear white hats and ride white horses, "bad guys" wear black hats and ride black horses. Angels are white, and devils are black. The definition of *black* includes "without any moral light or goodness, evil, wicked, indicating disgrace, sinful," while that of *white* includes "morally pure, spotless, innocent, free from evil intent."

A children's TV cartoon program, *Captain Scarlet,* is about an organization called Spectrum, whose purpose is to save the world from an evil extraterrestrial force called the Mysterons. Everyone in Spectrum has a color name—Captain Scarlet, Captain Blue, etc. The one Spectrum agent who has been mysteriously taken over by the Mysterons and works to advance their evil aims is Captain Black. The person who heads Spectrum, the good organization out to defend the world, is Colonel White.

Three of the dictionary definitions of white are "fairness of complexion, purity, innocence." These definitions affect the standards of beauty in our culture, in which whiteness represents the norm. "Blondes have more fun" and "Wouldn't you really rather be a blonde" are sexist in their attitudes toward women generally, but are racist white standards when applied to third world women. A 1971 *Mademoiselle* advertisement pictured a curly-headed, ivory-skinned woman over the caption, "When you go blonde go all the way," and asked: "Isn't this how, in the back of your mind, you always wanted to look? All wide-eyed and silky blonde down to there, and innocent?" Whatever the advertising people meant by this particular woman's innocence, one must remember that "innocent" is one of the definitions of the word white. This standard of beauty when preached to all women is racist. The statement "Isn't this how, in the back of your mind, you always wanted to look?" either ignores third world women or assumes they long to be white.

Time magazine in its coverage of the Wimbledon tennis competition between the black Australian Evonne Goolagong and the white American Chris Evert described Ms. Goolagong as "the dusky daughter of an Australian sheepshearer," while Ms. Evert was "a fair young girl from the middle-class groves of Florida." *Dusky* is a synonym of "black" and is defined as "having dark skin; of a dark color; gloomy; dark; swarthy." Its antonyms are "fair" and "blonde." *Fair* is defined in part as "free from blemish, imperfection, or anything that impairs the appearance, quality, or character; pleasing in appearance, attractive; clean; pretty; comely." By defining Evonne Goolagong as "dusky," *Time* technically defined her as the opposite of "pleasing in appearance; attractive; clean; pretty; comely."

The studies of Kenneth B. Clark, Mary Ellen Goodman, Judith Porter and others indicate that this persuasive "rightness of whiteness" in U.S. culture affects children before the age of four, providing white youngsters with a false sense of superiority and encouraging self-hatred among third world youngsters.

ETHNOCENTRISM OR FROM A WHITE PERSPECTIVE

Some words and phrases that are commonly used represent particular perspectives and frames of reference, and these often distort the understanding of the reader or listener. David R. Burgest[3] has written about the effect of using the terms "slave" or "master." He argues that the psychological impact of the statement referring to "the master raped his slave" is different from the impact of the same statement substituting the words: "the white captor raped an African woman held in captivity."

> Implicit in the English usage of the "master-slave" concept is ownership of the "slave" by the "master," therefore, the "master" is merely abusing his property (slave). In reality, the captives (slave) were African individuals with human worth, right and dignity and the term "slave" denounces that human quality thereby making the mass rape of African women by white captors more acceptable in the minds of people and setting a mental frame of reference for legitimizing the atrocities perpetuated against African people.

The term "slave" connotes a less than human quality and turns the captive person into a thing. For example, two McGraw-Hill Far Eastern Publishers textbooks (1970) stated, "At first it was the slaves who worked the cane and they got only food for it. Now men work cane and get money." Next time you write about slavery or read about it, try transposing all "slaves" into "African people held in captivity," "Black people forced to work for no pay" or "African people stolen from their families and societies." While it is more cumbersome, such phrasing conveys a different meaning.

PASSIVE TENSE

Another means by which language shapes our perspective has been noted by Thomas Greenfield,[4] who writes that the achievements of Black people—and Black people themselves—have been hidden in

> the linguistic ghetto of the passive voice, the subordinate clause, and the "understood" subject. The seemingly innocuous distinction (between active/passive voice) holds enormous implications for writers and speakers. When it is effectively applied, the rhetorical impact of the passive voice—the art of making the creator or instigator of action totally disappear from a reader's perception—can be devastating.

For instance, some history texts will discuss how European immigrants came to the United States seeking a better life and expanded opportunities, but will note that "slaves *were brought* to America." Not only does this omit the destruction of African societies and families, but it ignores the role of northern merchants and southern slaveholders in the profitable trade in human beings. Other books will state that "the continental railroad *was built,*" conveniently omitting information about the Chinese laborers who built much of it or the oppression they suffered.

Another example. While touring Monticello, Greenfield noted that the tour guide

> made all the black people at Monticello disappear through her use of the passive voice. While speaking of the architectural achievements of Jefferson in the active voice, she unfailingly shifted to passive when speaking of the work performed by Negro slaves and skilled servants.

Noting a type of door that after 166 years continued to operate without need for repair, Greenfield remarks that the design aspect of the door was much simpler than the actual skill and work involved in building and installing it. Yet his guide stated: "Mr. Jefferson designed these doors . . ." while "the doors **were installed** in 1809." The workers who installed those doors were African people whom Jefferson held in bondage. The guide's use of the passive tense enabled her to dismiss the reality of Jefferson's slaveholding. It also meant that she did not have to make any mention of the skills of those people held in bondage.

POLITICS AND TERMINOLOGY

"Culturally deprived," "economically disadvantaged" and "underdeveloped" are other terms which mislead and distort our awareness of reality. The application of the term "culturally deprived" and third world children in this society reflects a value judgment. It assumes that the dominant whites are cultured and all others without culture. In fact, third world children generally are bicultural, and many are bilingual, having grown up in their own culture as well as absorbing the dominant culture. In many ways, they are equipped with skills and experiences which white youth have been deprived of, since most white youth develop in a monocultural, monolingual environment. Burgest[5] suggests that the term "culturally deprived" be replaced by "culturally dispossessed," and that the term "economically disadvantaged" be replaced by "economically exploited." Both these terms present a perspective and implication that provide an entirely different frame of reference as to the reality of the third world experience in U.S. society.

Similarly, many nations of the third world are described as "underdeveloped." These less wealthy nations are generally those that suffered under colonialism and neo-colonialism. The "developed" nations are those that exploited their resources and wealth. Therefore, rather than referring to these countries as "underdeveloped," a more appropriate and meaningful designation might be "over exploited." Again, transpose this term next time you read about "underdeveloped nations" and note the different meaning that results.

Terms such as "culturally deprived," "economically disadvantaged" and "underdeveloped" place the responsibility for their own conditions on those being so described. This is known as "Blaming the Victim."[6] It places responsibility for poverty on the victims of poverty. It removes the blame from those in power who benefit from, and continue to permit, poverty.

Still another example involves the use of "non-white," "minority" or "third world." While people of color are a minority in the U.S., they are part of the vast majority of the world's population, in which white people are a distinct minority. Thus, by utilizing the term minority to describe people of color in the U.S., we can lose sight of the global majority/minority reality—a fact of some importance in the increasing and interconnected struggles of people of color inside and outside the U.S.

To describe people of color as "non-white" is to use whiteness as the standard and norm against which to measure all others. Use of the term "third world" to describe all people of color overcomes the inherent bias of "minority" and "nonwhite." Moreover, it connects the struggles of third world people in the U.S. with the freedom struggles around the globe.

The term "third world" gained increasing usage after the 1955 Bandung Conference of "non-aligned" nations, which represented a third force outside of the two world superpowers. The "first world" represents the United States, Western Europe and their sphere of influence. The "second world" represents the Soviet Union and its sphere. The "third world" represents, for the most part, nations that were, or are, controlled by the "first world" or West. For the most part, these are nations of Africa, Asia and Latin America.

"LOADED" WORDS AND NATIVE AMERICANS

Many words lead to a demeaning characterization of groups of people. For instance, Columbus, it is said, "discovered" America. The word *discover* is defined as "to gain sight or knowledge of something previously unseen or unknown; to discover may be to find some existent thing that was previously unknown." Thus, a continent inhabited by millions of human beings cannot be "discovered." For history books to continue this usage represents a Eurocentric (white European) perspective on world history and ignores the existence of, and the perspective of, Native Americans. "Discovery," as used in the Euro-American context, implies the right to take what one finds, ignoring the rights of those who already inhabit or own the "discovered" thing.

Eurocentrism is also apparent in the usage of "victory" and "massacre" to describe the battles between Native Americans and whites. *Victory* is defined in the dictionary as "a success or triumph over an enemy in battle or war; the decisive defeat of an opponent." *Conquest* denotes the "taking over of control by the victor, and the obedience of the conquered." *Massacre* is defined as "the unnecessary, indiscriminate killing of a number of human beings, as in barbarous warfare or persecution, or for revenge or plunder." *Defend* is described as "to ward off attack from; guard against assault or injury; to strive to keep safe by resisting attack."

Eurocentrism turns these definitions around to serve the purpose of distorting history and justifying Euro-American conquest of the Native American homelands. Euro-Americans are not described in history books as invading Native American lands, but rather as defending *their* homes against "Indian" attacks. Since European communities were constantly encroaching on land already occupied, then a more honest interpretation would state that it was the Native Americans who were "warding off," "guarding" and "defending" their homelands.

Native American victories are invariably defined as "massacres," while the indiscriminate killing, extermination and plunder of Native American nations by Euro-Americans is defined as "victory." Distortion of history by the choice of "loaded" words used to describe historical events is a common racist practice. Rather than portraying Native Americans as human beings in highly defined and complex societies, cultures and civilizations, history books use such adjectives as "savages," "beasts," "primitive," and "backward." Native people are referred to as "squaw," "brave," or "papoose" instead of "woman," "man," or "baby."

Another term that has questionable connotations is *tribe*. The Oxford English Dictionary defines this noun as "a race of people; now applied especially to a primary aggregate of people in a primitive or barbarous condition, under a headman or chief." Morton Fried,[7] discussing "The Myth of Tribe," states that the word "did not become a general term of reference to American Indian society until the nineteenth century. Previously, the words commonly used for Indian populations were 'nation' and 'people.'" Since "tribe" has assumed a connotation of primitiveness or backwardness, it is suggested that the use of "nation" or "people" replace the term whenever possible in referring to Native American peoples.

The term *tribe* invokes even more negative implications when used in reference to American peoples. As Evelyn Jones Rich[8] has noted, the term is "almost always used to refer to third world people and it implies a stage of development which is, in short, a put-down."

"LOADED" WORDS AND AFRICANS

Conflicts among diverse peoples within African nations are often referred to as "tribal warfare," while conflicts among the diverse peoples within European countries are never described in such terms. If the rivalries between the Ibo and the Hausa and Yoruba in Nigeria are described as "tribal," why not the rivalries between Serbs and Slavs in Yugoslavia, or Scots and English in Great Britain, Protestants and Catholics in Ireland, or the Basques and the Southern Spaniards in Spain? Conflicts among African peoples in a particular nation have religious, cultural, economic and/or political roots. If we can analyze the roots of conflicts among European peoples in terms other than "tribal warfare," certainly we can do the same with African peoples, including correct reference to the ethnic groups or nations involved. For example, the terms "Kaffirs," "Hottentot" or "Bushmen" are names imposed by white Europeans. The correct names are always those by which a people refer to themselves. (In these instances Xhosa, Khoi-Khoin and San are correct.[9])

The generalized application of "tribal" in reference to Africans—as well as the failure to acknowledge the religious, cultural and social diversity of African peoples—is a decidedly racist dynamic. It is part of the process whereby

Euro-Americans justify, or avoid confronting, their oppression of third world peoples. Africa has been particularly insulted by this dynamic, as witness the pervasive "darkest Africa" image. This image, widespread in Western culture, evokes an Africa covered by jungles and inhibited by "uncivilized," "cannibalistic," "pagan," "savage" peoples. This "darkest Africa" image avoids the geographical reality. Less than 20 percent of the African continent is wooded savanna, for example. The image also ignores the history of African cultures and civilizations. Ample evidence suggests this distortion of reality was developed as a convenient rationale for the European and American slave trade. The Western powers, rather than exploiting, were civilizing and christianizing "uncivilized" and "pagan savages" (so the rationalization went). This dynamic also served to justify Western colonialism. From Tarzan movies to racist children's books like *Doctor Dolittle* and *Charlie and the Chocolate Factory,* the image of "savage" Africa and the myth of "the white man's burden" has been perpetuated in Western culture.

A 1972 *Time* magazine editorial lamenting the demise of *Life* magazine, stated that the "lavishness" of *Life*'s enterprises included "organizing safaris into darkest Africa." The same year, the *New York Times'* C. L. Sulzberger wrote that "Africa has a history as dark as the skins of many of its people." Terms such as "darkest Africa," "primitive," "tribe" ("tribal") or "jungle," in reference to Africa, perpetuate myths and are especially inexcusable in such large circulation publications.

Ethnocentrism is similarly reflected in the term "pagan" to describe traditional religions. A February 1973 *Time* magazine article on Uganda stated, "Moslems account for only 500,000 of Uganda's 10 million people. Of the remainder, 5,000,000 are Christians and the rest pagan." *Pagan* is defined as "Heathen, a follower of a polytheistic religion; one that has little or no religion and that is marked by a frank delight in and uninhibited seeking after sensual pleasures and material goods." *Heathen* is defined as "Unenlightened; an unconverted member of a people or nation that does not acknowledge the God of the Bible. A person whose culture or enlightenment is of an inferior grade, especially an irreligious person." Now, the people of Uganda, like almost all Africans, have serious religious beliefs and practices. As used by Westerners, "pagan" connotes something wild, primitive and inferior—another term to watch out for.

The variety of traditional structures that African people live in are their "houses," not "huts." A *hut* is "an often small and temporary dwelling of simple construction." And to describe Africans as "natives" (noun) is derogatory terminology—as in, "the natives are restless." The dictionary definition of *native* includes: "one of a people inhabiting a territorial area at the time of its discovery or becoming familiar to a foreigner; one belonging to a people having a less complex civilization." Therefore, use of "native," like use of "pagan" often implies a value judgment of white superiority.

QUALIFYING ADJECTIVES

Words that would normally have positive connotations can have entirely different meanings when used in a racial context. For example, C. L. Sulzberger, the columnist of the *New York Times,* wrote in January 1975, about conversations he had with two people in Namibia. One was the white South African administrator of the country and the other a member of SWAPO, the Namibian liberation movement. The first is described as "Dirk Mudge, who as senior elected member of the administration is a kind of acting Prime Minister. . . . " But the second person is introduced as "Daniel Tijongarero, an intelligent Herero tribesman who is a member of SWAPO. . . ." What need was there for Sulzberger to state that Daniel Tijongarero is "intelligent"? Why not also state that Dirk Mudge was "intelligent"—or do we assume he wasn't?

A similar example from a 1968 *New York Times* article reporting on an address by Lyndon Johnson stated, "The President spoke to the well-dressed Negro officials and their wives." In what similar circumstances can one imagine a reporter finding it necessary to note that an audience of white government officials was "well-dressed?"

Still another word often used in a racist context is "qualified." In the 1960s white Americans often questioned whether Black people were "qualified" to hold public office, a question that was never raised (until too late) about white officials like Wallace, Maddox, Nixon, Agnew, Mitchell, et al. The question of qualifications has been raised even more frequently in recent years as white people question whether Black people are "qualified" to be hired for positions in industry and educational institutions. "We're looking for a qualified Black" has been heard again and again as institutions are confronted with affirmative action goals. Why stipulate that Blacks must be "qualified," when for others it is taken for granted that applicants must be "qualified."

SPEAKING ENGLISH

Finally, the depiction in movies and children's books of third world people speaking English is often itself racist. Children's books about Puerto Ricans or Chicanos often connect poverty with a failure to speak English or to speak it well, thus blaming the victim and ignoring the racism which affects third world people regardless of their proficiency in English. Asian characters speak a stilted English ("Honorable so and so" or "Confucius say") or have a speech impediment ("roots or ruck," "very solly," "flied lice"). Native American characters speak another variation of stilted English ("Boy not hide. Indian take boy."), repeat certain Hollywood-Indian phrases ("Heap big" and "Many moons") or simply grunt out "Ugh" or "How." The repeated use of these language characterizations functions to make third world people seem less intelligent and less capable than the English-speaking white characters.

WRAP-UP

A *Saturday Review* editorial[10] on "The Environment of Language" stated that language

> . . . has as much to do with the philosophical and political conditioning of a society as geography or climate. . . . people in Western cultures do not realize the extent to which their racial attitudes have been conditioned since early childhood by the power of words to ennoble or condemn, augment or detract, glorify or demean. Negative language infects the subconscious of most Western people from the time they first learn to speak. Prejudice is not merely imparted or superimposed. It is metabolized in the bloodstream of society. What is needed is not so much a change in language as an awareness of the power of words to condition attitudes. If we can at least recognize the underpinnings of prejudice, we may be in a position to deal with the effects.

To recognize the racism in language is an important first step. Consciousness of the influence of language on our perceptions can help to negate much of that influence. But it is not enough to simply become aware of the affects of racism in conditioning attitudes. While we may not be able to change the language, we can definitely change our usage of the language. We can avoid using words that degrade people. We can make a conscious effort to use terminology that reflects a progressive perspective, as opposed to a distorting perspective. It is important for educators to provide students with opportunities to explore racism in language and to increase their awareness of it, as well as learning terminology that is positive and does not perpetuate negative human values.

NOTES

1. Simon Podair, "How Bigotry Builds Through Language," *Negro Digest,* March 1967.
2. Jose Armas, "Antonio and the Mayor: A Cultural Review of the Film," *The Journal of Ethnic Studies,* Fall, 1975.
3. David R. Burgest, "The Racist Use of the English Language," *Black Scholar,* Sept. 1973.

4. Thomas Greenfield, "Race and Passive Voice at Monticello," *Crisis,* April 1975.
5. David R. Burgest, "Racism in Everyday Speech and Social Work Jargon," *Social Work,* July 1973.
6. William Ryan, *Blaming the Victim,* Pantheon Books, 1971.
7. Morton Fried, "The Myth of Tribe," *National History,* April 1975.
8. Evelyn Jones Rich, "Mind Your Language," *Africa Report,* Sept./Oct. 1974.
9. Steve Wolf, "Catalogers in Revolt Against LC's Racist, Sexist Headings," *Bulletin of Interracial Books for Children,* Vol. 6, Nos. 3&4, 1975.
10. "The Environment of Language," *Saturday Review,* April 8, 1967.

Also see:

Roger Bastide, "Color, Racism and Christianity," *Daedalus,* Spring 1967.

Kenneth J. Gergen, "The Significance of Skin Color in Human Relations," *Daedalus,* Spring 1967.

Lloyd Yabura, "Towards a Language of Humanism," *Rhythm,* Summer 1971.

UNESCO, "Recommendations Concerning Terminology in Education on Race Questions," June 1968.

READING 47

Gender Stereotyping in the English Language

Laurel Richardson*

Everyone in our society, regardless of class, ethnicity, sex, age, or race, is exposed to the same language, the language of the dominant culture. Analysis of verbal language can tell us a great deal about a people's fears, prejudices, anxieties, and interests. A rich vocabulary on a particular subject indicates societal interests or obsessions (e.g., the extensive vocabulary about cars in America). And different words for the same subject (such as *freedom fighter* and *terrorist, passed away* and *croaked, make love* and *ball*) show that there is a range of attitudes and feelings in the society toward that subject.

It should not be surprising, then, to find differential attitudes and feelings about men and women rooted in the English language. Although the English language has not been completely analyzed, six general propositions concerning these attitudes and feelings about males and females can be made.

First, in terms of grammatical and semantic structure, women do not have a fully autonomous, independent existence; they are part of man. The language is not divided into male and female with distinct conjugations and declensions, as many other languages are. Rather, *women* are included under the generic *man.* Grammar books specify that the pronoun *he* can be used generically to mean *he* or *she.* Further, *man,* when used as an indefinite pronoun, grammatically refers to both men and women. So, for example, when we read *man* in the following phrases we are to interpret it as applying to both men and women: "man the oars," "one small step for man, one giant step for mankind," "man, that's tough," "man overboard," "man the toolmaker," "alienated man," "garbageman." Our rules of etiquette complete the grammatical presumption of inclusivity. When two persons are pronounced "man and wife," Miss Susan Jones changes her entire name to Mrs. Robert Gordon (Vanderbilt, 1972). In each of these correct usages, women are a part of man; they do not exist autonomously. The exclusion of women is well expressed in Mary Daly's ear-jarring slogan "the sisterhood of man" (1973:7–21).

However, there is some question as to whether the theory that *man* means everybody is carried out in practice (see Bendix, 1979; Martyna, 1980). For example, an eight-year-old interrupts

*Adapted from Laurel Richardson, *The Dynamics of Sex and Gender: A Sociological Perspective* (New York: Harper & Row, 1987), by permission of the author.

Laurel Richardson is emeritus professor, Ohio State University.

her reading of "The Story of the Cavemen" to ask how we got here without cavewomen. A ten-year-old thinks it is dumb to have a woman post*man.* A beginning anthropology student believes (incorrectly) that all shamans ("witch doctors") are males because her textbook and professor use the referential pronoun *he.*

But beginning language learners are not the only ones who visualize males when they see the word *man.* Research has consistently demonstrated that when the generic *man* is used, people visualize men, not women (Schneider & Hacker, 1973; DeStefano, 1976; Martyna, 1978; Hamilton & Henley, 1982). DeStafano, for example, reports that college students choose silhouettes of males for sentences with the word *man* or *men* in them. Similarly, the presumably generic *he* elicits images of men rather than women. The finding is so persistent that linguists doubt whether there actually is a semantic generic in English (MacKay, 1983).

Man, then, suggests not humanity but rather male images. Moreover, over one's lifetime, an educated American will be exposed to the prescriptive *he* more than a million times (MacKay, 1983). One consequence is the exclusion of women in the visualization, imagination, and thought of males and females. Most likely this linguistic practice perpetuates in men their feelings of dominance over and responsibility for women, feelings that interfere with the development of equality in relationships.

Second, in actual practice, our pronoun usage perpetuates different personality attributes and career aspirations for men and women. Nurses, secretaries, and elementary school teachers are almost invariably referred to as *she;* doctors, engineers, electricians, and presidents as *he.* In one classroom, students referred to an unidentified child as *he* but shifted to *she* when discussing the child's parent. In a faculty discussion of the problems of acquiring new staff, all architects, engineers, security officers, faculty, and computer programmers were referred to as *he;* secretaries and file clerks were referred to as *she.* Martyna (1978) has noted that speakers consistently use *he* when the referent has a high-status occupation (e.g., doctor, lawyer, judge) but shift to *she* when the occupations have lower status (e.g., nurse, secretary).

Even our choice of sex ascription to nonhuman objects subtly reinforces different personalities for males and females. It seems as though the small (e.g., kittens), the graceful (e.g., poetry), the unpredictable (e.g., the fates), the nurturant (e.g., the church, the school), and that which is owned and/or controlled by men (e.g., boats, cars, governments, nations) represent the feminine, whereas that which is a controlling forceful power in and of itself (e.g., God, Satan, tiger) primarily represents the masculine. Even athletic teams are not immune. In one college, the men's teams are called the Bearcats and the women's teams the Bearkittens.

Some of you may wonder whether it matters that the female is linguistically included in the male. The inclusion of women under the pseudogeneric *man* and the prescriptive *he,* however, is not a trivial issue. Language has tremendous power to shape attitudes and influence behavior. Indeed, MacKay (1983) argues that the prescriptive *he* "has all the characteristics of a highly effective propaganda technique": frequent repetition, early age of acquisition (before age 6), covertness (*he* is not thought of as propaganda), use by high-prestige sources (including university texts and professors), and indirectness (presented as though it were a matter of common knowledge). As a result, the prescriptive affects females' sense of life options and feelings of well-being. For example, Adamsky (1981) found that women's sense of power and importance was enhanced when the prescriptive *he* was replaced by *she.*

Awareness of the impact of the generic *man* and prescriptive *he* has generated considerable activity to change the language. One change, approved by the Modern Language Association, is to replace the prescriptive *he* with the plural *they*—as was accepted practice before the 18th century. Another is the use of *he or she.* Although it sounds awkward at first, the *he or she* designation is increasingly being used in the media and among people who have recognized the power of the pronoun to perpetuate sex stereotyping. When a professor, for example, talks about "the lawyer" as "he or she," a speech pattern that counteracts sex stereotyping is modeled. This drive to neutralize the impact of pronouns is evidenced further in the renaming of occupations: a policeman is now a police officer, a postman is a mail carrier, a stewardess is a flight attendant.

Third, linguistic practice defines females as immature, incompetent, and incapable and males as mature, complete, and competent. Because the words *man* and *woman* tend to connote sexual and human maturity, common speech, organizational titles, public addresses, and bathroom doors frequently designate the women in question as *ladies.* Simply contrast the different connotations of *lady* and *woman* in the following common phrases:

> Luck, be a lady (woman) tonight.
>
> Barbara's a little lady (woman).
>
> Ladies' (Women's) Air Corps.

In the first two examples, the use of *lady* desexualizes the contextual meaning of *woman.* So trivializing is the use of *lady* in the last phrase that the second is wholly anomalous. The male equivalent, *lord,* is never used; and its synonym, *gentleman,* is used infrequently. When *gentleman,* is used, the assumption seems to be that certain culturally condoned aspects of masculinity (e.g., aggressivity, activity, and strength) should be set aside in the interests of maturity and order, as in the following phrases:

> A gentlemen's (men's) agreement.
>
> A duel between gentlemen (men).
>
> He's a real gentleman (man).

Rather than feeling constrained to set aside the stereotypes associated with *man,* males frequently find the opposite process occurring. The contextual connotation of *man* places a strain on males to be continuously sexually and socially potent, as the following examples reveal:

> I was not a man (gentleman) with her tonight.
>
> This is a man's (gentleman's) job.
>
> Be a man (gentleman).

Whether males, therefore, feel competent or anxious, valuable or worthless in particular contexts is influenced by the demands placed on them by the expectations of the language.

Not only are men infrequently labeled *gentlemen,* but they are infrequently labeled *boys.* The term *boy* is reserved for young males, bellhops, car attendants, and as a putdown to those males judged inferior. *Boy* connotes immaturity and powerlessness. Only occasionally do males "have a night out with the boys." They do not talk "boy talk" at the office. Rarely does our language legitimize carefreeness in males. Rather, they are expected, linguistically, to adopt the responsibilities of manhood.

On the other hand, women of all ages may be called *girls.* Grown females "play bridge with the girls" and indulge in "girl talk." They are encouraged to remain childlike, and the implication is that they are basically immature and without power. Men can become men, linguistically, putting aside the immaturity of childhood; indeed, for them to retain the openness and playfulness of boyhood is linguistically difficult.

Further, the presumed incompetence and immaturity of women are evidenced by the linguistic company they keep. Women are categorized with children ("women and children first"), the infirm ("the blind, the lame, the women"), and the incompetent ("women, convicts, and idiots"). The use of these categorical designations is not accidental happenstance; "rather these selectional groupings are powerful forces behind the actual expressions of language and are based on distinctions which are not regarded as trivial by the speakers of the language" (Key, 1975:82). A total language analysis of categorical groupings is not available, yet it seems likely that women tend to be included in groupings that designate incompleteness, ineptitude, and immaturity. On the other hand, it is difficult for us to conceive of the word *man* in any categorical grouping other than one that extends beyond humanity, such as "Man, apes, and angels" or "Man and Superman." That is, men do exist as an independent category capable of autonomy; women are grouped with the stigmatized, the immature, and the foolish. Moreover, when men are in human groupings, males are invariably first on the list ("men and women," "he and she," "man and wife"). This order is not accidental but was prescribed in the 16th century to honor the worthier party.

Fourth, in practice women are defined in terms of their sexual desirability (to men); men are defined in terms of their sexual prowess (over women). Most slang words in reference to women refer to their sexual desirability to men (e.g., *dog, fox, broad, ass, chick*). Slang about men refers to their sexual prowess over women (e.g., *dude, stud, hunk*). The fewer examples given for men is not an oversight. An analysis of sexual slang, for example, listed more than 1,000 words and phrases that derogate women sexually but found "nowhere near this multitude for describing men" (Kramarae, 1975:72). Farmer and Henley (cited in Schulz, 1975) list 500 synonyms for *prostitute,* for example, and only 65 for *whoremonger.* Stanley (1977) reports 220 terms for a sexually promiscuous woman and only 22 for a sexually promiscuous man. Shuster (1973) reports that the passive verb form is used in reference to women's sexual experiences (e.g., *to be laid, to be had, to be taken*), whereas the active tense is used in reference to the male's sexual experience (e.g., *lay, take, have*). Being sexually attractive to males is culturally condoned for women and being sexually powerful is approved for males. In this regard, the slang of the street is certainly not countercultural; rather it perpetuates and reinforces different expectations in females and males as sexual objects and performers.

Further, we find sexual connotations associated with neutral words applied to women. A few examples should suffice. A male academician questioned the title of a new course, asserting it was "too suggestive." The title? "The Position of Women in the Social Order." A male tramp is simply a hobo, but a female tramp is a slut. And consider the difference in connotation of the following expressions:

It's easy.
He's easy.
She's easy.

In the first, we assume something is "easy to do"; in the second, we might assume a professor is an "easy grader" or a man is "easygoing." But when we read "she's easy," the connotation is "she's an easy lay."

In the world of slang, men are defined by their sexual prowess. In the world of slang and proper speech, women are defined as sexual objects. The rule in practice seems to be: If in doubt, assume that *any* reference to a women has a sexual connotation. For both genders, the constant bombardment of prescribed sexuality is bound to have real consequences.

Fifth, women are defined in terms of their relations to men; men are defined in terms of their relations to the world at large. A good example is seen in the words *master* and *mistress.* Originally these words had the same meaning—"a person who holds power over servants." With the demise of the feudal system, however, these words took on different meanings. The masculine variant metaphorically refers to power over something; as in "He is the master of his trade"; the feminine variant metaphorically (although probably not in actuality) refers to power over a man sexually, as in "She is Tom's mistress." Men are defined in terms of their power in the occupational world, women in terms of their sexual power over men.

The existence of two contractions for Mistress *(Miss* and *Mrs.)* and but one for Mister *(Mr.)* underscores the cultural concern and linguistic practice: women are defined in relation to men. Even a divorced woman is defined in terms of her no-longer-existing relation to a man (she is still *Mrs. Man's Name*). But apparently the divorced state is not relevant enough to the man or to the society to require a label. A divorced woman is a *divorcee,* but what do you call a divorced man? The recent preference of many women to be called *Ms.* is an attempt to provide for women an equivalency title that is not dependent on marital status.

Sixth, a historical pattern can be seen in the meanings that come to be attached to words that originally were neutral: those that apply to women acquire obscene and/or debased connotations but no such pattern of derogation holds for neutral words referring to men. The processes of *pejoration* (the acquiring of an obscene or debased connotation) and *amelioration* (the reacquiring of a neutral or positive connotation) in the English language in regard to terms for males and females have been studied extensively by Muriel Schulz (1975).

Leveling is the least derogative form of pejoration. Through leveling, titles that originally referred to an elite class of persons come to include a wider class of persons. Such democratic leveling is more common for female designates than for males. For example, contrast the following: *lord-lady (lady); baronet-dame (dame); governor-governess (governess).*

Most frequently what happens to words designating women as they become pejorated, however, is that they come to denote or connote sexual wantonness. *Sir* and *mister,* for example, remain titles of courtesy, but at some time *madam, miss,* and *mistress* have come to designate, respectively, a brothelkeeper, a prostitute, and an unmarried sexual partner of a male (Schulz, 1975:66).

Names for domestic helpers, if they are females, are frequently derogated. *Hussy,* for example, originally meant "housewife." *Laundress, needlewoman, spinster* ("tender of the spinning wheel"), and *nurse* all referred to domestic occupations within the home, and all at some point became slang expressions for prostitute or mistress.

Even kinship terms referring to women become denigrated. During the 17th century, *mother* was used to mean "a bawd"; more recently *mother (mothuh f——)* has become a common derogatory epithet (Cameron, 1974). Probably at some point in history every kinship term for females has been derogated (Schulz, 1975:66).

Terms of endearment for women also seem to follow a downward path. Such pet names as Tart, Dolly, Kitty, Polly, Mopsy, Biddy, and Jill all eventually became sexually derogatory (Schulz, 1975:67). *Whore* comes from the same Latin root as *care* and once meant "a lover of either sex."

Indeed, even the most neutral categorical designations—*girl, female, woman, lady*—at some point in their history have been used to connote sexual immorality. *Girl* originally meant "a child of either sex"; through the process of semantic degeneration it eventually meant "a prostitute." Although *girl* has lost this meaning, *girlie* still retains sexual connotations. *Woman* connoted "a mistress" in the early 19th century; *female* was a degrading epithet in the latter part of the 19th century; and when *lady* was introduced as a euphemism, it too became deprecatory. "Even so neutral a term as *person,* when it was used as substitute for *woman,* suffered [vulgarization]" (Mencken, 1963: 350, quoted in Schulz, 1975:71).

Whether one looks at elite titles, occupational roles, kinship relationships, endearments, or age-sex categorical designations, the pattern is clear. Terms referring to females are pejorated—"become negative in the middle instances and abusive in the extremes" (Schulz, 1975:69). Such semantic derogation, however, is not evidenced for male referents. *Lord, baronet, father, brother, nephew, footman, bowman, boy, lad, fellow, gentleman, man, male,* and so on "have failed to undergo the derogation found in the history of their corresponding feminine designations" (Schulz, 1975:67). Interestingly, the male word, rather than undergoing derogation, frequently is replaced by a female referent when the speaker wants to debase a male. A weak man, for example, is referred to as a *sissy* (diminutive of *sister*), and an army recruit during basic training is called a *pussy.* And when one is swearing at a male, he is referred to as a *bastard* or a *son-of-a-bitch*—both appellations that impugn the dignity of a man's mother.

In summary, these verbal practices are consistent with the gender stereotypes that we encounter in everyday life. Women are thought to be a part of man, nonautonomous, dependent, relegated to roles that require few skills, characteristically incompetent and immature, sexual objects, best defined in terms of their relations to men. Males are visible, autonomous and independent, responsible for the protection and containment of women, expected to occupy positions on the basis of their high achievement or physical power, assumed to be sexually potent, and defined primarily by their relations to the world of work. The use of the language perpetuates the stereotypes for both genders and limits the options available for self-definition.

REFERENCES

Adamsky, C. 1981. "Changes in pronominal usage in a classroom situation." *Psychology of Women Quarterly* 5:773–79.

Bendix, J. 1979. "Linguistic models as political symbols: Gender and the generic 'he' in English." In J. Orasanu, M. Slater, and L. L. Adler, eds., *Language, sex and gender; Does la différence make a difference?* pp. 23–42. New York: New Academy of Science Annuals.

Cameron, P. 1974. "Frequency and kinds of words in various social settings, or What the hell's going on?" In M. Truzzi, ed., *Sociology for pleasure,* pp. 31–37. Englewood Cliffs, N.J.: Prentice-Hall.

Daly, M. 1973. *Beyond God the father.* Boston: Beacon Press.

DeStefano, J. S. 1976. Personal communication. Columbus: Ohio State University.

Hamilton, N., & Henley, N. 1982. "Detrimental consequences of the generic masculine usage." Paper presented to the Western Psychological Association meetings, Sacramento.

Key, M. R. 1975. *Male/female language.* Metuchen, N.J.: Scarecrow Press.

Kramarae, Cheris. 1975. "Woman's speech: Separate but unequal?" In Barrie Thorne and Nancy Henley, eds., *Language and sex: Difference and dominance,* pp. 43–56. Rowley, Mass.: Newbury House.

MacKay, D. G. 1983. "Prescriptive grammar and the pronoun problem." In B. Thorne, C. Kramarae, and N. Henley, eds., *Language, gender, and society,* pp. 38–53. Rowley, Mass.: Newbury House.

Martyna, W. 1978. "What does 'he' mean? Use of the generic masculine." *Journal of Communication* 28:131–38.

Martyna, W. 1980. "Beyond the 'he/man' approach: The case for nonsexist language." *Signs* 5:482–93.

Mencken, H. L. 1963. *The American language.* 4th ed. with supplements. Abr. and ed. R. I. McDavis. New York: Knopf.

Schneider, J., & Hacker, S. 1973. "Sex role imagery in the use of the generic 'man' in introductory texts: A case in the sociology of sociology." *American Sociologist* 8:12–18.

Schulz, M. R. 1975. "The semantic derogation of women." In B. Thorne and N. Henley, eds., *Language and sex: Difference and dominance,* pp. 64–75. Rowley, Mass.: Newbury House.

Shuster, Janet. 1973. "Grammatical forms marked for male and female in English." Unpublished paper. Chicago: University of Chicago.

Stanley, J. P. 1977. "Paradigmatic woman: The prostitute." In D. L. Shores, ed., *Papers in language variation.* Birmingham: University of Alabama Press.

Vanderbilt, A. 1972. *Amy Vanderbilt's etiquette.* Garden City, N.Y.: Doubleday.

PERSONAL ACCOUNT

Becoming a Minority

"Sticks and stones may break my bones, but names will never hurt me." Names *will* hurt me, I thought to myself as the young girl across from me yelled, "I'm not like *them!* I'm normal, I don't have *their* problem!" Contrary to the childhood rhyme, her words did indeed hurt me. Those words created an emotional pain that exceeded any physical pain I had endured. They made me feel inferior and different from the rest of the world.

After a week at the hospital I had become accustomed to the daily group meetings, the morning weigh-ins, the scheduled meals, and the strict rules for all patients. I came to accept my problem: I was anorexic. The other patients had similar problems. They suffered the same loneliness and confusion that I suffered. They fought the same battle I fought every day. As we helped each other, we became a community. I was accepted in these walls.

This was shattered by a girl who was admitted to the hospital with a bingeing problem. We all had our own problems. Some were anorexic, bulimic, or bingers; others were suicidal, suffered from obsessive-compulsive disorders, or were addicted to alcohol or drugs. Therapy and support were there for everyone. Since we were understanding of each other, I never once thought of myself as a minority, different from anyone I had met. I figured that we were all people who were there for the same reason—until the day those words of criticism hit me.

All members of the eating disorder group had three meals to eat together every day. You had to eat everything on your tray in a half-hour. Any patient who failed to do so had to drink two "Ensures," which were loaded with fat and calories. The young girl sat across from me, ate half of the food on her plate, then exclaimed that she was done. I looked at her in horror because I was aware of what awaited her. I wondered if she had any idea what she was dong to herself by breaking the rules. She was told to eat the rest of her food but she refused, saying that she was full and had had enough. After a verbal exchange, she got up in exasperation and said that she wasn't like us. She didn't have our problem, she wasn't so crazy that she would deprive herself of food. She claimed that she was there because she ate too much and should be eating less, not more. After her offensive speech, she left the table. Her parents checked her out the next day.

Tears came to my eyes as her words hit me. I remembered the stares I got before coming into the hospital, the snickering and whispering I heard from behind me. Then I remembered the television talk shows I had seen about people suffering from eating disorders. I remembered my disgust and confusion and my belief that they were different from me. And now, without warning, I too was part of that minority. A rush of emotions came to me. I felt angry for ever looking at those people as different or with disgust; I felt lonely because I was now part of a minority. I felt angry because this girl was heartless and weak. I had allowed her actions to make me feel different, not good enough, not acceptable.

I suffer from an eating disorder, something most people are not able to understand. Something I myself don't quite understand. I may be different in the fact that I suffer this ongoing battle, but this disorder does not make me different from others because we are all people.

Elizabeth Lukos

READING 48

To Be and Be Seen: The Politics of Reality*

Marilyn Frye

. . . Reality is that which is.

The English word 'real' stems from a word which meant *regal,* of or pertaining to the king.

'Real' in Spanish means *royal.*

Real property is that which is proper to the king.

Real estate is the estate of the king.

Reality is that which pertains to the one in power, is that over which he has power, is his domain, his estate, is proper to him.

The ideal king reigns over everything as far as the eye can see. His eye. What he cannot see is not royal, not real.

He sees what is proper to him.

To be real is to be visible to the king.

The king is in his counting house.

I say, "I am a lesbian. The king does not count lesbians. Lesbians are not real. There are no lesbians." To say this, I use the word 'lesbian', and hence one might think that there is a word for this thing, and thus that the thing must have a place in the conceptual scheme. But this is not so. Let me take you on a guided tour of a few standard dictionaries, to display some reasons for saying that lesbians are not named in the lexicon of the King's English.

If you look up the word 'lesbian' in *The Oxford English Dictionary,* you find an entry that says it is an adjective that means *of or pertaining to the island of Lesbos,* and an entry describing at length and favorably an implement called a lesbian rule, which is a flexible measuring device used by carpenters. Period.

Webster's Third International offers a more pertinent definition. It tells us that a lesbian is a homosexual female. And going on, one finds that 'homosexual' means *of or pertaining to the same sex.* The elucidating example provided is the phrase 'homosexual twins' which means *same-sex twins.* The alert scholar can conclude that a lesbian is a same-sex female.

A recent edition of *Webster's Collegiate Dictionary* tells us that a lesbian is a woman who has sex, or sexual relations, with other women. Such a definition would be accepted by many speakers of the language and at least seems to be coherent, even if too narrow. But the appearance is deceptive, for this account collapses into nonsense, too. The key word in this definition is 'sex': having sex or having sexual relations. But what is having sex? It is worthwhile to follow this up because the pertinent dictionary entries obscure an important point about the logic of sex. Getting clear about that point helps one see that there is semantic closure against recognition of the existence of lesbians, and it also prepares the way for understanding the connection between the place of *woman* and the place of *lesbian* with respect to the phallocratic scheme of things.[1]

Dictionaries generally agree that 'sexual' means something on the order of *pertaining to the genital union of a female and a male animal,* and that "having sex" is having intercourse—intercourse being defined as the penetration of a vagina by a penis, with ejaculation. My own observation of usage leads me to think these accounts are inadequate and misleading. Some uses of these terms do fit this dictionary account. For instance, parents and counselors standardly remind young women that if they are going to be sexually active they must deal responsibly with the possibility of becoming pregnant. In this context, the word 'sexually' is pretty clearly being used in a way that accords with the given definition. But many activities and events fall under

*This is a very slightly revised version of the essay which appeared in *Sinister Wisdom 17* with the title, "To Be and Be Seen: Metaphysical Misogyny."
Marilyn Frye is a feminist philosopher and theorist.

the rubric 'sexual', apparently without semantic deviance, though they do not involve penile penetration of the vagina of a female human being. Penile penetration of almost anything, especially if it is accompanied by ejaculation, counts as having sex or being sexual. Moreover, events which cannot plausibly be seen as pertaining to penile erection, penetration and ejaculation will, in general, not be counted as sexual, and events that do not involve penile penetration or ejaculation will not be counted as having sex. For instance, if a girlchild is fondled and aroused by a man, and comes to orgasm, but the man refrains from penetration and ejaculation, the man can say, and speakers of English will generally agree, that he did not have sex with her. No matter what is going on, or (it must be mentioned) *not* going on, with respect to female arousal or orgasm, or in connection with the vagina, a pair can be said without semantic deviance to have had sex, or not to have had sex; the use of that term turns entirely on what was going on with respect to the penis.

When one first considers the dictionary definitions of 'sex' and 'sexual', it seems that all sexuality is heterosexuality, by definition, and that the term 'homosexual' would be internally contradictory. There are uses of the term according to which this is exactly so. But in the usual and standard use, there is nothing semantically odd in describing two men as having sex with each other. According to that usage, any situation in which one or more penises are present is one in which something could happen which could be called having sex. But on this apparently "broader" definition there is nothing women could do in the absence of men that could, without semantic oddity, be called "having sex." Speaking of women who have sex with other women is like speaking of ducks who engage in arm wrestling.

When the dictionary defines lesbians as women who have sex or sexual relations with other women, it defines lesbians as logically impossible.

Looking for other words in the lexicon which might denote these beings which are non-named 'lesbians', one thinks of terms in the vernacular, like 'dyke', 'bulldagger' and so on. Perhaps it is just as well that standard dictionaries do not pretend to provide relevant definitions of such terms. Generally, these two terms are used to denote women who are perceived as imitating, dressing up like, or trying to be men. Whatever the extent of the class of women who are perceived to do such things, it obviously is not coextensive with the class of lesbians. Nearly every feminist, and many other women as well, have been perceived as wishing to be men, and a great many lesbians are not so perceived. The term 'dyke' has been appropriated by some lesbians as a term of pride and solidarity, but in that use it is unintelligible to most speakers of English.

One of the current definitions of 'lesbianism' among lesbians is *woman-loving*—the polar opposite of misogyny. Several dictionaries I checked have entries for 'misogyny' (hatred of women), but not for 'philogyny' (love of women). I found one which defines 'philogyny' as *fondness for women,* and another dictionary defines 'philogyny' as *Don Juanism.* Obviously neither of these means *love of women* as it is intended by lesbians combing the vocabulary for ways to refer to themselves. According to the dictionaries, there is no term in English for the polar opposite of misogyny nor for persons whose characteristic orientation toward women is the polar opposite of misogyny.

Flinging the net wider, one can look up the more Victorian words, like sapphism and sapphist. In *Webster's Collegiate,* 'sapphism' is defined just as *lesbianism.* But *The Oxford English Dictionary* introduces another twist. Under the heading of 'sapphism' is an entry for 'sapphist' according to which sapphists are those addicted to unnatural sexual relations between women. The fact that these relations are characterized as unnatural is revealing. For what is unnatural is contrary to the laws of nature, or contrary to the nature of the substance of entity in question. But what is contrary to the laws of nature cannot happen: that is what it means to call these laws the laws of nature. And I cannot do what is contrary to my nature, for if I could do it, it would be in my nature to do it. To call something "unnatural" is to say it cannot be. This definition defines sapphists, that is lesbians, as *naturally* impossible as well as *logically* impossible. . . .

Lesbian.

One of the people of the Isle of Lesbos.

It is bizarre that when I try to name myself and explain myself, my native tongue provides me with a word that is so foreign, so false, so hopelessly inappropriate. Why am I referred to by a term which means *one of the people of Lesbos?*

The use of the word 'lesbian' to name us is a quadrifold evasion, a laminated euphemism. To name us, one goes by way of a reference to the island of Lesbos, which in turn is an indirect reference to the poet Sappho (who used to live there, they say), which in turn is itself an indirect reference to what fragments of her poetry have survived a few millenia of patriarchy, and this in turn (if we have not lost you by now) is a prophylactic avoidance of direct mention of the sort of creature who would write such poems or to whom such poems would be written . . . assuming you happen to know what is in those poems written in a dialect of Greek over two thousand five hundred years ago on some small island somewhere in the wine dark Aegean Sea.

This is a truly remarkable feat of silence.

. . . I think there is much truth in the claim that the phallocratic scheme does not include women. But while women are erased in history and in speculation, physically liquidated in gynocidal purges and banished from the community of those with perceptual and semantic authority, we are on the other hand regularly and systematically invited, seduced, cajoled, coerced and even paid to be in intimate and constant association with men and their projects. In this, the situation of women generally is radically different from the situation of lesbians. Lesbians are not invited to join—the family, the party, the project, the procession, the war effort. There is a place for a woman in every game. Wife, secretary, servant, prostitute, daughter, assistant, babysitter, mistress, seamstress, proofreader, nurse, confidante, masseusse, indexer, typist, mother. Any of these is a place for a woman, and women are much encouraged to fill them. None of these is a place for a lesbian.

The exclusion of women from the phallocratic scheme is impressive, frightening and often fatal, but it is not simple and absolute. Women's existence is both absolutely necessary to and irresolvably problematic for the dominant reality and those committed to it, for our existence is *presupposed* by phallocratic reality, but it is not and cannot be *encompassed* by or countenanced by that reality. Women's existence is a background against which phallocratic reality is a foreground.

A foreground scene is created by the motion of foreground figures against a static background. Foreground figures are perceptible, are defined, have identity, only in virtue of their movement against a background. The space in which the motion of foreground figures takes place is created and defined by their movement with respect to each other and against the background. But nothing of the background is *in* or is *part of* or is *encompassed* by the foreground scene and space. The background is unseen by the eye which is focused on foreground figures, and if anything somehow draws the eye to the background, the foreground dissolves. What would draw the eye to the background would be any sudden or well-defined motion in the background. Hence there must be either no motion at all in the background, or an unchanging buzz of small, regular and repetitive motions. The background must be utterly un*event*ful if the foreground is to continue to hang together, that is, if it is to endure as *a space* within which there are discrete *objects* in relation to each other.

I imagine phallocratic reality to be the space and figures and motion which constitute the foreground, and the constant repetitive uneventful activities of women to constitute and maintain the background against which this foreground plays. It is essential to the maintenance of the foreground reality that nothing within it refer in any way to anything in the background, and yet it depends absolutely upon the existence of the background. It is useful to carry this metaphor on in a more concrete mode—thinking of phallocratic reality as a dramatic production on a stage.

The motions of the actors against the stage settings and backdrop constitute and maintain the existence and identities of the characters in a play. The stage setting, props, lights and so forth are created, provided, maintained and occasionally rearranged (according to the script) by stagehands. The stagehands, their motions and the products of those motions, are neither in nor part of the play, are neither in nor part of the reality of the characters. The reality in the framework of which Hamlet's actions have their meaning would be rent or shattered if anything Hamlet did or thought referred in any way to the stagehands or their activities, or if that background blur of activity were in any other way to be resolved into attention-catching events.

The situation of the actors is desperately paradoxical. The actors are absolutely committed to the maintenance of the characters and the characters' reality: participation as characters in the ongoing creation of Reality is their *raison d'etre.* The reality of the character must be lived with fierce concentration. The actor must be immersed in the play and undistracted by any thought for the scenery, props or stagehands, lest the continuity of the characters and the integrity of their reality be dissolved or broken. But if the character must be lived so intently, who will supervise the stagehands to make sure they don't get rowdy, leave early, fall asleep or walk off the job? (Alas, there is no god nor heavenly host to serve as Director and Stage Managers.) Those with the most intense commitment to the maintenance of the reality of the play are precisely those most interested in the proper deportment of the stagehands, and this interest competes directly with that commitment. There is nothing the actor would like better than that there be no such thing as stagehands, posing as they do a constant threat to the very existence, the very life, of the character and hence to the meaning of the life of the actor; and yet the actor is irrevocably tied to the stagehands by his commitment to the play. Hamlet, of course, has no such problems; there are no stagehands in the play.

To escape his dilemma, the actor may throw caution to the wind and lose himself in the character, whereupon stagehands are unthinkable, hence unproblematic. Or he may construct and embrace the belief that the stagehands share exactly his own perceptions and interests and that they are as committed to the play as he—that they are like robots. On such a hypothesis he can assume them to be absolutely dependable and go on about his business single-mindedly and without existential anxiety. A third strategy, which is in a macabre way more sane, is that of trying to solve the problem technologically by constructing actual robots to serve as stagehands.[2] Given the primacy of his commitment to the play, all solutions must involve one form or another of annihilation of the stagehands. Yet all three require the existence of stagehands; the third, he would hope, requiring it only for a while longer.

The solution to the actor's problem which will appear most benign with respect to the stagehands because it erases the erasure, is that of training, persuading and seducing the stagehands into *loving* the actors and taking actors' interests and commitments unto themselves as their own. One significant advantage to this solution is that the actors can carry on without the guilt or confusion that might come with annihilating, replacing or falsely forgetting the stagehands. As it turns out, of course, even this is a less than perfect solution. Stagehands, in the thrall of their commitment, can become confused and think of themselves as actors—and then they may disturb the play by trying to enter it as characters, by trying to participate in the creation and maintainance of Reality. But there are various well-known ways to handle these intrusions and this seems to be, generally speaking, the most popular solution to the actor's dilemma.

. . . The king is in his counting house. The king is greedy and will count for himself everything he dares to. But his greed itself imposes limits on what he dares to count.

What the king cannot count is a seer whose perception passes the plane of the foreground Reality and focuses upon the background. A seer whose eye is attracted to the ones working as stagehands—the women. A seer in whose eye the woman has authority, has interests of her own, is not a robot. A seer who has no motive for wanting there to be no women; a seer who is not loyal to Reality. We can take the account of the seer who must be unthinkable if Reality is to be kept afloat as the beginning of an account of what a lesbian is. One might try saying that a lesbian is one who, by virtue of her focus, her attention, her attachment, is disloyal to phallocratic reality. She is not committed to its maintenance and the maintenance of those who maintain it, and worse, her mode of disloyalty threatens its utter dissolution in the mere flick of the eye. This sounds extreme, of course, perhaps even hysterical. But listening carefully to the rhetoric of the fanatic fringe of the phallocratic loyalists, one hears that they do think that feminists, whom they fairly reasonably judge to be lesbians, have the power to bring down civilization, to dissolve the social order as we know it, to cause the demise of the species, by our mere existence.

Even the fanatics do not really believe that a lone maverick lesbian can in a flick of her evil eye atomize civilization, of course. Given the collectivity of conceptual schemes, the way they rest on agreement, a maverick perceiver does not have the power to bring one tumbling down—a point also verified by my own experience as a not-so-powerful maverick. What the loyalists fear, and in this I think they are more-or-less right, is a contagion of the maverick perception to the point where the agreement in perception which keeps Reality afloat begins to disintegrate.

The event of becoming a lesbian is a reorientation of attention in a kind of ontological conversion. It is characterized by a feeling of a world dissolving, and by a feeling of disengagement and re-engagement of one's power as a perceiver. That such conversion happens signals its possibility to others.

Heterosexuality for women is not simply a matter of sexual preference, any more than lesbianism is. It is a matter of orientation of attention, as is lesbianism, in a metaphysical context controlled by neither heterosexual nor lesbian women. Attention is a kind of passion. When one's attention is on something, one is present in a particular way with respect to that thing. This presence is, among other things, an element of erotic presence. The orientation of one's attention is also what fixes and directs the application of one's physical and emotional work.

If the lesbian sees the women, the woman may see the lesbian seeing her. With this, there is a flowering of possibilities. The woman, feeling herself seen, may learn that she *can be* seen; she may also be able to know that a woman can see, that is, can author perception. With this, there enters for the woman the logical possibility of assuming her authority as a perceiver and of shifting her own attention. With that there is the dawn of choice, and it opens out over the whole world of women. The lesbian's seeing undercuts the mechanism by which the production and constant reproduction of heterosexuality for women was to be rendered *automatic*. The nonexistence of lesbians is a piece in the mechanism which is supposed to cut off the possibility of choice or alternative at the root, namely at the point of conception.

The maintenance of phallocratic reality requires that the attention of women be focused on men and men's projects—the play; and that attention not be focused on women—the stagehands. Woman-loving, as a spontaneous and habitual orientation of attention is then, both directly and indirectly, inimical to the maintenance of that reality. And therein lies the reason for the thoroughness of the ontological closure against lesbians, the power of those closed out, and perhaps the key to the liberation of women from oppression in a male-dominated culture.

My primary goal here has not been to state and prove some rigid thesis, but simply to *say* something clearly enough, intelligibly enough, so that it can be understood and thought about. Lesbians are outside the conceptual scheme, and this is something done, not just the way things are. One can begin to see that lesbians are excluded by the scheme, and that this is *motivated,* when one begins to see what purpose the exclusion might serve in connection with keeping women generally in their metaphysical place. It is also true that lesbians are in a position to see things that cannot be seen from within the system. What lesbians see is what makes them lesbians and their seeing is why they have to be excluded. Lesbians are woman-seers. When one is suspected of seeing women, one is spat summarily out of reality, through the cognitive gap and into the negative semantic space. If you ask what became of such a woman, you may be told she became a lesbian, and if you try to find out what a lesbian is, you will be told there is no such thing.

But there is.

NOTES

1. The analysis that follows is my own rendering of an account developed by Carolyn Shafer. My version of it is informed also by my reading of "Sex and Reference," by Janice Moulton, *Philosophy and Sex,* edited by Robert Baker and Frederick Elliston (Prometheus Books, Buffalo, New York, 1975).
2. This solution is discussed in *The Transexual Empire: The Making of the She-Male,* by Janice G. Raymond (Beacon Press, Boston, 1979).

PERMISSIONS

F. James Davis, "Who Is Black? One Nation's Definition" (originally titled "The Nation's Rule") from *Who Is Black? One Nation's Definition.* Copyright © 1991 by The Pennsylvania State University. Reprinted with the permission of The Pennsylvania State University Press.

Jon Michael Spencer, excerpts from the Introduction and selected bibliography from *Colored-People: The Mixed-Race Movement in America.* Copyright © 1997 by Jon Michael Spencer. Reprinted with the permission of New York University Press.

M. Annette Jaimes, "Federal Indian Identification Policy: A Usurpation of Indigenous Sovereignty in North America" (including notes) from M. Annette Jaimes (ed.), *The State of Native America: Genocide, Colonization, and Resistance.* Copyright © 1992 by M. Annette Jaimes. Reprinted with the permission of South End Press, Cambridge, Mass.

Carlos A. Fernandez, "La Raza and the Melting Pot: A Comparative Look at Multiethnicity" from *Racially Mixed People in America,* edited by Maria P. P. Root. Copyright © 1992 by Sage Publications, Inc. Reprinted with the permission of the publishers.

Yen Le Espiritu, "Asian-American Panethnicity" from *Asian American Panethnicity: Bridging Institutions and Identities.* Copyright © 1992 by Temple University. Reprinted with the permission of Temple University Press.

Ruth Frankenberg, "The Social Construction of Whiteness" from *White Women, Race Matters.* Copyright © 1993 by the Regents of the University of Minnesota. Reprinted with the permission of the University of Minnesota Press.

Anne Fausto-Sterling, "The Five Sexes: Why Male and Female Are Not Enough," *The Sciences* 22, no. 2 (March/April 1993). Reprinted with the permission of *The Sciences.*

Walter L. Williams, "Of Religions and Dreams: The Spiritual Basis of the Berdache Tradition" from *The Spirit and the Flesh.* Copyright © 1986, 1992 by Walter L. Williams. Reprinted with the permission of Beacon Press, Boston.

Susan Basow, "Gender Stereotypes and Roles" from *Gender Stereotypes and Roles,* Third Edition. Copyright © 1992, 1980, 1966 by Wadsworth, Inc. Reprinted with the permission of Wadsworth Publishing, a division of International Thomson Publishing.

Richard D. Kahlenberg, excerpt and chapter notes from "The Case for Class-Based Affirmative Action" from *The Remedy: Class, Race, and Affirmative Action.* Copyright © 1997 by Richard D. Kahlenberg. Reprinted with the permission of Basic Books, a member of Perseus Books, L.L.C.

Ronald B. Mincy, "The Underclass: Concept, Controversy, and Evidence" from Sheldon H. Danziger, Gary Sandefur, and Daniel H. Weinberg (eds.), *Confronting Poverty: Prescriptions for Change.* Copyright © 1994 by the President and Fellows of Harvard College. Reprinted with the permission of Harvard University Press.

Jonathan Ned Katz, excerpts from *The Invention of Heterosexuality.* Copyright © 1995 by Jonathan Ned Katz. Reprinted with the permission of Dutton, a division of Penguin Putnam Inc.

Barbara Sherman Heyl, "Homosexuality: A Social Phenomenon" from *Human Sexuality: The Societal and Interpersonal Context,* edited by Kathleen McKinney and Susan Sprecher (Norwood, NJ: Ablex, 1989). Reprinted with the permission of Ablex Publishing Corporation.

Heidi Levine and Nancy J. Evans, "The Development of Gay, Lesbian, and Bisexual Identities" from *Beyond Tolerance: Gays, Lesbians and Bisexuals on Campus.* Copyright © 1991 by the American College Personnel Association. Reprinted with the permission of the American College Personnel Association.

Joanne Nobuko Miyamoto, "What Are You?" from *Asian Women* (Berkeley: Asian American Studies Program/University of California–Berkeley). Reprinted by permission.

Marilyn Frye, "Oppression" from *The Politics of Reality: Essays in Feminist Theory,* edited by Marilyn Frye. Copyright © 1983 by Marilyn Frye. Reprinted with the permission of The Crossing Press, Freedom, CA.

Sally French, "'Can You See the Rainbow?' The Roots of Denial" from John Swain, Vic Finkelstein, Sally French, and Mike Oliver (eds.), *Disabling Barriers, Enabling Environments.* Copyright © 1993 by The Open University. Reprinted with the permission of Sage Publications, Ltd.

Michelle Fine and Adrienne Asch, "Disability beyond Stigma: Social Interaction, Discrimination, and Activism" from *Journal of Social Issues* 44, no. 1 (1988). Copyright © 1988 Reprinted with the permission of the publishers.

Magdoline Asfahani, "Time to Look and Listen" from *Newsweek* (December 2, 1996). Reprinted with the permission of *Newsweek.* All rights reserved.

Eric Liu, excerpt from *The Accidental Asian: Notes of a Native Speaker.* Copyright © 1998 by Eric Liu. Reprinted with the permission of Random House, Inc.

Helen Zia, "Can Asian-Americans Turn the Media Tide?" from *The Nation* (December 22, 1997). Copyright © 1997 by Helen Zia. Reprinted with the permission of the author.

Arturo Madrid, "Diversity and Its Discontents" from *Academe* 76, no. 6 (November–December 1990). Copyright © 1990 by Arturo Madrid. Reprinted with the permission of the author.

Bob Blauner, "Talking Past Each Other: Black and White Languages of Race," *The American Prospect* (Summer 1992). Copyright © 1992

New Prospect, Inc. Reprinted with the permission of the author and *The American Prospect.*

John Lamberth, "Driving While Black" from *The Washington Post* (August 16, 1998). Copyright © 1998 by John Lamberth. Reprinted with the permission of the author.

D. Marvin Jones, excerpts from "Darkness Made Visible: Law, Metaphor and the Racial Self" from *Georgetown Law Journal,* 82 (1993). Copyright © 1993. Reprinted with the permission of the author and publishers.

Patricia J. Williams, "Of Race and Risk" from *Nation* (December 29, 1997). Copyright © 1997 by Patricia J. Williams. Reprinted with the permission of Brandt & Brandt Literary Agents, Inc.

Deborah Tannen, "Wears Jump Suit. Sensible Shoes. Uses Husband's Last Name," *The New York Times Magazine* (June 20, 1993). Copyright © 1993 by Deborah Tannen. Reprinted with the permission of the author.

Judith Lorber, excerpt from *Paradoxes of Gender.* Copyright © 1994 by Yale University. Reprinted with the permission of Yale University Press.

Dorothy Allison, "A Question of Class" from *Sisters, Sexperts, Queers,* edited by Arlene Stein. Copyright © 1993 by Arlene Stein. Reprinted with the permission of Dutton Signet, a division of Penguin Putnam Inc.

John Larew, "Why Are Droves of Unqualified, Unprepared Kids Getting into Our Colleges? Because Their Dads Are Alumni," *The Washington Monthly* (June 1991). Copyright © 1991 The Washington Monthly Company. Reprinted with the permission of *The Washington Monthly,* 1611 Connecticut Avenue, N.W., Washington, DC 20009.

James E. Jones, Jr., "The Rise and Fall of Affirmative Action" from *Race in America: The Struggle for Equality,* edited by Herbert Hill and James E. Jones, Jr. Copyright © 1993 by The Board of Regents of the University of Wisconsin System. Reprinted with the permission of The University of Wisconsin Press.

William G. Bowen and Derek Bok, excerpts from "Summing Up" from *The Shape of the River: Long-Term Consequences of Considering Race in College and University Admissions.* Copyright © 1998 by Princeton University Press. Reprinted with the permission of the publisher.

Cheryl Zarlenga Kerchis and Iris Marion Young, excerpts from "Social Movements and the Politics of Difference" from Dean A. Harris (ed.), *Multiculturalism from the Margins: Non-Dominant Voices on Difference and Diversity.* Copyright © 1995 by Bifocal Publications. Reprinted with the permission of Greenwood Publishing Group, Inc., Westport, CT.

George Lipsitz, excerpt and chapter notes from "The Possessive Investment in Whiteness" from *The Possessive Investment in Whiteness: How White People Profit from Identity Politics.* Copyright © 1998 by Temple University. Reprinted with the permission of Temple University Press. All Rights Reserved.

Roberto Suro, excerpts from "Children of the Future" from *Strangers Among Us: How Latino Immigration Is Transforming America.* Copyright © 1998 by Roberto Suro. Reprinted with the permission of Alfred A. Knopf, Inc.

Andrew Hacker, excerpts from "The Gender Gap: Contours and Causes" from *Money: Who Has How Much and Why.* Copyright © 1997 by Andrew Hacker. Reprinted with the permission of Scribner, a division of Simon & Schuster.

Dorothy Nelkin and M. Susan Lindee, excerpts from "Creating Natural Distinctions" and "The Supergene" from *The DNA Mystique: The Gene as a Cultural Icon.* Copyright © 1995 by W. H.

Freeman and Company. Reprinted with the permission of the publishers.

Nancy Krieger and Mary Bassett, "The Health of Black Folk: Disease, Class, and Ideology in Science," *Monthly Review* 38, no. 3 (July–August 1986). Copyright © 1986 by Monthly Review, Inc. Reprinted with the permission of Monthly Review Foundation.

Gilbert Zicklin, "Media, Science, and Sexual Ideology: The Promotion of Sexual Stability" (including notes) from Martin B. Duberman (ed.), *Queer World: The Center for Lesbian and Gay Studies Reader.* Copyright © 1997 by Gilbert Zicklin. Reprinted with the permission of New York University Press and Martin B. Duberman.

Michael Oliver, excerpts from "Disability Definitions: The Politics of Meaning" and "The Cultural Production of Impairment and Disability" from *The Politics of Disablement: A Sociological Approach.* Copyright © 1990 by Michael Oliver. Reprinted with the permission of St. Martin's Press, Incorporated.

Susan Faludi, "Backlash" (originally titled "The 'Trends' of Antifeminism: The Media and the Backlash") from *Backlash: The Undeclared War.* Copyright © 1992 by Susan Faludi. Reprinted with the permission of Crown Publishers, Inc.

Yen Le Espiritu, excerpts from "Ideological Racism and Cultural Resistance: Constructing Our Own Images" from *Asian American Women and Men: Labor, Laws and Love.* Copyright © 1997 by Sage Publications, Inc. Reprinted with the permission of the publishers.

Jerry Mander, excerpts from "What Americans Don't Know about Indians" from *In the Absence of the Sacred: The Failure of Technology and the Survival of the Indian Nations.* Copyright © 1991 by Jerry Mander. Reprinted with the permission of Sierra Club Books.

Dennis Baron, "English in a Multicultural America," *Social Policy* (Spring 1991). Copyright © 1991 by Social Policy Corporation. Reprinted with the permission of *Social Policy.*

Robert B. Moore, "Racism in the English Language" from *Racism in the English Language* (New York: Council on Interracial Books for Children, 1976). Reprinted with the permission of Lawrence Jordan, Literary Agency, 250 West 57th Street, Suite 1527, New York, NY 10107.

Laurel Richardson, "Gender Stereotyping in the English Language" from *Feminist Frontiers IV,* edited by Laurel Richardson, Verta Taylor, and Nancy Whittier (New York: McGraw-Hill, 1997). Originally appeared in Laurel Richardson, *The Dynamics of Sex and Gender: A Sociological Perspective* (New York: Harper, 1987). Reprinted with the permission of the author.

Marilyn Frye, "To See and Be Seen" from *The Politics of Reality: Essays in Feminist Theory,* edited by Marilyn Frye. Copyright © 1983 by Marilyn Frye. Reprinted with the permission of The Crossing Press, Freedom, CA.